Depraved - Fred & Rose

C G C COOK

ISBN: 1727271904
ISBN-13: 978-1727271904

DEDICATION

This book is dedicated to all of the victims of Fred and Rose West; both known and unknown.

CONTENTS

Warning: This book contains graphic details and descriptions of abuse, rape and torture that some may find disturbing.

Introduction

It has been 25 years since the police first knocked at 25 Cromwell Street looking for Heather West. What they found there hadn't been seen since the case of John Christie and 10 Rillington Place in 1953. The police had gone looking for Heather West's remains as she hadn't been seen for quite some years and some of her siblings, who were in care, had joked to social workers about Heather being 'buried under the patio'. What they eventually discovered was a case of abuse, rape, abduction and mass murder dating back to 1966, with bodies being found in the cellar, the garden, and at two further sites.

Speculation remains as to exactly how many women and children Fred and Rose West killed, and when they first started. It is a fact that Fred had already killed before he met Rose, although Fred denied that right up until his suicide in 1995. When he was arrested, and the first body was found in the garden of his home, he admitted to the killing but told the police that he had acted alone and that Rose had known nothing. He kept this stance on each subsequent discovery of a body, right up until Rose blanked him at a joint court appearance in July 1994. Then it was all Rose's fault and he knew nothing about the murders.

After his suicide in 1995, the police had to shift all of their efforts in to getting the case against Rosemary to court. After all, there was no physical evidence to link her to any of the murders. The police were unable to say how the victims were killed. All they could say for certain was that they had been decapitated, had their legs disarticulated at the hips and that they all had bones that were missing. Most were discovered with masks and restraints in the graves alongside them, indicating that torture and acts of sadomasochism had taken place before the girls were killed.

The police had to prove that Rosemary West alone was responsible for killing her step-daughter Charmaine and getting the court to agree to allow 'similar fact' evidence to be heard in the case. Rosemary West had said very little in her police interviews and denied all knowledge of how the bodies came to be in her basement and garden. To this day she still denies murdering anybody.

In writing this book, my aim has been to give a full account of what is known to have taken place through the life of both Rose and Fred West. From early childhood, to love, to murder, to death and through to the present day. I have given you, the reader, the opportunity to hear them in their own words as much as possible to allow you access to their minds. You will hear from police, family and friends of both the Wests and the victims in their own words to help you understand the pain caused by these acts.

ACKNOWLEDGMENTS

This book wouldn't have been possible without the close support and encouragement of my friends and family.

1 FRED WEST

Frederick Walter Stephen West was born on the 29th September 1941 at Bickerton Cottage in Much Marcle, Herefordshire, to Daisy Hannah West and Walter Stephen West. He was born with curly blonde hair and big blue eyes.

Just a few weeks after he was born Fred West was baptized at Much Marcle Parish Church.

Daisy West gave birth regularly and by 1945 she had given birth three more times: to John Charles Edward West, David Henry George West and Daisy West. Unfortunately, David had a heart defect and passed away within a month of being born.

Daisy quickly became a very large woman and violence was a way of life in their household. In particular, violence towards the West children was an accepted part of life. Daisy wore a large leather belt and would use it to beat the children with when they were badly behaved.

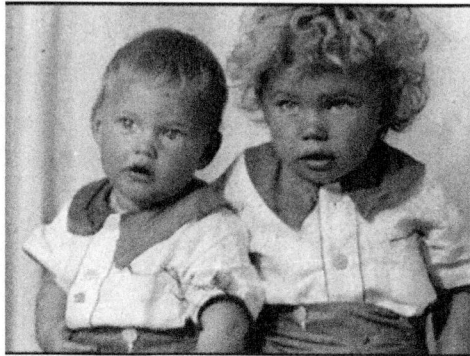

John and Fred West

In 1946, the West family moved to Moorcourt Farm in Much Marcle, where Walter got himself a job as a Milking Herdsman and Harvest Hand. As before, it was a tied cottage but this time it was owned by Frank Brooke, the farmer for whom Walter worked. It was crowded, having just two bedrooms until Mr Brooke added a third. The cottage had no electricity and the only source of heat came from a log fireplace. It had views across to Letterbox Field, Fingerpost Field and the surrounding countryside.

Fred was an ordinary young boy. He was small with a crop of curly hair and took after his mother in looks. He was cheeky, mouthy but also a bit naïve and easily led.

In November Daisy had yet another son, Doug. She grew tired of the boys getting under her feet and as well as beating them, she would send them outside in the middle of winter for getting under her feet.

Fred was her favourite and the only one who could get away with teasing her. In interviews he would say: "We used to have a fir tree by our back door, and we had the top cut out where the electric came through and we made a house up in there. When my mother used to get at us we'd shoot straight up this tree. My mother was a big woman, and she used to say: 'you'll come down when you get hungry.' She wouldn't bother with you, but when you came down, she'd have you.

"Whatever mother said went. You didn't answer mother back or she grabbed you and wopped you a bit quick. I mean, sixteen or sixty, didn't matter. She was a pillar of steel. There was no messing. She'd sort anything out. No problem. Mother was a bit of a neurotic about things. She used to shout a lot really when she was talking to you. She was very dominant, like, and you didn't get a chance to get a word in. She would tell you and that was the story, like. My mother knew exactly what was going on. You could tell her the biggest lie you ever thought up, my mother would listen and tell you the truth.

"Me and my father got on great together. There was no doubt about that. He was a massive man, mind, big man, tall, you know, massive hands on him. But he wouldn't hurt a fly. He was the most understanding person you'd ever met. You could go to Dad and ask him anything. He was always calm, and he always understood you.

"My mother was very old fashioned in her ways about sex and things like that. Dad was different altogether. If it's on offer, take it, son. That was my father's idea. Whatever you enjoy, do, only make sure you don't get caught doing it. That was Dad, like. Dad got on with anybody, he didn't judge nobody. If you went to the old man and said: 'so-and-so is doing something', he would say: 'That's their business, son. What you worrying about? You're not doing it.' That was his attitude to life. Just did his own thing…He was so placid it was unreal."

In November 1947 Daisy gave birth to her second daughter, Kathleen (or Kitty as she was known). At school Fred was listed as 'retarded'. He did possess artistic skills and was always making gifts for his mother. He was good at art and enjoyed drawing and sketching. Everyone knew that Fred was his mother's favourite and he used to get teased about it at school. Ann Colburn, who went to school with Fred, remembered: "Mrs West was very protective of Fred, more than any of her children. The highlight of our summer days was to see Mrs West coming down the road in her pretty dress to sort out one of the teachers who had been giving Fred a hard time."

Fred admitted that he was "thick as two short planks" and wasn't interested in school. He wanted to learn about farming and used to go lambing with his father and to hunt foxes with him.

Before going to school the children had to get up early and help to milk the cows and see to the other animals, and when it was lambing season they would be up at all hours of the night tending to the sheep. By the time he was eight-years-old he had been taught how to have sex with sheep by his father.

Daisy gave birth to another child, Gwendoline, in February 1951 and within two years it is believed that Fred had started to have sex with his mother. He would later claim that his belief in incest being 'normal' stemmed from his father's incest with his own daughters, but his brother Doug later dismissed these claims as 'pure fantasy'.

School Photo 1954. Fred is bottom row, second from the right

In December 1956 Fred left school uneducated and could barely read or write. It is believed that he had an IQ of just 80. He went to work on the farm full time but grew bored after 18 months. He gave half of his wages to his mother, kept some for himself and put the rest into a savings account so that he could get the motorbike he was desperate for.

On Saturday nights Fred and his brother John would meet other

3

young men from the village and go out together usually to the youth club in nearby Ledbury. Fred would pester the women there and given half a chance would fondle them too. Fred's brother, John, would later say: "Fred was always a ladies man. I never stood much of a chance." Despite being a year younger than Fred, John had grown to be much bigger and stronger and if Fred got into trouble with the boyfriends or brothers of these girls John would step in if the situation threatened to turn violent.

When they went out Fred almost always wore a suit. He said that it used to impress the girls and helped him to attract them. When he did meet a girl, the practice (according to him) was to meet up later "somewhere in the woods, or anywhere quiet in the fields. You just went with them, and that was it. You enjoyed yourself that time, and then it was finished until you met them again."

Fred soon grew desperate to get away from home and the farm that he had grown tired of and in the summer of 1957 he disappeared. He cycled to Hereford and took a job on a building site. Barely a month later he returned home with a gift of a watch each for his parents. He took a job in a cider factory and began to save even harder for his motorbike.

He carried on his womanising ways and his favourite place to take them was Fingerpost Field. His usual trick to get a girl to sleep with him was to propose first. Once she had a ring on her finger and he'd had what he wanted from her, he would quickly break off the engagement and move on to the next woman.

After a couple of months working at the cider factory he had enough money saved up and bought himself a 98cc Bantam motorbike. This offered him the freedom he was looking for and on Saturday's he would ride down to Ledbury and park up outside the cafes there and talk to the women and girls and then on Sundays do the same in Gloucester. At this time Fred got his first proper girlfriend and it was on his way home from seeing her that he had a major accident on the 28th November.

Fred West on his bike shortly before his accident. Also pictured are Daisy, Gwen, Kitty and Doug

He ran over a bicycle that was left partly in the road on the bend between Fingerpost Field and Moorcourt Cottages. The bicycle belonged to a girl he knew, Pat Mann, and he later said that she had stopped to "drop her knickers" at the side of the road. He was taken unconscious to Ledbury Cottage Hospital, but was immediately transferred to the larger Hereford Hospital. He suffered multiple injuries including a fractured skull and lay unconscious for several days. He suffered damage to his brain, most notably to his frontal cortex. His nose was broken, as was a leg and one of his arms. The leg was shortened making him walk with a pronounced limp for the rest of his life and he had to walk with braces for several months.

After the accident members of Fred's family noticed that Fred's personality had changed. His brother, John, would remember that he would sit in the living room staring at the wall and not talk to anyone. If anyone spoke to him he would shout and bite their heads off. Later, in interviews, Fred denied this was because of his accident and insisted "Half the bloody problem of what changed me was John, because he kept stirring the shit for me all the time. He was always top monkey, like, couldn't do anything but he had plenty of talk, and he always reported on everything. If you broke a spade handle and skived off, he would tell the old man 'Fred's gone'."

While Fred was recovering at home, he would go up to the fields with his father and it's believed that this was when Walter told him that it was a father's duty to 'break in' his daughters.

The following spring Fred packed a suitcase and went looking for

5

work down at the docks. Whilst working on the boats he used his shore leave to get a job as a delivery driver in Cheltenham delivering bread for Sunblest. He later boasted that he got a redheaded woman pregnant after she seduced him and made love to him on a rug in her living room. When she saw him again and told him she was pregnant with his child he quit the job immediately.

In 1960 he signed on as crew on the oil-boats under a series of different names. When he returned home he bought himself another motorbike, a grey 1000-cc Triumph. He returned home at Christmas and began working the fields again with his father. Daisy made Fred give up his motorbike and, with the money, he and John bought a car. Fred used it almost exclusively and at weekends would disappear with girls. His behavior became more and more erratic and he started to rape his 13-year-old sister Kitty.

He also began thieving and in early 1961 he and his friend, Brian Hill, were arrested. They had stolen two ladies cigarette cases and a rolled-gold watch-strap from shops in Ledbury. On the 17th April, Fred appeared at Ledbury Magistrates Court charged with the crimes and was fined £4.

He was by now aged nineteen but started to date a girl aged just fourteen. He met her at a dance in the Memorial Hall and then at the Rendezvous Café in Newent, where she worked at weekends as a waitress. His brother, John, began dating her sister and shortly after her 15th birthday Fred started to talk about marrying her and produced an engagement ring. This failed to get her to sleep with him so Fred started to see other girls at the same time. Fred would say: "I used to drop one off and then pop round to the other".

If he saw a girl he liked he would go straight over and talk to her, whether she had a boyfriend or not, but one day his luck ran out. Fred took his mum and John in to Newent and then drove back to a local youth club in Ledbury. He saw a girl he fancied and managed to get her to go outside on to the fire escape with him for some 'fresh air'. He tried to put his hand up her skirt but she immediately pushed him away and he fell down the fire escape stairs head-first. He was knocked unconscious and spent the night in the local hospital.

On the 14th June 1961, Fred's 13-year-old sister Kitty told their mother Daisy that Fred had had sex with her four or five times since the previous December when he had returned and she had become pregnant. The baby was later aborted. Fred was arrested and freely admitted to police that he had been molesting young girls since his early teens and asked: "Doesn't everybody do it?" Most of Fred's family disowned him and his mother banished him from her house. He moved into his Aunt Violet's home called Daisy Cottage in Much Marcle. His father also banned him from working on the farm with him so he took a job on a building site in Newent.

Not long after, on the 18ᵗʰ October, Fred appeared at Newent Magistrates Court where he was found guilty of 'Larceny as a servant'. He was fined £20 for stealing materials from the building site he had been working on. His only explanation was: "Everybody else was doing it".

It wasn't long before Fred appeared in court again, only this time he got very lucky. On the 9ᵗʰ November he stood trial at Hereford Assizes for the "illegal carnal knowledge" of his 13-year-old sister Kitty. At the trial, his physician, Dr Hardy, claimed that Fred was suffering from epileptic fits. Daisy, Fred's mother, surprisingly testified in his defence and when Kitty entered the witness box she refused to answer any of the questions put to her. Had Fred threatened her not to say anything? Had her parents told her to keep quiet so as not to break the family up? She was asked by Mr Justice Sachs, the trial judge, if it was her boyfriend or her brother who was responsible for her pregnancy. She shook her head. The judge asked her to speak up and, barely audible, she answered 'No' to both questions. The judge then passed her a pencil and piece of paper and asked her to write down the name of the person responsible. There was a long pause and she simply looked down at the floor. She was asked again to write the name of the person responsible but again she just stared at the floor. The judge sent her out of court for a few minutes to 'consider her decision'. When the court re-convened ten minutes later she still refused to say anything.

The judge then asked her "has someone told you not to say anything?" but still the girl didn't reply. He then asked the defence and prosecution if they 'felt it was safe' to continue to hear the case on the basis of a 'suspicion' that Fred West was guilty of incest. After a brief retirement, they announced that they did not wish to go on with the case. Ted Lewis, one of the jurors, recalled: "The reaction in the court was one of disbelief and despair. I couldn't believe it. The case should have gone on, we felt sure of that. Fred West had defeated the law. There's no doubt about it, that boy was guilty. Justice failed." Because the case against him had been dismissed, it did not appear on his criminal record.

Shortly after the trial, Fred celebrated with the local girl he had asked to marry him. He gave her a lift home one evening in his car but stopped suddenly at a gate and got out. Curious to know what was going on, the 15-year-old got out too and followed him. He told her that she had to marry him as soon as she turned 16 but she refused. All of a sudden he pushed her back on the bank and raped her. He then fell on his back on the floor, appearing to be unwell. When he had recovered, he apologized to her and told her not to be scared. They both then got back in the car and he drove her home.

7

Just after Christmas, Fred moved into a friends flat above an ice-cream parlour in Gloucester and got a new job at the local power station as a labourer. He continued to see his girlfriend and she turned up at the flat looking for her sister, who was going out with the friend Fred was sharing the flat with. "He pushed his way into the flat, threw me on to the bed and raped me", she was to recall some years later. As soon as the attack was over he said they should just sit and wait for her sister to arrive. Again, this attack went unreported.

In the last years of his life, Fred insisted that the girl "was mad in love with me, mind" and had become "one of the first big sex symbols for me...I had other girls but she was my first serious girlfriend...I was going to marry her, live in her house".

By now Fred, had heard that lorry-drivers were always picking up young hitchhikers so in the spring of 1962 he took a job driving for Ledbury Farmers, delivering grain from Avonmouth Docks to and from farms all over Herefordshire. He was allowed to move back home to Moorcourt Cottage as he had been found 'not guilty' at the trial and he wanted to save money.

In September 1962 Fred met his first wife. He had stopped in the town centre for a cup of tea and sandwich at The Milk Bar café and one of the waitresses was a 19-year-old girl he knew from school called Margaret Mackintosh. He knew her by her nickname of "Haggis" because she had spent so much of her life in Scotland. She had recently returned after a period of time in a borstal in Greenock on the Clyde. Another waitress in the café was a friend of hers she had met whilst in there and who had come down to try to start a new life for herself. Her name was Catherine Costello, but she was known to everyone as Rena.

Rena was born on the 14th April 1944 in Coatbridge, Scotland. Aged just 11, she appeared at Coatbridge Juvenile Court charged with theft. She was reprimanded and sent home. Less than a year later, she again appeared at Coatbridge Juvenile Court charged with theft. She appeared there for a third time charged with theft in 1957 and was given a two-year probationary sentence, but the following year was back in the court on another theft charge. She was found guilty and sent to an approved school.

In 1960, she started to work as a prostitute aged just 16. In December of the same year she and a friend were convicted of attempted burglary. She was sentenced at Airdrie Juvenile Court to borstal and she served 17 months.

In November 1961 she appeared in court in Glasgow charged with soliciting and was released with a caution. She started to hang around with a biker gang called 'The Skulls' and they were quite heavily in to drugs. She tried to go straight and got herself a job as a bus conductor in Glasgow while still at the approved school. It was here that she met Margaret Mackintosh. Shortly before Rena's 18th birthday in 1962 she was released and moved to Florence Street, where she began to train as a nurse whilst still working on the buses. She quickly became pregnant by one of the Pakistani bus drivers and in July she was convicted of theft and fined £2.

Margaret had by now moved back down to Herefordshire and was living with her parents and had got a job in the local café. She kept in contact with Rena and Rena decided that a change of scenery might do her good so in September she moved south to Ledbury and Margaret got her a job in the same café.

"Margaret was serving, and Rena was on a half-day off" Fred later recalled. "She said, 'This is my mate Rena' and Rena looked a fair picture. Fair play, she was a beautiful looking woman, girl, like. Well, Rena said, 'Can I come with you, like?' and she did. I delivered, then picked up another load, then went back to the café and dropped her off."

The following day Fred took Rena out with him again. They drove from Avonmouth to the Severn delivering his load of grain and on the way back they stopped off in a lay-by. "Rena told me she was 'on the run' from a convent in Glasgow", where she was supposed to be living under the terms of her parole, "and that she was pregnant". Fred told her that he had "learned to do abortions" during his time "away at sea" and that he could "help her out".

A few days later Margaret, Rena and Fred went to Dog Hill, near Much Marcle, and he tried to abort Rena's baby. He failed to do so and within a few days proposed to Rena. Fred introduced his brother John to the two women at this point and he started to date Margaret.

Rena agreed to marry Fred, probably more because she was looking for a way out of raising a baby on her own in a strange part of the country than because she was in love with him, but for Fred it "was only to get her out of the shit!"

On the 17th November 1962 they married at Ledbury Register Office, Herefordshire. The sole guests were Fred's brother John and Rena's friend Margaret. Five minutes before the ceremony was due to start Fred got cold feet and offered his brother £5 if he would take his place but John refused. "I'd be lying if I said I loved her", Fred would recall many years later. There was no party or reception. Instead, they stood in the street and drank a bottle of Bristol Cream Sherry that John had brought with him.

Fred's other brother, Doug, recalled: "We didn't know Fred was getting married until afterwards. He came back and said he had got married. He didn't tell the family; only John knew about the wedding. He was best man. When he came back and said that he had got married we thought he

9

was joking. That was Fred all over. If he decided to do it he just went ahead and did it. He was a bit secretive. He would go and do things without thinking and that was that."

Fred and Rena on their wedding day

Doug West would later recall going on a night out with the newly-wed couple: "We went out and we was at the pub and a bloke tried to chat her up and she'd just about had enough and she warned him and he wouldn't take the warning and that was it. The next thing he was getting up off the floor. I mean, she did literally lay him out, I mean fair do's, she did pack a wallop. Otherwise, she was very friendly."

Fred moved in with Rena and stayed in the flat she shared with Margaret Mackintosh. After ten days staying at the tiny flat above the New Inn at Ledbury they decided to move to Glasgow. Fred's brother, John, drove them to Birmingham where they caught a train for the rest of the journey. Fred would maintain the lie that the father of Rena's baby "ran a string of corner shops", and had "offered him a job as her minder" before they left Ledbury.

On the 28th November Fred and Rena moved into a flat at 46 Hospital Street in Coatbridge. It wasn't long before Fred started to beat his pregnant wife, not because they drank, even though Fred reckoned that Rena could "sink a bottle of Johnnie Walker Red Label a day", but because she refused to give in to his sexual demands. "That is when I realized that I was the bloody keeper of her. I didn't own her." He would bruise her around the face first and act as her pimp although he would say that he was more her driver than her pimp as she worked for the father of Rena's baby. "I was mixed up with these bloody Indians and that. But I got the motor and the money, and I played it through."

Fred was known to have had a string of affairs while in Scotland and one of these affairs was with a young girl who had been injured in a factory. As a result of this she had lost all of her fingers and both thumbs in a guillotine. This would later bear a distinguishing similarity to how some of his victims were found in 1994. He is also believed to have fathered a child (possible named Gareth) from another affair.

In 1963 Rena wrote to Walter and Daisy West to tell them that she had "lost the baby" she had been expecting; but barely a month later she wrote again, this time to tell them that she and Fred had "adopted" another baby, a mixed-race child whom they had christened Charmaine. It is believed that this was because Fred had told Rena that his family would never accept that she had become pregnant by a Pakistani and that the baby wasn't white, and therefore could not be his. Claiming that the baby was adopted meant they could overcome that hurdle.

Charmaine Carol May West was born at the Alexander Hospital, Glasgow, on the 22nd March 1963. No fathers name appears on her birth certificate. Fred didn't attend the birth and he actually spent the night in bed with one of Rena's sisters. Rena originally called the baby Mary but Fred didn't like the name and it was changed to Charmaine.

She was christened on the 9th June at St Mary's Roman Catholic Church. "The registrar of births threatened to take me to court" Fred insisted years later, because he wouldn't register her name as 'West', and he did so only after repeated threats from the Scottish authorities.

After bringing Charmaine home, Rena began working again as a prostitute and Fred's sexual demands started to increase. He demanded it at any time of day no matter where they were or what they were doing. If she refused he would beat her in to submission and taunt her that "she only liked doing it with other men", though he seemed to find that arousing.

He soon found himself a job working as a 'Mr Whippy' ice cream man, renting his van directly from Walls. He would often not get home until the early hours of the morning and neighbours gossiped about his night-time activities. In the first few weeks of his new job he and Rena moved into Glasgow itself, first to Shettleston and then in to a dilapidated flat at 25 Savoy Street, Bridgeton, on one of the most decayed areas at the city's heart, not far from St Enoch's station in the early summer of 1963.

The new flat was close to the home of two notorious paedophiles: James Gallogley, a church elder who was later jailed for 10 years, and bus driver Alexander Gartshore, who would have stood trial for the murder of 11-year-old Moira Anderson on the 23rd February 1957, before he died in 2006 after a cold-case review.

Sandra Brown, Alexander Gartshore's daughter, recalled many years later: "My dad would be ten years older than Jimmy Gallogley. Fred West would be younger than Jimmy Gallogley but my mother never understood what the friendship was all about. I've no idea how paedophiles in those days would have found each other. It's very clear now the internet plays a big part in that. I think this gang preyed on that type of child (from troubled backgrounds) knowing that questions would not be asked."

As a child, Sandra knew Rena and their fathers also knew each other. They lived very close by and Rena and her friends, who were a couple of years older, taught Sandra and her friends games to play. Years later, as Rena had returned to Glasgow and had Charmaine, Sandra recalled seeing her again one day on a bus, but they didn't talk to each other and Rena was watching for the reactions of the other passengers to her mixed-race baby.

When Fred was not working on his ice-cream van he would drive Rena to her clients, leaving one of her sisters (probably the one he was having an affair with) or a friend to look after Charmaine. Fred would recall: "Whenever these certain blokes walked in I was given £5 to fuck off, and I went."

Even though Fred would beat Rena with astonishing regularity she would often give as good as she'd got. "She knocked me out cold on three occasions, with one blow." He also noticed that she was now carrying a cut-throat razor and another knife for protection. "You didn't mess with Rena. Nobody did. No matter how big they were, she'd drop 'em. She was a vicious type if she wanted to be", Fred would later recall.

Rena was well aware that Fred's rounds on his ice-cream van meant that he met many young women with young children. Fred's old habits had not died away. He would park up in a side street, look out for a particular young woman that took his fancy, then engage her in conversation and offer her a lift. "I had masses of girlfriends at the time, hundreds of them", he would later boast. But it wasn't just women he was interested in…

Colin MacFarlane, then aged 10, recalled: "It (the Gorbals) was very, very rough at the time so for a little English man to arrive there in an ice cream van… it was a completely incongruous thing to do. Word had got around that he had a fascination with girls aged 12 or so." He was given the nickname of 'Fred the Perv'. One day Colin called him that and Fred grabbed a rope and threatened to strangle him. "All of a sudden I just realized that I was perhaps looking into the eyes of a potential murderer."

Fred and Rena had started to get on a little better and started to go out to pubs and clubs. Rena even tattooed her name on Fred's arm in blue Indian ink. In October of the same year Fred took Rena to Barrowland, Glasgow's dance hall, where Rena got very drunk while Fred stuck to his one glass of Shandy. "We stopped off half-way home and I give her one in

12

the back of the car" he would later recall. By the time Fred took Rena and Charmaine back to Much Marcle for Christmas, Rena was pregnant with their first child together. Rena didn't want Fred's baby and attempted an abortion, only this time without Fred's help. "I think she shoved a knitting-needle up herself" Fred recalled. She was taken to Bells Hill Maternity Hospital, where staff managed to save the baby.

Rena knew that Fred would not forgive her for attempting to abort his child. Afraid of a violent retaliation, she decided to leave Glasgow and went to Much Marcle to visit Fred's sister Daisy. Fred enjoyed having time to himself and "spent the rest of the week in bed with one of the beautifulest women in Scotland", a girl he insisted was "a mate of the pop singer Lulu." He assumed that Rena would be gone for at least a fortnight but, aware the baby was due any time, Rena returned to Glasgow early in order to get things sorted out for the arrival of the baby. On the train home, however, Rena went in to labour. When she got off the train she took a taxi home and found Fred in bed with the woman he had spent the week with.

According to Fred, Rena burst in to the bedroom and said: "You two better get out of that bloody bed and let me in!" They sent the girl to the phone box in the street to call the midwife, but by the time she returned Fred himself had delivered the baby. On the 6th July 1964 Anne Marie Kathleen Daisy West was born, although she was originally named Hannah.

On the 28th August Rena wrote a letter to Fred's mother Daisy. The contents showed how Rena was struggling to cope with the new baby. "Hannah does nothing but cry day and night." As the new baby was his own flesh and blood Fred took more of an interest in her than he ever did in Charmaine. Charmaine had become a nuisance to him and he didn't think twice about hitting her, as he hit Rena, but never laid a finger on Anne Marie. He made her a cot out of a wooden orange box and put it under the counter of his ice-cream van and took her with him when he went out on his rounds, leaving Charmaine with Rena.

When Fred got home in the early hours of the morning he would demand sex from Rena, whether she was in the mood or not. There would be arguments, often violent, and reconciliation sex. Fred would insist: "Me and Rena would always make love after, no matter how bad we fell out with each other."

Rena took to drink to help her cope (a bottle of Scotch a day, according to Fred) but he insisted that, rather than make her aggressive, she became "rather loving actually".

She took Anne Marie and Charmaine with her to Much Marcle to show them off to Fred's parents, and a strange bond began to develop between Fred's father Walter and Rena. He began to call her 'Cath' rather than 'Rena' and the rest of the family noticed how close they became.

13

A few months later, at Christmas, Fred took his family back to Much Marcle, as he always did, and was introduced for the first time to his brother John's fiancé. She had been badly burned in an accident when her night-dress caught fire. John took Fred, Rena and the children up to Birmingham, where she had been sent due to the severity of her injuries, and Fred's first remark when he met her in her hospital bed was "Christ, you're not marrying that, are you?" Rena told her privately that she should be thankful she was engaged to John and not his brother Fred.

When Fred and Rena returned to Glasgow shortly after Christmas they moved for the third time into a tenement flat at 241 McLellan Street in Kinning Park, one of the longest streets in Glasgow. Beyond the flat was a set of allotments on which families could grow vegetables and flowers. Fred hired a plot but barely bothered to cultivate the land. Instead he used the small shed, which came with it, as a hideaway to have sex with the various girls he had picked up on his ice-cream rounds. Despite hardly using the land, he is remembered for guarding a specific part of it jealously but no-one could figure out why. He told one of his neighbours that he was saving that section of the land for "something special" and was seen working over the soil in the early hours of the morning.

Could he have started killing and burying bodies there? Four young girls similar in age and physical characteristics to those Fred was later charged with murdering in Gloucestershire are known to have disappeared during the time Fred lived in Glasgow. However, the only real possibility of a search by Strathclyde Police at the site would arise if Rose West were to pass on the crucial information that her husband had boasted of earlier killings in Glasgow. Police were unable to search here during the original investigation in 1994 as the allotments were concreted over in the 1970's as a section of the M8 motorway expansion.

Rena would normally only work in the evenings so her daytime was spent looking after the children and shopping. She would sometimes visit the local bookmakers called Telky's and it was here that she met a man named John McLachlan, a local bus driver.

He vividly recalled their first meeting in the bookies which left him asking a friend: "Who was that smasher?" Although a married man, he was introduced to Rena a few days later in a mutual friends flat below where she was staying with Fred. Norrie Mason lived in the flat with his wife Sarah and when Norrie and John went back to the flat after a day in the bookies they found Rena in there talking to Sarah. They all had a drink and a laugh together, but then John recalled: "I remember seeing a face at the window, a dark face, a head of curly hair", and he opened the door to see who it was. Fred then "came charging in and grabbed Rena, and pulled her up the stairs. He was belting her on the way up." John then went upstairs and witnessed Fred beating Rena. "He was kicking the shit out of her. She had bruises everywhere. It was sadism."

John and Rena soon began an affair and he grew increasingly shocked at Rena's bruises and black eyes. But John stood up for Rena, and every time it was obvious that she had been hit John would find Fred and beat him. On one occasion Fred discovered the pair in an embrace. He punched Rena, making her scream. John then punched Fred, but Fred drew a knife and grazed John's stomach with it. John managed to hit Fred a second time and Fred backed off. John recollected that "He couldn't tackle a man, but he wasn't so slow in attacking women."

On a further occasion, John McLachlan witnessed Charmaine – little older than a toddler – ask Fred for an ice cream from his van and in response, Fred slapped her across the head, resulting in John beating Fred up again. "Any ordinary man would have given the child some ice cream, but instead he smashed her round the head with his hand... he was a violent and sadistic bastard who enjoyed beating up women and kids."

Rena had grown tired of Fred and his violent and sexual demands. She would spend as much time as she could with John McLachlan, but if he was busy then she would spend time in the nearby Victoria Café in Scotland Street. That spring she met two young women at the café. Isa McNeil and Ann McFall worked together at Livingston Industrial Clothing on Kilmarnock Road and had known each other since childhood. Isa was the older of the two at 18 while Ann was just 16. Ann was despondent over the recent death of her boyfriend Duncan McLeish. He had been electrocuted at work while climbing into the cabin of a crane. The voltage was so high that the coins in his pockets were burned into his thighs.

Isa and Ann spent a lot of their time at the West's flat. When they went out they would wheel Anne Marie in her pram while Charmaine walked along beside them holding their hands.

Isa was going out with a friend of John McLachlan's called John Trotter, and she and Rena started going out together in the evenings to the pubs along Paisley Road with their boyfriends.

In July, Rena invited the older of the two girls, Isa, to move in with her, Fred and the children to work as their 'Nanny'. After just a week, Isa had seen the violence that Fred would reign on Rena and Charmaine and described his as like 'Jekyll and Hyde'.

Fred insisted that his daughters should sleep together on the bottom mattress of a pair of bunkbeds, and he nailed a set of vertical slats across the space between the upper and lower bunks so that they couldn't get out. He insisted to Isa that the two girls were to stay in there while he was in the flat and they should be fed, changed and made to play there. He would sometimes allow Anne Marie out but never Charmaine.

Rena seemed to cling to John McLachlan for support and their sexual relationship contributed to the break-up of his marriage. Rena talked about leaving Fred and moving in with him and she would often tell him about Fred's obsession with sex. She kept telling John that all she wanted was to be allowed to live in peace with her kids. John would later recall that Rena had told him that "He (Fred) knew a lot of the women. He'd talk to them, and fanny about. He would be away till all hours. Most of the (ice cream) drivers brought their van back at eleven or twelve, but he was out in his till three or four in the morning."

Ann McFall

Fred started to spend entire nights away from the flat. One reason was that he was involved with one of the young women he had picked up on his rounds, a 20-year-old Scottish woman called Margaret McAvoy. "She'd walk hundreds of miles just to be with me", he would recall and later on she started to "help on the van at nights when I was busy." She became pregnant by Fred in the autumn on 1965. Margaret, who worked in a factory bottling mineral water went on to give birth to a boy named Steven. In 1995, Margaret said of this time: "He was my first love and I will always love him." She said she ended the affair when she discovered that Fred was married to Rena. She recalled how she met Fred when he was working one day. "He was fantastically good looking. He had some kind of magnetism. He was a real charmer." She said they first had sex after Fred had knocked down a 4-year-old boy with his van. She said he turned up at the house of one of her friends in his car. "The police knew it was an accident and Fred wasn't charged but he was terribly upset. It was the first time I made love to anyone but Fred was very caring and gentle, not at all perverted like it said on the news."

It was 15:10 on the 4th November 1965 when Fred ran over and killed a 4-year-old boy called Henry Feeney with his ice-cream van near Stravanan Road in Castlemilk. Although cleared of any wrongdoing by the police, Fred feared the hostile reaction and potential reprisals for the accident. Fred would recall this incident in later interviews. He said that he had grown to view the boy "like a son" and had bought him a ball the day before the accident. Fred said that when he drove into the cul-de-sac he saw the boy playing with it and it went over the hedge into a garden. Fred reversed the ice-cream van and went back a couple of feet when he heard "an almighty bang." He looked in the mirror and could see the boy laying under the back axel. He remembered that the child's father came to see what the commotion was and that the crowd had to hold him back from getting to him. "At first I thought it was a bad dream. I dashed from the house to the accident but there was nothing I could do", the boys father remembered. Robert Riley, who was there at the time recalled: "The ice cream van came up and then reversed over the wee boy and went over his head. There was a great deal of hysteria at the time." Another witness, Tom McGougan, recalled: "There was an angry mob and they didn't believe Wests story that it was an accident. They began shouting and swearing and banging on the van windows. The crowd was going to lynch him."

Fred was taken to hospital. "I was put under sedatives in Glasgow Royal, and then I discharged myself after a while and I went home."

What happened next isn't entirely clear. What is known for sure is that Fred hurriedly left Scotland and took Anne Marie and Charmaine with him, but left Rena behind. Fred gave conflicting accounts of what happened when he left the hospital. One account he gave was that he went straight home and found his flat full of a motorcycle gang called 'The Skulls'. He said that both John McLachlan and John Trotter were members of the gang and he said he found Rena "starkers" in bed with two of the gang and with another two sat on the end of the bed. He said he tried to hit one of them but ended up accidentally punching Rena and "she went out cold." He said the shock made him pass out and when he came too the police and ambulance were there and the gang had disappeared. The police then arrested him, but let him go and told him to go back to the hospital, which he did. Whilst there he was very upset and ended up assaulting a nurse, which lead to him being arrested for a second time and put in "Barlinnie prison for the night." The following morning, in court, he said that the judge cleared him but advised him to get legal advice regarding his marriage. But when he got outside the court Rena and the gang were there waiting for him and told him that he was "a dead man." He said he was so scared that he went to live with Margaret McAvoy and took a job delivering timber for a timber yard rather than return to his round for Walls.

In his second version of what happened Fred said that Rena's former lover, the father of Charmaine, threw him out of the house when he discovered that Anne Marie was not mixed-race and therefore wasn't his. He said that The Pakistani 'Billy Boy' threw Anne Marie's clothes into the car and Rena came down from the flat with Anne Marie in her arms and "chucked her in through the window to me and said 'Get out before he gets you'." In this version there is no mention of how he came to end up with Charmaine, which he certainly did, and Charmaine's father was actually a student studying for his degree at this time, so it can be discounted.

The third version he gave, in the book he started to write while in prison, stated that it was Ann McFall who helped him to leave and helped him to take the children from Rena. He said that Rena was out selling her body until 4 or 5 in the morning and would come home drunk. He said that Ann rang him at work to tell him when Rena was out with the biker gang so he went home and they came up with a plan where he would have to hit her so that she could say Fred took the children by force.

However, Colin MacFarlane remembered Fred's departure differently. "If you had a complaint about a suspected paedophile you could actually approach gang members who would sort them out for you." He recalled a senior gang member searching for Fred at the time and asked Colin if he had seen Fred. Colin replied that Fred hadn't been on his rounds for a few days and he was told to tell him if he came back. The gang promised any young members who 'did Fred in' would be rewarded. Minutes later, Fred appeared in his van. "The guys saw him and they all ran towards the van with their big knives and razors. Fred saw this, panicked, and sped off."

On the 11th December 1965 Fred returned to Much Marcle with Charmaine and Anne Marie, but without Rena. He told his parents about his accident and the death of the young boy and then asked his mother and sisters if they would look after the two girls while he went out and got a job to pay them for doing so. But his mother Daisy did not like Charmaine and refused to accept her because she was mixed-race.

Fred got a job trimming and skinning hides and drove the truck for the abattoir. Just three days later Fred asked Hereford Social Services to take Charmaine and Anne Marie in to care. The two girls were in 'a deplorable state' and social services had to "clothe them pretty well from scratch."

Fred recalled that "When I got back I went round all my old girlfriends", even "making love to one on the altar of the church down the road." His methods hadn't changed. He would tour the area in his car, looking for a young woman who he would follow until he decided she might be tempted, or physically persuaded, to have sex with him.

In early February 1966 Fred persuaded his sister Daisy and her husband Frank to act as guarantors for a new caravan for him to live in. He sold his blue Vauxhall Viva that he had bought in Scotland to make up the rest. The caravan was delivered to The Willows Caravan Site, Sandhurst Lane, just outside Gloucester.

On the 23rd February Rena joined Fred. He drove his abattoir truck to collect her from Gloucester Railway Station. She had reluctantly agreed to move south, provided Isa McNeil could come with her, as her relationship with John McLachlan was on the verge of breaking up and she desperately wanted to see her children. Ann McFall also joined them as she wanted the chance to start a new life, but she had already hinted to Isa that she was infatuated with Fred and Isa recalls that "she kinda flaunted herself at him."

Charmaine and Anne Marie were returned to Fred and Rena from care. Fred insisted that "Ann got hold of Anne Marie and was kissing her for about 20 minutes… I could feel her love."

Fred and Rena shared the small bedroom at the front of the caravan, while Isa and Ann slept on the U-shaped sofa in the lounge. The children slept together in a single bed that pulled out from the wall. As in Glasgow, the three women were told not to take the children far off the caravan site while he was at work. Fred said that he would pop back at random times during the day to make sure they were where they should be, and if they were not where he expected them to be he would scream at them.

It wasn't long before the violence returned. He would return from work covered in blood and offal and demand his dinner. If it wasn't immediately available he would hit Rena or throw boiling hot water over her. If Rena tried to stop him hitting Charmaine for any reason he would hit them both even harder. Isa and Ann would take the children out of the caravan so they didn't witness Fred hitting their mother.

By April Fred had begun to demonstrate even more dominance over the three women. This was probably due to the fact that the three women didn't have anyone to stand up to him, as John McLachlan had done for them in Glasgow. He was prone to violent mood swings and it was almost always Rena and Isa who bore the brunt of his anger, although he physically attacked Charmaine on more than one occasion. He was encouraging Rena to turn back to prostitution and he was also starting to sexually abuse Charmaine.

Within six weeks Rena had decided that she couldn't take any more. Isa McNeil telephoned the Victoria Café in Scotland from the phone box at the entrance to the caravan site and left a message for John McLachlan, asking him to phone her back on that number later in the evening. When he did so she pleaded with him to come and collect her, Ann, Rena and the children as soon as he could. He said he would and they arranged a time when Fred was going to be out at work.

A few days later John McLachlan phoned again, at a pre-arranged time, and told her that he and John Trotter would be down later that week and asked her to meet them beside the telephone box at the entrance to the caravan site.

In spite of the beatings, in spite of the abuse of his children, in spite of his boasting about how other women found him attractive, Ann McFall had convinced herself that she could change Fred. She could make him happy. When Isa had told her of the plan to leave, Ann absorbed every detail and then betrayed her friends by telling Fred.

When John McLachlan and John Trotter arrived at the entrance to the caravan site on the pre-arranged morning in a borrowed Mini, Rena and Isa were ready, but Ann was slower and dragging her heels. Within fifteen minutes Fred suddenly appeared. She had delayed them for long enough. He walked calmly onto the site but an argument quickly broke out. Rena ran into the caravan to collect her coat but Fred followed her inside and started hitting her. When he re-emerged holding Charmaine, John McLachlan punched him in the stomach hoping that he would let her go. Isa could see that Fred wasn't about to let her go and set off with her suitcase for the car. She told Ann to hurry up and get her belongings but she just stood at the entrance to the caravan with Anne Marie in her arms, shaking her head slowly. Rena tried to pry Charmaine from Fred but not even a second punch from John McLachlan could make him let go. Isa shouted at Ann to get moving but she said she was going to say and be the girls 'nanny'.

A uniformed police constable suddenly appeared on a bicycle and the argument came to an abrupt end. Rena and Isa climbed into the back of the Mini, while the two John's got in the front. They then sped off before the policeman could get off his bicycle.

Fred and Ann then became a couple. Fred's brother Doug recalled: "Fred used to come home with her and she was a sweet girl, I suppose. But she used to follow me around the garden like a puppy dog. And I mean, I wasn't all that worried at the time and then of course she went with Fred and that was the end, I never seen her then."

Ann McFall

By the beginning of July 1966 Fred and Ann McFall had come to the attention of the Gloucester Children's Department. An internal memorandum suggested that Ann McFall was being difficult and that Fred was anxious for her to leave the caravan as there was not much room. It also suggested that although Rena had left the family home in the caravan, she was planning to return. Whenever child care officers visited the caravan, the children greeted Fred with lots of affection and reported that Fred was the one stable and caring factor in their lives.

Rena spent part of the intervening months living with Isa McNeil in a tiny flat in Arden Street in Maryhill, Glasgow and had taken a job as a bus conductor at the same depot that John McLachlan worked from as a driver. She rapidly got herself a dubious reputation at the bus depot by offering to have sex with any driver or conductor who was interested, but on the 29th July Rena returned to Fred alone. Isa McNeil couldn't be persuaded to join her due to her upcoming wedding. Fred reassured Ann that Rena would not be staying for long in Gloucester, but he also warned her that Rena could be dangerous. He suggested that she should stay in a friends caravan on the site while his wife was back. Ann did as she was told and even found herself a job in a bakery in Court's Road, Gloucester.

On the 1st August Fred and Rena were visited by a child care officer. Gloucester Children's Department reported that Fred's 'little angel' (Ann McFall) had returned to Glasgow, but according to Fred: "Rena and the yobs came down" and Rena threw Ann McFall out of the caravan. "I felt

21

sorry for Anna. The only thing Anna had done wrong in her life was to fall in love with me."

Fred's perverted sexual practices continued and it's believed that he was sleeping with both Rena, Ann and possibly various young girls. John West's wife, Catherine, remembered: "John used to go and see him." After one of these visits John told her that Fred liked to "tie women up and have sex with them", and that "Rena would be present and participate." He went on to explain that Fred and Rena were befriending the young girls they treated in this way. It is widely believed that Rena was sleeping with John but Ann McFall refused. This may be what eventually cost her her life.

Around this time Fred became friendly with a boy called Robin Holt who knew Ann Mcfall. He was a "nice looking" 15-year-old boy who Fred found "sat on a gate crying" on the lane that led to The Willows Caravan Site. Fred became friendly with him and often took him out in his lorry when he went out picking up hides, skins and offal.

Rena went back to Scotland and on the late August Bank Holiday Fred took advantage of her absence to tow his caravan to another site where he hoped she would not be able to track him and Ann McFall down. The site he chose was behind 'The Flying Machine Pub' in Brockworth called Watermead. Here, he met a man named Terrence Crick. Shortly afterwards, Fred also got a new job in the hope that Rena wouldn't be able to trace him. He left his job at the slaughterhouse and took to driving a sewage lorry, emptying septic tanks.

He didn't manage to hide for long and barely a month later Rena turned up at the Watermead caravan site. Fred went to great pains to disguise his relationship with Ann and he sent her to live with a friend back at Sandhurst Lane. In the weeks to come Fred split his time between the two caravan sites and women.

Despite juggling the two women and having Robin Holt with him when he was working, he still went out touring the countryside in search of young women. There were more than half a dozen violent sexual assaults on young women in the Gloucester area during the time that Fred was a resident at the two caravan sites, including one on a 15-year-old girl in the city. Many of them were carried out by a man whose description fitted Fred West, but at the time he was never suspected or questioned.

One night Fred went out with Rena and a man who he would describe as his wife's pimp, Rolf. They went to the Bamboo Club in Bristol where they had a drink and a dance. He said that when they left the club Rena announced that she was taking him to a party, but that he needed to be blindfolded. Fred said that "We went down some steps and in the basement of a house. Rena took off the blindfold. I cold not see, it was so dark. There were flashing lights, red, blue and yellow. It was full of black people and a smell of drugs. There were four small tables in two rooms with what looked like Christmas cakes made with Christmas paper. Two spotlights came on. The paper was ripped up. There were these young girls in them. They were drugged. They were handed round to drugged and drunken men…I got out of there after fourteen hours."

Fred mention 'Rolf' a few times when talking about his past, and usually when something bad had happened. There has never been any indication that this person ever existed.

Rena found out that Fred was still seeing Ann McFall and on the 11th October Rena stole an iron, some cigarettes and money from Ann's caravan and fled back to Glasgow. She was arrested on the 16th November and returned to Gloucester to face justice. In one of the many coincidences of this case it was a young WPC Hazel Savage who was sent up to Scotland to bring Rena back. On the journey back Rena confided to her that Fred was a sexual pervert and unfit to raise their children. Hazel Savage would be the officer who wouldn't let the case drop of Fred's missing daughter Heather and go on to arrest him in 1994.

On the 29th November Rena stood trial for housebreaking and theft at Gloucester Quarter Sessions. Her counsel, John McNaught, pleaded for leniency, saying "this offence was the actions of a jealous woman", and adding that if she were sent to prison "her children must go in to care." Fred testified at the hearing, where he admitted that he and Ann McFall were living together, but added that he intended to pay her fare back to Scotland. Rena was sentenced to three years' probation. He had succeeded in pulling the wool over the courts eyes. Rena moved back to Scotland and he moved Ann McFall back in with him at Watermead.

In December, in order to keep up the pretence, Ann McFall told a social worker that there was now nothing between her and Fred and she suggested that the best thing was "to leave the caravan." She even told the social worker that Fred planned to 'artificially inseminate' her if she didn't fall pregnant with his child soon.

Fred's version of the next few weeks was as follows: He took Ann to his parents in Much Marcle together with Charmaine and Anne Marie. He drove them there in his tanker and then went off to make a series of deliveries before going back to collect them. When he arrived back "Ann was talking to my mother in the front room… You had to be special for my mother to let you in there. Rena had never been in the front room. We were never allowed in there." Ann and his mother "got on well. That was the first girl I had my mother took to. I felt wonderful about it."

There were a number of attacks on women at this time, and other mysterious events, that are of particular interest and were looked at by detectives working on the later murder enquiry. Eight violent sex assaults were committed on young women in the Gloucestershire area between December 1965 and January 1967 by men fitting Fred's description. These include a girl in Cheltenham who was struck on the head when walking near her home, a 15-year-old who was grabbed in Gloucester and a nurse who had her jaw broken during an attack.

Janette Clarke, 16 at the time, recalled that she was stalked by a man she later identified as Fred West in Gloucester in November or December 1966. On her way home, she found herself walking close to his car and glanced at him. "He just glanced at me. I did not feel comfortable because there was nobody else about". Moments later he pulled up in front of her, flung open the door and said: 'Have you got the time?' "I felt uneasy and I ran. I didn't know what fear was until then" she explained. Two nights later the man followed her again in his car, and this time she froze. "I didn't know what to do. I just froze. I couldn't move. I couldn't scream." It was only the arrival of her younger sister that frightened him away. "She ran up and banged on the car door and told him to bugger off." When shown a photograph of Fred West in court at Rose West's trial in 1995 she said: "Oh God, that's the one." She said she screamed at the TV and dropped some mugs of tea when his face flashed up on the screen at home. "I have never forgotten him. It was something from the past, and I never forgot his face."

At about the same time in 1966, another young woman (known only as 'Mrs C' at Rose West's trial) accepted a lift from a man she later identified as Fred West when she was hitchhiking from a bus stop to Cheltenham to see her boyfriend. During the journey he pulled into a lane and stopped the car. He told her to remove her knickers but she refused. He then exposed himself, but when she tried to get out of the car to run, he hauled her back by throwing his arm around her throat. "He pulled into a lane. He grabbed my body. I can't remember the precise details but it was a sexual and physical attack…I managed to get halfway out of the car and he had his arm around my throat dragging me back into the car." She then told how he masturbated in front of her. Afterwards "he was charming, pleasant, laughing." Both young women reported the attacks to the police, but no policeman ever questioned Fred West.

On the 18th February 1967 Robin Holt was seen in Much Marcle. Fred had taken him to Moorcourt Cottage and was seen by Fred's sister and other members of his family. No-one saw him after this and he was reported missing two days later. On the 1st March his half-naked body was found hanged in a disused cow shed near The Willows caravan site and the

Longford Inn on the Tewkesbury Road near Gloucester. He was discovered by a farm worker who had gone looking for firewood. Pornographic magazines with nooses drawn around the necks of the models were found on a manger near his body. The pathologist who inspected the body said he had been dead for around ten days. His death was treated as suicide, but the possibility remains that Robin Holt was murdered by Fred West, as no one could figure out exactly how he could have hung himself.

Shortly after Ann McFall's 18th birthday in April, the Gloucester Authorities were indicating their concern about the children in writing. An official reported that they were 'extremely worried about these children, who are being looked after by Annie McFall, who is expecting Mr West's baby.' The report also noted that the caravan 'had become dilapidated'.

On the 1st July Rena returned to Fred, Charmaine and Anne Marie at the Watermead Caravan Site. Fred again moved his pregnant girlfriend out of his caravan, firstly to another caravan on the site, and then back to a smaller caravan at The Willows. Rena stayed less than a fortnight, as on the 12th July Charmaine and Anne Marie were sent to live with a short-term foster family. The local authority reported that, understandably, the children 'are now thoroughly confused'.

Letters posted by Ann McFall to both her family and Isa McNeil in Glasgow between 1966 and 1967 indicated that she believed a relationship with Fred would offer her a better life than that she had experienced in Scotland and she is known to have tried to persuade Fred to get a divorce from Rena in order that he could then marry her. It may have been her insistence that he divorce Rena that lead to her murder, as it appears to have happened again years later, when Shirley Robinson fell pregnant to Fred and she insisted that she should be the next 'Mrs West'.

In August, a seven-month's pregnant Ann McFall went missing. She was last seen at a fair in Gloucester. Her disappearance was not reported to the police. Although Fred went to great pains to deny that he had murdered her to the police and his solicitor, he did confide to one visitor whilst he was in prison during the final investigation in 1994 that he had stabbed her to death following an argument. Nonetheless, this explanation is inconsistent with the fact that Ann's wrists were found with sections of dressing gown cord wrapped around them, suggesting she had been restrained prior to her murder. It has been suggested that Fred and Ann had been arguing towards the end and that at least one reason for these arguments was her refusal to sleep with Fred's brother John.

Whatever the reason, Fred would tell the police and his solicitor in 1994 that she was already dead when he found her. While on remand in

Winson Green Prison he told his solicitor, Howard Ogden, that Ann used to accuse him of thinking of Rena and putting her first. He admitted that he and Ann had made plans to run away together and that he was all for it, but when Rena was around he wasn't so keen.

He said that he told Rena that Ann had left him, but as usual he had just moved her to a different caravan site while Rena was back. He said that he got home from work at around 23:30 and parked his lorry in the road as it wasn't allowed on the site. He said he went in the back way towards Ann's caravan and found Rena and his friend 'Rolf' there. He noticed a large suitcase in the caravan and Rena was "absolutely out of her brains". He claimed he asked where Ann was and Rolf told him to join him outside. He said that once there, 'Rolf' told him that Rena had stabbed Ann by accident, and he believed him because Rena was "so drugged out of her brains". He said he didn't know whether Rolf was there when Rena stabbed Ann but he had never seen the suitcase before, and that Rolf told him that was where they had put Ann. He told Fred that they had no choice but to take the suitcase containing Ann's body and dump it on Gloucester tip, but Fred said they couldn't do that and she would have to be buried at their 'special place'.

He said they drove out to Fingerpost Field in Much Marcle, where he and Rolf dug a hole while Rena sat in the car with Ann's body. He said that once they'd dug the hole he and 'Rolf' walked back over the field to collect Ann's body but it was actually 'Rolf' and Rena who drove the car over the field, put Ann in the hole and then drove back up to him. He was sat by a water tank where he was splashing his face with water. He insisted then that they went back to Gloucester and the case disappeared, but he insisted that her body hadn't been touched in anyway.

The following day Fred said that he went to his parents house and he told his father, Walter, what had happened and they both walked up to where Ann was buried. He then contradicted himself by admitting that "when I buried Ann I went straight to Dad." Walter apparently told him "I'm your father, I'm not going to turn you in…if you can live with it I'll say nothing."

What is known is that within a few days Walter had told his wife Daisy about what had happened to Ann McFall as one evening, later in the month, Daisy went to see Fred's brother John and his wife at Bushy Cottage where she broke down and cried at the kitchen table. She told them: "Freddie's killed the girl and buried her in Kempley Woods." After she left, John's wife kept asking him if she meant he had killed the girl who was pregnant. John told her that Fred had thrown Ann out after she had already packed her bags. He then refused to discuss it with her any further.

Just a few weeks later Fred, Rena, Charmaine and Anne Marie moved to number 17, Lake House Caravan Park in Bishop's Cleeve and Fred got a new job working at an animal feed in the village. Rena went back to prostitution, sometimes using the caravan as her base and Fred went out looking for young girls again. He would tell them that they were "sitting on a fortune", but that they "don't always know about it." He would insinuate that he knew more about sex than the girls' boyfriends and started to invite them back to his caravan to see his 'pictures'. As they climbed in to the caravan, Fred would quickly lock the door behind him and peer through the drawn curtains to see if anyone had seen them. More often than not, the 'pictures' showed his wife Rena in sexually explicit poses.

Michael Newman, who lived in a caravan on the site, recalled that Fred "was in a dark, strange mood at times. He was almost in a dream world." There is also an eyewitness account of Fred inappropriately touching Charmaine around this time. Rena's friend Margaret saw him lying on his back in the caravan with Charmaine, naked and aged about five, astride his crotch. "She'll cum if I carry on", Fred told her.

2 MARY BASTHOLM

In 1967, when she was aged just 15, Mary Jane Bastholm was often seen in the company of teenagers who frequented a café on Southgate Street, Gloucester, known as the 'Pop-in' and during the course of that year she took a job there as a waitress. Fred West was a regular visitor to the café and he did some building work behind it. Mary was seen in the company of a young woman who resembled Ann McFall and there was a witness who has claimed to have seen Mary in Fred's car on more than one occasion.

Within a few weeks of Ann McFall's murder, Fred turned up at his parents' cottage in Much Marcle with another young woman, but no-one commented. The girl was slim, short and blonde, with hair shorter than Ann McFall's, 5'3" tall and aged 15 or 16. It's possible that this girl was Mary Bastholm.

At 20:15 on the 6th January 1968, Mary went missing from a bus stop on Bristol Road in Gloucester. She was on her way to her 19-year-old boyfriend Tim Merrett's house in the village of Quedgeley. The last time she was seen, she was wearing a knee-length navy blue coat with vertical pin stripes and a navy jumper with blue cardigan along with a lime green pleated mini-skirt and navy blue shoes. She was carrying a royal blue umbrella as sleet and snow was forecast for that evening. She also had a navy blue handbag and a white bag that contained a game of Monopoly that she had borrowed from her boyfriend for Christmas.

Tim Merrett had arranged to be at the bus stop to meet Mary but when the bus arrived and Mary was not on it he became concerned. He waited but when the next two buses arrived and departed with no sign of Mary he got his sister to take him to her home, only to find that she wasn't there either.

Tim Merrett

Mary was reported missing to the police that night and a local search for her began. By the following morning she still had not been found and the concern for her grew, so the search was widened. A young policeman named John Bennett (who would later become the Senior Investigating Officer in 1994 when Fred and Rose were investigated for their crimes) joined the search on the now snow-covered ground above Painswick Beacon, which looked down onto Gloucester. They walked the area from late morning until darkness fell, and then carried on again the next day.

The search for Mary was both extensive and relentless. Gloucester police sought the assistance of the South-West Regional Crime Squad and eventually called in Scotland Yard. The search, which was lead by the squad's Deputy Co-Ordinator Detective Chief Superintendent Kenneth Clark, was being directed from a mobile police unit near The Avenue Hotel.

Volunteers searched the local waste land and the police searched factory sites and at a gas works in the Tuffley district, near Mary's home. A police roadblock was also put up on Bristol Road to ask passing motorists if they had seen anything. The local press covered the story and soon a witness was found that had seen Mary at the bus stop in Bristol Road at around 20:15. She was never seen again.

On the 8th January 1968, 300 officers searched for Mary. The Deputy Chief Constable of Gloucestershire, Mr H.D.J Smith, told a press conference "It is pushing things a bit too far to say we are treating this case as suspected murder, but we are very concerned that the girl has not been found. She comes from a good home background and is not the type of girl to go missing. She has never gone off before."

Mary's mother commented: "I cannot understand it. There was no family quarrel or anything like that. She had no reason to go away."

Enquiries continued throughout the following week and when a number of Monopoly pieces were discovered not far from where she would have waited for the bus the decision was made to call in Scotland Yard.

With the arrival of Detective Chief Superintendent William Marchand and Detective Sergeant Morris Wenham the investigation intensified. Every aspect of Mary and her background was gone in to. There were house-to-house enquiries in the Bristol Road area and in Hardwicke. Police officers with dogs searched the surrounding countryside, which still had a light covering of snow and was frozen hard. Thanks to Marchand's influence, a helicopter joined the search – a rare sight in those days – and John Bennett was pressed into action to search beneath the bridges that crossed the Gloucester-Sharpness canal.

At a press conference, Gloucester Chief Inspector Kenneth Barker said the time factor had played an important part in the decision to call in Scotland Yard. "The position still has not changed and we are still investigating a missing person. But obviously it could change to something else and it is much better that the 'Yard' be informed at this stage. Time is going on. Nothing has been discovered." Detective Chief Superintendent Marchand added: "I am here because there is a possibility that we are dealing with something more serious than a missing person and if such is the case I shall be here when it comes to light."

The following day police became aware of a car-prowler in the area near Mary's home after a 19-year-old woman came forward to tell them that a man had tried to entice her in to his car in Tuffley Avenue, only a few hundred yards from Mary's home, less than an hour before Mary Bastholm disappeared. The woman chose to stay anonymous, but her father told the press: "My daughter was walking up Tuffley Avenue at about 18:30 when a dark coloured saloon car approached from the opposite direction travelling towards Bristol Road. There were two men in the car and a driver, who was getting on in years, slowed down and shouted to her asking if she wanted a lift. Wisely, my daughter hurried on without stopping and the car carried on towards Bristol Road."

One of the detectives on the case gave a television interview where he linked this case with previous sexual attacks in the area:

Detective: We are very concerned at the moment. She has been missing since Saturday evening and it's causing us a great deal of concern.
Reporter: Have you any reason at all to suppose that she's still alive?
Detective: Well we're hoping so, of course, but earlier in 1966 there were two rather serious sexual assaults in this particular area which are bound to have some relevance in this inquiry.
Reporter: Does this mean that these two particular assaults were never solved?
Detective: This is true.

One man went to the police to report that he had seen her four or five times in the autumn before she disappeared. He knew her well, as Mary used to go to his house to play with his daughters. He was a 45-year-old Joiner named Vincent Oakes, who lived a few doors away from Mary's home. She had, he said, always been with the same man, and once he saw her sitting in a car with him. He described the man as a "swarthy builder type. There was no cuddling or anything like that. They just sat there, deep in conversation." He described the car as a sandy-coloured, bulbous shape. In 1994, when newspaper photographs of Fred West began to appear, Vincent Oakes told a newspaper that he was the man he had seen with Mary. "It was always parked in the same place, about two or three hundred yards from her home in Rosebury Avenue. I thought it strange that she didn't acknowledge me. I'm certain it was Mary and 99.9% sure the man was Fred."

The following day, police said that the discovery of Monopoly money was being treated "very cautiously". Police received some of the money in an anonymous letter saying it had been found in the Tredworth district of Gloucester. The rest was found in two different areas of Barnwood, 2 miles from the city. Chief Superintendent Marchand said: "It was pouring with rain on Saturday night and we have had snow and ice ever since then. But two lots of this money were bone dry. The rest was found on top of the snow. We are investigating it, but I do not see how it can have anything to do with the missing girl."

By the 13th January, police had issued an appeal for a girl who was seen talking to Mary Bastholm at the bus stop just before she went missing and the police believed that she had been told not to speak to them by her mother. The police had also stopped searching the waterways and instead 60 police officers with 5 sniffer dogs went over the ground close to where Mary was last seen as the snow had began to thaw. Between 19:30 and 20:30 that evening police stopped everybody, both pedestrians and drivers, passing the bus stop where Mary was last seen to ask if they had seen anything the previous week.

Jewellers and second-hand dealers were asked by police to keep their eyes open for jewellery Mary was wearing when she disappeared. She was wearing a gold, heart shaped locket with a fine chain, a yellow metal watch with gold batons in place of numerals on the face and a gold buckle ring. Her ears were pierced and she was wearing a pair of gold sleeper earrings. A watch identical to that worn by Mary was found in Tobyfield Road, Bishop's Cleeve. In years to come, and in another coincidence of this case, Rosemary Letts would come to live at number 96 Tobyfield Road.

The possibility that Mary might never come home wasn't lost on her family. Her father, Christian, told the press: "If Mary has gone off – and I doubt that she has – I can only say that I would be grateful. I would rather have an erring one than a dead one."

The search for Mary expanded and police as far afield as London were handed copies of her description for them to keep a look-out for her.

Sergeant John Watkins was a member of the search team looking for Mary. His job in the Incident Room was to co-ordinate the card indexing system, a facility that was the backbone of police investigation methods in pre-computer days. He remembered: "As the inquiry stretched from days into weeks, the files grew so large that I used to go home to my workshop and construct timber trays to hold the cards…All this was in vain – it was as if the girl had never existed." He remains convinced that it was Fred West who took and ultimately murdered her. "Knowing now how West lured many of his victims by targeting bus stops, I feel sure she was a victim of his evil. I know this is circumstantial, but the hallmarks of the West method are plain to see."

By the 31st January, the inquiry was scaled down and the two detectives from Scotland Yard returned to London.

Stephen West, Fred's son, would recall in 1995: "From as far back as I can remember, Dad always brought things home like women's jewellery, women's purses, women's handbags, suitcases, stuff that he said he found, which, looking back now it seems it was quite impossible that he could find so many things. He used to give the purses to the younger children. He used to give the rings to the girls, which now they've handed over to the police. Some of the victims' jewellery have now been found and identified as that what he gave to his young daughters."

Years later, Mary's brother Peter said: "My wife and I went down to the police station to view a lot of things that had been taken from the West's house. My wife picked out a silver locket on a chain and she said that was Mary's because she wore it as a bridesmaid at our wedding. We had a photo of it and the police took it away to examine, but because it was a black and white picture they said they could not tell if the locket was silver or gold, so nothing came of it, but it was exactly like the one found at Cromwell Street."

During the course of the investigation into Mary's disappearance over 250 different lines of inquiry were pursued. Following a complete review of the missing person file in 1994, which had been retained, over 100 people who had either initially been seen by the original investigation team, or people found by the inquiry then, were interviewed. Some people in the original enquiry, who may have been of assistance, were found to have died. Despite these enquiries, no evidence was found to support arresting Fred West for any offence whatsoever in connection with Mary Bastholm, although he was questioned in 1994 but denied any involvement. The file in relation to her disappearance has been retained and kept open.

In the first week of February 1968, Fred gave up his job driving the lorry and got a job in the packing department of Oldacres, working on a bagging machine. He could walk the distance from his caravan to work and had no means of transport. Fred said that he got the new job because "there was nowhere to park a lorry at Lake House", but this seems like a very odd reason. The possibility remains that his transport at the time may have become compromised, either with the DNA of Mary, or because his car matched a description given by police as one they wanted to trace. By changing jobs and getting rid of evidence it would have proved much harder for the police to trace him.

He obviously wanted a new car and to make as much money as quickly as he could so Fred also started doing odd jobs and maintenance work for Mrs Dukes, the owner of the caravan site.

Just a few days after starting his new job, Fred's mother Daisy died of a sudden heart-attack, at the age of 44, in Hereford Hospital. Her funeral was held on the 9th February and she was buried in Much Marcle. Fred didn't cry at her funeral and actually whispered to Rena: "We should sell her clothes." The rest of the West family were horrified.

With Daisy dead, Fred took Rena and the children to Moorcourt Cottage more often and Rena's relationship with Walter deepened still further. In the summer of 1968 Rena taught Fred's youngest sister Gwen how to drive. She borrowed a car from some of her clients for the trips to Much Marcle and during the investigation into Mary Bastholm's disappearance Fred and Rena were stopped by the police in a Volkswagen Beetle. They were questioned regarding her disappearance during a random check at Westgate Bridge in Gloucester.

As he had no means of transport, Fred contented himself with inviting young girls to his caravan. He met the girls in the village, offering to help with odd jobs and would use exactly the same excuse that he had used in Scotland to tempt them back to his caravan. He would tell them that he was looking for someone to help him take care of his two girls, Charmaine and Anne Marie, who were now aged five and four respectively.

Rena meanwhile, took a job near Tewkesbury as a waitress in a mobile canteen for the workers on the M5 motorway which was being constructed. She used this job to expand her list of clientele to add to the regulars she had from around the lanes and villages. Charmaine and Anne Marie were looked after during the day by Mrs Nock, one of Fred's old bread-round customers, nearby at Stoke Orchard.

Fred repeatedly asked the men at Oldacres whether they were interested in sex and where he could meet girls. The older girls at Bishop's Cleeve School soon began to talk about him amongst themselves and swapped stories of what happened to them when they went in to Fred's caravan after school. They told stories of photographic sessions, the offers of abortions should they "find themselves in trouble" and of how much a girl could make "on the streets of Cheltenham". One girl gave him the nickname of 'Weird Freddie'.

Rena was still leaving for a time and coming back to Fred. There was still violence and sex, and often together, but it was when Rena had left and Fred was alone that he would get these young girls back to his caravan. "He could be very, very persuasive", one young woman remembered from that time. He took photographs of the girls, and more often than not of their vaginas, with a black and white Polaroid camera he had stolen.

Rena set out to find clients for herself and gave herself the working name of 'Mandy James'. She took out an advertisement in the local paper and it read: "Young, attractive lady looking for employment. Anything considered…" Fred would later tell that Rena had quite a response. Some of the letters were offering her actual jobs, but she was more interested in the ones from men offering sex. According to him "she had quite a round going on."

Fred was arrested on the 15th May for stealing a cheque and using it to buy a £10 record-player for his caravan. He appeared at Cheltenham Magistrates Court on the 10th June charged with 'Theft' and 'Obtain by deception.' He was fined £10 for each offence. He claimed he had been battling to pay back £2,000 of business debts.

Rena's job in the canteen gave her plenty of opportunities to find more clients, and for a time Fred joined her there, not only to help her gather more clients but also to work as a trench digger for Costain's, the motorway construction firm. He became known as 'the best trench digger on the M5, a man who would keep on digging when everyone else had stopped.' But then "Rena got pally with one of the big boys on the motorway, and she pissed off with him and left me again." He found himself on the dole and determined to find someone to look after the children after school so he could go out and find work. The attraction of looking after the young children to 13 and 14-year-old girls Fred targeted, in return for cash and the suggestion that they might earn even more, or learn "something about sex", proved irresistible to them.

A woman named Alison Clinton said that she had been grabbed by a man in 1968, when she was aged 13, and that she thought her assailant was Fred West. She said she was walking home alone when a car passed her and pulled up in front. The driver got out and opened the bonnet. As she walked past "He grabbed my wrist. I got free and ran to the nearest house". Twenty six years later she recognised Fred West's face on television after his arrest. She reported the details of the attack to the police at the time, but Fred was not identified or questioned.

3 ROSEMARY LETTS

Rosemary Pauline Letts was born at the Highfield Maternity Hospital in Barnstaple, Devon, on the 29th November 1953 to Daisy Gwendoline Letts and William (Bill) Andrew Letts, where she showed signs of mental disturbance from an early age. She would develop the habit of rocking herself in her cot and at night she would keep her older siblings awake as she bashed her head against it.

Bill had been a seafarer and naval man since being called up in 1943. He was a short, violent man and had been diagnosed as a Paranoid Schizophrenic whilst in the Navy, but he didn't tell anyone. His wife, Daisy, only found out when she was going through his belongings after his death. Daisy found it hard to cope with all of her children and a violent husband and suffered from depression. When Bill was at work she would shout at the children and sometimes hit them with a copper stick as she wanted the house kept spotless for one of Bill's inspections. Bill managed to send his two oldest daughters, patsy and Joyce, to be educated at a boarding school in Cornwall.

In March 1952, Daisy and Bill had their first son together and called him Andrew. Just six months after his birth, Daisy became ill (possibly with post-natal depression), and Bill had to leave the Navy and it's financial security. He was discharged on compassionate grounds after nine years of service.

In the spring of 1953 Daisy's depression deepened, no doubt aided by her husbands' violent attacks and she became increasingly anxious. She developed agoraphobia and soon had a breakdown. She was referred to a psychiatric hospital in nearby Bideford, where the psychiatrist suggested a course of electroconvulsive therapy (ECT). It was during the beginning of her course that she fell pregnant with Rosemary.

After the first course it was decided that Daisy was worse than first suspected and the doctor decided to continue the therapy throughout her pregnancy with Rose. The sixth and final course was given to her just days before she gave birth to Rose.

As well as banging her head on her cot, Rose rarely cried and as she got older she would swing her head in front of her and put herself in to a trance-like state.

Bill was still hitting Daisy, but neighbours had no idea and only noticed Daisy being cruel to the older children, who were in their teens at the time. A neighbour recalled: "When the girls arrived home from school she had them in the back yard checking their hair for nits. You could hear their screams next door. She'd go out and hose them down in the back yard... with all the washing and scrubbing she did, it's a wonder they had any skin left."

In the autumn of 1957 Daisy gave birth to another son, Graham. Andrew recalled years later that Rose played by herself when she was younger and that she struggled to grasp things. "It was frustrating trying to teach her anything and you had to show her several times. You'd be fed up by then. My parents shouted at her to try to make it sink in." Things like this earned her the nickname of 'Dozy Rosie'.

Despite not being the brightest, her family and friends remember her as being polite and always doing as she was told. Andrew remembered her as being "so quiet and obedient that Dad didn't notice her to tell her off."

On one occasion Bill returned home early from work to find Daisy exchanging the time of day with other women outside the house. He immediately flew in to a rage and punched Daisy in the face. He then grabbed her by the hair and dragged her back into the house where he continued to beat her. The neighbours were shocked and called the police, but they took no further action.

He made the school aged children do chores, which he called their 'duties', and expected them to be done before and after school each day. If the children didn't wake up on time then Bill threw a bucket of icy water over them as they slept, and if the chores weren't done to Bill's satisfaction he would make them clean the entire house. Andrew later recalled: "You didn't dare argue with him. One look from him would send the fear of God through you."

Of Rose, he recalled: "She was a lovely little thing with a pony tail, who was pampered by mum and dad. Rosie was very clever as a young child in learning how to manipulate dad." She soon became known as a 'Daddy's girl', but only his daughters knew that the kind of love Rose received from her father was both distorted and perverted.

When a 15-year-old Patricia (Patsy) Letts got out of the bath one day her father Bill followed her into her bedroom where he pushed her onto the bed and tried to remove her bathrobe. Patsy screamed as he tried to touch her and she pushed him away. She then rushed out to the landing, where Bill caught up with her and threw her down the stairs. Her injuries were so severe that she had to be treated at the Casualty Department at Barnstable Hospital. After she came home he made another attempt to molest her and when she resisted he beat her. Soon after this she fled Northam and joined the Wrens with the help of a friends father. With her gone, Bill then bullied his next eldest daughter, Joyce. He took her out in the van one day and they went to a pub. Bill hardly ever drank but gave her gin masked in orange juice. When he tried it on with her back at home she stood up to him and he beat her.

Not long after this Daisy and the younger children helped Joyce move to her friend Diane Glover's house. Diane remembered sharing her room with Joyce for several weeks and she told her that her father "had turned strange" and she needed to get away from him.

Andrew Letts remembered that at this time his father "was a mad man, a complete mad man when he was in this rage of tempered fits or whatever. We tried to stay out of his way really." His brother Graham recalled "Nobody was excluded from it, my mother included and we all lived under this threat of what he would do next."

Joyce began work in Bideford soon afterwards and moved back home, but Bill started beating her again so she moved out to live with another friend. This left Glenys as next in his firing line, but Bill didn't touch her. He began looking elsewhere for opportunities to satisfy his lust for young girls. He set up a youth club in the local hall with his friend, Ronnie Lloyd, where they played records which became popular amongst the young locals.

In 1959 Rose started school at Northam Primary, but wasn't very bright. She was often sent to the corner of the room and made to wear a dunce's hat. She was also held back a year. While she was at school Bill and Daisy continued to sleep together and the following year Daisy gave birth to another son, Gordon.

At home Rose was given chores to do, but she was slow in doing them. To spare her a beating from their father when he got home the other children did her chores for her. Bill then began allowing her to skip her chores all together and started to turn a blind eye to her breaking the rules at the dinner table, where she would play with her food. For the other children that would have lead to a severe beating at his hands, but Rose was allowed to carry on. Andrew would recall that their father "felt sorry for her and would let her off." It's believed that now Rose was of school age Bill let her off because he was sexually abusing her.

Leo Goatley, Rose's defence solicitor from 1992 onwards said: "Her father was very, very abusive to his daughters, and the other daughters wouldn't tolerate it and moved out. Even the mother moved out at one stage. He would have been having sex with her (Rose) and she would have been accepting of it. The relationship with her father continued after Fred and Rose got together and, in fact, Rose's father would turn up at Cromwell Street even after Rose had had four children to have sex with her and then Fred would send her into the bedroom with Anne Marie. I think Rose's sisters just wanted to get away from there. Whereas, curiously, Rose just kind of accepted the regime and was the subject of terrible sexual abuse from Bill Letts. When I took a 'Proof of Evidence' from her it was a sanitized version of her early life that she gave where the darker, sinister side was dealt with by symbols almost. This man in a dark cape and dark hat, almost a shadow, would follow her when she walked. That was about as near as she'd get."

By February 1962, Bill Letts had fallen behind with the rent on the house. Whatever income he was making he was spending on himself rather than the rent and he bought some modern recording equipment for the youth club, but the club soon closed down amidst rumours in the village of Bill's fancy for young girls. A former neighbour recalled: "Social Services stepped in and stopped the youth club, then they flitted off." Bill Letts moved his family to Benbow Street, Plymouth. They left in the middle of the night, leaving most of their belongings behind.

At the new house Rose began to suffer with nightmares and was being bullied at school. She also started to exhibit disturbed behavior by cutting up bedclothes when she came home from school to make clothes for her dolls and she frequently told transparent and pointless lies. It's quite possible that Rose's grandfather, as well as her father, was also sexually abusing her at this time. Rose's brother-in-law Jim Tyler remembered: "There was something about her father and grandfather that just wasn't right."

In July 1964 Bill and Daisy Letts moved the family to Bishop's Cleeve, Gloucestershire, after Bill found work with an electronics firm called Smith's Aerospace on the outskirts of Cheltenham. They moved in to 96 Tobyfield Road. Rose's sister Patsy went to live in Australia with her new husband and Joyce started a family and trained as a nurse. Neither had any contact with the family.

By July of the following year Rose had grown into quite a large girl and wasn't afraid of throwing her weight around at school. She would turn on her bully's and became known on the estate as someone to avoid. If anyone picked on her brothers Graham or Gordon she would go after them too.

Daisy Letts got herself a job in the canteen at Whitbread's brewery in the village. The job started in the afternoon and went on until late evening. Andrew was working in Cheltenham and staying over at his girlfriend's house a lot and Bill was barely home in the evenings as Smith's Aerospace had a social club where he would go after work. This meant that Daisy had to rely on Rose to get the little boys – Graham, 10, and Gordon, 7 - their tea when they came home from school. Rose also had to get them ready for bed on time and then babysit them. During the school summer holidays of 1967 Rose helped her mother with the boys' care, but she also began to masturbate her 7-year-old brother Gordon as she towel dried him when he got out of the bath. At 13-years-old she began taking herself off in to the village in the evenings, leaving her brothers to look after themselves. Soon, the two boys also began to wander off to the village in the evenings once Rose had gone out. Rose started to hang out by the shops where she took up smoking to look older and chatted and laughed with bus drivers and the local boys. Her little brothers, however, soon began stealing whatever small goods took their fancy to sell on and buy alcohol with.

Rose began practicing the sexuality she had picked up from her father, grandfather, local boys and bus drivers on her brothers. She would walk around the house naked after a bath and on one occasion she even stripped off and stood naked in front of her father, telling him about all the children she was going to have one day.

When her parents were out Rose took to inviting some of the local boys around to the house where she would invite them to touch her sexually. She would also sometimes go around to their houses for the same reasons but when she returned home at night she would climb in to bed with Gordon and Graham.

So by now both Fred and Rose had grown up in households where their parents were strict in regards to household chores. Rose's father Bill made the children do chores from a young age, as Rose would insist her own children do later, and in both cases, if any chore was not done to the required standard then the punishment would be a severe beating.

Violence and cruelty was an everyday occurrence in both families. The children had been beaten with shovels and belts, as well as being hit with fists and feet, and both parents were violent towards each other. Fred and Rose would go on to hit their own children with belts, mallets and even sledge-hammers and among other items even attack them with knives. There were also many reports of Fred and Rose hitting each other.

Incest was rife in both families, with Rose being abused by her father and grandfather and in turn going on to abuse her younger brothers and then eventually her own children. Fred was made to sleep with his mother at a young age, he raped his own 13-year-old sister and was told by his own father that "it was a father's duty to break in his daughters", which he proceeded to do.

In December 1968, Rose left school and went to work at a bread shop in Cheltenham. She was still sharing a bed with her brother Graham, and she masturbated him in the mornings and again late at night, graduating to having full sexual intercourse with him when he was twelve. This continued right up until she moved out to live with Fred.

In January 1969 Rose said that she was raped for the first time after a Christmas party. She had gone to the party with a friend at the place where the friend's mother worked. She was aware of a man whose eyes had been on her all night. At the end of the party her friend, who was supposed to be giving her a lift home, had gone off with a boy, and she was wandering around outside on her own when a man pulled up and said he would give her a lift home to Bishop's Cleeve. The last bus had gone and she was alone so she got in. Instead of turning off, he went on past her home and on to the hills above where she lived. They stopped on the golf course on Cleeve Hill. She said that she feared for her life as she was ordered to take off all of her clothes and get in to the back seat, where the man raped her. Afterwards, he took her back to her house and dropped her off outside. She didn't tell anybody what had happened to her until 1995.

Later in the year Daisy turned up out of the blue at Glenys' house. She was black and blue following a particularly heavy beating given to her by Bill and she had Rose, Graham and Gordon in tow. Glenys and her husband Jim Tyler made room for them to stay.

Jim was a car mechanic and worked at the Audi garage in Cheltenham but he and Glenys also ran a roadside refreshment business up at the village of Seven Springs on the Cirencester Road. Jim would tow their caravan up to an area of wasteland by the gravel pits each morning and he would then set off for work. Glenys would then spend her days serving the customers that stopped off there.

As Glenys was only weeks away from giving birth, Rose ran the refreshment bar while her sister took maternity leave in March of that year. When Jim was test-driving a car he'd serviced, he used the chance to replenish the snack bar with supplies. Each time he turned up unannounced he would find the hatch closed and Rose would emerge from the cab of a parked-up lorry with her clothes unbuttoned and with messy hair. Jim would later refer to Rose as "a hot-arsed little sod". He even found her once climbing out of a car that was full of gas fitters and said that they had driven her down to the shops as she had run out of hotdogs, which he knew to be a lie.

When Glenys was in hospital having just given birth, Jim was awoken one night by the sound of crying. He walked down the hallway and found Rose in her bed rocking and sucking her thumb. He said he put his arm around her to comfort her and she told him that she was in love with an older man who visited the refreshment bar but that he didn't love her. She then told him how lucky her sister was to have a man like him and ran her hand along the inside of his thigh. Jim then said that he jumped up and left.

However, there is another version of this story. Some members of the family believe that Daisy came home and caught the pair in bed together, leading to a fight between Rose and Glenys. Soon after, Daisy and the younger children moved out.

At her trial, Rose said she'd returned home from work one day to find her mother and brothers had packed up and gone. She'd asked Glenys where they'd gone, but her sister had been instructed not to tell her. Andrew Letts refutes this story. He recalled his mother buying a copy of The Lady and a week or two later finding a job in the countryside, with a tied cottage for herself and all the younger children. Rose, however, hadn't wanted to go with them. "Mum begged her to go to Teddington, but Rosie said she was going home to live with Dad. We just couldn't believe it. After all of the violence, and everything, she wanted to go back. She wouldn't listen to Mum."

At the time, Rose was staying out late with different men she was seeing. Some of these men she charged for sex, others she didn't. She didn't want to rush back to live with her father, who she knew would try to restrict her going out, so she preferred instead to wander the streets where, according to Jim Tyler "the police picked her up for street-walking in Cheltenham. She was only 15."

One Sunday evening, as she walked the streets with her bag, she was offered a lift by an older Irish man called Ken who she'd briefly met at her sister's house. He offered her a cup of tea at his flat and she accepted. Rose then had sex with him that night. At 30-years-old he was twice her age. He offered her a place to stay in return for rent when she got a job – and probably also sex. Soon after, Rose found work at Sketchley Dry Cleaners and from there moved on to train as a seamstress at the County Clothes shop in Cheltenham.

She found out from her brother Andrew's girlfriend, Jacquie, where her mother and brothers had gone. She turned up out of the blue to visit them, bringing her new boyfriend along with her, a soldier from the local army barracks. She also brought other men there too, having sex with them in the fields around Teddington, followed by a drink in the local pub, before setting off again for home.

Since her first brush with the law, the police had begun keeping an eye on her. She was now working at a bakers-cum-teashop in Cheltenham, where for several weeks, a policeman would wait outside until she left for the day and then take her in for questioning. The police knew she was seeing a lot of older men and were particularly interested in the one whose flat she went back to each night, Ken. They wanted to know whether an offence had been committed as she was still under age. In the end, the police did not charge Ken, but neither did Rose stay away from him or any of the others as she promised the police she would. A Police Constable continued to wait outside the bakers until Rose finally gave in and returned home to her father. "Hello, Mr Plod. Cunt" she would often whisper under her breath.

After returning home to live with her father, she reported him to Social Services and told them that he was being 'restrictive'. After they visited the house life carried on as before.

During the summer, Daisy was unable to meet the costs of her growing children and they reluctantly moved back in with Bill in Tobyfield Road. Bill soon started to beat her again, only this time even harder to teach her a lesson for leaving him.

One evening, as Rose waited at a bus stop in the dark having just finished work, she claimed to have been frightened by a man who was also waiting there and who'd told her he'd been in the Army. The bus stop, on the Evesham Road, was opposite Cheltenham's famous Pump Rooms and Pittville Park (the same bus stop that her and Fred would later abduct Lucy Partington from). Being scared, she ran away from the man, across the road towards the park, but he chased after her. The park gates were locked, but the soldier, she said, "just smashed the padlock off with his fists", before dragging her under some trees and raping her. This claim did not come to light until she mentioned it at her trial in 1995. After the second attack, Rose said that she began to catch the bus home in the evening from the main bus station in Cheltenham.

4 WHEN FRED MET ROSE

In early 1969, just after her 15th Birthday, Rosemary Letts met Frederick West at a bus stop in Cheltenham whilst waiting for a bus to Bishop's Cleeve. Fred had been at the bus stop because he had just been released from hospital following an accident whilst driving a truck on the construction site of the M5.

Rose recalled: "I was waiting at the bus stop when I noticed this man looking at me. I didn't take to him at all, he was dirty and had work clothes on and looked quite old. I had just finished my day's work in a bread shop, it was dark and I was waiting to catch a bus to my parents' house in Bishop's Cleeve, a few miles out of Cheltenham. This man started talking to me on the bus and just sat next to me without asking my permission. Within a few minutes he had asked me out. He was like a tramp, a real mess, and I said 'No'. I thought that was the end of that. Soon after our first meeting I saw him again at the bus stop. He got on the bus with me and started asking me out to pubs which were near where I was working in the bread shop. One day a lady came into the shop and gave me a present, saying a man had given it to her to give to me. It was something stupid, I can't remember what. Then Fred came in himself and shouted across the counter 'The Swallow – 8pm'. That was my local pub and just a few minutes from where I lived. He'd obviously worked out that this was the best place for him to meet me." It would appear that Fred had been stalking her and found out where she lived. He would later confess "You could see the pub from her house. That's the reason I chose it."

Rose: "Curiosity got the better of me and I went to the pub, thinking I'd give him back the present he had given me." (The gift was a fur coat and lace dress. Fred would later photograph Rose standing on a deserted road, striking obscene poses and wearing nothing but this fur coat). "I didn't have any feelings for him. We sat talking and drinking, that was all."

Fred gathered from the conversation that Rose was no stranger to sex and sexual practices and he used his sympathy vote on her by claiming that his wife had abandoned him and left him struggling to look after two young girls.

Rose: "He asked me out again and I agreed, so he took me home to his caravan where he lived with his daughters Charmaine and Anne Marie."

Fred said in interviews later that they went back to his caravan but "there was a girl staying there…staying in the caravan, but she was on drugs and I couldn't allow her near the children. But Rose refused to come in the van because the girl was there. She knew her. They went to school together." He said he then walked Rose part of the way back to Tobyfield Road, before he returned to his caravan, woke up the sleeping girl and told her that he was "taking her back to her mother" the next morning.

Fred then said that "the next day I came home. Rose had been down and stripped the caravan – cleared it completely out. Loads of girls had been staying there. But Rose puts all the girls' clothes and that…she put it all in a big tea-chest and said 'Dump that'." He said he gave the clothes, which included "knickers, bras, pants, God knows what" – which he had been keeping as trophies – to another girl he knew. "There were loads of Rena's clothes as well, 'cause Rena never wore the same clothes twice. She never washed a pair of knickers in her life. When she took a pair off, she'd put a brand-new pair on."

Rose and Fred then began a relationship, with Rose becoming a frequent visitor at the Lake House Caravan Park. In a letter to a penpal written in 2005, Rose recalled: "I started to believe this was my way out of the oppression my parents had kept me under for so long."

Almost immediately Rose started taking time off from work and sneaking down to the caravan rather than catching the bus to work. She spent the daytime looking after the children and in the evening sleeping with Fred when he got back from work. Fred was still seeing other girls and one morning Rose was met at the caravan door by some girls her own age who were babysitting. She recognized them from her school and realized that she wasn't Fred's only lover, but she gave them what for and they left immediately.

Within weeks of her first meeting Fred, Rose quit her job at the bread shop in order to become the full-time nanny for Charmaine and Anne Marie. This decision was made with the agreement that Fred would give her sufficient money for her to give to her parents on Fridays to convince them she was still working at the bread shop.

Several months later, Rose chose to introduce Fred to her family but they were horrified by her choice of partner. Rose's mother Daisy was unimpressed with Fred's obvious lies, and correctly concluded that he was a pathological liar. Daisy had heard through village gossips that Rose was no longer going to work at the bread shop. "Immediately we thought he was an older man. He was twenty-seven, but he did not look young for his age", she would later recall. Her father Bill strongly disapproved of the relationship and threatened Fred directly. He promised to call Social Services if he continued to date his daughter. Rose recalled that "I asked Fred to meet my parents and they took a dislike when he came to the house. Mom said that he was ugly and had a bad attitude and was old with two kids whilst I was only fifteen." Daisy explained that "Dad (Bill) said he did not want that gypsy anywhere near his daughter." Bill also called him a "grubby, lying little tramp." Daisy noticed a scar on Fred's nose that he had got from his motorbike crash years earlier, but he told her that "In Scotland, some woman had chased him and then he fell down a manhole cover, and this woman smashed him across the face with a chain."

Rose was forced to break off the relationship, and Bill made her write him a letter telling him to 'Go back to your wife and try and make a go of it.' Rose remembered: "But he didn't take any notice of the letter and turned up again at our door. I began to fall in love with him; he was so persistent and I was so flattered by his determination to be with me. I started to see him in secret. Often when I went to the caravan Fred would have women there who were supposed to be looking after Charmaine and Anne Marie. But most of them were sleeping with Fred. A lot of them were girls from my school. I chucked them all out, together with the trunk of women's underwear he had at the back of the caravan."

Rose's brother Andrew remembered when his family found out that Fred was married: "We only found out some months later when there were various other things that kept cropping up that we were finding out about. One was his marriage, there was another one about he'd been in prison."

Her other brother, Graham, said: "I think after maybe 6 months of going with him, I think she had actually fallen head over heels for him."

On the 30th June, Fred West appeared at Cheltenham Magistrates Court charged with 4 motoring offences. He was ordered to pay a fine of £22 and to pay £12 in back duty.

Around this time Rose agreed to Fred's suggestion that she take over Rena's role as a prostitute. She even took over Rena's working name of 'Mandy'. Fred began advertising her services by word of mouth at first, and soon a steady stream of customers began to call at his caravan. Bill Letts had heard all about Rena's services from his workmates who lived at the same Lake House Caravan Site but now rumour had it that his own daughter was selling her services there too. He visited the Bakery where he thought Rose was still working but the staff there confirmed his worst fears – Rose hadn't worked there for quite some time. When he confronted Rose she tried to explain that she was now employed as Fred's 'nanny', but Bill knew that wasn't the whole truth. Daisy recalled that: "There was no way Dad (Bill) was going to allow her, at her age, to go down to a caravan with a man who had two children."

Although Bill and Daisy forbade Rose from ever seeing Fred again, she defied their wishes, which prompted them to visit Gloucestershire Social Services to explain that their 15-year-old daughter was dating an older man, and that in addition, they had heard rumours that Rose had begun to engage in prostitution at his caravan. Social Services placed Rose in a home for troubled teenagers in Cheltenham in August 1969, and she was only allowed to leave those premises under controlled conditions.

Rose's brother Graham recalled: "They went to Social Services and actually got Rosemary put into care. Now, at the time, she was 15 and a half, so the very worst that could happen is that she would stay in care until she was 16, which is what happened eventually. But it didn't deter her one little bit. In fact, if anything, it made her more determined to stay with Fred."

Neither her parents or her siblings visited her in the whole time she was staying there and she couldn't even speak to them on the phone as the house at Tobyfield Road wasn't connected up. Although allowed to return home to visit her parents at weekends, Rose almost always used the opportunity to visit Fred. She began writing to Fred while she was in the home and she had heard from her Aunt Eileen that Rena had gone back to Fred in her absence. One letter read:

Dear Fred,

I am glad you came to see me. Last night made me realise we are two people, not two soft chairs to be sat on…about us meeting this week, it could be Sunday afternoon. I will have to get Lynda to say I'm going with her. You know we won't be able to meet so often, that's why I can't get the idea out of my head that you are going with someone else…You told my Aunt about Rena, but what about telling me the whole story even if it takes all day. I love you, Fred, but if anything goes wrong it will be the end of both of us for good. We will have to go somewhere far away where nobody knows us.

I will always love you.

Rose

With Rose not around, Fred went back to trying to get Rena to stay with him and the children. He had more time on his hands now that Rose wasn't around and went back to both thieving and luring young girls back to his caravan. On the 28th August, Fred appeared at Cheltenham Magistrates Court charged with theft after he stole some fencing panels from his employer. He was fined £50 and given 6 months imprisonment, suspended for 2 years.

Rena briefly returned to stay with Fred but left again on the 20th October. A week later Social Services called at Lake House Caravan Site and found a young woman looking after Charmaine and Anne Marie 'in a very satisfactory manner.' Rena had moved into a caravan with the site foreman from Costain's at Sandhurst Lane, but continued to offer her services to a number of Costain's workers.

On the 18th November Fred was imprisoned for 3 days for the non-payment of the fine for the fencing panels and Charmaine and Anne Marie were taken back in to care. When Fred was released, Rena moved back in with him in order to have the children released from care, but she left them again three days later and on the 28th November Charmaine and Anne Marie were taken back into care, first with foster parents and then at a children's home not far from Whitminster.

The following day Rose turned 16 and she left the home to move back in with her parents. She had an almighty row with Bill almost straight away as he tried to tell her that she could no longer see Fred now that she was back under his roof and he told her that he would disown her if she disobeyed his orders, but she could stay if she found herself a good job and stopped seeing him. It was so ferocious that the police were called. A social worker who subsequently visited them said in his report that the family "presented as quite reasonable."

Just before Christmas, on the 10th December, Rena was arrested for soliciting in Gloucester. She went up to Glasgow for Christmas with her boyfriend from Costain's, but Rose wasn't so lucky. She was locked in her room where she was not allowed to see anyone or to give or receive any presents. Now she was back home she carried on abusing her younger brothers.

In early January 1970, Fred met Rose at the Swallow Pub in Bishop's Cleeve, but Bill had followed her and confronted the pair. Fred said that he encountered "her father standing there, with his crash helmet on, and a big coat, wanting to fight me. I couldn't do nothing. So anyway he hit me on the jaw and I walked away, and he took Rose home, and shouted down the road 'I'm gonna burn you alive in the caravan tonight' or summat like that."

The following evening Fred went round to Tobyfield Road and "Rose came to the door and nearly passed out with fright when she seen me stood there. I said 'Can I see your parents and let's talk this over?' but they wouldn't come out."

Two days later the meeting did take place. The more Fred boasted about the "hotel and caravan site" that he owned in Scotland, the more incensed Bill Letts became. As Fred left his house, he instructed his daughter that she was never to see that 'dirty gypsy again'. He then locked her back in her bedroom and told her that she would not be allowed to leave the house again until she agreed to his terms.

One day Rose did manage to escape the house and she met Fred at his work. He was working as a driver delivering sand to building sites and remembered that his foreman told him that he had a visitor in the cabin. Rose told him "we've got to do something, 'cause Mum and Dad's going to get a court order on me." She told him that "The only answer to it is…for you to get me pregnant." He asked her if that was what she really wanted and she told him that it was.

However, Rose wasn't Fred's only sexual partner at the time. The Full Moon Pub in Cheltenham High Street attracted crowds of young people and he would sit at the corner of the bar and engage them in conversation. He was specifically looking for female companionship and especially of the type where they might need a bed for the night. One evening he ran in to Terrence Crick, a young man who had lived at Watermead Caravan Site in Brockworth at the same time as him. Terrence was hitchhiking with his girlfriend and Fred offered them both a bed for a few nights at Lake House. Many years later, Terrence explained that Fred seemed "like a very nice bloke. I thought it would be fun."

Fred's caravan had grown gloomy since Rose wasn't around to tidy up for him and Anne Marie and Charmaine were in care. There were tools, piles of clothes and pieces of metal strewn around the small rooms where children's toys had once been. The atmosphere was downcast and made even more so when Fred started to boast to them about his skills as an abortionist. He told them that if they "ever got in to trouble" he could sort it out for them. He then produced his 'tools' to prove it.

One of the tools was a steel rod about a foot long with "something that looked like a corkscrew" attached to the top of it. Fred then produced a set of black and white Polaroid photographs of what he said were the "vaginas of the girls" he had operated on, and went on to inform Terrence and his girlfriend that if "things went wrong" during one of his operations, he would "sort the girls out once and for all."

The next morning Fred took Terrence to a large wooden shed with a dirt floor on the caravan site and showed him a set of oxy-acetylene bottles and equipment. Many years later Terrence said: "He showed me the garage next door. It was cold and eerie. The place was dirty and damp, and there were stains all over the place." Fred then pulled out a tray containing an oxy-acetylene burner, a large knife, two bottles of antiseptic, and a ten inch tube with a corkscrew at one end. Under these tools were photographs of women. Terrence remembered the "gruesome Polaroid photographs of bloodstained women. He laughed as he showed me the photos, as if they turned him on." Fred then went on to explain exactly how he performed abortions, and asked Terry to help him recruit girls who needed his services. "I took him to the Full Moon Pub in Cheltenham that night, and watched him leave with a girl."

On their third night in the caravan, Terrence and his girlfriend were introduced to Rose. He remembered that they laid awake at night listening to Fred and his 16-year-old girlfriend talking, giggling and making love. He was later convinced that during the night he had heard Fred and Rose plan to commit murder, although he did not report the events to the police at the time. Instead, he and his girlfriend left the caravan early the next morning. Terrence never returned , but his girlfriend did as one of the many young girls brought under Fred West's charm.

In February, Rose became pregnant for the first time. "I told my parents and I got a beating that I'll never forget", she recalled. Bill made one final effort to prevent Rose from seeing Fred. He told the police that Fred had been having sex with his daughter while she had been under the age of sixteen, thereby breaking the law. At the insistence of the police, the local authorities intervened and placed Anne Marie and Charmaine back in a foster home, but when a police surgeon examined Rose, it was discovered that she had not conceived before her sixteenth birthday. As a result, Fred was interviewed only briefly, and neither detained or charged.

In response, Rose was sent to a mother and baby unit for teenage girls, but was discharged on the 6th March on the understanding that she would terminate her pregnancy and return to her family. Rose recalled: "Without discussing it with me, my father booked me into an abortion clinic. I decided I had to meet Fred and tell him what was happening. I made an excuse that I needed to go into town to buy some things for the hospital and they believed me and gave me some money. Fred was working at a tyre fitters (Cotswold Tyres) and I met up with him. We hatched this plan where, instead of getting into the ambulance that my parents had arranged, I would run round the corner and meet him in his car. That was our plan but it didn't go like that."

Just as Rose had decide to leave home Rena reappeared. She turned up at Cotswold Tyres and told Fred that she had come back to him and wanted to give their relationship another go. She wanted them to immediately go and get the children out of care. Rena moved back in to the caravan at Lake House and the children were reclaimed from Parklands Children's Home. But then, according to Fred, Rena "did the dirtiest trick she's ever done on me in her whole life." After collecting the girls: "we took 'em home, put them to bed. I got up the next morning and Rena had scarpered. So I had to put them back again."

Social Services grew tired of the amount of times the children were handed over in to their care and insisted that Fred should find a 'permanent home' for the girls. They warned him that if he failed to do so, it would take them into care formally, rather than offering them foster-homes whenever he ran into difficulties. Fred told them that his brother John and his wife would soon be moving in to a small flat in Clarence Road, Cheltenham with him and provide a permanent home for the children. John's wife would act as babysitter while he and John went to work. It was yet another lie but he had calculated it would keep them quiet until he and Rose were together.

Rose would then tell of the day she came to leave home: "Dad came up to my room later that day and gave me an ultimatum. He said 'you can get rid of the baby, stay at home with your Mum and Dad, have no boyfriends, pay your own way, and everything will be all right. Or you can leave now with this Fred West bloke and you will never see your Mum and Dad again. And if I see you in the street, I'll knife you.' Dad had made these threats before and had once said he would burn down Fred's caravan with us both in it if he caught us together there. Staying at home didn't sound much fun, so I packed two carrier bags, kissed Dad goodbye and then went to the kitchen and tried to cuddle Mum. But she was furious and said to me: 'What do you think you're doing?' My brothers Gordon and Graham waved me off, we were quite close."

Rose's mother, Daisy, remembered: "She came down the stairs with her little bits and pieces and my sister who was staying with us then, she looked at Rose and said: 'You're not going, are you Rose?' She laughed 'Yeah I am'. She looked lovely, her hair was lovely…she looked so lovely on the day she left…she went straight from school to him."

Fred had a night job at this point, working in a pub called The Gamecock in Cheltenham. Rose turned up there looking for him, and when the landlady told him that his 'floozy' was at the door he became incensed and gave her a load of foul mouthed abuse and told her where to stick her job.

It was around this time that Fred's brother Doug first met Rose. "He said she was the new nanny, but she was too loud for my opinion. We never hit it off from the start." He then said that with the children Rose was "a bit abrupt. If she had of been my nanny I'd have clobbered her!"

Fred was annoyed both with Rena, who had visited her daughters whilst they were in care, and Bill for shopping him to the police, so he decided to disappear. He collected Anne Marie and Charmaine on the morning of 27th March 1970 from the local authorities and he, Rose and the children moved in to 9 Clarence Road, Cheltenham.

He said that he took both of the girls with him because when Rena came down to visit she was "only taking Charmaine out…not Anna Marie. I mean, Anna Marie was a complete failure as far as she was concerned, never should have happened."

9 Clarence Road was well known to the police. It was owned by a Greek Cypriot called Costa, who had previously let the property out to bikers, and with them had come drug dealers, alcoholics and runaways. Fred got the keys to the property a few days before letting Rose and the children move in so that he could do some minor repair work. On one of these days, Fred had to call the police because a girl from Bishops Cleeve School had followed him to the property. She stood outside shouting all day and followed him to his job where she stood outside shouting again. It is not

known why this girl was there, but it is almost certain that he had attempted to interfere with her in some way. He said that he had her removed for her own safety because he knew what Rose could do.

According to Rose, 9 Clarence Road was "a real pit. We were in this little room together; me, Fred and his kids…It was impossible to live there because it was so small. There was just a tiny sink in the corner. It was hopeless. Fred suggested we move to Gloucester because Cheltenham folk didn't take kindly to unmarried families."

Clarence Road joined at the junction with Evesham Road, along which Lucy Partington would later go missing and where Rose claimed to have once been chased from and raped. Rose would later confess to her daughter, Mae, that she found this period of her life very difficult. "I hadn't the faintest idea what I was letting myself in for…It was worse than you can possibly imagine, Mae. Much worse."

The new family stayed in the property for just a week and, in the first week in April, they moved to a ground floor, one bedroomed flat at 10 Midland Road, Gloucester. The other flats were all rented out to Jamaicans by the landlord, Frank Zygmunt, and although Fred and Rose had 2 rooms this time, they still had to share the kitchen, bathroom and garden with the other tenants. Rose refused to stay in the flat for more than a couple of weeks. "It was the first experience Rose ever had of coloured people, and she didn't enjoy it", Fred later recalled.

The bathroom in the property was on the first floor, and Rose would later recall that a young Jamaican who lived in the flat on that floor had tried it on with her when she was four months pregnant with Heather. She said he forced her into a corner and tried to force himself on her and she had to fight him off.

Just a week later, Fred arranged for the family to move to 4 Park End Road, another of Frank Zygmunt's properties which was just a few hundred yards away. This time they were in the middle flat of the house, and the school that Charmaine and Anne Marie were about to go to was just around the corner.

Again, this property proved unsuitable so in July Fred, Rose and the two children moved back to Midland Road, but this time to number 25. Rose recalled: "We moved to Midland Road, just outside the town centre, where there were a lot of Jamaicans living. That was my first experience of coloured people. My parents came to visit us there and tried to make up with us."

25 Midland Road

The flat was on the ground floor with a bedroom, living-room and small kitchen. The bathroom was shared on the first floor. There were two other flats in the house and a basement, which was occupied by an elderly Polish gentleman when they moved in, but the basement was inhabitable and he soon moved out. At the rear of the property was a small, unkept garden where an elderly coal cellar was attached to the house. Their flat was compact and Anne Marie recalls it being cold and dark. It was sparsely furnished with some shabby curtains and bare carpets left by the Polish owner Frank Zygmunt when he moved out. The view opposite was of Gloucester Park.

Fred was still working at the tyre fitters but spending more time each evening working for Frank Zygmunt, the owner of the flat and he was encouraging Fred to learn more about the building trade. The harder Fred worked, the more work Fred would be given. According to Rose's brother, Andrew: "Fred saw it as Rose's job to look after the kids" while he went out to work.

It didn't take long for the violence that Rose had learned from her father to come out. Anne Marie recalled that at this time when Fred was out at work, Rose would tell her and Charmaine that they were difficult children and that Charmaine reacted by telling her that her real mum would be back one day to take her away. Charmaine hated Rose and never shied away from telling her so. Anne Marie remembered that Fred had ordered them to call Rose 'Mum' but that they were both reluctant to do so which caused more arguments. She remembered fighting with Rose for Fred's affection and

Rose would tell Fred that Anne Marie was being naughty and doing things that she hadn't which caused Fred to shout at her.

She recalled Rose's uncontrollable temper and times when she would froth at the mouth and stab repeatedly at her arm with a knife. She also recalled both her and Charmaine being made to stand naked on chairs and hit with a wet leather belt.

Rose made the girls do most of the household chores. They did the vacuuming, cleaning, dusting and washing up, as well as setting the dinner table and helping with the cooking. If the jobs weren't done to Rose's satisfaction she would beat the children. Anne Marie recalled that Rose "didn't try to hide the beatings from Dad. It was rare for him to lose his temper with us or hit us himself, but he never, ever objected to Rose doing so. In later years his only comment would be: 'Make sure you hit them where it doesn't show'."

She recalled an incident which is still held on her medical records which show that she had a number of stitches in a head wound after a 'fall'. One morning Rose instructed the children to get up and wash their breakfast bowls before going to school but Charmaine was in an antagonistic mood and slowly dragged her chair across the floor to make as much nose as possible. Rose swore at them both and told them to get a move on but Charmaine replied: "My real mother wouldn't swear or shout at us!" Anne Marie could sense the fury building in Rose and quickly queued up behind Charmaine at the sink. Charmaine was playing with the water to annoy Rose and Rose shouted at Anne Marie "What are you doing there?" She replied that she was just waiting to wash her bowl in the sink. Rose snapped and ripped the bowl from her hands and broke it across her head.

There were other incidents too, where the children would be dragged across the floor by their hair, have their mouths taped up, be gagged and have their hands tied up with ripped-up old sheets or with washing line cord. She would tie them together, or tie them to the bed separately. If they spoke in anything other than a quiet whisper and they would be gagged. If they carried on annoying Rose then the beatings would begin. Rose could then hit them as hard as she liked with whatever she liked.

Shirley Giles, her husband, and their two daughters Tracey and Janet moved in to the flat above Fred and Rose shortly after. They were buying their own house and needed somewhere to live while the deal went through. Shirley grew to become a good friend of Rose's and Charmaine became good friends with the two girls.

Fred expected Rose to continue to ply her trade as a prostitute while the children were at school. He told her to start working the bus garage as Rena had done in Glasgow. She was more than happy to go along with the plan. Fred got himself another job, as a Milkman, for Model Dairies in the early mornings before going on to his main job as a tyre fitter. He would leave home at 3am, do his milk round, and then go straight to work at Cotswold Tyres, rush home for dinner and then go straight out again to do work for Frank Zygmunt or to repair someone's car. Rose and the children hardly saw him.

Rose was really struggling to look after the children, after all she was still a child herself. On one occasion she accidently left a paraffin heater tilted on a carpet and the paraffin spilled out, setting the children's bedroom alight. She immediately rang Fred at work to ask what to do but just told her "You'll just have to get on with it. I'm not leaving work." Eventually the fire brigade came after Rose asked her neighbour Shirley Giles to help her.

At the end of September Rose's parents Bill and Daisy Letts turned up at Midland Road without warning, having discovered from one of her sisters where she was now living. It was a rare occasion when Fred was at home too and he recalled: "There was a knock at the door, and Rose went to the door. She was very near due to have her baby. Rose come back to me and she looked white as a sheet…and she said 'Mum and Dad's at the door'." Fred then went to the front door himself and said: "Look, I've got nothing against you whatsoever, but give me any trouble and I'll give you more trouble than you brought me." He then invited them in. "We got on quite well…it was only a matter of days before Rose fell in to labour, and her mother and father said they would have the children…Charmaine and Anne Marie, while she was in hospital." Bill and Fred became quite close after this and Fred would go on to say: "He was bloody everlasting there after that."

At 02:45 on the 17th October Rose gave birth to her first child, Heather Ann West, at Gloucester Royal Hospital. As Rose was still living at home when she fell pregnant there is a possibility that her father Bill was actually Heather's father.

Rose chose to bottle feed her baby as she struggled to bring up the other two children as well. Her solicitor, Leo Goatley, would later recall asking Rose if she ever breastfed her children. Her reply was succinct: "Tits are for fucking!" At this stage, being a 16-year-old first time mother looking after two other children as well, she should have been brought under the watch of Social Services and monitored but she wasn't. And so began a pattern that would persist throughout the West story as the warning signs went unheeded by family members, teachers, neighbours, social services and the police.

Fred wasn't much help with the new baby and in early November he was arrested for 'swapping' a vehicle excise disc from one of Frank

Zygmunt's vans to his own and changing the details. He was arrested again a couple of weeks later, this time for the theft of four tyres from his employers at Cotswold Tyres, Albion Street, Cheltenham. As a result, Fred was sacked and he went to work for Frank Zygmunt every day after his milk round.

He appeared at Gloucester Magistrates Court on the 4th December, charged with 'Theft', 'No Insurance', 'No Test Certificate, 'No Vehicle Excise License' and had the charge of 'Theft' of the fencing panels from his suspended sentence of 28th August 1969 added. He was imprisoned in Gloucester Prison leaving Rose to look after the three girls alone. He was given 3 months imprisonment for each case of the theft of car tyres and having no insurance, and disqualified from driving for 9 months. He was fined £3 for having no Test Certificate. He was also fined £5 and told to pay £10.8s.4d in back duty. He was imprisoned for 6 months for the theft of the fencing panels.

While he was in prison Rose struggled to pay the bills and the rent. The only income she had would have been from prostitution, but with 3 small children it would have been hard for her to earn much. It's widely believed that she was having sex with the elderly Frank Zygmunt at this point as a way of paying the rent.

During his prison sentence, Rose beat the children even more harshly. She would hit Charmaine and Anne Marie for not mashing potatoes properly or for not stirring the gravy the right way. "Your fucking fault. You should have done it properly", she would tell them. She would grab them by their hair and drag them across the floor, as well as scream and shout at them. The girls would be locked in their room and sometimes tied together. At times they would be tied naked to their bed and threatened to be silent. She would even lock Charmaine in her room for an entire day, with her hands tied behind her back and her legs spread-eagled and strapped to the bed. Rose would go out and deliberately leave Charmaine alone in the flat in this predicament. If the girls made a noise they would be slapped across the face or have a wet belt beaten across their legs.

"Sometimes you felt the back of her hand, but if she wanted to give you a good going-over, she would grab the nearest weapon, so she didn't hurt herself. I was hit across the head with a broom on more than one occasion, and I still have a small scar where she knifed my hand", recalled Anne Marie. "To watch her go into one of her major rages was like watching a horror movie. Her expression would change: you would see a coolness transforming her face. It would go like porcelain, very cold and translucent. Then her eyes would disconnect. When she got really angry and began to hit you, she would froth at the mouth and spit. She was like a wild dog. Evil, truly evil. If she was going to use the belt to give you a thrashing, Rose would wet it first. Damp leather stings, and she liked to inflict as much pain as possible. She would use both ends of the belt. Once she lashed me between the legs with the buckle end and I was bruised and bleeding by the time she had finished."

That last statement is very reminiscent of what Fred would later do to their babysitter Caroline Owens after he and Rose abducted her.

Fred's brother John had been having an affair and asked Rose if he could move his girlfriend into her flat. In a letter to Fred over Christmas 1970, which was later found amongst his belongings, Rose wrote to him about 'John's girlfriend' coming to stay at the flat, saying: "Is it alright if she comes to stay with me. It'll be company for me and she's great fun". The letter concluded: "Keep happy. Keep writing them letters. Keep kissing me. With all the love I have in my heart. Your ever worshipping wife. Rose." Interestingly, Rose had already started to call herself Fred's 'wife' and also Rose had written in the letter: "I give you my solemn word that John won't stay here under any circumstances. I think, like I told John, I'd be violently sick if anyone tried to touch me. I think I'd be that sick I wouldn't have any insides left. Just think when you come out it'll be like when we first met."

Rose was actually lying to Fred and was sleeping with John. He admitted as much when he was interviewed by the police in 1994 and Rose later said that she was having an affair with a man at this time and was trying to find a way to leave Fred.

A week after Christmas, on the 31st December, Fred appeared at Cheltenham Magistrates Court, where he received an additional 1 months' prison sentence for the theft of the car tyres.

In early 1971, Charmaine started to say that she wanted to go and live with her real mother, Rena. At every opportunity she would tell Rose: "You're not my Mum. You can't tell me what to do!" This was corroborated by Rose's sister Glenys, Mrs Giles upstairs, Anne Marie and even Rose herself. It became common knowledge in the family that Charmaine was unhappy and that it would be better for everyone if a way could be found for her to live with Rena. Charmaine repeatedly infuriated Rose by her refusal to neither cry or display any sign of grief or servitude no matter how severely she was beaten or what punishment she was subjected to. Rose was constantly trying to 'break' her. Despite the years of neglect and abuse she had endured, Charmaine would tell Anne Marie that her "mummy will come and save me."

Charmaine's best friend was Tracey Giles who lived upstairs. One day Tracey was asked by her mother to pop downstairs to borrow something from Rose. She did as asked, but instead of knocking on the door, she burst in and saw Charmaine standing on a chair with her hands tied behind her back and Rose poised with a wooden spoon as if about to hit her. She ran upstairs in tears and her mother went downstairs to confront Rose. She simply told Mrs Giles that "Charmaine had been very naughty" and she had to "teach her right from wrong."

On the 27th January Fred was transferred from prison in Gloucester to Leyhill Open Prison, Wotton-under-Edge.

Fred and Rose wrote to each other and in letters from prisoner 401317 to Rose he wrote: "You can bring Char and Anna as it is open prison. Please bring them with you my darling. You are my precious diamond never to be lost or hurt. A star fell from Heaven right into my arms. Give Heather a big cuddle, the biggest one you can…I know you have a hard life without me. Thank Anna and Char for their letters."

The letters they swapped spoke of their future lives together, where he told Rose that when he was released he would have fifty-two weeks in bed with her, and produce two sons. "The honour of having our son is yours, or there will be no son for me."

In one of her letters to Fred, Rose exposed the possibility that Fred looked at Anne Marie as more than just a daughter. "If you ask me your whole life is Anna. Remember darling you can't fall in love with your own daughter, nor spend the rest of your life with her…I reckon that when you come home and there's something wrong that she don't like, you'll chuck me out."

Rose visited Fred every four weeks, and Fred remembered: "Rose used to come down and see me in prison regular, and she told me that Rena was seeing the girls at school…Charmaine used to say to Rose: 'I'm going with my mammie shortly, so I'm not taking no orders off you'."

While Fred was in prison, Daisy, Bill, Glenys and Graham went to visit Rose. They were shocked by the condition of the flat. The wooden floorboards were stained and dirty, there were used nappies all over the floor and there was crockery piled high in the sink. "The place was a shambles, you wouldn't want your dog to live in it", Graham went on to say. With Bill's OCD he couldn't bring himself to sit down and Daisy was shocked by Rose's foul language. She also noticed Rose's eyes were red from crying and that she'd lost a lot of weight. Graham remembered: "Rosemary couldn't cope; it hit her all of a sudden and she got run down." She admitted to Glenys that she did not like Charmaine because the child wet the bed and told her that she smacked her when she did this. Daisy called round twice after this, on both occasions unannounced, and on one of these visits she found Rose had gone out with Anne Marie and baby Heather, but had left Charmaine alone in the flat.

Rose later told her daughter Mae about this period in her life. "Heather was born and Fred started doing repair work for the man we rented the flat from. Then Fred went to prison for crimes. I was only eighteen, and I was pregnant with you, I had a twelve-month old baby, Heather and I had Charmaine and Anne Marie to look after, all in a one-bedroom flat. I made a good friend with the lady upstairs, but I felt very alone, especially at night, and money was really tight."

On the 4th March, Rose wrote a letter to Fred:

To My Darling,

What was you on about at the beginning of your letter. I just can't make it out for trying. Hey love that's great, three more visits, it'll take up half the time I've got to wait for you. Blinking base peoples get's on my nerves. Darling, about Char. I think she likes to be handled rough. But darling, why do I have to be the one to do it. I would keep her for her own sake, if it wasn't for the rest of the children. You can see Char coming out in Anna now. And I hate it.

She later carried on:

About our son, I'll see the doctor about the pill. And then we'll be safe to decide about it when you come home.

This letter shows how she was struggling to look after the children. She was obviously annoyed with the neighbours playing loud music, and by saying that Charmaine "like's to be handled rough", shows how Rose would beat the child in an attempt to make her cry. By asking "why do I have to be the one to do it?" the question must be asked who else would discipline her? Rena was not around and Fred was in prison. The sentence "I would keep her for her own sake…you can see her coming out in Anna now. And I hate it", tends to give credence to Rose's defence at her trial where she told the court that her and Fred had discussed letting her go back to stay with her mother Rena and how she didn't want the younger children to turn out like her. However, the prosecution used this letter to show that Rose wanted rid of Charmaine.

The other question that needs to be asked is why would Rose need to go on the pill to ensure that she only gave birth to Fred's son when he came out of prison? This comment adds more weight to John West's claims that at this time he was sleeping with her and also that she was sleeping with her landlord and possibly her father still. In later police interviews, Fred would say: "making love to your father, you don't have a chat-up, I shouldn't think. So she lost that part of her life. Rose didn't want foreplay; she wanted rough sex."

At her trial in 1995, she admitted that she was having an affair. "I was in a difficult position. I had had an affair with a man. I wanted this man but I was not sure whether I could split up my home without hurting the children."

Shirley Giles, Rose's neighbour at Midland Road recalled: "Rose would say that she couldn't cope with Charmaine. She ruled Anna Marie and Charmaine with a steel rod, but Charmaine had a rebellious nature which she didn't like." She also remembered Rose adding that she "had had enough of Charmaine"; she was "at the end of her tether" with the girl and could not wait to get rid of her.

Hospital records reveal that Charmaine had received treatment for a severe puncture wound to her left ankle in the casualty unit of Gloucester Royal Hospital at 18:50 on the 28th March 1971. This incident was explained by Rose to have resulted from a household accident, but it is now believed that Rose had used a knife to either jab at her or had thrown it at her when she wouldn't do as she was told.

A few weeks after this incident, Anne Marie recalls that she opened the door to their bedroom and found her big sister naked and tied to the bed by her wrists and ankles. She looked terrified and her hair was wet, as if she had been sweating or crying.

In April, Mrs Giles, her husband Ronald and two children Janet and Tracey, moved out of Midland Road to their new home in Cinderford. She promised her daughter Tracey that they could go back and visit Charmaine. When they returned later in June, Charmaine was no longer there, and was told by Rose that Charmaine had already gone to live with her mother. Tracey burst into tears and was comforted by Anne Marie. Rose did not offer them a drink and they got no further than the hallway. Mrs Giles noticed a model caravan made by Fred in prison from matchsticks and sent him a letter asking if he could make one for her.

He sent a letter to Rose in reply to her letter regarding Charmaine being treated rough. He wrote:

Now about Char, yes or no. I say yes but it is up to you darling, and then we can have our SON, ha ha, darling and we will keep our own darling.

He concluded:

I love you and Anna and Heather forever my darling

At Rose's trial in 1995, Rose's defence argued that this letter meant that Fred and Rose were discussing sending Charmaine to live with her mother Rena and that Fred thought it was a good idea but wanted Rose to have the final say. He wanted them to have a son and to keep their own

60

children, not Charmaine who was not related by blood to either of them and proved the point by not saying that he loved her as he signed off his letter. The prosecution successfully argued that this letter actually meant that yes, Rose should get rid of Charmaine, and he would sort it out later.

On the 29th April, Rose arranged for a photographer to come to Midland Road and take photographs of the children. A photograph of Charmaine, showing the gap in her front teeth, was taken and this photo would later be used to identify her remains.

Charmaine, Heather and Anne Marie

On the 7th May, Rose took the three children to see Fred in prison. Just two days later, Fred wrote to Rose saying:

You say yes to Char. That's good. I will see to it when I get out but don't tell her for you know what she's like, and you can have our son as soon as I come out.

61

In interviews years later, when Fred was accusing Rose of carrying out all of the murders, Fred would say about this letter: "We were going to let Charmaine go off with Rena…'cause what I wanted to do was to just come home, grab the kids, get another place, and forget about it. But Rose didn't fucking want that because Charmaine was giving Rose a hard time."

At the beginning of June, Charmaine appeared in a school end of year photograph and on the 15th June Rose took the children to visit Fred in prison.

Around this time Rose told one of her neighbours, a Polish lady named Mrs Jagura, that she could not 'wait to get rid of Charmaine', and was waiting for the child's mother to come and take her away.

Anne Marie remembered: "One day I went to school and Charmaine didn't and when I came home Rosemary was putting nappies out on the line…and I said: 'Where's Charmaine?' I remember our bedroom, the door was locked and the key was always at the top. So I went and opened the door and I actually saw Charmaine tied to the bed and I'll never forget she looked at me and she had pleading eyes and I shut the door and locked it and later when I went to bed she wasn't there."

Rose is believed to have killed Charmaine shortly before Fred was released from prison on the 24th June 1971. In addition to later forensic odontology confirmation, Charmaine had died while Fred was still incarcerated, and further testimony from Tracey Giles' mother, Shirley, would corroborate the fact Charmaine had been murdered before Fred had been released. Shirley Giles would state that after her family had vacated the upper flat of 25 Midland Road in April 1971, that on one day in June, she had taken her eldest daughter Tracey to visit Charmaine, only for Tracey to be told by Rose: "She's gone to live with her mother, and bloody good riddance."

Rose has never said what actually happened to Charmaine but she was probably either battered or stabbed to death. She would stick to a carefully prepared story for the next twenty-four years; Rena had collected Charmaine and she had gone to live with her.

As with the Giles family, Rose explained Charmaine's disappearance to others who enquired as to her whereabouts by claiming that Rena had taken her to live in Bristol, although she informed staff at her primary school that Charmaine had moved with her mother to London. When Fred was released from prison on the 24th June, he told Anne Marie that her mother had collected Charmaine and returned to Scotland. She asked Fred why Rena had taken Charmaine and not her and he callously replied: "She wouldn't want you, love. You're the wrong colour."

Rose's brother Graham remembered: "Charmaine, we was told,

preferred to be with her mother and that was the reason why she had disappeared, and Scotland was a very, very long way at the time, although we love Charmaine, all of us dearly, but it was maybe a little bit strange that she suddenly wanted to go back and not say 'cheerio'."

The body of Charmaine was initially stowed in the coal cellar of Midland Road until Fred was released from prison. He buried Charmaine's naked body in the back garden, close to the back door of the flat, and although he remained adamant he had not dismembered this particular victim, a subsequent autopsy suggested Charmaine's body had been severed at the hips. In addition, several bones – kneecaps, finger bones, wrist bones, toe bones and ankle bones – were missing from her skeleton. This would prove to be a distinctive discovery in all of the autopsies of the victims exhumed in 1994.

Once out of prison, he wasted no time in drilling holes in the bedroom door and lining up men for Rose to 'perform' with. These men were mostly Jamaicans with whom he had made friends with whilst in prison and whilst working at various sites for Frank Zygmunt. As soon as Rose's client had finished and left, Fred would then have sex with her. He told her that by coating himself in the superior sperm from another man it would help him delay ejaculation.

This picture was taken shortly after Fred's release from prison and after Charmaine's murder. Rose is 17 and Fred is 29.

On the 2nd August, Fred started a new job at Simon Gloster SARO and by the end of August, Rena had become concerned as to the whereabouts of Charmaine. By now Rena was living in Reading and she had travelled regularly to Gloucester to take Charmaine for days out when she was supposed to be at school. According to Fred: "She would visit Charmaine at school, and take her out for the day." Rena was so concerned that she couldn't visit Charmaine that she visited Fred's father Walter at Moorcourt Cottage in late August to find out if he knew where her children were. Fred's sister-in-law, Christine, would recall that Rena was both depressed and extremely anxious about her children's welfare. Christine had recently married Fred's brother Doug and they were living at the cottage at the time. When Rena turned up Christine told her that Walter was down on the farm so Rena went down and helped him bring in the corn. Rena managed to get Fred's home address from him and she set off to confront him. This was the last time she was seen alive.

It is believed Fred agreed to meet Rena at the East End Tavern in Barton Street in Gloucester at 21:30. According to Fred: "She was with a gang of Irish blokes" and was drunk by the time he got there. He continued to buy her drinks until she was paralytic and incapable of resisting him. He said he offered her a lift and she was "very loving when she got drunk" and helped her to get in to the passenger seat. He decided to take her to Much Marcle, and halfway there he had to help her in to the back because "she was so drunk".

When they arrived at the entrance to Letterbox Field it was dark. He said that they used to make love all the time in that field so that's why he took her there. He helped her out of the car, took a rug out of the boot and walked up the field to an Oak Tree on the edge of the field. He said he woke her up and "we made love against…by the tree there, just on the edge of the field." According to him, shortly afterwards they walked halfway back to the car, sat on the bank "and made love again there."

He said that they went back to the car but "I lost my head with her a bit and we had a right set-to, and a right row…and that was when she ended up getting killed…I just smashed her against the gate." He said that he ended his wife's life by kicking her to death on the ground.

After his arrest in 1994, he maintained that "I didn't know what to do then. It was the first time I'd ever been mixed up in anything like that, so the only thing I could think of was to bury her in the field." He then added that he just happened to have a pickaxe and spade in the boot of his car, as well as a curved two-and-a-half foot long Jamaican sabre knife, which he used to dismember the body. He said that the ground was hard due to the time of year and it took him around half an hour to dig a hole, but then "the problem was it wasn't big enough…and then I realized that I couldn't get her in there, so I then decided to cut her up and put her in there." It was now just after 23:00 and Fred "took her legs off and her head off", and buried her body in the hole in Letterbox Field.

After he had finished he went to the cattle trough and washed his hands and upper body, because he had been in just his trousers. He then had a cigarette before putting "all her clothes in a big chunky sweater she wore" and "chucked them over into a fire" that he insisted was alight in a nearby field, which he knew as "The Allotments".

Rena Costello

After Rena's murder, Fred and Rose became keen to involve others in their sex lives. They made friends with a neighbour who lived in the house next door and she was called Elizabeth Agius. She was 19-years-old and had married a Maltese man and had 2 children. They met when Fred noticed her struggling to get up the stairs with her pram and so rushed to her assistance. They got talking and he invited her over to meet Rose and have a cup of tea. She remembered that when she first met Rose, she thought that she was only about 14-years-old but that she was obviously pregnant. They got on well and so she went to visit them regularly.

Fred once helped to decorate a room for her, as her husband was away in Malta. Elizabeth Agius said in a statement to police: "That was the sort of person he was, always helpful if he could be. He was a real sweet talker. He would charm most women, a real gentleman." She said she first became aware of Fred and Rose's unusual sex life when Rose told her that Fred wanted her to join them in a three-in-a-bed session. "She said Fred was falling in love with me and desperate to have sex with me. She did her best to encourage me. She told me she had sex with other men. There were condoms and rubber things. I told her I wasn't interested. She told me she liked Fred to watch her having sex and there was a hole in the wall. If Fred wasn't there she had to tell him about it." She told the police that by the time she had known the couple about nine months Fred's remarks got more and more suggestive. He told her he would like to tie her to the bed; he said she could burn him with a cigarette or whip him. He would say all of this in front of Rose, but Elizabeth said that she just "used to laugh it off."

Elizabeth Agius in 1995

In November, a neighbour complained to Social Services of naked sex romps at 25 Midland Road and that an unusually large number of young women were visiting late at night and early in the morning. A district nurse, who was responsible for maternity care for Heather and school checks on her step-sisters was sent to investigate, but she found nothing to justify alerting other agencies.

At 11:00 on the 29th January 1972, Fred and Rose married at Gloucester Registry Office. Rose recalled that "Even the marriage was rushed. Fred was fixing an old car half an hour before we were due at the Registry Office. I had to beg him to take off his overalls. His brother John witnessed the marriage, and another friend of Fred's who had so many aliases he had to scribble out the first name he wrote on the certificate." Fred apparently found some money in the street on the way home which he used to pay for the marriage license. Rose remembered: "We had no honeymoon. We just went to the Wellington Pub and he bought me one drink. He asked me what I wanted, and I said a lager and lime. He said: 'you have a bloody Coke and like it.'"

Fred put himself down as a bachelor on the certificate. This was seen and signed by Rose, along with John West and Mick Thornbrook. Either they were aware that Fred had killed Rena, or Fred had told them that he had divorced her. I suspect that in the case of Rose and John, they were fully aware that Fred had killed Rena.

19.1.. Marriage solemnized at .... the Register Office .... in the .... County Borough .. of .. Gloucester .... in the

No.	When married	Name and surname	Age.	Condition	Rank or profession	Residence at the time of marriage	Father's name and surname	Rank or profession of father
181	Twenty sixth January 191..	Frederick Malin	30 years	Bachelor	Glazier Plate glass labourer	26. Midland Road WEST.	Walter Maple	Draper
		Rosemary Pauline WEST	18 years	Spinster	—	56 midland Road LEYS.	William Andrew Quaman	Blacksmith Engineer

Married in the Register Office

This marriage was solemnized between us, { Frederick Malin / R.P. West }

in the presence of us, { ... R. Mumbert / L.B.E. West }
Justice E.G.

MXH 349325

CERTIFIED to be a true copy of an entry in the certified copy of a register of Marriages in the Registration District of Gloucester City

Given at the GENERAL REGISTER OFFICE, under the Seal of the said Office, the   4th   day of   May   2018

One evening shortly after their wedding, Fred and Rose told Elizabeth Agius that they had been out looking for young female hitchhikers. Fred claimed that he got them into prostitution and that he liked them to be between fifteen and seventeen-years-old because they were more likely to be virgins and that way he could get more money for them.

In her statement to police, Mrs Agius said that Fred and Rose had told her it was easier to get the girls into the car with Rose present. Often the girls had run away from home and had no money and would do anything for cash and a place to live. She said: "I babysat when they were out. Once they came back very late. It was in the early hours of the morning. They had been as far as London looking. Fred said the best pick-up place was Bristol, because there were a lot of young girls trying to get to the bright lights of London." She said she just dismissed this as Fred's smutty talk and laughed it off but then Rose told her that Fred was actually telling the truth, and went on to tell her that she was working as a prostitute herself. She earned "extra money that way" and "Fred didn't mind one bit." In fact, he "liked to watch and listen" to know exactly what she did with her clients. "There was a hole through the wall" so that he could watch whenever he wanted to, but if he was at work "she'd tell him exactly what happened."

Elizabeth later said: "As time went by, as I got to know Rosemary and Fred West, Rose started talking to me about her personal life, how did I feel about it? By she was a prostitute. I just told her it was her business and nothing to do with me. She did go into details that she had microphones or something in the bedroom because if she ever had clients there, Fred was always on the other side, listening in the next room. He liked to listen to things like that…I never took no notice really. I liked her for what she was, as a friend. What she did in her own life was her own business, not mine.

He started off a casual conversation like 'How are you?', 'Where have you been?', then as time went by, it got to sex. He always talked about sex. He used to say to me: 'What I could do with you in bed.' Would I like to try it with him? If I liked it, I could have three-in-a-bed with him, Rose and myself. How would I feel if I went on the game? It was just sex, sex, sex. Sex mad!

He said to me that he likes to go around finding young girls. Because they'd run away they've got no homes, he would support them by giving them a roof over their heads, and if they wanna go on the game work for him. One day, Rose knocked on the door. She said she was going out with Fred, and I said: 'Well why are you going with him?' and she turned around and she said to me 'as long as there's a woman in the car with a male, there's always an easy chance that another girl they are going to pick up will get in the car because she will be with him."

With the report of young girls going in and out of the flat often it begs the question of how many women and young girls were abused in this flat?

One afternoon Rose showed Elizabeth two small shoe boxes she kept under the double bed in the front room at Midland Road. One contained an assortment of different coloured capsules, while the other was filled with sugar cubes wrapped in silver paper. Rose told her that they were both "for protection against disease". When she visited Rose soon afterwards, she began to feel drowsy shortly after having a cup of tea they had given her. The next thing she remembered, she was to confess to the police two decades later, was "coming to" naked and in bed with both Fred and Rose.

The relationship between the neighbours changed when Elizabeth's husband returned from Malta and she tried to introduce him to Fred. "Fred got quite funny and stormed off into the kitchen. He said: 'I'll kill him and put him down there', indicating the cellar. He said: 'If I can't have you, why can he?' I said he was nuts."

Elizabeth also recalled the violent side shown by Rose. "When Fred was there she was alright, but when he wasn't there, she seemed to pick on Anna a lot. This one day, for no particular reason, she got hold of Anna's hair and she dragged her from one side of the room to the other, screaming, shouting and punching her. I just couldn't believe it. I said to Rose West once when I caught her hitting her I said 'If I ever see you marking them I would report you.' She said 'No Liz, I wouldn't do that.' I said: 'You wouldn't do that? Look how you treat them…you pull their bloody hair' and she said 'But she makes me mad. Don't your kids ever make you mad?' I said 'Well yeah, but not like you'."

Despite being several months pregnant, Rose still entertained her clients in the afternoons. They were usually from the local bus garage, although she would also sleep with a couple of Fred's friends, including a well-known burglar who had stayed with them in the flat from time to time, as well as their landlord. Fred insisted that Rose talk suggestively to her clients and made as much noise as possible when making love. "And I always made love to her again, after they'd gone, like. That was part of the deal", Fred revealed.

On the 1st June, Rose gave birth to May June West. After the court case in 1995 she would change the spelling of her name to Mae. Rose stayed in hospital for ten days after the birth, waiting and waiting for Fred to visit her and then take her home, but he never turned up when he said he would. Eventually she gave up waiting and made her own way back to the flat with Mae, against the doctors' advice. When she got home Rose claims that she found Fred in bed with Elizabeth Agius. She said that when she got back to her flat "Anna Marie was dirty and Heather was a mess." She went around to Elizabeth Agius' house, where she said the front door was open. She climbed the stairs to the top floor and hammered on the door. There was a lengthy silence until, eventually, Fred emerged "flushed and hassled."

Around this time, their landlord Frank Zygmunt proposed that the ever increasing family should move to a bigger property. He offered them another of his properties, a house at 25 Cromwell Street, which had 6 rooms on 3 floors, a back garden and a basement. The house was in a state of disrepair and it would take Fred many years to get it up to scratch. The price was £6,500. Frank offered to lend them £500 for the deposit, and he agreed to help Fred apply to Gloucester City Council for a mortgage for the remainder. Frank had previously rented the house out as bedsits to students but had then quickly had to evict them for mess, nuisance and non-payment of rent. He had done the absolute minimum to make the house suitable for quick multi-occupation.

Leo Goatley later recalled: "The house was on 3 floors, and as it turned out a basement as well. The rooms were very small and very close together and to have a family there, then half a dozen lodgers, then the place would have been packed and it would have been very difficult to come and go without hearing footsteps on the stairs."

To make it up to Rose for not bringing her and Mae back from the hospital, Fred took her on a belated honeymoon to North Devon. They stopped off at The Golden Lion Pub in Northam where Rose chatted to some of her former neighbours. Rita New, a chalet cleaner from Westward Ho! Holiday camp and former friend of both Joyce and Patricia Letts, later explained: "I had my daughter Tracy with me... I sat with Margaret Wilcox – Barry Seathe and his wife were sat by the bar. The door opened and in walked a slim man in a tank top...He had two young women with him – one with a blonde bob and one with long dark hair, who was about eighteen. Barry chatted to them then brought the dark one over to me and said: 'Do you know who this is?' I didn't recognize her, it'd been some years since she'd left but she said: 'It's Rose'. She was smiling and looked lovely – she was a beautiful girl. She said: 'I don't have anything to do with them now (meaning her family). This is my husband (pointing to the man at the bar).' I saw him at the bar with the blonde. He was all fidgety and on edge. She said they'd got married and couldn't have a honeymoon at the time for some reason, so they were taking a belated one. After a while Rose said: 'We've got to go now – I've taken them to Exeter, now I'm going to show them Ilfracombe.' When they went Barry came over to us. He said that blonde with him at the bar, that's his ex-missus. 'I find it awful funny', Barry said, 'he takes his ex-missus on a belated honeymoon...I find it most weird that's his ex-missus'."

The blonde lady was not with them by the time they reached Plymouth, and to this day, no-one has been able to identify her. It certainly couldn't have been Fred's ex-wife Rena as he had already killed and buried her. Could it have been Elizabeth Agius?

Rose then took the family on to Benbow Street to see her old friend Joan Scobbling. Joan invited them in, but Fred wouldn't get out of the car. He sat with the children as Joan passed orange squash through the car window to them while she and Rose chatted.

Once back from their honeymoon, Fred and Rose decided to move to 25 Cromwell Street. Fred asked Elizabeth Agius if she wanted to move in with them. He told her that she could go on the game and that the Social Security would pay her rent. But only if she agreed to leave her husband, but Elizabeth just laughed off his suggestion. He also told others that he could use the basement as a bar and have card schools there. He also suggested that it could be turned in to a children's play area, and even boasted to one that he was going to make home-made pornographic movies down there using prostitutes from Birmingham and elsewhere.

Fred needed more income to pay off the mortgage so he took a new job as a Fibreglass Presser at Permali's factory on Bristol Road. He worked mainly during the nights and worked for Frank Zygmunt during the day.

Even though he was married, it appears that Fred carried on approaching women on his own. Caroline Langman said in a statement in 1995 that in 1972 when she was just 16-years-old she was repeatedly followed by a blue van as she cycled home from school in Gloucester and that she later received an obscene telephone call. Her brother answered the phone to a man who asked for her by name. The caller subjected her to a stream of sexual abuse, using phrases such as "I would like to do to you" (as Fred had previously said to Elizabeth Agius). She said she was once too terrified to ride past his van. She went to a nearby house where police were called. When she saw Fred West's photograph in 1994 she "went very cold and felt very strange. All of this incident immediately came back to me. The photo was that man who followed me all those years ago."

5 25 CROMWELL STREET

In September 1972, Fred and Rose officially moved in to 25 Cromwell Street, Gloucester. Cromwell Street was not regarded as a good area. Most of the houses in the street had been sub-divided into flats and bedsits and a single-storey corrugated hut stood at the side of the house, used as a church by Seventh Day Adventist's. (The church was later turned into a brick building, as can be seen on the right of the picture above).

In order to pay Frank Zygmunt back as quickly as possible, and save money to pay off the mortgage, Fred decided to rent out the top two floors of the house as bedsits. Rose didn't get much of a say. He advertised the rooms through word of mouth at first, letting it be known that he had rooms going for cheap around the cafes and local pubs that he frequented.

It wasn't long before the first group of young men moved in. They brought with them drugs and troubled friends. It didn't take long for the word to get around that 25 Cromwell Street was a place where you could crash and get up to almost anything you want, and where the landlord didn't ask questions.

Mike Yost, a policeman at the time, recalled: "I knew Fred. I met Fred many times in the Pop-In Café, a little café in Southgate Street, where the youngsters used to congregate, Fred being a little older than them, where I used to pick up snips of information, listen, find out what was going on and I also met Fred when he had been brought into custody for petty things, where he was fingerprinted and photographed…Fred was well known to the police as a petty criminal."

Elizabeth Agius continued to visit Fred and Rose and she remembered being shown around. "We went down there (the basement) and Fred said he wasn't sure what to make of this yet. He said: 'I don't know whether to make it a playing area for the children' he nudged me and used to say 'or else I could make this into my torture room' and things like that. He said: 'and just think what I could do to you down here. Nobody would hear me 'cause I would make it soundproof'.

Once, I was in what they called the sitting room but there was beds as well inside there. I was sitting on the settee and Rose was making a cup of tea and the next thing Fred come from behind the door, put these handcuffs on me, and I was quite nervous, and Rose turned around and said: 'Get those fucking off her!' and just like that, and without any hesitation, he took them off. When he put the handcuffs on me he said: 'now I've got you. This is what I could do to you and you couldn't do anything about it.' All I knew is that Rose was a prostitute and they both had other women as prostitutes, but I didn't see any, it was only what they told me."

Just a few weeks after moving in, Rose left Fred and went back to live with her parents. Rose would later suggest, after her arrest in 1994, that she left because Fred had tried to strangle her. She was unhappy because Fred was never around and it was she who had to deal with the noise of the tenants and people going in and out of the house at all hours. She wanted her part of the house kept separate, but he refused to listen. He started to show his violent side towards her at this point, and began punching and kicking her when he 'lost it' over her nagging him about the lodgers. Rose also claimed that he had tried to strangle her with her own clothing after an argument, and that he only released her after he made her take back her words. He then picked up a cup of hot tea and threw it over her.

In the last months of his life, Fred described what happened next. "Rose was actually treated like a schoolgirl by me, and this came to a head in Cromwell Street. Rose was sort of Anna Marie's schoolgirl mate, and more or less acted like a schoolgirl sort of thing. That went right on up until she'd had Mae, and suddenly one morning Rose had obviously realised that she was a schoolgirl part of this marriage. What she did was, she didn't get any shopping in on Friday, and on the Sunday morning she got up early and said: 'I'm going out for the day'." This was a surprise to him as "Sunday dinner was always something really special." Anne Marie chose to stay with Fred, but Rose took Heather and Mae out with her and didn't tell Fred where she was going. When she hadn't returned by 17:00, Fred took Anne Marie with him to go and find her. "I mean, I knew exactly where she'd be. I gets there, and I jumps out the van, because you had to go across the green to her place in Tobyfield Road, and I crossed the green. By the time I'd got to the door, her father's standing there, protecting his daughter, and he says: 'Rose has left you'. So I said: 'What's the crack then? What's wrong?' and he says: 'You treat her like a child'. I said: 'Right, tell Rose that I'm going to sit in the van out the front there for ten minutes, and if she ain't there, there'll be somebody else in her bed tonight.' Within four minutes Rose was in the van with me and her father's following her, and he's saying: 'Oh, he's only kidding, he's only kidding'. Rose turned around and said: 'I know him, you don't, so shut up, Dad.' And so we went back home and we sorted it out. And from then on, that was where Rose had always had the say in the house, and I've had the say outside, work, my work, and everything."

One of the main points the prosecution focused on in the 1995 trial was the discussion had as Rose got back into the van. According to Daisy Letts, Rose's mother, as Rose left the house with the two children she told her "You don't know him. You don't know him. There's nothing he wouldn't do. Even murder!"

Rose's brother, Andrew Letts, also later recalled this incident. "There was one occasion that come to light when Rosemary did leave Fred. I think it was a couple of years after they got together and she came back home. I think it was just for the night, and Fred came round to fetch her and said: 'Come on Rosemary, you know what we've got between us. Come on back home.' And Rosemary, as she was leaving the house said: 'Mum, Dad, you don't know what he's really like, he's even capable of murder'."

If these are the words that Rosemary spoke, and it is odd that both her mother and brother say she did when she denies it, then it is clear that she already knew that Fred had killed. Had he told her about Ann McFall? Or Rena? Or Mary Bastholm? Or was there somebody else that we don't yet know about? Maybe after she had confessed to him that she had murdered Charmaine, he then opened up and excused it by admitting to her that he too had killed before. We simply don't know. And unless Rosemary West decides to change her stance of insisting that she knew nothing of the murders, we will probably never know.

As part of their new agreement, Fred handed over his pay packet at the end of every week to Rose and told her to use it for the food shopping and clothes for the children. In return, Rose insisted that she wanted a bedroom of her own to 'entertain her clients'. She now also started to give in to Fred's demands and agreed to sleep with some of his black friends, who, he assured her, were massive.

Fred was still working on the house and he divided the cellar into three interconnecting rooms. In the back room, nearest the garden, he kept his tools; the middle room where the stairs came down from the hallway, he left empty; and the front room he began to convert in to a playroom for his three children. He would work down there all day, after getting just a little sleep after his job at Permali's.

The main entrance to the house was at the side of the building and because street lighting was poor, number 25 was particularly dark at night. To maintain some privacy for his own family, Fred installed a cooker and a washbasin on the first-floor landing so that the lodgers didn't have to enter the ground floor where the West family lived, and only he and his family were allowed access to the rear garden.

The first two lodgers were Ben Stanniland and Alan 'Dapper' Davis. On the night they moved in, Fred invited them both out for a drink with him and Rose. The conversation was laced with sexual innuendo's, and Fred's questions about their 'girlfriends'. He was full of suggestions and told them that he had no objections to them bringing their girlfriends back to spend the night. When they returned back to Cromwell Street that night, Rose appeared upstairs in the top back room that the two men shared and climbed into bed with Ben Stanniland. After they had sex, she climbed out of his bed and into the bed of Alan Davis and had sex with him too. "In the morning we were a bit dubious about going downstairs", Ben later recalled, but Fred "made it clear it was OK". What they did not know was that Fred had been watching them through a hole he had drilled in the door. He also told two of his later lodgers that "if they couldn't pay the rent they would have to have sex with Rose." She also slept with the next batch of male lodgers David Evans and Charlie Knight, amongst others, in their top floor front bedroom.

Rose continued to work as a prostitute, and she later engaged in sexual relationships with several male and female lodgers who either lived in the house, or who Fred encountered via his work. She is also known to have bragged to several individuals that no man or woman could ever completely satisfy her.

The room Rose used for prostitution was known throughout the West household as 'Rose's Room', and had several hidden peepholes allowing Fred to watch her entertain her clients. He would also later install a baby monitor in the room, allowing him to listen from elsewhere in the house. The room included a private bar, and a red light outside the door warned when Rose was not to be disturbed. Rose carried the only key to this room around her neck, and Fred installed a separate doorbell to the household which Rose's clients were instructed to ring whenever they called around.

Rose didn't charge the men that Fred arranged for her to sleep with, she did it because she enjoyed it and because it was a turn-on for Fred.

The physical abuse of the children was still going on and Anne Marie recalled a time when she had made a cup of tea for Fred, Rose and some guests. As she was bringing the tea in for them she tripped and the tray containing the tea went all over her, scalding her. She remembered being quite badly burned and instead of helping her, Fred and Rose just laughed and made her start all over again.

It wasn't long before the abuse turned sexual, and in September 1972, Fred and Rose took 8-year-old Anne Marie down to the cellar. As she was lead down the stairs she noticed a number of items on the floor. She asked Fred: "What's going on? What are you doing?" Rose was smirking and Fred told her to "Just do as you're told. Take your clothes off and put them on the floor. Go on, get on with it!" In almost one movement Rose ripped Anne Marie's dress off. "You heard your father. Get that off!" They then grabbed her and pinned her down on a mattress. She started to struggle and Rose told her to "shut up and be quiet" as she laughed.

Anne Marie remembered that she could see a glass mixing bowl with some water in, some black tape, some strips of torn cotton sheets and a large vibrator. Fred tied her hands together with the black sticky tape and used sheeting to secure her hands and arms to an iron object above her head.

Fred was quiet but Rose was urging him to get on with it. Rose sat on Anne Marie's head in order to keep her still and she struggled to breathe. Rose, who had an evil look in her eye, started to paw and scratch at her and Anne Marie started to scream and cry because it hurt her so much. Anne Marie asked her father why he was doing this and told him that it hurt. Fred replied: "Shut up! It is going to help you in later life. I'm just doing what all fathers have to. It's a normal thing, so stop carrying on. This will make sure you get a husband when you're older. You'll be ready for him and you'll be able to have children."

Fred shouted at Rose to hold her so she got more sheeting and tied it around Anne Marie's mouth as a gag. They then inserted the vibrator and Anne Marie remembered that it hurt so much that she wanted to die. They pulled her legs apart and secured them with the rest of the sheets. By now the glass bowl has turned red and the pain level meant Anne Marie almost lost consciousness. Rose was laughing and telling her to stop being silly as it was for her own good.

After a while they got up and went upstairs, leaving Anne Marie still tied up, but without her gag. She remembered she screamed and cried but no-one could hear her. She was shivering both from the cold and from sheer fright. Eventually, Fred and Rose went back down to the basement and carried on where they left off.

This time, when they finished they released her and sent her upstairs. Rose laughed at her as she struggled to walk and stumble back up the stairs.

When she made it to the bathroom and tried to clean herself up Rose pushed her way in and gave her a sanitary towel to put in her underwear because she was bleeding so much.

Fred later adapted the large vibrator used to abuse Anne Marie with and added a belt to it and forced her to wear it while she did the housework in a mini-skirt. Rose found this hilarious and Fred joined in laughing at her. They told her that the sexual assaults would continue and they then threatened her and told her that she would receive severe beatings if they ever heard of her telling anyone about what went on in their house.

Anne Marie West

Anne Marie recalled: "The abuse continued for the rest of my childhood and well into my teenage years. I had no choice but to suffer it. I was a victim of my parents' sexual fantasies. To complain was to increase the torture and provoke severe beatings." Fred would continue to rape her when Rose was not around. "My father's abuse continued without a break until I ran away from the house at fifteen." Fred raped her in various places, including an old mattress in the back of his van, in fields, in old houses Fred was working on and even once back at 25 Midland Road, when Fred took the opportunity to re-bury Charmaine when he built an extension for the owner.

I firmly believe that the assault on Anne Marie in the basement was a dry-run for the future abductions and tortures that they were to carry out. They took Anne Marie down to the basement as she was easily accessible, and both abused her. They tried out their restraints on her, and which was the best way to gag and bind a victim. After the first assault, they ungagged her and both went upstairs. I believe that this was so that they could test if the sound-proofing in the cellar had worked. They were soon ready for their next victim...

In later September, Caroline Owens first met Fred and Rose West while she was hitchhiking. She was standing opposite the Gupshill Manor Pub on the Gloucester Road. She always waited there because she knew a telephone engineer who would always give her a lift for the 23-mile trip if he was passing on his night shift. Caroline recalled noticing a grey-colored Ford Popular going in the opposite direction minutes before it pulled up alongside her. She recalled feeling anxious but then relaxing when she saw there was a girl in the passenger seat (just as Rose had told Elizabeth Agius previously).

Caroline Owens – shortly before she met The Wests

They offered her a lift and Rose got out so Caroline could climb in to the back. When they pulled off they told Caroline their names and that they were married. They asked her a lot of questions about where she had been and who with, and did she have a job. Caroline told them that she had been away to Portsmouth for six months and that she had come back because her stepfather had suffered a heart attack.

Caroline told them that she didn't really get on well with him and spent a lot of time out of the house in order to avoid him because he kept on at her to get a job. As soon as she said that, Fred and Rose looked at each other and said: "We need a nanny to look after our three daughters." They went on to sell the idea to her by telling her that they owned a big house and if she wanted to she could move in with them and they would give her her own room. They offered her £8 a week plus free board and lodgings.

Caroline was very tempted by this but said that she would need to discuss it with her mum before she could agree to it and that her mum would want to meet them both. Fred and Rose agreed to meet her mother and step father and drove her all the way home. They told her that they would go to meet her parents the following Sunday afternoon. The following day after the meeting took place Caroline moved in to 25 Cromwell Street.

By now it was October and it didn't take long for Fred to start bragging to Caroline about the abortions he had performed for girls in trouble and he told her that the girls were usually so grateful that they would offer themselves to him as soon as the abortion had been performed. He told her that he'd had sex with thousands of women, and according to him he was God's gift to women. "Once you'd been with Freddie, you wouldn't go anywhere else", he told her.

Caroline was told that Anne Marie was Fred's daughter from a previous marriage and she was told by Anne Marie that she had a big sister called Charmaine who had "gone away", back to Scotland, with her mother. Fred told her that he wouldn't let Rena take Anne Marie with her because she was not a "fit mother".

She was disappointed that she did not get her own room when she moved in as promised, and instead had to share with Anne Marie. She and Rose would go shopping together, do the housework and cook together and quickly settled in to a routine. Caroline was only really allowed on the ground floor of the house, which meant she only had access to the bedroom she shared with Anne Marie, the kitchen and the living room.

Caroline had friends working in a café on Clarence Street, which was virtually around the corner and would sometimes meet friends there or go to the Dirty Duck pub off Southgate Street. There was also a nightclub called Tracy's below the car park on the bus station that she used to sneak in to sometimes.

Caroline remembered that Rose often told her that she was pretty and played with her hair when they watched TV. She was always complimenting her on her looks and appearance and they soon became friends. She became friends with the lodgers too and one day she went up to Ben Stanniland's room where she smoked her first joint. Soon they were listening to music and making love.

Once a week, Caroline's boyfriend Tony would stay and Fred and Rose would go out for the evening. Sometimes they would go out for a drink, or Rose would help Fred on a job or to steal some building materials.

It's quite possible that Fred and Rose were also engaging in what today would be described as 'Dogging' during this period. Fred would later tell anyone who would listen that he and Rose would go out in his van up to the hills where various men would have sex with Rose while he filmed it.

While Caroline was at Cromwell Street she also had a sexual relationship with an old flame from Portsmouth, called Steve, who Fred and Rose suggested stay over for Caroline's seventeenth birthday.

It didn't take long for Caroline to discover the weirdness of the West's.

One night, a tall, buxom blonde girl named Dee went to the house and started shouting and swearing at Caroline, accusing her of stealing her babysitting job. Fred went to the door and led her into the bedroom, trying to calm her down, and Rose followed. After ten minutes, all three of them went in to the living room and Dee apologized to Caroline.

Dee then asked Caroline if she would like to go out with her that night to the Jamaican Club. Her boyfriend was in a reggae band and they were rehearsing there. Caroline said that she was weary of black men – the only ones she had spoken to were the two that regularly visited the house once or twice a week, and even then she hardly spoke to them. These were Rose's clients, but she told Caroline that she worked as a masseuse when she asked her why these men came over. One was in his 70's and the other, Roy Morgan, was much younger.

After encouragement from Fred and Rose, Caroline agreed to go with Dee to the Jamaica Club that night. Once there, Dee soon disappeared with her boyfriend in to a back room where they had sex, leaving Caroline alone at the bar. She felt uncomfortable, and left soon after Dee had come back. She decided to run home and ended up being chased by one of the men from the club.

The following day, while Fred was at work and Rose was out shopping, Dee called round. She told Caroline how she had got to know Fred when he came over to her workplace for some DIY materials. Fred had invited her and her Jamaican boyfriend back to the house for some supper. Dee then asked Caroline if Rose had tried it on with her yet. Caroline said she hadn't and would reject any advance if she ever did. Dee then told her that Rose liked women and warned her: "She'll have you in bed before long". Dee then told Caroline that she had once brought a black man back to Cromwell Street one night and Rose jumped in to bed with both of them.

"After Dee's revelations, I started to look at all the visitors in a different light – the old Polish guy (Frank Zygmunt) they had bought the house from, the old black man, even nice Roy no longer seemed so nice. In my mind's eye, I started to look upon Fred's brother, John West, who called around every teatime, with suspicion too. I began to watch him out of the corner of my eye as he chatted to Fred at the kitchen table, and many a time I caught him looking me up and down. John was quiet, not like Fred, but I remember my mum telling me: 'The quiet ones are always the worst.'

I started to think of the times Rose had come into the bathroom while I was bathing. She always had an excuse, like needing the baby soap or that she was dying for a pee. She always stayed for a minute or two, talking to me. I had found it highly embarrassing but, naively, I never thought she was just coming in to look at my body."

Then one day, Fred started talking about sex again. This time he told

Caroline that: "Anna's not a virgin, you know!" When she questioned him, and he noted the concern in her voice, he replied that the saddle had come off her bike and she sat down on the bar and it went up inside her. He said she was messed up for a while "but at least she'll not have any pain now when she has sex!"

The next day, Fred and Rose sat down on either side of her on the sofa. Fred said: "We've got something to ask you Caroline. We'd like you to join our 'sex circle'. You like sex now, so how about it?" She asked: "What do you mean, 'sex circle'." He replied: "You know – me, you, Rose. You like Rose, don't you? Yeah, you, me and Rose and a few men friends of ours, you'd enjoy it. You haven't tried a black man yet, have you? You wouldn't want a white man again after being spoilt by a black man, they have bigger dicks, you know, and they know how to fuck. They'd fuck the arse off you. How about it then? Are you game for it?"

Caroline said that she felt uncomfortable and looked to Rose for support, but Rose replied: "Oh, go on Car, you'll enjoy it, give it a try." Caroline told them she wasn't into that kind of thing, lost her temper and told them she thought she should leave and move back home.

Fred then turned nasty and threatened her: "Do you want me to tell your mum and Tony what you've been up to? 'Cause if I do they won't want anything to do with you any more, will they? And that stepfather of yours won't want you back living in his house, will he?" Caroline started to cry and Rose put her arm around her and told her to have a think about it. Fred got up and left the room, muttering something about "fucking lesbians", and he told Rose to have it sorted by the time he came back.

Rose then had a client arrive and she went to her room with him, leaving Caroline downstairs. While she was still busy, Roy Morgan arrived. Caroline burst into tears and he asked her what was wrong. She told him about the proposition she had just been given and he offered her a lift home if she wanted it. She sneaked up to her room, packed what she could and Roy drove her back to her parents' house in Cinderford.

When she arrived home, her mother was surprised to see her and asked her why she'd left the job. Caroline told her that she hadn't got on with Fred and left it at that. It was now early November.

After Caroline left there was no one to keep an eye on Anne Marie or to look out for her. Rose asked her to go down to the basement to tidy up some toys, which she did, but when she tried to pass Rose on the stairs on the way up the 18-year-old blocked her way and forced her to strip off. Strapping a U-shaped sex gadget to Anne Marie, Rose then gagged her and began to whip her. Fred came home from work for some lunch, and when he went to the basement to see what was he going on he laughed loudly at the predicament his daughter was in, and instead of helping her, he raped her before going back to work for the afternoon. After screaming at Anne Marie and beating her, Rose lifted her skirts to reveal a vibrator attached to a belt with which she used to rape her. The internal cuts on Anne Marie were bad enough, but Rose then untied her and made her take a bath with salt in it.

On the 6th December Caroline Owens was abducted and physically and sexually assaulted by both Fred and Rose. Caroline had been to see her boyfriend Tony and they had already spotted the Wests drive past them while they were in Tewkesbury. She didn't think they had seen her, but when Tony left her at the Gupshill Manor to hitchhike home, they pulled up next to her.

She felt nervous because of the way she left and thought that they would have a go at her, but Rose got out of the car and asked how she was. Fred and Rose then told her that both them and the kids had missed her and Fred apologized for what he said to her before offering her a lift home.

Caroline remembered that her gut feeling was not to get in the car but it was cold and dark and they seemed genuinely sorry for what they had said to her. She climbed into the back seat and, unlike last time, Rose climbed in with her. They began chatting and Caroline began to relax but the mood soon changed.

Fred was looking in the rear-view mirror and began staring at Caroline. He then asked her: "Have you had sex with Tony tonight then, Caroline?" She felt uncomfortable and replied: "Oh, don't start all that again! Tell him to leave it Rose." Rose just smiled at her and Fred said to her: "Have a feel Rose, see if she's wet."

Rose then grabbed at her crotch. Caroline pushed her hand away and stared at her in disbelief. Rose started laughing and began groping at Caroline's breasts. Caroline was frightened and screamed at them to leave her alone and to let her out of the car, but her fear turned them on even more.

Caroline fought with Rose in the back of the car, but Rose was too strong for her. Caroline tugged at her hair and she gave out a yelp, which made Fred join in. He was trying to grab Caroline's hair while still driving. Fred violently pulled the car up on a grass verge and Caroline could see a five-bar gate in front of the car. This was later identified as Higham, in Mitcheldean. He turned around in his seat and started lashing out at Caroline, landing a punch on the side of her head. She felt several blows strike her before she then blacked out. When she came around, her hands were securely tied behind her back with her scarf. Rose was holding her in a bearhug, while Fred wrapped brown sticky tape around her head and mouth – gagging her. The drivers door of the car was open and Fred was squatting just inside while he taped her up. Rose had stopped laughing and was telling Caroline to be quiet and that she'd be "all right". It was now around 23:30 and Fred turned the car around and drove back to Cromwell Street.

Rose pushed Caroline down into the narrow foot well of the car and sat on her. The car came to a sudden stop outside the house; Fred went in to check there was no one about and then came back to give Rose the signal to take Caroline in. He told her to be good and added: "We'll let you go after we've tidied you up a bit."

She was led into the house and up to the first-floor front bedsit. Fred sat her on the sofa, told Rose to make a cup of tea and then kneeled down in front of Caroline and began talking to her softly: "Look, Caroline, this has all got out of hand, we didn't want to have to hurt you. If you just calm down, I'll take the tape off, but you have to promise to keep quiet." He took a knife and started to cut the tape away from the side of her head. She felt a burning sensation, and he stopped. "Oh shit! I'm sorry, I've cut you, it's a bloody double-sided knife!"

Rose then came in with three cups of tea. Fred went out of the room and came back with a pair of scissors and continued to cut the tape from Caroline. Rose was making soothing noises and saying: "There, there, don't cry, you'll be alright." Once the tape was off, Fred picked up his cup of tea, pulled a chair up and sat in front of her, while Rose sat on the sofa. "Guess what?" Fred said. "Rose has got a bun in the oven. She's three months gone now; we're hoping for a boy this time. Wouldn't you like to come back here to live? Rose really needs you now."

Rose snuggled up next to her and smiled as she said: "Go on, Car, say you'll come back. I've missed you and the kids have. It will be better this time, promise." They untied her hands so she could drink her tea, and they gave her a cigarette to calm her down. Rose finished her tea off by gulping the remains down and then put her arm around Caroline's shoulder and kissed her full on the mouth. Caroline moved away but he rejection only made things worse and she became angry. Pushing her away, Caroline shouted at her: "Fuck off! Fucking leave me alone!"

Angered, Fred grabbed her and held her down and pressed her head, face first, into the sofa, telling Rose to "get the cotton wool". She returned with the cotton wool and, as Fred lifted her head up, she rammed a large chunk of it into Caroline's mouth. Then they got what looked like a strip of torn-up white sheeting and tied it around her head to keep the cotton wool in place. As they did this they were cursing and calling her names.

They stood her up and started to undress her. "Keep fucking quiet, you stupid fucking bitch!" Fred raised his clenched fist and said: "Do you want some more of this, bitch? Just do as you're fucking told and you'll be alright". He then pulled her arms behind her back and bound her wrists together with some orange-coloured rope. Caroline realised by now that there was no way she could take both of them on and get out of the house safely, so she resigned herself to the fact that, if she wanted to get out of there in one piece, she would have to go along with whatever it was they were going to do to her.

Fred then led her over to the stained mattress and told her to lie down. Rose then stared at her as she got undressed herself. Caroline curled up into the foetal position. She then rolled over, half on her front, burying her face in the pillow, not wanting to see Rose naked. Rose then laid on the mattress next to her and rolled Caroline over on to her back. Her arms were under the weight of her body and she recalled that her shoulder blades hurt "like crazy". Rose's hands were running all over her body and Caroline turned away which angered Fred. He growled: "Keep fucking still, you bitch! Rose isn't going to hurt you!" Rose's fingers entered into every crevice of Caroline's body. She pinched her nipples hard and Caroline gave out a muffled shriek. Her searching fingers went deeper in between Caroline's legs and Caroline thought she was going to vomit and choke to death on it. She wriggled away from her again and Rose pulled her back to her.

"What's wrong with you? Haven't you ever had a woman before? Relax and enjoy", Rose would tell her over and over again. Rose moved down the mattress and wrenched Caroline's legs apart in a violent manner. Automatically, she closed them again. Rose looked up at Fred, who was stood up at the end of the mattress watching what was going on, at the same time rubbing his erect penis through his jeans. He asked: "You wanna hand there Rose?" as he got down on his knees. They each took one of her legs and prised them apart, and Caroline remembered Rose's hot breath between her legs as she took a good look.

Fred then said: "What do you think then Rose?" She grinned and replied: "Why don't you come and have a look for yourself?" Fred then picked up another strip of the white cloth and tied it around Caroline's head, covering her eyes.

Fred then climbed on to the mattress next to her and her legs were pulled apart once more. Rose and Fred's bodies were now both squeezed between her legs and she felt both of their hands on her. Rose's hands were stroking Caroline and Fred's was pulling and prodding at her. She remembered: "Two lots of fingers were forced inside my most intimate part, making me squeal out in agony as the faceless fingers searched and probed with an unrelenting fervor during this probing part of their molestation, all the while the two of them were discussing my genitals as if they were experts on the subject."

"She's big inside, ain't she, Rose?" Fred said. "Yeah, and she hasn't even had any kids yet", Rose replied. "Her lips are too fat", Fred said referring to her vulva. "They cover her clit, no wonder she doesn't enjoy sex!"

Caroline then began to fear that Fred might operate on her as she remembered the conversations they had had about him doing abortions, and then Fred told Rose: "I can put that right for her". Rose loosened her grip on Caroline's leg and she turned over on to her stomach. She was then pulled roughly back over onto her back again and Fred was stood there looking down on her holding his belt in his hand.

He said to Caroline: "This is for your own good, you'll enjoy sex much more after this." He dragged her to the edge of the mattress and said: "Hold her legs open, Rose" and she did as she was told. Fred then folded his leather belt in half, raised it above his head and brought it down in a hard frenzy upon Caroline's vagina. She remembered: "The blow sent a shockwave of pain through me…this was the first blow of what turned out to be a whipping frenzy. He struck me about six times…The buckle part of the belt was hitting its target with non-stop accuracy."

When he had finished, Rose went to the bathroom and came back with a bowl full of cold water. She now seem concerned and caring towards Caroline, and told her to turn over as she wanted to bathe her.

As this was going on, Fred then left the room and returned with three more cups of tea. "If you promise to be good I'll take the gag off so you can have a drink", he told her. He untied the gag and pulled the cotton wool out of her mouth. Caroline begged him to untie her hands and promised him that she wouldn't try anything.

Fred took her blindfold off, unfastened her hands and gave her a cigarette. He then explained to her that he beat her with the belt as it would flatten out her vaginal lips, exposing her clitoris, and how it would improve her sensitivity during sex. "You'll thank me for it one day", he told her with a wink and a smile.

Caroline tried to assure Fred and Rose that if they let her go they could trust her not to say anything about what had just happened, but Fred told her: "Just do as you're told and you'll be alright" as he re-tied her hands behind her back again. She pleaded with them not to gag her again and promised not to call for help, and Fred threatened her: "You shout and we'll fucking kill ya, bitch!"

He made her lay back down on the mattress and Rose lay beside her and kissed her full on the mouth. She then again squeezed her nipples hard and Fred grunted at her to keep still while he watched. Caroline's legs were then pulled apart again and Rose moved down the mattress and started to lick between her legs.

Fred was turned on by the noises Rose was making, as well as the pleasure she was clearly experiencing. He once again had an erection and started to openly masturbate. Fred and Rose then started to talk dirty to each other. Fred said to her: "You're enjoying that, aren't you…you dirty cow", to which his wife replied: "Yeah, you can join in now if you want."

Fred didn't need a second invitation and had sex with Rose from behind, doggy style, while Rose continued to perform cunnilingus on Caroline.

Caroline turned away, sickened by the noises and actions of the married couple, but when they had finished Caroline remembered that she could smell the semen that was running down Rose's legs. Rose went to the bathroom to wipe herself down and then her and Fred went to make another cup of tea. Caroline was left naked and tied to a chair.

After twenty minutes Fred and Rose came back and untied Caroline and removed her gag. "We think you should stay here for a few days, Car, till we know we can trust you. If you behave, you can stay in this room, if not...then you'll be kept in the cellar" Fred told her.

Caroline tried her best to convince them that she could be trusted and told them that her mum would call the police if she didn't hear from her soon. Fred and Rose then started on again about their 'sex circle' and how they thought she would soon get to enjoy it. Fred then said that he had to get some sleep as he had work in the morning. They tied Caroline's arms up, put her under the sheets and then climbed on to the mattress with her. Caroline pretended to go to sleep, while she was sandwiched between the couple, and tried to think of how she could escape. She then remembered that the milkman called around early and that she needed to get his attention.

Fred and Rose soon fell asleep and Caroline managed to extract herself from the mattress and walk over to the window. She managed to slip between the curtains and stood there naked...she tried to lift the window but her small frame wouldn't allow her to reach the latch to open it. She then climbed back on to the mattress and laid there for her chance to escape. She decided that she would make a run for it when they let her out of the room to take her to the cellar. It would be easier to escape when Anne Marie and the lodgers were awake. At least someone would see her then, even if she didn't make it out of the house.

Caroline drifted off to sleep as she was exhausted, but was then awoken by the doorbell. Fred jumped up and pulled his jeans on and then woke Rose and told her to keep Caroline quiet while he saw who was at the door.

Fred then walked back up the stairs whilst talking to the man who had rung the doorbell. He then walked back in to the room, leaving the man outside. Caroline thought that this was her chance of freedom and shouted out "Help me! Get..." Rose pressed a pillow over her face and put her entire upper body weight on her head in an attempt to smother her cries. At first Caroline struggled with her, but then chose to play dead in the hope that Rose would lift the pillow.

As she started to go dizzy, the pillow was suddenly lifted and Fred's angry face was right in hers. He grabbed her by the throat and lifted her up off the mattress. "You fucking stupid little bitch, you've had it now!"

Rose then grabbed her by the hair and pulled her towards her while swearing at her. They then started shouting at her at the same time and calling her names and threatened her. "We are going to keep you in the cellar and let our black friends use you and when they have finished with you, we will kill you and bury you under the paving stones of Gloucester. There are hundreds of girls there, the police haven't found them and they won't find you!"

A wad of fresh cotton wool was forced into Caroline's mouth and it was secured with some white material. Fred and Rose then hurriedly dressed themselves and Fred went outside on to the landing where Anne Marie told him that the baby needed feeding.

Rose went outside and ordered Anne Marie back to her bedroom, and then they whispered to each other. Fred returned to the room alone, shutting the door behind him and locking it. He knelt down next to Caroline and caressed her breasts. He kept saying to her that it was "OK, I'm not going to hurt you." He then thrust his hand between her legs and gently pulled her on to her back. Caroline remembered that he was in a trance-like state as he moved his hands all over her body. He looked behind him at the locked door and then took his jeans off.

"Don't cry" he told her as he positioned himself on her and entered her. He was stroking her hair and whispering "It's Ok, it's OK". After a minute or two he withdrew himself before he ejaculated.

He pulled his jeans back on and sat down next to her, patting her thigh. "I'm sorry Car, I shouldn't have done that." He then began to cry. "You mustn't tell Rose what I did, Car. She'll be really pissed off with both of us! You see, you were here solely for Rose's pleasure, not mine. When Rose is pregnant, she gets these lesbian urges and she has to have a woman, and she wanted you. She'll kill both of us if she finds out...if you don't tell her and promise me you'll come back here to live, I'll let you go...you know, if you do tell anyone or you don't come back, my black friends will come looking for you." Caroline agreed, so Fred said that he was off to tell Rose who he thought would be "so pleased".

As he stood up, he went to the door and then went back to Caroline and said: "I told Rose I was going to tie you to the chair, so I'll have to. Just now she's looking after the kids. I'll go and tell her that you want to come back here to live, OK?" Caroline was left naked, gagged and bound to the chair.

Ten minutes later Rose went in to the room with Fred behind her. She was happy and smiling and she ran over to Caroline and gave her a big hug. She then ran Caroline a bath and helped her to wash her hair, which was sticky from the gum on the tape that they had first gagged her with in the car. Fred brushed her hair to try to remove the gum, but it was too knotted and so she had to get back in the bath and lay down to soak the gum out of her hair. When that hadn't removed it all, Fred took some scissors and cut the remaining bits out.

Caroline noticed some bruising around one of her cheeks and she had rope burns around her wrists, her torso, under one of her breasts and around her back from where she had been tied to the chair.

An hour after being raped by Fred she was dressed and sitting on the sofa drinking tea and smoking a cigarette, with Rose sat next to her, stroking her hair and chatting to her as if nothing untoward had ever happened. Fred then brought the children into the room…

Anne Marie, who was already dressed for school, walked over to her and gave her a kiss and a hug. Heather then toddled over and gave her a cuddle while she finished her bottle of tea.

Fred then asked Caroline if she would help Rose out with the kids and the housework, while he dropped Anne Marie at school; then he would drop her, Rose and the kids off at the launderette. She did as he said and, while Rose fed Heather and Mae, she tidied up and vacuumed the room. She then sat on the sofa next to Rose while they waited for Fred to return.

Lodger Ben Stanniland then popped his head around the door and acknowledged Caroline. She looked at Rose, who was looking awkward and flustered, and Ben asked her if he could borrow the vacuum. Rose passed it to him and he left.

Caroline figured out that he wasn't part of the Wests 'sex circle' for two reasons. Firstly, because he looked as if he had walked in on something he shouldn't have, and secondly because of Rose's reaction; she looked guilty and frightened.

At about 09:30 Fred came back and the three of them sat and drank another cup of tea while they went over again how Caroline was not to tell anybody about what had gone on, and how Fred had friends that would come after her if she went to the police.

They all got in to the car and drove to the Launderette on Eastgate Street. Fred carried the bags in, Rose and Caroline carried the girls in, and Fred gave her a final warning: "I'll see you later then". Caroline held baby Mae while Rose sorted her washing into two machines, then she sat down next to Caroline, looking very nervous. She wasn't as confident now that Fred was out of the picture.

Caroline waited ten minutes, gave Mae to Rose to hold, told her she had to go and get some cigarettes and left before she could argue with her. She walked out of the launderette and just kept walking.

On the 9th December, Rose was arrested by PC Kevan Price. He and Detective Sergeant John Pearce called round to 25 Cromwell Street looking for Fred and Rose, but Fred had already left for work.

Caroline's mother had called the police after she finally opened up about what had happened to her at the hands of the Wests and when the police checked Caroline's clothes it was noticed that she had a button missing from her trousers. When Rose was told of the charge, she replied: "Don't be fucking daft, what do you think I am?" And when he the officer told her that they were gong to search the vehicle allegedly involved in the abduction, she replied: "Please your bloody self". The search of the car found Caroline's missing button, and a search of the house found a roll of partially used brown adhesive tape in the lounge and a large collection of pornographic photographs.

Fred wasn't arrested until he left his job at Permail's and 19:30 that evening. He told the officers in the interviews about Caroline sleeping with the two lodgers as well as her boyfriend Tony and the sailor from Portsmouth, Steve. "Look, to put it right, I kicked her out 'cause the blokes in the top flat was fucking her and I didn't want that in my house 'cause I was going to buy the place. That's why I told her to pack her bags and go. She's saying this now to get her own back on me and Rose." He denied the charges of indecent assault, but he did admit that Caroline had stayed the night in question but at her own request. He said that she had got stuck hitchhiking and had knocked on their door asking if she could stay. He said that she had slept with them both and then left the following morning.

When he was asked if Rose had "sucked Carol Raine's breasts and private parts" after he had tied her up, he replied: "All I want is to buy the house and settle down. Nothing like that happened. She is making it all up. The only thing is that some coloured blokes did it and she's trying to blame Rose and me."

In her own interviews, Rose told the police that she would not talk "because I told my husband I would say nothing", but then went on to admit performing lesbian acts on Caroline. When confronted with this Fred also then admitted assault.

On the 12th January 1973, Fred and Rose appeared before Gloucester Magistrates Court charged with rape. Inspector William Kingscott, prosecuting, told the court that Caroline was in fear of her life when Fred produced a knife, but this was used only to cut the tape from Caroline. He said that "in desperation, she agreed" to return as a 'nanny' for the Wests.

Mr Conrad Sheward, appearing for the defence, said: "It would have been very difficult if there had not been any passive co-operation. She made no attempt to call for assistance, the door was left unlocked throughout but she made no attempt to get away." When Rose appeared she said: "I don't know why I did it. It just happened."

Caroline Owens didn't appear in court herself. She found the whole process unbearable and had previously been intimidated by a police officer who had interviewed her in a very aggressive manner and who tried to make out that it was her fault and that she agreed to it. She knew that the Wests had pleaded 'guilty' to two charges each of Indecent Assault and Occasioning Actual Bodily Harm and was certain that they would be sent to prison so she didn't need to appear in court to push for a guilty verdict of Rape.

However, the Chairman of the Magistrates, John Smith, took a different view and told both Fred and Rose that although the court was bound to take a very serious view of "offences of this description, we do not think that sending you to prison will do you any good." Instead, he handed them a £25 fine for each charge, a total of £50 each.

Conrad Sheward recalled his astonishment of the leniency shown to his defendants: "I've been practicing in a Magistrate's Court for probably 30 years or so, and this was perhaps the most astonishing decision on the part of the prosecution that I've known during that time. It seemed to me to be a very serious case which I would not normally expect to be dealt with by magistrates. I would have expected the case to be dealt with by a Judge, and of course the Judge has more experience in sentencing in serious cases and of course has greater powers. The sentence that was imposed was one of the most extraordinary sentences that I can remember."

The Chairman of the Magistrates, John Smith, recalled in 1995 that "I dealt with hundreds of cases, but not one has haunted me quite like this. I regret not sending him to prison but it was a unanimous decision of the bench. Of course, if we knew then what we know now, we would have sent him to prison. But we gave him what we thought was quite a hefty fine. At that time we were not supposed to send people to prison for first offences if it could be avoided. I remember what a docile chap he was and the police said he was the same with them".

As Fred's son Stephen was to later say: "If I had got caught with what Mum and Dad did in the seventies with that girl Caroline Owens I would have expected to be put away, but all they got was a fine. It was like a green light. You know, go for it."

The case was prosecuted by the police as the Crown Prosecution Service did not exist. The prosecution file, including statements etc, was destroyed in accordance with the then Force policy and only the record of conviction now exists. It was a sign of the times that a person could be sent to prison for stealing car tyres or fence panels but wouldn't go to jail for abducting and sexually assaulting another person because you came across as a 'docile chap'. As a further tarnish on the judge, the fact that he said it was Fred and Rose West's first offence almost beggars belief, as Fred had a string of convictions for theft to his name and had been to prison before.

Bill Messer, who was a social worker from 1974-1984 in the Gloucester area, commented that "The fact that the magistrate didn't ask for a Social Inquiry Report almost beggars belief. I think if that case had been properly investigated and properly handled by the courts perhaps the Wests would have been stopped in their tracks at that point. We have a couple here who are accused of fairly serious sexual offences. Now, if the police discovered that there were young children in that family and that this couple had actually sexually abused a young person, and she was technically a young person, a lot of alarm bells should have been ringing, and they should have been getting in touch with, perhaps, several agencies. They should have been getting in touch certainly with Social Services."

There is no record of any police report to Social Services. Unbelievably, at that time there was no requirement for the police to report such matters to Social Services. During the 1970's there was little or no communication between the police and social workers. Now it is certain that there would be a referral to Social Services and it is possible the children would be put on the 'At Risk Register'. This would mean that any inquiries concerning them or the family would be registered and show up each time anyone checked the register.

Ricky Coleclough, a police officer with Gloucester Police from 1964-1988, said that at that time the relationship between the police and Social Services was "In a word, poor. I don't think many police officers had a great deal of time for Social Services. The dissemination of information between the two groups was negligible. From a basic working policeman's point of view I'd find that someone arrested would be taken before a court, social workers would interfere with excuses for his behavior and the man would leave court without, in my view I suppose, adequate punishment. A wrap on the wrist."

He recalled that Fred West viewed the police "with a hatred that seemed to be beyond the normal average criminals hatred. Most of that I learned from my mother with the fact that he would be always talking about the police and he would have, I suppose, a persecution complex, justified or otherwise. But he hated the police with a vehemence which is unusual."

Ricky Coleclough's mother, Anne, had stayed briefly at 25 Cromwell Street. Fred was taken to a rent tribunal by her as she was seeking a further extension of security of tenure. Fred went on to say at the tribunal while giving evidence: "I don't like the woman. She is a troublemaker. Her son is a police officer and she works for the police force. If she sees anything she thinks is a little outside the law she reports it to the police. I have been raided every time I turn my back."

In the weeks following the trial, Fred confessed to one of his male lodgers that he had decided to convert the "cellar into a dungeon" for sex parties. He told him that the court case had brought him "loads of kinky letters", which had convinced him there was an appetite for such 'parties'.

They continued to experiment on Anne Marie and she would go on to tell of the torture techniques and sexual abuse she suffered at the hands of Fred and Rose, and I believe shows, at least partly, what their later victims must have been put through. She believes that Fred and Rose perfected their techniques for torture and rape on her. They experimented with various methods of restraint and which methods would inflict the most pain.

It was normally Rose who tied her up. Sometimes she tied her hands behind her back and sometimes in front. She seemed to be trialing which way caused the most pain and which was the best for limiting her movements. Sometimes she was tied to a bed with her legs far apart, and other times with her legs tied together. Rose would use old sheets ripped into strips and tie them to her arms or legs and sometimes use them as gags. On other occasions she would use carpet tape to bind Anne Marie's arms and legs. She would use builder's rope or nylon clothesline tied so tight that her limbs went numb. When she had finished with the tape and wanted to remove it she would rip it off to cause as much pain as possible.

Once Anne Marie was trussed up Rose would use belts, canes, whips and even a cat-o'-nine-tales made by Fred to hit her with. When she had finished that she would then rape her with a vibrator, or if Fred were home, get him to rape his daughter.

After the court case, Fred and Rose must have discussed whether they should, or could, continue with their deplorable acts. I believe that they weighed up the good and bad parts of their techniques used so far and came to one conclusion. They had made only one mistake: Allowing Caroline Owens to live to tell the tale. They had enjoyed themselves too much to not do it again.

Lynda Gough

Lynda Carole Gough was born on the 1st May 1953 in Gloucester. She attended Calton Primary School and Longford School. She later went to a private girls school in Midland Road. She enjoyed a normal childhood but she did have some learning difficulties, and when she left school in 1969, she started work as a seamstress at the Co-Op in Brunswick Road, just two roads from Cromwell Street.

In October 1972, Lynda met Ben Stanniland in a local café. He introduced her to his lodgings on the top floor of 25 Cromwell Street and for the next six months she visited frequently and had a sexual relationship with Ben and other lodgers including Alan 'Dapper' Davis and David Evans.

On the 5th March 1973, Lynda's mother remembered a woman calling at her house and taking Lynda out for a drink, and that this woman was short, fat (Rose was pregnant with Stephen), with dark hair and older than Lynda. Rose told Fred that Lynda wanted a room at Cromwell Street and Lynda soon left home. She became a live-in 'nanny' for the Wests, just as Caroline Owens had a few months before.

On the 19th April, Lynda's mother returned home one lunchtime to find that her 19-year-old daughter had taken all of her possessions and left home. She left a simple note:

Dear Mum and Dad,

Please don't worry about me. I have got a flat and I will come and see you some time.

Love Lin

"Both her father and I felt, let her have her head for a bit, she'll come round", Lynda's mother June later explained.

Lynda had been the girlfriend of Ben Stanniland and it's believed that after they broke up she was seduced by Rose. She went on to share a bed with her and Fred. "Rose was knocking off Lynda before I was", Fred recalled after his eventual arrest. "She used to come there a lot…She had a massive bust on her, but the rest of her body was skinny." He would suggest that "Lynda was a bit kinked in different ways because she had black magic magazines. She was into virgin's blood and God knows what. She was a bit fucking weird." Fred and Rose began to extend their sexual experiments with Lynda into bondage and sado-masochism. Lynda may have been led into the basement willingly expecting kinky sex.

Fred gave slightly varying accounts of how she met her death in his first confessions to the police: "It was their fantasies I set up for them…it was new to me. I hadn't anything to do with that sort of thing much before." He said that Lynda wanted to "bathe in a virgin's blood. That was her fantasy and she was hell-bent on that." He insisted that "was building up for about three weeks and she was getting obsessed about it by the day. She was heavy into this kinky sex and all that, so we worked it out…or she worked out a bizarre thing to do with tying up, hanging up…She wanted to use her hair to bond herself with. She had such long hair." He recalled that they had "tried several times, different ways and that", but, "the problem was the basement wasn't high enough." He had already cut a slot in one of the beams in the basement – "for her hands and that to tie up to", but when he did so "she was standing on the floor." So he "dug a big piece out" of the brick and stones that lay on the basement floor at that time, so that he could suspend her body from the beam. Instead of hanging her by her hands, he suspended her body via her ankles, with her head hanging just above the hole he had dug.

"The bondage sex thing was planned with Lynda. She had no jewellery or glasses or nothing, they were all left in her room, 'cause she came down practically naked. She stripped off and oiled herself, and put funny markings on her face and body…off these books she had. Anyway, she was all roped up, and she kept laughing her head off, making weird noises and God knows what."

By this time, according to Fred, Lynda was tied up above the hole. He had attached a rope to her ankles and she was hanging on to it, supporting herself with her arms. "She had a rope around her neck and her arms were just up in the air for some reason, she was holding herself up like that…'cause then her legs went up and…she dropped down on her arms to hold her." Fred pulled the rope around Lynda's ankles and lifted her up until she was suspended upside down. "So anyway, she was just hanging there…and she was enjoying every minute of it. Then she wanted me to pour oil over her, and water, and God knows what over her, jelly or something she got, supposed to be love potions."

Fred never admitted exactly what happened. At one stage he explained that Lynda was "getting unbearable" and he just "lost the 'ead…put a rope around her neck and strangled her", but at another he suggested that she had strangled herself by accident. In this second version of events, he insisted that he was interrupted shortly after he had pulled her over the hole. "Somebody rang the bell, and somebody answered the door and somebody shouted 'Fred'. So I thought, bloody hell, I shall have to go up and see, 'cause they knew I was there…they could probably hear us. So anyway, I went up, and it was somebody come to see me…and I stood there talking to them for about twenty minutes, almost half an hour I suppose." He did not recall who that person was. All he could remember was: "I'm trying to get from them to get back to her because I had no shirt on. I only had just me jeans on, and anyway I finally got away…when I got back down, the flipping rope that was holding her legs…had snapped and she was hanging there. She was strangled. Hanging by this neck into this hole."

It's fair to say that none of this had happened. It would have been impossible for Lynda to have laughed, as either Fred or Rose had placed a surgical plaster over her mouth and then covered that with a length of two-inch-wide brown parcel tape, which they had wrapped around her head completely, to gag her. Nor was she tied only with rope; strips of fabric were also knotted and tied around her, as was a long length of string. The only kernel of truth may have been that she died as a result of strangulation.

She was certainly gagged and tied up. Lynda was probably abused sexually by both Fred and Rose. The sexual intercourse would probably have been followed by abuse with a vibrator and dildo, both in her vagina and her anus. It's possible that other people were invited to rape the helpless girl as she hung in the basement. She was probably whipped and had cigarettes stubbed out on her. Fred may even had had sex with her dead body, as he later admitted to his son that he was interested in Necrophilia.

I believe that once Fred and Rose, and possibly others, had had their fulfillment, Lynda was strangled and her body was then pulled up to hang above the hole that Fred had prepared. Her throat was then cut and the blood allowed to fill the hole. Her body was then dismembered. Several finger and toe bones were missing, as were some cervical vertebrae and chest bones. Her kneecaps were missing. He had decapitated her, disarticulated both of her legs at the hips leaving knife marks on the upper thighs, and removed bones he wanted as trophies.

He removed her body piece by piece by pushing it up through a small vent in the basement and threw them in to an inspection pit beneath the elderly garage attached to the back of the house. He even threw the dental plate she wore into the hole with its one tooth attached, although not her glasses.

Her body was excavated in 1994 from underneath a bathroom extension that Fred had built over the inspection pit. The pit could easily have taken Lynda's body whole.

Fred and Rose systematically went through Lynda's belongings, taking what they found to be useful for themselves. He collected almost three plastic bags full of her clothing and possessions, and he remembered that he discarded about twenty "witchcraft" books at the time and, unbelievably, "Lynda's bra and pants and all that got flushed down the toilet."

Rose took some of Lynda's clothes for herself along with some rings and necklaces. The clothes that were too bloodstained to wash were pushed into the plastic bags and Fred left them out with the household rubbish. The clothes she kept were put straight in to the washing machine for her to wear later. Fred later recalled: "I thought, fuck me, she'd killed her and had her fucking clothes on. She's wearing the girls' shoes and she'd killed her, and her dressing gown. I said 'you wore her fucking clothes after you killed her'. She said: 'I washed 'em'.

He went on to tell the police: "that was the first one at Cromwell Street. There ain't no doubt about that, because the basement was stones then, bricks, just bricks laid on that ash stuff."

On or about 20th April, other tenants, along with David Evans, were told that Lynda Gough had been told to leave after she had "hit our daughter while she was babysitting" and that "she wouldn't be coming round to the house again". By this time there were eight young men living in the four rooms on the top two floors, each paying £3 a week.

On the 5th May, Lynda's mother June visited 25 Cromwell Street in the search for her daughter. She had been asking around Lynda's friends and eventually got her home address from Lynda's boss, Mrs Ford, at the Co-Op. Rose answered the door and June Gough immediately recognized her as "the lady who called for Lynda when she went out for a drink" only a matter of weeks before. Fred quickly appeared and in no uncertain terms told her that her daughter was not there. "I told her mother she'd left. I told her she'd gone to Weston" he later admitted. However, June Gough noticed that Rose was wearing her daughter's slippers and was almost certain she was also wearing Lynda's cardigan. When she asked them why Rose was wearing them Fred told her that "She'd left them behind."

Her disappearance was reported to a neighbour of the Gough's, who was a policeman, but it is uncertain whether he officially reported it to anyone.

Whilst he was in prison in 1994, Fred recalled this time: "There were so many girls and so many blokes going in and out of the house that I hadn't got a bloody clue who they were. All the girls, all the blokes, in Cromwell Street, if they wanted to run somewhere, I would take them. All the girls I got on great with. I used to talk fucking dirty to them, and they'd talk dirty back."

Many years later, one lodger would recall: "People used to come and go at all hours of the day and night and Fred never seemed in the least bit concerned. There were girls on the run from local homes, boys who had nowhere to go for the night: endless parties. And there were always drugs if you wanted them."

Fred encouraged the 'hippy' lifestyle at his house. "It would be easier if people asked me who Rose didn't have sex with, not who she did. I mean there were so many. When I was in Permali's, the blokes were taking an hour off and going up and fucking Rose. I never thought nothing of it", he would later say. His fellow workers were not Rose's only lovers. There were also his lodgers and their friends. Fred even told one of his lodgers that if Rose looked 'moody' when he gave her his rent then he "should take her to bed."

Fred did not care if his lodgers smoked marijuana in their rooms or took hallucinogenic drugs. In fact, the police used to raid his house many times a month.

Sometimes, Fred's mood would suddenly switch. One evening, a lodger who had regular sex with Rose while Fred was at work woke up to find Fred's hands wrapped tightly around his throat. "Fred knew all about it, just like he knew all about everyone else". Fred had come home from work and found him asleep in his lounge after clearly having made love to his wife. A fight broke out, which resulted in the lodger being charged, and fined, for the assault on Fred. Once again, Fred had been beaten up by a man.

Pornographic photographs of Rose with her black lovers started to be passed around in the local pubs 'The Arthur', 'The Vauxhall', 'The Raglan Arms' and other Barton Street area pubs. Fred would show these same photographs to his workmates, and comment on the "massiveness" of the man and the thrill he got from watching another man "giving a good seeing to" to his wife. One of the Jamaicans, who was becoming a regular visitor to see Rose, recalled the story of going there one night when Fred was supposed to be away on a job in Cornwall but waking up with Fred in between him and Rose.

Janet Goodhall, a lodger at 25 Cromwell Street from 1973-1977, recalled that: "She (Rose) had a room on the middle floor, and it was her room and it was all done out with the red light bulb and whatever and there used to be men ringing the doorbell wanting to come in. She used to go around wearing a see-through negligee and that's what she was like when she decided to get up.

The police used to come there 'cause there was two students there called Ben and Dapper. They lived upstairs and they were doing dealings with drugs and there used to be about 2 or 3 policemen in the car and sometimes the paddy wagons used to come. That would be about twice a month they used to call there.

He (Fred) was making a washroom for Rosemary from the kitchen. He was extending it at the back, where he was up at the top. He was working all hours.

She treated her oldest one (Anne Marie) like a slave. If her mother was in bed she'd have to feed the kids and do the housework. One day I heard Rosemary asking Anna to do something, but I'm not quite sure what it was, and Anna happened to answer her back and Rosemary gave her a beating and it lasted for about 5 minutes but I didn't say anything because it's none of my business.

(The kids) didn't like him (Fred) at all. They were scared of him. He was like Jekyll and Hyde. One minute he'd be nice and the next he'd flip his lid for no reason at all. He'd beat them."

On the 6th July, records indicate that Anne Marie fainted at the swimming baths on her ninth birthday whilst on a school trip from St. Paul's School and was taken to the Gloucestershire Royal Hospital where she was examined by a consultant who noticed bruises (as did her teacher) and scratches on her chest. Rose was interviewed by a council welfare officer. She offered explanations for the marks and Anne Marie appeared to the officer to be a happy child who seemed fond of Rose.

During the summer of 1973 police raided 25 Cromwell Street for drugs. Detective Constables Castle and Price turned up "two or three times a month for years" Fred West later recalled. "That's where I come to know him (DC Castle) very well." Fred maintained that they had come round after Lynda Gough's disappearance to search one of her lovers' rooms "and they found heroin needles."

Major building work started on the Seventh-day Adventist's church next door. They tore down the old tin building and started to put up a new brick building in its place. In order to construct the church's south facing wall they had to put scaffolding in the Wests garden for what they said would be a few weeks but turned out to be several months.

Fred purchased a green Austin A35 van. He stopped his late-night searches for women and concentrated on building the extension to his house. He got several of his lodgers to help him move the elderly wooden garage from the back of the house to the bottom of the garden, and then he started to build an extension in its place. He told his lodgers that the idea was to create a small bathroom on the ground floor. He later told how Rose had helped him. "She could mix plaster all right. She dug holes, everything." One visitor to the house recalled seeing her putting tar on the roof of the extension by lamplight in the darkness, wearing a heavy coat and wellington boots, while heavily pregnant. He found it funny that Rose was up there as the roof looked to be unstable and was supported by only one wall and a telegraph pole. He was a workmate of Fred's from Permali's, and along with other workmates, would often go round to Cromwell Street to either borrow pornography or to have sex with Rose. He also recalled Anne Marie coming home and Fred accusing her of 'screwing in the park', which he thought was strange as she was only 9-years-old.

There was an outside toilet which he turned in to a shower and added a combination toilet-bathroom and put them all in the extension that was the same width as the kitchen. He put plastic membrane over the hole where Lynda Gough was buried when the shed/garage was removed and mixed and poured concrete for the floor. He then erected the building and when it was finished he referred to it as his conference room and his office. The extension was completed by the middle of August.

Before the ground-floor room at the front of the house became Rose's room, she shared it with Fred and a small time crook who was a friend of Fred's called Frank Stephens. Rose shared a bed with both of them. Fred wanted the three of them to sleep together, but Frank – so he maintained - wasn't prepared to go as far as that. Frank would eventually move out but he would often stay over until he fell out with Fred once and for all in 1980.

On the 19th August, Stephen Andrew West was born. "We were very pleased we had Stephen – our first boy", Rose recalled later. Fred was delighted and bought Rose a large bunch of flowers and a huge box of Terry's All Gold chocolates.

Just a couple of weeks later, Fred, Rose, Bill Letts and the kids went on holiday to Westward Ho! In Devon.

When they returned, an official from the Department of Health and Social Security knocked on the door of 25 Cromwell Street. One of Fred's former lovers in Scotland, Margaret McAvoy, had given birth to a son in July 1966. His son, who she had christened Steven. Unsettled, and increasingly unhappy, Margaret had traced Fred with he help of the DHSS. The official suggested to Fred that he might offer financial support to the child and mother. Fred refused, but Margaret had written to him herself, asking if he would look after Steven for a time. He reluctantly agreed.

Fred, Anne Marie, Heather, Mae and Rose

Margaret McAvoy would later say that she became ill about 5 years after giving birth to their son and sent him to Gloucester to live with Fred while she recovered. "I was sending letters, money and presents every week but Steven said he never got any of them. Rose was obviously just keeping it all for herself."

Fred would recall: "Margaret couldn't drive, except me up the wall. So we got a lift off Rose's Dad, who'd just been made redundant, to collect the boy. He took us to Preston in his new Mazda…She was on the verge of a nervous breakdown, that was the whole problem." They collected Steven in a car park from Margaret and another man.

When they got back to Gloucester and Rose unpacked his suitcase, she discovered that he still wore nappies in bed at night. Over the next few days she introduced Steven McAvoy to the weird ways of Cromwell Street. He was told not to contact his mother.

He was sent to the same school as Anne Marie and she remembers that she used to look after him. He missed his mother and it wasn't long before there was an incident of abuse that formed one of the charges against Rose in 1994.

Anne Marie was teaching Steven to read at home, as he was dyslexic, when she found an envelope on a shelf addressed to him. She opened it up and started to read it to him when Rose walked into the lounge and caught them. Rose realised they had opened the letter and launched herself at the children, who were laying on the floor, and started kicking and punching them. She grabbed hold of Steven and ground her stiletto heel into his face, just missing his eye and left a scar that is still visible to this day.

Steven's account of that incident formed one of the early charges against Rose, an assault on an 8-year-old boy. He would go on to explain that Rose had punched and kicked both him and Anne Marie repeatedly, dragging them by their hair around the sitting room at Cromwell Street. He also recalled getting up one night to go to the toilet, which was through the living room, where Fred and Rose were sleeping. When he walked in it was obvious they were having sex with each other but he was made to stay and watch. They laughed and seemed to enjoy him watching.

After his retirement, Bill Letts visited 25 Cromwell Street even more regularly. In the beginning, Fred was happy to tolerate Bill's sexual relationship with Rose. "Her father was making love to her…He was never sexually abusing her, my fucking arse. She was more willing than he was. I caught them at it at least half a dozen times, and she was enjoying it." He maintained later in life: "Rose's father was heavy into her, and she was heavy into him, because what Rose tried to do, I think, was to get me the same as him."

Fred's brother, John, also became a regular visitor to Cromwell Street. He had become a Gloucester council dustman, whose round included Cromwell Street, and he had taken to visiting his brothers house every afternoon after his round was over. Sometimes he would bring a toy he had found as a present for the children, and sometimes he would just go for a cup of tea. As Fred was normally at work it is believed that he was also having sex with Rose.

Barbara Jones was a lodger at 25 Cromwell Street. She had left home after an argument with her parents and she eventually ended up on a wall opposite the Wests house. She told how Fred approached her and offered her a room. She took a room and was given meals in exchange for babysitting and general house duties. She remembered "little Heather" being shy and quite nervous. She recalled never being propositioned or sexually abused and never knew of any underhand deeds. Looking back on it, she recalls: "I was one of the lucky ones. I escaped Cromwell Street." It is not known why Barbara was never propositioned. Maybe it's because she had people who would miss her if she suddenly disappeared or maybe the Wests just never got around to her.

Fred regarded any girl who found her way to Cromwell Street as "fair game" and "begging for it. 'Cause what we used to have in Cromwell

Street…from about eight o'clock in the morning you'd have girls from 17, 18, 19 leaving to go to work and they had their drug parties at night up there… then you'd get all the teeny-boppers coming in for the day…And then they'd disappear about half-four or five and then all the girls come back in. It was just a continuous flow going in and out all the time."

If they did not find their way to his door, he went searching for them again, exactly as he had done for more than a decade. He was quickly able to find the easiest targets, the vulnerable girls who needed someone to talk to and to listen to. He quickly figured out that one of the best places to find such girls were the local children's homes.

When he picked them up, he would often ask them gentle probing questions like: "oh, don't your boyfriend take you home?" In the last months of his life he recalled: "It was just conversation I made. It's a typical thing to say to a girl when you pick her up late at night, you know. Why ain't your boyfriend took you home? 'Cause normally a boyfriend takes them home. You don't leave them to thumb a lift on their own". If they proceeded to explain about how they had fallen out with their boyfriend or their parents, he would take care to appear sympathetic, anxious "to help 'em out in any way I could."

By this stage, the Wests had been living in Cromwell Street for just over a year and the builders were still working on the church next door. Fred had finished enlarging the basement and had dug down past the foundations to the main drain. Now a person could stand upright in the cellar without banging their head (or be hung from the beams with ease). Fred had carried out all of this work himself, using just a pick and shovel to move the tons of earth. He and Rose were now ready for more depravity.

Carol Cooper

On the 15th November 1973, 15-year-old Carol Ann Cooper went missing. She was born on the 10th April 1958 in Luton, Bedfordshire. Her parents separated in 1961 and she lived with her mother, but in 1967 Carol's mother died of an asthma attack so she went to live with her father but struggled to adapt to his re-marriage. Her step-mother, Barbara, recalled: "She was a rebellious girl, and used to say that I wasn't her real mum." When she became too rebellious she was put in Pines Children's Home in Bilton Road, Worcester, where her room was plastered with photographs of Elvis. She liked to be called 'Caz' and was known amongst her friends for her sparkle and good humour. She was known to have been friends with a couple of bikers from the Scorpion Gang whose members sometimes stayed at 25 Cromwell Street. She had used Indian ink and a needle to tattoo 'Caz' on her left forearm and a pattern of dots across the knuckles on her left hand and she was often seen wearing a jean jacket with the gang's 'patches'. Her Social Worker, Elspeth Keir, described her as "a lovely, intelligent girl", who had had a difficult life with many problems. "But I remember she had a sparkle in her blue eyes that said one day she intended to put it all behind her and make good."

Another friend remembered her and said: "All she wanted was to be loved", while someone from the home said that she "would do anything anyone asked her, right or wrong, because she was seeking attention all the time."

The day before she went missing she was given permission by the home to spend the weekend with her grandmother, Alice Tonks, in Warndon, Worcester, returning the next morning to keep a doctor's appointment.

On Bonfire Night, a firework had gone off in Carol's left hand, burning her as it did, and when she left that Friday night her hand was still bandaged.

She kept the appointment with her doctor and later met her boyfriend, Andrew Jones. During the afternoon she visited the Odeon cinema in Worcester with her friends. They then went to a fish and chip shop and ended the evening in a pub. "Carol and me had been getting a bit niggly with each other", her boyfriend admitted. "She put her arms around me and asked me to kiss her, but I wouldn't. She was standing opposite me. I think she was crying and I went over to her and made it up."

He saw her on to the number 15 bus at The Trinity, in the centre of Worcester, at around 21:10 to make the short journey back to Warndon. She never arrived. The bus journey wasn't long enough for Fred to have engaged her in conversation for the first time, like he had Rose. Maybe he just happened to drive past as she was getting off the bus and saw that she was alone, and faking a break-down, managed to get her to help him before abducting her, or maybe Fred had spotted her in town and decided to follow the bus until she got off. Or maybe he was out looking for a woman/girl with Rose and they simply offered her a lift which she accepted. The truth is that we simply do not know, and unless Rose changes her stance and tells all, we will never know.

After his arrest in 1994, Fred insisted that he had known Carol "for probably twelve months" and that he had "met her in a café in Tewkesbury", although he "didn't see her a lot…it was just a couple of times a week or something". He said that he had picked her up "when she was hitchhiking" from Worcester to the Pines Children's Home some time earlier that week in November.

Fred gave several different accounts of what happened to Carol once he got her to Cromwell Street, but he always maintained that he had known her before the night she disappeared. He had a nickname for her – "Skinny" – "for the simple reason that I didn't shout out her real name when I was making love to her and nobody else." He described her as a "fairly big girl" with a "DIY perm" and called her "a prostitute in Tewkesbury." He added that "She was quite professional in her job…making love." This was clearly a lie.

Her disappearance was reported to the West Murcia Police, who mounted a major investigation. Her family thought it was possible that she had run away but were not convinced as she hadn't taken any of her belongings with her.

When the remains of Carol Cooper were found in the basement of 25 Cromwell Street her skeleton was excavated from a depth of about 3ft. Her bones were layered, with the skull at the bottom. Around the skull was an elasticated cloth band 3" wide and 7" in diameter. It was wrapped around the lover part of her skull, covering the jaw, lower face and back of the head. A loop of fabric with a half-inch knot was tied under the forearms. There was also a clothesline nearby. Also present was a headband of surgical tape wound around itself several times and there were hair samples on the inside of the tape.

It was around this time that Rose started going to nightclubs in the search for lovers and introducing herself as 'Rose Letts'. She would make conversation with strangers and tell them about this family that she babysat for. If she managed to get people back to Cromwell Street then she would introduce Fred as her brother.

Fred made no secret of his obsession with sex at his workplace at Permali's. He would invite some of his fellow workers to "pornographic film shows" in his basement every Sunday from 12:00 – 18:00, and brag to them that he could "persuade" girls to go into prostitution by "keeping them locked up in a room without food and water", although he and Rose "would always have sex with them first". His workmates just thought that he was making it up.

Lucy Partington

Just a few weeks later, on the 27th December, 21-year-old Lucy Partington went missing after visiting her best friend, Helen Render, in Cheltenham.

Lucy was born on the 4th March 1952 in St Albans, Hertfordshire, and the following year the family moved to Bishop's Cleeve. She attended Gretton Infant School and later went to Pates Junior and Grammar Schools.

In August 1971, Lucy began studying Medieval English at Exeter University. Her father, Roger, was a lecturer in Industrial Chemistry and her uncle was the novelist Sir Kingsley Amis. Lucy was an extremely intelligent girl and had been on course to receive a First Class honours degree. She kept a diary in which she wrote about the impending finals: "The most enjoyable literature studies have been the lyric and the romance, and almost all of the art had been good. We went on a field trip to the Gloucester area for a weekend, and I was amazed how much we had absorbed, and could apply." The field trip included a visit to the Church of St Bartholomew in Much Marcle.

It wasn't learned until 2010 that during the week of 12-19th November 1973, just weeks before she went missing, Lucy and a student friend had been sitting on the floor by a fire in the living room of one of their tutors discussing the friend's intention to hitchhike home. Lucy was appalled by the idea, but her tutor remarked: "Well, I suppose it would be alright if there were a woman as well as a man in the car, especially if they had children with them." Coincidentally, Graham Lett's mother-in-law, Ellen White, claims to know that Fred and Rose had Stephen, who was just a 4-month-old baby, in the van with them on the night they picked up Lucy, but she is unwilling to say how she knows.

On the 20th December, Lucy returned home for the Christmas break to stay with her mother and siblings. Her parents had separated some years before and she had train tickets to go and see her father in Yorkshire on Friday 28th December.

On the 27th December, Lucy was given a lift into the centre of Cheltenham by her brother David and then made her own way to her friend Helen Render's house in Culross Close, next to Pittville Park. Whilst catching up they talked about their future's and Helen helped Lucy to write a letter of application for her to attend an MA course in Medieval Art at the Courtauld Institute of Art in London. Helen remembered that Lucy was "not being herself" that night but she didn't know why. Had Lucy already been spooked by someone on her journey to Helen's house?

Helen was disabled, and sadly passed away two years later, but that night her father told Lucy that if she missed the last bus home then she was to come back to the house and he would give her a lift. Lucy left to catch a Kersey bus, which was half the price of a normal bus, at 22:15, and it was sleeting out, but she assured the Render's that she would be OK as the bus stop was only 100 yards away.

She was last seen on the Evesham Road by a man out walking his dog. The roads were poorly lit, and in some cases not lit at all due to the fuel crisis that had gripped the nation. The bus was running ten minutes late, but Lucy never got on it.

Rose is known to have taken Fred and baby Stephen to visit her parents and brothers Gordon and Graham in Bishop's Cleeve earlier in the day, and Fred and Bill had disappeared from the Letts' house all that afternoon and most of the evening. The A435 where Lucy is thought to have gone missing from would have been on the route from Bishop's Cleeve to Cromwell Street.

Her disappearance was reported to the police who mounted a major investigation. The Head of Gloucestershire CID, Detective Chief Superintendent Bill Turner, led a major investigation involving more than 100 officers. Fields and estates were gone over with a fine toothcomb and there were house-to-house enquiries in Cheltenham, Gretton and Winchcombe. There were posters and appeals in the media, and the police searched every church but all they came up with was the witness who had seen her hurrying towards the bus stop while he was walking his dog.

MISSING

SINCE 10.15 p~ THURSDAY, 27ᵉ DEC. 1973.

WAS LAST SEEN IN . . . . .

ALBEMARLE
GATE, PITTVILLE,
CHELTENHAM.

21 yrs. 5'4" LONG DARK
CURLY HAIR, GOLD RIMMED
SPECS. DRESSED IN RUST
COLOURED RAINCOAT, PINK
JEANS. RED MITTENS.
CARRYING FADED ––

On the 30ᵗʰ December, Lucy's mother, Margaret told the media: "Lucy is a sensible girl who would not just go off without telling anyone. She travels everywhere on public transport and is terrified of hitchhiking. I am sure that if she had missed the bus home she would have gone back to her friend's house and stayed the night…as far as I know, she was under no stress. She didn't have any boyfriends."

By now, policeman John Bennett had been promoted to a Detective Sergeant at Stroud and he joined the frogmen who searched the lakes in Cheltenham's Pittville Park. Police also searched Cheltenham Racecourse but came up empty handed.

As part of their investigation, the police looked at the Mary Bastholm file and contacted Worcester Police about a girl called Carol Cooper who had gone missing the month before, but apart from the obvious similarities of the time of year and that the girls were either on or about to catch a bus when they were last seen, there was nothing. Worcester was more than 30 miles from Cheltenham, Gloucester nearly 10. There was nothing to link the three cases – and when Shirley Hubbard went missing from Worcester in similar circumstances eleven months later, the cases were compared again, but still there was no connection between any of them.

A television appeal was launched, and a reconstruction staged her trip to the bus stop, all in the hope of jogging the memory of passers-by. "How anyone could just vanish in three minutes completely baffles me", Lucy's mother Margaret would go on to say.

Unlike most of the other victims at Cromwell Street, Lucy had no known connection to either the property, owners or residents. She was sensible enough not to accept a lift from anyone and was terrified of hitchhiking. She had never visited the Wests. She had not visited any of their lodgers. She was not a resident of a local children's home. She was not a vulnerable teenage girl. Yet somehow, she came to be held prisoner in the basement of 25 Cromwell Street.

Fred had recently acquired an eight-millimetre movie camera and had made no secret amongst his friends that he "wanted to make movies."

He insisted that he had known Lucy for months before she disappeared. He also insisted that they used to 'make love' regularly in Pittville Park, and that he had given her the nickname of 'Juicy Lucy'. According to his first version of events, he had been waiting for her when she left her friend, and Lucy had been sitting in his van waiting for the bus to arrive when they had started to argue.

After his arrest, his solicitor Howard Ogden asked him how Lucy had been killed. Fred replied: "It must have been when I had taken her back to the bus stop. So I met her this night, and picked her up, and what she'd done, she'd found my phone number…'cause she was coming the loving racket. She was going to give up her boyfriend and wanted to come and live with me and all this rubbish…anyway, we had a row over it…I mean, it was always made clear to these girls that there was no affair, it was purely sex, end of story, and if they ever tried to threaten to tell my wife, they could be in serious trouble.

She was just sat there waiting for the bus and she said she wanted me to run her out near her home and what she was actually saying was come and meet her parents. I said to her that I had told her I didn't like any messing with my home and she got quite nasty about it. She said: 'I want to come and live with you' and all this and I just grabbed her by the throat and I drove back to Gloucester."

In all of his subsequent interviews he insisted that he and Lucy had been having an affair for months, and that she had a boyfriend who she wanted to leave for Fred. It was impossible that he had met Lucy when he said he did as they were in separate parts of the country and Lucy never had a boyfriend. Yet he did know things about her. He knew that she would "catch a bus from Pittville Park" because "she had a mate up there", yet he could easily have got this information from engaging her in conversation if he and Rose had got her into the car, or from the days she spent prisoner in his basement.

No clothes or belongings of any kind were discovered with her skeleton; not her rust-coloured knee-length raincoat, nor her pink, flared brushed denim jeans, not even the brown canvas satchel with the name L.K. Partington stenciled on it that she had been carrying on the night she disappeared. In the satchel was a book entitled 'Pearl' and her letter of application to the Courtauld Institute of Art, as well as a Victorian cut-glass jar that she had bought as a present for her sister Marian.

There is strong evidence to suggest Lucy had been kept alive for at least several days. Part of the evidence for this is that Fred remembered it was snowing on the night that he and Lucy had a row in Pittville Park, whereas in fact it didn't snow in Cheltenham until three days later. But more significantly still, although Fred had a hatred of hospitals since his motorcycle crash, he presented himself at Gloucester Royal Hospital at 00:25 on the 3rd January 1974 with a deep laceration to his right hand that required several stitches. It is believed that this injury occurred as he dismembered Lucy's body. The police even suggested to Rose after her arrest in 1994 that parts of Lucy's skin had been removed while she was still alive, and asked her if Lucy had been the subject of other forms of horrifying sadistic abuse involving the use of fire. Rose would only answer 'no comment'.

Lucy's remains were discovered buried 2'6" down in the basement in an area dubbed the 'nursery corner'. She had been decapitated and her skull was found upside down. Two pieces of woven cord, 0.25" thick, were knotted together below the jaw. A knife was also found alongside her remains. This is possibly the same knife that Fred cut himself on. It was made of stainless steel, honed down and was still sharp. There were three cut marks on her right femur and also on the left, sharp edges around the hip joints. 72 bones were missing. Her right shoulder blade, left knee cap and three ribs were some of those bones removed and are missing. 52 foot and toe bones were also removed, along with 11 ankle bones and 3 wrist bones.

Former Gloucester Police Officer Ricky Coleclough would tell in 1995 how the police linked the disappearances of Mary Bastholm, Lucy Partington and Carol Ann Cooper. Asked if police were looking for a killer, he replied: "Yes, after the disappearance of Mary Bastholm, although her body was never found, that was treated as a full scale murder inquiry and when Lucy Partington went missing there was an immediate link with Mary Bastholm and the girl from Worcester (Carol Ann Cooper)...so in police circles and local gossip between police officers we strongly believed that one person was responsible for all of those killings and presumption is that person would be local. Serial killers…wasn't a word banded about in the 70's, but yes you could call it that. It was quite firmly believed that one person was responsible and that he could well have been a local person. But who that person was, well, we didn't know it was Fred West that's for sure."

The sexual abuse of Anne Marie became a more regular occurrence at this time. She would recall times when Fred took her to work with him on various jobs to mix cement. Fred would do a lot of work for the West Indian community and the elderly, but when they went out and left him alone with Anne Marie, Fred would abuse her. He would also abuse her in the back of his work van. He would park up somewhere remote, abuse her, and then give her some money and tell her not to tell Rose. Anne Marie recalled that when he would rape her he would often kiss her on the mouth as though she were his girlfriend and not his daughter.

She also recalled occasions when Rose would make her take a bath in boiling water and then cover her in baby oil as soon as she got out. Rose also took photographs of her while she was naked. She made Anne Marie strip and stand against a wall while she used her Polaroid camera to take the photographs. The subsequent police search of the house in 1994 revealed similar photographs of all of the children at around the same age.

On one specific occasion Rose stripped Anne Marie naked and made the younger children paint pictures on her using paints. Rose then joined in and made Anne Marie get on all fours, and using black paint wrote the words 'black hole' on her bottom with an arrow. She was made to stay like that until Fred came home from work so that Rose could show him what she had been up to.

Shortly after this, Steven McAvoy managed to escape the Wests. Fred and Rose had refused to hand him back to his mother when she was feeling better and they refused to reply to her letters and phone calls. One day, when they were out, Margaret managed to break in to the house and take Steven back.

Rose West holding baby Stephen shortly before Therese Siegenthaler went missing

Therese Siegenthaler

On the 16th April 1974, Swiss student Therese Siegenthaler, 21, went missing. She was born on the 27th November 1952, in Trub, Switzerland, before moving to Berne. In 1969, at the age of sixteen, Therese left school and studied for a diploma in secretarial studies.

In early 1973 she moved to London to continue her studies and became a student in Sociology at Woolwich College of Further Education. She found accommodation in a flat with another Swiss student in Caterham Road, Lewisham, South London and at the weekends she worked in a 'Bally' shoe shop in the Swiss Centre, Leicester Square in the heart of London's West End.

On the 15th April, the day before she went missing, Therese attended a friend's party in Deptford, South London, where she told friends she planned to hitchhike to Holyhead to catch a ferry over to Ireland to meet up with a priest with whom she shared an interest in South African politics. It was only going to be a brief visit as she had bought tickets for a West End show and plane tickets to Zurich to see her family. After her friend Edward Simmons warned her of the dangers of hitchhiking, she laughingly replied: "I can look after myself. I am a Judo expert." She was last seen the following day as she left London.

No one will ever know how Therese came to be in the basement of 25 Cromwell Street. Fred West would insist through all of his interviews that he had given her a lift in his van, that he had taken her back to Cromwell Street alive, that she had been involved in a sexual experiment with him, and that he had buried her beneath the basement floor once the experiment had gone wrong. He insisted that he had never intended to murder her and she had died as the result of an accident. He also insisted that he and Therese had been lovers. "I had an affair with her. She was on holiday over here and she threatened to tell Rose...it was made quite clear that I was married to Rose...and every one of 'em did exactly the same thing... 'I love you, I'm pregnant, I'm gonna tell Rose, I want you to come and live with me'...and that was the problem." He also insisted that he had picked Therese up "just outside Worcester."

In his first version of events, Fred insisted that after he had picked her up they had made love, twice, in a lay-by and that she had then asked him for money. He said that "I just lost my head with her", hit her and took her back to Cromwell Street "after Rose had gone to the Bamboo Club." He said that he took her unconscious body and pushed it through the vent at the back of the house into the basement, where he went and strangled her "to make sure she was dead."

Just a couple of hours after giving this version of events, he gave another, in which he said that he had picked Therese up "outside Evesham" and that she had told him that she was from Amsterdam and liked Tulips, so he nicknamed her 'Tulip'. According to him, she told him that she "fancied sex" and as a result they had "pulled off down a lane". After having sex, he asked her where she wanted to go, and she apparently told him that "I'll just come home and stay with you". He said that he protested with her, but that she then said "I'm the one with the wet knickers...I've only to say you've raped me...you're in big trouble." As a result he said he agreed to take her home. After they arrived he decided to strangle her – but only after he had "made her a cup of tea" and they'd "made love again."

Under interrogation, however, it was suggested to him that Therese had been gagged with tape, which he hadn't mentioned to up to this point, and he said "it was...I think it was grey tape...what you seal boxes with, and then admitted that some of his victims were tied up.

Hours later, Fred expanded on his 'confession' and admitted that "The Dutch girl (as he called Therese) was the one I had the kinky bondage with...because that was what she wanted to do...she wanted a mask made on her face...and her nose trussed up and all this."

He then said that her 'fantasy' had got out of hand, and as a result he had taken her into the front room of the basement and laid her on the floor. "I tried to get the tape off. I couldn't even get it off her. I don't have nothing to rip it with...when you get two or three pieces together you can't rip it, and by this time she's in, you know, looking as though she's in some pain and that – so I just strangled her. I don't believe in suffering, anybody suffering, like myself. If anything happened to me I would rather somebody just end me there and then, than let me lie there and suffer, 'cause suffering is a thing I can't take, like with animals...Anything that's suffering should be put to sleep, not allowed to suffer." Yet it is very clear that his victims did suffer a great deal.

Fred then told the police that "After anything happened, when the girls died, I mean my stomach used to knot up and I felt sick and giddy and felt really ill, and I just wanted to get out of home, like, get out altogether, give myself a chance to try and get control of myself again. When I buried the girl and got rid of her clothes and that…I had to dive for it, the door, go out for a long ride somewhere."

Therese Siegenthaler's disappearance was reported to Lee Road Police Station on the 26th April. An investigation was carried out by the Metropolitan Police covering a number of years but without success.

Therese's remains were eventually discovered in 1994. Her body was compressed in a 2ft by 3ft area in front of an imitation fireplace in the basement. Her remains were in anatomical disarray, with her limbs on top of her trunk and head. One arm was above the skull, which was laying face down. In the grave with her was a knotted cloth loop made of something similar to stocking material, which had presumably slipped off her skull. There were numerous small injuries to her bones, with fine cuts to the left thigh bone, and multiple cuts to the vertebrae which pointed to decapitation. Forensic experts found threads of pink cloth, which could have been part of her clothing, and a hair decoration. Also discovered near the remains was a square silk scarf, folded or rolled to form a loop. Fragments of brown hair were trapped inside the knotted part of the material. Her left collarbone was missing, as were 5 ankle and 9 wrist bones, as well as 24 finger and toe bones.

In the early summer Fred left his job at Permali's for a new job nearby in the light fabrication shop at Muir Hill Wagon Works, where they made the shells for railway carriages and trains for the London Underground. Here, Fred was remembered as "a bragger and a liar", but also "a friendly sort who got on with most people." He made no secret that his wife was a prostitute "who liked women and blacks in particular", telling anyone who would listen that he made eight millimeter films of her having sex, which he "showed to friends" in his basement on Sunday afternoons.

Some of his new workmates accepted his offer and went to Cromwell Street, where they were shocked to find he had decorated the first floor bathroom with Polaroid pictures of Rose's "private parts". One of the regular white men who went was called Robert Jackson and who was known by the nickname of 'The Honey Monster'. He worked in the time clerk's office and was regarded as 'a bit weird' because he used to talk a lot about witchcraft and covens and sacrificing lambs. He was also known as 'Peardrop' due to his size and shape. He was always a good source for Fred for pornographic magazines, which he said he got from abroad. He claimed he had contacts in the modelling world and he persuaded at least one girl to pose topless for him at a friend's house and he carried the Polaroids of her around in his pocket.

Fred got on well with his boss, Ronnie Cooper. When Ronnie had to go into hospital for a week, Fred insisted on going to his house in Gibb Lane, Apperley, every night to check on his wife. Ronnie would go to Fred's house nearly every day, where they would sit in the back room and eat. Ronnie took his own sandwiches with him, and Rose would make him tea. He would later remember being shown the spy-hole in the side door and the Polaroids in the bathroom of Rose naked and in various poses. Fred told him that Rose was a model and showed him where the camera's were. Ronnie would be there for about half an hour a day, four or five days a week for five or six years.

Fred got some of his fellow workers to help him do work on the basement and the men were often introduced to some of the young female lodgers. Fred would brag to them that he would sometimes turn his lodgers "into prostitutes". One was a Swedish or Dutch girl who seemed to be pregnant, but there was also a girl called Marilyn from The Forest of Dean, together with a Gloucester girl, also called Marilyn, as well as the daughter of an American serviceman from the US Air Force base at Lakenheath in Suffolk, called Donna.

Years later, one visitor remembered that when one of the female lodgers, who was pregnant, had told her landlord and landlady in broken English "I am with child; it is Fred's", Rose snapped back "No it isn't, it's yours" and they both started laughing.

In June, a neighbour reported to the NSPCC that Anne Marie had spoken to other children about taking part in 'funny games' with a man. Anne Marie also spoke of watching men and women play 'mummies and daddies'. The details were passed on to Gloucestershire Social Services, but it later found no record of it.

Anne Marie and the other West children would often tell how Fred would sometimes provoke Rose until he got a reaction from her. One such occasion happened on the 13th August when Fred went up behind Rose while she was cooking dinner and began poking her in the back with his fingers and then jumping back out of the way. He kept on doing it and then started to taunt her by saying things such as: "Come on, come on, what's up Rose?" She turned and gave him a filthy look but he carried on doing it. Eventually she turned again and said: "Watch it, boy, just watch it or I'll fucking have you." But Fred just carried on.

He then started laughing and punching Rose gently and in a playful manner. Rose then snapped and said: "I fucking warned you fella!" She picked up a carving knife from the worktop and chased Fred up the stairs. Once he got to the top he slammed the door shut, just as Rose raised the knife and stabbed at him. The knife went halfway through the door but it also cut through her fingers. Rose didn't mutter a scream, shout or even cry. She walked calmly back down the stairs, picked up a kitchen towel and wrapped it around her hand to stem the bleeding. Fred then went down to see if she was alright and Rose told him: "Right, fella, you've got to take me down the hospital."

Her fingers were literally hanging off by the tendons and skin, but there was no reaction from her. At the hospital they had to sew all the tendons back together and even today Rose can only partly close that hand. When she arrived at the hospital she told the nurses that she had the 'accident' while "playing around with knives", but when she was on the ward she told the doctors that she got the wound from "cutting wood."

Rose was released from hospital the following day with her arm in plaster and was told to go back for a check-up and to have the stitches taken out but she didn't bother. She simply got Fred to cut the plaster off with some carpet scissors when she had had enough of it and then took the stitches out herself.

In interviews, Fred gave a slightly different account of what happened that night. It helps to show how everything he told his solicitor and the police was part truth and part fantasy. "I came in from work late, and she said: 'the children have broken the telly. I want a new one'." Fred said that he didn't take her complaint too seriously. But Rose grew angry when he refused to respond. Giggling, he picked up the broken television and ran towards the living-room door, only to see his wife run after him brandishing a kitchen knife.

"I slammed the fucking door straight in her face, and the knife came 'bang' straight in to the door. Next minute there's one almighty scream. So I put the television down and opened the door. One of Rose's fingers is hanging down and the other one is hanging off." She was not crying. "So I grabbed a towel, covered her hand, took her out the front. This is twelve o'clock at night." Oddly, he remembered his brother John had been "standing by the front gate" when they got outside. "We took her down the hospital."

Shirley Hubbard

On the 15th November 1974, 15-year-old Shirley Hubbard was reported missing to the police. She was born on the 26th June 1969 under the name Shirley Lloyd and she was also known as Shirley Owens. She was fostered by council worker Jim Hubbard and his wife Lina in Droitwich, and she was so happy with them that she announced her intention to change her surname to Hubbard; she never did, but in deference both to her and her family, it is as Shirley Hubbard that she is known on the files.

By October, Shirley, who had a broad smile and green eyes, was known as something of a flirt, and had once been found camping in a field with a soldier after running away from home. Before long she had found a regular boyfriend called Daniel Davies, aged 18. They had met at a fairground and Shirley had taken him home to meet her parents. She liked to hang around the fair when it came to Worcester and she "liked older men, who were strangers in the area", according to her friends. In the autumn there were rumours, for example, that she was seeing an older, married man working on some houses being built at Briar Hill in Droitwich, who "would take her out in his car."

On the 14th November, the day before she was reported missing, Shirley left work at the make-up counter in Debenhams as it was half-day closing and she and her boyfriend Daniel Davies, who worked at the John Collier tailor's shop, sat eating chips by the River Severn, cuddling and arranging further meetings. His brother Alan, who worked on the travelling

118

fair, had been one of Carol Cooper's boyfriends for a while the year before, but Carol and Shirley had never met. After seeing her on to the bus home to Droitwich, Daniel had arranged to meet her again the following day. In the morning, he waited at the bus-stop for every arrival from Droitwich, but Shirley never appeared and he never saw her again.

Her disappearance was reported to Droitwich Police, who mounted a major investigation.

Search continues for missing girl

THERE is still no sign of the young Droitwich girl who has been missing from her home for a month.

Shirley Hubbard, aged 15, of The Firs, Ombersley Road, was last seen in Worcester on November 14, and Worcester police have put out a fresh appeal for information that could lead to her whereabouts.

Shirley was a pupil at Droitwich High School, and had been attending a pre-leaving school employment course at a Worcester store for a month before her disappearance.

Worcester police have issued a picture of the girl, who they believe is still in the Worcester area.

She is described as 5ft 6ins tall, slimly built, with a roundish face, clear complexion,

SHIRLEY HUBBARD.

long, curly brown hair and blue eyes.

Supt. John Stanley said

today: "We are very concerned of the whereabouts of this girl, and we urgently appeal for anyone with information to come forward."

Shirley is one of three local girls who have been missing for some time. Worcester schoolgirl Carol Cooper, also 15, disappeared more than a year ago, and a nation wide search has failed to find her.

Lucy Partington, a 21 year-old university student from Cheltenham, also disappeared mysteriously a year ago, after apparently accepting a lift from a man. Her disappearance is still baffling Cheltenham police, who have given over a room in the headquarters to the case.

News in Brief

Evening News – 27/12/74

Fred West bracketed Carol Cooper and Shirley Hubbard together in police interviews, calling them "Worcester Girl One" and "Worcester Girl Two", and insisted that he did not even remember their names. He also told the police that their bodies were fully clothed, that they had not been mutilated, and that, once again, the only reason he had killed them was that they threatened to tell Rose about their relationship.

Fred continuously changed his version of what happened to his victims. At first, he suggested that he picked up both Carol and Shirley together "in Tewkesbury", but then changed his story and said he had picked up the "one without the fireworks burn" – that is Shirley Hubbard – "a few weeks later".

119

"I picked her up outside Worcester, and I was just generally talking to her as I was going along, and the next minute...she's got my fly undone and messing about...I just pulled in and...we made love. I think we made love twice...one after the other and then she said, that's right, then she said: 'That'll be ten quid' or something, and I said: 'Well, I don't carry money...and anyway I wouldn't pay a prostitute...if you'd said that in the first place, I'd have told you to get lost'...then she started shouting and she said: 'You're the sort of person who goes with slags' or something to that effect...And I just lost my head with her. Because as soon as she said that I thought of Rose, and Rose is no slag as far as I'm concerned. So I went for her."

He never gave any exact details of how Shirley Hubbard came to meet her death. However, at around this time, he did say to one of his workmates that he had worked as a pimp in Scotland, and that while there he had learned how to make girls do what he wanted them to. He told the worker that he would "lock them in a room for a couple of days without food and water, to make them behave." Fred told the man that he had recently picked up a 15-year-old girl outside the city and taken her back to Cromwell Street, where he had had sex with her. Rose had then joined in, and afterwards he had suggested that she should consider a career as a prostitute – presumably working for him and Rose. The girl had refused, so they had tied her to the bed and "sexually tortured her". Rose had used "instruments to penetrate the girl", Fred confided, but he had nevertheless left the girl tied up in his wife's hands and had gone to work. But when he had come home again "she was in a bad way". Unfortunately, the worker did not take Fred's story as the truth.

In police interviews he did not deny that he had "trussed the girl up" and "attempted to hang her upside down on a hook in the cellar ceiling" for "kinky sex". Yet again, he claimed that "enjoyment turned to disaster", and Shirley managed "to slip off, fall on the cellar floor" and "die as a result of her injuries". He could offer no explanation as to why 40 of Shirley's bones were missing when her remains were uncovered, including 7 wrist bones.

She had also been decapitated and her legs were buried separate from the rest of her body. Her skull was totally encased in a mask made from windings of brown tape from below her chin to eye level. Protruding from the front of the mask was a narrow plastic tube at nostril level. The tube on the other side of the tape would have entered her nostril to a depth of around 3 inches. There was also another tube found loose in the grave. There were fragments of her hair found in the mask and the police believed that the tubing was significant because it showed that Shirley had been kept alive and breathing through whatever cruelty she was put through by the Wests.

Anne Marie remembers at this time, Fred and Rose would often go out and leave her alone with the other children. "They never worried about leaving the children alone. If they fancied going out, they just went. I suppose I was babysitting for the rest of the family from the age of about ten."

Mae West

Fred continued to get in to trouble with the law as on the 25th March 1975 he appeared at Gloucester Magistrates Court charged with 'Theft' of a bicycle. He was found 'guilty' and fined £50 plus £10 compensation.

Just a week later, on the 1st April, Fred rented an allotment at Cheyney Close in Saintbridge, Gloucester, and went on to construct a small shed, 6ft x 3'6" on the site.

Juanita Mott

Juanita Marion Mott was born on the 1st March 1957. She was the daughter of an American serviceman called Ernest and her mother, Mary, lived locally in Newent, near Gloucester. She had two sisters. Juanita's parents separated when she was young and the girls all grew up with their mother.

At the end of May 1972, shortly after her 16th birthday, Juanita suffered an ectopic pregnancy. A month later, Juanita left Winifred Cullis Girls School at Coney Hill in Gloucester. She left home and took a bedsitting room in Stroud Road, Gloucester, while she found work in a nearby bottling factory. She went on to have a number of short-term jobs, including stints at Bird's Eye Walls and Cantrell & Cochrane at Eastern Avenue in Gloucester.

Juanita Mott (left) with her sisters Belinda and Mary-Ann

In early 1974, Juanita started living in a bed-sit at 4 Cromwell Street, where one friend remembered her as "not very bright, naïve and a bit dopey". While she was there she was charged with stealing a pension book and remanded to Pucklechurch Remand Centre. She received two years' probation, and moved into a flat in Stroud Road, and then into another in Albany Street, both only a few minutes' walk from Cromwell Street. She was a regular at the Pop-In Café in Southgate Street, where Mary Bastholm had worked and where Fred West was a regular visitor. In the summer of 1974, Juanita met a young man named Timothy 'Jasper' Davis who was also working at Cantrell & Cochrane. He was lodging at 25 Cromwell Street and, during the six weeks he came to know her, she also moved in to 25 Cromwell Street. In the middle of 1974 Juanita confided in a friend that she had met a man called 'Freddie', who looked like a gypsy and wore an ear-ring in one ear.

On the 1st March 1975, Juanita moved out of 25 Cromwell Street and went to stay with a friend of her mother's, Jennifer Baldwin, who lived in Horse Fair Bungalow, Horse Fair Lane in Newent.

Just six weeks later, on the 11th April, 18-year-old Juanita Mott went missing. She left Jenny Baldwin's house to hitchhike into Gloucester, which she often did at the weekends, and stood thumbing for a lift at the side of the B4215 road. This road also happens to be the most direct route between Gloucester and Much Marcle. She was due back that night as Jenny was getting married the next day and Juanita had promised to look after her children while the wedding took place, but she never returned.

Juanita was described as being a "very strong-willed, independent girl" who was "always on the go – nobody would know where she was". "She was leggy and gangly" according to a friend, with skin that always "looked tanned." Her sister commented that "She didn't like doing what anyone told her."

Her disappearance was not reported to the police, but her family did contact the Missing Persons Bureau and the media. Juanita's details were included in missing persons articles, magazines and newspapers. Had she been reported to the police then her link's with Cromwell Street might have been investigated.

Presumably, Fred recognized Juanita when he saw her standing by the side of the road and persuaded her to get in to the car. When Rose was shown a photograph of her at her trial, she said she had never seen her before.

Fred maintained that Juanita "used to come and visit" Cromwell Street, but that "she never lived there". He described her to the police as a "black-haired girl, fairly big built", who had an "American father", and he suggested that she "might have had a baby 'cause she had stretch marks." He insisted that she used to "come and visit friends at Cromwell Street", and that she had then become friendly with him over a period of "probably a couple of months". He said that Juanita used to come "down the basement helping me and that…when there was nobody there, like."

He said that they had become lovers and insisted that shortly after the affair had started they were "making love two or three times a day". In his first explanation to the police he suggested that he had killed her after they finished making love on a mattress in the basement. He said she had been helping him lay carpet tiles but then "we were both undressed. I never made love with clothes on…and she was undressed. As the erection went so I slid out of her, and then I still lay on top of her talking…I said something to the effect of 'oh, this is getting serious' or something – and she said 'oh, yer I think it's about time that I told Rose and we sorted it out.' I mean, I never had no inclination of that whatsoever. I got quite a shock when she said she was going to tell Rose and…start going together, making it serious…I thought, no way can I allow that to happen. I just lost me head. I just strangled her with me hand." He told police that "she enjoyed getting hurt when she was making love".

The other version he gave was to his solicitor, Howard Ogden, while he was on remand in 1994. Fred told him that he had taken "the Mott girl back to Stroud several times, and to Newent…Juanita used to come and talk to me quite regular." He insisted that he had not picked her up hitchhiking, and he "took the Mott girl out to Newent. She had been staying on and off for a considerable time, I think…she wanted to go to America to see her father, and I was helping her to make some money to go…giving her money when I could get a few bob on the side, without Rose knowing."

When Fred was giving his accounts of what fate befell the girls murdered at Cromwell Street to his solicitor, he was trying to shift all of the blame for the murders on to his wife Rose. He said: "We used to get loads of girls – but what I didn't realise was that Rose was enticing them there…I believe the girls ended up at these parties in Bristol. They were drugged. They were sexually abused. But I don't believe they were killed there. They were taken back to wherever Rose had 'em – and then they were tortured and killed by somebody else."

When Juanita Mott's remains were discovered, a pair of knickers, two pairs of tights – one within the other – a bra and two long white nylon socks (the sort that Rose West always wore) were found wrapped around her skull, "under the chin and over the top of the head."

I believe that Juanita was lured in to the cellar by Fred and possibly Rose on the pretense that they needed help with laying the floor, and once down there she was raped, tortured and murdered.

She had 88 bones missing. The upper part of her breastbone and her right first rib were missing, along with both kneecaps, 3 neck vertebrae (suggesting decapitation), her 11th thoracic vertebrae, 15 wrist bones, 6 ankle bones and 58 finger and toe bones. However, her fingernails were recovered, but not her finger bones, leading to the suspicion that they were pulled out while she was still alive.

Fred had perfected a sexual harness to keep his victim immobile while he and Rose abused her. A length of plastic-covered rope, like a clothesline and more than ten feet in length, was found knotted around Juanita's body, with two small loops for the ankles and wrists. There was another seven-foot length of rope in the grave too that may have been used to hang her body in the basement.

Juanita Mott

A couple of months later, in the summer of 1975, Rose went on holiday to Devon with an unnamed girl, believed to be one of her lesbian lovers, leaving Fred to look after the children with Anne Marie's help.

While she was gone, the local authority had been to visit Fred and inspected 25 Cromwell Street. They told him that he would have to install a fire-escape and a fire-alarm system if he was to continue to offer the house as a bed-sit, so when Rose returned, they threw all of the lodgers out.

He decided to wait until the authorities had returned for a second inspection, seen that there were no lodgers there, and left before he then started to advertise in the Gloucester Citizen for lodgers for £7 a week.

He also advertised for sexual partners for his wife and would arrange for the candidates to go to Cromwell Street to be vetted. If they proved acceptable and agreeable he would then film them with his wife. "He was always looking for people to be in one of his films", one fellow worker at the time remembered years later. Fred told one of his workmates at the time that he had "invited three lesbians down from Birmingham for Rose", but one of them had been so terrified when "her pubic hair had been bitten out" that she had "run out into the street half-naked". He said that he had been forced to "run down the street after her, catch her, calm her down and take her back inside."

He would also drive his wife to meet lesbians in other parts of the country. In the autumn of 1975, Rose embarked on an affair with a woman in Swindon who had replied to one of Fred's advertisements in a contact magazine. On the way back to Gloucester, Fred would insist that she tell him "every single detail."

One 17-year-old girl who found her way back to Cromwell Street in the second half of 1975 says she was first taken there by a friend. She

126

thought the Wests were "a very pleasant couple", especially when Fred offered "to run her home" in his A35 van. She went back a few weeks later and Rose invited her to her bedroom to see a jacket she had been making, and then persuaded the girl to take off her clothes and lie down on the bed. As Fred explained years afterwards: "Rose had terrific powers of persuasion over these girls. If you could persuade a girl to undress in a bedroom, and that you're measuring her up for a dress, you've got some power." When the girl was naked, Rose proceeded to kiss her neck, and then work down her body until she was sucking and licking her vagina.

"I was bewildered by it all", the girl later recalled. But, a few weeks afterwards, she returned to Cromwell Street, and on this occasion Rose took her down into the basement and laid her on a "single mattress on the floor". The rest of the room, she remembered, "was full of toys". Once again, Rose persuaded her to take off her clothes, and licked her vagina, but this time she went on to insert a vibrator into her. "She did it so quick, it hurt me a lot, and she held it up there inside me. I had to ask her to take it out because it was hurting so much."

The 17-year-old was a virgin and she ended up bleeding so badly that Rose handed her a baby's nappy to use as a sanitary towel. The girl did not report the assault to anyone.

It was around this time that Fred's brother John West started to sexually abuse and rape 11-year-old Anne Marie. He would go on to rape her on more than 300 separate occasions. He would usually have sex with Rose too when he visited during his lunch break. When Anne Marie told Rose what her Uncle John was doing to her, Rose replied: "He is your uncle, it is only natural."

The basement was now full up and there was no more room for any bodies. Fred concreted the floor and turned the basement into bedrooms for Heather, Mae and Stephen. Now that Anne Marie was of a sexual interest to both Fred and Rose, she was kept upstairs with them. Stephen slept in the back room almost exactly above the spot where Carol Cooper was buried, while Heather and Mae slept in the front part of the basement closest to the main street and directly under Rose's special room that she used for prostituting.

At this point, the only entrance to the basement was outside the house. Even in the coldest and wettest weather, the children were made to go outside and make their way to bed by way of concrete steps going down into the old coal hole around the back. It was cold and damp down there with one small window that had a view to the front street. Once the children had been sent down there to sleep they were not allowed back out. There was no toilet down there and the children were forced to use a bucket in the corner. Rose would tuck Heather, Mae and Stephen in tightly, unscrew the lightbulb and then lock the door behind her so it was pitch-black down there.

One night, Mae was trying to look out of the window when she slipped and fell onto the pointed bedpost of her bed and it went through her chin. She was bleeding and it wouldn't stop. Heather tried to help her but couldn't see due to the lack of light, so Mae climbed the steps and banged on the door to get Fred or Rose's attention but there was no response. Heather and Stephen began banging on the door too and all three started screaming but still no help was forthcoming. Eventually, a neighbour heard the commotion and knocked on the front door to tell Rose of the noise. She reluctantly took Mae to hospital for stitches.

A teacher at Anne Marie's school became annoyed at her bringing in yet another note to excuse her from taking part in a games lesson. The teacher noticed large bruises on her legs which was why Rose had written her the note. The teacher then made Anne Marie roll down her socks and hitch up her skirt which revealed further injuries. When she was asked how these injuries had occurred and if someone had given them to her Anne Marie was unable to bring herself to tell the truth. Instead, she told the teacher that she had fallen.

Not long after getting home that evening the doorbell rang and it was a woman from the Welfare Department who wanted to talk to Rose because they were concerned about Anne Marie. Rose sent her to her room while she invited the woman in, but by the time she returned, the woman was leaving and seemed happy with the explanation given to her that Anne Marie had fallen down the stairs. When she had left, Rose gave her one of the most savage beatings that she could remember.

Despite now having nowhere to bury any potential victim, Fred continued to attempt abductions while also continuing to thieve. On the 18th November, he appeared at Gloucester Magistrates Court charged with 'Receiving Stolen Goods', which was again a bicycle that was worth £44. He was fined £75.

Julie Coulson described in a statement given in 1994 how she was attacked in Tewkesbury, Gloucestershire, as a 15-year-old. "The man grabbed hold of my arm and tried to pull me into the car. I managed to get away and ran home."

Theresa Davies, a 24-year-old woman at the time, gave a statement at the trial of Rose West in 1995 in which she said she was assaulted by a man who gave her a lift near Stroud, Gloucestershire, in 1975 and who in 1994 she recognized as Fred West. She said she was hitchhiking and he gave her a lift. Suddenly, he stopped the car and lunged towards her. She started struggling with him and he locked the passenger door. "I continued to struggle and he became more and more violent, punching me in the abdomen several times. Somehow, I managed to unlock the door and struggle free." She flagged down a lorry driver who took her to a friend's house where the police were called.

Another woman (referred to only as Mrs D in the court case in 1995) said she had recognized Fred West on TV as the man who had masturbated in front of her and then assaulted her in Gloucester in 1975.

In early 1976 Fred started work on the basement with "the idea of making it in to a self-contained granny flat", for Rose's father Bill.

After taking voluntary redundancy at Smith's Aerospace, Bill Letts had taken his £3,000 redundancy money and disappeared. He was seen one day staring at his old house in Northam, Devon and then at his daughter Glenys' wedding but then formed a strange partnership with Fred. Bill moved in to 25 Cromwell Street soon after and he and Fred decided to launch a café together at 241 Southgate Street, Gloucester, no doubt as a place to meet young women. Bill used his retirement money to buy the lease and the catering equipment and Fred did all of the conversion and building work. The café was named 'The Green Lantern'. While Fred stayed behind to carry out the work, Bill took Rose and the children on holiday. The café finally opened on the 21st July 1977.

While Fred was working, Rose continued to sexually abuse Anne Marie. She caught her one day just after getting out of the bath and ordered her into her 'special room'. Anne Marie was made to get on the bed and Rose quickly joined her, while all the while calling her "a little bitch". Rose started to touch herself and Anne Marie's breasts, but became angry when Anne Marie didn't do likewise. She forced Anne Marie to give her oral sex and kept telling her to "do it properly...use your fingers". As this was happening Rose was grabbing at and scratching Anne Marie's breasts leaving deep marks which bled. She then grabbed the skin at the base of Anne Marie's throat and twisted it until she could hardly breathe.

As well as John and Fred West raping her, Rose's father Bill Letts had also been raping Anne Marie over a number of years. On one occasion, when she was twelve-years-old, Anne Marie ran into Rose's bedroom crying "Grampy's going to sleep with me!" Rose immediately snapped back: "Go back to bed. He's not going to eat you; he's only going to fuck you...I am sure you will love that." Soon after this, Bill moved out of Cromwell Street and went to live above the café. Both Fred and Bill would give conflicting reasons for his departure.

According to Bill (as heard by his son, Andrew) he had been kicked out by Fred when he objected to Anne Marie sleeping with a much older man. He had gone upstairs after hearing a lot of noise and there was a man up there. He told the man to get out of there, but on his way back down to his room he had met Fred who grabbed him and told him: "What goes on in my house is my business, Bill."

Fred's account, found amongst his prison jottings, said: "I stopped home to see Rose. It was about 11pm. Rose was in bed, so I went into the bedroom…I didn't put the light on in the room. I sat at the bottom of the bed. I was telling Rose what had happened to my hand (he had injured his thumb while using the drill). Then Anna came running downstairs and said to Rose 'Grampy's going to sleep with me'…I went upstairs to him and said 'What's going on?' Anna was with me. Bill said: 'Rose said Anna could sleep with me but Anna's playing up'…When I got home in the morning Rose and her dad was in the kitchen having breakfast…He said to me 'Do I have to go?' I said 'Yes'. 'Where can I go?' I said: 'To the café'. There was a flat at the top of the café."

As Fred would later explain: "It was a joint venture. I wanted to keep an eye on him, what he was up to…He was a devious bastard, and he was a bastard with young kids." He went on: "I was going home from work one morning. I stopped to see Bill. I went to the back door. I looked up to the roof at the back of the café. There was Bill in the bathroom window. He had sacking over him. I said: 'what you doing up there?' He said: 'Shhh.' He came down to me. He said: 'I picked up two young girls in Bristol. They were coming to Gloucester. And they stayed the night. And they're having a bath together. If you get up on the roof you can see them."

Fred resigned from the Muir Hill Wagon Works in the autumn of 1976 and devoted all of his time and energy to The Green Lantern café. His sister-in-law, Glenys Tyler, was also working at the café along with Bill.

As well as the green A35 van Fred had, he now also acquired a blue Transit van, which he used to indulge in his new past time in the evenings. As it was bigger, he would take Rose out with him to look for clients and allow them to have sex with Rose in the back of the van while he stood and watched. These sessions were usually video-recorded by Fred.

Stephen West, at just over 2-years-old, was treated in hospital for a flexor tendon injury and repair caused by a 'scissor cut'. Later, the explanation given was because he had 'fallen on a knife.' The truth is that he was attacked in one of Rose's rages. He wasn't the only one to be beaten. One day, Mae was putting the washing on when Rose shouted at her: "That's far too much washing powder, Mae! You're wasting it! Do you think I'm fucking made of money?" Mae apologized, but Rose said: "I'll give you fucking sorry, girl!" Rose started to slap and punch her and as she chased Mae out of the room she shouted "Fucking useless you are! Go on, get out! Go and help Heather clean the bathroom!"

Towards the end of 1976, Rose's brother Graham moved in with a 13-year-old girl. She would later be abused by both Fred and Rose after Graham had broken up with her, and it only came out after Fred's and Rose's arrest in 1994 that they had been in a relationship. She was only ever referred to up until then as 'Miss A'.

It was at this time that Anne Marie was forced to sleep with some of Rose's clients. She recalled one specific time when she was with a client and she wasn't allowed to speak or even make a noise. He was so big that he ripped her and when he had gone Rose made her get in a bath and then put salt in it.

The clients were told that Anne Marie was 16 and she was only introduced to them by their nicknames such as 'Bonnie', 'Sonny', 'Suncoo', 'Duke Roy' and 'Bigger'. Rose was always in the room when Anne Marie was forced to sleep with the men for fear that she might reveal her true age, despite it being obvious by looking at her body that she was a child. Rose had told her before that West Indian men were 'big down below' and preferred these to sleep with so Anne Marie had to sleep with them too. Rose loved it and couldn't get enough of them as they usually came closest to satisfying her.

One of the clients became keen on Anne Marie and brought her chocolates as a gift but Rose grew jealous and ate them all herself. He was never allowed to come back. Rose wasn't charging any of the men she slept with at this point and seemed to sleep with these men purely for hers and Fred's enjoyment. She would sometimes drop hints that she wanted presents instead and was often bought cigarettes or rum.

On one occasion when Anne Marie was aged either 13 or 14, Rose took her to a local pub. Fred dropped them both just outside the pub and then left. Rose, as usual, wasn't wearing any underwear and sat in the pub making it obvious to all who looked.

Anne Marie was brought barley wine, which she hated, but was forced to drink it. Various men were buying drinks for the pair and Anne Marie became quite drunk. Rose became annoyed by this and they left the pub. As they walked down a country lane on the way home, Fred's van pulled up alongside them and Rose suddenly became very angry with her. She grabbed Anne Marie and threw her into the back of the van, all the while shouting at her and screaming: "Do you think you could be my fucking friend? Who do you think you are?"

Rose and Fred had obviously thought that Rose didn't have to be alone anymore when she went out looking for men. I believe the plan was for them to both pick up a man to take back to Cromwell Street for Fred's visual pleasure, and when he pulled up in his van and the two women were without a man, Rose turned on her and made it all out to be her fault.

With Anne Marie now in the back of the van, Rose started to hit her and Fred pulled the van over into a layby. He jumped in the back of the van and, instead of protecting his daughter from Rose's onslaught, joined in with the beating. He then got Rose to hold her down while he raped her. When they had finished with her they drove back to Cromwell Street where the other children had been left unattended. As Mae would recall: "She always seemed to have a relationship with them that was private and that only the three of them understood. Above all, Anne Marie always gave me the impression of being troubled, lonely and very unhappy."

The sexual abuse of Heather also started around this time. In 1977, a teacher of 'Child X' (almost certainly Heather) reported to the NSPCC that the child was undressed and made to watch a couple having sex. The man told her: "this is what you will be doing soon. You are old enough." She was touched on her private parts by both the man and woman.

The following month, Rose became pregnant with Tara. Her father was not Fred West, but one of her clients. Fred and Rose had decided that they wanted mixed-race children as he believed that they were a superior race.

The pregnancy didn't stop Rose going out drinking in the various pubs and clubs while looking for new men to sleep with. On the 24th February, an entry in Rose West's diary states: "Went to Tracy's (a nightclub) with Anna (Anne Marie). Met two fellas. Not much good…12 o'clock got home. Hopeless! Fella not a lot of good. 12.30 o'clock with Fred, that's better. Got a cuddle!" Again, this adds weight to the theory that she would bring men back from the clubs and pubs for sex.

In the spring of 1977, Fred met a woman who was to become his next murder victim, Shirley Robinson. He said he met her in the café after Bill had picked her up in Bristol and brought her there because she was looking for a job. He said that he got to know her well and it wasn't long before he told her that she was a lesbian.

One morning, according to Fred, he went into the café where Shirley was sitting and she "was looking ill." She told him that Bill Letts was giving her a hard time and he had taken the lock off both the bathroom door and her bedroom door and he kept walking in and "touching me up…I only go with girls." She asked him if he had anywhere that she could stay, so he gave her a room at Cromwell Street.

Shirley Ann Robinson was born to RAF Corporal Royale 'Roy' Robinson and his partner Christa Carling in Leicestershire at RAF Cottesmore on the 8th October 1959. She later lived in both Germany and the West Midlands. In 1974, Shirley's parents split up and Christa left with

Shirley and moved to Hartlepool, but it did not work out and Shirley returned to live with her father, who was then based in Wolverhampton. She started to exhibit bad behavior and was selling her services as a prostitute at the age of thirteen. She was placed in to the care of Bristol Social Services and her mother lost touch with her. Shirley was sent to the Crescent School, Downend, Bristol and was originally housed in a secure unit. She was then transferred to the cottages used to accommodate the girls who had started work. A residential Social Worker there recalled her concern about Shirley, saying she was "extremely withdrawn and sullen" and whom she thought was beginning to show lesbian tendencies. The Social Worker noted that Shirley had lesbian girlfriends much older than herself.

In 1977, responsibility for Shirley Robinson's supervision was transferred to Gloucester Social Services. She then got a live-in job as a housemaid in Chipping Sodbury. How she got from there to be in Fred's café has never been established and we only have Fred's account to go by.

So it was, in April 1977, Shirley Robinson moved in to the small bedroom next to the bathroom on the first floor at 25 Cromwell Street. Anne Marie recalled of her: "She was nice and took me ice-skating so I remember her better than the others. Sometimes I would walk down to the unemployment office with her. She was a bubbly girl and I spent quite a lot of time talking to her. I would sit in her room and chat."

Shirley was in fact bi-sexual. "The Wests had told Shirley they had an open marriage", recalled former lodger Elizabeth Brewer. "Fred didn't seem to mind his wife with another man. Fred said prostitution was a good way of making money. Fred and Rose were very open about sex. Each knew the other's activities and discussed their exploits." She also recalled: "Out of the two of them, Rose would be expected to lose her temper." Elizabeth also remembered a conversation she had with Rose, when she told her that a relation of hers was leaving her husband. Rose commented that whatever Fred did, she would never leave him.

Elizabeth also said that the house was regularly targeted by the police for drugs raids and: "He thought she (Hazel Savage) was a hardened woman and made other unnecessary comments about her. Much the same as he did to other women really. He talked about her quite a lot actually. I got the feeling that she'd probably been investigating him and that's why he talked about her. And then of course there was Rose returning from nights out complaining that the 'fucking police' had been following her around and been accusing her of prostitution."

On the 21st June, Shirley Robinson registered with a Gloucester surgery as a patient, giving her address as 25 Cromwell Street. Shortly after, The Green Lantern café went out of business. Bill Letts had recruited the help of his wife, Daisy, and other family members to help him run it so he could save money on wages, but still the café could not support them all financially. Bill went back to live with Daisy.

With the café now closed, Fred recruited Shirley to work for him. He had been forced to go back to the Muir Hill Wagon Works, but he was still also working as a part-time builder, and he needed help. He was converting and refurbishing flats in Midland Road for his old landlord Frank Zygmunt's widow and son and he took Shirley with him. "She worked like a man. Shirley spent all her time on the job, seventeen hours a day. I worked on my job by day", and then "went to work with Shirley till we went home at eleven or twelve at night." It was while they were at Midland Road, adding an extension on to the back of a property, that they embarked on an affair.

Shirley Robinson

Fred nicknamed Shirley "Bones" because of her thinness. Three or four months after they started working together, Fred would recall: "Shirley was undressing to change out of her working clothes. She said: 'You want to have sex with me?' I said: 'You're a lesbian'. She said: "Lesbians have sex with men'. I had never made love to a lesbian. I wondered what it would be like. So I said yes."

According to Fred, Shirley then told him that she wanted a baby and told him that she had a girlfriend in Bristol and they wanted a baby together. Fred then said: "No baby. A baby has to have a mother and father, not two girls. What about when the child goes to school?" Shirley then countered and told him that "you can have sex with me when you want to", so he told her "we'll see".

A later job they worked on together was at 7 Cromwell Street, where

Fred recalled that Shirley was on a step ladder and told him to catch her overalls. He then said to her: "You got no pants on", to which she told him that it was too hot to wear them. She then jumped down on to him and they fell to the floor, where she asked Fred: "Please make love to me. I am in love with you." He said they then made love and got back to work.

At around the same time, during the summer of 1977, a girl known only as 'Miss A' in order to protect her identity, was tied up, beaten and raped by both Fred and Rose at 25 Cromwell Street. She had been a resident at Jordans Brook children's home and had been introduced to the Wests by a friend and told by Rose that she could visit whenever she wanted.

She was 13-years-old the first time that she went there. The conversations started off in a normal manner, normally revolving around her being in care. "At first we would talk about Jordans Brook. She seemed to know more about it than I did initially. She knew about the regime there, when you were allowed out and not allowed out. We talked about girls things like periods and puberty and how our bodies changed, and sex."

On one occasion, when she was 15-years-old, she ran away from the children's home with her best friend. They spent the first night hanging around the cafes and the bus station but on the second night they went to 25 Cromwell Street. She arrived around 23:00 and found Rose wearing just her underwear. She told her that she had run away from the home and Rose comforted her and put her arm around her. Rose then made them both a cup of tea and gave them blankets for the night and they slept on the sofa. In the morning Rose made them tea and toast and they left.

Not long after, 'Miss A' found herself back at Cromwell Street. She was feeling depressed and rejected by her family and was crying. Again, Rose put her arm around her. But then "Rose started kissing me on my neck. I sort of pushed her away. She was touching my breasts outside my clothes and saying: 'It's OK, this is what mum's and daughter's do when they get close'. I struggled and she got up and went and got me a drink and a blanket…she didn't say sorry or explain what she had done. She saw I didn't like it so she didn't do it. For once in my life an adult had done what I asked them to do…It may sound odd but, because she had stopped, I respected her even more. She was aware that her attention was unwelcome." 'Miss A' spent the night on the sofa, but soon afterwards was found by her father and returned to Jordans Brook but still continued to visit Fred and Rose.

One Friday morning, around six weeks later, she left Jordans Brook to go and visit her mother and called in to 25 Cromwell Street on the way. She recalled that Rose answered the door wearing a see-through blouse and skirt but no bra or tights. Rose called out to Fred to say that she had arrived and

Rose followed her up to the bathroom. Rose then invited her in to one of the bedrooms where there were already two girls of a similar age. The curtains were drawn and it was dark inside. The door then closed behind her.

"I was stunned to see two naked girls in the room, one on the floor and one on the bed. Fred was there too." She described the first girl as aged 12-14, 5ft tall with bleached blonde hair, a small bust and painted toenails. The second girl was sitting on the floor and looked older, maybe 15 or 16. She seemed quite comfortable and relaxed. She had jet-black hair cut in a short, spikey style, a well-developed bust and an Indian ink tattoo on her wrist. "I remember being struck by her calmness. It's hard to explain, but the way she looked was as if this was an everyday occurrence."

There is little doubt that this second girl was Anne Marie, but no-one knows who this blonde girl was. Anne Marie has no recollection of this incident but it's possible she has either blanked it from her memory, or more likely was drugged while the assaults took place.

'Miss A' then remembered that Rose put her arm around her and said: "It's alright to touch, to feel, enjoy, and show affection." Rose then stripped the girl and joked: "It's all girls together". Fred was still in the room, sitting and watching silently. He was wearing just a pair of shorts. Rose removed her own skirt and blouse and turned to the blonde girl who was on the bed, who struggled. Rose was calming her down but at the same time touching her breasts and vagina. "The girl was clearly upset, very distressed and scared."

The girls' hands were bound with wide sticky tape and she was turned on to her stomach by Fred and Rose. "Rose was reassuring us but Fred was silent. He spread the girls' legs apart and taped her ankles. Her legs were so far apart he almost split her." Rose then produced a vibrator, a white candle and some ointment and ran the vibrator along the girls back. She turned to Fred and asked: "Are you enjoying this now?" before inserting the vibrator into the girl, whose face was clearly scrunched up with pain. As it was being pushed in, Rose was saying things like "Enjoy" and "Does it feel good?" 'Miss A' remembered: "The girl had her head towards me as she was being hurt. She was crying in pain. It was Rose doing it. Fred had now taken his clothes off and she kept saying: 'Are you enjoying it, Fred?'

Fred had an erection and knelt behind the girl. He raised her buttocks off the bed and had intercourse with her from behind. Rose was stood behind Fred fondling his buttocks while this was going on. I looked at the girls face. She was in pain. She had a help-me look on her face. The other girl in the room was apparently taking the whole scene in her stride and not reacting. Fred then left the room and Rose un-taped the ankles of the girl on the bed, tearing at the tape to cause maximum pain. Rose turned her on to her back. The girl was crying and Rose was stroking her cheek, saying:

'There, there, it's OK'. The girl was just staring in front of her like she was in a trance. She virtually crawled away from the bed."

'Miss A' went to the bathroom and Rose followed her. "I was naked. I froze in fear. She started running her hands across my body and through my pubic hair. She was also necking me and whispering: 'Enjoy, it's alright.' I never encouraged or welcomed it. I remained frozen in fear. Rose commented: 'I like stiff ones!' Rose led me to the bed, where the other girl was seated. The dark girl was sitting on the floor with her legs drawn up to her chest. I sat on the bed. Rose got the tape. It was the same as before. Rose put the tape on. I can't understand why I let them do it. She wrapped the tape around my wrists similar to the way bandages go. The other girl got off the bed and leaned against the wall. She looked terrified.

Rose was very aggressive. Fred came back in and stood to the right of the bed masturbating himself. I put my head down on the sheets. Rose taped my ankles so they were apart. I couldn't move them.

Something moved down my back. It was cold, hard and vibrating. Rose stood by my left leg. The vibrator got close and was then taken away. She said: 'Is that nice, Fred?' and Fred grunted in reply. I felt Rose push two fingers in my vagina. I know it was Rose. She reached around my body and twisted my left nipple hard. I kept saying to myself, 'Why?' She kept saying 'Enjoy!' She called to the other girl and said it was great.

I felt something enter my anus. It was cold, about five or six inches in length and moved forwards and back. There was no lubricant. I felt my anus was being split. I think it was the candle. It was the right dimensions. I assumed it was Rose. It was in place for several minutes and then yanked out very fiercely. I heard a popping sound.

Someone climbed on the bed. I was entered in the vagina. He was moving in and out of me. Rose was fondling Fred as he was having sexual intercourse with me. Fred was telling Rose how close he was to coming. Rose said to come over my back. I felt warm droplets on my back and Rose rubbed it in."

'Miss A' told the police that someone went out of the room and she was left tied up for some minutes before Rose cut the tapes with nail scissors and tore them off roughly. Rose then threatened her: "We know what happens to little girls who tell." 'Miss A' went to the bathroom, found she was bleeding from her anus and washed herself, got dressed and then left the house. She said she could not run because she was so sore. She went on to visit her mother but told no one of what happened to her that day. "I felt so ashamed", she said in her police statement. She still remembered the sound of the tape being ripped off her body and added: "I am sure if I had offered any resistance I would have come to some harm."

She was left so distressed by the attack that some weeks later she stole a can of petrol and went to Cromwell Street intending to set fire to the property, but she lost her nerve.

On the 18th October, Shirley Robinson was confirmed to be pregnant and there are records of a positive test done on this date at the Health Centre.

She spent hours sitting on the wall in front of the house, devouring the red Mr Men lollies that she had a craving for and chatting openly to the neighbours about how she was expecting Fred's baby. On one occasion, Rose herself went outside and confirmed the news, pointing to Shirley's stomach and telling their neighbour Linda Greening: "It's Fred's". She then pointed to her own, more advanced pregnancy, and said: "I wonder what colour it will be?" Rose then told Linda that they were planning to bring up the two children together.

Rose's character and appearance became increasingly eccentric as her pregnancy developed. She took to wearing maternity dresses without underwear, and often sat on the back step of the house with her legs open and skirt up. There were other oddities, as one lodger remembered: "She dressed as a child, always wearing white schoolgirl socks. I didn't think she was quite right in the head."

Anne Marie recalled: "I was often aware as a child that dad was having affairs with other women. Sometimes they were women who came to the house; sometimes, like Shirley Robinson, they were lodgers...He used to put his arm around her and say: 'This is my next wife'. Rose's eyes would narrow, but she never said much about it."

On the 9th December, Rose gave birth to Tara Jayne West, who was given the nickname 'Mo'. She was with a client when she went in to labour. Tara was rarely told off to the extent of Fred's own children and she was never sexually abused. She was named after the hotel where Rose and her father (nicknamed Rosco) would meet, the Tara Hotel in Upton St. Leonards.

Just two months later, in February 1978, Rose became pregnant again, this time with Fred's child who they would call Louise. Tensions in the house had risen and Shirley and Rose had been arguing to the extent that their relationship had drastically deteriorated. When Shirley was 6 months pregnant she moved out of her tiny cramped room at Cromwell Street and moved in with another woman.

"I went to see her two or three times", Fred would later write. "I missed her. We got on so well together, and Shirley was having my baby. Shirley knew I was missing her. So as long as I went to see her, the longer she would stay away. So I stopped going to see her. Within a week Shirley was waiting for me outside my work...She said: 'Your baby is missing you and so am I'... We went to see Rose. Rose said: 'Shirley can have her old room back'."

At the beginning of May, and barely a month before she was due to give birth, Fred went to have a full-scale studio portrait of himself, dressed in his best suit, standing beside Shirley in her best dress. It looked just like a wedding photo. Fred later explained it by saying that Shirley had wanted it done "so she could send them to her father and friends."

At this time, Shirley wrote to her father, who was running an English pub in Cologne, Germany. She told him that she had met a wonderful man whom she was going to marry and that she had never been happier in her life. "I am expecting a child from Freddy. We are in love." She enclosed a smart photograph of herself and Fred together.

By the end of the month it appears that Fred had grown just as tired of Shirley as Rose had. He admitted to his brother-in-law, Jim Tyler, that: "She wants to get between me and Rose. She wants Rosie out so she can take over and take her place. I'm not having that. She's got to fucking go." Shirley had taken to staying in Elizabeth Brewer's room and sleeping on her sofa after she became frightened by both Fred and Rose. Rose had grown more and more antagonistic towards Shirley as her pregnancy progressed, and Shirley told Elizabeth that she "needed to keep away from them." Elizabeth recalled: "She was a lonely person who latched on to people. She didn't have many friends."

It was at this time that a man named Rikki Barnes recalled Fred and Shirley's relationship. Rikki met Anne Marie at a fairground and took her back to his caravan. Within a few days, he had moved in to 25 Cromwell Street. "I used to take Anne Marie to school in her uniform – and then take her to the pub at night." He said he got his marching orders from the house because he called Shirley Robinson 'love' so Fred threw him out. "She was in love with Fred and Rosemary knew Shirley was carrying his baby. It was an amazing relationship."

Shirley went to the health centre on the 2nd May to see her GP, Dr John Buckley, who told her about various other benefits she might be eligible for.

A week later, Shirley Robinson and Elizabeth Brewer posed for a picture in a photo-booth at Woolworth's in Gloucester.

On the 12th May, Shirley withdrew her claim for benefit because she said she was moving to Scotland. This was the last sighting of Shirley, and shortly after, Shirley disappeared while eight-and-a-half months pregnant. Her disappearance was not reported to the police. Both Fred and Rose caught Elizabeth Brewer and her boyfriend, Ped, in the hall at the foot of the stairs one morning after she had disappeared and Fred told her that Shirley had left to go and live with her father in Germany. Later that day,

Fred made a special visit up to Elizabeth's room to tell her privately that Shirley had to go because she was getting too randy and was planning to "rip Liz's knickers off".

When Fred confessed to the murder of Shirley, he deliberately avoided getting in to any detail of precisely what happened. In his first interviews he told almost nothing but blatant lies and was intent on maintaining that he alone had been involved, and no-one else. He told the police that he had "strangled her in the hall, in the living-room", when "Rose was in hospital having a baby". He also maintained that "I don't think Rose even knew Shirley...As far as I know Rose never met Shirley." He later added that Shirley was "pure lesbian" and then said "I don't know if she actually raped Anne (Anne Marie), but she had sex with Anna Marie."

He said Shirley had been waiting for him on his allotment in Saintbridge, and had wanted to have sex with him. He told her he didn't have time and wanted to get home, so they both got in the van, where "she was nagging on about me having sex with her." He said he then went upstairs when they got back to the house, but Shirley followed him and continued to nag him. "I turned round and hit her actually, smacked her across the floor, knocked her across the room. She went flying down on the floor.

She wasn't dead...so I got her outside and locked the back doors and stayed out with her. And I sat on the block there used to be...then I just sat there looking at her, and...it was going through me mind at the time, she's going to absolutely ruin me marriage...She's going to destroy the lot...There was loads of spare cable chucked on the floor there, all cut up. So I just went over and picked a piece of that up, and come back and just put it round her neck. I mean, I just didn't think to kill her, I wasn't thinking nothing."

All this took place "in the late evening", and after he had killed her he hid her body under "this big heap of cut-off cables...and left her there...locked the patio doors...and I picked up a bag and I went to the hospital." When he got back, Shirley was "stiff, cold" so he lifted a slab outside his back door. "But then I couldn't get the hole anywhere near big enough, because it was going to take too long. So I went in the back door and got the knife...and just cut Shirley up there, took her arms and legs off, and then I packed her up...just pushed her in with a spade. He admitted that he had ripped "a summer dress thing" from her body "to stop the blood getting on the patio, because I had nothing else."

He admitted that he was the father of Shirley's baby. "It had been carefully planned with Shirley not to say anything. I mean, I didn't want to get involved with Shirley or involved with any woman apart from Rose." He had even "chucked her out once" but "she would not bloody stop calling me, and coming and looking for me all the time." He insisted that he had no alternative other than to kill her. "I was aware that Shirley was carrying a child of mine…and I mean the last thing I wanted to do was hurt a child of mine." But Rose West, he insisted, "is the only thing that matters in my life, nothing else, not even my children."

In a second interview, he accepted that Rose had not been in hospital when he had killed Shirley. This time he maintained that Shirley had met him at his allotment and told him that she wanted him to live with her. He said he had made it clear to her that "I wasn't interested, no way, and she knew that…or it was made clear to her." He said he then took her back to Cromwell Street, where Rose had taken Tara, Heather, Mae and Stephen out to the park and he had killed Shirley because "What Shirley had done is gone upstairs and told Liz (Brewer)."

He said he had hit her and knocked her unconscious, and then put her body in the wash-room he had recently created at the back of the house. He then strangled her with a cable "to make sure she was dead", cut her up with a bread knife, dug a small hole "and carried the pieces out and dropped them in the hole…I took the big piece out first, and then the head, and then the legs. I didn't have much room to put it in, so it had to be packed." He had dismembered her body on her summer dress and washed the blood from his chest and arms in the sink. "Rose didn't know nothing", he insisted.

Both of Shirley's kneecaps were missing when her skeleton was recovered. Her unborn child's head was not in her pelvis, and it had not been left intact in the abdomen, suggesting that someone had tried to cut the baby out of her. Her right thigh bone had been severed with a heavy but very sharp weapon. 28 of Shirley's wrist and ankle bones, and 42 of her finger and toe bones were missing. 3 of Shirley's vertebrae were also missing. Her legs had been disarticulated at the hips. There were no fewer than 21 fine cut marks on her bones. There was no hair found in the grave, making it a distinct possibility that she had been scalped.

Mae West vaguely remembered Shirley as they only ever exchanged pleasantries now and again, but she did remember that it was Rose who told her that Shirley had "upped and offed". She told Mae that she had just gone and that sometimes young girls "clear off without so much as a by-your-leave and you never know why."

On the 25th May, a claim was made for unemployment benefit in Shirley's name. This could not have been made by Shirley, and the DHSS became suspicious as she had already told them that she was moving to Scotland. Three weeks later, on the 14th June, the Department for Health and Social Security sent a letter to Shirley at 25 Cromwell Street asking her to phone them. The letter went unanswered.

On the 4th August, Mr Peter Gregson, from the DHSS visited

Cromwell Street to enquire after Shirley Robinson. He was told by a lady who answered the door (undoubtedly Rose) that she had gone to live in Germany. He admitted that he was not authorized to question what he was told and had to accept the information given to him about Shirley going 'on face value'.

A few weeks later, Fred told Elizabeth Brewer that Shirley had given birth to a boy in Germany and had called him Barry. He told her that Rose was going to look after the baby for a while so Shirley could have a break.

The physical abuse of the children continued, and Anne Marie was treated in hospital for puncture wounds to both of her feet, similar to the wounds sustained by Charmaine when Fred was in prison.

Fred and Rose then decided to take the family on holiday. In October they went to Butlins in Barry Island, South Wales, where Fred had an affair with a worker called Lyn Barry and Fred got her pregnant. Lyn later recalled: "I was 18. I was young and naïve…He told me Rose was his sister. They had three kids with them. Two girls and a boy. He took me out drinking on the island. We got drunk and had sex in his chalet when Rose wasn't there…He stayed in Barry for a fortnight and we had a fling for 10-12 days of his holiday." She never told Fred of her pregnancy. Lyn remained convinced Rose knew he was sleeping with her. She said: "The three of us went out a couple of times. She was happy to go along with it. He wasn't rough with me – but he did turn nasty after he had a few drinks."

Just a couple of weeks after they got home, Rose gave birth to Louise Carol West on the 17th November.

In 1979, Juanita Mott's sister, Belinda, visited 25 Cromwell Street because she knew one of the lodgers and met (unbeknown to her at the time) both of her sisters killers, Fred and Rose. In 1995, Belinda commented: "When my eldest daughter was a baby I had a friend staying at 25 Cromwell Street and she introduced me to another girl and it just makes me feel sick to think that I was leaving my daughter there as a baby and I was staying down there having a laugh and a joke. To think that all that time my sister was buried below me."

At this time Fred embarked on a series of bizarre medical experiments designed to ensure that Rose would give birth to another mixed-race child. His plan was thus: If Rose had sex with a Jamaican client using a condom, he would take the condom away as soon as the client had left and protect its contents. He would then mix them with the contents of another black clients' condom, which he had stored earlier. A short time afterwards he would insert this newly mixed semen into Rose by means of a small syringe, in the hope that she might conceive. In order to store the semen from the first condom at the correct temperature, it was knotted and Anne Marie was forced to store it in her vagina.

If Rose's client didn't use a condom, he would insist that Rose allow the semen to dribble out into a small pot that he kept especially for the purpose before mixing it with other sperm and inserting it with a syringe back in to his wife. Anne Marie remembered: "I heard somebody say 'We will see if this works and gets you pregnant'."

During the last week of May 1979, Rose's father Bill Letts died aged 58 in Frenchay Hospital, Bristol, of Pleural Mesothelioma caused by asbestos a few days after being admitted. His funeral took place at Cheltenham Cemetery on the 5th June. It was paid for by his son Andrew and his wife Jackie. He left a lot of unpaid bills from his lifestyle, which Daisy spent the rest of her life working hard to pay off. One of Rose's older sisters said: "The only reason any of us went was to make sure he went down that hole." Some family members refused to follow the coffin into the chapel. The oldest children, Joyce and Pat, had a falling out before the funeral and sat away from each other and the main cortege; Graham followed the coffin behind Andrew, Daisy, her sisters Eileen and Dolly, while Jackie Letts and Jim Tyler sat it out at the back. Gordon arrived in handcuffs with police officers either side, which Daisy begged them to take off to no avail, while Bill's father, William, who had moved in with another woman and went on to live until he was 100-years-old, didn't turn up at all. Rose attended the funeral alone, as Fred refused to attend which led them to have some lively arguments. She wore provocative clothes, including a pair of black stiletto heels, schoolgirl white socks up to her knees and a miniskirt. As she went over to comfort her big sister Pat, it ended up in a fight, with Pat throwing Rose into the dirt. Years later, Gordon would say: "Everyone seemed so glad when he died. Gone and out of the way. My mother hated my dad intensely." To this day, Bill's grave is unmarked by a headstone.

A week after the funeral, Graham broke into his mother's flat, took what he could sell to fund his drug habit, and did the gas meter over while he was at it. Just after this, Daisy had read her husband's medical records. She found out for the first time that Bill had been diagnosed as a paranoid schizophrenic in his youth, before joining the Navy, and had suffered from 'severe psychotic' episodes ever since.

In the summer of 1979, Fred paid for Rose to have an abortion. It is believed that this is because they were sure that Fred's experiments had failed and they were sure that the baby would not be mixed-race. Fred would later tell his solicitor, Howard Ogden, that "She reckoned it was mine. So I went and paid for her to have an abortion."

In June, Rose took Anne Marie out to a pub called 'The Famous Pint

Pot'. Rose was 25 and Anne Marie was just a month short of her fifteenth birthday. When Rose saw two young men sitting together, she quickly asked if they could join them. One of them was a powerfully-built factory worker called Mike Spencer, who was 21-years-old. "From then on things moved very quickly. We chatted and were getting on quite well. Rosemary was quite well-dressed, making lots of sexy comments", he later said.

Before closing time, Anne Marie went to the toilets and Rose turned to Mike Spencer and asked: "Would you like to come and stay the night at our place? You can sleep with my daughter." When Anne Marie came back Rose nodded to her, and then Mike left the pub with them both. "My pal wasn't invited and when we got there I simply went straight to a downstairs bedroom, got undressed, and had straight sex with Anne.

I was 21 and she was about 18 (he thought) and seemed quite experienced. I regarded it as an easy lay because I was a young lad…In the morning I was a bit worried about what her father's reaction might be. I didn't have to be concerned because when he saw me the next morning there was no confrontation. He just seemed to accept that I had stayed the night with his daughter."

Mike went on to help Fred build a wall in his back garden and posed for a photograph with him.

Mike Spencer and Fred West

Mike continued to sleep with Anne Marie over the following three months, from June until August. He described how during one Sunday lunch Fred started talking about pimping and prostitution "and all types of sex. He talked about women, and what he liked doing to them in bed. I got the impression that there was prostitution going on but I was never charged for sex with Anne. I also remember the downstairs beds in the house had loads of pornographic books and material beneath the beds."

He noted that Anne Marie liked to wear a red outfit that struck him as

145

rather "tarty". He added: "But I didn't care, because I was getting what I wanted – sex."

The affair came to an end one day after a visit to a fairground. A man came over to Anne Marie and whispered to her. Anne Marie replied: "I don't do that kind of thing anymore." – which verified Mike's suspicion that she had been a prostitute. "It was then I thought I should get out of the relationship and left her a day later…I will never forget the night I met Rosemary and her step-daughter Anne."

At this time several lodgers remember a pregnant young woman with khaki shorts, hiking-boots and a German accent as having been at Cromwell Street. She was never traced and Fred West would never confirm who she was.

One day, Mae West recalled how Rose taught her and Heather about the facts of life. Rose was sitting on the sofa talking quite openly about sex. "What you two need to realise is that for a girl to understand her body she needs to explore it." Mae asked her what she meant and Rose lifted her skirt to reveal her vagina and said: "I want you to put your hands up there. You first, Mae." When Mae said she didn't want to, Rose shouted: "Do as I fucking well say, girl!" The girls were terrified but did as they were told. "That's what you'll be like down there when you're older. You need to know that", Rose told them.

Alison Chambers

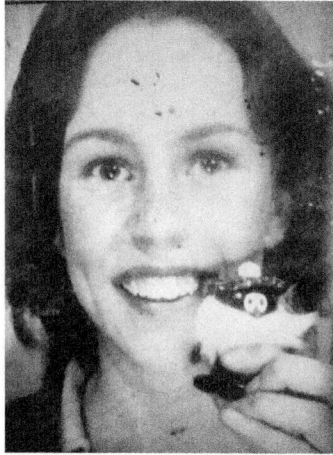

Alison Jane Chambers was born in Hannover, West Germany on the 8th September 1962, where her father was a sergeant in the Royal Army Ordnance Corps and her mother a WRAC Private. Her parents divorced and Alison went to live with her mother in Swansea, but she ran away so frequently that her mother didn't know how to handle her and her stepfather would sometimes be out late at night looking for her. Once, she managed to run away and got as far as Paddington Station in London with her friend, Helen Hulme. Her mother decided that she could no longer cope with her and that she would have to be placed in to care. She thought she would be safer there, and in 1977, Alison was taken in to care by Swansea Social Services and placed in a local children's home, from which she ran away on a number of occasions.

At the end of December 1978, when she was 16-years-old, she transferred to Jordans Brook children's home in Gloucester. Fred's Ford Transit van was often seen parked outside or cruising by.

She worked for a firm of solicitor's under a Youth Training Scheme and was described by a member of staff at the home as being "obviously insecure" and prone to exaggeration, particularly about her boyfriends. "It was as if she wanted constant attention." The girls at Jordans Brook remembered her as a fantasist, full of stories, hopes and plans. She spent hours drawing sketches, imagining the kind of life she wanted for herself. In the nine months she spent in care she absconded eight times. According to her friend Sharon Compton, on some of these occasions she went to 25 Cromwell Street, where she became familiar with both Fred and Rose. They showed her pictures of a farm that they said they owned, and told her that when she turned seventeen she could go and live there, which Alison was really looking forward to. In truth, however, the pictures came from an Estate Agent's leaflet.

Alison was friendly with a girl called Anne, who already had links with Cromwell Street and one day Alison and her room-mate Sharon Compton played truant from the home and met her outside a cinema in Gloucester. Anne then took them to Cromwell Street, where they had orange squash and biscuits with Rose.

It was at the beginning of 1979 when Sharon Compton and Alison Chambers again absconded from Jordans Brook and visited Cromwell Street, where Rose allowed them to stay the night, just as she had 'Miss A' and countless others. In the morning, they met a Dutch girl who was arguing with Rose about her rent. The girl wore the distinctive heavy walking boots and thick socks of a hiker, suggesting that the Wests were still meeting and picking up young women who were hitchhiking.

The theme of the Wests possibly drugging victims came up again at this time, as Anne Marie remembered: "One morning when I was about fourteen, probably not too long before I ran away, Rose offered to make me breakfast. I was staggered – normally you got your own, were quick about it and tried not to be noticed while you ate it. But today she handed me this bowl of Weetabix mashed up with hot milk…I was about half way through when I realised I was munching on something hard and chalky. I was too scared to spit it out, but I moved my spoon around my bowl to see if I could identify it. Rose sat opposite me watching every move. I put another spoonful into my mouth and began to retch, spitting part of it back into the bowl…She reached over the table and clipped me across the head. 'It's only a piece of grain. Put it in your mouth and eat it.'…My head lowered and my eyes downcast, I carried on eating, unable to avoid the partly crushed white tablets I could now make out in my cereal."

Anne Marie and Rose

Alison Chambers told the girls at Jordans Brook that she had met an older man and that he was in love with her and gave her gifts, including jewellery (Fred and Rose had given her various pieces of jewellery, including a necklace with her name on it). The girls thought that she was making it up. "Alison had a vivid imagination. When she was talking about this older man who loved her and was buying her this and that, nobody believed her", recalled one of the residents.

Carol Simms, who lived in the room next to Alison, remembered that Alison was "very unpopular". She would cry herself to sleep and was bullied by some of the other girls. She remembered that Alison was very clingy, almost needing constant attention from anyone who would give it. But things then all changed when she met "a really nice man, an older man" in Gloucester. She stopped fretting and proudly announced how her new-found friend was going to take her away and look after her. "I just remember she went away for a weekend and then never came back."

Alison wrote a letter, saying that she was being bullied by the other residents of Jordans Brook:

Dear Judy,

Please, please help me. I am at my wits end. I'm thinking of putting an end to my rotten worthless life.

My problem is one that I've had for almost 2 years now. Since I came into care, (I was 14 almost 15) I have developed bouts of depression. The least little thing makes me cry.

I am also very self-conscience about myself too, this is mainly because the girls in the 'home' I'm in at present, have all got boyfriends, except one who's just not interested and me.

I am not ugly, but I'm not brilliantly pretty either. I am big-boned and I'm always

149

complaining that I'm fat, although I exercise each night. I wear fairly fashionable clothes, although I can't really afford up-to-date clothes, because I am badly paid at work. I am a receptionist-telephonist.

Every time I meet a boy (I am quite shy), and they ask where I live, I am quite honest with them, and say I'm in care, they just clam up, and after one night they don't want to see me again.

Please help! I am getting desperate, not for boys, but through worry of thinking I'm abnormal.

I've known about this problem for ages, but I've no-one really close to talk to.

Thank you, Judy

Yours faithfully

Alison Chambers

On the 4th August 1979, Alison learned that she would not be released from Jordans Brook on her seventeenth birthday so she packed her bags and absconded from the home. She told her best friend that she was going to live at Cromwell Street, but asked her not to tell anyone. She asked her to tell the staff that she had "run away to Wales", and the two of them arranged to meet up the following afternoon so that Alison could collect the few clothes she had left behind. Alison Chambers did not turn up.

Ricky Coleclough, a former police officer, remembered how the police were never particularly bothered about children running away from homes. "They were happening so often, daily. Children would go out, sometimes in groups of 2,3,4,6,10 overnight missing from Jordans Brook. A majority would stay local in the Gloucester area.

There's not a great dissimilarity between a missing dog and a missing person. It's impossible with the number of missing people to actively investigate every one. 99.9% of missing people turn up in the next couple of days. Enquiries would be extended to nearer family, friends, where might they have gone to. They would have been checked. You would look at that but if the person was non-vulnerable, an adult and it would appear that they went off on their own accord, the immediate suspicion isn't that somebody has killed them."

The following day, the 5th August, Alison Chambers failed to turn up for work. Police were notified of her disappearance.

She wrote a letter to her mother and said the reason was:

To let you know exactly what I am at present doing with myself and my life…I can understand that this is little consolation to you, after my taking off from Jordans Brook

House, but I feel I owe you at least that.

I am at present staying with a homely family and look after their five children and do some of the housework. They have a child the same age as me who accepts me as a big sister and we get on great…the family own flats and I share with the oldest sister.

All I'm doing is trying and I might say succeeding in living a normal everyday life with worries that are shared and with happiness that is true. Also I'm living in a happy and relaxed atmosphere and not a strained and cold atmosphere. I cannot say I feel sorry for running away because that would be untrue, but I am sincerely sorry for any anxiety I've caused the family…I just wanted to let you know I'm safe, and shall continue to write to let you know how I'm coping.

One thing I don't want anyone to do is worry about me because I don't deserve it, so please don't. I love you and miss you all. Please believe that.

Until I write again, take care of yourselves.

All my fondest

Alison

It was due to this letter that she was officially discharged from care and the police no longer considered her a vulnerable person, but oddly the letter had been posted in Northampton.

Up until, and including September, 17-year-old Alison had been seen at 25 Cromwell Street several times over the summer. She then went missing. She is believed to have lived within the Wests household for several weeks before her murder, and before she ran away became obsessed with living at the 'farm' that Fred and Rose had promised her.

A lodger at 25 Cromwell Street, Gillian Britt, remembered a girl called 'Ali' who visited the house regularly at the time. She noted that the girl had lesbian tendencies and that sometimes she turned up wearing a suit and carrying a handbag looking almost professional.

Alison Chambers

At first, Fred West gave an extremely odd explanation for Alison's death. He insisted that she had turned up at Cromwell Street to blackmail him with a copy of the portrait photograph he had had taken sixteen months earlier with Shirley Robinson. He maintained that Alison, who had not even arrived in Gloucester when Shirley was murdered, was in fact "Shirley's mate". Clearly confusing her at first with another young woman, Fred described Shirley as "big boned" and "twenty-two years of age". He insisted that he never knew Alison's name, and was adamant that "Shirley's mate" had turned up at Cromwell Street "several years" after Shirley Robinson's death and said to him: "As far as I can gather you killed Shirley."

He then rapidly changed this story, suggesting instead that Alison had arrived "between twelve months and two years" after Shirley Robinson. "She came to the door and asked if Shirley was there." He said he told her that she didn't live there anymore, but that Alison told him "Yes, yes she does...I've got a photograph here of you with Shirley." He said he then told her to go and have a cup of tea in a café and to come back later because Rose was cooking dinner.

He then said that Alison was the girl that Shirley had told him she wanted to have the baby for, and that the café he told her to go to was the one he had owned, The Green Lantern, although it had closed down two years previously. He said that after dinner, he sent Rose out to spend the night with one of her clients and then went to the café and picked up Alison. According to him, Alison told him that Shirley had sent her a letter saying that if she didn't turn up within a certain amount of time, then Alison was to go to the address and find him as he would know where she was. She then said that if he didn't tell Alison where Shirley was then she was going to the police. "So we had an argument, a row, and I punched her on the jaw first, and knocked her on the floor and strangled her."

He said that he buried her body under a "big paddling pool" in his garden, which was made out of blue engineering bricks. He said that he had cut her body into four pieces, a head, torso and two legs, with his sheath knife.

A day after his confession, Fred changed his story once again. This time, he said: "I don't actually believe this girl was old enough to actually be associated with Shirley. She didn't seem to me to be. The only thing I can't understand is where she got the photograph from and the so-called letter. I never actually seen the letter but I've got the photograph off her." This time he said that Alison had turned up looking for "Cromwell Road and not Cromwell Street" and that he took her out driving around to look for the road. He said that while they were driving, Alison showed him the photograph, and he just "dropped her off". He said that she then turned up at his home again, and started to threaten him and demand money from him. He said that "Rose would definitely not have seen her" and that Alison never entered the house. He then claimed that he managed to get her into his car and that he was going to drive her back to Bristol, but on the way she started to threaten him. He then pulled in to a lay-by, "had a right shouting match" with her and then he drove back to Cromwell Street. When they were nearby, in a garage off St Michael's Square, behind his house "she set going again, so I grabbed her by the neck with me hands and choked her."

He then said that he put her "by the back door" and took some cable and twisted it around her neck because "I wasn't sure she was actually dead". He then said he cut her body up because he realised he couldn't get her in the hole under the paddling pool "without using a sledge hammer", and to use it would have made too much noise as Rose was upstairs in bed.

When the police finally identified the remains they had found as belonging to Alison Chambers Fred changed his story for a third time. He said that she had been living down the road at number 11 and he knew her because he had done her room up for her. He tried to make out that she wasn't very well off and had kept turning up at his home. "I think what she was really after was a handful of money off me 'cause she thought we got money, or I got money."

When the police suggested to Fred that the girl he was calling "Shirley's mate" was, in fact, Alison Chambers, he simply replied: "Don't mean a thing. I never asked her her name."

He admitted that some of the girls who arrived at Cromwell Street "were obviously trying to make money other ways", and added, "A lot of them were on the game". As a result, there were "girls that accepted what we did and, you know, and forgot about it, went home and on their

153

way…See, I had affairs with so many different girls, I mean, you're not talking one or two, and…every one didn't end up in disaster, by no means."

When Alison Chambers' body was recovered from beneath the rear bathroom window, her skull was found to be bound tightly with a one-and-three-quarter-inch-wide plastic belt, passing from under the chin to the top of her head. The buckle was still on the top of her head, with fragments of hair trapped in it. When Fred was confronted with this, he insisted: "She wasn't actually bondaged…it was just whatever was put on her…so I could keep her together and lift her…I can't even remember putting a belt on her head."

Her remains were jumbled. Both of her kneecaps were missing. Her upper breastbone had been removed, as had 63 finger and toe bones, but her toenails and fingernails were recovered. She had a total of 96 bones missing.

In the last months of his life Fred admitted to his solicitor, Howard Ogden, that Alison Chambers, whom he still described as "Shirley's mate" had, in fact, lived with him and Rose for "a month or more after she'd left Barnwood in Gloucester", and that she had befriended one of his lodgers. By this time, Fred was placing all of the blame for the killings at his wife's door, explaining only that: "When I caught them young girls there, they'd have to fucking go." He also suggested: "If the girl did stay at all at our place, I mean, I'm not saying she didn't because if anybody was in trouble…I helped them out the best I could with…no bad intentions whatsoever. I mean, I like people to look upon me as somebody they can trust."

Anne Marie started to see a man who was older than her, named Shaun Boyle, and he recalled a conversation they had where they talked about their first sexual experiences. "We were lying in bed the one time and the conversation came up and she asked me, and I said I think I was 15, 14, 15 I think I was and she said she was 8, which I tried to press and find out more about it. She did say something about her mother but then she just clammed up. I got dressed and went home. I didn't see her for a couple of days afterwards."

At the end of the year, Anne Marie became pregnant by her own father, Fred. She remembered that she was bleeding for about two months but was scared to say anything to anyone. Eventually she told Rose who took her to the doctors and after an examination the doctor sent her to Gloucester Hospital. Rose rang Fred and he took her, while Rose went out.

When at the hospital, the doctors consulted with Fred while Anne Marie was taken on to a ward. Shortly afterwards, Fred told her: "The doctors think there might be something wrong inside. They are going to put you to sleep and have a little look." Soon after he left the hospital.

He went back to visit her after the operation and he told her that he wasn't going to stay long as he hated hospitals and left just a few minutes later. In the following week that Anne Marie was kept in hospital, he visited just once more. No other member of the family visited her at all.

Anne Marie was never told that she had been pregnant - nor that she had suffered an ectopic pregnancy by any of the medical staff or members of her family. She only found out what had happened years later when she had her first daughter and discovered what had happened in her medical notes. She was never interviewed alone by the medical staff, even though she had suffered criminal, sexual abuse. Neither social workers or the police were informed. It is more than likely that during his meeting with the doctors, Fred told them that she had been sleeping with her boyfriend and that it must have been him that had got her pregnant.

Not long after she came out of hospital, Fred and Rose gave permission for Anne Marie's boyfriend, Phil, to go around to the house and meet them. After he had left, Fred told Anne Marie: "Well, he's a fucking divvy. You don't want no fucking schoolboy. Get a real man. You want someone who'll sort you out. He won't know what to fucking do with it." Rose laughed and told Fred: "Don't worry, I'll keep her busy. She won't have time for schoolboys."

Anne Marie was really upset and wrote a letter to Phil, saying: "I've had enough of what my Dad says and does to me." A few days later she was given such a severe beating by Rose that it made up her mind to finally get away.

Despite having just clips and stitches holding her wound closed and being doubled over in pain, Rose still made Anne Marie carry out the housework. She dusted, hoovered and polished but noticed that Rose was in one of her bad moods. Rose shoved Anne Marie and yelled at her: "You're not doing that right!" Anne Marie apologized, but Rose replied: "Don't be fucking sorry. Just do it fucking right!"

Rose then grabbed Anne Marie by her shoulder, shook her, and then pushed her to the floor. "Stupid cow! I'll teach you!" Rose said, as she repeatedly kicked her in the stomach. Anne Marie screamed out in pain and when Rose had finished Anne Marie struggled to her feet and went to her room. Rose then threatened her: "You wait until your fucking father gets home!"

Anne Marie stayed in her room until Fred got home, and as soon as he walked in from work Rose told him her version of events. He went up to Anne Marie's room and told her that she shouldn't provoke Rose and if she didn't go back downstairs immediately then he would give her "a bloody good hiding."

She did as she was told, but a few days later, feeling angry and abandoned by her parents, Anne Marie was put in the cells at Gloucester

155

Police Station for stabbing a girl. Police had picked her up with just a nightdress on, heading out on the A40 in the direction of the Forest of Dean. She had a stand-up fight with Fred outside in the street when he got her home, and Anne Marie ran away from home at 03:00 a couple of days after that.

The morning after she disappeared, Rose sent one of the children upstairs to wake Anne Marie. When the child came back without her, Fred went up to check for himself. When he came back alone, he said to Rose: "I don't think she'll be a problem, do you?" Mae asked Rose where she'd gone and she replied: "We haven't a fucking clue, Mae. And don't ask us again."

Later that day, Fred and Rose stripped Anne Marie's room bare. Some items they threw away, others they burned. They did their best to show that Anne Marie had never existed, just as they would in years to come with Heather.

6 MAE, HEATHER & STEPHEN

Both Heather and Mae West became the focus of Fred's incestuous sexual attentions after Anne Marie ran away from home. Fred was heard to say to one of his younger daughters: "It will be your turn next. If you don't lose your virginity young, then the older you get the more it will send you mental."

Maria Del Medico was just a child when she and her brother visited 25 Cromwell Street with their father. They lived nearby and Maria's father bought pornography from Fred, while she played outside in the street. Her dad had met Fred in one of the local pubs and they got on well. "There was a huge collection (of porn) in a box under our sofa. Dad had taken disgusting photos of me; I imagine they're in paedophile land now, being exchanged", she later recalled. "I remember Fred standing in that kitchen, pouring Corona into a glass. He had huge sideburns and yellow-green teeth. He smelled of body odour. He hadn't washed for years." She had been sexually abused by her father since the age of 5 and as a result "I was frightened of men – and I was very frightened of Fred West. Once when I was seven I found myself alone with him. Dad was upstairs. I don't know what he was saying, but a wave of fear came up from my chest and I ran outside. My father came out harassed; he shouted at us to get in the car and we drove away…I remember the West children particularly well. I'd see Stephen, Anne Marie and Mae most times but the one I got on best with was Heather. I remember loving her hairstyle. I admired her sense of independence and strong will…"

She recalled that her own father threatened her not to tell anyone about the sexual abuse he was subjecting her to. "If you ever tell anyone what I do to you I'll kill you and cut you up in little pieces and no one will ever find you."

In 1980, and when the elder children reached the age of seven, Rose demonstrated washing and ironing for them. From then on they were expected to do their own laundry. They were expected to do the ironing, scrub the kitchen, scour the toilet, feed the babies and change their nappies. Stephen West remembered his sister vacuuming at the age of eight. From the age of ten, the children cooked their own meals in the small kitchen Fred had built as part of the extension.

On one occasion, as Stephen was mopping the kitchen floor with a cloth, Rose accidently stepped in the bowl of water he had been using. In response, Rose smashed him over the head with the bowl, then repeatedly kicked him in the head and chest as she shouted at him. He remembered that Rose "boasted about the beating to Dad when he got home" and they both started to laugh. On another occasion, Rose became hysterical about a missing kitchen utensil, then grabbed a knife she had been using to cut a slab of meat, repeatedly inflicting light scour marks to Mae's chest until her rib cage was covered with light knife wounds.

On the 16th June, Rose gave birth to another son, Barry John West. His father was Fred and not one of Rose's clients. It is not known why Rose didn't have him aborted, unless she and Fred believed he had been conceived with one of her clients.

During the school summer holidays, Mae was raped. She was just 8-years-old. "I was playing happily in the garden when (her uncle John West) called me in to the bathroom and locked the door behind me. He picked me up and put me on top of the babies' changing board which Dad had made to fit on top of the bath. It was big and covered half of the bath because that's where Mum did the nappies. He made me lie down and tried to penetrate me. He didn't take his clothes off, he just unzipped himself. He didn't undress me, he just took off my knickers. I can't remember what he said or how I felt. I just remember what happened. I remember wriggling about, which made him annoyed. He told me: 'I can't do anything if you keep moving about'. I felt the weight of him, pressing down, crushing me. I tried to get out from under him, wriggling against him...he pressed down harder on me, lifting his revolting fat stomach out of the way as he pinned me down and carried on. It was actual rape, penetration, and it lasted several seconds. How long exactly, I don't know. I suppose I was just trying to fight him off and eventually he opened the door and I went out. It was during the school holidays because I know Stephen and Heather were in the house but I didn't go to them afterwards. I remember he smelt of cigars.

Afterwards he came up to me and started talking about money. He threw a ten pence at me and told me not to tell anyone, it was just between him and me or something. I didn't cry, I know that. I suppose it must have been painful but I have blocked it out of my mind...I didn't tell anyone about what happened until I was about 14 and went swimming with my half-sister, Anne Marie."

She later recalled him constantly smoking a pipe and stinking of stale, bitter tobacco and body odour. The children were scared of him because he used to tell them stories of how if cats went into his garden he would break their necks and throw them over the fence.

Mae recalled that "It was just one incident in a long line of being touched in inappropriate places by Dad's friends who came to the house; all I could ever do was wait for it to be over so that I could run back outside and play."

Her brother, Stephen, also recalled Fred raping both Heather and Mae. Mae has always denied it, but has admitted that "I block out a lot of things. Sometimes it seems as if I never lived at Cromwell Street". Stephen said: "He was raping Heather all her life. And Mae. I was in the same room. So I think I would remember that, yes."

Stephen also recalled a severe case of child abuse suffered by him, Heather and Mae. They were sleeping in the basement and there was a party going on above them. The noises and shrieks were keeping the three of them awake and then the trapdoor that Fred had built opened and Fred got them out of bed and led them up the stairs. Some of the people at the party were lodgers, but many of them were guests and of black origin. The room smelt of drugs and some of the party goers were naked and having sex. The three young children were then tied, by Rose, to a pole in the middle of the room which held the ceiling up and held their hands out as they had been ordered to do. They had rope looped around them. The children stared at the floor but when Heather fell asleep Rose woke her up by shouting "Wake up, you stupid bitch!" One of the guests said to Mae: "You're a pretty little girl". At the same time Heather was being raped by a black friend of Rose's, while Rose and another woman were touching him. Then one of the male guests, who Fred called 'Snooty' "started weeing all over Heather. Then he turned around and weed all over me…it never happened again and it never happened before…it's a terrible memory that I'd shut away…Mum was always tying us up with wire, electric cable, dressing gown belts. While we were tied up Dad would touch Heather and Mae. Mum would hit us and laugh as she did it."

Mae recalled: "There were visitors to the house all the time, and Heather and I used to get touched up regularly. Dad was the worst. His whole life revolved around sex…He wanted to know how often people were doing it and to whom. Anyone who came round to visit or anyone he'd known for a couple of minutes, he would ask about their sex life. Whenever he met a woman he would say they wanted him badly, he could tell. One of my aunties got so fed up and didn't come round again. A lot of people stopped coming. Sex had to be every night or he'd think Mum didn't love him. He'd come down in the morning and say: 'I had a good ride last night' or 'I screwed the arse off her'."

It is believed that around this time Anne Marie, who was working as a cleaner in a café, met a window cleaner named Erwin Marschall, and began a relationship with him. They spent one night together back at Cromwell Street, but Erwin could not sleep. In the middle of the night he heard a protracted scream, lasting between ten and twenty minutes. It was the voice of a young girl, and he could make out the words 'No, no, Please!' In the morning Rose told him that it was only Heather having one of her nightmares.

In October, Fred appeared at Gloucester Magistrates Court charged with 'Receiving Stolen Goods'. They were 5 tape recorders and a number of cassette tapes stolen from a local health centre in 1979. One of the tapes so shocked the police, that the contents were not read out in open court. Instead, the jury were handed a transcript. The jury also heard of his recording sexual relations between his wife and a black man in his van on audiotapes. The Wests confessed to the magistrate that they had "recorded themselves making love…in a van parked on a disused airfield in Stoke Orchard." Fred was given a 9 month prison sentence, suspended for 2 years. He was also fined £50 or one month extra in prison. He paid the fine.

In 1981 some lodgers were rehoused by Gloucester City Council due to overcrowding. Fred had refused to carry out an informal notice served on him by the local authority specifying that he repair parts of the upstairs of the house.

With less people in the house, it was even easier for Rose to attack and abuse her children. Mae would recall that when she was aged eight or nine she was getting changed into her vest and knickers when Rose was cutting some meat in the kitchen. Rose was shouting at her as usual and screamed: "I've fucking well had enough of you, Mae, do you hear?" Mae was scared and while backing away from Rose told her to stop it as she was scaring her. But then Rose started to move towards her and said: "Don't tell me what to do, you fucking little bitch!" She then started to slash at Mae and left little nicks all over her rib cage. Mae said: "I've got no scars, she just nicked me. She could be nasty and violent for no real reason. It lasted seconds, but I'll never forget it."

Stephen West's former girlfriend, Caroline Tonks, recalled a story that he had told her when they were dating about him having an accident with his finger. "I think it was around about the age seven or eight that he had this accident with his finger, that was supposed to have been cut off with a razor blade, but didn't seem to add up somehow. I was told he caught a razor blade, which I would have thought you would have tried to get out the way of, not try to catch it, even as a child...It later came to light that Rose liked to, if their fingers were up on the work top, she'd like 'get out of the way' with a knife."

Anne Marie still sent birthday and Christmas cards to Fred, Rose and the children. Her partner, Chris Davis, had been asking her about her parents and why she never saw them. She didn't tell him of the abuse she had suffered but did tell him that they were odd. She decided that the time was right to get back in contact and made a couple of phone calls to test the water. Anne Marie told Fred that she had a steady boyfriend and he seemed eager to meet him so invited them over.

After just twenty minutes Anne Marie wanted to leave. She still saw Fred from time to time around Gloucester and Fred found Chris odd jobs. When they went to visit, apart from saying 'hello', the other children were discouraged from joining them in conversation; most probably so that they couldn't tell Anne Marie of the abuse they were going through or to ask her how she managed to escape.

In March 1982, Anne Marie and Chris reluctantly moved into a bedroom on the first floor of 25 Cromwell Street. They had to use the bathroom downstairs as the one on their floor was now Rose's private bathroom and it was decorated with framed black-and-white photographs of Rose in explicit poses with black men. Anne Marie made Chris promise not to say anything to Fred and Rose, and never to leave her on her own with them. Chris noticed the profound effect living at 25 Cromwell Street was having on Anne Marie and she told him what had happened to her as a child. She begged Chris not to say anything to Fred and Rose. "Fucking weird bastards", said Chris. He told her that he was going to speak to them. "I said I'd had enough and was going to do something", recalled Chris. But

Anne Marie said: "For Christ's sake don't, because they'll kill us both!"

Chris had observed how withdrawn Heather was. She had bitten her nails until they bled and sat around the house day dreaming about leaving home. Heather had also developed the habit of watching Fred warily from a corner, or doorway, of whichever room he was in. Her stare unnerved Fred and he kept shouting at her wanting to know why she was so miserable.

After six weeks Fred got Chris and Anne Marie a bedsit at 31 Cromwell Street. They were on the other side of the church with Mrs Taylor. On Saturday nights they started going out with Rose to make up a threesome to hit the local pubs. Sometimes Rose and Anne Marie would end up going on to a club, but Rose was always up early on a Sunday preparing the big Sunday lunch that she always cooked.

On the 13th April, Rose gave birth to Rosemary (Ro-Ro) Ann West. Her father was not Fred, but a West Indian regular nicknamed 'Rosco', and he was one of the men that Rose had forced Anne Marie to sleep with.

Rose's mother Daisy became concerned at how regularly Rose was falling pregnant, and on the 16th July 1981 she wrote a letter to her:

I had a big family like you mainly because in those days there was no way not to. Then when I had all the misery with Dad and the boys doing things wrong, I just wished they had never been born. Now, Rosie, when I see you having babies I just can't think of you going through all that, you were married quite young and had no outside life at all. I feel Fred should make sure you don't have more babies...it's because I love you dear that I can't take seeing you like you are.
God bless you.

According to Mae: "Once Mum and Dad started having half-caste children, our grandmother asked Mum not to come around anymore. I know Mum tried writing to her, but the letters went unanswered. Mum had almost no contact at all with her Mum, which I know she regretted."

When the police raided 25 Cromwell Street in 1992, they discovered a document that had been written, and signed, by Rose and it was dated 1982:

I, Rosemary West, known as Fred's cow, give my cunt to be fucked by any prick at any time he so desires without ever saying no. My arse is to be smacked until I say I've had enough, my black hole is to be hurt until you say you've had enough. My tits I give to anyone that do not like them, to screw, to bite or suck them when I'm being cocked, apart from my husband who can have them at his pleasure. My baby box is to be filled by anyone who says so when I'm told. I give my mouth to be fucked by anyone I'm told and to be shut by Fred when I open it too wide. My tongue is to lick anything out when I'm told. My fingers is for wanking or fingering my cunt, or any other girl's cunt when I'm told. I must always dress and try to act like a cow for Fred, also to bathe and wash when I am told.

Signed MRS R.P. West

The police were contacted by a woman called Annie Smart after she had felt concerned by a conversation she had with Fred after telling him that her family ran a video store. She went round to Cromwell Street after one her children had been playing there and just happened to mention to Fred that her brother was the manager in a video shop. "He started asking questions about the video shop and who owned it and did they do blue movies down there and I said they had electric blue ones and he said 'no, the real thing'. That he could get hold of them and that he actually made them in his house and he said he done some involving his daughters.

He told me he had access to a helicopter and said: 'that's how I get some of my material into the country'. There were sex videos and lesbian romps and different things like that and then he got into a conversation 'had I heard of snuff movies?' I explained they had one down the shop called 'Snuff'. He said: 'No'. He could get hold of the real thing, the actual real snuff movies where they actually done it. I couldn't understand that a man could talk to somebody about things like that. It was just sickening. When I got home, we talked it over and I phoned the police the next morning and explained the conversation I had had with Fred West. I gave them his name and address and he said it would be investigated. I banned my children from going to the house."

In May 1983, allegations were made to the NSPCC outlining sexual abuse made by Heather and fears she had for her life, but these were not investigated properly.

Two months later, on the 16th July, Rose gave birth to Lucyanna 'Babs' Mary West. Her father was again not Fred, but her client nicknamed 'Rosco'. Rose decided to be sterilized after the birth.

One morning when Stephen was ten, Rose rang his school and demanded that he be sent home immediately. Fearing something was very wrong, he ran all the way home and when he reached it Rose told him to go into the bathroom, strip off and shut the door. Rose went in after him and tied his wrists together with wire which was already hanging in there. She then got him to lay on the floor and put his hands around the bottom of the toilet. She then tied his hands to the base so that he couldn't move. She then picked up a belt that was also in the room, stood on his legs and said to him: "Right then, what have you done wrong, son?" Stephen didn't know what he was supposed to have done wrong, but Rose told him that he had taken some pornographic magazines and wanted him to admit it. She kept beating him with the buckle end of the belt and kicking him in the stomach, trying to get him to confess.

Rose then stopped after a while, put the belt around her waist and left him tied up while she went downstairs. She eventually came back and untied him while telling him to go back to school. Stephen was bleeding from his bottom, backs of his legs and base of his spine from where Rose had been lashing him.

When he got back from school that afternoon, Heather arrived at around the same time and she gave Rose a note from school saying the teachers had caught her with the pornographic magazines. "Don't worry, Stephen got your beating", Rose told her whilst laughing. When Fred got home from work, Rose told him what had happened and Fred just laughed alongside her.

The abuse at 25 Cromwell Street was so intense after 1983 that Heather ran away but soon returned. Stephen ran away twice and was rewarded with a beating when he returned. After their attempts to escape, Fred created a device to strap Heather, Mae and Stephen to their beds. He would sneak downstairs and force himself on either Heather or Mae while they lay helpless on their fronts, bound to the bed with a rope.

Mae recalled: "Dad used to comment on our breast size. He thought if he created his daughter he should be able to look at his creation and touch it. He said a father's right is to break his daughters in and it was his privilege to do it by the time we were sixteen...he'd say: 'Your first baby should be your dads'." The two sisters became used to Fred bursting in on them early in the morning when they were getting dressed, or pulling the sheets from their beds. There was no lock on the bathroom door and Fred was able to reach around the shower and fondle Heather and her sister, Mae. "A groping could last twenty minutes, and in the end Heather and I would stand guard outside the shower and warn each other when he was coming... We had to almost parade in front of him. He said things like: 'Why don't you come out of the bathroom without a towel on?' If we wrapped one round us he would try and rip it off so he could see us naked."

If Fred called Heather or Mae to his room, they took a brother or sister with them. He also pestered Mae for sex and became enraged when she rejected his advances. On one occasion he "broke the door in when I slammed it in his face", Mae recalled. On another occasion, when Mae was cleaning her room, Fred came in and grabbed her breasts. She pushed him away and he said: "What's wrong with giving your dad a good old feel?" He went on to try to touch her again but Mae told him to go away and pushed him back. The look on his face turned from a grin into a threatening glare.

"Don't you dare speak to me like that, you little bitch!" As he was leaving he picked up a vacuum cleaner and threw it at her, hitting her hard.

From the age of thirteen, Fred had pestered Heather for sex. "It was really bad for me and Heather when we reached puberty, at about twelve or thirteen", recalled Mae. "Dad used to comment on our breast size or how they had grown a bit. He thought, if he created his daughter he should be able to look at his creation and touch it. He said a father's right is to break his daughters in…according to him, that was what his father had done. He also used to say he wanted us to have his baby. He'd say: Your first baby should be your Dad's.' He said if we got pregnant we could hand the baby over to Mum. I don't know why. He reckoned we would just be able to call it our brother or sister."

Stephen recalled that Fred "used to chase Mae and Heather around and touch them, grab their breasts or grab them between the legs. Mae was so against it she used to scream at him to get off. He would be alright at first, just messing around with her, but when she tried to run, he would get aggressive and call her a lesbian and stuff."

Fred often wrestled Heather to the floor and beat her if she resisted. "When she became a teenager Fred began to tease her, and I think that was the beginning of her slide into misery", recalled Anne Marie.

According to Mae: "The abuse really affected Heather. She just became really quiet and went into herself. She used to be moody. She never had boyfriends and at school she was always separate from everyone else. She used to rock on the chair for hours and not talk to anyone. And she'd bite her nails 'til she had none at all. She just got quieter and quieter and didn't even communicate with us a lot after that."

Some mornings Fred would sneak into Heather and Mae's bedroom and pull their bedclothes off and grope them. He was almost always the first to wake up in the mornings and used the opportunity to sneak in and

165

run his hands up his daughters' legs. In the end, the girls went to bed fully clothed.

In October 1983, Anne Marie discovered that she was pregnant with Chris Davis' baby, and just 3 months later, allegations were again made to the NSPCC outlining sexual abuse allegations made by Heather and the fears she had for her life. Again, these were not acted upon.

As time rolled on into 1984, Fred was made redundant from the Muir Hill works, which had closed, and on the 14th January, Anne Marie married Chris Davis against her better judgement at Gloucester Registry Office. Rose did not attend. The reception was held, at Fred's insistence, in the basement at 25 Cromwell Street. Among the guests were her grandfather Walter West and her uncle Doug West.

Anne Marie recalled: "I shudder when I look at those pictures now. To think that we were all there, drinking Sherry and eating wedding cake over the bodies of five women murdered by Fred and Rose."

The West family. From L-R. Rose (Holding Lucyanna (1)), Louise (6), Chris Davis, Barry (4), Anne Marie, Rosemary Jr (2), Fred, Stephen (11). Front row: Mae (12), Tara, (7) and Heather (14).

Fred talked endlessly about animals and their breeding habits. He told Mae that he had had sex with a sheep. He said there was an art to it and you needed long wellington boots. "You can put their back feet inside the wellies with yours, they can't move."

By the time Heather was fourteen and Mae was twelve, Fred had bored holes in the door and wall so he could watch his daughters dress and undress. He was always on at Heather about being a lesbian. "Did you know your sister was a lesbian? I caught her pissing on the bed", he told the other children.

Fred would call Heather and Mae "bitches" and "frigid" and Rose would just laugh. Lodgers and visitors noticed how Fred taunted Heather by saying she was ugly and was generally cruel to her. "There's my daughter, Heather. I think she's a lesbian", he would say. If Heather was moody or upset then it was because she was a lesbian, or as he termed it, "a lemon". If she was unhappy it was because she was "on". If she refused to eat, then it was because she needed a "bloody good sorting out by a man that knows what's what", he would say. When he told his daughters that it was a fathers right to take his daughters virginity, he would also sometimes add: "Only right and proper, it is. My old man did the same to my sisters. You see, I made you. You're my flesh and blood. It's only right that I get to see what I made." This may very well go on to explain, at least partly, why he never attempted to molest Rose's mixed-race children.

At meal times, no matter who was there, Fred would comment on the size of Heather and Mae's developing breasts, the hairiness of their vaginas and the colour of their pubic hair. He would also do things like walk out of the toilet, having just urinated, with his penis out and threaten to push it in the children's ears. He also started keeping a record of Mae's menstrual cycle, as he did for all of his natural daughters.

Although Anne Marie was the only child to have said that Rose took part in the sexual abuse in court in 1995, the other children have said that she turned a blind eye. Stephen was embarrassed by Rose's lack of intervention: "She never told him to stop doing it" and Mae recalled: "There was no point in appealing to Mum. She knew about it, but she ignored it. She'd just say that Dad was playing, she never really put it down to much. I think she thought that, as he wasn't really hurting us, there was nothing to worry about." Anne Marie recalled telling Rose about her own sexual abuse at the hands of her father, but Rose just said: "I'm sorry. Everybody does it to every girl. It's a fathers job. Don't worry, and don't say anything to anybody. It's something everybody does, but nobody talks about."

On the 17th June, Father's Day, Anne Marie gave birth to a girl and named her Michelle. Not long after, Chris Davis was up in the loft laying a floor, when Heather confided in him. She climbed up to be with him and smoked nervously as she spoke. She told him that she had had enough of life at home and wasn't going to take it. She said she was seriously thinking of running away and going to live in The Forest of Dean. She had recently been on a two-week school camping trip to Clearwell Caves and she explained that she had made up her mind.

Chris noticed how strained Heather looked and how shaky and tense she was as she spoke. He said that she could be unpredictable and sometimes was a "difficult character." When Heather was in a good mood she could be fun. But if she was in a bad mood then it was best if you made yourself scarce.

Before Heather left that day, Chris got her to promise that if she did run away to live in The Forest of Dean, she would contact him so he could reassure Anne Marie she was alright. Heather promised she would.

As Fred was not working steadily, just doing odd jobs for a man named Alex Palmer, he decided once again to start work on the house and the children were again sent to sleep in the basement. The four-poster bed was moved into the top-floor front bedroom. The 'Black Magic Bar' would eventually be installed underneath it, and Rose's visitors would be taken in there first and offered a dirty video to watch and a drink. Fred hid microphones in the headboards of the heavy oak bed and as soon as a red light went on in the family room to indicate Rose was with a customer, Fred would dive in there and listen.

Since Tara had been born Rose had become even more violent towards the rest of her children. At one point she knocked Stephen out cold by breaking a Pyrex dish over his head. She would throw kitchen stools at the children and even threw a television at Tara who luckily moved out of the way just in time.

With Fred not earning much money while doing odd jobs for Alex Palmer, he and Rose agreed that she should start to look for new clients and charge them. Mae recalled: "When I was 13 and studying for my mock exams, Mum started to advertise for clients, rather than sleeping with Dads friends. I saw the advert, they put an advert together for a sex magazine and put our phone number on." The advert read: "West Indian Well Endowed Male, Age 50-60 for sex with young housewife."

Mae recalls that Rose told her that her work as a prostitute disgusted her and that Fred had pressurized her into it as they were hard up for money, but Rose had a book where she kept a record of what she charged each individual and a mark out of ten for their sexual performance. Sometimes Rose wouldn't wait for the clients to call her and if she wanted sex she would call up one she fancied and soon enough there would be a knock at the door. In this book were the names of around 70 men with

169

photographs of their erect penises.

Stephen also recalled Rose keeping a red album and money box with a key. He opened it one day to find photographs of Fred laying naked on a bed and Rose naked with other men. There were close-up photographs of Rose having sex with 'Rosco' too.

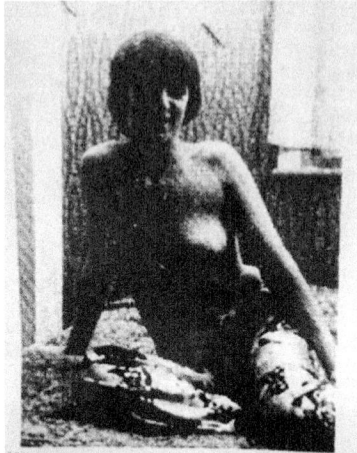

West Indian W.E. male. Age 50-60 for sex with young housewife with view to living in. See photo. Gloucester.

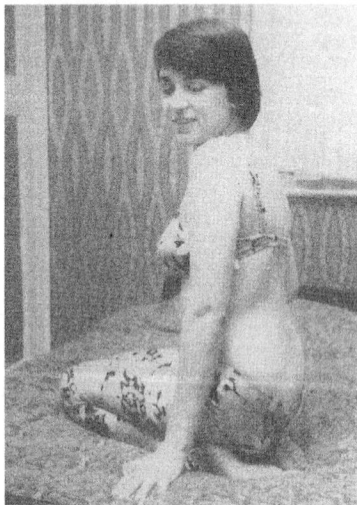

The photographs that accompanied Rose's adverts in 'Contact Magazines'

If a client stayed over, Fred would sleep on the sofa downstairs and listen to what was happening in the bedroom through the intercom he had fitted. The sessions were normally secretly video taped and Fred and Rose used to watch them back for memories. One of these video's showed Rose on the kitchen table with her legs apart using a vibrator. She then put some tea towels on the table and urinated on them. Another video was shot in the back of Fred's van where he tied Rose up before whipping her and having sex with her.

Some of the Wests children remember Fred and Rose's West Indian friends calling round on Saturday nights where they helped load the van up with sex aids and flasks of tea before heading out to the hills. Fred had already fitted it out with a carpet and a small gas fire that he put in to aid them to carry out their activities in the cold nights. The camera was usually set up on a tripod which Fred had bolted to the back and filmed Rose having sex as he drove along. While this was happening, the children were left alone at home to look after themselves.

Rose had become as obsessed with black men as Fred. "She was turned on by black men" recalled a former client called Andrew Angus. He recalled how, one afternoon, he was walking past 25 Cromwell Street when Rose came out and asked him if he knew anything about televisions. He went in to the house to see what was wrong. "When I turned around Rosemary was standing there in the living room, naked, apart from some revealing underwear. I remember she put a video on, which had some hardcore sex scenes in it, and she started to kiss me. Before I knew it, we were upstairs on her double bed. I put a condom on, and we began having sex. There was a huge mirror covering nearly all the ceiling and the bed itself was massive…I hardly knew her, and there we were in her bed having sex.

She showed me a picture of one of her children – a half-caste young girl – and seemed proud that she was half black. Her husband Fred knew I slept with his wife, but he didn't seem bothered by it at all. Rosemary said she had a very open relationship, and said her husband did not mind her sleeping with other men. Rosemary was totally sex mad. She always knew exactly what she wanted and how to get it. She loved sex. When I slept with her, she was very demanding. I was always exhausted afterwards."

Another of her clients, Market Trader John Holmes, remembered: "She's the best lover I've ever had. She had no inhibitions. She used to love watching herself in the mirror which was attached under the canopy over a four-poster bed."

Charlie Murphy, another client, said he saw an advertisement for 'Mandy' and telephoned the number. "She said it was £10 for everything. Rose was wearing a flimsy pink outfit fastened at the crotch. She was plump, with full breasts, and she knew how to excite a man. That first time she undressed me slowly, then we had oral sex. I was there for three-quarters of an hour and loved every minute. It was impossible for human beings to copulate in more ways. She was brilliant. The best sex ever." He went on seeing her once or twice a week for six months.

Of the customers that Rose saw, one had a hole in his hand, one a wooden leg, and another a glass eye. It wasn't always just sex that her punters were after either. One of her regular men liked Rose to sit in a clear Mac and talk to him, and Mae remembered that Rose took her all over Gloucester to find one.

Mae also remembered that when she was about thirteen she opened her bedroom door as one of Rose's clients was walking past and he asked Rose if she was available. Rose kicked him straight out of the house but when she told Fred he thought that it was a good idea.

One of the men that Rose saw on a regular basis was nicknamed 'Suncoo' because he nearly always went to the house when Rose was cooking the Sunday dinner. Rose never charged him because he was one of Fred's friends and he was told that he could use Rose whenever he wanted. Rose didn't like him and even told her children that it made her feel sick going to bed with him, but Fred made her do it.

Despite Fred wanting Rose to sleep with black men, he was known by his family as a racist. He wanted Rose to sleep with men with large penises and to help her get accustomed to them she used very large sex aides. One was a black 14" dildo which Fred called Rose's 'Cunt Buster'.

It was at this time that Stephen West recalled one of his worst beatings received from Rose. He was at home one day and sitting on a unit when Rose told him to get off of it, which he did, but then he sat on it again a few moments later. Rose grabbed him and dragged him into the living room. She grabbed him by the throat with one hand and with the other tried to pull his jeans down. As she struggled to do it she shouted at the other children to pull his jeans down for her. They were scared and crying and didn't want to get involved but Rose threatened to hit them too if they didn't do as she said. With both hands now grasped around Stephen's throat, she lifted him off the ground and held him there. Stephen was groaning and starting to lose consciousness, but Rose was still screaming at the girls to get his jeans off. He remembers that he kept blacking out and the more he struggled, the tighter Rose held him. Fred then walked in and Rose dropped Stephen on the floor and walked out. Rather than help his son, Fred just looked at him and followed Rose out of the room. Stephen was left with marks on his neck for weeks and the blood vessels in his eyes had burst. Rose wrote him a note for school to explain the marks by saying that Stephen had been in a tree playing with a rope when he fell out, which is how he got the spots on his forehead and in his eyes.

Fred was also violent towards his children, although he tended more to explode once or twice a year, rather than once a day like Rose. One day Stephen was fixing his sisters bicycle when Fred told him to leave it for him to fix when he got home from work. Thinking he was being helpful, Stephen went ahead and fixed it anyway, but when Fred got home he went ballistic. He started to shout at Stephen and punched him in the side of the face, knocking out his back tooth, and then walked away. Stephen then tried to run out of the back door but Rose got there first and locked it. Fred then ran after him and punched and kicked him when he caught him.

Stephen was seen in hospital because of injuries sustained because he 'ran into wall bars in a gym', although this was obviously a lie given to the hospital to cover up another particularly savage beating.

Heather, however, was beaten more than the other children. Rose laughed at her distress and called her a lesbian when she protested against Fred's abuse of her. She was beaten by Rose and because of this she refused to comply with the rule to shower after sports at school. Heather was self-conscious about her body and always wore "long-sleeved blouses and pulled her socks up way over her knees so that the bruises wouldn't show." She was frequently sent to the Headmasters office and given detention, yet still nobody at the school investigated further.

7 HEATHER BREAKS THE FAMILY CODE

Heather broke the unwritten West family rule that you don't tell anyone of what goes on behind closed doors at 25 Cromwell Street and she complained to friends about the abuse she and her siblings endured. Staff at Hucclecote Secondary School, which Heather and her siblings attended, are also known to have expressed concern as to why Heather – an otherwise obedient pupil – refused to obey orders either to change into sports attire for P.E classes or to comply with the school rule that all pupils must take a shower after these sports activities. On one occasion, she was forced to take a shower, resulting in both her friends and school staff noting her arms, legs and torso were covered in welts and bruises. Heather said that she had got these injuries from fights with her brothers and sisters, although she did tell her close friend, Denise Harrison (who was the daughter of Fred's Jamaican friend Ronalzo), that the injuries had been inflicted by her parents. She told her that her mother, Rose, considered her to be nothing more than "a little bitch" who deserved her beatings.

Heather was a bright pupil and her 97% attendance record was outstanding. One school friend, however, remembered Heather being "quite unhappy, particularly at home. She seemed desperately afraid of her parents" and was planning to "join the army or go and work in a holiday camp." Heather took to writing 'FODIWL' on the front of her school exercise books, her own books and on nearly everything she owned. It was later discovered this stood for 'Forest Of Dean I Will Live'.

Although one teacher at Hucclecote remembered Heather as "very pleasant and willing to participate" another described her as like "Jekyll and Hyde – one minute nice as pie and the next very aggressive", particularly out of school and in the company of older pupils. It was noted that Heather was uneasy in the company of men. She absconded from a school camping trip and did not return with the other children so a search was put out to find her. When she was found, Heather said she didn't like the male teachers. The headmaster suspended Heather but did not expel her. She wasn't given male teachers after that, but did receive a tremendous beating once Fred got her home.

"Heather became very withdrawn at school and was always getting into trouble", remembered Mae. "I used to hang around her in what was called the smoker's corner when she had a few crafty fags."

Rumours of Rose's sex life reached several of the children's classmates, and Heather did admit to her friends that many of the rumours were true. The father of one of these classmates was a friend of the Wests (Ronalzo Harrison); as such, word soon got back to Fred and Rose. Fred was so concerned that he started to take the children to and from school.

Heather's hatred of men was clear for everyone to see, and no wonder after what she had been put through in her short life. She was uneasy in male company and couldn't stand to be in a room with men or to have them near her. It showed in her actions and Stephen said he could read it in her face. Once, Heather's uncle, John West, began teasing her about boyfriends and warned her that she should "watch it like, because they get up to tricky things". Heather told him that "If any boy put his hand on my knee I'd put a fucking brick over his head!"

Fred and Rose seem to have genuinely believed that Heather had lesbian inclinations and were furious about it in spite of the fact that Rose was clearly bisexual. This anger almost certainly stemmed from the fact that Heather never gave in and accepted her abuse like Anne Marie had. She continued to try to fight off the advances of her father. Had Mae been killed, no doubt they would have said the same about her too. Rose believed that Heather was a lesbian because when she was still in junior school, she was able to describe to her what type of knickers the female teachers were wearing.

Rose's brother, Graham, recalled how "eerie" the atmosphere had become within the walls of 25 Cromwell Street. The children did not laugh and were unnaturally subdued. "Whenever we walked into the house, there was never any noise. Even with nine or ten children around, you could hear a pin drop. Barbara (his wife) and I felt that it was probably because Rose was so strict with them. If the children looked like playing up, just a half-glance from Rosie was enough. There was no screaming or shouting. It reminded me in some ways of our mom and when we were kids. Rosie was every bit as strict, and seemed to be using the same tactics. If you don't do as I say you'll regret it."

At this time another of Rose's brothers, Andrew, recalled going to 25 Cromwell Street for the first time. They had fallen out years before and he hadn't seen her since. "She came to the door in a see-through blouse, forty-inch bust, skirt round her arse, white socks, no decorum". As they were talking, the doorbell rang and Rose left him for half an hour to take a client. Their sister, Glenys, said the next time she saw her: "I think she's on the bloody game Andrew." After that visit, he thought Rose had her brains in her knickers, and wrote her off.

Every effort was made to keep the West children away from other adults or situations that might arouse suspicion. They were rarely allowed to play with other children and were confined instead to the back garden and basement play room. They visited the houses of other relatives only when Fred and Rose were there too. School friends were not allowed back to the house and the children were forbidden from visiting their friends' homes. If any children came to the door to ask to play with one of the Wests children then Rose would tell them to "Fuck off!"

When Fred's friends or Rose's clients came over, Fred used to embarrass Mae and Heather by saying things like "There's my daughter, I think she's a lesbian" or "This one hasn't had a man in weeks."

Rose used to love camping, but Fred wasn't too keen. She would nag at him until he gave in and took the family on holiday. For seven years in a row he took them to Butlins in Barry Island, Wales, in his transit van.

One year Fred got hold of a four-berth caravan and took them to a camping site in Shropshire called the Craven Arms. When the children would go out to play and make friends Fred and Rose would use the time alone to have sex. The children recalled on more than one occasion going back to the caravan to see it rocking and the loud screams of sex coming from the open windows. The children once asked Rose what all the noise was and she replied: "Well if you don't like it – go home. People don't have to listen, do they?"

On one of their trips away, Fred got Anne Marie and her husband to house sit for them. This badly affected Anne Marie. On the second or third day Chris had to pin her down on the breakfast counter because she was becoming so violent and moody. "It's the place. It gives me the shits", she told him. They were using the four-poster bed, which Fred had previously inscribed with the word 'Cunt', and in the corner of the room was a pile of pornographic magazines. They put a video on and quickly switched it off again when they realised it was a pornographic movie showing two women, one in an executioners mask, and with the other woman eating her faeces.

Mae West recalled: "In the corner of their bedroom were piles of porn magazines. Another time when Stephen and I were being nosy we found kinky rubber suits and masks under a mattress, and a lot of underwear...They had loads of other blue films which Dad insisted on loaning to everyone... Dad told me once that he had hidden in a tree with his video camera filming Mum having sex in the back of his van when the back doors were open. They had all sorts of sex aides piled into a black case which was full of dildos. He used to show us one called the 'Eiffel Tower' which he used to offer to lend my friends if they came round... He also had a cat-o'-nine-tails, which I remember seeing him make when I was about five or six.

They didn't care where they had sex. I know the younger ones saw them doing it on the big table downstairs and in the kitchen. They just didn't care who saw them or how much noise they made."

Fred was proud of what he had done to his house, and was known to invite people in off the street to give them a tour. One of those shown around was named Carol, and she had previously lived at number 19 a few years before but had since moved away. She recalled that her and her cousin Hayley went back to the street to try to find a girl they used to know and knocked at number 25. Fred was very friendly and welcoming and invited them in. Before they could say why they had come he took them on a tour of his house. He lead them through the kitchen at the rear where Rose was sitting surrounded by a lot of young children. It was tea-time but there was a pornographic video being shown on the television and the woman and children were watching it. He took them to a bedroom on the ground floor at the front of the house where there was a big camera mounted on a stand at the bottom of the bed. He opened a wooden trunk and a wicker basket which Carol saw were full of videotapes. On the walls of the room were Polaroid photographs of naked men and women in various poses. She could see from the satin-finish wallpaper in the background that the photographs had been taken in that room. Carol and Hayley became too embarrassed and told him that they had to leave.

On another occasion, when Fred was helping to move a fridge for a girl who was living in a bedsit at 4 Cromwell Street, he mentioned to her that he knew her mother and that he had had sex with her and so she could be his daughter. When the girl asked her mum, her mother told her that Fred was not her father, but that he had raped her when she was 15-years-old. Curiously, neither woman reported it to the police and even stranger still, the girl's only contact with Fred after that was when she went round to the house with her boyfriend to borrow pornographic videos from him.

As Heather's sixteenth birthday approached in 1986, Fred's attempts to rape her became more frequent and she began to fear for her safety. Like her half-sister Anne Marie, she began to think that "something terrible" was about to happen to her. She was finding it increasingly hard to cope with Fred's relentless sexual attentions and she hated his insistence on keeping a record of her periods and his threats that if she refused to allow him to have sex with her he would get "someone to sort her out."

Rose's sister-in-law, Barbara, recalled: "It was obvious that Fred had an abnormal sex drive. As time went on it got more and more out of control. If we stayed any length of time he and Rose would have to disappear upstairs for sex. They were quite open about it. One time they showed me a blue bottle which had been sealed. Inside was a pair of Rosemary's knickers. She said she'd worn them during a fantastic sex session with Fred. She wanted to preserve them as a souvenir."

Barbara and Graham Letts felt Fred and Rose were trying to draw them into their sordid world. They were invited to see the top floor of the house and discovered that it was decorated with framed pictures of Rose naked. There was a huge library of pornographic videos, including some involving animals. When Rose put one on for them to watch, the Letts' made their excuses and walked out.

"Another time we were sitting downstairs when Rose suddenly announced that she wanted to change her clothes. There and then she stripped right off. She wasn't wearing knickers – I don't think she ever did. I didn't know where to look. I think it was her way of trying to initiate us into their world."

Graham once confronted Rose after hearing rumours that she was prostituting herself and she confessed immediately. "What shocked me most was how casual she was about the whole thing…I was stunned, but Rose said I was overreacting. Quite often we'd go there and the phone would go and Rosie would have to disappear for half an hour."

On the 24th February 1987, Anne Marie gave birth to her second daughter, Carol, after she had had an affair with her long-time friend Phil. Not long after, Anne Marie had a full hysterectomy. Upset by this, and now fully aware that she had to have the procedure due to the sexual abuse she had suffered as a child, Anne Marie decided to confront Fred and Rose.

She telephoned them without saying why she wanted to see them and one afternoon they went to visit her. "Dad, I have to know why. I want to know why you did all those things to me when I was young. Why did you do it, Dad? You must have known it was wrong. You don't do things like that to children. I was just a child. I loved you. You abused me. I would kill anyone who touched my girls, but you were my father and you did it to me and let Rose do it, too."

Rose just stared at the floor and Fred didn't say anything. Eventually, Fred stood up and angrily shouted: "If you're going to bring up all that stuff – well, you're no bloody daughter of mine. I don't want to know. I'm not standing here and listening to this fucking rubbish. Things like that happen. They just do, alright?" They both then walked out.

A few months later, Fred called at her house and acted as though nothing had happened. Anne Marie then invited Fred, Rose and all of the children to her house to celebrate her daughter Michelle's 3rd birthday in June.

Before that party, Anne Marie and Mae went swimming together. After they got out of the pool and were changing, Anne Marie confessed to her that she'd been sexually assaulted by both Fred and Rose. She told her it had happened to her when Mae, Heather and Stephen were put to sleep in the basement and she was left upstairs with them. She warned Mae that they might try to do the same to her. Mae confided in her that Fred had already tried to grope her a few times and that Rose knew about it but hadn't taken part. Anne Marie then told her to watch out for their Uncle John as he had abused her. Mae told her that he had already raped her too. Mae then clammed up and the two of them never mentioned it between them again.

As Mae reached fifteen, the groping from Fred got worse. He used to tell Mae that it was wrong for a girl to be a virgin after sixteen and tell her that "Boys don't do it properly. Dads know how to do it right." It wasn't just his daughters that Fred molested either, sometimes it was their friends and he tried to make it look like an accident. Mae remembered that he once grabbed at one of her friends' breasts and another time he "put his hand up a friend's skirt when he gave us a lift in his van and we had to climb over the front seats in to the back."

She also recalled that when Rose went out and she was left alone with Fred she lived in fear that he would rape her. He would get out a pornographic video and make her watch it with him. He once even put on a video of Rose having sex with a man.

Fred used the video camera to record Rose in all sorts of situations. From her having sex with various men, to her inserting objects in to herself and her urinating. He would film her getting ready to spend the night with one of her clients and then film her undressing upon her return the next morning. He would show the semen stains in her black knickers and he would carry out a gynaecological examination of her, all in front of the camera. She would lie with her feet pulled backwards over her head and wide apart and he would film for four or five minutes.

Stephen West spoke to the NSPCC at his school after a particularly heavy beating from Fred and Rose. His girlfriend, Caroline Tonks, told teachers and she later recalled some of these meetings: "He'd just hang his head. He wouldn't say a word. They'd ask him about his legs and he'd say 'Yeah well, a lot of kids get beat, you know, it's nothing unusual.' He wouldn't elaborate on anything at all. We went to about three or four meetings together, then one day it, like, blew up in my face and he told me to 'butt out' and I said 'fair enough you carry on with it yourself'. He knew what the repercussions would be at home. I think the social worker we were talking to went to the house. I think his Dad shut the door in his face and told him to 'butt out' and mind his own business and it got worse. I think Steve got into quite a bit of trouble 'cause of that and I didn't wanna take it any further because I knew that it was gonna get worse for Stephen so I just butted out at that point."

She said of Stephen's injuries: "He wouldn't let you touch his head much. He had a lot of lumps and bumps on his head and his knees were a

179

weak point. He said they automatically hit at his knees to stop him running out of the front door 'cause at one time I know he was beaten and he did more or less jump the gates and escape. So from that point on his knees were a target to stop him running."

Bill Messer, a social worker from 1974-1984 in the Gloucester area, said: "I don't know whether the child was put on the 'at risk' register for instance. I imagine that he was. If he was not even put on the 'at risk' register, I would say that we have a clear indication of incompetence. Professional incompetence. And a standard of service far below what its users have a right to expect."

Heather was sixteen-and-a-half in the spring of 1987 and she had grown into a pretty teenager. She was 5'4" and slim with prominent front teeth. "She seemed more sexually aware than other girls our age", remembered one of her school friends and she got into trouble on more than one occasion for bringing pornographic magazines to school. Despite Fred and Rose's assertions that she was a lesbian, Heather developed an intense crush on a male teacher which led to Fred being called to the Headmasters office. "Mr West was very co-operative" a teacher later recalled.

Marie Gardner, to whom Heather confessed the extent of her parents' abuse, would later say: "One of the PE teachers took her into the little office that's in the changing rooms and...questioned her about the bruising because it was quite obvious. You couldn't miss it really. The bruising were in funny places. It was the inside of her legs and, like, the top of her arm, you know it was like hand-grip bruises". The 'Key Questions Answered – Contacts between the Public Services and the West family 1965-1994' issued by the Gloucester Area Child Protection Committee stated that "There is no record or recollection by teachers of bruising ever having been seen on Heather West."

During the last week of exams in 1987, a little less than a month before the official end of school, Heather finally opened up about what was happening at home. Denise Harrison was walking home through the Eastgate Shopping Centre one day when she saw Heather sitting on a wall and noticed that she was upset. She asked Heather what was wrong and Heather started to cry. She told her that she had just found out that her mother had been having a long affair with the father of a girl at school. 'Suncoo' was one of Rose's Jamaican regulars and was also the father of two of her sisters. Heather hadn't known. Fred and Rose had always explained that their mixed-race children were "throwbacks" to Fred's gypsy past. Heather had been extremely upset and confronted the daughter of 'Suncoo' who in turn went home and told her mother.

Heather West shortly before taking her exams

The following day 'Suncoo' turned up at Cromwell Street to confront Fred and Rose. Anne Marie recalled that: "Fred and Rose were furious that Heather had been discussing their business outside the family, and she suffered a tremendous beating."

Heather told Denise that her father came into her room at night. "She said he was having sex with her", recalled Denise. "I said 'haven't you told your Mum?' and she said her Mum didn't believe her." Denise encouraged Heather to go back to school and inform the teachers. Heather told Denise that her father was beating her and that Rose thought she was a "little bitch" who deserved her beatings. Anne Marie said that: "Denise never doubted her story. She had regularly noticed the severe bruising on Heather's arms and legs."

"I asked her whether she had told anyone", Denise said, "and she said she was too frightened." Denise told her parents, but Ronalzo and Gloria Harrison were friends of the Wests and didn't believe they were capable of such things. "We left school about three weeks after this so I never saw her again" recalled Denise.

Word quickly got back to Fred and Rose. From this point on they kept her under guard and made sure she spoke to no-one.

Heather found herself in a desperate situation at home. She knew she had to find a job to get away from Cromwell Street permanently but there were few jobs for school leavers. "I remember Heather was really miserable just before she disappeared, because Mum and Dad were nagging her about getting a job", recalled Mae. Fred would often tell her that it was "time you started paying your way, girl" and Rose would agree. "You can't expect us to keep you any longer", Rose would tell her. Heather was so depressed that "when she left school she just sat in the chair. She didn't want to know me anymore", Rose would say of her daughter.

Heather had previously told Anne Marie she was desperate to get out of Cromwell Street and asked if she could stay with her. Anne Marie, remembering the violent ways in which Fred would come and fetch her after she had run away, thought the same would happen if she encouraged Heather, so she refused.

Denise Harrison suspected that Fred and Rose waited for Heather to finish her last term at school before killing her because she would then not be missed by the school authorities.

Mae recalled that "Sometimes I found it hard to get on with Heather because she was so different. Stephen punched her on the nose just before she left. I think he feels a bit guilty about that now. She didn't cry though – she was hard. She was very similar to Mum, she could be hard towards us."

On the 29th May, Heather registered for unemployment benefit and she received a job offer cleaning holiday chalets for Butlins in Torquay, Devon, which she immediately accepted. She cheered up at the prospect of getting away from her abusers and Mae remembered her being: "More like her old self than I'd seen her in ages". But as the date of her leaving drew closer she became troubled and uncommunicative once again.

Her uncle, Graham Letts, recalled the last time he saw Heather: "I was at a family meal at Cromwell Street cooked by Rose. Heather kicked me under the table. She had a terrified, frightened look on her face. She was begging for help. I looked at her and I remember thinking if something was wrong, she would be better off talking with her parents. Little did I know they were the problem and they had put the fear of God into her. I have a constant picture of Heather looking at me, begging for help. It still haunts me. I feel a lot of guilt and can't get over that. I had a feeling that something was wrong but I never questioned their way of life. But that was the last time I saw Heather."

On the 17th June 1987, the whole West family went to Anne Marie's home at 52 Sapperton Road for her daughter Michelle's third birthday party. It was clear to everyone that Heather was quiet, upset and miserable from the moment she arrived. Fred bullied her and demanded that she join in with the celebrations. "Don't fucking stand there like a lemon" he shouted at her. "Why don't you leave me a-fucking-lone?!" Heather replied.

The last photo of Heather (Left), with Fred (Right) taken at the birthday party in Anne Marie's garden 2 days before she was killed.

Rose mentioned to Anne Marie that they'd had trouble with Heather before leaving home and Fred seemed to be keeping a very close eye on her all the time they were there. Heather went into the garden with the rest of the children but sat by herself at the far end while the other children played. Whenever Anne Marie approached her Fred or Rose quickly cut her off, so eventually she asked her husband to try to talk to her. Chris remembered that she hardly said anything to him and she just sat there looking sad. When Anne Marie got the family together for photographs Heather refused to participate.

Chris Davis had a friend called Charlie who filmed the party with his camera. He recalled how Fred approached him and asked him if he'd be interested in filming sex scenes at Cromwell Street. Charlie filmed Michelle and her friends in the house and garden but for a lot of the time Heather kept her back to the house.

There were complaints from some of the mothers of the attendees about Heather's language. To allay their displeasure, Anne Marie telephoned Fred that evening and told him. "She got told off by Mum and Dad and Heather cut Anna off for telling Mum, saying she was never going to speak to her again", recalled Mae.

The following day Heather received news that would wreck her dreams of escaping her present situation. Butlins contacted her and told her that there was no longer a position for her. She was stuck living with Fred and Rose. Mae, Stephen, Fred and Rose all confirmed that Heather spent the night in tears, and Mae said that she had never seen Heather so distressed. The next day Heather disappeared...

Mae recalled that in the morning Heather was "back to her usual self, looking miserable, biting her nails and sitting on the couch bouncing back and forth as she sat." Mae and Stephen left for school as normal at around 08:00 and Rose took the younger children to their school half an hour later. Fred had been working on an outside building job but couldn't work that day because it was raining so he was left alone in the house. Rose would normally get back to the house around 09:30 and then head out shopping.

When Mae and Stephen returned home at around 17:00, they were taken down to the basement and told that Heather had left home to take the job she had previously been refused in Torquay. "A girl picked her up in a mini, and she's gone to work at the holiday camp", explained Fred. He explained that he and Rose had given Heather some money to help her on her way. He also told them that he had put the clothes that Heather didn't take out for the bin men to collect and had packed her bed away. Anne Marie received a phone call from Fred telling her that Heather had left home to go to Torquay with a 'lemon' (Fred's usual term for a lesbian) and that Heather was one too, in order to look for a job there.

In what may be a nudge towards the truth of what happened to Heather, Rose told an enquiring neighbour that she and Heather had had "a hell of a row", and that Heather had run away from home. Anne Knight, who looked after two nearby houses and had an office in Cromwell Street was told: "There was a hell of a barney here a couple of nights ago. We found out that she was going with a lesbian from Wales, and she has gone to Wales with her."

Not long after, Ronalzo Harrison asked where Heather had gone and Fred informed him that Heather had been given a good hiding by Rose for assaulting the children "and putting scratches on their faces" while she was babysitting, and had left a few days later. When Ronalzo expressed to Fred how concerned he was about Heather, Fred told him that Heather was living somewhere in the nearby village of Brockworth and that she had telephoned them.

When Heather's remains were recovered there were two orange cords found, one 15" and the other 22" long. Orange, brown and green nylon carpet fibres were found trapped in the rope, suggesting that Heather had been held down on the floor as she was being tied up. There was no gag, but her remains were found without any clothing suggesting that she had been stripped naked before death, and that some sex act may have been forced upon her. 22 of her finger and toe bones were missing (out of a total of 76) and one kneecap. She was also missing 15 of her wrist and ankle bones. Her head had been severed with a sharp, fine-edged knife, her thighs had been chopped more crudely and her left one had been smashed in two near her pelvis by a sharp-edged object, such as a clever. Her legs were found on top, covering her chest, vertebrae, arms and skull at the bottom, with lots of hair and some loose finger or toe nails. Black plastic bin liners were found around her trunk. Part of a necklace was also discovered with her remains.

In the weeks that followed, Fred extended the patio at the back of the house. He got hold of several dozen square slabs, half coloured pink and the other half vanilla yellow. Stephen and Barry helped him and Barry remembered helping to lay the patio slabs and covering them over with some twigs.

Heather's murder was one of the few times Rose ever showed any remorse. She seemed genuinely upset that Heather had "runaway" and apparently cried a great deal. "Mum cried a lot when Heather left", recalled Mae. "We asked Dad why she was crying and he said it was because of Heather. It was an unusual sight because she was usually quite hard."

Mae found Rose in bed crying and asked her what was wrong. She asked if it was Heather, and Rose shouted at her: "Mind your own fucking business!"

Such was Rose's desire to escape from what she and Fred had done that they took a rare trip to see her brother Graham and his wife Barbara. "Heather's left us. She's disappeared. She's a lesbian. And that's it. Closed. I don't want you coming round in future if you mention Heather", Rose told the couple.

Samantha West, Doug and Christine West's daughter who was 7-years-old at the time, recalled: "I remember Grandad asking Fred once how she was getting on and Rose answering instead of Fred saying that she's got some job in some holiday camp somewhere and they got a letter 'If she felt like it' and they were letting her live her life."

With Mae now the oldest of his daughters still living at home, Fred touched her more and more. He would grab her, remove her bra and touch her breasts. If Mae and Stephen were playing together he would tell Stephen: "If you want to get Mae's knickers off, get in the bedroom and do it."

With Heather gone, Rose began to mellow according to Stephen and Mae. She never hit either of them again and they were brought presents and given bikes. The younger children were not quite so fortunate, and Barry remembered Rose tucking him and his siblings in at night and cuddling them, then the following morning "We'd wake up to her kicking us in our beds. She'd be shouting 'Wake up you little cunts!' There'd be no reason for it. We were terrified."

In December 1987, a school record shows that Fred West had been to see teachers at Stephen's school due to concerns that he appeared 'tired' and 'lethargic'. Fred told them quite openly that it was probably because he had hit his son and "laid him out." Stephen had already received hospital treatment earlier in the year for a fractured finger. Fred also instructed a teacher that some of his children should not see a speech therapist. Both Barry and Stephen were required to have a special education needs review, but Fred told the school that they were making a fuss. Barry was also referred to a pediatrician because of child protection concerns. None of these incidents were reported to either Social Services or the police.

Oddly, Fred and Rose began to make up stories that Heather had phoned them at home. Fred said that he had seen her around Gloucester and Birmingham, but someone started to ring the house and pretend to be Heather. Stephen recalled that one day in 1988, the telephone rang and Rose answered it. He was sitting nearby and witnessed Rose answer it and say "Hi Heather, it's your Mum". They were talking, but then Rose started to get upset and told the person on the other end of the phone that she was going to "get your father". She told Fred that the caller was "calling me every name under the bloody sun" and told Fred to talk to her. Fred talked to the caller and when he put the phone down he told Rose and the kids that he had calmed her down.

Anne Marie spent the following months searching for Heather and she travelled the West Country as well as contacting the Salvation Army. It was always Fred who claimed to have seen or had contact with Heather in the years after her disappearance. He claimed to have met Heather in Birmingham, Devizes, Bristol and Weston-Super-Mare. According to his stories, she had turned into a drug dealer and had dyed her hair blonde. Stephen and Mae grew so concerned that no-one else had seen Heather that they told Fred that they were going to report her as 'missing' to the police. Alarmed, he told them: "You'd better not do that...I've heard more rumours about her. Not just drugs. Someone told me she was involved in some kind of credit card fraud. You tell the police she's missing and they'll start poking their noses into all that. You could get her into real trouble. You definitely don't want to go bringing the police into this!"

In the first few months of 1988, Fred found himself a full-time job, working for Carson's, a firm of building contractors based in Stonehouse, just outside Gloucester, but he also kept up his part-time building work and odd-jobbing for the landlords of the properties in Cromwell Street.

One 16-year-old girl who moved to Cromwell Street at this time later remembered Fred and the area. She began by explaining that Cromwell Street was "a very rough, run-down area" where the majority of the houses were run as "bed-and-breakfast businesses", which meant that the

186

population was "transient...with a lot of movement between the various establishments on the street." This brought "a large number of young, single people" to Cromwell Street. "During the period I was resident there, I would say only three of the houses in that street were occupied as family residences." It was no time at all before she was introduced to Fred West, who was doing odd jobs for her landlord. By then, "Fred West was known to me by reputation." Her landlord had already told her cheerfully that he was 'kinky'.

"Apparently Fred would watch Rose having sex with other people" and was also "very interested in group sex and in making pornographic videos." It was also common knowledge among the young residents that "Rose would have sexual relationships with people other than Fred, both male and female" and that the West's would have "sex parties which involved visitors to the house watching videos made by Fred featuring Rose and various partners, and then going on to have sexual intercourse themselves.

When I first met Fred, my impression was that he was a very hard-working, caring man. Although I had initially been a little wary because of his reputation, I was quickly reassured by how kind and caring Fred appeared. When I met him, his main topics of conversation were his job, his family and his house."

Fred used his charm and he and the young woman became close friends. "I felt towards him like a father or a brother", although she admitted: "Fred loved to talk about sex, make sexualized comments. Even with all the sexual suggestion and innuendos that Fred made, I still felt safe with him." Safe enough to sit talking to him wearing "only pants and a short T-shirt, or sometimes just a short towel and nothing else.

As with Fred, I had a bit of a preconceived opinion of Rose, because of all the gossip I had heard about her." When they met, "My first impression of Rose was that she was very stern, with no sense of humour. She appeared to be a private, withdrawn sort of person. Fred was always the one everybody knew, liked and talked to; Rose was quieter altogether." As time went on, she realised that Rosemary West could also be a "very moody person, unlike Fred who was very even-tempered", and that she "would get bad-tempered for no reason", which meant that she could become "very nasty and vindictive". Nevertheless, the two women "quickly became very good friends".

It is believed that at this time, Rose was in the middle of a long-standing lesbian relationship with a much younger woman, who had been a resident at Jordans Brook Community Home. It had lasted for almost 2 years, and for a part of that time her lover had lived with her at Cromwell Street. Rose still had relationships with other young women, sometimes recorded on video, and she still worked as a prostitute, picking up clients in the local pubs.

The following is a typical exchange between Rose and one of her clients which appeared on a video recorded by Fred:

Rose: Fuckin' hell…It's fucked me for the night. You have an' all
Client: (Laughing) I can't help it, can I?
Rose: It's massive that…Is it classified as a dangerous weapon?
Client: (Laughing) Dunno. I wouldn't have thought so.
Rose: I should register it if I was you.

Stephen West recalled being made to watch pornographic videos with his parents. The films featured bestiality and adults abusing young children, and to stop him from turning away, Fred made him a metal head cage. The cage had a hook at the back and went over the sofa and if Stephen still tried to look away from the screen then Rose would hit him in the face with an ashtray.

Arthur Dobbs, a client of Rose West's, phoned Social Services reporting that the children were being abused. The council in 1995 later said that "an anonymous caller reported that the children were being left alone". There is no mention in their report of abuse. A social worker visited and stated that the children were "well and not neglected."

At this time a woman named Kathryn Halliday was befriended by the Wests. She met them for regular sex and bondage sessions until the middle of 1989. She was bisexual and had left her husband and moved into a rented flat at 11 Cromwell Street with her lesbian lover, Kimberley Stanton.

Kathryn recalled: "On Cromwell Street you could be anonymous because it was a lot of Bed & Breakfasts and DSS. People came and went all the time. You didn't stay in Cromwell Street for very long." She met Fred when her landlord appointed him to mend a leak in the roof at her flat. "He turned up in paint-spattered overalls and sandals…He was full of chat, a real Jack-the-Lad. By the time he finished, he had asked me to go round and meet 'the missus'…There was nothing at all in Fred's way to suggest anything but a bumbling, goofy builder and happy-go-lucky chap and that is how he came across. I liked the guy. When I first met him I liked him."

She told police that they went to the upstairs living room, where she noticed a unit full of video cassettes. Fred asked her what she wanted to watch and she told him a straight blue movie. He selected one and put it on for her and then Rose entered the room. She was wearing a very short skirt and a low-cut short-sleeved top. It was obvious that she was not wearing any underwear.

Kathryn remembered: "As soon as she walked in I wondered what I had got myself in to. She was plump, busty, not very attractive, and wearing dark-rimmed glasses and a tiny miniskirt. When she sat down next to me she wiggled down, so that her skirt slid up around the top of her thighs. She wasn't wearing anything underneath. She kept nestling up against me and getting closer. She couldn't walk past me without brushing up against me." Within minutes Rose had removed what few clothes she was wearing and was naked on the settee alongside her. "We chatted. We would laugh and talk and different things and we'd watch blue movies but then she started to get really, really heavy. About half an hour later, after Fred had poured me several large drinks, she took me by the hand and led me upstairs. Fred walked right behind me so I couldn't go back. Rose was very aggressive, by far the dominant one. We all took our clothes off, and had sex until three in the morning. It wasn't really human contact that Rose wanted. She liked pain. I wouldn't call it making love...She was very domineering. Very much so. She was quite domineering over Fred...She was very cold."

Part of her statement to the police reads:

Rose removed all my clothes. I was dragged rather than led to the bedroom. Fred followed behind with the drinks. He was still fully clothed. Rose started to make love to me. Fred was in the same room and took his clothes off. He was naked and he had a video camera. I felt Rose was getting me excited in preparation for Fred. After a short period Fred joined us on the bed and had sex with me. While Fred was making love to me I was still stimulating Rose.

Kathryn said that after Fred climaxed Rose's behavior changed. "She became the aggressor...she became more violent...more menacing...more abusive with my body."

After the first time, Kathryn then became a regular visitor to 25 Cromwell Street. She went most mornings when the children had left the house for school for sex with Rose, and there were evening visits too, when she would have sex with both Fred and Rose. She recalled that Rose particularly liked to use large sex aides.

On her second visit, the following day, Kathryn was taken down to the basement and shown the children's bedroom, after which they all went upstairs and had sex again. "Rose was absolutely insatiable. She used to say no woman or man could ever satisfy her. I don't think she got much sexual pleasure from Fred – he wasn't very well endowed. That time, Fred just wanted to watch. He walked around the bed, and on occasions would climb on to it, but just to get a closer look. Rose only had to look at my empty glass and he would go down and refill it."

Later that night, Fred asked her if she would like to see their "secret room". She was taken across the hallway and in to a room with a large four-poster bed.

Rose's four-poster bed that she used for 'entertaining'.

Rose took out a suitcase full of magazines from a wardrobe. It was full of pictures of black latex suits, with holes for the nose and mouth. Also in the suitcase were suits exactly like the pictures. Their worn appearance made it obvious that they had been used. "Rose and Fred described all the items in detail – they were very turned on by talking about them. We were all naked, and I felt embarrassed." The Wests wanted to know if she would be willing to wear one of the suits and "dish out punishment. The bedroom cupboard was filled with sex toys, and I realised I was totally out of my depth."

In the mornings, Rose would take the children to school, then knock on the window of Kathryn's flat at about 09:30. They would then go back to number 25, have a coffee, and then go upstairs and have sex until midday. "Fred used to come home in the evenings and join in. But I only had sex with him three or four times, because he preferred to watch. I never saw him and Rose make love, even when we were three in a bed. Their relationship was very strange. On the surface they seemed a normal, respectable couple. They were popular in the street, and people used to talk to them, or Fred would go to their houses to do odd jobs."

The Wests found out what Kathryn liked to drink and what brand of cigarettes she smoked, and stocked the bar with these items. "I'm afraid I used them for it. I was on the dole. I didn't have any money. Why not?", Kathryn later said.

In the evenings, Kathryn, Fred and Rose would sit and watch pornographic movies. Some of these unsettled Kathryn and showed women being abused in what she recognized as Fred and Rose's bedroom. One woman was tied hand and foot to the bed while a very large phallus was forced into her. The woman was clearly in pain, and Kathryn asked them if they had any normal sex films. He replied: "What do you mean 'normal'?" There was another movie of a girl with fair hair being whipped and tied to the bed by a man. There were others of girls being tied to beds with chains and straps.

Rose talked openly to her about her prostitution, giving Kathryn the impression that she enjoyed her work and was emotionally attached to some of her clients. There were photographs in the house of these men, and some were recognisable to Kathryn as respected and prominent members of the local community.

Kathryn recalled being tied up one evening and Rose holding a pillow over her head. "When you're tied up with a pillow over your head you don't know what's happening. All you think about is yourself and trying to get free. You don't think of what they are doing to you. Your mind and everything goes and you don't know where you are. It's a horrible, horrible feeling." Rose put her mouth next to Kathryn's ear and whispered: "What does it feel like not being able to see?" Then Rose pushed the pillow down harder, so that it folded over Kathryn's eyes and ears, muffling her hearing. "The next thing is she's having a go at me...he is...somebody is holding the pillow. She was talking to me and the next thing somebody, or something, is inside me."

Fred and Rose then had sex with Kathryn, who tried to get the pillow away from her face. Rose bent down and mocked: "Can't you breathe? Aren't you woman enough to take it?" Rose then said that, if she could not take it, she would be punished, and Kathryn felt something sharp and cold pressing against her stomach. When she was finally released she saw a half-inch cut near her navel. "She would cause as much physical pain as she possibly could. She had no limits to what she would do. Even then I knew they were dicing with death. They played with me and the idea that I was frightened. They got their thing from seeing other people frightened.

They got more and more violent. They wanted to do more and more all the time. They pushed me beyond my personal limits, and they hurt me...Rose West wanted me to do things to her which were very, very aggressive...She wanted orgasms all the time, like a machine."

During the summer Mae was effectively kicked out of home. She had been seeing a boy called Rob Williams for just three weeks and he had been staying over but they hadn't been sleeping together, although Mae had pretended that they were in order to stop Fred telling her that he was going to 'break her in'. Rob had a falling out with his parents and Fred and Rose agreed that he could move in to their house. "Mae can fuck who she likes

191

and if they want to do it under my roof, let them", Fred said.

Mae and Rob had met at the 'Paint Pot' pub when he was celebrating his 18th birthday. On his first visit to 25 Cromwell Street Rose walked out of the bathroom naked. He recalled that: "Everything was sagging and dangling everywhere. It was a pretty horrible sight." Mae gasped: "Mother!", but Rose commented: "He'll soon get used to it!" He then revealed that there was "a stream of black guys knocking at the door...She was a nymphomaniac – She just couldn't get enough." He recalled once when he was helping Fred lay a carpet, and Rose was sitting on the settee with her legs apart, he glanced up and realised that she wasn't wearing any knickers.

He also described how one day, Fred put on a film he had videoed for him and Mae, and how he inserted by mistake a video that showed Rose having sex with a black man. He also mentioned that Fred and Rose enjoyed driving out to the country for "sex parties", with the van loaded up with blankets and mattresses. "Fred let slip that there were others involved. They used to meet up with other men and go in to some remote hills for sex parties. Once, when I was driving with Fred, we went past a forest and he pointed to it and said that was where he was going to film his next orgy."

Fred and Rose got them a flat two streets away in Belgrave Road and told them that they were only allowed to visit on a Sunday afternoon between 14:00 and 15:00 and she had to hand her keys back. The other children were not allowed to visit her.

Mae was concerned that her sister Louise, who was now the oldest of Fred's girls still living at home, would now bear the brunt of Fred's sexual attention. He had already started to show a particular liking for her now she was getting older, and before she moved out she took Louise to one side and told her to watch out for their father, but Louise told her: "I know, I know what he's like."

On the 2nd February 1989, Rose received a letter from her mother, Daisy, asking: "Have you heard from Heather yet Rose? It's a worry when they go off. I would love to see her." A few days later, Fred and Rose took the remaining children to see Daisy. "I asked if she'd heard from Heather and she turned away and said 'No, she is off with her cronies'. Fred and Rose seemed to be content. Rose said 'I'm happy Mum'. She said that a couple of times." Not long after, Daisy went to Cromwell Street to visit Rose and caught her taking part in prostitution. She recalled: "We went to her place once and she came to the door with a dressing gown on. Before we stepped in, a man came out of the room and ran upstairs. I used to feel sorry for the children because they did not have a grandmother, but I felt I could not go to the house again." It would be the last time they would see each other until Daisy gave evidence against her daughter in 1995.

Kathryn Halliday's association with the Wests continued for a while until one day they went too far. Fred and Rose took her in to the back bedroom which had a large four-poster bed. Fred showed her the wardrobe which housed whips, a bullwhip and a cat-o'-nine-tails. He then showed her a catalogue of rubber clothing and latex suits. Some covered the eyes and head. Some had nose holes, others didn't. He then took out a suitcase which had similar outfits. Kathryn recalled: "He took out one suit but it smelled sweaty and had been worn. He wanted me to put it on but I refused". Rose then showed her a collection of sexy, revealing clothes.

Kathryn Halliday: "I felt on each occasion they were trying to take me to my physical and emotional limit. There was verbal abuse during the sex act about my inability to accept into my body the larger sex aides which Rose accepted more readily."

Years later, in her second statement to the police, she told them about being shown a pornographic movie by the couple which had obviously been filmed at the house. In it was a young woman who had been tied to a bed and was spread-eagled on her back. She was being abused with a large dildo and the camera was concentrating on her obvious distress. She continued:

What I didn't describe in my previous statement was the sheer terror and life-threatening situations Fred and Rose led me in to — nor did I give details of the full abuse. They became more and more violent, physically and mentally. Fred would beat me around the head with his fists and Rose slapped me. Each time they pushed me a little further. On numerous occasions I was tied up and blindfolded. Rose would lie across my face and they would put a pillow over my face so I couldn't breathe. On one occasion they threatened to cut my throat or stomach. Afterwards I found a half-inch cut close to my belly button, although it wasn't deep. I was so frightened I never went back."

She believed she was only allowed to escape because Fred and Rose knew she had family who would be suspicious if she disappeared. Whenever she saw Fred or Rose in the street they completely blanked her. They would just look straight through her.

Stephen West recalled a lesbian couple who lived on Cromwell Street: "Dad used to ask them around. They used to go upstairs into the middle front room where the bar is and do whatever they did with Mum and Dad. Dad said he hated lesbians, that they were too dry inside. Dad was never discreet. Mum never wore underwear, and the first thing he did when he came home was to stick his dirty hand straight up her skirt and smell it. Right in font of us." He would then wave his fingers under the children's noses and say "smell that, that's your mother."

In March, Kathryn Halliday moved away from Cromwell Street.

In regards to other videos which are known to have been in the possession of Fred and Rose, some were seen by his children. Some of these contained a woman performing oral sex on a horse before going on to have full intercourse with it, and another had a woman having sex with an Alsatian dog. Fred used to say that he was trying to get hold of a Bull for Rose as that was the only thing that would ever completely satisfy her.

In March 1989, Stephen West's school made a referral to the NSPCC about potential physical abuse suffered by him. The NSPCC investigated and established that Stephen was feeling threatened by his family and a teacher stated that the boy had been kept off school because he had been hit by his father with a mallet, although he later changed his story and stated that his injuries were caused by a friend. In fact, the previous day, Stephen had been seen in the A&E Department with an injury to an index finger and it was recorded that "the finger had been hit with a sledge-hammer". The NSPCC decided that this referral should be dealt with by counselling and support of the family, rather than dealing with potential physical abuse. Stephen was also seen in hospital for a head injury, and Fred told him, as he approached his sixteenth birthday. "You'll soon be ready to sleep with your mother."

Just five months later, as Stephen turned sixteen on the 19th August, Rose told him: "Got a good present for you this year – I want you out. You're on your own, fella. Sling your hook. You're out."

Stephen West

When he came home one day his things were packed and waiting by the door. He was told that from now on he was living in Mrs Taylor's house on the other side of the church. He was given the old room that Anne Marie and Chris Davis used to share.

Stephen and the rest of the younger children were made to carry his possessions to his new room where they were dumped and then Rose made the children leave straight away with her. Just like Mae before him, he was told to hand back his keys and was only allowed to visit for an hour or so on a Sunday afternoon.

By now, Mae and her partner Rob had bought a house together, with the help of his parents for the deposit. They stayed in Gloucester but moved a bit further away from Cromwell Street. This angered Fred, who wanted them to buy number 23 Cromwell Street. "You could at least have bought somewhere in Cromwell Street, girl. Next door even. Then we'd have been able to knock through and you could have stayed part of the family."

Fred was by now working full-time as a general maintenance man at a home for the autistic in Minchinhampton. Still working for the firm of Carson's Contractors, who had a contract to look after the home, he was on call "twenty-four hours a day, seven days a week for odd jobs" as he would put it. He would often disappear to the home at odd hours of the day and night in the red Vauxhall Astra van that he had recently been supplied with by the contactors. With thirty-two adult residents and sixty-one staff, Stroud Court was in the middle of a seventeen-acre estate, where Fred had access to all of the buildings. The main house itself had a series of cellars, which one resident described as "like a rabbit-warren", where Fred was more often than not to be found.

In 1990, Anne Marie and Chris Davis broke up. It had been a volatile and at times violent relationship where both liked to drink.

In October, David and Pauline Williams (who were friends with Fred and Rose) received a postcard from them. It was written to the West children who were staying with the Williams' and was addressed to the "West Williams Menagerie". The postcard refers to an unknown person called 'Colin'. At the time, Fred and Rose were reportedly regulars at the Prince Albert Pub in Gloucester, which was run by the Williams' and they lived just a couple of minutes away in Belgrave Road. The cryptic postcard, which showed four different images of the Cheshire canal ring, read:

Brilliant bit of canal, full of lagoons and things. Think Mae's nose would have frozen off by now, but weather actually very photographic. Colin says the 'birds' are very friendly here. Loads of wildlife – especially when the soup exploded all over the galley! Several fishermen have also lost their groundbait. Mum and Dad xx

It later emerged that David and Pauline Williams used the Prince Albert Pub, which was just around the corner from Cromwell Street, as their base to rape, sexually abuse and beat ten children.

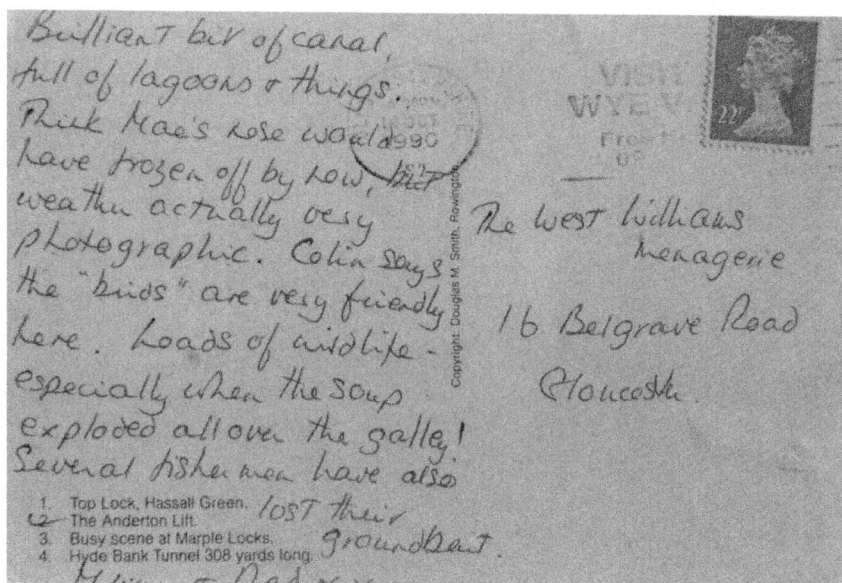

Brilliant bit of canal,
full of lagoons + things.
Think Mae's nose would
have frozen off by now, the
weather actually very
photographic. Colin says
the "birds" are very friendly
here. Loads of wildlife -
especially when the soup
exploded all over the galley!
Several fishermen have also
lost their
groundbait.

1. Top Lock, Hassall Green.
2. The Anderton Lift.
3. Busy scene at Marple Locks.
4. Hyde Bank Tunnel 308 yards long.

The West Midlands
menagerie
16 Belgrave Road
Gloucester

After their break away, Fred and Rose had begun to argue a lot more than usual and these arguments had turned violent. She told Fred that she wanted more than just having sex with other men, especially as she didn't need to be at home in the evenings as there were no babies for her to look after and the youngest child, Lucyanna, was seven-years-old. Fred didn't like the idea and wouldn't listen. He would punch and kick Rose every time she brought the subject up. She told Fred that she would no longer see the men he had picked for her unless he loosened his grip on her life and movements, so finally, he agreed.

Rose had a bicycle and would ride it over to Mae's house. She told Mae that she was envious of her situation, and when Mae asked her what she meant, Rose replied: "Having a place of your own. Decent job. Nice boyfriend. I wish I could get away from that fucking house too." When Mae asked her why, she replied: "That fucking father of yours, that's why. He's made my life a fucking misery. I hate everything about him. He's a filthy, disgusting, selfish pig. A stinking, horrible bully. I wish I'd never set eyes on him!" She went on to tell Mae that she hated his perverted sexual demands and her work as a prostitute. She then told her that she was thinking of leaving him.

Rose had read an advert in the local paper for a singles night at The Bristol Hotel, on the Bristol Road. She turned up when they were holding a Country & Western night and met the barman, Alan, and the landlady, Yvonne, who made her feel welcome. After a couple of drinks, Yvonne introduced her to the Cellar Man, Steve. He had bright ginger hair, his ears stuck out and he was known by the nickname 'Lurch'. Rose became a

197

regular at the bar in the hotel and started going to the Country and Western 'do's' there.

She was soon on first name terms with Yvonne and Alan and a few of the others, and she would often go up to Steve's room with him. Fred beat her black and blue when she returned home from a New Years Eve party on the 1st January 1991 at the hotel, despite her hitting him back.

It's very possible that Rose wanted to leave Fred to be with Steve. She had conversations with Mae later on where she told her that she wanted to be with someone 'normal' and who 'appreciated her.'

To get further away from Fred, Rose rented a bed-sitting room for herself in Stroud Road, not far from Cromwell Street, without telling Fred. She called herself 'Mandy West' and explained to her landlord that she was a 'nanny' at Cromwell Street, who "wanted to get away sometimes". She took Lucyanna with her to meet him. The top-floor flat cost her a little over £100 a month, and she furnished it herself with great care. She rented it for more than six months, visiting it regularly during the day when Fred was at work, and not leaving until late September. When she did leave, she left all of her possessions, including a brand new vacuum cleaner in it's box, behind.

After her sudden disappearance, the landlord went to 25 Cromwell Street in search of 'Mandy' West, but instead found Fred West, who knew nothing about the flat. He told the man that there was no 'Mandy' who lived there, but there were two Rosemary's. At that moment, Rose went to the front door to see who Fred was talking to. She was scared and embarrassed and denied that she had anything to do with the flat. Either Fred didn't believe Rose, or he saw an opportunity to get his hands on items he could sell on, but he told the man that he would "clear the place out in an hour" and kept his word.

In his interviews with his solicitor Howard Ogden in 1994, Fred claimed that "Rose had flats all over Gloucester" that he "knew nothing about."

Just as in Fred's previous relationship with Rena, him and Rose would have sex as a way of making up. Tara West recalled that when she was 10-years-old Fred sat the family down to watch a pornographic movie. "He called it sex education. I was a bit uncomfortable with it all", she recalled. But Tara and her siblings also had to get used to their parents having sex in front of them at any time of the day. "Dad would come into the kitchen and Mum would be cooking dinner. They would start having sex. We would just ignore them."

On the 28th March 1992, Walter West died at Ledbury Cottage Hospital, aged 78. He had been ill for a long time, since a farm accident left him with only one good lung. At the funeral five days later, John West vowed never to talk to Fred again as he was upset that Fred hadn't visited their father in hospital before he passed away. Fred attended the funeral with Rose and Anne Marie at St Bartholomew's church and Walter was laid to rest next to his wife, Daisy.

Between 1972 and 1992, there were 31 instances of the West children being treated at various A&E Departments, as well as contact with other health care departments and agencies. None of these resulted in a referral to Social Services. The West family members were treated for Thrush (including Fred) and a minor for Gonorrhoea, but there was a catalogue of injuries to tendons, fingers and chests. One child was seen with scratches and bruises around her breasts with three different explanations given for how they got there, including the child saying her mother did it when she was naughty. A child suffered a finger flexor tendon injury caused by a scissor cut – later described as falling on a knife – a child who hurt her chest and finger after "falling off a gate" as well as lacerations between the toes of the children, some supposedly self-inflicted. There was also a child with an injured finger, a different child with an injured finger caused by a sledgehammer, a child with a cut hand when it was said it was put through a plate glass window, a different child with a cut thumb seen on the same day and various ankle injuries. Explanations for these injuries were various and were somehow only later seen as unconvincing.

There were also frequent referrals of the children to Ophthalmology Departments with Squints, and a far from always co-operative response from Fred and Rose, with many missed appointments. A number of the children also required speech therapy, but Fred and Rose were hostile to the idea.

Mae had thrush once and Fred made her tell him all about it. She was also once reading a pamphlet on Cystitis and he completely took over and went through it all with her because there was a diagram of a woman's insides.

When Louise West was due to start secondary school, Fred and Rose decided not to send her. They told the authorities that she had moved away to live with a relative. She was sometimes sent to pick up her brothers and sisters from school, waiting around the corner so as not to be seen by any of her former teachers. Since the age of eleven, and Louise had started to have her periods, both Fred and Rose encouraged her to have boyfriends. Rose even put her hands on Louise's vagina to check how sexually developed she'd become.

She had been told that since Mae had moved out it was her responsibility to help Rose more around the house. The truth was that Fred had already started to sexually abuse her and didn't want the school to notice the signs. The abuse started out as touching and groping until one day it went further…

Rose West

Fred West

8 THE FINAL LET-OFF

One afternoon towards the end of May 1992, Rose went out of the house shopping, leaving Fred upstairs while the five young children sat downstairs watching television. Fred came down and asked Tara to make him a cup of tea. At the same time he made up an excuse to get his 13-year-old daughter, Louise, to follow him back upstairs. Once she had entered the Black Magic bar-room, he closed the door behind her and began his assault. He told her to sit on the small sofa under the window. Fred then adjusted the video camera opposite them and pointed it towards her. He laid her down, took off her clothes and knelt down in front of her after unzipping his own trousers, telling her to "look at the television". She was terrified and shouted: "Stop, Dad, it hurts". He then turned her over and abused her from behind, before turning her on her back again on the sofa and raping her a second time. He used lubricant, but no condom.

The other children were aware that something bad was happening and tried to find a way to intervene. Shortly after, the children heard her scream: "No, don't!" Tara got Barry to knock on the door, which he kept doing. Fred shouted out: "What do you fucking want?" Barry told him that his cup of tea was ready, and Fred grew annoyed at the interruption and stormed down the stairs. He started to shout at Barry, but Tara asked if she could go upstairs, which normally she wasn't allowed to, to see Louise who she realised had been raped. Louise told Tara that she had been penetrated four times, twice anally and twice vaginally, and at one point partially strangled. Tara later recalled: "All she said was, 'He's raped me'. She was hysterical. I couldn't get a word out of her." The girl was severely shaken.

When Rose returned home, Louise told her mother that she had been raped by Fred, but Rose didn't seem to care and simply replied: "Oh well! You were asking for it!"

Fred later attempted to blackmail Louise and warned her: "You mustn't say anything, you know, because I'll go to prison for five years. We'll all be split up, and you need a Mum and Dad at your stage of life." It is believed that threats like these are what caused her to eventually withdraw her complaint in 1993. Fred made no further approaches towards her, other than to ask her if she was "bigger" and whether she had "put anything inside herself".

The sofa in The Black Magic bar

The following week he took Louise to one side and told her he "Would have to do it again", because "there were two layers that needed breaking" and, as she recalled later, it "could be dangerous if he didn't do it" as a "man might hurt me in future." Later that week Fred kept his promise, repeating the rape in exactly the same way in the Black Magic bar. Throughout the ordeal, she was crying and begging Fred to stop, but he just replied that "It'll be OK this time. I wont need to do it again."

When she went back downstairs she found that Rose had returned. Louise went into the bathroom on the ground-floor, but Fred and Rose followed her inside. Fred told Rose what he had done and invited her to examine Louise to verify that she was no longer a virgin, which she gladly did. Rose then asked her: "Well, what did you expect?" and then told Louise to get off to bed.

Before she went to bed, Fred told her that he wanted her to go with him the following day, a Saturday, to a warehouse he was painting near Reading. When they arrived at the deserted building the following morning, he raped her again, despite her shouting and trying to push him off. After he had finished, and they were sitting in his van, he patted her thigh and said: "I'll leave it alone now".

Tara herself escaped her father's attentions and later said: "I realise now that Dad was only interested in his natural daughters. He thought they were his property. Because I wasn't his daughter he left me alone." Tara later revealed to one of her school friends the gist of what had occurred, and this friend went home and told her mother. The mother was sufficiently alarmed to inform Social Services, who in turn passed their concern on to the police. There were also suggestions of firearms and knives in the house.

Shortly after 18:00 on the 2nd August, Police Constable Steven Burnside was told about the possibility of Fred West sexually abusing one of his daughters. Whilst he was on patrol, a girl from Beaufort Comprehensive School was joking with him in Cromwell Street when one of a group of three twelve-year-olds talking to him suddenly asked him: "What would you do if your friend was being assaulted?" The banter continued for a moment, and then the constable asked who was being assaulted. The girl told him that she was worried that her friend might have been "mucked about with" by her father, who had taken a video while he was doing so. The children told the officer that the girls' surname was something like Guest or Chest. The following day, after checking the electoral role and educational records, the name was clarified as West.

A case conference was held by police and Social Services on the 4th August, and a joint investigation was agreed upon. Social Services were to deal with an Emergency Protection Order regarding the children, and the police were to obtain a search warrant, which was granted the following day.

On the 6th August, the search warrant was executed at 09:00 by two detectives and four police women. The officers told Rose that they wanted to speak to Fred, but he was not there as he had already left for work. As the female police officers filed past Rose and into the ground-floor living room where the children were watching TV, one of the officers explained that they had come to search the premises for pornographic material following a serious allegation of child abuse.

Rose flew into a rage. While the first police officer was still trying to explain what was happening, she started shouting abuse at the officers at the door, and then turned and ran into the downstairs living room, where she screamed at her five children. "You don't have to say anything!", she told them. She told Louise to keep her "fucking mouth shut". She then started to lash out at a woman police officer, hitting her repeatedly, first with her fists and then with her feet. Finally, one of the male detectives grabbed her arm, twisted it behind her back, and arrested her for obstruction. Rose's reply was succinct: "Fuck off, you bastard!"

At 09:05 Rose was further arrested for aiding and abetting the rape of a young girl. Tara remembered: "We had just got up. There was a loud knock on the front door and somebody shouted 'Police, Open Up!' A few minutes later I heard Mum scream 'You're not taking my kids'. The police drove her away in a van."

Immediately after her arrest she was taken to Gloucester police station, while the first search of the house was started by the male detectives while the female constables tried to comfort the Wests children. They explained to Tara, Louise, Barry, Rosemary and Lucyanna why they had come and then gave them breakfast. They arranged for them to be taken to a local authority home nearby to be introduced to the team of Social Workers who would be looking after them.

Rose's Solicitor, Leo Goatley, recalled: "She was quite agitated at being at a police station and asking what on Earth this was all about. It was as though this was an unwanted and unnecessary interlude or interruption in her life. At that stage there was nothing to suggest she was lying and it didn't make me think that something terrible had happened to Heather and that she was no longer alive."

In interviews with DC Hazel Savage that day, Rose remained evasive, even on basic questions such as Heather's age and if she had been reported as missing. She told the detective that on the day Heather left, she had come home from doing her shopping one Friday "as per usual" and Heather had simply gone. "She took whatever she had in her room. Her personal things. Clothing…She refused to know about all the normal things of living…She went off to Devon with a lady…I didn't want her to stay here, not in those circumstances, not if she was going to practice what she was doing. She was a lesbian…And that was why she wanted to leave. She said it wasn't good for the rest of the children."

It was not until after 14:00 that the police finally located Fred. He was carrying out general repairs at a home for autistic people, the Stroud Court Community Trust, near the village of Nailsworth. He was on-call to perform routine maintenance there, retained his own set of keys and often worked unsupervised late into the night. At 14:15 he was arrested for rape in the small village of Bisley. When he was cautioned, he replied: "What…fucking hell, I know what this is – it's down to jealousy." When he was in the police car, he laughed at the charges. "Absolute rubbish. Lies, all lies…I never touched her."

Although numerous objects of sexual paraphernalia – including 99 pornographic videos of both home-made and commercial nature – were discovered in the house, police did not find the video showing Fred raping his daughter Louise. They did, however, find photographs of two of the West children posing naked.

Louise West made a full statement through a specially-trained Solicitor, describing her father's actions, the fact the sexual abuse had begun 2 years previously when she was aged just 11, and that her mother had been indifferent to her plight. The five children were removed and an Emergency Protection Order was granted at Tewkesbury Magistrates Court.

Police found a note in Rose's handwriting, signed by both her and Fred, which said:

I, Rose, will do exactly what I am told, when I am told, without questions, without losing my temper, for a period of three months from the end of my next period, as I think I owe this to Fred

R.P *West*
F. *West*

Stephen West recalls: "I was at work and got a phone call from a CID officer who said they wanted to see me about a serious matter. He told me Dad had been arrested for raping a girl, and Mum had been taken into custody as well. I rang Mae and she picked me up from work and we went home. We weren't too surprised because we knew what he was like."

That evening, Fred was interviewed by the police. He was represented by local Solicitor Howard Ogden. "I first got to know Fred West through representing him in 1992 in linked criminal and care proceedings. The allegation in the Crown Court was of rape and buggery of one of his daughters who was brought up with the purpose of being 'broken in' by their dad." He later recalled: "The earliest recollections of Fred are of this quite jovial chap who was obviously quite outgoing, who worked hard and he was just an ordinary bloke."

Howard Ogden

Fred painted a picture of himself to the police as a straight-forward, ordinary, working man who loved his wife and family and who was the victim of vicious and un-founded allegations. "I left home this morning with a bloody family and a home and tonight I'm in prison and I ain't done nothing…I mean, we got what we want. We don't mess with our kids. We've got everything." He suggested that Louise had made up the allegations to get attention. "I got no problems with my children at all. They think the world of their father as far as I know, all of them, I mean."

To the shock of the police interviewing him, Fred began to reveal some extraordinary and bizarre details, such as the dates of Rose's and his children's periods. "Like, my wife's on now. I think Louise is due because Louise is normally with her mother."

He told the interviewing officers that "Me and my wife leads an active sex life...We make love every night, I mean perhaps twice, it just depends on what happens...I mean you'll find harnesses, you'll find bloody God knows what in my home that we make up and things we do. You'll find tapes where we've been out in the van, out in the lanes, making love, and we're not frightened to show it. We enjoy our sex life, but not with our children." They also, he explained, had "mates that come in and share our life with us...come in and sit with us, and perhaps make love with us, like."

At 21:30 that evening, as his second formal police interview finished, he suddenly announced that "As far as I know, Tara, Louise, Rosemary and Babs should still be virgins. Nobody should ever have gone near them." When he was told that his daughter Louise was saying that he had taken her virginity, he replied: "Well, prove it then, if she says that."

On the 7th August, all of the children were removed jointly by the police and Social Services and lodged at Cowley Manor in Cheltenham (then a County Council conference centre), in order to keep them together. They were medically examined and the results showed disturbing signs of both physical and sexual abuse.

The children were interviewed jointly by police and Social Services. The interviews of some of the children took a long time; in one case the interview took approximately one and a half days to complete. One of the children mentioned a family joke to a Social Worker, that "Heather is under the patio" of 25 Cromwell Street. The police officer who was present does not, however, recall the comment being made and at a time when the focus of the investigation was on the child protection issues, such a brief and out of context comment was neither recorded or followed up. At the time, Heather's whereabouts were only of interest because she could have provided additional information regarding the investigation.

From this time no further comment was made to either police or Social Services staff regarding Heather and the patio until the late spring/early summer of 1993.

Anne Marie was taken to Tuffley Police Station to make a statement by DC Hazel Savage and another detective. She was upset that Fred and Rose were trying were trying to make Louise out to be a liar and treat her the same way they had treated her. She told the detectives how Fred raped her when she was just 8-years-old and how Rose had helped him. She also told them about Fred and Rose experimenting with semen and artificial insemination but left a lot out. She also told the detectives about Heather disappearing in strange circumstances and how she hadn't been able to find any trace of her. Because she was co-operating with the police, Mae recalled that "Anna was effectively kicked out of the family. Mum put the phone down every time she rang up."

DC Savage then went to interview Anne Marie's former husband, Chris Davis, who also told her that she should find and interview Heather. He told her that Heather would know more than anyone, but had disappeared and that he and Anne Marie had tried to find her but came up empty handed.

Fred West was later confronted with details of Anne Marie's first 25-page statement and called it: "Rubbish. Absolute lies", and said that "I never touched her". He then suggested that Anne Marie had taken the wording of the statement from a book. "It's all made up…she's copied it from somewhere…there ain't one blade of truth in it as far as I'm concerned." He then told the police to go to Cromwell Street and "Knock on any door and they'll tell you those children are looked after."

During his three police interviews that day, Fred denied everything and chose to instead play the victim, condemning the children for "ganging up" on him as it became clear that they were supporting Louise's allegations. He said that two of his daughters may have wanted to "go into care" and had made up the story in order to get there. He suggested that Louise was making the allegation up because she was jealous that he was paying more attention to one of her younger sisters than to her. He even told the police that he had found Louise in bed with a boyfriend and that she was angry with him for "grounding her" after a gang of girls at her school had threatened her with a knife because she had stolen one of their boyfriends.

He challenged the police to charge him and take the case to court, claiming that the 'lie' had "damn near been rehearsed." He said: "I'll tell you what, this has got to go to court, and they have all got to stand up there and be counted on why these lies have come out like this, or who is instigating them…I never thought my children would tell lies about me." He then blamed the case on their "jealousy" of the better conditions of his "flat upstairs" in Cromwell Street. He was finally charged on three counts of rape and one count of buggery against his daughter.

He was later seen by his son, Stephen. Fred was worked up and crying in a way that Stephen had never seen him before. He seemed to Stephen to be scared to death.

Fred: They've got medical evidence that I touched your sister, but I haven't touched her, it was one of her boyfriends.
Stephen: Well, I doubt it, she's only a schoolgirl, Dad
Fred: No, c'mon, it is one of them. But they're going to have me for it. You've got to say you done it when you were a kid. I'm telling you. You've got to say it! (He then turned nasty) Look, you either do it, or I'll kill you

when I get out of here

Stephen: Don't be stupid. I'm not sticking my neck out. I'll get put in prison

Fred: No, you won't

Fred told him that if he said he was only 12-years-old when he did it, the police wouldn't be able to touch him and the case would crumble. As Stephen got up to leave, Fred hugged him and said to him: "I mean it boy, I mean it".

To take the burden off his Dad, Stephen made a statement to the police claiming that it was him who had committed the offences against his sister Louise, as he thought he would be better able to serve the time in prison than his father. The police officers laughed at his attempt to get Fred off the hook. He was later charged with wasting police time.

Rose West was interviewed by the police and she insisted that she had never sexually abused her children. Then she exercised her right to remain silent during her interrogation. The police were left with no choice other than to release her pending further investigations.

When she got home she told Mae to leave and disappear as the police would want to interview her and was worried that she might say something incriminating. Stephen and Mae were threatened and told to keep their mouths shut and to not say anything about what they saw or experienced in the house. "We knew what the consequences were. We knew we would get the worst beating of our lives", recalled Stephen.

Rose told Mae: "It's not that I don't know he's tried it on with you girls. But to say I'd help him do something like that. It's horrible, Mae! Fucking police, they haven't got a clue! Nor have Social Services! All they want to do is break up this family. They want to take my babies away from me. I haven't done anything!"

Rose's sister-in-law, Barbara Letts, went to 25 Cromwell Street to help Rose pack some clothes to send to the children in care. Rose broke down and cried. She was able to continue living at Cromwell Street and Mae and Stephen returned home to live with her while she and Fred awaited their trial.

That night, Rose telephoned Anne Marie (who was going to be used as a witness for the prosecution) and threatened her. There was no greeting, just the threat: "If you think anything of me or your Dad, especially your Dad, you'll keep your mouth shut!" she then slammed the phone down.

Mae recalled that: "I went with Mum to see her solicitor and he read Louise's statement to us. It was awful. I realised what she had suffered could easily have happened to me, and I felt that I could almost have signed my own name at the bottom."

Stephen asked Louise "if it was true, and she said 'Yes, it is.' I believed her because I knew what Dad was like and how he often threatened to have young girls."

During the police investigations, Rose's brother, Andrew Letts, was made to strip naked by the police. One of the younger children in care had reported being raped by one of the Letts brothers, and they were looking for a distinguishing feature that she'd reported. Andrew didn't have this feature and the police immediately apologized. None of the Letts brothers were ever charged.

On the 8th August, Fred West was remanded in custody in Gloucester Prison as a Rule 43 prisoner, a category reserved for sexual offenders who are segregated from the rest of the prison population. He was concerned for his own welfare whilst in prison on these charges and had asked the authorities to be segregated.

His son, Stephen, went to see him. "He started saying that he had been covering up stuff from all of us. He said that his life began when we went to sleep at night. I asked him what he meant but he wouldn't elaborate. He said it had been going on for years and went back to when he was in Scotland. He said it was a worse crime than anyone could imagine and the police would find out soon and he would never leave prison again."

Discussions began between the police and the Crown Prosecution Service in regards to tracing Heather West to see if she had been abused and they resulted in an agreement not to pursue this, in light of the investigation of other serious allegations.

Fred West admitted in police interviews to his experimentation with semen from Rose's clients. He admitted to police that all he and his wife used to do was: "Just shove it in the bag and take it with us. We go up the hills…and use it the same night…within an hour and a half", because "What you must remember is whenever a coloured bloke makes love to her, then I make love to her within half an hour of that…because that is our thing, like." He also explained to the police that he had been experimenting with ways to film inside a woman's vagina, and had even found a medical device for the purpose. "It was left at home by a midwife one time", and he and Rose adapted it to their own purpose. "We put it in her, look in with a torch and things like that, and try to film inside as well. It shows the womb, like, inside."

The following day Rose visited Fred. One topic of quiet conversation concerned the whereabouts of the missing incriminating videotapes. Amid a discussion of whether their son Stephen would be capable of a plumbing repair that seemed to be necessary on the top floor of their house, there seemed to be the suggestion that some videotapes might need to be removed.

Following this suggestion, on the 11th August, 25 Cromwell Street was searched again by the police. At 08:30 Rose was re-arrested and interviewed on ten separate occasions throughout the day. When it was put to Rose that her children had at various times been beaten in front of other men, had their bottoms painted with rude words, had photographs taken while they were naked, had been made to watch pornographic videos, had been put in boiling water, had had their trousers pulled down and been whipped, their mother called the allegations "rubbish, absolute rubbish". The police then asked her to explain the vast collection of rubber masks and suits, vibrators and dildos, and other sexual paraphernalia that they had recovered from Cromwell Street, but she refused to discuss the matter. When they asked her about a video that had been found showing her being tied up in the back of a van and sexually assaulted, she declined to answer. When the officers asked her whether she had helped Fred in the rape of Louise, she denied it.

The police decided to try to trace Heather in an effort to corroborate Anne Marie's claims of sexual abuse, but enquiries with the Inland Revenue and the Social Security found no records which showed Heather was alive.

Rose told the police that she had no idea of the whereabouts of her eldest daughter, Heather. She said that Heather had "hung around the house for six months and then left." The police then asked her where Heather was now, and she replied "I don't know". She was then asked whether she had any contact with Heather and bluntly replied: "Not since she's left home, none." She told the police officers that "I went out shopping one day, as per usual on a Friday, and come back home and she'd gone." She was unsure whether Heather had ever been reported officially as a missing person. "As far as I'm concerned she hasn't just disappeared, she made a conscious decision to leave." DC Savage then suggested that losing contact with her first-born child must have been distressing, to which Rose replied: "It's been awful." DC Savage then revealed that the results of her checks using Heather's National Insurance number and the records of the DSS and Tax Office had shown there to be no trace of Heather for four years, which meant that she had not taken a regular job, claimed any sort of state benefit or even visited a doctor in that time. This was almost impossible unless Heather had completely changed her identity, left the country illegally, or was dead. Rose replied that the police must "believe what they want". Rose said that Heather had told her that she intended to leave home, and she claimed she had said to Heather "Please don't do so – we've got more to talk over". Rose then claimed that she had gone out shopping for approximately two hours and when she came back, Heather had gone. DC Savage asked her if Heather had any money when she left, to which she replied: "I don't know."

After lunch, the police tried again. This time Rose said that she believed Heather had left home in a Mini driven by another woman. This had apparently happened while she was out shopping. It was suggested to Rose that she did not know whether her daughter was alive or dead. "Is there any reason why she shouldn't be alive, apart from having accidents and stuff? If my child don't want to know, what can I do about it?", she said.

In an interview at 17:22, Rose claimed she could "remember now" why Heather had left home:

Rose: Why I didn't pursue Heather to sort of stay home was Heather had told me, and certain things pointed to the fact, that Heather was a lesbian…and wanted a life of her own…And that was why she wanted to leave. She said it wasn't good for the rest of the children.
DC Savage: Are you a lesbian?
Rose: No
DC Savage: Have you ever been a lesbian?
Rose: No…I know in my own mind that she's getting on with her own life…One of her friends told me.

Rose added that she did not want the other children being exposed to Heather's sexuality and had given her £600 to help her on her way, completely contradicting what she had earlier told the police about not knowing if Heather had any money when she left.

She contradicted herself even further when she maintained that she had heard from Heather on the telephone "a while ago", adding that "she just rings to say she's all right", but that Fred might not be aware of it because "she doesn't want to speak to him."

Charmaine's whereabouts were also discussed and Rose told the officers that "She went with her mother and stayed with her Mum…because it's what she requested."

Further enquiries conducted with Chris Davis revealed that Heather had confided in him just how unhappy she was shortly before her disappearance and of her desire to leave home. He elaborated that although Heather had not divulged any details as to her enduring any sexual abuse, he had been so concerned about her welfare that he had offered to confront Fred and Rose, although Heather had dissuaded him from doing so. He then suggested that the police may wish to speak to Heather to get further details about the abuse she suffered.

Rose was formally charged with 'causing or encouraging the commission of unlawful sexual intercourse with a girl under the age of sixteen' and with 'Cruelty to a child'.

After spending the night in the cells at Gloucester police station, Rose appeared at Gloucester Magistrates Court on the 12th August. She was granted bail on condition that she did not communicate with her younger children, her step-daughter Anne Marie or her husband, Fred.

Mae recalled: "Mum was in a bit of a state and said she wanted to sleep on her own upstairs. She wandered into the living room as if she was drunk and called out my name. She fell on the settee and was mumbling. I checked the bar to see what she'd drunk but nothing had been touched. I looked by the side of her bed and saw an empty box of Anadin with all 48 tablets gone". At 01:50 on the 13th August, Rose had her stomach pumped at Gloucestershire Royal Hospital. Mae remembered: "She looked old and frail, and nothing like Mum. It was as if all the energy had drained from her body."

On the 14th August, Fred and Rose were interviewed further about Heather's whereabouts and both said she had gone to a holiday camp in Devon.

During an interview, Fred told the police more about his sexual life with Rose and that he had tied her to a five-barred gate in Minchinhampton late one night and made love to her. "She wanted me too, but there were other blokes doing it to her. Sometimes she came home and she'd been well fucking beaten, mind. She had some deep fucking cuts in her arse and back and that, where she'd been whipped."

He continued with the same lie in regards to Heather's disappearance too. "She went through the door laughing her head off, and she said: 'Tell Mae and Stephen I'll get in touch with them or something'." When he was asked if Heather had got in touch with them, he replied: "I don't think so", and then added that he had seen her himself "about twelve months ago" in Gloucester, when she had been "dealing in drugs" with Shirley, whose surname he had "the vague idea was Robinson."

When Mae and Stephen visited him, Stephen remembered: "He started talking really strangely. He was crying and said that he'd done stupid things at night…the worst crime that we could ever imagine. He became all pathetic, and for the first time in our lives said 'I love you'. It was the first time I had seen him cry. He seemed scared to death."

In their efforts to gather further evidence, police and Social Services also spoke with Mae, who, having spoken with Louise and having learned that she no longer wanted to see her father Fred charged, denied that she had suffered any sexual molestation.

Louise began to backtrack on her story, later saying that she didn't want to be responsible for breaking up her family and she missed her parents, so Mae withdrew her statement too. Mae commented: "She didn't want Dad charged. She thought that she would be allowed to go back to her home if the whole thing went away. I was in a similar position so we agreed that, to keep the family together, I'd lie to the police. We thought that if the charges were dropped then all our younger brothers and sisters could come back to Cromwell Street and we'd be a family again...she didn't want to give evidence against Dad, and she wanted her life to return to normal. I couldn't say anything against him myself because I thought – well, he's our Dad after all. I was also scared of losing my Mum, who was sticking by Dad. It put us all in a very difficult position over loyalties and doing the right thing."

Anne Marie also retracted her statement, calling it "a figment of my imagination". She had become scared that Fred would get off after Mae and Louise had withdrawn their statements. "I knew who Fred and Rose could get at – me and my two children. And I knew that they wouldn't hesitate to do it."

When Chris Davis found out that she had retracted her statement, he said: "We had one helluva fight in the street about it. One fuckin' helluva row...I wouldn't say that she had been threatened by them. What I would say was that she was scared shitless of Fred and Rose. If they got off, she was dead. That's how she put it...DC Savage came to see me at my mother's. I told her if she wanted any information about what went on from 1987 onwards she better find Heather. I said Anne and me had tried to track Heather down without any success. I'd made inquiries up and down the fence. She gave me a very knowing look."

DC Hazel Savage was not convinced and believed that Anne Marie's allegations were true. She was 49-years-old and had been involved on and off with the West family since she was sent to Glasgow to fetch Rena Costello as a young WPC. She had been in and out of 25 Cromwell Street over the years investigating drug related offences involving the lodgers there. Rose was known especially to despise her and referred to her within the family as "a bitch and an arsehole."

The children had always been told that the police were not to be trusted and were the enemy. As such, they didn't like the police either, but despite being upset about them withdrawing their statements, DC Savage told them that "one good thing that's going to come out of this is that I'm going to find your sister." Mae recalled: "We didn't like Hazel, but we thought that if she'd find Heather, then that was alright with us."

In an interview with DC Savage on the 18th August, Fred told her that Rose was not responsible for anything that went on in his house. "I'm the boss and she follows. We've always lived that way...I control Rose's sex life." When he was told that Rose had been charged with sex offences, Fred was shocked, and kept repeating "this is crazy", and blaming Anne Marie for "trying to get her Mum done as well."

He said that he arranged for Rose to sleep with other men because: "I rarely get an erection...because I got injured some years ago on a motor

213

bike. I mean, it'll come up and suddenly it'll go boom…And that was how it all started with these men and because Rose likes sex…I mean if I can get an erection once a month I'm bloody lucky, you know."

He said that his children resulted from good fortune. "It sort of caught at the right time and everything connected up right." He said that after he came out of prison in 1971 he had "got lucky" and managed to father Mae and Stephen, but "then it just died. There was nothing. I mean I never got an erection then for something like about four years, five years….As far as I'm concerned if I can't do it then I should help her to get someone else to do it."

During the search of the house, police took away trunkloads of dildo's, leather underwear, whips, a bull whip, a rice flail, straps, photographs showing the erect penises of a number of naked men, photographs of two of the West children naked, a photograph of Rose sitting on a gear stick of a car, as well as photographs of her in a variety of sexual poses, including one close up of a naked, pregnant Rose exposing her vagina to the camera, having written the words 'black hole' across her stomach in lipstick. "She was expecting a black child, that's why", Fred would say when confronted with this photo in an interview. They also found pornographic magazines, some of which involved bestiality, and 99 pornographic videos. Fred's brother John may have also featured in some of the home movies. Among the videotapes was one which had a sequence called 'Fuck My Uncle'. It featured an older man with a beard – the type John West sported – and included the line: "I always thought I'd have it off with my niece one day – I didn't think you were ready for it yet."

Another videotape was of a young woman, drugged and bound, who had a clear plastic tube inserted into her vagina, through which two live mice were encouraged to enter her. Before the tube was inserted, she was raped by two men, who then had sex with each other. The film ended with them leaving the girl tied up with a lit cigarette inserted into her vagina.

Of the videotapes of Rose, they showed that she derived sexual excitement from inserting the largest vibrators and dildos into her vagina, as well as cucumbers, oranges and pint glasses. She would also urinate over a towel, or into a glass, and pour or wipe it over her naked body.

Fred is known to have told a woman friend that he had been paid £150 a time for some of his home-made tapes, which involved the humiliation and beating of women, and told her that he "didn't understand how some women survived the beatings."

Much of the collection of videotapes featured the abuse of women by groups of men, including scenes of bondage, where the victim was bound and gagged by her attackers, and then subjected to repeated sexual abuse. Several of the tapes showed a 'teacher' instructing pupils on the elements of

214

sexuality. One tape showed a young girl hung up by her arms from a beam in a basement and being abused by two men, one white, one black.

Another showed a young woman apparently drugged and gagged with masking tape, before being abused by two men. Other tapes showed lesbian scenes, scenes of bestiality, as well as scenes of 'schoolgirls' having sex with several 'teachers' at the same time and often featured anal sex.

Of the home-made tapes, all of which featured Rose (either alone or with another partner other than Fred), many centered on her love of urinating on herself in front of the camera.

Significantly, the collection of home-made videos had been updated at the beginning of 1992. One videotape in particular, made between February and March, featured timed and dated occasions in which Rose got dressed to go out, and then returned either later that evening or early the next morning, and undressed in front of the camera to show the semen stains in her underwear. On one occasion, Rose held up a small note to the camera along with her underwear showing her score out of ten for the mans performance. Straight after that, there was a sequence showing Rose urinating on a tea towel in her kitchen and wiping herself with it.

With Fred now in prison, there was no steady money coming in to the house, so Rose took a cleaning job at the Gloucester College of Art and Technology, just a five minute walk from Cromwell Street. She still had a mortgage to pay and she never charged her clients enough to get by on that income alone.

She missed Fred and for company she bought a tank of tropical fish and two mongrel dogs from a local rescue centre. One was called Benji and the other was called Oscar.

On the 9th September, Fred West was released on bail to a hostel called Carpenter House, in Edgbaston, Birmingham. Rose was allowed to visit Fred here, and did so no less than fourteen times over the next five months. Fred was even given special dispensation to return to his home at Cromwell Street for Christmas.

Inmates at Carpenter House were allowed to come and go as they pleased, provided they were back in the hostel by 23:00. Fred could receive visitors and spend his time as he chose. He went out after breakfast, sometimes returning at lunch-time, and would then go out again until late evening.

When he returned in the evenings, he always had a plastic bag with him that often contained coins and notes. "That was money I picked up on the streets during the day", he would later recall. He said he collected "near bus stops and telephone boxes" and maintained that he could "pick up £10 on a good day" and never collected less than £30 a week. His bag also contained credit cards which he said he "found in wallets lying all over the place."

He was seen talking to a number of young women during his time at the hostel, one of whom he helped when her car broke down not far from the hostel. Although he would later tell the police that he "stopped killing altogether after Heather", many of the people involved in the case remain convinced that he committed at least one murder during his time there, in spite of the fact that the police were now clearly taking a far greater interest in him.

Throughout his time in Birmingham, Fred went to great lengths to point out to the Psychologists and Social Workers who visited him that he was a man "wronged" by false accusations. He told them that he would contest the care proceedings "to show the children that he cared about them". He told a Psychologist that "I wish to clarify, in respect of our sex life, which I admit is not conventional, we have never involved the children". Professionals who interviewed him described him as "friendly and cooperative throughout."

Throughout the autumn of 1992, Fred and Rose made a determined effort to persuade the local authority to give them their children back. They presented themselves as a "caring couple" who did not argue and "discussed everything" and made all their decisions jointly. Fred and Rose also cast doubt on Anne Marie's evidence by saying that she was "living in her own fantasies" and that she had "always rejected Rose as a mother." Fred even said that if Anne Marie "got a chance to back her into a corner and have a go at her she would." He told the police that "Anna thought she was miles above Rose because Rose had half-caste children", and believed that Anne Marie had been "coerced into making these allegations" out of jealousy. He said that she "had got in with the wrong crowd" and described her as "an old baby who has always had a real mouth on her."

On the 19th November, Fred and Rose West were committed for trial on the charges against them.

Five days later, Full Care Orders were made in respect of Tara, Louise, Barry, Rosemary and Lucyanna West at Bristol County Court. Fred and Rose were denied contact with their five youngest children, unless the children themselves officially requested it. One factor that weighed against them was the fact that the children had responded favourably to being away from Cromwell Street. Another was the photographs of the naked West children as well as the huge collection of pornographic items found.

One Social Worker who dealt with Fred at the time recalled: "Fred didn't seem too bothered. Perhaps because it meant that he could do what he wanted to when he was at home without worrying about the children, but Rose clearly minded a great deal. She missed them; without them there wasn't very much to do."

But knowing how upset Rose was by the court's decision, he became un-cooperative with Social Services. He resented that for now neither he nor Rose were allowed to see their children at any time without a Social Worker present during a 'supervised' visit. A Social Worker recalled that "For the first time, Fred shut down completely. He wanted to see his children alone, and that was all he wanted. He refused to compromise." This was no doubt so he could make sure that the children did as he told them and made sure that the case against him was dropped.

The Wests did see the five children later. Rose, in particular, saw them in the park at the end of Cromwell Street, and there were also occasions on which some of the children found their way back to Cromwell Street for short, unofficial visits.

1993 soon came around, and whether or not he had, as he claimed, "stopped all that girlfriend business" and "never had no girlfriends up in Birmingham at all", he still had his Rose. She "came up by train, two or three times a week", as he would tell the police just a year later. "I had no worries". He and Rose took to camping near Edgbaston reservoir, using a small blue tent their son Stephen had given them, as well as a "green sleeping bag for a bit of a mattress. It was for me and Rose to go and make love in the woods. It was the only place we had."

Stephen recalled buying the tent because whether he and Mae were visiting with Rose or not, they would often just start to have sex outdoors more or less in full public view. They would just jump in a bush down by Edgbaston reservoir leaving Mae and Stephen to just stand there and look embarrassed. "We bought them a little tent in the end…and said 'Right, fucking go in there and stop embarrassing everybody, for Christ's sake'."

After one of these visits, Rose wrote a letter to Fred:

To my darling,

Well, you really tired me out on Saturday, but it was a wonderful day...Remember I will love you always and everything will be alright. Goodnight sweetheart.

Lots of love,

Rose

Fred was also seen carrying the tent, together with the sleeping bag, during his daily tours around the centre of Birmingham when his wife was not present. Fred would later claim that he murdered a girl while on remand in Birmingham, but he never gave any further detail and this has never been proven.

In the eyes of the bail hostel staff, Fred was a model inhabitant and in March 1993 he was allowed to move to the even less disciplined regime of a 'cluster house' in Handsworth. There was the minimum of supervision here and the house was subjected to only random checks. Rose continued to visit him here too, right up until the trial in June.

As the regime was more relaxed here, it was easier for Fred to slip back to Gloucester and Cromwell Street without permission to see Rose, Stephen and Mae. "Dad would suddenly turn up out of the blue even though he wasn't supposed to", recalled Mae.

Rose's brother, Graham, said that: "One of the children actually told me that they were threatened while Fred was in custody. He actually managed to get a letter to them saying that their lives were in danger if they carried on. They were just too scared. This is what they told me afterwards, which horrifies me to be quite honest."

Between the end of April and the beginning of May, residential Social Workers caring for the West children started to pick up on brief comments made by the children about the patio being laid at the same time as Heather left home, and also the 'family joke' of Heather being under the patio. As these comments were being made only very occasionally, to different staff and with little weight by the children, the staff in the home were unsure whether or not to treat them seriously, bearing in mind the mental state of the children.

On the 7th June 1993, Fred and Rose West faced trial at Gloucester Crown Court before Judge Gabriel Hutton. Fred faced three counts of rape and one of buggery against his daughter, while Rose faced one count of encouraging the commission of unlawful sexual intercourse and of cruelty to a child. Tara, Barry and Louise, who were to be witnesses in the trial, were prepared for their evidence by staff at the home they were staying in (they were to give evidence via video link) but on the day itself they refused to give evidence against them; Judge Hutton entered formal verdicts of 'not guilty'. Having escaped justice once again, the Wests embraced each other in the dock.

When Fred got back to Cromwell Street, he told Mae and Stephen that he had changed, and everything "would be different". Mae recalled: "He treated me like a real person. He brushed past me a couple of times as though he was thinking of trying it on, but nothing more than that. It wasn't his fault. Sexually, he was weird."

All of the younger children remained in foster care, albeit with permitted supervised visitations to Cromwell Street. Fred and Rose were unhappy that the children were not released back to them. "They're our fucking children, Rose! I am not going to sit in some fucking meeting room with some fucking busybodies just to see my own children. I want them back home and that's that!" He refused to go but Rose accepted the conditions.

When Rose met Louise, Louise recalled that she was careful with what she said. Rose came across as a caring mother who missed her children to the authorities. Louise felt guilty about breaking the family up (as she saw it) and missed her brothers and sisters but was careful not to say anything that meant Rose and Fred could get her back. She saw herself as "the pig that squealed" and was scared of what would happen to her if she ended up back in their care. Rose was offered another similar visit but Fred told her it was a waste of time. "I told you it was a waste of fucking time! You're not going again, Rose. We'll just have to forget we ever had them and that's that!" Rose said she felt the same and said if she couldn't be in control of her children then she didn't want them. They went and cleared out the children's bedrooms and threw their clothes and belongings away. "They've only got themselves to blame, haven't they, for telling a load of fucking lies", Rose told Mae.

Despite claiming to the few relatives with whom they were not already estranged by 1993 that the charges had been fabricated by police, almost all of their remaining family members severed contact with Fred and Rose.

Shortly thereafter, Anne Marie spoke again with DC Hazel Savage, further emphasizing that her mother, Rena, and half-sister, Charmaine, were also missing, as well as Heather.

With the case having collapsed, one of the first things Rose did was to sign an authorization for the police to destroy all 99 pornographic video tapes, and all sex aides that had been seized during the police search of 1992. As Mae put it: "She didn't want them in the house again because it had lost her her children. Dad was livid about losing his stuff." As the police destroyed these videotapes, it will never be known whether the torture or murder of any of the Wests victims had been recorded.

Fred thought life could carry on as before as though nothing had changed, but Rose had other ideas. Fred wanted Rose to go back on the game but she refused outright. She even refused to sleep with the father of her mixed-race children and banned him from coming to the house, which caused a lot of arguments and tension in the house. Fred stayed away a lot on various building projects and even though Rose wasn't supposed to see the younger children, Tara began to sneak away from the home she was in. Neither of them had ever paid much attention to her before and didn't mind her hanging around the house. Due to her skin colour Fred wasn't interested in her sexually, and due to her feisty nature Rose couldn't control her.

Around this time, Fred and Rose decided to have her sterilization reversed. Rose was 40-years-old, and it may well have been a way of cheering Rose up as she was missing the younger children, or more likely she and Fred wanted to forget about the children in care, pretend that they never existed, and start afresh. God only knows what kind of torture and abuse those children would have been subjected to had Rose fallen pregnant.

They visited a venereal diseases clinic in Cheltenham to ensure they were not suffering from any sexually transmitted diseases, as Fred had once contracted Thrush. "I knew we didn't have an ordinary sex life, like. That's why me and Rose went along in the first place", Fred recalled years later.

Rose discussed the idea of getting pregnant with Mae, who was against the idea. Apart from Rose's age, she knew that Social Services wouldn't let her keep a new baby. "They don't trust you to have your other children at home with you", she told her. Rose replied in her usual tone: "Fuck Social Services! It's none of their fucking business!"

Rose soon fell pregnant but the baby was growing in her fallopian tube which left her house-bound and depressed.

Fred went back to working for Carson's Contractors and now drove a white Bedford Midi van. He went back to offering lifts to young female hitchhikers on his travels around Gloucester. He picked up a "new age traveller" who told him that she "liked a bit of violence with her sex", as he told police a few months later. He again offered rooms in Cromwell Street to young girls who might need a "place to stay for a while".

Mae recalled: "We were suspicious of Mum and Dad and at that time the other children were coming back to visit and when they visited we said to them that we think the police think that Heather is under the patio. They obviously went back and told their care-workers, and them care-workers then told the Social Workers and Social Services told the police."

On the 20th August 1993, Gloucestershire Social Services held a planning meeting about the West children in care. A legal executive representing the department and the residential Social Workers caring for the West children who had been living apart attended, but the police were not in attendance. During a break, when most of those attending the meeting had broken up into small groups, the residential care workers began to talk to one another in general, discussing how the children were progressing and how they had coped with what had happened to them. Comparing stories, the Social Workers noted how the patio at home seemed to keep cropping up in conversation with the children: how it had been laid at the time their sister Heather had left and how it had become "a family joke" she was buried underneath. It appeared that the children had only mentioned it briefly and did not take it seriously, though it did appear to be on their minds. Thinking back, members of the group reckoned at least one of the children had mentioned it the first time when the inquiry began in 1992, and that it had arisen again around April or May of that year and had kept cropping up ever since.

The conversations concerning Heather were not discussed or minuted formally, but both Gloucestershire Social Services staff and the legal executive there had become sufficiently concerned to make contact with the police. Later that day the legal executive telephoned Gloucester CID to speak to DC Hazel Savage, but as she was not available had left her a message covering the conversations and comments made during the break.

Fred and Rose in the Malvern Hills in 1993

On the 23rd August, DC Savage returned the call, after which she made further enquiries to trace Heather. At her request, concerns now emerging about Heather West were set down in a letter from Gloucestershire Social Services.

DI Tony James and DC Hazel Savage had a meeting with DSI John Bennett, who asked if everything had been done to find Heather, to which they replied that it had and there was still no trace of her. "There is always the chance, Sir, she could have gone abroad, but if she has then she's managed it without having a passport in her name", he was told. DSI Bennett made some suggestions, including research of the Wests and their family tree, and DC Savage then said: "Once we've done that, Sir, the only thing left is to go and search the garden."

The detectives knew that they were listening to third-party information and needed to get something on the record, and to do that, DSI Bennett said he would get permission to interview the residential Care Workers and get access to any relevant information that might be of use. Meanwhile, the search for Heather would continue, and if they still couldn't find her, or if the Social Workers confirmed the 'patio joke', he would have the West children interviewed as well. If, after all of that, everyone stood by what they were supposed to have said and there was still no trace of Heather, then he would seriously consider a search warrant.

DC Hazel Savage went to see Anne Marie and asked her about a family joke that the children in care had mentioned to the Social Workers. The carers believed that the children were genuinely afraid of Fred and Rose and said that they didn't want to end up under the patio like their big sister Heather. Anne Marie had mentioned the same thing to the police previously which was why DC Savage wanted to clarify its origins. She told the officers that the first time she had heard it a number of the children had been sat around the kitchen table in Cromwell Street and Fred had told them that Heather was under the patio and then laughed.

On the 12th October, DC Savage discussed the lack of progress in finding Heather with DI Tony James, and six days later she submitted a written report to him seeking advice. At an impromptu meeting, DSI Bennett considered the report and discussed it with DI James and DC Savage. Further enquiries were directed and a strategy to pursue them was outlined, but the investigation was not considered to be a high priority.

Fred was still telling Mae and Stephen that he had seen Heather, once at a community centre in Gloucester and once when she had supposedly gone to visit him while he was in Birmingham.

The Wests had become paranoid about who they could trust, and who was talking about them to the police. They knew that Anne Marie was helping DC Savage, so Fred and Rose decided to sever all links with their families. Even Graham Letts found himself turned away at the door. The last to be rejected was Graham's wife, Barbara, who had been Rose's closest friend in recent years and had stood by her throughout the child abuse case. Shortly after Christmas, Barbara and her two children were visiting 25 Cromwell Street when Rose suddenly ordered them to get their coats and leave. Barbara believed it was Fred's idea. "He didn't like her having any friends. She had told Fred that she wanted to keep me as a friend. She had no others left that I know of. Then she told me that Fred didn't like me and didn't want me around. She started being funny, telling me to go."

Graham and Barbara Letts

By the 15th January 1994, the results of further enquiries regarding the whereabouts of Heather proved negative. DSI Bennett instructed the detectives to get written statements from Social Workers and then arrange for the West children in care to be interviewed.

The children in care were interviewed on video in Gloucester by both police and Social Workers following a meeting between DCI Terry Moore, DI Tony James and DC Hazel Savage on the 12th February. Following information that had been gathered from the interviews, on the 23rd February a Section 8 Police and Criminal Evidence Search Warrant was obtained to search the garden of 25 Cromwell Street for evidence of the remains of Heather West.

The Cromwell Street investigation was about to begin...

The West children in care were taken to Gloucester to be interviewed further. DC Savage called Anne Marie at home as she was getting her children ready for school and told her that police would be digging up the patio at 25 Cromwell Street later that day to look for Heather's body.

Mae was walking back to Cromwell Street from work for lunch and remembered "There was a big police van on the corner. It wasn't that close to the house and I didn't take much notice of it. As usual the door was open and I walked straight through in to find Mum lounging around."

At 13:25 the search warrant was executed at 25 Cromwell Street by Detective Chief Inspector Terry Moore, Detective Inspector Tony James and approximately 15 other officers drawn from the Gloucester Division Support Group and Operation Gemini team. The Cromwell Street investigation officially began. Mae answered the door to DCI Moore, DI James and Police Sergeant Tony Jay, who pushed straight past her and went in to the living room to find Rose, who was sat on the sofa watching an episode of 'Neighbours'. She was told that her rear garden was going to be searched in connection with the disappearance of her daughter, Heather West. She read the warrant, handed it back and told DCI Moore that "this is stupid". As he placed the warrant on the table in front her, she became hysterical, hurling foul abuse at the policemen, calling them 'bastards' and 'cunts', who she claimed were invading her home. Mae was told that she couldn't go back to work, but instead had to go and make a statement at the police station. Stephen then turned up and began shouting at the police officers and demanding that they wait until Fred arrived. Stephen had the day off from work and had gone out for a look around the shops. The police told him that they were digging up the patio whether his father was there or not.

Stephen told Mae to refuse to go to the police station, while he tried to call Fred on his mobile phone, but Fred was out of range for his phone to work. Rose was just sat, looking at the floor in a state of shock. She then phoned Fred's boss, Derek Thompson, and said: "I don't care where he is. I want him home now."

Fred was finally located at 13:50, 25 minutes after the police arrived. Derek Thompson had rung Mr Gerrard, who looked after the house where Fred was working and asked to speak to Fred. He told Fred to ring home immediately as his wife wanted him. Fred then called home and said he would leave the job he was doing and go straight home. He was barely a dozen miles from his house in Cromwell Street, working alone on the loft of an address called Hatton House in the village of Frampton Mansell. They expected him within 20 minutes. What is known for sure is that he did not go straight home.

Stephen recalled: "I kept calling Dad and although the phone was ringing, he didn't answer it. I finally got through to him just after 15:00 and he was driving. He said he would be home shortly. I asked him where he had been but he just told me not to worry. He asked what was going on, and was really calm and polite, which was very unusual for him...When I told him what was happening he asked me how Mum was and said he'd be home soon."

Under the supervision of Police Sergeant Tony Jay, police were taking both photographs and videos of the back garden, preparing to excavate, and they could see that the large patio slabs would have to be removed first, but there was little chance of much work that evening as it was due to get dark just after 16:00.

The patio. Heather's body would be found half way down on the left hand side

Kitchen of 25 Cromwell Street. Shirley Robinson's body would be discovered just below the door on the right.

The view from the kitchen to the 'children's area'

The Black Magic Bar

Rose's bedroom

The children's bedroom in the basement

The Excavation Team

DC Savage told Mae that quite frankly they were looking for her sister's body. Mae asked if that meant Heather was dead, to which Hazel replied: "I think you know what I'm on about."

17:30

The team assigned to the garden eventually left, with one officer left on the spot to stand guard all night. Fred's boss reported that he had left the site where he was working about an hour after he had been told to rush home and it was about 3 hours after that when he did finally arrive. It has never been established what he did or where he went during this period. DSI John Bennett gave the opinion that this was 'thinking time' for him. Fred's own account of passing out in a lay-by, after inhaling the fumes having left the lids off some paint pots, is quite frankly laughable.

17:40

Fred finally returned home ten minutes after the police left. Stephen recalled: "He didn't whistle or call out as he usually did. He just strolled in." As Stephen told him what had been going on, he appeared to be more worried about the electricity meter, which he had been routing directly from source in such a way that it did not show on the meter. "Mum started doing the washing up and he went over to talk to her. They were whispering all the time and went upstairs for a bit so that they could talk on their own. I don't know what was said but I went down to the station to make my statement."

Different interview teams were set up to interview Fred and Rose West when they were to be brought in for questioning. Lines of questioning were determined by the Senior Investigating Officer, who was Detective Superintendent John Bennett. After each interview, the relevant team was debriefed initially by the office manager, DI Mike Wilson. Significant events were then immediately brought to the attention of the Senior Investigating Officer.

The tape recording of the interview was first entered into a paper system in the Major Incident Room and recorded as an exhibit and then transcribed at either Gloucester, Cheltenham or Tewkesbury Police Stations and then entered on to the HOLMES computer network.

The transcriptions were reviewed by the Senior Investigating Officer and if necessary the interview strategy was changed or actions raised for detectives to explore and validate what was being said in the interview. Despite the volume of tapes, the transcribers were rarely more than 2 x 45 minute interviews behind.

All interviews with Fred and Rose were to be tape recorded in purpose built interview rooms at either Gloucester or Cheltenham Police Stations. They were conducted in the presence of a solicitor or other legal representative and appropriate adults. Appropriate adults, under the Code of Practice of the Police and Criminal Evidence Act 1984, are people who are not police officers or solicitors who have a responsibility to safeguard the rights and welfare of suspects held at police stations.

19:40

Fred presented himself at Gloucester Police Station, where he was voluntarily interviewed by DC Hazel Savage and DC Robert Vesty ten minutes later. He was confident that he could put the police off the scent and declined to have his solicitor present. In the interview he couldn't remember Heather's date of birth or her age, and he had "no idea" where she was. All he knew was that she had left home years before to go away with her "lesbian friend", a girl who had gone to his house to collect her. He remembered this girl clearly: "She had a red miniskirt on just about to the bottom of her knickers. You know, if she bent, it lifted like that – you could see everything", he winked. "Heather obviously didn't want nothing to do with us, or she'd have been back home. I mean, Stephen left home, Mae left home, but they've all come back. I don't want any of my children to leave home", he explained. He later added that he had even been considering buying 23 Cromwell Street for Mae and Stephen, now that his own mortgage was almost paid off.

"I've no idea where she is...I think I've seen her quite a few times, actually", he told the interviewing officers. He said he had seen Heather recently in Birmingham. "She was more of a lady...Her hair was expensively done". He claimed that Heather was his biggest fan, but "Heather had summat against Rose, for some unknown reason. Every time Rose spoke to her, she bloody insulted her, and walked away. But me and Heather was *very* close, which all of them will tell you. I mean, me and Heather built half our home together."

Fred then told DC Savage that he didn't want to snitch on Heather by reporting her missing to the police and then suggested that she had become a prostitute and a drug dealer.

DC Savage: You don't go inside just because you're a missing person.
Fred: Ah! What Heather's up to is a different story. You name it, Heather's up to it...I think Heather was supplying the whole of Cromwell Street, somehow...Lots of different girls who disappear take different names and go into prostitution.

He said that he had learnt through speaking to Heather on the phone that she had "umpteen names". He told the interviewing officers that Heather was "into drugs...because she gave bloody drugs" to her brother Barry when she was just 7-years-old. "He went up on the flipping church roof and thought he could fly."

He then told the police that Rose had given him £600 to give to Heather to help her get started, but he had only given £100 to her and spent the rest of it on a Transit van, telling Rose that he was paying for it by weekly installments.

DC Savage: Is she under the patio at your house?
Fred: No!
DC Savage: I cannot rest until I know Heather is safe and well…That's all I want.
Fred: If I knew that I'd be the first one to tell you.

DC Savage then asked him why there seemed to be a 'family joke' amongst his children that Heather was 'underneath the patio'. Fred then laughed loudly.

Fred: Oh, for God's sake! I mean, you believe it? Just suppose you did (murder her). I mean, you're not going to sit there and say "you're sister's under the patio". I mean, I think we better pack it up, Hazel. We're talking rubbish, aren't we? I mean, you're digging me place up. Carry on doing it!
DC Savage: Where is she Fred?
Fred: You find her, and then I'll be happy. That's all I can say. You'd have dug that up for nothing. But you put my patio back level!

Fred was interviewed for a second time a while later. Again, he refused the offer of a solicitor and began rambling on about his last contacts with Heather and why he didn't report her as 'missing'. "She was bringing drugs from somewhere and taking them up to schools, recruiting schoolkids." He didn't report her as missing because he didn't want her to be arrested. He again said that he had seen her in Birmingham, and that she had once threatened his brother John with a "two by four" piece of wood because he had "put his hand on her head", which he described "as the reason I thought she was a lesbian" and that he had heard from her on the telephone.

He then started to ramble on about his previous meetings with DC Savage regarding a thief called Frankie Stephens and the previous drug dependent lodgers he had once housed. DC Savage grew tired of Fred deflecting her questions and brought the interview back on track.

DC Savage: What can we do to find Heather and find Heather quickly?
Fred: I'm going out from here in a few minutes and see what I can do. If you want me I'll be at home all day tomorrow. I ain't going to work tomorrow.

Rose West was interviewed voluntarily using a portable tape recorder by DS Terence Onions and WPC Deborah Willetts in the Black Magic Bar room on the first floor of 25 Cromwell Street. The interview lasted until 20:41. DS Onions told Rose that the police were there because they were concerned about where Heather might be, and in all of the questions asked to her, Rose's replies were always kept as short as possible and she never went in to any great detail. She said that Heather had left because she was unhappy at school and was "having arguments with the teachers…she got suspended…"

She confirmed that she withdrew £600 from a bank account, but couldn't remember which one. "I gave it to my husband. I had shopping to do that day. Things were pretty tricky. She said she would speak to him and sort things out. I went and did my shopping and when I came back she had gone."

Rose said that there may have been raised voices over Heather wanting to leave, and then told a ridiculous story about why she thought her daughter was a lesbian:

Rose: I had a problem with her because I knew what she was. That was what made it tricky with the other children. She was a lesbian, as far as I know.

DS Onions: She was a very young girl. How did you know that?

Rose: One particular incident, her uncle was talking to her. He said to her about boyfriends or something and he said, you know, you had better watch it like, because they get up to tricky things. She said "If any boy put his hand on my knee I'd put a fucking brick over his head."

Rose was then asked again about which bank account the £600 came out of and claimed that she could not remember. "I was upset at the time. I was upset…What do you think? I'm a fucking computer? In the last 18 months I have had fucking hell! What more do you want?"

She then explained that Heather refused to even talk to her before she left and "just sat in the chair". She said that Heather never told her where she was going, but did tell Fred, and that she never asked Fred where their daughter had gone.

DS Onions then pleaded with Rose to tell them where Heather was. "The reason why we have come round here is because there have been extensive inquiries since the inquiry two years ago and from that inquiry came Heather – nobody knew where she was, or whatever. Since then, checks have been done – marriages, deaths, nationwide. Her National

Insurance number stops with you from birth. They are not all-consuming and she could have gone away and changed her identity completely. Possibly. But she wasn't particularly streetwise. She hasn't contacted – to our knowledge – another living person. Tomorrow there will be a lot of officers out there, digging that garden. If you can point us in any direction as to where she could be. Even if you can say she is anywhere in the world, it would be cheaper than having the inquiry going on. If you know where she is, I beg of you to tell us. Have you *any* idea where she is?" Rose's reply was blatant and pointed: "No".

She told the interviewing officers that neither she nor Fred ever hit their children, and that the first she heard of Heather being 'under the patio' was when Anne Marie had mentioned it.

DS Onions asked Rose if she would tell the police if she knew where Heather was, to which she replied: "I don't know".

She basically said everything that she had already said in her 1992 police interviews, except for one detail. In her 1992 interviews, she said that Heather refused to speak to Fred and would only talk to her, however, now here she was saying the complete opposite.

21:30

Fred returned home and re-connected the electricity supply to the meter in the hall. He had been fiddling it for years, routing the supply to a faulty meter, and then re-routing it again just before it was meant to be read. "God knows why, it was all Dad was concerned about", recalled his son Stephen. He then went upstairs and took a shower, came back downstairs and watched the news on TV in just his underpants. Stephen and Mae recalled how their parents had many whispered conversations that evening. He then took the dogs for a walk in the park with Rose for roughly 45 minutes, which Stephen and Mae found odd as they had never seen them walk the dogs together before. When they returned, Fred and Rose went upstairs to bed, for what would be their last night together.

25th February 1994

PC Andrew Ewens, a trained Accident Investigation Officer, was called to Cromwell Street to prepare plans of the garden. He would go on to prepare plans of the search of the house which were used in conjunction with original plans to construct a scale model. His involvement continued for around 120 days and his expertise were also used at 25 Midland Road and at Kempley. As the work was outside the normal experience of PC Andrew Ewens, McCarthy Taylor Systems Ltd acted as a back-up providing theoretical and practical advice whenever problems arose.

Word of an investigation had leaked out and the press started to get wind of something potentially large about to happen in Cromwell Street. Slowly but surely, they began to appear at the address.

Stephen recalled of that morning: "I decided to go to work...as normal, but as I went out Dad asked me to look after Mum. I asked him where he was going and he just repeated himself."

11:15

DC Savage and DC Law went to Cromwell Street and spoke to Fred at his front door. He invited them in and they were lead into the living room where Rose was sat watching TV. The officers explained that they were going to question other members of the family, including Rose's mother, Daisy. At that, Rose exploded in anger and shouted: "I'll kill that bitch Hazel Savage if she ever speaks to my Mum. Nan is ill and I don't want her to be involved." Fred took her aside and went with her into the hallway, closing the door behind them. Rose recalled: "The police were in the living-room. Fred came into the hall and told me to go upstairs. So I did, and I waited. Nothing happened."

Stephen then went home early from work, worried about his earlier conversation with his Dad. "Dad asked me to clear all the tools out of his van, which was parked outside the house. Dad sat there playing with an old lighter and then said: 'Look, Son, look after your Mum and Mae. I'm going away for a bit.' I didn't understand and told him the police had got nothing on him. He said: 'They don't need anything to arrest and charge you', and got up and walked away. Derek rang and asked us to move the van away because the press, who were camped outside on the doorstep, had seen the number on the side and had started calling him. Just before I left I saw Dad staring out of the bathroom window, looking out into the garden where the digging had started again. He gave me a look that sent a shiver down my spine. His eyes bore straight through me. It definitely wasn't normal."

Fred then said: "I shall be going away for a while. Look after Mum and sell the house. I've done something really bad. I want you to go to the papers and make as much money as you can and start a new life." Fred then presented himself to the police officers with the words "Can we go to the police station?" As they were walking out to the car, Fred saw a local reporter standing outside and started shouting "I didn't kill her!!!" Once in the CID car, he admitted for the first time that his daughter Heather was buried in the garden, but said that the police were digging in the wrong place. Fred West was immediately arrested by DC Savage and taken to Gloucester Police Station.

11:30

Fred arrived back at Gloucester Police Station unaided and unhandcuffed. When he was asked to empty his pockets, he became unsteady on his feet and was helped to sit down on a wooden chair. Asked what was wrong, he replied: "I feel sick and I've got a pain in my head."

Meanwhile Rose, who was still at the house, was crying heavily. "I don't know what's happening, I don't know what's going on. He told me to go upstairs and keep out of the way", she told DS Onions.

12:25

Rose West was arrested by DS Onions on the suspicion of Heather's murder, after word of Fred's confession reached them. She told the police they were "taking a fucking liberty".

Stephen recalled: "I started crying, and she went upstairs to get dressed. When she came down again, Mum took her cigarettes and lighter and went out the door without looking at me or saying 'goodbye'. I rang Mae and she came home immediately." Rose was taken to Cheltenham Police Station, where she arrived at 12:45.

Shortly before 12:30, Fred was examined by a police doctor, and then allowed into the station's exercise yard for a cigarette with a uniformed constable. For the next 80 minutes, he walked around holding his head and looking into space. When the constable asked him if he was OK, Fred told him: "My head hurts and I keep seeing stars." He also told him that he had killed his daughter Heather.

Mae and Stephen remained at the house watching the police dig the garden. While they were eating crisps and drinking tea in the kitchen, the police unearthed a bone. When it was confirmed that it was from a chicken, they laughed and Stephen made clucking noises and motions.

Sergeant Peter Maunder, a Police Search Advisor, was directed to take charge of the search operation at 25 Cromwell Street.

Fred's solicitor, Howard Ogden, recalled: "My secretary rang and said that there's been a bit of bother at Gloucester Police Station that I think you should know about. She said it was Fred West and he'd been arrested for murder. And so I did the standard patter along the lines of 'Oh I'm sure it's all just some big misunderstanding Fred. Don't you worry, you wait until I get there, we'll get it sorted out'. To which he replied that fatal words no criminal lawyer wants to hear... 'Well I've admitted it'."

16:57

Fred West was interviewed by DC Savage and DC Law about the murder of Heather West. Howard Ogden was now present, as was his appointed 'Appropriate Adult', Janet Leach.

Janet recalled how her appointment came about: "Normally they give you a name of the person that you're actually going to sit in with. This time they just said a 52-year-old male. So I said 'yeah, fine'. I just assumed it was somebody with learning difficulties or something like that, because I did subsequently discover he had difficulty in reading and writing, to which I did quite a bit of work with him on that."

Fred went in to detail in the interview about what he and Rose had discussed the previous night. He said his exact words to her when he left Cromwell Street that morning were: "I'll go and talk to Hazel and persuade her not to go up and see your Mum." He then went on to insist that "Rose shouldn't be under stress, because she hasn't done anything."

Fred: "Through the past eight years, there's quite a few times that I've actually decided I was going to come down to see you personally", he told DC Savage. "I mean, when I was in Birmingham my sole intention was to get back home, put my home all back together and then sort it out once and for all." He made the point that he hadn't told his family anything about his confession or the murder of his daughter.

When questioned about Heather, and when she lost her job offer in Torquay and the events leading up to her death, Fred said: "Right, what happened was Heather was going to leave home the day before and we stopped her and said give it the night, give it the night to talk it over with us because you're too young to leave home anyway and we'll talk it over, right? Well we talked it over most of the night. The next morning Mae – Heather's sister – came up and told Mam and told me that Heather had cried all night and Heather looked as though her had had a rough night. So Rose said 'I'll go and draw the money out, £600, and give it her and let her go'. Rose said 'I want to go shopping' and I said 'don't hurry back. Give me a chance to talk to Heather, right'."

Later, he said: "When Rose goes shopping you can guarantee three to four hours, I mean she looks around the shops. Heather said 'If you don't let me go I'll give all the kids acid and they'll jump off the church roof and be dead on the floor'."

He then said that they had an argument and "I brought my two hands up and grabbed her round the neck. But I mean, I didn't grab her, grab her round the neck to choke her or do nothing, all I was gonna do was grab her around the neck and shake her. It's surprising how long somebody can hold you round the neck before...before you erm...you really have to do something I suppose. I mean I can undo three quarter nuts without a spanner when we've just locked them on turn them and I can undo them."

He said that after Heather was dead "I put the children to bed, locked the back door, went down behind the fence with a torch and dug the hole."

It took him "two and a half hours perhaps". He said the digging happened at night after he had sent Rose out to spend the night with one of her clients. "I dug this hole and buried her down behind the fence, then…we had some of the blue membrane polythene, you know they use on floors and blue that blue stuff think blue plastic…I put her on the top to cover up, to show there hadn't been any digging done there, to cover up the digging." He then told the detectives that they were "digging in the wrong place". They asked him what sort of grave they should be looking for. He said just a hole in the ground. This was the first time that the police realised that Fred had mutilated the body:

DC Savage: And what's going to be in this hole in the ground?
Fred: Heather.
DC Savage: In how many pieces?
Fred: Three. Two legs and a head and a body.
DC Savage: What?
Fred: I think the main bulk of her body is in the middle and legs are on the side, and head's on the front.
DC Savage: Did you not get stained at all?

Fred: No, not to my knowledge. Anyway, I think I got blood on my hands, not anywhere else.
DC Savage: What, no blood on you then?
Fred: No, because she was quite cold and that. Really cold before I decided what to do with her.
DC Savage: What have you told Rose about Heather's whereabouts ever since?
Fred: Rose accepted it then, that she had gone, that she had left home. I would like to stress Rose knew nothing at all. Whenever Rose brought it up years later, Rose used to say 'Christ, I wish we'd try and get in contact and find out where Heather is'. Although they didn't get on, she still loved her, same as the rest. And then that's when I used to make excuses up.

He said that he was most worried about his standing within the family if the investigation were to uncover the truth.

Fred: Once Rose finds out about this, then I'm finished. At least I had her behind me before with the other case, somebody, but now I mean my daughter and son and wife, I mean they made it quite clear last night. Me marriage has gone, me home's gone, but at least me home's done up that they've got something to sell or keep. The thing I'd like to stress, I mean, Rose knew nothing at all…she hasn't done anything."

He then went over what happened to Heather again:

Fred: I just wanted to shake her, or wanted to take that smirk off her face.
DC Savage: But as a result of what you did…she died.
Fred: Yeah, and that's the bad part of it.
DC Savage: Right, who else knows what you've told us?
Fred: Nobody…nobody at all. That is something I've had to live with for eight years. It's not easy, I'll tell you, because I loved Heather. That's why I was trying to persuade her not to go – I mean, what happened…in the brief moment when she was laughing about going to kill the rest of the children with acid, I couldn't believe it was Heather.

Howard Ogden later commented: "The first taped interview was chilling. This was Fred telling in a wholly dispassionate, unemotional way, with the cold, dark eyes that he had, this account as though anybody else would say 'cheers for that'. There was a silence. We all rose as a group…we shared a common human bond in terms of the shock and horror at what we had just heard."

17:25

Stephen West recalled: "Hazel Savage rang saying Dad's solicitor Howard Ogden wanted to speak to us. A copper called Bob, who had been friendly towards us, gave us a lift and we walked into Gloucester Police Station." Janet Leach and Fred's solicitor Howard Ogden walked into the pink interview room at the station and Howard Ogden told Mae and Stephen: "I'm sorry to tell you this, but your Dad has admitted to the killing of Heather."

"We couldn't believe it. I slipped down the wall and sat on the floor crying. It was such a shock and we were not prepared for it", recalled Stephen. "I felt someone had hit me with a hammer".

"I just went quiet", recalled Mae. "We asked how he did it, and Howard said she had been strangled. I found it hard to accept and didn't break down at all." She refused to accept it and said that Fred must have been making it up. But Howard Ogden shook his head and told them: "He's gone to Cromwell Street with the police to show them where he buried the body."

When Fred was told that Stephen and Mae had gone to the police station he told the police to keep his son away from him. "Be careful with him. I mean, so what if I injure one of them badly?"

18:34

DC Law and DC Savage took Fred to the back garden of 25 Cromwell Street. Fred was handcuffed to DC Law throughout. He pointed out the exact spot, half-way down the garden under a line of small fir trees, where he had buried Heather. Fred was unsteady on his feet and kept slipping off the wooden boards put down by the search team.

20:27

Rose West was interviewed by DS Onions and DC Smurthwaite. Her solicitor, Leo Goatley, was present and the interview started late as they had trouble locating an 'Appropriate Adult' for her. Again, she didn't really offer up any information, and was evasive in her answers. Not how a caring mother would really react when told that police were digging up her garden to search for her daughter's body.

The questions asked by the officers were mainly a repeat of the interview they had conducted at Cromwell Street previously, but when they asked Rose what had been spoken about in the house last night, she replied: "That she must be around somewhere. We were getting some publicity out of what was going to happen, that we were going to come out in the news."

Later that evening she stuck to the story that she knew nothing about Heather's disappearance. "Fred just said she'd left", and he wouldn't tell her where she lived. "I don't know anything about it. I was not aware of it." She told the officers that Fred was the dominant partner in the relationship "in lots of ways".

Fred was interviewed again about the murder of his daughter, Heather, and gave more of a detailed account. After he put his hands around her throat "She fell back on to the drier and then slid forward, she was making funny noises from her throat or chest for a little while. It is surprising how long you can hold someone round the neck before…you know…I had one heck of a job to pick her up." He said that at one point he had left Heather's body in the bath and gone into the tool room to look for something to take her head and legs off with. "I looked up and I seen this knife sticking out and he was brand new. He came with something from Icelandic (Iceland Supermarket) – summat we bought from Icelandic and the knife was free with it. And he was put up there out of the way of the children. Because he was deadly, this thing was. I mean the blade on it was terrible…so I just shoved him up in there. What I was going to use him for was trimming the trees. That's what I was actually going to use him for…I was going to try and break him up, just bust him through and chuck him in

239

the bin, because it was such a deadly weapon to have about... (But) it just ripped. It didn't actually cut across. It just ripped across the skin, like. Cut bits out. So I went in the kitchen and got the bread knife...I run the knife round the neck through the skin, and then just twisted the head round. And whatever bits was left, just cut that off."

He told police that he regarded Heather's death as an accident. "I've spent more time standing in that garden by her than I like to think. I used to go out there and stand and say prayers for her and all that. I used to actually, you know, tell her to rise and come up. That's a secret I've kept to myself for eight years and I never told anybody."

He explained that although he tried to "revive" Heather for two or three hours he never considered calling an ambulance or a doctor. All he could think to do was to dismember her body and hide it "in case Rose came back from the shops or the children came back from school."

He said he chose a knife, rather than an axe, because it minimized the potential of any damage to his bath. "The body was in an enamel bath. Pressed-steel enamel bath. So if you tried chopping in that, the thing would splinter all over you. The enamel..."

He said that he had strangled Heather with a length of flex "to make sure she was dead. It was 13-amp, ring-main cable. Grey. Three-core. Plain copper wire...We use it for pulling posts out of the ground, things like that. All you do is just pull it round and twist it. You can't tie knots in it...I may have chucked it in with her; I don't know what I done with it. Because there would have been blood on it...I mean, I knew she was dead before I did it, or as good as...It was a bit I'd cut off when I was rewiring a house. Probably two feet to a metre long."

He then said he had rolled the dustbin containing Heather's remains outside and hidden it behind the Wendy house at the bottom of the garden. "I put her behind the Wendy house and covered it over with that blue polythene again...That blue membrane polythene, you know, they use on the floors."

After he had buried her, he said: "I took the dustbin to the house and washed him, because we had a tap on the side...and put him back out the front. I washed off at the hosepipe outside. Washed Wellington's and that in the bin full of water and then tipped him over across the yard."

Later that night, Stephen and Mae were allowed home and spent it trying to get some sleep in the same room. Stephen: "They had marked the spot where Dad said she was buried, and they dug until quite late under a huge floodlight."

26th February 1994

An incident room was set up on the fourth floor of Gloucester Police Station. This was led by Detective Superintendent John Bennett, the Senior Investigating Officer, and Detective Chief Inspector Terry Moore, acting as Deputy Senior Investigating Officer.

DSI John Bennett

11:19

Authority was given by an Acting Superintendent to extend Fred West's detention in custody over 24 hours until up to a period of 36 hours from his arrest, and at 11:34 Rosemary West's detention was also extended to over 24 hours.

11:50

Rose was interviewed again and arrested by DS Onions and DC Smurthwaite.

DS Onions: Why do you think you've been arrested today? For the most grave of offences. There has been a major development this morning. A major development. Fred has confessed to murdering Heather.
Rose: What? So you know where she is?
DS Onions: He has told us where she is.
Rose: So she is dead, is that right?
DS Onions: I'm telling you, and we're on tape, I'm telling you Fred has confessed to murdering Heather.

Rose: What?

DS Onions: And that automatically implicates you.

Rose: (Crying) Why does it automatically implicate me?

DS Onions: I am just saying our suspicions are aroused automatically that you are implicated, that you are involved.

Rose: It's a lie.

DS Onions: Is there anything you can say to us? Perhaps to help us? Fred's told us where she is. Where do you think she is? Did you know you have been living with a murderer for the past eight years?

Rose: NO!

DS Onions: But you have been living with someone with an odd appetite for sex most of your marriage. He has been making you prostitute yourself with black men…

Rose: Yeah

She then denied assisting Fred in killing Heather and denied that he had told her that he would keep her out of it. The interview then ended.

Leo Goatley, Rose's solicitor, recalled the moment when Rose was told of Fred's confession: "That drew a huge and shocked gasp from Rose and she was disturbed and trembling at that point. It was probably one of the most emotional points that I witnessed with Rose in the whole enquiry. Her venom turned to Fred and that was the narrative right the way through and Fred was the enemy. Fred was the betrayer. Fred was this evil person who'd manipulated and exploited her and killed her daughter."

13:32

In an interview, DC Savage admitted to Fred that her colleagues digging in his garden had found nothing. "Did I ask them to go and dig my garden up? Let them keep digging", he said. He then broke off the interview after just eight minutes.

14:05

Fred asked to resume the interview. Scott Canavan, standing in for Howard Ogden as Fred's legal representative, remembered: "He already admitted to the murder of his daughter, Heather, the day before. They were interviewing him further about this and he was obviously distressed. The police doctor was called and gave him some Diazepam. This reacted with him kind of funny. He started telling a story of Heather being involved in and running drugs."

Fred grew anxious and upset most of all when he learned the police officers were tearing apart his home. He retracted his earlier confession and insisted that Heather wasn't dead after all:

Fred: Heather is not in the garden. Heather's alive and well. She's possibly at this moment in Bahrain. She works for a drugs cartel.

According to him, she had a Mercedes, a chauffeur and a new birth certificate. They even had lunch together recently in Devizes in Wiltshire.

Fred: She's got no identification – that's why you can't find her…They're looked after like queens. I have no idea what her name is, because I will not let her tell me. She contacts me whenever she's in this country. Now, whether you believe it or not is entirely up to you. As far as I'm concerned, I'd like to see them all still over there digging in my garden because they tore my house apart eighteen months ago, and they weren't satisfied with that, they had to come back and rip my home apart. Then you came in yesterday and upset Rose over her mother and all that…That's the reason I made up that story…She begged you not to have nothing to do with her mother 'cause her mother was an old lady…Rose was so upset over her mother, and mind I love Rose, and no messing. We're devoted. And when I see anybody hurt that woman then I want to get them back and make sure they pay hard for touching her. She's an angel…If Rose was all right, then I was quite prepared to go on with it. Let them go on digging out there…I feel a lot better for it. There ain't nothing in my garden. They can dig there for evermore. I've never harmed anybody in my life…I do not believe in it, hurting people.

When he was asked what benefit there had been for him in the admission of Heather's murder, he smirked and said: "The police are out there digging…I feel a lot better for it. How many months will they carry on digging for?" He then asked: "All right, how many weeks?"

DC Savage: Was Heather buried in the garden at Cromwell Street?
Fred: No! They can dig there for evermore. Nobody or nothings under my patio. I mean, I know Heather ain't there. Nobody's in there. So what am I bothered about?

Finally, he called the whole matter "a joke…it always has been". He then tried to deflect some of the attention away from the investigation and condemned DC Savage for waging a "personal vendetta" against him. "Because you seem to want to get me for some unknown reason, well, not me quite so much, but Rose. We've always had the feeling that you wanted to get me and Rose."

14:52

DSI John Bennett and DCI Terry Moore visited 25 Cromwell Street. They noticed some members of the Gloucester Division Support Group, a Sergeant and six Constables digging in the garden. Every spadesful was carefully scrutinized by Acting Detective Sergeant Bob Beetham and DC John Rouse who were both Scenes Of Crime Officers. Other members of the group were removing slabs by hand.

16:03

A bone was found in the garden of 25 Cromwell Street, in a part of the garden where Fred had insisted the police were searching was the wrong area. The support group officers stopped digging and informed a Scenes of Crime Officer. Acting DS Beetham had decided to remove the bone found near the extension. He put it in a brown paper exhibit bag and took it to Gloucester Police Station where it was examined by the Home Office Pathologist, Professor Bernard Knight. He confirmed that the bone was a female human femur (thigh bone). He believed that it hadn't been in the ground that long, and that it likely came from quite a young person possibly aged 15-25.

This bone, found under a window outside the extension, was subsequently found to belong to Alison Chambers. Due to the initial find it became obvious that there might be a second set of remains buried in the garden.

The remains of all subsequent victims were initially taken to Gloucester Police Station and then taken to the University of Wales, College of Medicine at Cardiff where they were handed to Professor Knight. After his examination they were then passed to Doctor David Whittaker for the purpose of establishing the person's identity.

Dr Whittaker revealed his technique in identifying skulls: "Providing we can get a photograph of them smiling and showing their teeth, those teeth have an incredible amount of information in them in terms of height, tilt, and roundness. All of these will show up in a good photograph and so we assess those in the laboratory and then we sort of fuse simply a photograph that comes in to me from the police with an image of the person's skull and if we've got it right it sort of goes 'click'.

16:32

Fred was interviewed again, and the first thing he did was to apologise to DC Savage for the previous interview. "I got nothing personal against her at all. I don't know what happened. When I walked in here and sat down there, I could feel my head lifting up, and I was going in to space. And I could see diggers and everything all ploughing round and ripping the house up and tearing floorboards up and bulldozing the house down and it was all weird and...I could see it all in me mind and everything had gone wrong."

He then retracted his earlier retraction when he learnt that the police had recovered human remains and admitted to the murder of his daughter Heather. "Heather's where I told you she is, and I mean they should have found her anyway by now, because she's there."

DC Savage: I understand that you have been told by your solicitor that we have found something?
Fred: Yeah. Bones.
DC Savage: Would there be anybody else's bones there? Would there be anybody else's bones in any other part of the garden?
Fred: (after a short hesitation) Well, that's a peculiar question to ask, ain't it? Heather is in there, and there ain't no more. There's nothing else.

Half an hour later DC Savage asked Fred who else was aware that Heather was buried in the garden, to which he replied: "Nobody". He knew that Rose was under increasing suspicion and again insisted that she knew nothing. "I love my wife...but I mean I don't want to destroy the love that I had there when I've destroyed one love already, you know...I mean, Heather's gone...Rose is not going to let me say to her "I've strangled Heather" without coming straight to the police."

18:55

Professor Bernard Knight was taken to Cromwell Street to examine the rest of the remains found so far.

A view of the garden under the tarpaulin.

The garden area was by now covered in a well-used crime scene tenting that formed a canopy over the pathway. DSI Bennett and DCI Moore positioned themselves alongside the video cameraman, giving themselves a clear view of what the pathologist was doing. Crouching to examine the excavated area, he immediately confirmed the presence of what appeared to be further human skeletal remains.

Each bone was handed to a Scenes of Crime Officer to be recorded and prepared for removal so it could be examined in greater detail later. The visible part of the remains were found around 2ft below the surface and had been pushed down to a depth of another foot or so.

Professor Knight gave a running commentary as to what he was finding and his initial opinions. As he continued, the smell of adiopocere, a wax-like organic substance formed by the decay of a dead body's fat, was becoming more evident. It could be seen, too, in the form of traces of a soapy, off-white liquid and traces of it were easily visible. The surrounding mud was also darker, no doubt due to further decomposition.

While the leg bones were in some semblance of anatomical order, they appeared to have been separated from the torso and placed on it. Further down in the ground, a black polythene bin liner was found partially underneath the torso. Close by were two lengths of cord. The head also seemed to have been separated and was found with its hair still in place, though heavily matted in mud. By the time he had completed recovering what bones and fingernails there were, there appeared no evidence whatsoever of any clothing. It appeared the girl had been buried naked.

Professor Knight leaned forward and pulled out another bone. It was part of a left thighbone – another femur. He could see it was obviously broken, though he couldn't tell how at that stage. Then he pulled out another, longer portion that had a number of cuts near to where it had been broken.

Whilst he was there, police found what they thought were different remains roughly in the position where Fred had indicated Heather would be found. Moments later, professor Knight pulled out another bone, this time a complete right femur. "Well, either we have found the world's first three-legged woman or there's another victim around here somewhere", he said. These remains transpired to be those of Heather West.

There were 2 orange cords found with Heather's remains, one 15" and the other 22" long. Fred West maintained that the chord "was what I tied the dustbin lid with". Orange, green and brown nylon carpet fibres were found trapped in the rope, suggesting that Heather had been held down on the floor as she was being tied up. There was no gag and her remains were found without any clothing, suggesting that she had been stripped naked before death, and that some sex act may have been forced upon her. 22 of her finger and toe bones were missing (out of a total of 76) and one kneecap. She was also missing 15 of her wrist and ankle bones. Her head had been severed with a sharp, fine-edged knife, the thighs had been chopped more crudely. Her legs were found on top, covering her chest, vertebrae, arms and skull at the bottom, with lots of hair and some loose finger or toe nails. Black plastic bin liners were found around her trunk. Part of a necklace was also discovered with her body. Her left thigh had been smashed in two near her pelvis by a sharp-edged object, which Professor Knight believed had been done with a cleaver.

"I was just really shocked when they told me about Heather", recalled Mae. "A lot of it just didn't sink in. Just too unbelievable. I was shocked because it could so easily have been me. And I started to hate my Dad from there."

Anne Marie was told in a phone call from the police that they had found remains that they believed to be those of Heather in the garden at 25 Cromwell Street. She bought some flowers and placed them at the gate. Her note with the flowers read:

To my sister Heather,

I've searched and sought, I've wept and prayed we'd meet again some sunny day. Missing you so very much. Will always love and remember you.

All my fondest love

Big Sis

Anne Marie

18:45

Rose West was interviewed and updated on the latest discoveries.

DS Onions: A short while ago human remains have been recovered from the area which Mr West has indicated and for obvious reasons we believe those human remains to be your daughter Heather. Is there anything you want to say about that?

(Rose shook her head but did not reply. Leo Goatley recalled: "There was a gasp of shock and Rose remained in a brittle and distressed state from then on in".)

DS Onions: We just want to get to the bottom of it. There's no charades now. What do you know about it all? Or what have you known about it over the last eight years?

Rose: I don't know anything about it. I was not aware of it.

DS Onions: Are you protecting him?

Rose: What's the point? Protecting him from what?

DS Onions: Was Heather killed because, as you said, she was different from the rest because she was going to blow the whistle on what happened in your house? Which, from statements I have read from your children, was a bit like a prison for them.

Rose: I do not know nothing about it. Why do we have to go through this again?

DS Onions: Do you feel that perhaps you've been a bit naïve over this eight-year period?

Rose: Looks like it, don't it...I feel a bit of a cunt, to be blunt about it.

DS Onions: What's your feeling towards Fred now? Now that you know he's slain your eldest daughter?

Rose: Put it this way. He's a dead man if I ever get my hands on him.

DS Onions: You are the wife of the person who's confessed to killing her. You live in the house on whose land the body is allegedly lying at this very moment...Fred has described to us the steps taken and what's happened to Heather, and that it didn't take minutes, it took somewhat longer, and you'd have been in that house in between time, or at the time things were happening, and either you're blind, extremely naïve, or totally trusting of your husband – or you're a liar.

Rose: Or I was sent out...I was more or less given a certain time to come back in.

Later in the interview, DS Onions told Rose that there might be more human remains in her back garden, to which she sighed and said: "Oh, this is getting too much".

Mae recalled: "When I start to forgive him I remind myself of what he's done, and then I hate him again. I heard that he was angry with me when I told the police about him abusing us, after the final investigation began and the police were digging up the garden. But when Heather's body was discovered I didn't want him to get out again, so I told the truth about his abuse of us kids.

I'm still angry about what happened to her. I keep thinking how scared she must have been in the last two minutes of her life. That upsets me."

19:17

Fred West was interviewed again. He gave details of the disposal of Heather's body in the garden. He claimed that Heather was standing with her hands in her pockets against the washing machine: "And I said to her ...

248

now what's this about you leaving home! ... You know you're too young. You're a lesbian and there's AIDS and all that. I mean, you're vulnerable to anything". He told them that he had said: "Well, Heather, I'm not going to let you go," and she had replied 'if you don't fucking let me go I'll give all the kids acid (LSD) and they'll all jump off the church roof and be dead on the floor.' So she stood there and she had a smile and a sort of smirk on her face like 'you try me, I'll do it'. I lunged at her like that and grabbed her round the throat. I held her for a minute, how long I held her for, I don't know. I can't remember because for that few minutes I can't even remember what happened. I can just remember lunging for her throat and the next minute she's gone blue. I looked at her and I mean I was shaking from head to foot, I mean what the heck had gone wrong? I'm strong in the hands because of the job I do ... When you're using big spanners and things like that, you get strong ... in the arms ... I spotted she'd gone blue and so I let go of her quick and, of course, she just started to fall backwards on to the washing machine and slid forwards. I put her on the floor, blowed air into her mouth and that, and pumped her chest and she just kept going bluer, so I mean at this point I didn't know what to do. I mean Rose was due back, I mean I didn't know when Rose was due to walk in or when anybody else was due to walk in...and I've got her on the floor there and I mean I tried everything to try and get her to breathe again, but she just couldn't breathe. So anyway, I tried to put her in the dustbin to cover, to get her out of the way...till I could get to do something about it...she started to go cold by then and she already wet the floor...I mean I never intended to hurt her I mean I just went to grab her and shake her and say take that stupid smirk off your face, you know, because I was going to smack her across the face, but some years before that me and Rose had a word or two and I smacked Rose across the face and dislocated her jaw, so from that day on I'm always nervous of slapping them across the face. I do a heavy job so I've got plenty of strength in me. Then I got Heather and there was no way I could get any life back in her, she was just flat out and I thought 'Jeez – I've got to do something'. I was going to put her in the Wendy house because I don't know whether I was going to bring her to the police or nothing. I was so scared of what was going to happen, so anyway I tried to get her in to the dustbin, I couldn't get her in there, so at that time we used to have one of those big ice saws for cutting big blocks of ice, so I cut her legs off with that and I'm telling you, I have lived that a million times doing that since then and then I cut her head off and then I put her in the bin and put the lid on and rolled it down the bottom of the garden behind the Wendy house and covered it up and left it there. Then I got all her stuff, which was by the door and the cases and bags and I took it over and put it by the wall at Brunswick Road – no, St. Michael's Square."

He went on to explain that it was bin day and he'd left Heather's belongings and other rubbish in a "big heap. Then Rose come back, must have been an hour or more later, and she said: "Oh, didn't you persuade Heather to stay?" or something, and I said: "No".

That evening he said he sent his wife out to spend the night with a black man and buried Heather in the garden while she was away. He used a heavy serrated knife from the food shop Iceland, chopping her left thigh clean in two. He then held Heather face down and cut through the back of her neck while her chin was pushed into her chest, decapitating her. He then removed her kneecaps and parts of her hands and feet.

It was not implied that Heather had been subjected to torture before she died but two pieces of cord found with her remains suggest that her father had attempted to rape her. It was, as Mae believes, Heather's resistance which lead to her death. Several loose finger nails were also unearthed with Heather's remains. Although the possibility that they were pulled out while she was still alive is not corroborated by the evidence, it cannot be ruled out.

After almost twenty minutes DC Hazel Savage told Fred that the police had found more remains.

DC Savage: This is the third femur, a leg bone, Fred. The question is, is there anybody else buried in your garden?
Fred: Only Heather.
DC Savage: You never said to us that you scattered Heather all over the garden. And Heather didn't have three legs!

"Have you any knowledge of where this other bone might have come from at all?" asked the solicitor's clerk after a long silence.

Fred: Yes, Shirley (almost inaudibly)
DC Savage: Shirley who?
Fred: Robinson. The girl who caused the problem.

Fred West was arrested for the murder of Shirley Robinson. He suggested that Shirley and Heather had been friends, and that Rose had been in hospital when he had killed Shirley Robinson.

After suggesting that Shirley Robinson had been only six months' pregnant when she died, he maintained: "She was going to have the baby for another girl, in Bristol." Then he offered a motive for the killing. "Shirley was the one who was supplying the dope to Heather to take to the schools, and that was the reason we fell out." Shirley Robinson was described by Fred West as a lesbian. She was a former tenant at 25 Cromwell Street who was expecting his child when she disappeared.

20:00

Fred West arrived in the dock at Gloucester Magistrates' Court. News reached the court that he had admitted to the further murder of Shirley Robinson. The clerk of the court offered Howard Ogden the opportunity of a short adjournment due to the change in circumstances and Fred then left the dock to go back to the cells, under escort. It is believed that it was at this time that Fred said to one of the guards "They don't know the half of what I've done."

20:34

Fred West was brought up from the cells and appeared before Gloucester Magistrates' Court. He looked pale, almost green. The guard called DSI Bennett and DCI Moore over. He whispered that Fred was now saying there was yet another person buried in the garden. Heather and two others. A warrant of further detention for a period of 36 hours was obtained.

Howard Ogden: "In between police interviews, he told me there was another one out there, he called 'Shirley's mate'. It seemed that both women were buried in the garden. The murder of 'Shirley's mate' was by strangulation using a flex."

21:11

Fred West was interviewed about the death of Shirley Robinson and at the end he admitted killing and strangling a third person whom he described as a friend of Shirley Robinson (Alison Chambers). The investigation was never able to establish a link between Alison Chambers and Shirley Robinson. In fact Shirley Robinson disappeared in May 1978 and Alison Chambers did not arrive in Gloucester until January 1979.

Fred went on to state that he needed to conceal that he was the father of Shirley's baby from Rose. With regards to Shirley's death, he said that he met Shirley at an allotment and then went first to Painswick Beacon and then back to Cromwell Street where a row developed. According to Fred, Shirley had called Rose a bitch and a cow "and I had warned her a lot of times about that". When they got back to the house, Rose had taken the kids to the park (there were four of them, ranging from Heather (7) to Tara (6 months), and only Anne Marie was at home. She was shut in her room, and being by this time deaf in one ear, she would not hear what was going on in the back room on the ground floor. The row continued and Fred claimed that Shirley had threatened him. 'I'm going to tell Rose that this (the baby) is yours', she said. He was furious, because "it was stated right from the word go that the baby that she was carrying was not to be mentioned to Rose and it was hers, nothing to do with me. It was going through me mind at the time, she's going to absolutely ruin my marriage. I hit her on to the floor and then I strangled her. I wasn't that bothered whether she were dead or alive, you know, I mean it was just to get rid of them". He then shocked the interviewing officers by the manner in which he recounted how he dismembered and disposed of his former lover and the mother of his unborn child. Fred also revealed that there were further remains which he could only identify as belonging to "Shirley's mate...Shirley's lesbian lover from Bristol."

At first, he gave an unexpected explanation for her death. He insisted that Alison Chambers had turned up at Cromwell Street to blackmail him with a copy of the portrait photograph he had had taken sixteen months earlier with Shirley Robinson. He maintained that the sixteen-year-old from Swansea, who had not even arrived in Gloucester when Shirley Robinson disappeared, was, in fact, "Shirley's mate". Clearly confusing her at first with another young woman, who Fred said was "big-boned" and twenty-two years of age, he went on to insist that the girl he only ever knew as "Shirley's mate" had turned up at Cromwell Street "several years" after Shirley Robinson's death and said to him: "As far as I can gather you killed Shirley."

He explained that she had come to Cromwell Street looking for Shirley. She showed him a photograph of the two of them together. He told her that she no longer lived there and she seemed to accept this explanation and went away. However, the girl returned a few weeks later and said she knew that he had killed Shirley and she was going to the police. Fred said he had persuaded her not to go to the police and offered her a lift back to Bristol in his van. As they drove out of Gloucester along the A38 he stopped in a lay-by, strangled her and took her back to Cromwell Street where, just as he had with the other two, he cut her body into pieces and buried them in the garden.

Fred then went on to expand on the lies that he had told earlier in the evening about his killing of Shirley Robinson. "Shirley's mate", he explained, was about "twelve months to two years later", and their bodies were "by the bathroom window" and "where the bins were" in his back garden.

He continued to deny that Rose knew anything about the bodies and said in interview: "Don't get Rose wrong, Rose lives by the law properly, I mean although she doesn't like the law she will not have it broken you know".

At the end of the interview, after his admission of the killing of Shirley

Robinson, he asked: "Has Rose been told yet?" adding "How did she take it? I expect she hates me now."

21:35

Rosemary West was arrested for the murders of Shirley Robinson and an unknown female and at 21:36 she was taken to Gloucester Magistrates' Court for application for a warrant of further detention.

27th February 1994

10:15

Fred West was taken back to 25 Cromwell Street by the police. In the convoy of vehicles were Fred, his legal representative Howard Ogden, the 'appropriate adult' Janet Leach and the interviewing officers Hazel Savage and Darren Law. The video recordist was already there along with scenes of crimes officers Beetham and Rouse and the seven-man Gloucester Support Group. The whole of the West's garden was now covered by white tenting with access into it where the back gate had been. He was asked to identify the sites of the remains of Shirley Robinson and the other as yet unidentified female (Alison Chambers) who he described as "Shirley's mate". With the video officer recording every footstep, Fred stopped, looked around and pointed to an area immediately in front of the back door to his house. The spot where he had buried Shirley Robinson. Moving to his right, towards the extension, he pointed again to just in front of the bathroom window. That was where they would find her "mate".

Howard Ogden: "When confronted with the fact that a body was about to be revealed then Fred would occasionally go weak at the knees and that happened in the garden and he was quite swiftly removed from it. I remained and I looked into my first grave which was that of Heather. Seeing a skeleton with hair and what turns out to be a young woman. So it was a telling experience."

11:45

Rose West was further interviewed. She maintained: "The only Shirley I knew used to come to the house when we had tenants." She did not remember Shirley Robinson's pregnancy, she denied that the tenants ever paid their rent to her "because they had drugs and that up there, so I didn't go near them", and she denied that she was covering up for her husband. When told that Fred had 'seen sense and told the police all', it was suggested that she do the same. Her only comment was that there was "something wrong with the bloke altogether".

Rose became more withdrawn as the interview progressed. Her head dropped, and she turned away from the table to look at the floor, refusing to make eye contact with anyone. When Hazel Savage travelled from Gloucester to see her and tell her that her husband had specifically asked for her to be told about his confession, she hardly acknowledged it. A few moments later she denied again that she was covering up for her husband, and ended the interview by saying: "I told you what I know, and that's it."

12:02

Fred was again interviewed. He talked about his visit earlier in the day to the garden of his home and said: "You know I looked straight across and I could see her. I think she is in a plastic bag, I think. You could actually see it in the corner. See, there's a big hollowing behind it. If you look underneath the step you can see straight underneath, there's a big hole." He maintained fiercely that there was "no question of anybody else", and in particular he denied that he knew anything about the whereabouts of his first wife and his stepdaughter. "Now Rena and Charmaine, I have no idea where they went."

As far as he was concerned, he told the police, he was going to leave his house to "Stephen, Mae and Rose. The rest gets nothing."

Scott Canavan: "Myself and Janet (Leach) took Fred aside between interviews in to a separate cell and spoke with him telling him that they (the police) weren't messing him about. If there are any bodies, from the defence point of view, it would be better if he tells us who they are and where they are."

Janet Leach: "I just said 'look, enough's enough. I can't cope with it. If there's more you've got to tell them there's more'. He said 'No, I've told you everything and there's not any more.' I said, 'I don't believe you and I'm going.' As I got up to walk out he said 'no, there is.'

Scott Canavan: "His words were 'there's a fucking load more'. I was really quite shocked and I had a cold shiver going down my spine. About two minutes later I said 'Look, Fred. Explain to me what you mean by 'there's a load more bodies down there. How many?' He said, 'Well, five or six."

Janet Leach: "I said 'well we'll draw the cellar, which I did, and he pin pointed where the victims were.'

Scott Canavan: "I again left the police station to phone my boss Howard Ogden because I didn't have a clue what to do in that situation."

14:12

Fred was interviewed again and he gave further details regarding the death of Heather West, which he said was without Rose West's knowledge. In this interview, he was confronted with a drawing of his daughter showing in detail which bones were missing from her body after it was recovered. He could barely bring himself to look at it. When he was asked if there was any possibility that she may have been alive when the bones were removed, he refused to offer an explanation. "I've no comment on that."

Fred gave a lurid and graphic account (below) of what had happened to Heather in the presence of his solicitor Howard Ogden and his appropriate adult Janet Leach. Later, he proudly declared that: "Janet had turned green".

Fred was anxious to avoid any suggestions that sexual abuse might have played a part in Heather's death. "She's still dressed. I hadn't touched her clothes, because there was no sexual motives at all. I mean, I wouldn't do nothing like that".

"I called her into the hallway and I said to her...now what's this about your leaving home...You know you're too young. You're a lesbian and there's AIDS and all that. I mean, you're vulnerable for anything." But Heather "just stood there and looked at me. I said, 'Well, Heather, I'm not going to let you go. Anyway, Heather's standin' by the washing machine. In the 'allway then but it's not there now. Enterin' the 'ouse through the front door the washin' machine and dryer used to be there. So she's standin' there against the dryer by the washin' machine like that, doing the 'big lady' business. And I said to 'er about getting a flat up the road if 'er wanted girlfriends up there. It would be no problem to us, which was what we'd 'ave done for the other two. And she said 'If you don't fucking let me go I'll give all the kids acid and they'll all jump off the church roof and be dead on the floor'. I already known she 'ad given it to Barry as 'e 'ad already jumped off the church roof for that reason – which we didn't know for some time after the school reported 'im. Well, we knew 'e was walkin' a bit funny. 'E jarred all 'is 'ips and 'is speech was gone funny and anyway it was traced back to Heather who'd given him acid on sugar or summat and then e'd mat 'her and 'er told 'im to fly off the church roof: so that was it.

But Heather's standing there grinning all over her face, with her hands in her pockets shaking her trousers. So then I grabbed her by the throat and I'm shouting at her in anger really, you know, 'How dare you say that about your brothers and sisters?' She stood there and she 'ad a smile with a sort of a smirk on 'er face that said summat like "you try me and I'll do it".

Heather then tried to get past him, but he grabbed her. "First of all I went to slap her across the face. Then I suddenly stopped and thought on a previous occasion me and Rose had had an argument and I slapped her across the face and I dislocated her jaw…so I mean the last thing on my mind was to hurt Heather in any way.

I lunged at 'er and grabbed 'er round the throat and I 'eld 'er for a bit. 'Ow long I held 'er for I don't know, I can't remember 'cos for that few minutes I can't even remember what 'appened to that extent. I just remember lunging for 'er throat and the next minute she'd gone blue. I looked at 'er and I mean I was shakin' from 'ead to foot. What the 'eck had gone wrong?"

He told the police that he kept his hands on his daughter's throat and she still "Had this grin on her face" until it got to a point where "I was actually still looking at her but couldn't see her for some reason…So I let go of her quick and, of course, she just started to fall backwards on to the washing-machine and slide forward."

He said he tried to give his daughter mouth-to-mouth resuscitation. "I tried, you know, pressing her chest and that to make her breathe again." But, as he confessed to the police, although he had "seen it on the telly" he had "never actually gone to classes or learned how to do this type of thing…and there was no way I could get anything out of Heather. She was making funny noises, whether it was coming from her throat or her chest for a little while", and he dragged her into the living room and got some wet cloths to put on her face. He even "tried to get a drink of water into her mouth".

"By this time I'm panicking like anything. I mean, I'm literally a nervous wreck at this stage because of what had happened. I had no intention whatsoever of hurting Heather because I think the world of her." But he did not call an ambulance, nor did he telephone the police. Instead he took a brass mirror off the living-room wall "and put it over her mouth" to see if she was breathing, "and there was nothing on it."

He then dragged her body into the bathroom near the kitchen on the ground floor and as he did so "she wet all over the floor", he told the police. "I put her in the bath and I ran the cold water on her and I still couldn't get nothing, no life out of her. So I can remember standing there and thinking, how do you know when somebody's dead?"

Heather West was now lying naked in the bath at 25 Cromwell Street. Her father told the police that he had removed the culottes his daughter had been wearing because they were "soaking wet", and he had previously taken off her blouse in the living-room. Heather had not been wearing a bra or pants. He took his daughter's naked body out of the bath and dried it.

Fred then told police that he "put something round her neck…to make sure she was dead. I know I put something round Heather's neck…I can see that knot…in the front of her neck. That's what I picked up the knife for, to cut whatever she had round her neck…'cause I had no intention at the time of cutting Heather at all. I was just going to put

Heather in the dustbin. And that was the whole idea. I didn't want to touch her while she was alive. I mean...if I'd have started cutting her leg or her throat or something and she'd have suddenly come alive...that's what I was thinking. I tried everything to try and get 'er to breathe again, but she just couldn't. I can still see her. I can see her sat there in the bath."

He then said he went to get a dustbin from the garden. "I put the dustbin flat...tipped on its side on the floor...and I folded Heather and tried to slide her in...and lift the dustbin back up."

But that did not work. When he lifted the dustbin back on to its base, Heather's body was sticking out. "No way you'd get the lid on or nothing. I mean, she was a good foot, two foot above, above the thing, and I mean her legs were even farther up than that.

So then I...put her back on the floor and pulled the dustbin back off her and then rolled her back into the bath and then I...then I did the rest."

He then told the police exactly how he had dismembered his daughter. He began by closing his daughter's eyes before he started. "She's looking at me, I thought no. If somebody's sat there looking at you, you're not going to use a knife on a person are you? And I just went like that and I closed her eyes and they stayed shut and that was that."

Fred had intended to use an 'ice knife' but it was not sharp enough, so he threw the knife to one side and found another, sharper knife in the kitchen of Cromwell Street to use in its place.

He cut and twisted off his daughter's head. He described the sound. "I remember it made a heck of a noise when it was breaking, horrible noise...like scrunching...I suppose...I had my eyes closed. I just couldn't look at her face and do it to her, you know what I mean. I just couldn't look at her...how I cut round I've no real idea."

He then cut off Heather's legs, cutting her groin with a knife and then twisting her foot until he heard "one almighty crack and the leg come loose, like". Then he left his daughter's two legs in the bath, and lifted her "main body and put it in the bin". She "filled the bin shoulder-ways".

Howard Ogden: "He had a strange way about him, in that he would see something as significant, that perhaps he might think I might be able to use in his mitigation, because somebody might actually agree with him and feel sorry for him. So in this particular instance he's explaining the severing of the head from the torso, but of course he had gone to the trouble of making sure that her eyes were shut, because it wouldn't be right for her to see it."

When the police officers asked him how he felt, he told them: "I was absolutely dead. I couldn't think of nothing. I mean, I was trembling. I mean, I was absolutely trembling."

Nevertheless, he was able to put the lid on the dustbin, which now contained his daughter's dismembered body, and "using it like a steering wheel to roll him out down into the garden…Then I spotted this rope hanging out of the tree, so I went down and cut two pieces off it and then tied the handles on the bin." He said he then rolled the dustbin "down the garden round the back of the Wendy house, covered her with a sheet. Then I went back in the house and washed everything…There was no blood anywhere…no marks anywhere."

As soon as he had finished and had cleaned the urine from the living-room floor with a dishcloth from the kitchen sink, he picked up the case and plastic carrier bags containing all his daughter's belongings, which were sitting in the hall, stuffed everything into black plastic bags and "put them out for the dustman".

"Then Rose came back, must have been an hour or more later," and shortly afterwards his other children started coming home from school.

That night, after his children had gone to bed, he told the police he sent his wife out for the evening with a man and set about burying his daughter's body in the back garden. He started digging a hole, after putting polythene around the sides to protect his clothes. He wore wellington boots. But before he got far, he hit water.

"The wind was blowing like anything and the amount of water that was in there. I mean the water was making a noise." He pushed his daughter's naked and dismembered body into the small hole, about four feet deep, with water at the bottom, with his spade. "I then backfilled the hole, levelled it out…rolled this big piece of plastic out and put it on top." He did that "to cover up the digging."

He was then asked by the interviewing officers if there was any sexual motive for the killing. He replied "No, nothin' like that."

16:13

Fred West was charged with the murder of his daughter, Heather West, by Detective Constable Law. He made no reply after charge.

Fred was then keen to present himself as a man so overcome with grief at the death of his daughter that he was unable to think: "I mean, with Shirley and that it didn't matter. I wasn't bothered whether they were dead or alive, you know. I mean, it was just to get rid of them".

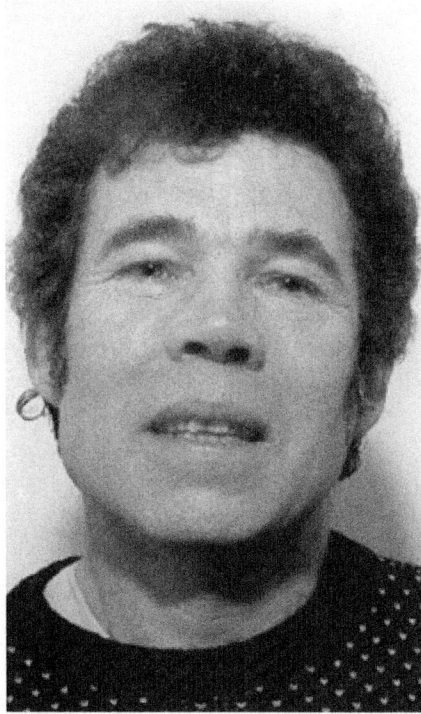

Fred West's mug shot having being charged with Heather's murder.

16:32

Fred described how he got rid of Heather's body, but accidentally gave away the possibility of there being more bodies to find. "It was a bright moonlit night. I remember that, the moon was shining bright, so there was no need for any lights or any at the bottom, dug the middle of this pool out quietly, took the top off it, and dug it out. But as I said, there was already a fair hole under there. So I thought, well gee, I can't get her down there and then I was looking at her body and I thought, gee, I'm going to cut her up again. Where's this gonna end? By this time I am realising that three...two, sorry that's two not three. Where is this gonna stop? I have got to give myself up. I've gotta tell Rose so she can get somebody to help me that I don't do this again. The problem I have, and I know it's a problem, and I knew I should have got help with it."

Later that day, Fred said: "I looked around everywhere, trying to find a knife or summat. I mean, I looked at the axe. I mean there was no way I could touch her with it. I just couldn't do it so I looked up and see this knife sticking out that had like two prongs and it had big serrated edges all along it. You could saw blocks of ice with it. So I finally managed to do it…unbearable…I can hear that now in my sleep. I wake up very often screaming."

The Gloucester Constabulary gave their first media release. It was held in the canteen at Gloucester police station. Present were local photographers and journalists, regional radio and TV stations with the usual London agencies and a couple of Bristol-based national journalists:

Police investigating the disappearance of Heather West have charged a 52-year-old Gloucester man with her murder. He will appear before the city magistrates tomorrow, accused of killing Heather between May 28th 1987 and February 27th 1994.

A 40-year-old Gloucester woman who was arrested on Friday in connection with Heather's disappearance is still being questioned by officers in the city.

Late yesterday police search teams searching a house and garden at 25 Cromwell Street discovered what appeared to be human remains. As a result Professor Bernard Knight has visited the scene and confirmed that they are the remains of a young female.

The remains were removed with the authority of HM Coroner Mr David Gibbons and are now undergoing examination at Gloucester Police Station. They will later be taken to Cardiff University to be examined by forensic experts.

The search of the house and the garden in Cromwell Street, Gloucester, has continued today and will continue tomorrow. We will seek further advice from the city council's engineers and surveyors department in connection with excavations there.

We would like to appeal to anyone who knows anything about Heather's whereabouts since May 28th 1987 to contact us at Gloucester Police Station.

An incident room has been set up in Gloucester Police Station led by DSI John Bennett and DCI Terry Moore.

In fact, Rose was being questioned in Cheltenham, seven miles away. The official press release did not name Fred West, but the following morning both the Daily Telegraph and the Western Daily Press named him as the man due to appear in court that morning charged with her murder.

18:56

Rosemary West was further interviewed before her release, but nothing of interest was garnered.

DSI Bennett knew that during the 1992 investigation Rose West had tried to commit suicide and he was concerned she might try again. This was why he had directed she be interviewed in the presence of an appropriate adult. Now his thoughts switched to where she would go and who would care for her – and if necessary prevent her harming herself again. So, while the bail forms were being typed, he told of his concerns to DC Hazel Savage and asked her to accompany him to the cells where they could raise the issue with Rose's solicitor Leo Goatley.

At first, Leo Goatley argued that there was no need to tell the police of her plans. DSI Bennett replied that he would release her for the matters for which she was under arrest but would immediately detain her for her own safety until he was satisfied that a responsible person would be with her – at least in the short term. At that the solicitor revealed she intended going back to Cromwell Street and promised to make sure her family would be there to look after her when she did.

One officer said: "She insists on staying in the house with all this going on around her."

20:30

Rose West was released on police bail under Section 47 (3) of the Police and Criminal Evidence Act 1984, to report back on 25th April. Throughout her two nights in custody she refused to eat anything, and she was examined by a doctor before being allowed to return home. She remained in the police station while her solicitor Leo Goatley checked out her domestic arrangements. Another 51 minutes elapsed before he returned to collect her.

21:22

Rose West was released from the police station and taken to 25 Cromwell Street to her family. She spent the evening with Mae, Stephen and his girlfriend Andrea all sleeping in the same room. According to Stephen and Mae, they could hear the sound of digging outside, but could see nothing as the windows had been covered with black plastic.

Mae: "When she came in she looked a bit of a mess. She was very quiet and she just sat down. Then she said: 'I'm spending one night here and then we are off, and we're never coming back to Cromwell Street again.'

Rose continued to sound off about Fred. "I can't believe this! That fucking man! That horrible, lying, evil fucking man! How could he do this? How could he do this to all of us? I knew he was a nasty piece of work but this…I'd never ever have imagined he could do something like this!"

28th February 1994

DSI Bennett had become unhappy that all of the paperwork and case files from the previous 1992 case had been destroyed shortly after the case had collapsed. He decided to apply for another search warrant, this time for the house, to enable the police to carry out a detailed forensic search of the ground floor and bathroom area to see if there was any evidence to support Fred West's account of where he had dismembered Heather and his two other victims. He knew the search would take a long time – perhaps a week or more – and that Rose, Mae, Stephen and his girlfriend Andrea would have to move out while the work was carried out. He also felt that everything in the house would now have to be gone through, especially any papers or photographs and anything that had been given back to them in 1992.

In a police briefing, DSI Bennett said that the main lines of inquiry should be to identify the other victims that Fred West had admitted to killing as well as finding and recovering them. 25 Cromwell Street would also be searched and the Wests rehoused. Completing the West family tree was most important in order to fill the gaps, as was tracing the rest of the West family to see if they were 'safe and well'. The immediate response from the floor was that they were already having problems tracing Fred's first wife Rena and her daughter Charmaine. DSI Bennett then handed over to the detectives who had been interviewing Fred West so they could add their views and perspectives. DC's Geoff Morgan and Barbara Harrison had now joined DC's Hazel Savage and Darren Law. "After he had killed Heather and cut her up, he was more concerned about his hedge than anything", said DC Savage. "When we hadn't found her we took him back to show us where he had buried her – he said we were looking in the wrong place as he wouldn't have dug that close to his hedge as it might have damaged it!"

10:00

Fred West appeared at Gloucester Magistrates' Court charged with the murder of his daughter, Heather West. His solicitor, Howard Ogden, told the court that Fred had admitted to killing his daughter, was being "utterly co-operative", and was also helping the police with two other murder enquiries. He was remanded in police custody for three days.

11:59

Fred West was interviewed and explained how he killed Shirley Robinson. Almost his first words were: "I've got to be straight and honest with you. I've no idea when. I know Rose was carrying one of the half-caste children…We wanted a half-caste child…and it was planned. So, I mean, I was quite excited about it." When he confessed to the murder of Shirley Robinson, he deliberately avoided getting in to any detail of precisely what happened. In his first interviews he was intent on maintaining that he alone had been involved, and no-one else. He told the police that he had "strangled her in the hall, in the living-room", when "Rose was in hospital having a baby." He also maintained that "I don't think Rose even knew Shirley…As far as I know Rose never met Shirley." He later added that Shirley was "pure lesbian" and then told another lie in saying "I don't know if she actually raped Anna, but she had sex with Anna-Marie."

He said the girl had been waiting for him on his allotment at Saintbridge, and had wanted to have sex with him. "I said, "I aint got time to mess with you. I got to get home….So we got in the van…We went home…and she was nagging on about me having sex with her…I remember I kept saying to her all the time, "keep to the agreement, the baby is yours" and that was the end of it." When they got back to Cromwell Street, Fred explained that Shirley had gone upstairs, but when he had joined her she had continued to nag him and had threatened to tell Rose that he was the father of her baby. "I looked at her and I thought, Gee, I've got to stop this bitch telling Rose, because Rose is the only thing that matters in my life, nothing else, not even my children." Then "I turned round and hit her actually, smacked her across the floor, knocked her across the room. She went flying down on the floor.

She wasn't dead…so I got her outside and locked the back doors and stayed out with her. And I sat on a block there used to be…Then I just sat there looking at her, and…it was going through me mind at the time, she's going to absolutely ruin me marriage…She's going to destroy the lot…There was loads of spare cable chucked on the floor there, all cut up. So I just went over and picked a piece of that up, and come back and just put it round her neck. I mean, I just didn't think to kill her, I wasn't thinking nothing."

All this took place "in the late evening", Fred maintained, and after he had killed the girl he had hidden her body under "this big heap of cut-off cables…and left her there…locked the patio doors…and I picked up a bag and I went to the hospital." When he got back, Shirley Robinson was "stiff, cold", so he lifted a slab outside his back door and beside the wall of the neighbouring church. "But then I couldn't get the hole anywhere near big enough, because it was going to take too long. So I went in the back door and got the knife…and just cut Shirley up there, took her arms and legs off, and then I packed her up…just pushed her in with a spade". He admitted that he had ripped "a summer dress thing" from her body "to stop the blood getting on the patio, because I had nothing else."

He claimed that he did it because "It had been carefully planned with Shirley not to say anything. I mean, I didn't want to get involved with Shirley or involved with any woman apart from Rose." He admitted he had "chucked her out once" but "she would not bloody stop calling me, and

263

coming and looking for me all the time." Finally, he insisted she had given him no alternative other than to kill her. "I was aware that Shirley was carrying a child of mine…and I mean the last thing I wanted to do was hurt a child of mine."

When DC Savage asked him if Shirley Robinson was the first person that he had killed, Fred replied quickly: "Yeah, yeah, yeah, yeah. There's only three. There's no more." He also insisted that he did not 'mutilate' her as such, just "pushed her in with a spade". Then once again he repeated: "Rose had no suspicion I was doing anything apart from building the wash-room" while he was dismembering Shirley Robinson's naked and pregnant body, although he admitted: "The ball joint makes a noise anyway…with the muscle and that pulling away."

Arrangements were made to re-house Rose West, Mae and Stephen. They were re-housed in police accommodation in Longlevens, Gloucester. The removals were carried out by members of the Force's Operations Department, using some furniture and effects from 25 Cromwell Street and other items supplied by Gloucestershire County Council's Social Services Department. In the hope that Rose might say something to her family that would incriminate her, the police had been in and bugged the flat.

Stephen was seen by the police as a volatile character and his lack of judgement soon disturbed the peace, and there were squabbles, rising to physical fights with his sister and girlfriend. Rose told him: "this isn't what we need right now. We should be sticking together." She even called the police at one point to say she would rather be behind bars if her son was going to act like his father and said to his face "You're as nuts as he is".

By this point, the national press were in contact with some of the key characters in this case. Unbeknown to the police, Stephen had made an arrangement with the 'News of The World' newspaper and seemed only interested in his own gain. He said he wanted to visit his father in prison, but Rose thought that this was only for commercial gain as the newspaper owners wanted him to report back to them after the visit.

The Daily Star was in contact with Anne Marie, against all legal rules governing interference with potential witnesses, and some newspapers placed anonymous advertisements in the local press asking for anyone who knew the Wests and could 'help with their enquiries' to contact a certain number.

15:32

Fred West was again interviewed and explained how he had killed Shirley Robinson without Rose West's knowledge. He gave a cold and detailed account to police of how he strangled, dismembered and disposed of Shirley Robinson in a style so bereft of any feeling that DC Hazel Savage admitted to being shocked. In this version, he accepted that his wife had not been in hospital at the time of Shirley Robinson's death, and that the girl had wanted him to pose for a photograph with her as "the father of the baby". This time he maintained that Shirley had met him at his allotment after he had left the Wagon Works for the day. "Shirley wanted me to go and live with her...so we went up to Painswick Hill...to talk it over right...She came up with "you love me" and all that...but I mean I wasn't interested, no way, and she knew that...or it was made clear to her." He then said that he took her back to Cromwell Street, only to find that his wife had gone out for a walk in the park with Tara, Heather, Mae and Stephen. He then insisted that he had killed her because "What Shirley had done is gone upstairs and told Liz (Brewer)."

He said that he hit her and then claimed that he had put her unconscious body in the wash-room he had recently created at the back of the house, and strangled her with a cable "to make sure she was dead". He used a brown serrated bread knife to cut her up – "that was how I found out that the bone would come out" - dug a small hole "and carried the pieces out and dropped them in the hole...I took the big piece out first, and then the head, and then the legs. I didn't have much room to put it in, so it had to be packed." He had dismembered the girl's body on her own summer dress, and washed her blood from his chest and arms in the sink. "If Rose had come out, she had no suspicion that I was doing anything, apart from building that wash-room...Rose didn't know nothing."

The dismemberment had been ferocious. The thigh bones had been chopped through with nine heavy strikes of a meat cleaver, as if the murderer were in a hurry or in a rage, and several bones, including kneecaps and finger-bones, had been removed. Fred's child, the eight-month old foetus, had been removed from her body and interred with her, mimicking what had happened eleven years earlier with Ann McFall and her baby. "If Rose had come out at all I could have said make a cup of tea and she'd have went straight back in and made it...she had no suspicion I was doing anything apart from building the washroom". Rose proceeded in years to come to "bathe the little ones and everything there, with Shirley just behind the wall, not even knowing".

17:20

A support group officer digging in the back garden of 25 Cromwell Street found the skull of a person, who was subsequently identified as Alison Chambers, under the patio and by the extension wall. It was in the area where the third femur had been recovered earlier. The Coroner David Gibbons was informed.

17:42

Fred was again interviewed and explained how he killed and buried Shirley's friend, later identified as Alison Chambers.

19:45

DSI Bennett and DCI Moore returned to Cromwell Street. They were shown an area just in front of the extension's bathroom window, not far below the surface and certainly no more than 2ft or so down in the glutinous mud. Along with clear evidence of human remains there was the faint smell of adiopocere. Where the mud had been moved back, an off-white to yellow area of bone and the mostly hidden but still recognisable features of a skull with hair matted in mud showed through.

21:00

A support group officer digging in the back garden of 25 Cromwell Street found the remains of a person who was subsequently identified as Shirley Robinson. Shirley's body would be the only one found at Cromwell Street without any form of tape or rope on the body.

1st March 1994

09:00

Professor Bernard Knight attended at the house to examine the remains of Alison Chambers and Shirley Robinson prior to their removal for forensic examination.

Professor Knight began with the remains of Alison Chambers. As he began to remove the skull, its hair slid to one side. Everyone there could see there was something wound beneath the chin and up around the top of the head though it was masked by black slime. Professor Knight gently scraped at the surface with his fingers until it was obvious it was a wide belt with a large buckle. Even though it was now quite loose, it would have prevented her from opening her mouth because the presence of flesh and hair would have made it much tighter. There were hair fragments still attached to the buckle. Unlike the other bodies, there were no obvious injuries to the bones, but the pathologist concluded that the body had still been cut up before burial.

Her remains were jumbled. Both her kneecaps were missing. Her upper breastbone had been removed, as had 63 finger and toe bones. Oddly, her fingernails and toenails were recovered. A total of 96 bones were missing. There was no evidence Alison Chambers was clothed when buried.

DSI Bennett said: "Well, unless Fred is telling another story today then he has got some explaining to do. He's made no mention of this belt, just that he used his hands to kill her like he did Heather – that's if this is the girl who came to find Shirley. It will be interesting to see what story he comes up with to get round this."

When Fred was confronted with this, he insisted: "She wasn't actually bondaged...it was just whatever was put on her...so I could keep her together and lift her... I can't even remember putting a belt on her head."

Moving across the boards to the third set of remains, those of Shirley Robinson, Professor Knight could see that the hole was wedged between the wall of the Seventh Day Adventist church and the doorstep of the house. The bone and shape of the back of a human skull was just visible. There appeared to be no hair this time which lead to the police and the pathologist wondering if she had been scalped.

He retrieved some vertebrae, and then came some leg bones including a femur. As the mud was scraped from the bone it exposed a number of deep black marks, some of which penetrated right through, along with a larger number of finer ones. Professor Knight said they had probably been made with a very sharp blade such as that of a cleaver or heavy knife. There were twenty-one fine cuts slicing the fifth cervical vertebra, which indicated that she had been decapitated. Both of Shirley's kneecaps were missing when her skeleton was discovered. Her unborn child's head was not in Shirley Robinson's pelvis, and it had not been left intact in the abdomen. Fred West would later suggest that he had cut the baby from her womb in an effort to keep it alive, but missing fingers and toes suggested otherwise. Her right thigh bone had been severed with a heavy but very sharp weapon. 28 of Shirley's wrist and ankle bones, and 42 of her finger and toe bones were missing. 3 of Shirley's vertebrae were also missing. Her legs had been disarticulated at the hips. Some brain tissue remained with the skull. Once again, there was no evidence of her being clothed when buried.

11:30

Fred West was interviewed regarding the murder of the person who transpired to be Alison Chambers. He denied that the police would find any more victims and insisted "there's three in the garden and that's it". He also denied that he may have become confused over the identity of 'Shirley's mate'.

At first, he gave an unexpected explanation for Alison Chambers' death. He insisted that she had turned up at Cromwell Street to blackmail him with a copy of the portrait photograph he had had taken sixteen months earlier with Shirley Robinson. He maintained that the sixteen-year-old from Swansea, who had not even arrived in Gloucester when Shirley Robinson disappeared, was, in fact, 'Shirley's mate'. Clearly confusing her at first with another young woman, who he said was "big-boned" and twenty-two years of age, he went on to insist that the girl he only ever knew as "Shirley's mate" had turned up at Cromwell Street "several years" after Shirley Robinson's death and said to him: "As far as I can gather you killed Shirley."

Details of what had been found in the grave with the remains of 'Shirley's mate' began to emerge. There had been bindings. DC Savage did not go into detail, asking only "What are they for?" He sidestepped quickly. He accepted that he may have "put straps" around the girl's body to "help him carry" her. And when DC Hazel Savage asked him why she had a piece of belt tied around her skull, he still stuck to his story. He said instantly: "Well, that probably had another piece through it. Holding her head forward."

15:32

Fred West was again interviewed and gave further details about the remains found. He rapidly changed his story, suggesting instead that "Shirley's mate" had arrived "between twelve months and two years" after Shirley Robinson. "She came to the door and asked if Shirley was there, and I said, "Shirley don't live here now", and she said, "Yes, yes, she does…I've got a photograph here of you with Shirley". Fred said he then told her to "go to a café or something and have a cup of tea and come back later", because "Rose was cooking the dinner."

Fred then began to heap lie upon lie. He suggested that "Shirley's mate" was the girl Shirley Robinson had told him she was "having the baby for", and that he had sent her down to his café in Southgate Street (though it had closed two years earlier). I said: "I'll come down and pick you up"…So anyway I…sent Rose out to sleep for the night…went down with the van, drove past the café, she came out and…went back home with her to try and sort it out". Back in Cromwell Street, he explained: "She said that Shirley said in her letter that if she didn't turn up in so long or something then to come and get me and I'd know where she was. I said, "What do you mean by that?" and she said… "That you could have knocked her off, killed her." She was telling me about Shirley, and if she didn't find her she'd go round and get the police, and all this lot, so we had an argument, a row, and I punched her on the jaw first, and knocked her on the floor and strangled her."

He went on to tell the police that he had buried the girl's body under a "big paddling-pool" in his garden, which was made out of blue engineering bricks. "All I done was lifted them up and packed her underneath him, and dropped him back on top of her." Finally, he confessed that he had cut the girl's body up into four pieces, a head, torso and two legs, with his sheath knife.

Fred could not come up with a plausible explanation for why the baby was not found in Shirley's womb and laughably suggested that the baby might have fallen out. "I never touched the baby at all".

That afternoon he finally accepted that he had made admissions of his own guilt only when he had been trapped in a corner. When DC Hazel Savage pointed out that he had made his confession about three bodies only after he had seen the extent of the police excavations at Cromwell Street, he muttered: "Well?"

DC Savage: What did you mutter to me when I was fingerprinting you? You said, "Did you blame me for trying it on?"
Fred: But when I realised they were going the whole way, then what's the point?

DC Savage leaned across the desk.

DC Savage: Right, so you haven't been totally cooperative, have you? It's been a bit like pulling teeth.
Fred: Well, were you expecting it any other way?

Detective Superintendent Bennett met with Paul Britton, a Consultant Clinical Psychologist with the Trent Regional Psychology Unit at Leicester in a hope to further understand the crimes of Fred and Rose, and ask for advice on the best ways to proceed with questioning.

18:00

The police briefing began. DS Roger Kelland, who was trying to establish the identity of remains thought to be those of Shirley Robinson, said they were making progress towards identifying her father and tracing her mother, who, it appeared, were no longer together. Others who knew her had not seen her since May 1978, though she was never reported as missing.

As for the other set of remains (Alison Chambers), it was looking more likely she too may have been in care as 25 Cromwell Street seemed to be a magnet for girls with no real roots. They already knew that Fred West's first wife was named Rena Costello and that she had at least two daughters,

Anne Marie who was Fred's and the older Charmaine who wasn't. A priority now was to track them down and, even more important, find out if they were safe and well.

A press conference was then held, during which a poster was released asking for information on Rena Costello and her whereabouts. The force's Press Officer Hilary Allison asked DSI Bennett to hold it due to the amount of calls and questions they were facing.

APPEALS

MISSING
can you help?

CATHERINE COSTELLO

Gloucester Police have asked the national charity the Missing Persons Helpline to try and make contact with Catherine Costello.

Relatives have not heard from her for over 20 years.

Catherine Costello may be living somewhere in Scotland, but could be anywhere.

WE WOULD APPEAL TO CATHERINE COSTELLO OR ANYONE WHO KNOWS HER OR HAS ANY INFORMATION TO CALL THE 24 HOUR MISSING PERSONS HELPLINE ON (081) 392 2000.

Posters supported by *Today*

081-392 2000
24 HOURS
MISSING PERSONS HELPLINE

MISSING PERSONS BUREAU

The missing poster for Rena Costello

270

DSI Bennett began with a brief statement that covered the finding of the remains but he quickly moved on to taking questions. DCI Terry Moore was sat alongside him. He confirmed the find of "two further sets of remains, possibly those of young women, having been recovered from the garden of 25 Cromwell Street that morning."

The questions he then faced included:

"Who are these young women?" and "Can't you give us photographs, we might be able to help you find who they are?" DSI Bennett calmly reiterated that what had been found were "remains" – resisting the use of 'bones' in deference to the victim's relatives. "The state of the remains is such that any conventional means of identification like photographs are out of the question."

Press: How did they die?

DSI Bennett: At present we do not know and factually we might never know.

Press: You must know whether they were stabbed, shot or strangled? Any knife wounds, bullet holes?

DSI Bennett: Human remains have been found, not bodies. We hope the media will report it that way so as to save unnecessary work and calls coming in to the investigation from those who have lost loved ones and want to try and identify them. What we are engaged in is similar to an archaeological dig.

He confirmed that one skull had been found and that "They are not complete skeletons."

DSI Bennett: At this stage it is impossible to tell the age of the people we have found, how long they have been dead or how they died. We are having difficulty with identification due to the condition of the remains. There are, however, positive lines of inquiry in respect of two of the remains. One of these centres in Gloucester in relation to Heather West. We don't feel able at this moment to give specific information on the other regions in which inquiries are being made. We have no wish to cause undue anxiety for any family which may be unfortunate enough to have a missing person as a relative. It would be very helpful if people who are concerned, or feel they may have any information, to contact us.

Around this time, Dean Barry, Fred's son from his affair at a Barry Island Holiday Centre, recalled: "We were in the front room watching the news. A picture of Fred West came up on screen. All the colour drained from Mum's face and she ran out of the room. I could not understand why.

271

It was only later it made complete sense." His mother agonised over whether to tell him the truth. He had grown up believing his dad was the man Lyn cheated on at the time of her fling and who went on to become her husband. She said: "It was eating away at me so it took a while to pluck up the courage to tell Dean. I still don't know whether I did the right thing in telling him."

"We went into the kitchen and she said she had something important to tell me", recalled Dean. "She looked at me and said, 'Dean, I'm sorry to tell you, but that man who did all those murders — he's your real father'. I couldn't believe my ears. I didn't really understand what she was saying. She was crying and I started to cry too. I don't think she wanted to tell me, but she thought I had a right to know. I was totally shocked."

Fred's brother, Doug West, told the local press: "I can't believe the news. Fred has always been such a gentle guy. He would not hurt a fly. He just did his work and loved his family. They were the two loves of his life and now he's supposed to be a murderer." His wife Christine described Fred as "like Heather – gentle and quiet."

A woman in the local area told reporters from the Daily Express: "I used to go there when I was 16 – that's 17 years ago – to look after the children. It makes me shudder now when I think about it. Looking back, I remember there used to be a lot of comings and goings late at night. I was told at the time that people were playing cards in the house. It makes you wonder now."

Retired Joe Heffernan, 67, was a neighbour in Cromwell Street for 22 years. "Fred used to work at a concrete works called Dowmac. His first wife was blonde and quite a looker but she ran off with an engineer. Then he met Rosemary. They were a lovely family. I used to say hello to the children as they were coming and going from the house to school. They were always immaculately dressed and turned out. I knew Heather, and I was shocked when I heard what had happened. I used to see Fred working all hours. He never went to the pub. He just worked and spent time with his family. I used to see him working for the neighbours. He seemed very regimental. It is terrible – I still can't believe it. It is just an ordinary street."

Tina Waugh, a school friend of Heather's, remembered her as being "very insecure. She was a funny, lonely type. She always said she wanted to join the army or something like that. I never thought much about her after that, because I never saw her. I hope it's not her body they have found."

One neighbour, who would only identify herself as 'Meg' and was in her 30's, said: "It is terrible living here now. We are being called the Street of Death. I live at the opposite end, but if my husband knocked me off and buried me in the garden, nobody would know about it – That's the sort of street it is. I won't let my kids stay out in the street anymore. I want to move."

2nd March 1994

A phone call was put through to DSI Bennett in the Senior Investigating Officer's office. The caller asked if he could remember a fire officer called Gough who had worked in fire prevention at the Cheltenham fire headquarters. "Did he ever mention that his daughter went missing some time ago?" He then related how Lynda Gough had left home in Gloucester in the early 1970's when she was about 20 to live with a man and woman in the city whom he was sure lived in Cromwell Street. After a while, her parents went to the address and although they were told their daughter had left, they noticed that the woman who came to the door was wearing some of their daughter's clothes and that some of her other things were on a washing line. He had not spoken to the Gough's and wondered whether the police knew. DSI Bennett asked if the girl's disappearance had ever been reported. The caller was not sure though he thought that it had been mentioned to a police officer neighbour.

A Forensic examination of the two sets of remains found on 28th February confirmed them to be those of two women.

Word had started to spread and the national press, as well as the local papers tried to gather as much information about the occupants of 25 Cromwell Street as possible. Interviewed in the 'Today' newspaper, Doug West would say: "Fred was such a gentle guy – he wouldn't hurt a fly. He was often bullied at school, and our other brother John would have to stick up for him. He was a superb dad. His work and his family were the two great loves in his life. He loved those kids and he would give you his last shilling if you needed it."

A young mother who lived further down the road, and did not want to be named, said one of her daughters had been to the Wests' house to play. "She used to come home and tell me about playing in their garden and how they had a cellar with a trap door covered by a carpet."

A neighbour said: "They were a quiet family who kept themselves to themselves. You couldn't just go and knock on their door. They had an extra set of gates put up with a bell on, so if you went through them they always looked through the window. This was just a typical inner-city street, but you never know what goes on behind closed doors."

Shopkeeper Imtiaz Kholwadia said: "The family were regular customers – the woman used to come in with six or seven children around her. The boys did not play out so much and when we kicked a ball in the park they did not join in."

Another neighbour said: "Heather was just an ordinary girl. We heard she wanted to work in a holiday camp – but we did not think much about it after that."

Stephen West was quoted as saying "She just wanted to be independent – that's the way she was… She always kept herself to herself. It wasn't surprising she didn't keep in touch – she was a loner."

John West, Fred's brother and Heather's uncle, told of when he last saw her. She was "happy and full of hope." He said that she was "very excited" because she had just fixed up a job in a holiday camp. "She was with her mother in the centre of Gloucester. She told me she had just fixed up a job in the camp – I don't know which one. I pulled her leg because she was so happy and said 'you must have been spending a lot of money'. Heather was such a pretty girl and a happy one as far as I know. I last visited Fred's house about four years ago. It is hard to imagine what they are saying about Heather being buried in the back garden of their home. Everything seemed so normal. I did ask Fred over the years how Heather was getting on. He always said he thought she was doing fine."

11:50

Fred West was interviewed regarding his background history. He said: "I met Rose at sixteen and trained her to what I wanted". He would often talk about the men Rose would sleep with. "Rose only had big fucking blokes. She didn't want little worms playing about with her." She didn't like "some little thing wriggling about" in her.

DC Savage: You find Rose so perfect for your needs, and the fear of losing her is beyond belief to you?
Fred: Yes…yes
DC Savage: Because for all those years, as you say, you've trained her, down to letters and commands, and she's complied, and she's got a very wide and open… (The officer is about to say 'attitude to sexual matters')
Fred: (interrupting) Vagina, isn't it what they call it?
DC Savage: And that pleases you?
Fred: Yep
DC Savage: And that has taken a lot of years for you to perfect?
Fred: Yep

15:30

Fred West was charged with the murders of Shirley Robinson between 1st January 1972 and 27th February 1994 and an unknown female (Alison Chambers) between the same dates. A day after his confession, Fred changed his story again. "I don't actually believe this girl was old enough to actually be associated with Shirley. She didn't seem to me to be. The only thing I can't understand is where she got the photograph from and the so-called letter. I never actually seen the letter but I've got the photograph off her." This time, he explained that the girl had turned up looking for "Cromwell Road and not Cromwell Street" and that he had been driving her around looking for "Cromwell Road" when "she produced this photograph, because I think what she was doing was building up courage" to ask him. In this second version, he suggested the girl was "too young-looking" to be Shirley Robinson's "lesbian friend", and that he had simply "dropped her off". "Then she turns up again, later, and she starts the same crack again, and she starts putting threats. She wanted money to go off somewhere." Fred still maintained that he never knew her name.

"Rose would definitely not have seen her". He described Alison Chambers as: "about five feet two", with "blonde crinkly hair...just to her ears", and "blue eyes", estimating her age as "fourteen, fifteen, sixteen, if that." In this second version the girl had turned up "a month or two" later, but he had prevented her from even entering Cromwell Street, and had instead set off to drive her back to Bristol when she started demanding money. "Then she starts giving me all that, evil of the day, all she could think of. What she was going to do to me and what she was going to tell the police that I'd done." He pulled into a lay-by, "had a right shouting match" with her, then decided to drive her back towards Cromwell Street. When they were nearby, in a garage off Saint Michael's Square, behind his house, "She set going again, so I grabbed her by the neck with me hands and choked her."

He claimed that by now it was after midnight, "So I...put her along under the window by the back door", took a piece of "thirty amp cable" and twisted it around her neck because "I wasn't sure she was actually dead". He then claimed to the police that he could not make the hole under the paddling-pool in the garden any bigger "without using a sledge-hammer" – "plus the fact that Rose is in bed" – and so had been forced to cut her up into the four pieces he had originally described.

18:00

During the police briefing, DS Roger Kelland, who had been working on finding Shirley Robinson's relatives, believed that by the next day he would succeed. Her father was thought to be in Germany, divorced from Shirley's mother, and there were new leads that would help him trace her, too.

Lynda Gough's father had been in touch and confirmed much of what the police were told on the phone earlier in the day. Meeting both Lynda's parents was now a priority.

A media briefing was then held, where DSI Bennett confirmed that Fred West had been charged with the murder of two other women…

"…following the discovery of human remains in the garden of a house in Cromwell Street. The forensic examination of the remains is ongoing. It is still too early to say how the women died. Examination of the remains by Home Office pathologist Professor Bernard Knight has revealed that one of the women was in her late teens. We believe she was using the name Shirley Robinson and was aged 18, although the remains have not yet been formally identified. We believe she was in the latter stages of pregnancy when she died and had been living in Gloucester for some time. We can't say who the father of the unborn baby was… She was a lodger at 25 Cromwell Street. Inquiries are still active to trace any relatives but at this time we are not aware of any living in this country. However, if anyone knows of a person of that name or any relatives, we would like to hear from them. We know that she spent some of her life in Leicestershire, Wolverhampton and Bristol."

DSI Bennett also said that police were checking dental records for a formal identification of Shirley and to help identify the third woman. He said that the remains of the third victim were believed to be those of a woman in her early twenties. "The search at the house is continuing. We have removed documentation from it to help us understand the family history. We have not found evidence of other bodies, despite speculation." He also said that inquiries were being carried out in Scotland.

By this time, the team of investigating officers had expanded from fifteen to thirty, DSI Bennett explained, and this was apart from the search teams still working at Cromwell Street. The police had also decided to empty the house entirely of its contents.

Some of the questions centered on Shirley Robinson but there were more about Rena West and Charmaine and the fact that neither had been seen for many years.

DSI Bennett said that what appeared to be positive lines of inquiry were being followed up as regards to Shirley Robinson's relatives. He also appealed for Rena West, formerly Costello, or anyone who knew her or had seen her, to come forward.

A police spokesman added: "It would be fair to say that the women were probably lesbians. They were not relatives of the accused man."

Police brought back the previous tenants of 25 Cromwell Street. "We wanted them to cast their minds back and describe what changes there have been in the lay-out", said a detective.

Chief Inspector Colin Handy appealed for more information about

Shirley Robinson. "She lived for some time as a lodger at the West's home but we are not sure when or for how long."

3rd March 1994

10:00

Fred West was further remanded in police custody for three days at Gloucester Magistrates Court. As the clerk was reading out the second charge, the murder of Shirley Robinson, Fred West's face turned white and then green. His knees buckled and he grabbed on to the rail in front of him until he was helped into his seat by the uniformed police officer who was guarding him.

Statements had now been taken from Lynda Gough's parents and they made interesting reading. Lynda Gough had left home and later gone missing but before she actually went a woman had called at their home to take her for a drink. She left with her in a car that was waiting nearby. Lynda had been telling her parents she wanted to move out to get some experience of life. Although they were not in favour they accepted she had to go and get it out of her system. June Gough, Lynda's mum, was sure it was mid-April 1972 when her daughter left. She had taken everything she owned, leaving behind a note, which they had kept. It read:

Dear Mum and Dad

Please don't worry about me, I have got a flat and I will come and see you sometime,

love Lyn

In order to make sure she was OK, her parents found out where she was living and checked to see if she had kept up her work as a seamstress, but when, after a few weeks, she did not return home as they had hoped, June Gough had gone to the address where she believed Lynda was staying. She was sure it was 25 Cromwell Street.

She recalled it was on a Saturday morning and she saw the same dark-haired woman who had called for Lynda before she had left home. She was with a man who also had dark hair who, from the way he talked and acted, she thought was the woman's husband. When June Gough asked them about her daughter they told her she had "left and gone to Weston-Super-Mare" – a Bristol Channel resort some 50 miles away. As they spoke, she noticed the woman was wearing slippers that she recognised as Lynda's. She was also wearing a blouse or cardigan, she was not sure which now, that also belonged to her daughter, and on a washing line were other items of clothing she recognised as Lynda's. When she mentioned this the couple passed it off by saying: "She just left this all behind when she left."

Most, if not all, of what had taken place they had told a neighbouring police officer and friend, whom they thought had noted it but they hadn't formally reported Lynda missing because they accepted that as she was in her late teens and regarded as an adult there was little they could do to make her return home, and despite making enquiries through the Salvation Army they never heard from her again.

Fred West was interviewed about his time in Scotland working as an ice cream seller. He went on to tell of the accident in which a young boy died. "This little lad got to like it (ice cream) and he come every day and I bought him a bright coloured ball, about that big, about four-or-five-inch ball, and I gave it him the day before... and in this cul-de-sac they had hedges which was about three foot high". He backed his van up to park and heard "one almighty bang and I stopped there and then and it was on top of his head and it was his head that had made the bang".

He talked about having "hundreds of girls" while he was in the Merchant Navy, and on several occasions being in bed with three or four girls at the same time and making love "at least twice with each a night." He explained that he disliked homosexuals – "I mean, I couldn't kiss a man" – but felt that lesbians were a different matter – "There's nothing dirty about two women being attracted to each other, is there?" He told the officers interviewing him that he liked to watch his wife with other men – "It's a turn on" – and that "It was important to keep our sex life alive and changing." But he insisted "I haven't touched other girls since Shirley, because it was causing slight problems with Rose."

He was asked if he could remember some of the residents of Cromwell Street, whose names the police had discovered. He managed to remember many young people – except a girl named Lynda Gough: "Don't ring a bell. I mean, there were dozens of girls staying there that shouldn't have been there. They were using the address", he said. When he was told that her parents had even come to look for her after she had stayed at Cromwell Street, he replied cheerfully: "I...we had hundreds of parents coming asking...Hazel (Savage) was there very often, fetching girls from there." When Detective Constable Savage suggested that Lynda Gough could be the third girl in the garden, Fred West said only: "Wouldn't have thought so."

When told that the police had a statement from Lynda Gough's parents, he claimed that someone was "making it up", "getting on the band wagon" to make money out of the press. Mocking his interrogators he argued that he could not have been in Cromwell Street in April 1972 because he hadn't bought it then.

Digging at 25 Cromwell Street continued as well as numerous enquiries from the incident room set up at Gloucester Police Station. At the evening police briefing it was confirmed that Shirley Robinson's mother had been found and interviewed.

4th March 1994

In the morning police briefing, it was agreed that finding Lynda Gough was a top priority. DSI Bennett outlined their intentions to search the whole of 25 Cromwell Street "properly", which meant that once they had excavated under the extension they would move on to the cellar because "It would be unthinkable for someone in the future to find evidence of more victims that we had not found."

DC's Savage and Law mentioned how Fred West regularly asked about his home and what sort of condition it was in. News that the extension may have to come down and the floor dug up, said DC Law, might give him something more to think about and knock his confidence – especially when he learned of the ground-penetrating radar equipment.

Specialist ground scanning equipment, which indicated any disturbance behind solid matter, was used at 25 Cromwell Street. Arrangements had also been made to X-Ray the walls. ERA Technology Ltd of Leatherhead, Surrey, carried out the search of 25 Cromwell Street. Their surface penetrating radar was developed originally for the detection of buried plastic mines.

At this stage, Mary Bastholm and Lucy Partington had almost been dismissed as being the second set of remains found, while the combination of date and forensics they had so far gathered seemed to rule out Lynda Gough as well.

14:18

Fred West was interviewed and this time admitted knowing Lynda Gough. He said that Lynda Gough had been seeing one of his lodgers, and had then asked if she could move in. "The room by the bathroom was empty, so I said yes." He even admitted that he and his wife had gone to pick up Lynda's belongings from her parents' house. But he then maintained that she had been involved with a lodger called Terry who had "smashed me straight on the top of the head" with an ashtray when he had asked him about her, injuring him so badly that he had "to go to hospital for stitches". After that, Terry and Lynda had left for Weston-Super-Mare, "as far as I know." As the interview drew to a close at 15.17, Detective Constable Savage told Fred that the police intended to "dig up the whole of the basement".

16:32

DSI Bennett and DCI Moore arrived at Cromwell Street. The house had been stripped of all of the West's belongings. The upper floors had been cleared and every feature now exposed was being systematically logged. The narrow staircase leading to the cellar was steeply angled, making it necessary for most people to bend slightly to prevent banging their heads as they went down.

It was the same in the cellar where the two men from ERA Technology Ltd dragged their machine to and fro across the bare, grey concrete floor, stooping slightly to avoid the low ceiling and beams that ran across it. The floor extended throughout the cellar and was partially divided into three: a large area to the rear of the property, a smaller area in the centre partially enclosed by part walls and the stairs, and another larger area similar in size to that at the rear.

The walls of the rooms were almost bare of paper. Children's drawings and paintings on the plaster added to the eerie atmosphere.

When DSI Bennett and DCI Moore got back to the police station, DC's Hazel Savage and Darren Law approached them. "Something's up. Now he says he doesn't want to be interviewed anymore, at least not until he's seen Ogden. Canavan (one of Ogden's clerks) is with him now, and Janet Leach. We don't know whether he wants to make a complaint or what."

They also updated DSI Bennett on the interviews so far during the day and how Fred now remembered Lynda Gough, though she wasn't there in 1972 but a long time later, and that she had gone off to Weston-Super-Mare with another tenant called Terry.

DSI Bennett and DCI Moore then left them and went into their office where a few minutes later DSI Bennett took a call telling him that Howard Ogden was in the building and wanted to see him urgently. DSI Bennett agreed and arranged for him to be brought up.

The three men met on the landing. Howard Ogden's face was pale, deadpan and serious. "You may like to sit down before reading this" he said as he handed over a lined piece of paper torn from a notebook.

9 THE CONFESSION

I, Frederick West, authorise my solicitor, Howard Ogden, to advise Detective Superintendent Bennett that I wish to admit to a further (approx.) 9 killings expressly Charmaine, Rena, Lynda Gough and others to be identified.

DSI Bennett asked DCI Moore to find DC's Hazel Savage and Darren Law and within seconds there were five in the office. Howard Ogden said that Fred would go into more detail later but that the victims had been buried in Cromwell Street and Midland Road and included, he thought, Lucy Partington.

18:10

Fred West was interviewed and admitted killing and burying Lynda

Gough, Rena West and her daughter Charmaine. When the confession note was read out in the formal interview, DC Savage asked Fred exactly how many bodies there were in Cromwell Street. He replied calmly: "That's the ones I can remember."

In the first minutes of the interview, Fred confidently explained: "I got it in me mind in a certain way and I don't want to change that if I can help it." He told the officers first that Lynda Gough was under the bathroom, "quite deep...'cause there was a big cellar underneath originally". Then he told the police that they needed to move on to the cellar. He explained that they needed to look for a series of graves, adding: "Now these, I'm not a hundred percent sure on some of these."

He identified the first body as being buried by the false fireplace he had put in the front cellar room: "I think she was Dutch or summat". Another girl in the cellar was from Newent, but he could not remember her name. But he could remember that another was called Lucy Partington, although he was not sure exactly which of the graves contained her body. He also gave an explanation about how Lucy Partington was killed. He insisted that he had known Lucy Partington for some months before she disappeared. He also insisted that they used to make love regularly in Cheltenham's nearby Pittville Park (less than a 5 minute walk from where she was last seen), and that he had even given her a name, "Juicy Lucy", due to the amount of vaginal fluids that she had. According to his first version of events, he had been waiting for her when she left her friend, and Lucy Partington had been sitting in his van waiting for the bus to arrive when they started to argue. "She said she wanted me to run her out near her home or summat, and what she was actually saying was "come and meet my parents. So I met her this night, and picked her up, and what she'd done, she'd found my phone number...'cause she come the loving racket...and wanted to come and live with me and all this rubbish...anyway, we had a row over it...I mean, it was always made clear to these girls that there was no affair, it was purely sex, end of story, and if they ever tried to threaten to tell my wife, they could be in serious trouble.

Anyway, I reminded her that I said...like, any messing with my home and you're in deep trouble...and, oh, she got quite nasty about it. She said I wanna come and live with you and all this crap, and I just grabbed her by the throat."

He then suggested that he had killed Lucy in his van that evening, driven her body back to Cromwell Street, and pushed it down into his cellar through the vent in the back wall. Throughout this, and subsequent police interviews, he insistently repeated that he and Lucy has been "having an affair" for several months, and that he first met her "in the early summer" when he had taken his children to the boating-lake in Pittville Park on a Sunday afternoon. "I got going with her after. It was all secret, hush, hush.

I met Lucy as I said in the first place, in the park, right, in Pittville Park…when I was walking the children. I was sat on the seat talking to her, and they were playing, throwing stuff in the lake, you know, and feeding the ducks and all that. And then I took the children home and I arranged to meet her back at night, and I came and met her on that hill, and, um, we had a bit of a sex romp and that, and that was it. Then I didn't see her again for a long time, for a while, quite some time, then I met her again, that was on the other side of the park…I was there with the children then again, and Rose was somewhere. But I think Rose was down on the swings…and I took them up to see the peacocks up at the top and…I seen her and I went across and had a chat to her…and then I met her the following night again. Then I didn't see her for a while after that."

He seemed to remember her well: "Fairly slim, shoulder-length black hair, a student. I had the children with me when I met her, and that's what fascinated her towards me. I think it was the children; she came talking to them and that." He certainly knew that she "used to catch a bus from Pittville Park", because "She had a mate up there", and he maintained that she would meet him either before or after she "had been to see her mate." He said that he used to "park in Pittville Park and wait for her…I met her quite a few times", keeping the van out of sight.

"I mean when we met, like…it was sex and virtually straight away, and then had a chat, used to lie on the grass and have a chat, and then probably sex again…because we only met more or less in the dark, like, in late evening…She was a very talkative girl, actually; she used to try and cram I suppose a week's news into a couple of hours, like…'cause we get on well together, I mean, too well, that was the problem." He said he agreed to meet Lucy in the park because he was afraid that his wife's parents, or her brothers, might see him. "Her brother used to walk that road regular, all hours of the day and night, to his girlfriends in Cheltenham…and he did catch me and Rose once in the park, or seen us, and went back and reported it to his parents…And the last thing I wanted them to do was to go and tell Rose I was meeting another girl in Cheltenham."

He claimed that he would never risk taking Lucy Partington to a pub or a café, or anywhere else in Cheltenham, in case he encountered his brother-in-law. It was this fear of discovery that had caused the difficulties that night. He said that she had "got my phone number and address from somewhere, her wanted me to see her parents, her wanted me to do bloody everything. Then she was going to ring up Rose, go and see my wife, tell her we were having an affair…because she reckoned I was taking advantage of her." It was this threat, he maintained, that led to him strangling her in the park, putting her body in the van, and taking her back to Cromwell Street. "Don't forget once I'd beat their brains out they wouldn't know what time of day it was. Whether they were girls or boys they hadn't got a clue what they were doing."

He was asked if all the bodies were dismembered. His reply was shocking and succinct. "To my memory, yes."

Fred then went on to give a graphic and blunt account of Rena's death. He said Rena had threatened Rose when she went to collect Charmaine. "It was Rena threatened Rose and Rena come and see me about it and I told her she couldn't have Charmaine". He then claimed that Rena went to the child's school to collect her. "I went and found Rena and then Charmaine was in the back of the car asleep. He said he took Rena to the East End Tavern in Barton Street in Gloucester one night in August. "I took Rena in the pub and got her absolutely paralytic and then took her out to Dymock in the country where I know and I strangled her and buried her." He said she had passed out in the car from all the alcohol, and when he stopped he dragged her unconscious body out of the car, dragged her over to the field and then "I just smashed her against the gate". He then strangled her with his belt. He dragged her over to the tree he knew as the marker in the hedge, and using a "massive" Jamaican sabre knife, a two-and-a-half-feet-long sugar-beet scythe that somebody had given him once for chopping nettles, he took off her legs and her head and jammed the trunk of her body into the ground. Using the sheath knife that he always carried on his belt, he removed a kneecap and a number of fingers and toes and set them aside to bring away with him. He recalled the ground was hard, which pointed to high summer, probably July or August. He washed his hands and chest in a cattle trough and then took Rena's clothes and bundled them and threw them over into an adjoining field where there was a fire burning.

"I think Rena had given Charmaine a drink of some sort, a bottle of lager or something. And then she drank that and she was sound asleep and I had forgotten all about her. I went back to the van and I found her [Rena's] car. There was Charmaine in the back of it, and I thought 'shit, what am I going to do now?' She must have been about six or seven, perhaps eight, summat like that, but she was only little for her age.

Anyway, I strangled her while she was still sleeping because there is no way I could have touched her any other way, and wrapped her up in the back and drove back to Midland Road. By that time Midland Road had a garage up the side of the house. I used to use it and you could go out of the back of the garage into a little workshop and then into the underneath of the house, the basement. I put her in there."

Years later, after he had moved to Cromwell Street, the landlord asked Fred to build an extension at Midland Road. This was, he said, a perfect opportunity to rebury his stepdaughter's remains further down in the foundations. "I had the perfect opportunity to make sure of it then." The police asked where they would find her body. "You won't" he said. "Not without taking the building down, cos she's in the footings".

In his usual fashion, in order to give himself time to think, he then went off on a story of how a hitman called Norman White had worked with him on that job. He told how he knew Norman (a Jamaican) and his family. "He worked with me in Midland Road, putting up ceilings. When I did the six flats there. Me an' him got on great together. He was a great guy, till he got on that ganja…He always treated me like a gentleman. Still does to this day. Always called me Mister West. If anyone said anything about me…He thought the world of me…I've known his sisters since years. I mean, Marcia's about the same age as Anna. Very big fat girl she is, ever so pleasant…Lives there on her own. I know why an' all. (Her father) potted two of his daughters. One was shipped off to America. The other daughter lost the baby in the bathroom of that house, on the floor…I did the whole of that house inside, decorated it some years back when Euan got married, married a Welsh girl…"

Later on he added that he was worried about Rosemary finding out, because "what's she gonna say"? He claimed that "I had too many people to watch at once. That's what went wrong."

22:20

Detectives took Fred back to 25 Cromwell Street dressed in similar overalls to those worn by the police search team so as not to be recognised by the press. He indicated the areas where the bodies were buried in the basement using an aerosol paint spray, marking eighteen-inch squares to indicate where he remembered four of the bodies were buried. He then returned to the police station at 23:25.

Howard Ogden recalled from his defence files: "This was very eerie. Required to dress in boiler suits to preserve anonymity. Two police officers guarding the scene. Had to wait until the press had left the scene thinking there was no activity. Noted flowers in the doorway of the house. Fred could 'feel' where the bodies were. They were coming up out of the ground at him, as though they were at a party. He knew them all individually, albeit they were coming at him thick and fast. They wanted to reassure him that they were better off where they were. He had regretted telling the police where they were all in one go since he had been able to handle Heather coming up at him on an individual basis, but it was very difficult when the spirits were all together present in the basement. They said it was alright what he had done and they would wait for him. This frightened him. It was a new experience. They were reassuring him. The reaction obviously surprised him as he could not understand it. They were all smiling when they left him that night in the basement."

A search warrant was obtained under the Police & Criminal Evidence Act 1984 to search 25 Midland Road, Gloucester.

A police officer told the Daily Express: "We suspect very strongly we will find a body or bodies under the concrete floor of the extension and that is what we are working on." They also reported that the bodies of Shirley Robinson and the unknown girl (Alison Chambers) were wrapped in pink blankets.

Lucy Partington's step-father, David Righton, told the press: "Margaret (Lucy's mum) has been quietly knitting and making marmalade. She finds it some comfort to get on with normal things. It would be too much to bear if we just sat in the house all day waiting for a phone call or a knock at the door from the police. We've been out shopping together to try and relieve some of the stress. It is not easy – it's very painful, but it's something we have to come to terms with." He told how police had visited in the week previous and broke the news that one of the bodies dug up could be Lucy. "They came one day last week. It is distressing that I can't even remember when. The waiting is the worst part. We are just about to drive to Gloucester police station to see if there is any more news."

5th March 1994

In the morning police briefing, new teams of officers were allocated to each of the new victims. DSI Bennett said he would soon be briefing the Chief Constable and asking for the investigation to be managed under the contingency plans for a major incident.

Mr and Mrs Gough, he said, had now been told that Fred West had admitted killing their daughter, Lynda.

DCI Terry Moore explained what happened when Fred West was taken back to 25 Cromwell Street, for although he claimed to be still unsure of exactly how many he had killed, he was able to indicate where he had buried four of his victims in the cellar: "Lucy" (Partington), "a Worcester girl", "a girl from Newent", "a Dutch girl", and another under the bathroom – "Lynda Gough".

He also told them Charmaine, the other missing daughter, was buried at 25 Midland Road in Gloucester, and Rena, his first wife, in a field at Kempley near the village of Much Marcle on the Gloucestershire – Herefordshire border. This made the number still to be found seven and, with the other three already recovered, ten victims in all.

At Cromwell Street, the ground-penetrating radar was being trawled across the area where Fred West had painted the red-circle markers. Initial soundings indicated the earth beneath the concrete was different in composition to other parts of the cellar.

The search inside the house required further trained officers and the Cheltenham Support Division Support Group was called in and given responsibility for the inside of the house.

Fred West was interviewed several times during the day and insisted that the spirits of his victims had visited him whilst he was in the basement. In regards to last night's visit to the basement of 25 Cromwell Street, Fred said: "There is one more girl in there and I just cannot pinpoint where she is because there was far too much in there last night, I could not stop any of it. I couldn't trap her to where she was and hold her there so that I could trace her you know, go back because when you get these things like that the person will actually come out and float round with you and you can actually send them back to where they are. Wherever they're buried you can go back. She was flying around the room and I couldn't hold her to what she looked like. She would not come in to my mind to hold her and see what she was. I mean, to be honest, it could be any of the girls. It's not the Dutch girl I know that and I mean it could be any of the other girls. There is a girl flying around that room. Why she's doing it is what I'm trying to work out. When they come up in to you, when the visions come into you it's beautiful mind, ain't no messin' that's lovely, but it's when they die away from you 'cause you're trying to hold them, you know you just got 'em and then they sort of...you can feel them pulling away from you and you're trying to struggle to stop 'em and that's where I think you get the ill feeling from."

Asked if he could remember the name of one victim, he replied: "I did know it at the time, but I forgot it now. There's so many. I mean, I knew her well because we had had an affair. All these girls I've had affairs with and that's why they ended up this way, because they threatened to tell Rose. Every one of them did exactly the same thing. 'I love you, I'm pregnant, I'm going to tell Rose, I want you to come and live with me', and that was the problem. My main problem was Rose not finding out what was going on."

Howard Ogden: "Fred had this notion in his fanciful way that if he could take responsibility, Rose would be safe as a result. She'd be able to buy a lovely little house just down the road from the prison where he would be and she'd be able to come and visit him and bake him a couple of pies and that sort of thing. It really was as ridiculous as that."

Fred went on to give a further account of the death of his stepdaughter Charmaine. "She was fully clothed and everything...There was no clothes taken off her or nothing". He went on to maintain: "She wasn't dismembered at all". He said he had killed her "about a week" after he had been released from Leyhill Prison in June 1971.

In another interview regarding the death of Lucy Partington, Fred West went on to suggest that Lucy Partington was pregnant when she confronted him on the night of her death. In his expanded version he said they made love, and then she told him: "I'm pregnant and I want a thousand pound off you...or eight hundred pound...for an abortion. That's where the row took up there, because I don't reckon she was pregnant. I think she was having me on. So then we had a violent row, and that's how it all happened...All I can remember. We had one almighty row...argument and practically a fight in the back of that park, 'cause she was threatening me."

He maintained that Juanita Mott "used to come and visit" Cromwell Street, but that "she never lived there". He described her to the police as a "black-haired girl, fairly big built", who had an "American father", although he also suggested that she "might have had a baby, 'cause she had stretch marks." He insisted that she used to "come and visit friends at Cromwell Street", and that she had then become friendly with him over a period of "probably a couple of months." He said Juanita Mott used to come "down the basement helping me and that...when there was nobody there, like"- insinuating that they had sex there.

He boasted that he and Juanita had become lovers. He insisted that shortly after the affair had started they were "making love two or three times a day" in the basement. In his first explanation of her death to the police, he even suggested that he had killed her after they had finished making love on a mattress on the cellar floor. He said that they had been in the basement laying carpet tiles and she "could have tied something round her head to keep her hair away from the glue" they were using. "We were both undressed. I never made love with clothes on...and she was undressed.

As the erection went, so I slid out of her, and then I still lay on top of her talking...I said something to the effect. "Oh, this is getting serious", or something – and she said, "Oh, yer, I think it's about time that I told Rose and we sorted it out." I mean, I never had no inclination of that whatever. I got quite a shock when she said she was going to tell Rose and...start going together, making it serious...I thought, no way can I allow that to happen. I just lost me head. I just strangled her with me hand."

He told the police that "she enjoyed getting hurt when she was making love." He went on: "I don't think any of them were cut up," he announced, but adding "I ain't sure, I wouldn't be one hundred per cent on that, mind."

Because of media interest in the site, police officers were posted to Finger Post Field and Letter Box Field to maintain security. The police guards were largely drawn from the Forest of Dean Division.

11:47

The remains of a person subsequently identified as Therese Siegenthaler were found in the cellar area of 25 Cromwell Street. Therese's body was found compressed in a 2ft by 3ft area in front of an imitation fireplace in the cellar. Professor Knight said that the remains were in anatomical disarray, with the limbs on top of the trunk and head. One arm was above the skull, which was lying face down. In the grave with her was a knotted cloth loop made of something similar to stocking material, which had presumably slipped off the skull. There were numerous small injuries to the bones, with fine cuts to the left thigh bone, and multiple cuts to the vertebrae which pointed to decapitation. Forensic experts found threads of pink cloth, which could have been part of her clothing, and a hair decoration. Also discovered near the body was a square silk scarf, folded or rolled to form a loop. Fragments of brown hair were trapped inside the knotted part of the material. Dental examination put the victim's age at twenty plus. Therese was twenty-one. Her left collarbone was missing, as were 5 ankle and 9 wrist bones and 24 finger and toe bones.

13:56

Fred West was taken to Letterbox Field where he pointed out where he buried Rena. The police investigation referred to the location as 'Kempley A'.

The spot where Ann McFall was found in Fingerpost Field

The spot where Rena Costello was found in Letterbox Field

Howard Ogden: "We looked at Ordinance Sheet 149. The hill is called 'The Fingerpost'. There are woods up on the right. Fred said he used to work these fields when he was young. He buried her by a tree in the hedgerow, since "being a farmer myself" he did not wish to "destroy the crop". So this was a spot where corn would not grow. DC Morgan marked the spot by driving a steak in to the ground."

Scott Canavan: "He was taken off the handcuffs and allowed to wander to do his spiritual bit again and feel where the bodies are. That's how he used to say where the bodies were."

Howard Ogden: "He could feel she was by this tree."

14:51

The remains of a person subsequently identified as Shirley Hubbard were found in the cellar area of 25 Cromwell Street. This grave was directly opposite the previous one, against the other wall adjacent to the fireplace decorated with Marilyn Monroe wallpaper. She had been decapitated and her legs were separate from the rest of her body. Professor Knight also found some significant evidence, which was present again two days later with the discovery of Lynda Gough, when he examined the skull. It was totally encased in a mask made from windings of brown tape from below the chin to eye level. Inserted into the front of the mask was a narrow plastic tube at nostril level. There were three inches of tubing inside which would have entered the nostril. Also found with the body was a second length of tubing. Forensic experts later confirmed that a length of pale grey or brown tape had been wrapped round the skull in an overlapping manner from the chin to the top of the skull. They found hair fragments inside the mask. The police believed that the tubing was significant because it showed that the victim had been alive when the mask was applied. It had been used to keep her living and breathing throughout whatever cruelty it was that she experienced at the hands of the Wests. 40 of Shirley Hubbard's bones were missing when her remains were unearthed, including 7 wrist bones.

Howard Ogden: "It was more chilling than that of Heather because it was something I really wasn't ready for and it hadn't figured in terms of anything Fred had had to say or anything the police had had to say and I was looking at a masked, as in taped up, skull from the nostrils of which two small plastic tubes were emerging. That clearly was the only way in which the deceased had been assisted to breathe. I also recollect that there was a little toy of some description in there as well and for me it took everything to another level. In terms of murder you think of somebody shot or you think that they've been stabbed or knifed, but here somebody had clearly been tortured."

17:46

Fred West, with the help of Janet Leach, prepared a sketch showing where bodies had been buried at his home.

DC Savage: Who's that under the floor in the bathroom?
Fred: Lynda
DC Savage: Lynda who?
Fred: Gough, is it?

Fred then went on: "Yeah, but there was this rape thing that she was on about in the, in the van. She was going to say I'd raped her and everything else and the whole fear, and this is something we've gotta go in to, was the, the biggest fear that was in me was Rose finding out that I was messing with other women. So I brought the girl in. I brought her in in a box. So anyway, I put her in there and carried her in and down the stairs and at that time the hole that she's in was already dug out. There was a big piece dug out there. But see, like at that time a noise in the basement meant nothing because I was there every night digging and raking concrete and get these stones out and throwing out through the window. I felt terrible after,

291

all of them. I felt really ill. Really ill. It was just this urge at that time when they upset me that I went for them and suddenly it was over and I thought 'what the hell did I do that for?' It weren't what I meant to do at all."

Scott Canavan: "Those interviews, that's where it became apparent that there was sexual motives in the killings, which to me, put a different light on Fred...I did start to see him quite differently at that point. It all became real and I started to imagine what those poor victims had actually gone through before they died."

The evening police briefing began with DC Malcolm Wood, the video recordist, showing pictures of Fred West being taken back to Cromwell Street.

DSI Bennett told them of his meeting with the Chief Constable earlier in the day and that the media now knew that Fred West had admitted more killings.

The different teams were also gathering information about their allocated victims:

- The 'Worcester girl': there was a girl outstanding from a children's home and Fred West said he knew where this girl lived in Worcester.
- The 'Dutch girl': Fred West said she was a hitch-hiker. She came from Holland. She had a badge with a truck on it so he caller her 'Truck'. They would follow it up through Interpol...
- The 'Newent girl': from what Fred West had said, she was living there, had a father in America and relatives in Gloucester. There was a possibility her name was Juanita Mott. It wasn't definite but a sister had been found and she was being seen.

Someone also mentioned that Fred regularly talked about a girl he knew and referred to as 'Annie', an Ann McFall who had apparently been living with him at Much Marcle in the mid-sixties, near where he said Rena was buried.

Fred was again interviewed, and talked about both Rena and Ann McFall: "I got such an experience when Rena came up in to me in that field. I mean that was summat else. I mean I never gone through anything like that in my life...She had a smile on her face and Ann was in my mind there with her you know? And as Rena went away Ann sort of stayed there and for the life of me I couldn't think who the hell Ann was. I mean, I said I got the name Ann in my head but I ain't got a clue who it is. So then of course that night it all come back to me. I went and sat on the step, lit the fag and I felt terrible, really felt ill and I went to put my hand like that and suddenly I'm in between it and more or less pushed her in to my head and I knew who it was, you know, straight away. So I got in touch with everybody to get everybody there because I felt her."

Fred had said: "I never touched Ann in my life. Never even laid a finger on her. I thought the world of her and anybody will tell you that. I would not have harmed a hair on her head."

Janet Leach: "When we were in the cell he would talk about Ann McFall, that he had visions of her in a white dress, silvery dress and that she was just floating above him...He was talking about Ann McFall and how I reminded him so much of Ann McFall and he said 'just wait until you see a photograph'. They showed me a photograph of her. When I looked at the photograph the hairs on the back of my neck stood on end because the resemblance was just uncanny. Then I could realise why he was sort of offloading, so I think he thought he was talking to her, not me."

Fred also said that Charmaine's body would not be found as she might have been removed when the foundations were dug out for an extension at Midland Road. He said that he was there then, and had looked for her, but had been unable to find her.

Later in the day, Fred had asked to see DC's Hazel Savage and Darren Law and told them more details of two more victims, one of them another girl from Worcester. He said that he had picked up three women hitchhikers in the Worcester area, one of them a 'Dutch girl'. It was later established that the 'Dutch girl' was in fact the Swiss Therese Siegenthaler. "I have no description whatsoever of them because I never actually saw them in daylight as such.

Fred West bracketed Carol Ann Cooper and Shirley Hubbard together in police interviews, calling them "Worcester Girl One" and "Worcester Girl Two", and insisted he did not even remember their names. He also told police that their bodies were fully clothed, that they had not been mutilated, and that, once again, the only reason that he killed them was that they threatened to tell his wife of their relationship with him.

Time after time he would amend and modify his version of their deaths. Indeed, throughout the first stages of his police interviews he would even suggest that he picked them both up together "in Tewkesbury" one day, but that he had then picked up the "one without the firework burn (Shirley Hubbard) a few weeks later.

I picked her up outside Worcester and I was just generally talking to her as I was going along and the next minute she sat on the engine, and the next minute she had got my fly undone and messing about. So I did the same. We made love, I think we made love twice, I think we did one after the other, and then she said, 'that'll be ten quid, or something'. And I said, 'well, I don't carry money. And anyway, I wouldn't pay a prostitute. She started shouting and she said, 'you're the sort of person who goes with slags or something. As soon as she said that I thought of Rose, and Rose is no slag as far as I was concerned, so I went for her and then the same thing happened with her. I smacked her up against the [lorry] window and she just dropped. I strangled her, or held my hands around her neck anyway, and that was it."

In police interviews he did not deny that he had "trussed the girl up" and "attempted to hang her upside-down on a hook in the cellar ceiling" for "kinky sex". Yet again, he claimed, "enjoyment turned to disaster", as the girl managed "to slip off", "fall on to the cellar floor" and "die as a result of her injuries".

DC Savage: Are you responsible for killing all of these people, Fred? Can you tell me whether the way you killed them was different?
Fred: No, they're all exactly the same.
DC Savage: As what?
Fred: I strangled them and then cut them up
DC Savage: Are you responsible for burying them all in there?
Fred: Yes
DC Savage: Is there anybody else involved with you?
Fred: Nobody at all

Peter Bastholm, Mary's brother, told the press: "We are dreading the knock on the door and I hate it every time the phone rings. I have tried to get on with my life these 25 years, but all this brings it home. I just want an answer about what happened to my sister. If we know for sure that Mary is dead we can start to grieve properly. She was a lovely, lovely girl. The memories fade but they will never disappear."

May Lappin, one of Rena Costello's sisters, said that she had been trying to contact her sister for 25 years since learning through another sister that Rena was going to Saudi Arabia. "I hoped the publicity would bring some news that somebody might recognise her or she would turn up again." Mrs Lappin's husband said his wife and another sister, Isobella Prentice, were trying not to think the worst. He said there were five sisters and added: "We were naturally hoping for good news. The last we heard of Rena was when her marriage finished in 1969, but she just disappeared. We just thought they had gone their separate ways, but when she didn't get in touch we did worry. We tried to find her. The Gloucester police have been to speak to May. Now we don't know what to think."

19:30

DSI Bennett announced to a packed press conference:

"This afternoon, police searching 25 Cromwell Street Gloucester, discovered what they suspect are the remains of two further human beings. Excavations will stop shortly (in about half an hour) and will begin again tomorrow.

Home Office Pathologist, Professor Bernard Knight, will not be attending the scene until Monday at the earliest, when the latest findings will be confirmed or otherwise.

While the identities of these suspected remains haven't been established, we have contacted relatives of two people who we believe may be able to help us if the remains are identified as human. Both of these families are from Gloucestershire and only one of the two people has been officially reported to the police as missing. At the request of the families, we are unable to elaborate further on the question of identification at this time."

He went on to explain that the specialist equipment had indicated a number of readings in the ground-floor area but the results were still to be analysed. The ground radar only detected disturbances in the ground and was not "a body or skeleton detector." The whole of 25 Cromwell Street would be methodically searched, though how long that would take was impossible to tell. Only when that was done would they search in two other, for now unspecified, areas of Gloucestershire.

Relatives of Lucy Partington were contacted and told that Fred West had admitted killing their daughter. Lucy's sister, Marian Partington, wrote in her diary: "10.15am phone call from the police saying that they would like to come over to talk to us. They have some 'news' for us. That half hour of waiting for them to arrive was full of a terrible restlessness and anxiety – palpitations and nausea. The numbness and muteness of shock began to invade. Two youngish plain-clothes policemen arrive. They introduce themselves as Brian Smith and Russell Williams. I notice Brian's polished brown shoes and his red tie and the scar on Russell's face. There is a pause. Then Russell confirms our worst fears. Fred West has been talking to the police and has told them that there are more bodies in the basement and that one of them is called Lucy. They have begun to dig. It was a lovely sunny afternoon and I felt like going for a walk up Gretton Hill. However we went shopping in Cheltenham. Denial was setting in. Numerous messages on the answering machine on our return. The Pain Vultures sound as if it's unquestionable that we should call them back (TV and major tabloids). We don't. By now they know that three more bodies have been recovered and that two families in Gloucestershire have been informed. Talk to Dad, he will come by train on Monday. Phoned Nick to say what has happened and that I must stay longer. I hardly slept that night. A paralysing feeling of weight, fear and a pain in my heart. This is enormous. Shock brings you into focussing on surviving. Some people die of it."

6th March 1994

The Sunday Mirror confirmed by what they printed in that mornings papers that there was a leak in the police department. The newspaper reported not only how many victims there were buried at 25 Cromwell Street, but it also published a diagrammatic plan of the three-storey house, pointing out exactly where each of them was buried. It also coined the headline 'The House of Horrors'.

There was concern, too, at the pressure the media was mounting on the West family. Rose, Stephen and Mae may have been under police protection but that did not stop reporters trying to track them down. Their safe house had become more like a prison. Contact with the outside world was restricted to the telephone or Stephen and Mae's liaison officer, DC Clive Stephens. Rarely did either of the children venture out and never at the same time for fear that their mother might harm herself.

The investigation was finally declared a major incident by the Chief Constable Tony Butler at the request of Detective Superintendent John Bennett, through Detective Chief Superintendent Ken Daun. Additional staff were drawn in from around the constabulary. At this stage they compromised: 2 Detective Inspectors, 2 Police Sergeants, 3 Detective Sergeants, 12 Police Constables, 23 Detective Constables and 5 civilians. These figures related to the Incident Room and did not include officers involved in searches and guard duties at the various sites. General working hours were 08.00-22.30 but this was often exceeded.

A police presence was posted to 25 Midland Road to protect the house from media intrusion before the search commenced. This presence was maintained 24 hours a day, 7 days a week until 25th April 1994, when a full guard was posted to protect equipment which had been delivered to the site.

The Police Search Advisor for 25 Midland Road, Gloucester, was Sergeant David Cooper from Cirencester Police Station. He was in charge of a team of five officers, drawn from the Cotswold and Stroud Division. They were trained in search techniques and had not previously been involved in the operation.

In the early morning police briefing it was revealed:
- When mentioning Ann McFall, Fred West had talked about her being somewhere in the same field as Rena – and that it was Rena who killed her not him!

- It was decided there and then that Ann McFall should be the subject of further detailed investigations and 'owned' by an inquiry team – just like all the other victims.
- Fred West also said he was wrong about the 'Dutch girl', she was still alive. The dead girl might be German.
- He accepted that Juanita Mott was one of his victims as he could remember a girl with a distinctive name like that.
- As for his admission there were 'two Worcester girls', West Mercia Police had records of three young women who were missing, though they could only find details of a girl named Carol Cooper who had disappeared in 1973.

09:02

The remains of a person subsequently identified as Lucy Partington were found in the cellar area of 25 Cromwell Street. She was buried 2ft 6ins down in the basement. Her body was discovered in what was known as the 'nursery corner' of the cellar, where the wallpaper was decorated with cartoon and nursery characters. Professor Knight's examination found the skull upside down. Two pieces of woven cord, 0.25" thick, were knotted together below the jaw. A knife was also found alongside the remains. It was made of stainless steel, honed down and still sharp. There were three cut marks on the right femur and also on the left, sharp edges around the hip joints and signs of decapitation. Dental examination put the age of the victim at twenty plus. Lucy was twenty-one when she vanished. 72 of her bones were removed. Her right shoulder blade, left knee cap and three ribs were some of those bones removed. 52 foot and toe bones were also removed, along with 11 ankle bones and 3 wrist bones. No clothes or belongings of any kind were discovered with her skeleton; not her rust-coloured knee-length raincoat, nor her pink, flared brushed denim jeans, not even the brown canvas satchel with the name L.K. Partington stenciled on it that she had been carrying on the night she disappeared.

DSI Bennett decided that double-checking the reviews of the missing person files on Mary Bastholm and Lucy Partington was even more of a priority since Fred West had confessed to killing Lucy. Uppermost in his mind was whether the investigation in 1973 had made any mistakes and missed something that connected the young student with Fred or Rose or Cromwell Street. The similarity in both girls' disappearance was obvious and one the media had already picked up on, though Fred himself had not, as yet, admitted even knowing Mary Bastholm.

Mary Bastholm's brother Peter, her only surviving close relative, had been told of the lines the police were following, although it was extremely unlikely his sister was buried at Cromwell Street since the Wests didn't begin living there until some years after her disappearance.

Neighbours of 25 Midland Road told reporters about the police outside. Clair Elkins, 20, said: "The police have been sitting outside the house in unmarked cars for the past three days. I thought they were burglars until I found out who they were."

Another neighbour, Heather Warren, said: "I heard they might be digging there but I couldn't believe it when I was told the police definitely will be excavating."

11:50

The remains of a person subsequently identified as Juanita Mott were found in the cellar area of 25 Cromwell Street, in an alcove by the wall, where a staircase had once been. The pathologist reported that the bones were in disarray and a clothes-line type rope was wound around the body. There were two small wrist-sized loops in the rope. Around the skull was a band of fabric, running around the jaw to the top of the head and round the back of it. It was formed from a continuous length of material made from bits of clothing knotted together to form a makeshift mask.

There were signs that the body had been cut up at the hips and decapitated. At the top of the skull was a depressed fracture where the bone was cracked and crushed inwards. Professor Knight said that this could have been caused by a heavy blow from a circular object similar to a ball-headed hammer, but he stressed that the fracture could have been inflicted after decapitation.

The forensic experts who examined the ropes and mask found in the grave with Juanita described them as two pieces of grey plastic cord similar to washing line, one measuring 10ft and the other 7ft. The ropes contained a series of loops made with slip knots and one had a piece of ribbon tied to it.

Two pairs of tights, one within the other, a bra and two long white nylon socks (the sort that Rose West always wore) were found wrapped around her skull, "under the chin and over the top of the head". There was also a pair of knickers.

She had 88 bones missing. The upper part of her breastbone and her right first rib were missing, along with both kneecaps, 15 wrist bones, 6 ankle bones and 58 finger and toe bones. Her fingernails were recovered.

Fred West was interviewed several times during the day. In an interview, DC Morgan grew tired of Fred's myth-making: "I don't want you making up a story to keep me happy because that wouldn't keep me happy at all. Can you look at me, Fred, when you're working this out. I prefer to sort of have eye contact with people when I'm talking to them and then we can assess things, can't we?"

14:20

Fred West was taken in a car to the Worcester area where he pointed out where he said he had dropped off hitchhikers.

DSI John Bennett told a press conference:

"Officers searching in 25 Cromwell Street have discovered what they believe to be another set of human remains in the cellar. This brings the total to six – three in the garden and three in the cellar. Inquiries in respect of the latest remains are continuing and we have some positive lines in all three of the latest discoveries."

He was asked if he was re-opening the cases of Mary Bastholm and Lucy Partington. He replied: "Our investigations into missing persons are gone into in great detail. We are certainly not ruling them out." In regards to Rena and Charmaine, he said: "We are still making inquiries in all parts of the country to find them."

7ᵗʰ March 1994

09:26

Professor Knight began his work on the holes thought to contain the remains of Therese Siegenthaler, Lucy Partington, Shirley Hubbard and Juanita Mott.

The hole where Therese Siegenthaler was found was full of semi-liquid mud. The Professor felt inside and pulled out the bones one by one. He pointed out cut marks on both femurs, some quite fine, saying they were definitely female and that dismemberment had probably occurred there. Next, he brought out a blackened, waterlogged, mud-soaked knotted loop approximately 14" in diameter, which looked as though it was made of cloth. Then, close by, he removed a skull and some hair. There was little doubt that the cloth loop had been around the skull and at some point had either come off during decomposition, had moved in the mud or had been thrown in with the remains. Two vertebrae from around the neck also seemed to have cut marks on them, making it likely that decapitation had taken place there.

10:00

Fred West appeared at Gloucester Magistrates' Court and was further remanded in custody to police cells until Friday, 11th March 1994.

14:25

The remains subsequently identified as Lynda Gough were found deep below the bathroom inside 25 Cromwell Street.

Professor Knight decided that he would first inspect the hole in front of the open fire place, with pictures of Marilyn Monroe on the walls. This is where the remains subsequently identified as Shirley Hubbard were buried. There were fine cut marks on the upper part of the femurs and a deeper mark on one. Next came bones from the trunk along with some of the vertebrae, together identifiable as belonging to a young woman.

Professor Knight then moved more sludge until the top of a skull came into view. The victim had been dismembered into three parts, just like all the others found so far.

There seemed to be something around the skull. It was completely encircled in a mask made of overlapping tape – from around the forehead to down below the jaw. Every part of the head and face was covered, making it a blindfold as well. Sticking out from between the lower layers was a length of discoloured plastic tube about 1ft long. He turned the skull so that he could look up and inside from the base, pointing out as he did so that the tube went through the tape into the area where the girl's nostrils would have been, making it another 6 or 7" long.

Professor Knight then brought out another piece of plastic tube from where the skull had been found which matched the tube in the mask and looked about the same length, 16-17". There was little doubt that this one also went through the tape to act as a crude breathing pipe but had become dislodged.

The hole containing the remains later identified as Lucy Partington was inspected next. They were in the alcove on the main wall. The Marilyn Monroe wallpaper had been replaced by children's nursery figures.

Professor Knight excavated leg bones, femurs, some with fine cut marks, all belonging to a young woman. Other bones followed and then a 6" black-handled kitchen knife.

Having recovered some vertebrae the Professor then found the skull. Close by was a length of thick cord made from two pieces knotted together in the middle, about 1ft in total.

After slowly removing the skull he produced a 16-17" loop of light-coloured tape, which had been wound round and round until it was about 4" wide. As he gently removed it he pointed out hairgrips and what looked like hair inside the loop where there would have been adhesive. Satisfied that there were only small bones and teeth left in the hole, the Professor climbed out and left the rest of the work to the scenes of crime officers.

The Professor then moved directly across to the opposite wall to the matching alcove under the stairwell to begin the retrieval of the remains later identified as Juanita Mott.

As he leaned forward, he struggled to pull some of the bones free from the hole. Slowly some bones emerged, pulling with them others connected by something. He went deeper into the hole and gradually pulled out an upper arm bone which had some knotted plastic-covered rope attached, like a clothes line. It was wrapped around the bone near the elbow and at the other end, close to where it would have met the shoulder. It continued under what would have been the trunk, where there were two small loops about 18" apart, across to the bones of the right arm, around to the right knee and back around the femur in a loop. There was another piece of rope with loops but not now attached to anything.

The Professor could tell from the thigh bones that her remains had either been folded or dismembered. No cut marks could be seen; she appeared to have been hog-tied, arms to legs, and the plastic rope bindings were only loose now because the flesh around the bones had decomposed.

As the Professor removed the skull, it was obvious that a loop, made by entwining a number of different pieces of material, was wound around the skull from the top, down under the jaw then round to the back. Nearby was a pair of knickers. Examining the skull more closely, he pointed to an area below and behind the right ear that looked like a depressed fracture. Whether it occurred before or after death would only be established through closer forensic examination back at the lab.

Professor Knight then climbed down the metal ladder in the bathroom extension into the narrow oblong pit. The hole was about 6ft deep and contained the remains later identified as Lynda Gough.

He found the bones to not be in any anatomical order and were possibly even more jumbled than the other remains he had removed that day; many of them were missing, including some vertebrae – more, in fact, than elsewhere.

The leg bones and femurs were slightly curved, confirming this was another young woman. Both had many fine cut marks around where they would have joined the hip so almost certainly she was dismembered and, as he delicately brought out the skull, there were more signs that she too had been gagged and possibly bound. There was an oval-shaped ring of overlapping tape around 15" in circumference, which seemed to be made up of a mixture of parcel tape and some other type of tape. A piece of material about 2" wide and 5" long was also found nearby.

The remains were discovered beneath the bathroom, which had

previously been a garage. She had been dumped in what had once been the inspection pit, which had been filled in with earth, metal and other debris.

A ring mask of adhesive tape was found close to the skull. There were two long pieces of tape, a long piece of string and fragments of dark, knotted fabric. There were many fine cut marks near the upper thigh bones, suggesting disarticulation of the hip joints and dismemberment of the body. The skull was found separately. A number of vertebrae were missing and the body had been decapitated. More than 120 of her bones had been removed.

A dental expert put the age of the victim at nineteen plus, Lynda's age when she vanished.

The ring mask was examined by forensic scientists, who said that a piece of 2" wide brown tape had been wound in a circle in an overlapping fashion with white tape and some 1.5" wide surgical tape. The ring mask was 15" in circumference. Small tubes found by the body were also examined. The experts formed the opinion that the tape was used to gag the victim and bind up the head.

18:55

Fred West was taken to Fingerpost Field near Kempley and there he explained that he knew Ann McFall but did not kill her. He indicated the position where he thought she may be. Fred said: "I have got a horrible feeling that she was stabbed through the heart" and hinted that his first wife Rena was responsible. The police investigation referred to the location as 'Kempley B'.

Janet Leach: "When we came out he went right over the field. We were looking around for quite some time and one of the officers was getting quite annoyed…He said she was the only one he ever loved and that she was special to him. There was no way that he would have done anything to her and he wanted to be with her. It was frightening because I don't like the dark anyway and he kept saying 'my handcuffs are loose. I can easily get out of them and go in them woods. Nobody would ever find me."

Christa Carling, the mother of Shirley Robinson, told a newspaper reporter: "I am deeply upset and distraught. I am in a state of shock. The news about Shirley hasn't sunk in yet. I need to be left alone in peace to grieve."

Chief Inspector Colin Handy told the Daily Express: "The specialist equipment we have used in the house has been right four times. It also tells us there are other places in the house where we should be digging and that is what we will be doing."

A police source also told the Daily Express: "It is a gruesome task working in the heat of powerful lights with exposed remains all around. The cellar was converted in to bedrooms. Now it is a crypt full of bodies. The men are doing a fantastic job in the most appalling circumstances. Tragically they have an eighth set of remains, the skeleton of a baby unborn at eight months that cannot be the subject of a charge under the law."

8th March 1994

Fred West was interviewed five times during the day regarding the murders of the various victims. He gave his first account of the death of Carol Ann Cooper. He suggested that he killed her after picking her up in his lorry and making love in a "lay-by on the Worcester Road" near the Bunch of Grapes pub.

"She's sat in the lorry. She didn't put her clothes back on. She just sat on her clothes in the lorry naked…and I said, "What do you want to sit like that?" or something…and I said, "You're going to have to get dressed…because we're going out into the lights now"… and she said, "Oh, let's make love once more" and then we made love again…and then she said, "Of course, this will cost you double", and I said, "What do you mean, cost me?"…and she said, "Well, it will, or I'll scream rape on you"…I hit her straight over without even thinking."

He maintained that then he took her body back to Cromwell Street, where his wife was asleep in the ground-floor front room.

"Anyway, I checked that Rose was asleep and there was nobody about, and I went down in there and dug a hole and put her in." He then suggested that he "cut her up" with his nine-inch-long sheath knife, which he kept "on the right-hand side of me belt." The reason he bought her back to Cromwell Street , he said, was that he had no means of digging a hole; otherwise he "would probably have buried her on the way back somewhere…out round Tewkesbury somewhere…I wouldn't have taken the risk of bringing her back if I'd have had…something to bury her with".

He also maintained that he did not know she was only fifteen years of age. "She certainly looked a lot older than that to me, and she acted a lot older, I mean sexual-wise."

He again insisted that "Rose had nothing to do with it. Rose didn't even know nothing."

The police also asked him if he had been able to bury somebody else somewhere else. "No, No," he quickly replied.

It was not until he knew for certain that the police had discovered bindings with some of the remains that he suddenly admitted that the girls had been tied up. DC Hazel Savage put it to her fellow officer during an interview: "He didn't want to talk about bondage in the beginning. We've been here for days. He's never talked about it…he is now saying: "I'd better think up this story that she hung herself".

At the end of that evening he told the police confidently: "I mean, every girl I picked up I didn't put in the basement." When he was asked where he did put them, he laughed out loud, and replied: "I dropped them off where they wanted to go."

Acting Sergeant Jim McCarthy carried the first of the remaining exhibit boxes from the front door of 25 Cromwell Street to the waiting vehicle outside. As he passed, the uniformed officers on guard outside spontaneously bowed their heads and saluted. The process was repeated for each of the boxes and became one of the most enduring images of the entire investigation. Each box that contained human remains had a black cloth laid over it.

In regards to the torture of the victims, Stephen West recalled: "My understanding of it was that the holes in the ceiling were big enough to get hands and wrists through. All he would do was to make two nooses round the legs and pull them up through the holes. That would allow him to muck around with them when the bodies were upside down. He only did things to them when they were dead. Dad said to me: 'I hung them from the beams. It wasn't when they were alive. I cut their legs off to get them in a bin. Then I'd take them out afterwards to do something to them.'

He even became a third person describing someone else as the murderer, saying he had to protect him. He'd say: 'Don't you know whoever killed them took them away in black dustbins to a farmhouse. They were put in a vehicle'. But half way through his story he kept saying: 'And then I did this and I did that.' He said it was at this farmhouse, they were taken there to be cut up and tortured and whatever and to be brought back from there to be put in the garden at home.

I asked: 'Where is it, where is it?' He didn't tell me at first, but several visits later said: 'I know where it is. I followed someone there once. It must have been this person all along.' I asked again: 'Where is it?' He said it was towards Berkeley power station. I decided on my way home to have a look and sure enough it was there."

19:10

The remains of a person subsequently identified as Carol Ann Cooper were found in the cellar area of 25 Cromwell Street, away from the wall and adjacent to a wash-basin. Her skeleton was excavated from a depth of about 3ft. The bones were layered, with the skull at the bottom. Around the skull was an elasticated cloth band 3" wide and up to 7" in diameter. It was wrapped around the lower part of the skull, covering the jaw, lower face and back of the head. A loop of fabric with a half-inch knot was tied under the forearms. There was a clothesline rope nearby. Also present was a headband of surgical tape wound around itself several times and there were several hair samples on the inside of the tape. The band covered the lower part of the face as a gag.

21:15

Fred West was taken to 25 Cromwell Street and he pointed out where a "Worcester Girl" was buried in the cellar. He had a feeling there was still another victim in the cellar, though he couldn't be sure where.

Professor Knight arrived at 25 Cromwell Street in the late afternoon to remove the remains later identified as Carol Cooper. The hole in the room at the garden end of the cellar was near a sink. The search team had gone 3ft down before they made their discovery. The hole dug was larger than the rest, an indication of how difficult it had been to find what they were looking for. The Professor slowly pulled out, one by one, lower leg bones and then a femur, again belonging to a young woman. Next came the pelvis and trunk.

A short time later a skull was recovered with some black hair still intact. Wrapped horizontally around what would have been the lower face, mouth and jaws was an elasticated cloth band, about 3" wide. The skull was upright and from where it had been found the Professor concluded it had been decapitated. Then came shoulder bones.

The Professor delicately removed one bone after another until he brought out two separate pieces of cord. One was around 6" long, the other over 1ft with a 3" knotted loop. The looped cord appeared to be near the arm bones but not around them.

The Professor then climbed out of the pit and cleaned off some of the larger bones with his hands to reveal deep cut marks on both femurs – the victim appeared to have been severed in three as before.

Professor Knight estimated the age of the skeletal remains to be between fifteen and seventeen years of age. The upper end of the thigh bone showed fine cut marks, there was a gouge in the left femur and the hip joints had been severed with a sharp blade. There were also cuts on the neck and evidence of decapitation. The bones were jumbled in a random way which suggested dismemberment. 50 of her bones were missing, including most of her wrist bones, and 35 finger and toe bones. The lower third of her breastbone was entirely removed.

A dental examination of the skull agreed that the victim was between fifteen and a half and nineteen years of age. Carol was fifteen and a half when she disappeared.

Shaun Boyle, a former boyfriend of Anne Marie's, gave an interview to the Daily Mirror. He told of how he was shown the cellar on his first visit there. "There must have been six or seven mattresses down there. We started making love at one end and worked our way round all of them. We went down there at every opportunity to be on our own. We used to scream and yell.

You would never have known the room was there. They used it to store beds for the bedsitters, and the local kids would play there. They would jump down the steps on to a mattress and there were toys piled in one corner. It was completely bare. The walls and ceilings were plastered, the floor was concrete with a carpet on it and for ventilation there were air bricks up into the lounge. I certainly never saw any group sex going on. There were no orgies or threesomes – nothing like that."

In regards to Fred, he recalled: "In his spare time he did a lot of DIY. He was a workaholic. It was a very easy going, relaxed household. We would go out with all the tenants to the American bar in the market for drinks. There was Shirley Robinson, a girl we called Huggy Bear, Liz Brewer and another chap of 20. It was just like a work mate who would nudge you in the ribs and make coarse jokes to you. I found Fred over-friendly. He was always all over you, joking and jolly. He wasn't special to look at – a small bloke with sideburns and a rock-and-roll hairstyle. Most of the time he wore scruffy builders clothes. He was very strong, with sturdy shoulders and good muscles. I just can't take in what happened at number 25. I mean, there were bodies buried there and I made love a few feet above them. I had to confess to my wife about it."

Former neighbour, 19-year-old Roger Hawkins, recalled: "It seemed there was drilling and banging going on at all times of the night. One evening I went round at about 11pm and told Fred West about the noise. He was alright about it and didn't say much."

Rena's cousin, Annie Graham, 69, told The Daily Mirror: "If she was alive she'd have come forward. She was that kind of girl – she'd have wanted to put the minds of her family at rest…All this has been a shock and we would dearly love to know what happened to Rena. I watch all the news programmes. We are just waiting for news."

Annie Graham's brother, John Costello, added: "Surely if she was alive she would have got in touch with one of us over the years?"

Rena's sister Georgina McCann travelled from Ireland to be with her three other sisters. Her daughter Joanne said: "She was the type of person that if she was still living she'd be in contact. Before all this news about West, my mother sometimes said she thought Rena was dead."

Alex Palmer, a friend of Fred West's who owned 3 neighbouring properties, told the Daily Express: "It has turned my life into one big nightmare. I always thought Fred was a great guy who would help anyone in a crisis. But because of our friendship people suspect I might have been involved. I first met Fred and his wife about nine years ago. He used to carry out repairs for me. He never went out drinking and always stayed in with his children in the evening. People in the street regarded him as a real family man. The police have interviewed me about my friendship with him."

In regards to the remains so far discovered, Chief Inspector Colin Handy said: "We have positive lines on the identification of most of them except the third, the woman in her 20's. The majority are dominantly local."

Graham Letts told the Daily Express that he helped to concrete over the basement floor in 1987. "I'm haunted by the thought that I helped. It was explained a lorry would be pulling up with the cement and it had to be laid quickly or it would set. I agreed to help as a favour. I worked in the cellar while someone was on top shovelling the cement in down the makeshift shoot through the basement window. Work started at around

10am and it went on all day. By the time it was finished the cement was about a foot deep. My accidental role in it will haunt me until my dying day. I keep thinking 'My God, what have I done?'

"We still can't believe it. Heather was such a lovely girl, a dream child. She was pretty, polite and full of life. She was always immaculately dressed and loved school. She had finished her exams and talked of wanting to join the army. Then she suddenly vanished. We frantically tried to find out where she was but we always drew a blank. It all remained a mystery although we never gave up hope she would one day come home. Now we know that she is dead we are all devastated."

He went on to tell how he and his wife Barbara had been forced in to moving because of a backlash by the locals. "We felt it was only a question of time before one of us got hurt. I've got to protect my family. This is an absolute nightmare."

9ᵗʰ March 1994

Positive lines of enquiry were being followed up in an attempt to identify the remains found so far. To date there had been no positive identification. This would take some time and would involve the Home Office Pathologist and other specialists. Meanwhile, ground scanning equipment was used on the waste ground at the rear of 25 Cromwell Street and at the fields in Kempley.

DSI Bennett sent a fax request to the Home Office for Fred West to be remanded in police cells for further questioning, instead of being sent to prison under Section 29 of the Criminal Justice Act 1961. Local MP Douglas French appealed to the Home Secretary for extra police funding to pay for the murder enquiry, described as Britain's biggest ever.

Fred West was interviewed during the day. He would insist through all of his interviews that he had given Therese Siegenthaler a lift in his van, that he had taken her back to Cromwell Street alive, that she had been involved in a sexual experiment with him, and that he had buried her beneath the cellar floor once the experiment had gone wrong. As ever, he was also at pains to suggest that he had never intended to murder her; it was all an unfortunate accident. He was also anxious to insist that he and Therese had been lovers.

"I had an affair with her. She was on holiday over here, and she threatened to tell Rose…It was made quite clear that I was married to Rose…and every one of 'em did exactly the same thing… 'I love you, I'm pregnant, I'm gonna tell Rose, I want you to come and live with me'…and that was the problem."

He maintained that she had a "nice figure, petite" with "blondish/mousy hair" and that he had picked her up "just outside Worcester."

In his first version of events he went on to suggest that they had then twice made love in a lay-by, and that shortly afterwards she had asked him for money. "I just lost my head with her", he said, explaining that he had hit her, and then taken her home to Cromwell Street "after Rose had gone to the Bamboo Club." He suggested that he had driven his green A35 van round the back of his house in Cromwell Street, and had put the Swiss girl's unconscious body through the vent into the cellar at the back of the house. Soon after he had joined her there and explained that he strangled her "to make sure she was dead."

Within a matter of hours, he altered that version of events, and explained instead that he had picked up the girl "outside Evesham" and that she was heading for Cheltenham. In this second version she had told him about Amsterdam, and tulips, and had then told him that "she fancied sex." As a result they had "pulled off down a lane. It was dark." Afterwards, he had asked her: "Where do you want me to take you? The other side of Gloucester? Because it would be good to get a lift." But the student had replied: "Oh no, I'll just come home and stay with you…because I've got nowhere to go." He said that he had protested, but the young Swiss girl had threatened him, saying: "I'm the one with the wet knickers…I've only to say you've raped me…you're in big trouble." As a result he had agreed to take her home to Cromwell Street. After they arrived he decided to strangle her – but only after he had "made her a cup of tea and they'd made love again."

Under interrogation, however, Fred West admitted that not even this second version of events was the truth. When it was suggested to him that Therese Siegenthaler may have been gagged with tape, he suddenly volunteered the fact that "it was…I think it was grey tape…what you seal boxes with" and went on to admit, unprompted, that some of his victims were tied up.

A matter of hours later he even expanded on that explanation and said "the Dutch girl (as he called Therese Siegenthaler) was the one I had the kinky bondage with…because that was what she wanted to do…She wanted a mask made on her face…and her nose trussed up and all this."

A few hours later he refined his version of events still further, this time to explain that he had picked her up in his van in Evesham, and had given her a lift to the Trustee Savings Bank in Barton Street, Gloucester, so that she could change some money. He had then arranged to meet her again a week later: "She said: "I'll go on to Monmouth and that and then I'll meet you back here at the end of the week"…She was touring, like." It was only when she had come back that he had taken her to Cromwell Street, "where it all went wrong." In this version, Therese "walked in" to Cromwell Street because she "wanted bondage, and I mean that was arranged and we did it."

He said that she "was too excited to get this flipping bondage thing going. I mean, she was all sort of geared up when she come back. I mean, when we finally got into the basement...I mean I looked round and she was absolutely starkers except for her ear-rings...I mean, that's how geared up she was." He now claimed that every single one of the victims that he buried in the cellar had "wanted to have bondage sex, or kinky sex, and that's all it was...It was their thing. They wanted to try or do it...each one was their own fantasy."

In this version the fantasy had once again got out of hand, and as a result he had taken Therese into the front room of the cellar in Cromwell Street and laid her on the floor. "I tried to get the taping off. I couldn't even get it off her. I don't have nothing to rip it with...When you get two or three pieces together you can't rip it, and by this time she's in, you know, looking as though she's in some pain and that – so I just strangled her." Fred West then gave his reason" "I don't believe in suffering, anybody suffering, like myself. If anything happened to me I would rather somebody just end me there and then, than let me lie there and suffer, 'cause suffering is a thing I can't take, like with animals...Anything that's suffering should be put to sleep, not allowed to suffer."

He then told the police: "After anything happened, when the girls died, I mean my stomach used to knot up and I felt sick and giddy and felt really ill, and I just wanted to get out from home like, get out altogether, give myself a chance to try and get control of myself again." He then explained: "When I buried the girl and got rid of her clothes and that...I had to dive for it, the door, go out for a long ride somewhere."

Frankie McIntosh, a 37-year-old former neighbour, told the Daily Express of her experiences with the Wests. "I didn't want to go into the house. I didn't know him. I simply lived across the street at 30 Cromwell Street. His wife Rosemary was doing the ironing and didn't even look up. I thought that was strange, seeing her husband was showing a woman into their bedroom. It had a mirrored ceiling and mirrors on the wardrobe. The camera was pointing to the bed. West told me 'Rosemary and I like to film each other.' I think he just wanted me to react. If I was in to anything like that I thought he would be the last person I would tell. I just walked out of the room, but I could not get out of the house. It had been made in to a rabbit warren with walls in the way of rooms and the corridor. He showed me his work-room, which was amazing. It was crammed from floor to ceiling with tools, electric saws and drills. I remember wondering what he needed it all for. The house was full of children. I know he had nine there and they were everywhere. But he said they were never allowed into his private room, which was near the bedroom. He took me in and showed me a bar he had built. He said he liked to go in there on his own and have a drink. He asked me to have one, but I was worried about my two sons who were asleep across the street. I told him I had to go. We walked in to the back garden, which had been completely paved over. There wasn't a blade of grass to be seen. He said, 'Come back another time, or I can come to your place.'

Former lodger Gloria Langdon stayed in the house from the end of 1977 to 1980 and she was friendly with Shirley Robinson. Gloria was never given a key and Fred and Rose told her to never lock her bedroom door at night. After suffering a brain hemorrhage in 1988, it left her almost completely paralysed. Her sister Debbie, who often stayed with her at 25 Cromwell Street, told the Daily Express: "It gives me shivers to think we were there. Gloria is still petrified about what she has heard. And to think she lived there when all this was going on. I remember the fireplace in Gloria's room was blocked up. I used to imagine there were bodies behind it. I used to think I heard voices – we both felt very uneasy about being there. It was very creepy. A couple of neighbours complained about the noise, and there was always a funny stale smell in the air. Sometimes it was so strong it would make us feel sick. Fred would not allow Gloria to have a front-door key, or a key for her own bedroom. She was unable to lock the door. It was a strict house rule. Gloria was very timid, and wouldn't stand up for herself. But she was never asked to take part in any funny business. Shirley always seemed terrified of Fred West, but through that fear, he seemed to have an amazing hold over her. Out of all the girls who lodged there she seemed to be his favourite, and the one he talked to the most. Gloria always told us of strange noises that came up through the house at night from the basement. There were always bangs and crashes, but she was too terrified to leave her room. The next morning Fred always said he was doing some DIY work." She went on to explain how Gloria and Shirley Robinson quickly became friends and spent many evenings chatting in each other's rooms. "One day Shirley just disappeared. We were told she had gone to Germany and everyone accepted that."

Gloria's mother, Joan Galvin, added: "Rosemary was jealous there was something going on between Shirley and Fred. Towards the end Gloria was terrified to be in the house. She never really said why. Fred invited us around for tea one night and he seemed a nice person. But when I started to hear how Rosemary would answer the door stark naked, the whole thing started sounding very weird. Gloria told us Fred was often busy digging in the garden. He offered to do some work for us, but we didn't need him."

The Basement

10th March 1994

Detectives began to enquire deeper into the missing person, Alison Chambers, as a possible victim. The eight sets of remains so far discovered had now been moved to The College of Medicine at the University of Cardiff in Wales and police had liaised with other forces throughout the country and also contacted Holland, Germany and Switzerland in an effort to identify the victims.

09:34

A warrant under Section 8 of the Police and Criminal Evidence Act was issued by Gloucester Magistrates for a search of Letterbox Field at Kempley, for the remains of Ann McFall. A second warrant was also obtained to search for the remains of Catherine (Rena) West in Fingerpost Field at Kempley.

In his 49th interview, Fred West said that he had fathered at least 3 children while in Scotland. Steven McAvoy (who came to stay with Fred and Rose for a time), another boy called Gareth and a daughter called Anne.

11:30

A press conference was organised at the Brunswick Road Campus of Gloucester College of Art and Design, just 200 yards from St. Michael's Square and Cromwell Street.

DSI Bennett was asked if ligatures had been found on the bodies. He replied: "I can't comment on matters that are evidential. We have eight sets of remains and as far as I am concerned the term 'remains' encompasses anything we find." He went on to reveal that Interpol had now stepped into the case after fears that women from Germany and Holland may be among the victims. "We are in touch with five families in this country whose identities I cannot disclose in respect for their own wishes".

He went on to appeal for anyone who had left home and vanished for their own reasons to contact the Bureau to advise them, in confidence, that they were safe and well. "It would help considerably if relatives and friends would now try to contact people who have left home. People who are aware that they are reported missing could help by making some contact with relatives and friends, even if they do not wish to return."

He said that the excavation work at Cromwell Street was likely to go on for some time. "The speed of excavations of the cellar area has been slowed following the continual finds and the need to prevent structural problems by infilling stage by stage with concrete. Despite extensive excavations there is still a large area to be explored. There is also the ground floor extension and further areas in the bathroom. This is expected to take several days and we will not be excavating any other sites until we have completed our work."

Discussing the finds of all of the bodies so far, Professor Knight dismissed the likelihood of large bones decomposing though he accepted some of the smaller ones might have, adding that some of the vertebrae were missing where decapitation had taken place. Some remains even had the same bones missing. He would do a complete bone count for each set of remains and put it in his report.

11th March 1994

The Chief Constable of Gloucestershire, Tony Butler, stood in front of Gloucester Police Station in front of camera crews and reporters. His statement read:

"Following a formal complaint to the Attorney-General by Mr West's legal advisers concerning press coverage of this investigation the following warning is considered appropriate.

Our attention has been drawn to the extensive media coverage afforded to the circumstances leading up to and surrounding the arrest and subsequent court appearances of Frederick West. We have noted that in particular, background material relating to Frederick West includes reference to the nature of the evidence said to be available against him, and alleged past misconduct towards members of his family. There has also been much speculation about possible offences going well beyond those with which he is charged. Frederick West was arrested on 25th February 1994 and at that point the proceedings became 'active' within the meaning of Paragraph 4 of Schedule 1 to the Contempt of Court Act 1987. We would like to take this opportunity to remind editors of their obligation not, at any time, to publish material which gives a 'substantial risk' of serious prejudice in the proceedings."

10:00

Fred West appeared at Gloucester Magistrates' Court on eight separate charges of murder. He was remanded in custody to Gloucester Prison for 28 days, to reappear at Gloucester Magistrates' Court on Thursday, 7th April 1994.

The Home Office Prison Department inspected the cell complex regarding the continued detention of Fred West. Fred's solicitor, Howard Ogden, gave written approval for him to be remanded in police cells, rather than taken to prison. Fred was then taken to HM Prison, Gloucester to await a Home Office decision regarding where he would be held. The Home Office gave consent for Fred West to be held at Gloucester Police Station under Section 29 of the Criminal Justice Act 1961 from Friday, 11th March until further notice, under normal remand conditions.

Stephen West: "I saw him when he appeared in court. I was sitting there with my girlfriend, and didn't feel too bad. He came up the stairs from beneath the court, and I felt sick and went cold. He looked withdrawn and had lost a lot of weight. He didn't see me. I wasn't crying or anything. All the reporters were staring at me and making me feel uncomfortable. I was staring at Dad when they read out the charges, and they said: 'Do you understand the charges?' and he said: 'Yes.' That was it, I was crying then. I couldn't believe that he understood what they had just said to him…For him to say yes, he understood he was being tried for murder, made it hit home that he might actually have done it. He still hadn't seen me. They told him he was being remanded in custody and he was taken down the stairs. I lifted my head up as he went out of view, and then at last he saw me. He put his head back and his hands up, and I winked at him, then he carried on walking down the stairs".

Fred West was interviewed just once during the day. For once, Fred wasn't happy to talk about his crimes. Howard Ogden recalled from his defence file: "Total change of officers and attitude. DI James accompanied by DC Harris. The attitude of these two officers was much more 'professional', being hard and direct and of a more formal attitude. So that we were referred to as 'gentlemen' as a group and Fred was referred to as 'Mr. West'. He was shown a series of what are medical type diagrams of skeletons referred to as 'speculative chart of bones missing' which have been prepared by a particular police officer in each case and have shown, in red, the areas where bones are missing."

Fred: Could the appropriate adult just slip down to my cell and get my glasses please?

Howard Ogden recalled: "The diagrams are gone through in the order of their death. In general it shows that the striking feature is that the majority are missing kneecaps, hands and feet."

Officer: 113 missing bones. Can you explain where the missing bones are?
Fred: No explanation for that whatsoever
Officer: 49 missing bones, the majority from the hands and feet.
Fred: No comment on that, sir.

Officer: 72 bones missing. Shoulder blade, a large bone, missing. Majority of bones missing are from hands and feet.
Fred: No idea.

Howard Ogden: "At this point Fred becomes very distressed. He cannot look at the diagram. He turns it over and lays over it crying. He is given time to recover composure. He indicates to me that he wants to carry on."

Officer: Six out of the nine referred to have missing kneecaps. You haven't kept them, have you? Like souvenirs?
Fred: I mean, I keep souvenirs but it's of old time things, not…
Officer: Eight out of the nine have got various articles with them which are used for bondage.
Fred: No comment
Officer: Did you tie them up before killing them?
Fred: No comment
Officer: Did you tie them up before dismembering them?
Fred: Well, I recognise what the cord is, but I don't recognise that particular piece. It's a special nylon cord which is unbreakable. I always carried a roll of that on the van.
Officer: Did you torture them?
Fred: No
Officer: Were there acts of sadism?
Fred: No
Officer: Is there someone else involved?
Fred: No comment

(Fred is then shown a knife found in Lucy Partington's grave)

Fred: I've never seen a knife like that

(Fred is then shown photos of the various views of the masks made from tape with the skull inserted and as recovered from the grave)

Fred: No idea
Officer: Were any of the victims hung up from the beams?
Fred: No comment, sir.
Officer: Were they taped up?
Fred: No comment, sir
Officer: Were they masked up for bondage?
Fred: No comment

Howard Ogden: "At this stage I noticed that Fred was staring intently across the table at DC Harris, who was staring back. It was like one of those situations of trying to stare out the other. I'd never noticed this in Fred previously."

Officer: I have to ask if parts were cut off as part of a sado-masochistic ritual?
Fred: No comment
Officer: Would you accept it seemingly occurred in your home?
Fred: No comment
Officer: These girls all found their way in to your cellar where they were tortured and mutilated
Fred: No comment
Officer: Was someone taped up and hung upside down on a hook in your basement? Do you remember saying that?
Fred: No comment
Officer: Did it happen to all of the girls?
Fred: No comment

(He said he had nothing to do with the missing bones. He denied amputation even before he was asked about it)

Fred: 'Cause I mean I never, I never cut no toes and fingers off.
Officer: Did I suggest you had?
Fred: Well, I mean you said they're missing, so –
Officer: Yeah?
Fred: Well I mean you –
Officer: They might be in another place?
Fred: No, no, no, no.
Officer: That's what I'm asking you.
Fred: No, no, every, everything is in one place, there ain't no, there wasn't, all, all if they were cut up it was just their head and arms, and legs, nothing else took off.
Officer: You're sure about that?
Fred: Yeah…when you push them down with a spade I mean it's quite possible for something like that to happen.

The ninth set of remains had now been removed to Cardiff for forensic examination. Excavations at the house continued, concluding at approximately 20:00.

12th March 1994

No excavations and no work were carried out at 25 Cromwell Street for the first time since the enquiry commenced. This allowed the officers involved in the work to take a break. Other enquiries, however, still continued from the Murder Incident Room.

A report in the Daily Mirror identified a site in Upper Apperly as one which could be searched in the hunt for more bodies. Fred West was known to have had a girlfriend in the village and lived on the outskirts of the village in the late 60's and early 70's. A 'police insider' was quoted as saying: "We have been interviewing various people in the village who are known to have wells, after receiving certain information. There is no suggestion anyone had any idea of what we are told happened years ago." One villager said: "Police told me they had information that the concrete filling of the well was done by a man at night. It's certainly a funny time of the day to be doing work like that."

Rose's mother, Daisy Letts, told the Daily Mirror that she remembered meeting a 'son' of Fred West's once but never seeing him again. She remembered it was about 20 years ago and he was a "very polite little boy" aged about 6. She said that Fred had told her that the young boy, who she remembered had a Scottish accent, was his and Rena's son. "Fred brought the lad back after going to Scotland on business. I asked if he was keeping him – but he said he had to go back to his mother. I can't remember his name – but I didn't believe he was Fred and Rena's. He looked foreign – and Fred was such a terrible liar anyway." This was almost undoubtedly Steven McAvoy.

13th March 1994

09:00

Police Officers commenced digging in the cellar area of the house. There were no further developments. The Odontologist, Dr Whittaker, was confident he knew who four of the victims were and was able to give the approximate age of four of the others. Professor Knight had sent him the skulls from the eight sets of remains. Dr Whittaker's analysis showed the skull from the first set of remains was that of Heather West, the third found was Shirley Robinson, the sixth was Lucy Partington and the eighth was Lynda Gough.

Regarding Lucy Partington, Dr Whittaker later said: "This girl must have had some damage to her two front teeth. They had crowns on them and these crowns were temporary crowns. Now, to a dentist this means she had an accident probably, she had the work done to make new crowns. She had temporary ones put on and she died and was unable to go back for the fitting." A policewoman remembered an incident from a hockey match many years before when a local girl had her teeth knocked out and she asked if it could be the same girl.

Dr Whittaker: "We had 10,000 missing girls in Britain. They were in the frame and a woman police detective says "Do you think it could be this girl who was playing hockey?" And of course the answer has to be that it's incredibly unlikely, but we ought to check it out. The team was put on to sort this out and it turned out to be her!"

As for the others at this stage, the second was a girl approximately 17-18 years old, the fourth a woman in her early twenties – but not Juanita Mott – the fifth were not those of Carol Cooper but a girl aged about 16, and the seventh a girl aged approximately 17-18 who might be Juanita Mott. Then again, either Juanita or Carol could have been the ninth.

Dr Whittaker's research was based on a combination of the information supplied by Professor Knight and available dental records. If there were no dental records or only old or partial ones then he would use his photographic imaging comparison system.

The police had a lot of information about Juanita Mott and Carol Cooper, including dental records, but still very little was known about Alison Chambers and virtually nothing of Shirley Hubbard that would take their identification further.

As for the 'Dutch girl', 'Tulip', or 'Truck' as Fred West was now calling the hitch-hiker he had picked up near Monmouth, there was even the possibility he was referring to two girls rather than one. There were already over 130 possibilities, all of them foreign nationals whose details had come from various sources including Interpol, other police forces, direct from families, the Metropolitan Police Missing Persons Bureau, the National Missing Persons Helpline charity, Salvation Army and the media.

Gloria Langdon, a former lodger, told The News of The World newspaper that Fred West had tried to get her to sleep with him and Rose. "Fred would say to me 'you don't have to go back upstairs if you don't want to'. I knew exactly what he meant. But it didn't bother me because I was used to them both and I suppose they didn't shock me after a while. Another girl lodger called Liz told me Fred was always going on about sex to her. Fred never knew when to stop. They'd joke about sex all the time in front of the kids, who seemed quite used to it. I dreaded seeing Rose because she'd often have no clothes on. She always had men in and out of the house. Fred and Rose were always friendly towards me. But I wasn't allowed anywhere near the cellar. Whenever I went down towards it I was told to stay away. That was their private room and I had no idea what went on there… Shirley Robinson was a friend and Heather West played around my feet. It haunts me to think what became of them."

A former client of Rose's, 67-year-old John Homes, also gave an interview to The News of The World. "She was bloody good at it. It's the best sex I've had for years. We used to do it in her four-poster bed upstairs. I'm much older than her but I gave her a good seeing to and she never complained. Fred must have known I was sleeping with his wife but I don't think he minded. Once when I was in the Wellington pub where we used to meet, Rose came in and said Fred wanted to meet me. I thought 'here we go' but he was as nice as pie. Rose sat next to me on the sofa and we all had a drink and smoked rolled up cigarettes together. I couldn't believe it. There I am shagging his wife, and he's ordering beer for me.

It was great fun while it lasted. She had a good body with bumps in all the right places. Sometimes it would last half an hour, or we'd stay together making love for two hours. She was brilliant. Very good. It was straight sex, nothing sordid. We just used to have a few drinks and then go back to her house for sex."

He said the affair ended in 1992 when he objected to Rose seeing other men. "One night I had sex with her and was about to go when another bloke turned up. I was very cross and said I wasn't having that. After all, you don't know what you might catch do you? Also I felt a bit jealous. I walked out and we've never spoken since. When I look back, it gives me the creeps. I've had sex in a house full of bodies. I never knew anything about them. Now it sends a shiver down my spine."

14th March 1994

Fred was interviewed four times during the day. He started by reminiscing about his early life and recalled the day Rose moved in with him. He recalled that Rose said that she had a tearful farewell with her brothers Gordon and Graham, who had accompanied her to the bus-stop, and having met Fred, walked with him to a five-bar gate by a field, which she found romantic. "We stood at that gate and something happened to us both, we crashed into each other and just locked so solid in each other's mind, it was just unreal I mean. Rose knew that something had happened at that gate and so did I but we weren't a hundred per cent sure what had gone on, and from that time we have absolutely been locked into each other. We can virtually read each other's minds at all times". He went on to say that Rose wanted to commemorate the moment by taking the gate home. "Rose always wanted that gate, a big farm gate. To have as an ornament at home. A big five-bar gate! It was a couple of years later before we went back there and the gateway was filled in and the gate was gone, and

320

Rose actually stood there and cried. It was only a farm gate, you know, but it meant so much to her because she realised that was the start of our life together."

Fred described his mother as 'dominant'. "My mother knew exactly what was going on. You never kept nothing from my mother. You could tell her the biggest lie you ever thought up, Mother would just listen and then tell you the truth and that was it, finished". He described his father as "the most understanding person you'd ever meet. You could go to dad and ask him anything. He was always calm. He was a massive man, mind, big man, tall, you know, massive hands on him but he wouldn't hurt a fly and he always understood you whenever we had problems…he was so placid it was unreal".

Fred was then told that the police would be meeting with Rose, Mae and Stephen. "Mae's certainly not going to lie anyway. Whatever Mae says will be the dead truth…Mae will tell you exactly what she knows and it will be the truth…there's nothing about Mae that's false…she's a very educated young lady".

The search continued at 25 Cromwell Street but again there were no new developments. Six square metres of concrete was delivered to infill the cellar area to ensure the house was structurally safe.

In the afternoon DSI Bennett met with Rose, Stephen, Mae and one of Mae's friends at Gloucester Police Station. They were told that soon the fields at Kempley and the flat at 25 Midland Road would be searched and that he would also be seeing Anne Marie.

Throughout the meeting, DSI Bennett aimed his words at Rose. From behind her big, horn-rimmed glasses came a penetrating stare that betrayed hatred either of him or all he stood for. It really didn't matter which. She barely uttered a word, leaving what little was said to Stephen and Mae.

15th March 1994

Fred's daughter Mae made a ten-page statement to the police in which she said that her father had regularly touched her in a sexual manner.

DSI John Bennett and DCI Terry Moore visited 25 Cromwell Street to view the progress, while Stephen West visited Fred in prison. Fred told him that "I only made love to them when I thought they were dead…When they start telling you that snuff movies are involved, don't believe them. It was not quite like that." In regards to why he killed them, he told Stephen: "They all deserved to die. They were slags". He said that the victims had their nails pulled out and fingers cut off while they were hung up, and had

321

cigarettes stubbed out on them. But he told Stephen that all of the victims were cut up away from Cromwell Street. He sexually assaulted them in the house, tied them up, tortured them, killed them, took them away and cut them up and then brought them back to bury them.

16th March 1994

10:37

Fred West was interviewed by police artist, Detective Constable Bob Wilcox, to obtain an artist's impression of the victims. Digging and the search of 25 Cromwell Street continued and was expected to continue for a few more days, although there were no new developments.

DCI Terry Moore told the press that five families had been reunited with their missing loved ones since their earlier appeal. He told how the police had been working closely with the Missing Persons Bureau to trace as many missing people as possible. He said that he was pleased that his officers' work had made "several families a great deal happier. With their help we have put five families back in contact with their loved ones, some of whom have been missing for a considerable time. Obviously, we need to eliminate as many missing women as possible from our inquiries to help us make positive identifications of the remains we have found."

"If any good can come from this case, it is that someone will be reunited with their son or daughter", Chief Inspector Colin Handy added.

17th March 1994

The police finally identified Alison Chambers as "the girl under the pond" and Fred West changed his story for a third time. This time he claimed that she had been living at number 11 Cromwell Street, and that he had "done her room up for her and she stayed there for a while...'cause she had nowhere to stay". When the house had first been converted to multiple occupancy, he went on to explain: "There was a load of girls ran away from Jordans Brook and was there...I mean, it used to be a regular place for them to go."

He continued: "She was looking scruffy. She wasn't scruffy in the first place. No, she was quite well dressed, but she'd worn the same clothes over and over...and she had an iron mark on her jumper." He then insisted that the girl "was turning up too often, watching me", and "I think what she was really after was a handful of money off me 'cause she thought we got money, or I got money."

He said that some of the girls who arrived at Cromwell Street "were obviously trying to make money other ways", and added, "A lot of them were on the game." He was trying to say that most of the girls who went to his home were sexually open-minded and had agreed to all sorts of variations of sex with him and Rose. As a result, there were "girls that accepted what we did and, you know, and forgot about it, went home and on their way…See, I had affairs with so many different girls, I mean, you're not talking one or two, and…every one didn't end up in disaster, by no means."

When he was asked why he had not killed in the last years of his life, he replied: "Why did I stop for eight years and not do anymore? There's a simple answer for that. When I attacked Heather I got such a shock that I didn't know how the hell to get over it…Then I sorted it out, what the problem was, and it was messing about with other girls, with the fear of Rose catching me."

When the police suggested that the girl he was calling 'Shirley's mate' was in fact called Alison Chambers, he simply replied: "Don't mean a thing. I never asked her her name." But he went on to insist: "This girl never stayed with us."

Detective Superintendent Bennett again met with Paul Britton, a Consultant Clinical Psychologist with the Trent Regional Psychology Unit at Leicester. Paul Britton gave his advice on what avenues of enquiry to follow and what lines of questioning the interviewers should try.

20:33

Fred was charged with the murder of Carol Ann Cooper. He was interviewed regarding Heather's disappearance and he said he found it difficult "to have to lie to Rose and Mae and Stephen, especially Mae, even more so…I mean Rose believe anything I tell her anyway, always have done, I mean that, done ever since I can remember with Rose, so I mean but with Mae, I mean it was, Mae was always a bit special to me because of her being educated and she was going places".

18th March 1994

09:30

The morning's news conference was arranged at the Brunswick Road Campus of GLOSCAT, the city's arts and technology centre. There was an accompanying statement giving details of the new charge against Fred West and the circumstances of Carol Ann Cooper's disappearance. The statement also included an update on the search at Cromwell Street, the plan to use a police artist for facial reconstruction, and the information that no further sites would be searched until at least 28th March when the investigation would move to Kempley.

Speaking to news reporters, Carol Ann Cooper's step-mother, Barbara Monro said: "I am horrified. I never believed she had been killed. She was a rebellious girl and used to say I wasn't her real mum, but I did my bit for her."

Carol's closest childhood friend, Kim Porter, said: "This is just so horrible, a big shock. My parents spoke to Carol on the day she disappeared. We were very good friends and had some happy times together."

Carol's great aunt, Ruth Brazier, said: "We were all dreadfully upset when she went missing. Her grandmother, Alice, who died several years ago, lived very close to the home where Carol was put in to care. In the evenings she religiously stood by her front window to watch for Carol after she went out. They would wave at each other and Alice knew she was safely home. The night she didn't turn up, Alice ran into the street and asked everyone if they had seen Carol. She was beside herself with worry. Alice spoiled her as if she was her own daughter. After she went missing, Alice couldn't talk to anyone without breaking in to tears. It broke her heart."

The enquiries into Fred and Rose West's previous convictions for indecent assault and physical assault on Caroline Owens were continuing. In keeping with force procedure, the file had been destroyed long ago and the prosecuting police inspector was now dead. There was little detail of the case in the court records and the magistrate who had dealt with it only had a vague recollection.

DSI Bennett read Caroline Owens's statements but had seen no official detailed description of the offences, as they had all been destroyed. To get that detail detectives went to the offices of The Gloucester Citizen and found a full report of the case. This corroborated what Caroline alleged.

The criminal records of Fred and Rose West at Scotland Yard included a note of the case and although details were scant, it did at least name the officers involved. One had retired and was unable to remember anything, while the other, Detective Constable Kevan Price, was still serving.

He had searched his old pocket books and found the entries for the arrest and interviews of both Fred and Rose West. These were revealing. After both had continually denied the allegations, Fred eventually admitted sexual and physical assault and implicated Rose. When she was told, Rose simply responded that if her husband had said that was what had happened, it had!

Kevan Price also remembered photographs were taken of Caroline Owens's injuries and the marks the tape had left when she was bound and gagged. He could offer no explanation for the relatively minor charges that were preferred. He could only say that the decision in respect was made way above him.

A search through a large number of old police photographic negatives sent to headquarters for archiving uncovered the original negatives of the offence. These included photographs of Caroline's injuries and the marks left by the tape, as well as the side of 25 Cromwell Street showing how, at that time, a car could be driven between the house and the church, along with photographs of the car she had been picked up in.

In an interview Fred was asked about an incident with a neighbour opposite who collapsed. "I mean that man practically died in my arms you know". He went on to tell the police how his wife saw as little of him as anyone, because there only had to be knock on the door and he would be off helping someone out of a fix.

In a later interview, the police were trying to establish if there could be any other places where Fred could have buried a body. He said: "I tell you what, I can't remember half the places I've been laying concrete and patios. It's an everyday thing for me." And then he burst out in a fit of laughter. "I mean, when they talk about going through places that I've been, I mean you're going to be here for a month…Every day's a different place, and two or three places a day, like. Asda stores, Gateway stores, offices all over England." He had been in Reading and Leicester, Nottinghamshire and Newmarket, he told them with a grin on his face. "I shall have done me life sentence and back out or buried or something by the time you got round to it."

At one point, Fred chatted to guards and his 'Appropriate Adult', Janet Leach. "I can now think of what Rose is feeling now that I've got that out of my mind, and Stephen and Mae, what everyone is feeling at this moment in time. You know, as before I couldn't think of what they felt, I was making sure they didn't know".

Stephen West went to visit Fred in prison again. Fred had lost weight and was now chain smoking. He told Stephen that the police were trying to get evidence against Rose and told him to make sure that Rose didn't go back to the police station when she was summoned. He even suggested that Rose should "get out of the country". Stephen told Mae to pass the message on as Rose wasn't talking to him at the time.

19th March 1994

Rose West's accommodation was compromised as the police learned of Stephen West's deal with the News of The World. They were rehoused to a former police house at the back of the police station at Dursley. The covert listening operation continued there and Stephen was banished. For weeks, Mae and Rose wouldn't tell him where they were. He sent flowers to Rose via the police in an attempt to gain favour but she was having none of it. Rose and Mae were afraid to go out in case they were recognised. They stayed at home and played Scrabble, watched TV, cooked and phoned anyone they could. They did not know that all of their conversations were recorded. "Mum knew she was going to face the same charges as Dad. He was being charged with new murders almost daily. I think she was sort of waiting for it, knowing it was inevitable. She said if she ever did time and was sent to prison, she was always going to say she was innocent, right to the end".

The Sun Newspaper quoted Carol Cooper's mother-in-law, Barbara Cooper as saying: "I never believed she had been killed. I always thought she was living somewhere else. She was a rebellious girl and used to say I wasn't her real mum, but I did my best for her. I'm glad that it's all over now." Her uncle, Ken Brazier said: "At least this has put our minds at rest. I hope now we can get together as a family and plan a little service in her memory."

Elspeth Keir, a retired social worker who cared for her at the time, said: "Carol was a lovely, intelligent girl. She was not the sort you expect to end up in a home. She was such a pretty girl and never gave us any trouble at all."

20th March 1994

No work was carried out at 25 Cromwell Street for only the second day since the inquiry started and Fred was taken to 25 Midland Road, where he again said the police would not find Charmaine, and then to Bristol Road, Gloucester (the site where Mary Bastholm went missing). In between, he was taken to a nearby allotment he had used, a ploy to see if it jogged his memory about other possible victims.

Back at the police station, he was interviewed regarding the disappearance of Mary Bastholm but he denied any involvement. When the questioning moved on to the remains of Charmaine, he told police that his stepdaughter's body could not be there at 25 Midland Road, as she must have been taken away "during the demolition. They can go and dig the whole of Midland Road up, but they won't find nothing there, because there's nothing there."

News reports started to name Alison Chambers as a possible victim. Her mother, Joan Owens, said: "They tell me they are 70 per cent certain she is a victim. As soon as I heard bodies had been found, I started to wonder if Alison could be one of them."

Alison's best friend, Helen Hulme, said she last saw Alison at Paddington Station in London after they had hitchhiked there. Alison left, saying she would return within the hour, but she never came back.

Stephen West had an interview printed in The News of The World which had obviously been conducted some weeks before. "There are times I hate my father's guts for what our family has been put through, and never want to see him again. But he's my dad. People might not understand, but I still love him. I care about him... I guess I just want to see him. I don't know whether it would do me any good, but I want to see if I can look at him in the same way as before, though I doubt it. He's asked to see me several times, but the solicitor has advised against it, saying it's in his best interests to see no one. I've been told he's eating and sleeping and he's got a psychiatrist there when they feel he needs one."

He then told of his reaction when the police discovered Heather's remains in the garden. "I felt dizzy and really sick that I could ever have played there in the garden above my sisters' body. We used to have barbeques in the summer, and enjoy a laugh and a joke out there. I feel so guilty that we were playing at happy families while she was there all the time. Now I have the most dreadful recurring nightmares all the time. I wake up with a start and find myself crying and sweating all over. I've imagined myself in the garden looking down at a big hole and seeing my poor sister's bones. Mum has been having nightmares as well, but she won't talk about them.

Mum and Mae don't even want to see Dad any more. Mum even wants to change her name. I'm so confused I don't know what to think. Sometimes I feel like running away. I don't know what the future holds. Dad's written two letters to the three of us. He said sorry our lives had been messed up, and advised we sell the house, move away and start again. Both letters said the same thing and were about a hundred words long. He dictated them to his solicitor and signed them. Mum read them, folded the letters up and put them upstairs in her room. She's quite hard in her personality, she showed no reaction. Dad said he loved us all, and that upset me. I really want to see how he is."

He said that he and Mae had asked Rose if she had anything to do with the murders, and she replied: "No way, I don't know anything." He said she told him "The only thing that worries me is what you and Mae feel". He said "Her reactions have convinced us she knew nothing about what happened. We still love her and will give her every support we can. When we told her that, she smiled and was pleased.

Mum used to get up at 5.30am for work and she can't get out of the habit, but when she starts to think about Heather she goes back to sleep and the feelings go away. It's her way of coping with the stress of it all. Mum cries a lot for no reason. She hasn't called anyone or seen any of her friends. She just wants to be on her own. She says she wants to live on her own with her collie dogs Benji and Oscar. Mae wants to go and live with a friend. Nobody wants me. I just don't know what to do now – I've lost everything.

The police are paying the bills. They visit us once in the morning and once in the afternoon. We've also had visits from a doctor and the victim support people. We have our ups and downs and arguments – you're bound to get that when you're living together 24 hours a day. We've been told to stay in for our own safety. When I go out I feel people are staring at me. Mum and Mae have been in the papers a lot and I think they'll be recognised straight away if they go out, so they stay in."

He said that he had tried to hide from Rose's previous activities as a prostitute. "I tell myself it's her private life, but it's hard to look at her knowing the truth. Still, it's not changed my feelings towards her – although it's difficult to see her in the same light. At home, Mum had a flat upstairs to get away from the rest of us. She needed her time and space. There was nothing really hidden away in our family. But we didn't want to nose too much into each other's business. Mum and Dad used two bedrooms, one with a four-poster at the front of the house, and the other at the back which I remember had a kingsize bed. Although Mum had her own flat, she and Dad always slept together. I wasn't aware they were making blue movies."

Of his father, he said: "I look a lot like him but that's where it stops. We have very different ideas on life. We don't have many things in common, but we both love to work, and in the past ten months we've been together quite a bit. I've been helping him at work and he let me rewire the house. He never used to let me do things like that before and it was as though I had become a man for the first time. He was treating me like an equal and he taught me everything I know."

He said he was brought up strictly by his parents, but had been treated well as a child. "There was no tension in the house, although I always had to behave myself. But Mum told me I had to leave home as soon as I was 16. There was a bedsit down the road which she'd found for me. I had to do a paper round and things to pay for it. Mum said it was time I stood on my own two feet.

When I was 12 I had to do my own washing and ironing, and we kids cooked our own tea when I was 12. When we got home from school we would get changed and there would be jobs to do. Then we would do our homework and go to bed. I knew it was stricter for me at home than it was for my school friends, but I was happy and it didn't cause me any problems."

He then told how his fiancé, Andrea, had been supportive of him. "She's been very good and supportive to me, but it's put a lot of pressure on our relationship. I've not had time to stop and think about the future. I've become much harder over the past couple of weeks and I feel bitter towards everyone."

Andrea said: "I just want to be with Stephen and help him. I want to talk to Stephen and to be there for him when he gets upset."

Stephen then said that police had been in contact with him. "They've asked me to make a full statement. It's entirely voluntary. They've told me they're going to ask me very intimate sexual questions... I wish I could have been born into another family. Sometimes I wake up and think I'm a kid again, back in my old bedroom at Cromwell Street, and everything is OK. But it doesn't take long for me to realise that we can never again have our home life together. This nightmare is true."

21st March 1994

Fred was asked about the letters that the police had found in the attic of 25 Cromwell Street, and more specifically about the one which said "Yes or not to Char? I say Yes but it is up to you." Fred explained how he and Rose wanted to avoid Rena: "Rose come to me and say that Rena had been for Charmaine and that what Rose said in her letter was whether she was gonna let Rena have her or not or whether we were going to dive off a bit quick before she come back... what I said to her was if Rena took Charmaine would it be all right with her, and for a while she didn't want to know, and then I said to her we will have a son of our own... What I didn't want her to do was to tell Charmaine so Charmaine goes and tells Rena that we move and Rena is sat there waiting for us". According to this version, they were prevented from moving anyway, because their gas and electricity had been cut off due to non-payment of bills. He later added that he had made love to Rena before murdering her. He again mentioned that Charmaine's skeleton had been dug out by a bulldozer during the building work and taken away in a skip. He said after killing Rena he had cleaned himself up in a cattle tank at the edge of the field and burnt her clothes on a fire.

He said that the body of Charmaine "was wrapped up in a lot of blankets, 'cause she wasn't cut up or nothing, she was just as she was." He also confided in the police that: "I make sure nobody harms Rose. I worship that girl, my wife. We've got a very special thing in our own minds…it's got stronger."

The search continued at 25 Cromwell Street. More concrete was delivered to make the house structurally safe – the total amount of concrete delivered so far was 17.3 cubic metres.

Shirley Robinson   Alison Chambers   Heather West

22nd March 1994

The second of Caroline Owens' statements that was used in court was written and work continued at the house in the afternoon.

Fred denied that Rose was a lesbian, and that she had had lesbian relationships. He said in interview that Rose had never "had any sexual relations with any girls, 'cause I would have known that".

23rd March 1994

Digging work in the kitchen and basement area was carried out and advice was taken from civil engineers regarding the safety of the house.

In interview, Fred West again denied that Rose was a lesbian, or had any lesbian tendencies. He stated that "Rose was not a lesbian. I've tried several times to get her into it, but without success."

A file was discovered that included details of the disappearance of Therese Siegenthaler at the Metropolitan Police Missing Persons Bureau. The file was at Lewisham, South London, and contained photographs and a dental record.

Fred West was becoming annoyed at the amount of letters he was receiving and asked his solicitor Howard Ogden if there was something he could do. Howard Ogden wrote to the Governor of the prison asking for his advice, and also to make a complaint after a photograph of Fred had apparently been illegally leaked to the press.

The photo in question

24th March 1994

Fred's brother John West was arrested in connection with the sexual abuse of his niece, Anne Marie. A search was carried out of his home and it was found to contain a large number of bondage and humiliation videotapes and magazines, which John West claimed to have picked up on his rounds as a dustman. He admitted during police interviews that he went to 25 Cromwell Street to have sex with his sister-in-law Rosemary.

Digging continued at 25 Cromwell Street and more concrete was delivered.

Janet Leach had been the only person who had attended 100% of Fred West's interviews following his arrest. Concern was growing that her attitude towards him had changed and that she may even have become a victim of 'Stockholm Syndrome'. DSI Bennett decided it was time for a change and for her to step down. A document was drawn up and backdated to the 24th February when the investigation began. It spelled out her legal responsibility to keep everything she had seen and heard confidential until she was officially released from her undertaking, in writing, by the constabulary, which would at the earliest be the conclusion of any court proceedings. It underlined what she had already agreed verbally and covered every conceivable aspect of her role as an appropriate adult. Janet Leach signed the document with the proviso she might be asked to come back at a later date. Arrangements were then made with the probation service to find a replacement.

25th March 1994

A warrant under Section 8 of the Police and Criminal Evidence Act was issued by Gloucester Magistrates for a search of 25 Midland Road in connection with the disappearance of Charmaine West and no work was carried out at 25 Cromwell Street.

Rose West was photographed by the media while out shopping at KwikSave while living in Dursley. Because of this, she was shortly afterwards moved to other police accommodation in Hales Close, Cheltenham.

During her time in police accommodation, Rose West said nothing to implicate her in any of the murders. When she was asked about them by Mae, a recording picked up Rose's reply: "Fuck off! Of course I'm angry with him Mae. What do you think? I mean look, if I got near the bastard now, I'd put me fucking hands round his throat and somebody would have to fucking pry them off. Mae, he's taken your sisters and my daughters fucking life. This is something you don't fucking forgive. I'd never forgive that. You never forget it. See Mae, look, I told you, as you well know, I told you I thought your dad was a very sick man and the worst liar I ever could have dreamed of but nobody could have known. They'll never get a confession out of me for something I haven't fucking done. If they think I've got fuck all to do with this then the best thing they can do is put me in the cells and fucking throw the key away because I shall always protest my fucking innocence. No matter if I do spend the rest of my life in fucking nick." She continued…

"You gotta remember that I am sixteen, right, now I've got this man that, Fred West, right, right? And he's an older man which my mum always told me 'get an older man, he'll look after you, he's had his life, he's had his flings, you know, you'll be alright' and I'm with this man and I'm almost completely brainwashed and I'm doing what he says…I was in love with your father. Whenever I made love with your father that was it for me. I didn't make love with anybody else and it mean anything. I had to adapt my mind to that, Mae. I had to be able to say oh, you know, make excuses. Yeah, fine and literally psych myself up to go. Mae, it's all very well and I'm…but I had to go out with this bloke I didn't like and climb in to his bed and make love all night and come home in the morning. Now, your mind just…see, nobody knows that. He was sending me fucking out with them, yeah? And it was just fucking crazy for him to say that I couldn't choose another man when he was lining them all fucking up for me and I wasn't allowed to choose. I've told you, haven't I? You know, it wouldn't have been so bad if I liked the people I was sat in the fucking pub with for, you know, for hours every week, you know."

26th March 1994

In interviews the following day, Fred was asked about Rose's violent nature and her treatment of the children who she had physically beaten. Fred said: "Rose wouldn't harm anybody. I mean, Rose didn't have a violent nature at all. I mean she used to shout at the children and things like that, but all mothers do."

He also tried to convince the police that his wife did not even enjoy her relationships with other men. "She was just doing it, because I wanted her to."

Getting back on to the murders, Fred told in a callous manner how one of his dismemberments had taken him an hour and a half. He said: "I used to put their head over the hole and cut their head off, and of course that was most, the bulk, of the blood gone…it would just rush out…Once you've cut the jugular vein, blood just rushes out." He told the police that he made sure "always" to cut his victim's heads off first, because that way he kept the bloodstains to a minimum. "There are no words to describe it, actually. You feel terrible. There is just no words to explain what you go through…Both mentally and physically, like, you are absolutely shattered. Once you go to cut somebody's head off, you then freeze mentally, and you just carry on and...from then on you don't know what you're doing...your mind is gone...and you're in so much pain in your stomach and you're shaking so much...I mean, like people say once you've done a thing it becomes easier. It does not – believe me, I can tell you that it does not get easier."

When it was pointed out to Fred that he might have disposed of the bodies of his victims in a different way, for example by burying them in larger holes that did not demand the he decapitate them, he dismissed the idea at once. "It don't work like that...When it happens you panic there and then. You got to do summat quick." He insisted that his idea was always the same. That he "always wanted to make the body fit the hole."

When DC Savage confronted him, telling him that she could not understand how his wife, "the lady of the house", could have nine bodies buried in her house and not have "a clue" they were there, Fred didn't budge. "Well, that's the truth", he told her. And when she suggested that she found it hard to believe in the light of their joint attack on Caroline Raine in 1972, he insisted: "I set Rose up to do that, that was my fault...Rose was pregnant practically all the time...She had more to do than to bother with that sort of thing."

No work was carried out at 25 Cromwell Street.

27th March 1994

No work was carried out at 25 Cromwell Street for the third successive day, but enquiries continued within the incident room at Gloucester.

Stephen West gave another interview to The News of The World, this time talking about his parents' sex lives. "My parents are total nymphomaniacs. They're totally barmy as far as sex is concerned. They didn't give a damn what we saw or heard. If one of Mum's men came round on a Sunday she'd break off from cooking the dinner and go upstairs with him. The meal would be ruined. My dad would be listening to what she was getting up to through a speaker which he kept in a cupboard. It had an extension lead on it and he'd hold it up to his ear as he pretended to watch TV. No one was allowed to speak and we could hear everything that was going on upstairs. My dad had connected a hi-tech baby intercom system in every room of the house. He said he's installed it to make sure we weren't misbehaving but really it was so he could listen to mum and her men. He fitted bugs into mum's kingsize bed and also a vent in the ceiling with a video camera hidden in a cupboard which had a hole in it.

They were mainly black men who came into the house, although there were white men as well. It would start about 9am and would possibly still be going on until six the next morning. The men would be all ages, but mostly in their 50's, 60's and 70's. Mum would sometimes have as many as eight different blokes coming in and out of the house in a single night.

She'd keep a big black book and used to record the men's name and which magazine advert he'd responded to, whether he was black or white, how old and how well endowed. In fact, all the personal details. It would all be written like an accounting book. And if she fancied one of them back again she'd just ring them up and they'd be down a bit later.

My parents were into making videos in a big way. My dad would take my mum and another man for a drive in the back of his work van. He'd put carpet in the back and bolt down a video camera and as he was driving along he'd film mum and this bloke in the back. They'd take some rope and a whip and also a flask of tea. It was their idea of a good night out. We were always woken when they came back in. They'd make so much noise at whatever they did. They'd be laughing and joking and the three of them would go upstairs. My mother was so loud making love you could hear her about 200 metres away. Once, when we went on a caravan holiday, I could hear a sound as though someone was in agony…and it was getting louder and louder as my two sisters and I walked to the caravan. I said to them 'What the hell is that noise?' Then we got close and realised it was my mum and dad. There was an audience outside, people just couldn't believe it. But she didn't give a damn and when I complained she said: 'Well if you don't like it, go home. You don't have to listen.'

There were loads of sex toys in the house. There were 30-odd different things really grotesque, with strap-on bits and pieces and whips. My dad made a cat-of-nine-tails with leather straps. He once put a video of my mum on TV accidentally and I just watched it stunned. She was on a kitchen table and it was really disgusting. I'd say to myself 'You weird bastards' and leave it at that. I never got used to any of this, although it became a way of life. Whenever my dad came home from work, he'd always grope my mum in front of me. She never wore any underwear and he would just stick his hands up her skirt.

The first time I brought a girlfriend home my mother came downstairs in her dressing gown. She totally ignored my girlfriend and went for a shower, and then my mother simply walked out naked across the living room. I was so embarrassed. Other times she would just sit there with her legs wide open and no knickers on. Her answer to it all was 'If you don't like what you're looking at then you shouldn't be looking'. I'm ashamed of what went on in our house. It's not nice and I knew that at the time. You should protect your children from that kind of stuff.

My father would always use crude language in front of us. It was effing this and effing that and every other word was a swear word. And when he ran out of them he would make them up himself. If he met someone new he'd pass comment about them. Once, when he was doing a job for a 94-

year-old lady he said: 'I'm going to have an affair with her. I think she likes me.' My dad also used to tell dirty jokes but they were lost on me. He had his own sense of humour which was difficult to understand."

He went on to tell about his childhood: "I remember eating some eggs but I hate the yoke part and went and threw it in the bin. I was only 11 and then I went out to play. But my mum called me back in, grabbed me by the neck and took me to the bin and showed me the parts of the egg that were in it. She pushed my head over the bin and said to me 'Now, eat it all up.' The egg bits were in all the slops and she made me get a fork and eat it out of the bin. It was vile and I was really sick. But she just sat there until I'd eaten it all. I was very quiet and kept myself to myself after that. I never fought back because it just wasn't worth it."

He then said that for 6 months, Rose wanted nothing to do with the family. "I was 13 at the time and my dad just said to me 'your mum is having a break, you won't see much of her around. We had to get all our own tea and carry on ourselves. After the initial shock it was good because we were on our own a lot."

He said that since his interview in last week's paper, Rose had disowned him. "She just turned on me and said 'You can get out. I never want to see you again. I don't care if you're dead'. That, as far as I'm concerned, is the last thing I will remember her saying."

28th March 1994

Fred West had the existing charges of murder of 'unknown females' amended to murders of Alison Chambers, Lucy Partington, Juanita Mott and Lynda Gough. In interview, when police challenged his assertion that he and Rose had been 'locked into' one another, which they thought might be interpreted as becoming accomplices in crime, he responded: "We're not evilly locked together at all, I mean Rose might look a bit hard-faced and that but Rose is as soft as a kitten, and I mean I know that because I've lived with her so long… I've been tempted over the years to tell Rose I must admit, but I never ever did, I always backed off it". He went on to say that had Rose known what he had been up to, she would have reported him for the safety of her own children.

DSI John Bennett, DCI Terry Moore and police press officers Colin Handy, Hilary Allison and David Morgan held a press conference at GLOSCAT. DSI Bennett said: "Ladies and gentlemen, I will read a statement regarding police investigations at Cromwell Street and the situation to date. There will be no questions. Copies of this statement will be available and I will do one-to-one reading for television and radio stations at the end of the proceedings. But I repeat, there will be no questions taken or answered today." A silence hung over the hall as he announced: "18-year-old Juanita Mott...19-year-old Lynda Gough...17-year-old Alison Chambers...21-year-old Lucy Partington".

Juanita Mott's sister, Belinda, told reporters: "I didn't want to believe she could be one of the bodies, but now the police have said they are sure she is, I feel numb. My mum is almost having a nervous breakdown over this. I had two friends there and used to visit them. I feel sick to think I was sitting in a bedroom and Juanita might have been below. I can't bear to think about it...Juanita was my big sister. We shared a bedroom until she left home and she would say 'I will always be here to look after you'. I will always remember that. I knew she wouldn't run off. We searched high and low for her. When I heard about Cromwell Street, it sent a shiver down my spine."

Joan Owen, Alison Chambers' mother: "It's going to take a long time to sink in, even after all these years. Alison will always be with me. I just can't put in to words the pain I feel. I always prayed that Alison had married and settled down to a new life somewhere. It gave me some comfort. At least the waiting is over at last. My thoughts and sorrow are now with the other poor families who are in the same boat as me. For the last 15 years we haven't celebrated Alison's birthday. We were hoping to make up for everything when we found her. In my mind, she will always be 15. I can't imagine her any other way. "

Lucy Partington's father, Roger, said: "The grief is still there, but uncertainty is worse. It is something that has been living with us for 20 years. It has been a harrowing time for us all."

Lynda Gough's parents, John and June, issued a joint statement saying: "Our daughter left just two weeks before her 20th birthday. All our efforts to trace her failed. Down all the years since, we have lived in the hope that she would come home. Now we know that she will not. It is very painful for us and our family to relive this grief now, and will be again at court proceedings and at Lynda's funeral."

Fred was interviewed regarding the attack on Caroline Owens again, but this time he said that Rose wanted it to happen. Fred said that Rose had wanted to have sex with Caroline and was frustrated by her departure. He said that she had told him that they would have to 'get' her – and over a period of a few days, they formulated a plan to abduct and rape Caroline. He said the attack on Caroline had been a test to see if Rose could help abduct a girl. He also made it clear that murder was going to be the likely outcome.

DC Geoff Morgan told the other interviewing officers that Fred had become upset in a previous interview when they asked about Rose's involvement. To push this, they then asked him about bondage. "The bondage side of it was mine – Rose never had nothing to do with it", he said. Asked again about Caroline Owens, he indicated that she had indeed almost died. "I think I would have went too far with it if Rose had been willing." He added that he had been "trying to get Rose involved with my sex life". Fred also claimed that Caroline Owens had wanted to have intercourse with him the night they abducted her. He said: "I was trying to get her (Rose) on lesbian and see how she reacted. I mean it went wrong anyway...I probably would have took her back home and put her in bondage or something but I mean Rose just didn't want to know about it...that was the reason why the lady went home...it all ended when Rose backed off...once Rose touched her and she screamed then that was Rose finished...Rose had her untied as soon as we got in the house. And Rose sat on the bed with her for a long time talking to her." As for the rape:

DC Savage: Are you saying she agreed to it?
Fred: Well, she didn't do a lot about it, put it that way. I mean she could have screamed then and the whole house would have heard her
DC Savage: Women don't always scream when they're being raped – they're terrified very often
Fred: Rubbish!

Later on in the interview:

Fred: Rose said what about some breakfast, So Rose went and got some breakfast for her and then her and Rose spent the rest of the day downstairs
DC Savage: You find things like that very difficult to cope with, don't you?
Fred: What?
DC Savage: Allegations of rape.
Fred: Well, yeah, 'cos I never raped nobody.
DC Savage: And yet you killed people.
Fred: You see, you've even got the killing wrong. You're trying to make out that I just went out and blatantly killed somebody...
DC Savage: No I'm not. They went through hell actually
Fred: No, nobody went through hell. Enjoyment turned to disaster.

DC Savage told Fred bluntly that she found it unbelievable – and so did the experts the police had consulted – that he had stopped killing for periods of six years: between 1967 and 1973, and then between 1987 and

1994. She added that the only reason she suspected he was claiming this was his fear of implicating his wife in any killing. In response, he screamed at his interrogator: "Rubbish. Because Rose had nothing to do with it at all…Rose knew nothing of what I was doing at all, ever….all Rose wants is to be a mother, and that's all she's ever been…an absolutely perfect mother."

Digging and searching resumed at 25 Cromwell Street.

29th March 1994

A search warrant was executed and the search began at Letterbox Field (Kempley A) for the remains of Rena Costello. The excavations commenced under the direction of Police Search Advisor (POLSA) Sergeant John Pickersgill. The team of officers involved were members of the force underwater search team which was subsequently disbanded for financial reasons.

Equipment, including a portable building, trackway and pedestrian walkway, were delivered to the site. An incident support unit, supplied by the Gloucestershire Fire and Rescue Service, was also set up at the site to provide the search officers with hot meals.

EMRAD Ltd used their 'Pipe Hawk' radar system to check for soil disturbances. It was designed to detect pipes down to 18mm in diameter at depths ranging from 5cm to 3 metres

Work continued at 25 Cromwell Street, but there were no further developments. Fred West was then interviewed again regarding the previous court case with Caroline Owens:

Fred: We were asked by the prosecution not to put the girl in the stands, so we pleaded guilty

DC Savage: You've got that silly look on your face again, that sort of gawky look that always brings, I'm just about to shoot off on another story now. I've got to recognize it over these weeks. You tell us nothing at all until we plug you. It's like pulling teeth.

Fred then told DC Savage of his technique to confuse the police:

Fred: What happens is, I'm talking away to them…and suddenly it comes into my mind, shit, I'm telling them the truth, you know what's been going on…So then I shove something in there…to get away from it."

The use of irrelevant detail, he admitted, was "because I want to get

339

away from it, to give me a chance to think."

This was the only occasion on which Fred West admitted that he knew when he was lying and when he was not, and how he managed to cope with the situation. The only difficulty he encountered was "that you get to a stage where you…just don't know what you are actually saying…you've got everything mixed up. So you've got to try and get out of it, to give your mind a chance. When you've got so much on your mind, it, well, suddenly runs into each other in your mind and…the only thing you can think of is to dive out of it, to give you a chance…because the last thing I want is for you to be able to come back and say, "you lied to me about that"."

30th March 1994

The police continued to ask Fred about Rose's involvement in a subtle way, in the hope that he would give something away and implicate her.

DC Morgan: There was a girl (Shirley Robinson) that even Rose had taken to, and that you wanted, yet you killed her because you'd got all worked up and you didn't know what you were doing half the time, do you remember you said that?
Fred: That's quite true

Work at 25 Cromwell Street continued. Two further deliveries of concrete were made to infill the areas previously excavated.

5th April 1994

Marian Partington, Lucy's sister, arranged to travel to Cardiff to see her sisters remains with two of her closest friends. The mortician unscrewed the lid on the coffin which revealed two cardboard boxes. Lucy's skull was in the smaller of the two boxes and Marian was allowed to wrap it in her childhood blanket and place a branch of Heather entwined with sheep's wool into the box.
Beryl, Lucy's childhood friend from Gretton Farm, placed a couple of soft toys either side of her skull and Marian placed a hand painted egg into one of Lucy's curved hip sockets.

After a short break for Easter, work resumed at 25 Cromwell Street and Letterbox Field. A portable tent was erected over the area being excavated and moved when necessary to provide privacy from the media who had gathered in a field opposite.

Fred West was allocated his Probation Officer - R. W. Anderson from Cinderford. He was given access to Fred West's criminal record.

6th April 1994

Fred West was taken back to Letterbox Field, where he indicated again where he buried Rena's remains. A further 11 tons of concrete were delivered to 25 Cromwell Street.

7th April 1994

Fred West appeared at Gloucester Magistrates' Court and was remanded in custody until Thursday 5th May 1994. Searching continued at 25 Cromwell Street.

8th April 1994

09:05

Fred West was served with amended charges naming Therese Siegenthaler and Shirley Hubbard while Detective Superintendent Bennett held a media briefing at GLOSCAT with an update of the current progress of the enquiry.

10th April 1994

11:12

The remains of Rena Costello were discovered at Letterbox Field (Kempley A). The search was halted and Scenes of Crime Officers called when the mechanical digger brought up bones in one of the scoops.

Howard Ogden: "I got a call from DSI Bennett that afternoon on the basis that they believed that they had found Rena. We were up to nine murders at that point. The next day he'd want to go out to Kempley in an effort to find Ann McFall's remains but at this point they believed they had found Rena."

Searching continued at 25 Cromwell Street but was now nearing completion.

11ᵗʰ April 1994

Professor Knight attended the excavation site of Rena Costello's remains. About two feet below the surface the left thigh bone, and other remains were uncovered. The jawbone, the base of the skull and teeth were also present. He confirmed they were female and that they had eroded and were in poor condition. As he pulled the femurs out, he pointed out faint, fine marks where they would have joined the pelvis. Among the other bones he found a small rectangular piece of cloth and a piece of corroded metal that looked like a broken knife blade. Close to a piece of skull was a bright-red plastic boomerang with the words 'Woomerang Boomerang' in gold lettering – a catchphrase from a 1960's children's television programme. And, mixed in with more jumbled-up bones, a small piece of metal tube that looked as though it was chrome-plated. The skull appeared to have corroded and come apart during decomposition and broke into more pieces during recovery.

The remains were taken to the University of Wales, College of Medicine where they were examined by Professor Knight and Doctor David Whittaker, a Forensic Odontologist. It was clear that dismemberment had taken place at the thighs and the neck and 35 of the expected 76 toe and fingers joints were missing. A dental examination revealed that the woman was aged between twenty-three and thirty when she died. There were no dental records available for Rena Costello, but using photo and video technology to recreate an image from the skull, it was later concluded that the remains were indeed hers.

Work at 25 Cromwell Street continued.

Fred West's probation officer, R. W. Anderson: "Frederick West was allocated to me following being charged with murder. This is in accord with Home Office Circular 55/1984 which requires immediate allocation of anyone charged with murder or manslaughter.

So far, West has been charged with nine murders, all of women. I plan to initiate contact with him once the police have completed their daily questioning and he is remanded in prison.

Our Cheltenham office apparently had contact with him 20 years ago but those records have been destroyed. On 7th June, 1993, at Gloucester Crown Court, a Not Guilty verdict was directed for Rape x3. His wife had also been charged with Causing Unlawful Sexual Intercourse and Cruelty to a Child and a Not Guilty verdict was also ordered for her."

A warrant to search an area next to Stonehouse Coppice (Fingerpost Field) was granted.

12th April 1994

Work continued at 25 Cromwell Street. By this point, the police enquiry believed that friends of Fred and Rose, as well as two other family members, may also have committed sexual offences and needed to be interviewed. Some of the new allegations involved Fred's younger brother John and a couple of long-term friends of the Wests. There was no suggestion they were involved in any of the murders but there was a strong possibility they may have committed serious sexual offences.

Now that the police knew who his victims were, they no longer had to sit through Fred's accounts of how he met them and how they died. They decided to change approach as of more importance now were Rose's sexual activities. The investigation had discovered she had had other sexual encounters he knew nothing about which had upset him.

Mary Bastholm's disappearance would also be put to him again, along with any other sexual offences or even killings they knew of. Speculation was rife that he had been responsible for a number of attacks on women in Gloucester at the time Mary disappeared and witnesses said they might have known one another as they both used the Pop-In Café.

In interviews, Fred completely changed his story regarding Charmaine.

"Charmaine is not dead. Charmaine is well, and that I can assure you of...I never touched Charmaine." He was then told that Midland Road was about to be excavated. "I can state this on my life that they will not find anything at Midland Road at all. And I would like that to go on the record as said."

He then went on to explain how Rena died: "Anyway, she...she drank as though there was no yesterday and she was well drunk, and when Rena got the drink in her she got very loving and she started mucking about and that so anyway that was how we decided to go out to the field to our favourite spot. So anyway, we got out there. We made love again there and then we went back to the car and then I lost the 'ead with her a bit and we had a right set to and a right row there and that was when she ended up getting killed against the gate. I just smashed her against the gate. It was the first time I'd ever been mixed up in anything like that so the only thing I could think of was to bury her in the field. I mean it was the middle of the Summer and the ground was rock hard...so...I...the one that was in there as well as one of those, it's like a pick axe. It's got like an axe on the one side of it and like a blade on the other side, it's like a pick axe...Chopped it up mostly that and then shovelled it out with a spade. Then the problem was it wasn't half big enough 'cause by this time Rena was lay just inside the gate way. Anyway, so I went down there and picked her up and carried her up and then I realised I couldn't get her in there."

Howard Ogden: "He therefore decided to dismember the body, cutting off the head and legs. The arms were left on the torso. When asked what happened next, Fred said that he filled the hole back in. He said that the hole was in the turf at the edge of the field and when he finished it looked like it hadn't been touched. He said that he washed himself down as he had no shirt on."

Fred: "Anyway, I washed up...and I got back in the car. I had a cigarette and I just sat there wondering what to do. Then I went and gathered all her clothes up and tied it all up. I could see this fire in the distance, all the time – glowing and I drove down to that. I took the clothes out, jumped over the ditch into the hedge and threw it over in to the middle of the fire. So that was the end of that."

Anne Marie was taken to Letterbox Field at her own insistence. She remembered wooden boards covering the hole where they had excavated Rena's remains from. She was asked by a police officer if she wanted the boards removed but she declined. She then laid the flowers she had brought with her against a near-by tree. The card with the flowers said:

To my mum, wanting, missing, hurting and needing you so very much. Will always love and remember you.'

09:30

The media was informed that work was now starting on a second field site adjacent to Stonehouse Coppice. The search warrant was executed at Fingerpost Field (Kempley B), where Fred West 'believed' Ann McFall had been buried. This proved to be a difficult area to search as the farmer had recently amalgamated two fields into one and levelled the land, thereby transforming its appearance. Because the search team were excavating to a depth of six feet at times, the sides of the workings had to be shored up using sheeting and hydraulic supports to prevent their collapse. The excavations were based on an engineering plan drawn up with the advice of the Forest of Dean District Council.

EMRAD Ltd once again used their 'Pipe Hawk' radar system to check for soil disturbances.

The dig for Ann McFall's remains

The top soil was removed by machine and the search teams then took over excavating the various search areas by hand. Often the search was hampered by rain, which flooded the workings and had to be pumped out before digging could start again.

17:40

Fred West was charged with the murder of Catherine Bernadette West between 1st January 1969 and 27th February 1994.

Bricklaying took place at 25 Cromwell Street in preparation for removing the extension. More concrete was delivered.

15th April 1994

11:00

HM Coroner David Gibbons opened inquests at Shire Hall into the identification of the nine remains found at Cromwell Street and adjourned proceedings *sine die*.

Stephen West: "When I went to the opening of the inquests, it was terrible…it was very hard when I walked into the waiting room. It all went quiet and everyone looked at me. I felt low, embarrassed, and wanted to run out. At the same time I wanted to show my face. I had nothing to hide and I was in the same boat as everyone else. They had all lost somebody and I was a victim as much as they were.

Then Belinda, one of Juanita Mott's sisters, came over to me and asked if I was alright. She started crying because she didn't know what to say to me. It was very awkward. Her mum was terribly upset and being there made me feel sick.

It was heart-breaking when Heather's dental records were read out. I could visualise the teeth they were talking about because her front ones stuck out a bit. She was meant to wear a brace, but she never had one. Afterwards Belinda came up to me, gave me a kiss and shook my hand. Then the other sister came up and said: 'Don't blame yourself.' Then the mum came up and she was really crying, so I gave her a kiss and I think I mumbled: 'It will be alright.' It meant so much to me – it meant they didn't all hate me and blame me for what had happened. I respected them so much for that, because I knew what they were going through."

The rear extension at 25 Cromwell Street was demolished by workers from Gloucester City Council. Work continued at 25 Cromwell Street and the area on which the extension stood was searched on the 17th April.

Two days later, Detective Superintendent Bennett held a media briefing to update the press on developments so far.

09:25

Rose West was arrested at the Cheltenham safe house by Detective Constables Steve Harris and Barbara Harrison on two charges of rape against the same victim (the 13-year-old Anne Marie) and the physical assault of an eight-year-old boy (Steven McAvoy) — both charges dating from the mid-1970's, in company with two separate men. As such, the covert listening operation ended after 885 45-minute tapes had been recorded.

Mae and Rose were allowed to spend a few moments together before Rose was taken to the police station. Rose told her that her wedding ring was in a pocket in her coat in the wardrobe and asked her to keep it safe. "I'm not taking it to the police station, those bloody idiots will only lose it."

Mae: "She quietly got dressed while I ran upstairs and sat in a bedroom. I didn't want her to go. I rang Stephen and told him what had happened, and we sort of made it up." As the police were taking her to the car she told them: "You've no fucking right whatsoever to treat me like this! Fuck you, fuck the lot of you!" She was taken to Cheltenham Police Station. Mae was told that she had until the end of the day to find somewhere to live. She had nowhere to go and was told that she was no longer the responsibility of the police. She rang Stephen and was allowed to stay with him, Andrea and her parents for a short time.

Rose West

At first she was questioned only about allegations of child abuse and of acting as a prostitute at Cromwell Street, and throughout four interviews that day she answered the questions evasively rather than aggressively. She admitted that her sexual relationship with John West "went on over years, on and off" and that her husband had not only been aware of it but had encouraged it. When the police asked her when it began, she didn't hesitate: "When I was in Midland Road."

Preparations were made for the search of 25 Midland Road and a portable building was erected there. The search continued at 25 Cromwell Street.

21st April 1994

Rose West appeared before Gloucester Magistrates Court charged with 2 counts of rape against the same person, a 13-year-old Anne Marie, alongside Whitley George Purcell (64) between July 1976 and July 1980. She was jointly accused of the same offence against Anne Marie at an earlier date, between 1974 and 1976 alongside William Smith (67) and was remanded into police custody. These proceedings against Rose were later dropped by the Criminal Prosecution Service. Both men were friends of the Wests.

She was later questioned more closely about the murders, in particular those of her daughter Heather and Lynda Gough. For thirteen minutes she refused even to agree that her name was Rosemary West, admitting only: "I've just got nothing to say." Those are the last words she spoke in the remaining 59 police interviews, until her last one on 2nd June 1994, other than to declare her innocence of charges as they were brought against her.

Fred West was interviewed, and explained that his wife had started to have sex with other men "only as a turn-on for me and herself", but he made sure always to make love to her either before she went out with another man or when she came back. As for the deaths, "it had been a long secret, longer than I believed", he confessed.

22nd April 1994

The well found at the back of 25 Cromwell Street was searched but nothing found. The entire ground floor and the garden had been excavated to the depth of the Severn clay, often 6-8 feet from ground level. This was how the well was discovered.

23rd April 1994

15:40

Rose West was arrested by DC Stephen Harris and DC Barbara Harrison 'on the suspicion of the murder of Lynda Gough'. In interviews she was asked:

DC Harris: Would you accept that the remains of Lynda Gough were found in your former home at 25 Cromwell Street, Gloucester, Mrs West?
Rose: No comment
DC Harris: Would you accept that Lynda Gough lived in your house at 25 Cromwell Street, Gloucester, Mrs West?
Rose: No comment
DC Harris: Would you accept that, following the disappearance of Lynda Gough, you were seen wearing her slippers?
Rose: No comment
DC Harris: Would you accept that you seemingly told lies to Lynda Gough's mother when she called to speak to you at 25 Cromwell Street, Gloucester, following the disappearance of her daughter?
Rose: No comment
DC Harris: Do you accept that you told Mrs Gough that her daughter had gone to Weston?
Rose: No comment
DC Harris: Were you told by your husband, Frederick West, to tell Mrs Gough that Lynda Gough had gone to Weston?
Rose: No comment
DC Harris: Were you threatened or pressurized in any way by your husband, Frederick West, to tell Mrs Gough that her daughter, Lynda, had gone to Weston?
Rose: No comment
DC Harris: Was it your idea to tell Mrs Gough that her daughter, Lynda, had gone to Weston?
Rose: No comment
DC Harris: Would you accept that Mrs Gough pointed out to you that her daughter's clothing was on your washing-line?
Rose: No comment

Whitley George Purcell appeared before Magistrates charged with raping a 13-year-old girl (Anne Marie West) between July 1976 and July 1980. He was granted bail until 16th June.

24th April 1994

18:15

Rose West was charged with the murder of Lynda Gough between 1st April 1973 and 27th February 1994. She simply replied: "I'm innocent".

Work continued at 25 Cromwell Street throughout the day but there were no further developments.

Stephen West again showed his violent side. He was living with his girlfriend Andrea when he reversed his van over his tool box and threw them all over the road, which lead to an argument with Andrea. Not long after he had a row with her and ended up grabbing her around the throat all because she had gone to use the phone in a phone box without him.

The following day Andrea found out that she was pregnant but that didn't stop him being violent towards her. He hit her and gave her a black eye. Mae left with Andrea and went to Andrea's parents in Brockworth. He phoned them there and blamed everything on Mae and threatened to kill them both. They phoned the police and a WPC arrived and told them that if he turned up to lock the doors and leave her outside to talk to him. Sure enough Stephen turned up and was warned that if he didn't calm down he would be arrested. He calmed down and a few hours later left with Andrea in tow.

25th April 1994

09:00

Detective Superintendent Bennett held a media briefing outside 25 Midland Road, Gloucester, where the details of the search that was to take place there were outlined:

"We will be searching part of the garden and one specific area on the ground floor near to where the extension meets the house at the rear. This will be an extremely difficult operation as large amounts of concrete, hard core and ballast were used to build the extension foundations. It is possible that what we are looking for could have been removed when builders were excavating the footings prior to building the extension. We have no indication at present as to how long this search will take."

Six male students who were living in bedsits at the house were found alternative accommodation.

Rose West appeared at Gloucester Magistrates' Court where she faced the one charge of murder (Lynda Gough) and was immediately remanded in custody until 29th April. It was noted that she still was not wearing her wedding ring. Meanwhile at Cromwell Street, the final stages of the search were taking place prior to the building being handed over to the solicitors representing Rose West.

In interview, Fred West was explaining to DC Savage his plans for having his children "baptised together", and how his wife had written to him when she was a young woman of fifteen, telling him to meet her in Pittville Park in Cheltenham on a Sunday afternoon to make love, and finishing her letter: "Keep saying your prayers and remember I'll always love you. Lots of love, Rose."

When DC Savage suggested to him that he seemed to be enjoying the questioning, he replied: "Yeah, why not?"

DC Savage: I don't know. I don't understand it really
Fred: You will in the end
DC Savage: Will I? When will I understand it?
Fred: I don't know. At the end, whenever that is.

Then, with a big grin on his face:

Fred: You're the love of my life, Hazel. I can't even remember Gloucester police station without Hazel.

Back at the police station, Rose was interviewed about a second murder, that of Carol Cooper. Again Rose said nothing. DC Barbara Harrison asked:

"Mrs West, would you accept that you have an unnatural interest in sex?"

"Do you accept that you have featured in sex sessions recorded on video tape?"

"Were you forced in to making these sex videos, Mrs West?"

"Did your husband force you to make these sex videos, Mrs West?"

"The police are in possession of a copy of a videotape seized from your home at 25 Cromwell Street, in 1992. This video depicts a female being tied to the ceiling of a room and then abused by two men. Do you know the film I am talking about?"

"In the cellar area of your home at 25 Cromwell Street, Gloucester, there are two holes in the rafters. These seemingly are similar to the scene depicted in the film. Is that what those holes were used for, Mrs West?"

"Were any of the holes used to facilitate the torture of Carol Cooper?"

"Were any of the holes used to facilitate sex with Carol Cooper?"

"When you picked up Caroline Raine in the car with Fred, was that a practice session?"

"Was that a practice session with her before you started killing people?"

"Had you done acts of lesbianism before Caroline Raine?"

"Fred has told me that the incident with Caroline was a practice session. Is that right?"

"We also have some other videos seized from your house in 1992 and they could be described as porn videos. Did you get your ideas for sex from these porn videos?"

"Did you practice anything that you saw in the porn videos?"

"There are some unusual acts shown on the films, such as someone being tied up. Is that an idea that you got from a video?"

"One of the videos shows a woman seemingly in a cellar and she's having sex with a black man and a white man and she doesn't appear to be enjoying the experience at all times. Do you remember that video?"

"She is then whipped with I think you'd describe as a cat-o'-nine-tails whip and whipped with a cloth. Do you remember that on the video?"

"Did you take ideas from that video and put them in to practice in your own basement at 25 Cromwell Street?"

"Did you kill Carol Cooper?"

"Were you present when Carol Cooper was killed?"

"Was Carol Cooper tied up in your house in Cromwell Street?"

"Was she taken down to the basement and held there as a prisoner?"

"Did you tie her up?"

"Did you tie her hands with rope?"

"Did you tie her feet with rope?"

"Did Fred tie her up with rope?"

"Were you present when she was being tied up?"

"Did you gag her?"

"Did you put cloth round her face or over her eyes?"

"Did Fred put any cloth round her face or eyes?"

"Was she tortured while she was still alive?"

"Was she cut at all while she was still alive?"

"Did you take part in cutting her head off?"

"Did you take part in cutting her head off after she was dead?"

"Did you cut her legs?"

"Did you cut off her legs?"

"Did you cut off her arms?"

"Did Fred cut off her legs?"

"Were you forced to do any of these things to Carol Cooper?"

"Did you bury Carol Cooper?"

"Did you assist in the burial of Carol Cooper?"

"Did you dig the hole in your basement where Carol Cooper was buried?"

"Were you present when that hole was being dug?"

"Did Fred dig the hole?"

"Was the hole prepared already?"

"While Carol Cooper was still alive, did you cut her hands?"

"Did you cut her fingers?"

"Did you cut any part of her hand off?"

"Did you cut off her feet?"

"Did you cut off any part of her feet?"

"Did you cut off her toes?"

"Were you present while any of Carol Cooper's fingers or toes were cut off by another person?"

"Were you forced to cut off Carol Cooper's fingers or toes?"

"Some of Carol Cooper's bones are missing. Can you explain what happened to them?"

"Did you assist in the disposal of any parts of her body?"

"Did you assist in the disposal of them in a place other than in your basement?"

"Fred has told us that he had control over you. I think the time is now if you could perhaps confirm that to us, if that is the case…"

"We've spoken about some horrific things and we've heard some horrific things in these interviews and if there's anything you can tell us which might help us understand what happened there, then we'd be grateful to you for an explanation. Is there anything you would like to tell us about your relationship with Fred and any force that may or may not have been used on you to perform any of these awful things?"

"No comment", was all Rose would say.

26th April 1994

11:00

The search warrant was executed and the search began at 25 Midland Road, Gloucester. EMRAD Ltd again used their 'Pipe Hawk' radar system to check for soil disturbances.

19:47

Rose West was charged with the murder of Carol Ann Cooper. She simply replied: "I'm innocent".

27th April 1994

The search commenced on the rear garden and the adjoining rear garden of number 25 Midland Road.

Police searching the back garden of 25 Midland Road

Shortly before lunch Fred was told that Rose was facing two further charges of murder (Lucy Partington and Carol Cooper).

28ᵗʰ April 1994

Fred was due to be interviewed but oddly asked for time to consult with his lawyers and had a meeting with his solicitor Howard Ogden and counsel.

15:22

Rose West was charged with the murders of Lucy Katherine Partington between 26ᵗʰ December 1973 and 27ᵗʰ February 1994 and of Carol Ann Cooper between December 1973 and 27ᵗʰ February 1994. She replied: "I'm innocent".

The search continued at 25 Midland Road. Excavation of the kitchen area required a concrete floor to be removed and metal sheet reinforcing cut through, then impacted rubble to a depth of about five feet removed before the previous coal cellar area could be searched.

At Cromwell Street, the work was concluded and the building handed over to the Wests solicitors Howard Ogden and Leo Goatley. Rose West had made it clear that no matter the outcome of her case, she would never live there again.

29ᵗʰ April 1994

Rose West appeared at Gloucester Magistrates' Court and was again remanded in police custody for three days.

09:38

In an astounding manoeuvre, Fred West retracted his earlier confessions. After learning that Rose was to be charged alongside himself, he may well have thought that the best way out of it for her was for him to change his story and say that other people committed the murders, and he was just an accomplice, therefore lessening Rose's possible involvement even further. He first asked Howard Ogden to write out another note, a counterpart to his 4ᵗʰ March confession of nine murders. Then, in a two-minute interview, he put the note into his own words, telling the police: "I have not, and still not tell you the whole truth about these matter. The reason for this is that from the very first day of this enquiry my main concern has been to protect other person or persons, and there is nothing else I wish to say at this time."

As soon as he had finished, DC Hazel Savage asked him if he was feeling alright. "Yeah, perfect", he replied. "That's what the doctor just said".

Howard Ogden: "I saw Rose as interested in violence and lesbian sex pretty much in equal measure and preferably together and that Fred's role was, in many ways, to assist her to fulfil her fantasies."

Searching continued in the garden area of 25 Midland Road but nothing significant had been found thus far.

30th April 1994

13:51

Rose West was charged with the murder of Therese Siegenthaler and replied: "I'm innocent".

No work was carried out at 25 Midland Road.

1st May 1994

The News of The World printed two letters sent by Fred to Rose, Stephen and Mae:

The first letter read:

Dear Rose, Mae and Stephen,
Sorry for everything that has happened.
Please look after Mam. Don't go back to Cromwell Street, sell it. I will sign any papers over to you.
Help Mae to clear off her debts to the house. I don't mean pay the house off. Carry on letting the house. You will then have enough money left for the three of you to decide what new life you are going to make.
I hope you will all stay together, because you need each other's help.
I realise it will be hard for you to come and see me at the moment, but maybe it would be possible sometime in the future.
You are the only family I have left.
LOVE FOR EVER
Fred

The second letter said:

To my darling wife, Mae and Stephen,
Would you contact Mr Ogden so that we can sort things out regarding Heather, the house

and any other matters which are very important. I hope you received my last letter.
Could one of you please write to me to let me know if you are alright.
Sorry for messing up all your lives, it will all sort itself out in the end.
Mae and Stephen please look after Mam.
Love you forever, Fred.
P.S. Rose, please can you get the fish moved from Cromwell Street.

Mae commented: "It's unbelievable that my dad is still trying to run our lives. He is living in a dream world and simply can't accept that things will never be the same. He's always been the boss of the house and he can't accept that it's never going to be the same again.

What really hurts is that my dad thinks he's going to have control over Heather's funeral. He wants Heather to be buried in his family's grave in Much Marcle where he lived as a child. There's no way that's going to happen.

My dad still seems to think that we can all play happy families. Dad says in one of his letters 'Sorry for messing up all your lives, it will sort itself out in the end.' I don't know what my dad means. I can't even guess. It is as if he thinks that he will always be the head of the family and we will always do things his way."

3rd May 1994

Rose West appeared at Gloucester Magistrates' Court and was further remanded in police custody until Friday, 6th May 1994.

Searching resumed at 25 Midland Road following the Bank Holiday break. Council engineers prepared an area to search in the kitchen of 25 Midland Road and the concrete floor was removed. Nothing of evidential value had been found so far.

4th May 1994

15:55

Rose West was charged with the murder of Shirley Hubbard. She made no reply.

19:10

PC George Sharpe, excavating below the kitchen area at 25 Midland

Road, found human remains at a depth of 2.19m. The coroner was informed and so too was Professor Knight. The area was secured to await his arrival the next day. It also meant the whole of the cellar would have to be scanned by the ground-penetrating radar and then excavated down to the hard clay, just as at Cromwell Street.

The kitchen extension area of 25 Midland Road before police started to dig. Charmaine's body was found below the table area.

5th May 1994

DSI Bennett made the formal announcement of the discovery of more human remains at a news conference.

Pathologist Professor Bernard Knight examined the bones and noticed that the two thigh bones were sticking up vertically, separate and at some distance from the main body, which appeared to be slumped in a sitting position. He was at a loss to explain how these bones could have moved through soil displacement after burial and wondered if their position indicated dismemberment. Both of Charmaine's knee caps were missing, and a total of 47 out of a possible 76 finger and toe bones were missing along with the lower part of the breast bone. The body had been naked when placed in the ground. Pieces of coal around the body indicated that she had been killed and hidden elsewhere first, possibly in a coal shed or bunker, and buried later. The remains were subsequently removed to The College of Medicine at the University of Wales, Cardiff, for further forensic examination.

359

DC Hazel Savage interviewed Fred West regarding the discovery of Charmaine's remains

DC Savage: What happened to her clothes when this poor little mite went down there? Where are they? Who undressed her? Why was she undressed?

Later on...

DC Savage: This is a child. You told us that other people wanted your body, wanted sex, fell in love with you, threatened to tell Rose that they were pregnant by you. Charmaine doesn't fit in to that story to me. Does she to you? What went on there that night? Where did you undress her, this little girl, your daughter? You didn't cover her up or anything in that hole, you stuffed her in there. She's not wrapped, she's not clothed, and she's not in one piece.

He was asked if sex or bondage had anything to do with the child's death, and, although he refused to answer the question directly, he nodded his head. Fred started to cry and mumbled "Charmaine my child...I just got the fear that you're gonna take Charmaine away...I mean, I'm the only Dad she's had."

6th May 1994

09:00

Detective Superintendent Bennett held a media briefing outside 25 Midland Road where the press were updated. It was also announced that Rose West had been charged with the murder of Shirley Louise Hubbard between 14th November 1974 and 27th February 1994.

Rose West appeared at Gloucester Magistrates' Court charged with five murders. She was remanded until 3rd June.

16:34

Rose West was charged with the murder of Juanita Mott. She replied: "I'm innocent by the way".

8th May 1994

As no work was carried out at 25 Midland Road, Anne Marie went back to lay some flowers. A note attached to the bouquet read:

To my sister Charmaine.

We played, we cried, we laughed and sang – but how I've prayed we'd be together again.

Missing you so very much,

Will always love and remember you.

All my fondest love,

Anna-Marie.

9th May 1994

11:30

Detective Superintendent Bennett held a media briefing to update the press on progress at 25 Midland Road. Work continued at 25 Midland Road but there were no further developments.

Fred West was interviewed about the death of his daughter Charmaine but he refused to explain anything regarding her death.

11th May 1994

14:35

Fred West was charged with the murder of Charmaine West. He said nothing in reply. He then refused to return to Fingerpost Field to assist the police search for the body of Ann McFall.

More concrete was delivered to 25 Midland Road.

12th May 1994

In interviews, Fred refused to comment on questions about the missing bones, the masks, gags and bindings, and the cuts in the bones found on the victims. He remained silent as two officers asked him whether he had attacked the young women found beneath his house and garden at Cromwell Street before or after their deaths.

Fred denied he had anything to do with the murders and then came out with a curious statement:

Fred: I had nothing to do with these girls death at all. I have lied through the statements and at this moment I am not prepared to change that… I am not prepared to say who I am protecting in this case. You do know a vast amount of the truth. And what I'm saying is, for God's sake, put it together…My life means nothing to you, but it means a lot to me…and if the police sorts it out then I haven't said anything, it's as simple as that.

Asked if he was frightened, Fred pointed to a folder showing where the victims' skeletons were found, and replied: "Just look at that – do you need anymore?" A detective asked: "What are you suggesting?" Fred replied: "No comment."

A little later he added: "I am not so worried for myself, probably, but I have eight children out there." When he was asked if his reply meant that he thought the "person or persons" he was referring to might harm his children he replied: "I suppose".

He was then asked what misgivings he had about talking fully about other people, and he said: "I have got to do summat. I can't do anything at this time. It's too dangerous for me and for everybody."

13th May 1994

11:56

In what was Fred West's 132nd and final interview at Gloucester Police station, DI James changed tact and started to call Fred 'Mr. West'. He asked Fred if he was still thinking about what to do. Fred replied: "Yeah, yeah, got to do summat". Then, "No I can't do anything at the moment, it's too dangerous to try, too dangerous". He then begged for the interview to be terminated, and as it was he muttered: "Nobody spares a thought for what I've lost in this. I've lost more than anybody else… My ex-wife, my daughter, my daughter, two unborn children, how much more do I need to go?"

He was taken to Winson Green Prison in Birmingham as a 'Category A' prisoner charged with 12 counts of murder. Information provided by the police indicated he may have had suicidal tendencies. He was located in the Health Care Centre and placed on 15 minute observations, but no suicidal indications were evident.

14th May 1994

Fred West was moved to the Category 'A' landing after special observation was withdrawn. As a category 'A' prisoner, he was subject to much closer observation and supervision than average. His prison notes stated: "Will staff please monitor this man's behaviour. May be suicidal. No association for two weeks."

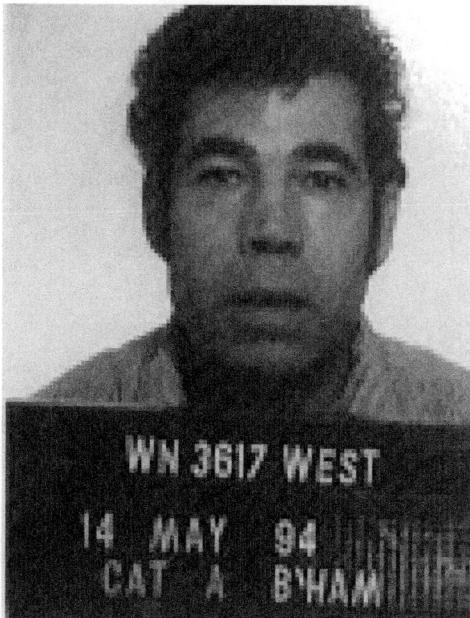

WN 3617 WEST
14 MAY 94
CAT A B'HAM

15th May 1994

Fred West was checked over at HMP Birmingham Health Care Centre.

Christine West gave an interview to The News of The World: "It's been very difficult for us since the police investigation started. Doug took it very hard to begin with, although he's a little better now. We've been trying to live a normal life since all this happened and we've had to try and protect the children who've had a bit of a miserable time at school.

Doug has lived in the village all his life and knows everybody, but the worst thing is that he thinks they're looking at him in a different light. But everyone's been marvellous. We've had letters and cards from family, friends and neighbours wishing us well.

Doug has now more or less accepted that Fred and his wife have been charged with all those murders. In the beginning he just didn't want to believe it was true that all those girls and women had gone missing and were now dead. Doug, of course, knew Fred's first wife Catherine, and the children Charmaine and Heather and it's hard to accept they've been dead for so long. He also knew that families nanny, Ann, who is also thought to be a victim. All this is swimming around in his head and it's affected us all. We still have bad days thinking about everything."

16th May 1994

Rose West was charged with the murder of Juanita Mott between 1st April 1975 and 27th February 1994. She replied "I'm innocent". Meanwhile, the cellar at 25 Midland Road continued to be searched.

The police believed that Fred might tell family and other visitors more about the case and reveal unknown facts. They asked the prison service to monitor and report anything they considered to be useful.

18th May 1994

Rose West was charged with the murder of Shirley Ann Robinson. She replied: "I'm innocent" and Inspector Ted Kania took over as the Police

Search Advisor at Kempley.

Fred West gave his first interview at Winson Green Prison to his solicitor Howard Ogden. Ceaselessly rolling hand-made cigarettes, Fred set about describing his first meeting with his wife Rose, and how she had "taken over from Rena", who "kept disappearing for a week or a fortnight at a time – after she'd had Charmaine."

He told Howard Ogden that Rena had been "supplying girls for these parties" given by Rolf (her supposed pimp), at which girls were used for the sexual gratification of the guests. He claimed that he had known Rolf first, and had then introduced him to Rena, who begun to use him as her pimp before they went back to Scotland together. He went on to deny that he had killed her, but then he specifically accused Rena of killing his 'angel', Ann McFall, and went on to claim – quite suddenly – that Rolf had "recruited Rose" to "get" his first wife.

Fred: I am not lying to you in any way. Anything I say to you can be backed up. What I tell you is the gospel truth. Ann thought the world of me. She was mine. She belonged to me. I mean, Rena wasn't belonged to me. Rena belonged to whoever she was with at the moment and I mean Rena always looked after me, don't get me wrong. I mean she was never unkind to me in any way.

Howard Ogden: The allegation is that you've killed her isn't it?

Fred: Yeah

19th May 1994

Information and intelligence was gathered at Winson Green Prison about an attempt by an inmate(s) to photograph Fred West and sell the photo to the press. The reported asking price was £50,000.

Fred West's Probation Officer, R. W. Anderson, made first contact with him and Fred was interviewed a second time by his solicitor, Howard Ogden:

Fred: I had a chat with the Salvation Army bloke in here the other day about how people become criminals. And this all started from home. It's

365

Moorcourt Cottages, but it's Moorcourt Farm. We used to go for long walks round the fields…

I wanted to be Dad. I admired all he stood for. He was my God, like. He was tall, big, big man, like. Could handle himself no problem. Mother was very old fashioned in her ways. I mean, like, if you had a girlfriend. Girlfriends were strictly out until you were twenty-one, not sixteen…Whereas Dad was different altogether. 'If it was on offer, take it son'.

Howard Ogden then read statements to Fred, from his family, about how his motorbike accident affected him.

Howard Ogden: 'It was noticed by the family over a period of time that Fred had changed. His personality was changing. He started lying, boasting, bragging and stealing. He was not the same person.' Do you think that's fair?
Fred: Yeah

Howard Ogden then read his brother John's statement to him.

Howard Ogden: 'Fred was always a ladies man. He was always the smart one who got all the good looking ladies and I never stood much of a chance.'
Fred: (Laughing) Alright then. I wouldn't go out in a pair of trousers unless you could cut your wrists on the seams.

Fred then went on to describe how he first met Rena:

Fred: Rena was telling me she was on the run from a home in whatsitsname and she was expecting a baby and all that. And that's all there was to it. She was just generally telling me her life story. So anyways, as the bloody CID shot in front of me and I stopped in the middle of the fucking street Rena said: 'Shit, they're gonna have me' and I said 'Just tell them that I'm the father of the baby and that you've come down to find the father of the baby. And she got away with it. Rena said: 'Look, I'm gonna have to disappear…or if we get married and then I'll get rid of the marriage after.' And I said 'alright then'. So it was only about a fortnight and we were

366

married."

Howard Ogden would later tell how Fred explained the reasons for them moving to Scotland: "Fred was later offered a job to become Rena's minder/chauffeur in Scotland by a Pakistani man who was the father of Charmaine. One night Rena and Fred went to Barrowland in Glasgow."

Fred: I mean that's when all the trouble came up when she got drunk that night and in that Barrowland. We went to Barrowland, big dance hall up there, and she got drunk and stopped half way back home and then I give her one, give her one right an' all. It's Anne Marie.

23rd May 1994

17:08

Rose West was charged with the murder of Alison Jane Chambers.

24th May 1994

20:05

Fred West's younger brother John was arrested on charges of rape and indecent assault against his nieces Anne Marie and Mae.

In the bedroom he shared with his wife was a Betamax video machine containing a pornographic videotape as well as a collection of other pornographic videotapes that featured group sex and oral sex. Significantly, one of these videotapes also featured a girl kidnapped in a van. When he was questioned about it, he said: "I haven't got to that one. There's a lot, a lot of them in there."

One family friend recalled how John West had shown him "dozens of porno films" which featured "bestiality, young girls and violent sex scenes", adding, "It looked to me as if the films were home-made."

His bedroom was also found to contain more than a hundred pornographic magazines, many of them featuring scenes of "spanking", as well as three riding-crops, a pair of rubber shackles for the arms or legs, and five vibrators. He explained this collection by saying that he had picked them all up "at various times on my wagon." He also maintained that none of the vibrators, not even the big one, worked, or at least it did not work half the time.

In police interviews, he told how he hadn't spoken to Fred since their father's funeral. "As far as I'm concerned he no longer exists". He went on to admit that he had seen Rose "a few times" at Midland Road, and that his new girlfriend had stayed there for "a couple of nights", adding, "Fred said that she could stay but I couldn't". He also explained that he had soon learned that "Rose had a very quick temper, like."

He fiercely and repeatedly denied that he had seen his brother at all during the following four years – the years which saw the deaths of at least six young women in Cromwell Street. He maintained firmly that he had seen his brother Fred "less than ten times" in 1972, and, because he was "courting and working" from 1973 to 1978, "I never saw him once." He admitted only coming into contact with him again "in late '77 when Rose was pregnant with Tara".

His partner Polly, however, remembered going to 25 Cromwell Street during this period with John West and their babies. Even after their relationship had broken up, she and her two children stayed there with Fred and Rose for a time, on one occasion "house-sitting" for them when they went away for a holiday to Rose's birthplace in Devon. Afterwards, Fred West invited her to move in permanently, but she declined.

John West insisted that he went to Midland Road only "four or five times" and that the sexual relationship he had with Rose had taken place "in the middle of the eighties" and there had been only "six or seven times" over a period of about "six to twelve months." He explained the reasons for it: "It just sort of happened. She used to sit there, no knickers on and that. I mean, you've got to be a saint, haven't you?"

He admitted that his brother Fred had offered him the seventeen-year-old Rosemary Letts at their Midland Road flat in 1971. "One Sunday lunch-time I called in to have a cup of tea while I was waiting to go out with a girlfriend…and he said to me, "Oh, take Rose in the bedroom and screw her". "I couldn't believe me ears and said: "I've got to go." But Rosemary Letts did not say no, even though "she was only a young girl then". Instead, "she just sat there". Fred, he maintained, had been to his home only "twice in all the time I've known him."

His reason for severing all ties with Fred and Rose, according to him, was that he "fell out with Rose" in 1988 over her "chasing" her second son Barry, then aged eight, "down the garden with a wooden spoon and beating him." He maintained that he did not argue with his sister-in-law: "I just didn't go there."

He was charged with the rape and indecent assault of a girl aged 11-16 (Anne Marie) between 1976 and 1979, and the same charge again against a girl aged 7 or 8 (Mae) between 1980 and 1981. He laid great emphasis on how little contact he had had with his brother "for years". Even when he was visiting Cromwell Street regularly, he told police, it was only "Saturdays" and "odd nights in the summer", and "Fred was never there."

When he appeared before Gloucester Magistrates Court he was remanded on bail to be dealt with after the trial of Rosemary West.

25th May 1994

Fred gave another interview to Howard Ogden. He had prepared his new sanitised version of events. He began by portraying himself as just an innocent victim, just like those found buried and then began trying to spread the guilt for the killing of the young women in Cromwell Street far and wide, and maintaining that the accounts of his own sexual appetite were "fantasy". It would seem that when he said he was trying to protect 'certain people' in his police interviews to get Rose out of trouble, now he was claiming that it was actually Rose who was in control the whole time. He said that Rose, not he, was guilty of the killings. He also implied that his younger brother John had been involved, "'cause John was shagging Rose for fucking years...I knew that. John's up to his fucking neck in it, with Rose. John goes back a bloody long time in this thing, mind. He goes right back to Rena". He told his solicitor that John had "fetched" his first wife's body and that he "hated" his stepdaughter Charmaine. "He would never let her sit on him, or by him or anything, because John is colour prejudiced completely. Whenever he walked by her he kicked her, caught his toe in her...John is Rose's partner in all this," he added coldly. He blamed his Rose's sadistic sexual nature for the murders, and insisted that he had "deliberately mixed things up for the police". "I know Rose was into sadistic love – violent sex. The only person I can tie that up with is John. John is well into bloody violence, and that's why Rose got on so well with 'im." He then added: "John was always on to me about tying women up…John was beating Rose. He was tying her to gates and beating her arse and her back and that. Rose would come home back and blue…But she loved it. John had no words for girls, he treated a woman like a dog. He still does to this day."

He said that his brother had had a sexual relationship with Rena almost from the beginning and that this continued "after I had left her", and that he would take her to "one of his caravans" to have sex with her. "John had two caravans, touring vans. They were parked up in various places."

Fred then implicated his brother in at least one of the murders at Cromwell Street: "It was John that dug one of the holes in the basement. It was John that levelled the basement out, and put the membrane down for the concreting, and helped me concrete it." He then proceeded to associate his younger brother with Rosemary West's father, Bill Letts, whom he had also implicated in the killings. He suggested that John and Bill had procured the girls for Rose's use and then murdered them. "He was well in with John at Midland Road", and at Cromwell Street. "Rose's father had been there all the time, and him and John got on great. They were always going out together, and Rose."

He denied that he had any kind of sex life with his wife. "I hated it. I hated the smell of her at times as well." He denied that he liked bondage: "I put it on Rose once, and even then I didn't like the idea of it, and I didn't ever have anything to do with it." He denied any attacks on his other daughter Heather: "All I did was kick her in the fucking arse at the gate, a few nights before, for being with a drug addict." He denied any attacks on either Anne Marie or Mae. He even denied that Heather West was his daughter, claiming that she could well have been the result of an incestuous relationship between Rose and her father. He denied that he had attacked Caroline Raine: "That was Rose attacked her, not me." He denied that the cellar at Cromwell Street had been kept locked: "The basement was always wide open. Anybody who wanted to go down there could." He denied that "it was kitted out for sex games". He denied that he was interested in pornographic films. He denied that he ever knew that his wife advertised in contact magazines, and he denied that he had ever encouraged her to have sex with any other man. "Rose fucking ruled me, I didn't rule Rose. Everybody knows that", he told Howard Ogden. "Every penny I earned she had. She searched my clothes to make sure I didn't have any money."

He then accused her of having "new clothes all the time", when "most of my clothes was off building sites." He claimed that his wife "laid roofs" and "could mix plaster all night. She dug holes and everything." She was also "a brilliant cook", but "had special food of her own, kept the best of everything for herself." Most of all, he insisted, "Rose must be cool, calm and collected. When Rose told me where the bodies were and everything, I died at that moment. Every feeling dropped out of me body." Fred then claimed: "I didn't suspect Rose of anything" and went on: "I was quite prepared to take it. It was my fault that these girls got too vulnerable. I should have checked on my own home more."

He then tried to sustain the lie that he "fell asleep" in a lay-by for "two or three hours" on his way back to Cromwell Street that afternoon. He remembered: "Rose was in some kind of state. She was crying and shaking and God knows what, and that ain't Rose, believe me. She's a hard case, no messing with her." He went on to tell Howard Ogden that he "couldn't quite catch on why" she was so upset, but that he had gone to the police station to tell "Hazel Savage about Heather – what I knew". When he returned home again he maintained that he caught up with his wife in the bar room on the first floor and told her: "There's piss-all out there. What are you worrying about?" In this version of events, Rosemary West told him: "What the hell do you mean? Heather's out there."

Trying to sound like the innocent victim and hero of the story, he said that he told Rose: "I shall have to take it. You say nothing". But "I wanted to get out of the house there and then. It seemed as though my whole life stopped there, finished…I drank my tea, took a couple of paracetamol and I said: "Right, what happened, then?" She wouldn't tell me no more, nothing. I said: "Is that it?" She said: "Oh no. There's Shirley and Shirley's mate."

Fred said that he had then asked his wife: "How many is there? She says "I don't know, seven, or eight, or nine, something like that." According to him, Rose then pointed out where each of the bodies was buried, and "she named them all." She also told him that "Charmaine's in the cellar at the back of Midland Road", and "Rena's out at her beauty-spot."

Fred told his solicitor that Rosemary's explanation for the deaths were "sex acts that went wrong, bondage that went wrong." That night he lay on the bed, "I was in a trance, in limbo, like," but he was sure that the police would "just dig the bodies up and leave Rose, Mae and Stephen" living there in peace.

26th May 1994

Rose West was charged with the murder of Heather Ann West between 28th May 1987 and 27th February 1994. She replied: "I'm innocent".

27th May 1994

The search team completed their work at 25 Midland Road.

28th May 1994

Scott Canavan, the legal clerk who had sat in on some of Fred West's police interviews, was arrested by police. A highly confidential letter written by Howard Ogden to Fred West was being sold around the pubs at £25 a copy. Howard Ogden and his secretary called the police after claiming that Scott had stolen it after being given the job of delivering it to Fred West in person. He was arrested and questioned for four hours but was released on police bail. The case was later dropped.

31st May 1994

Howard Ogden again met with Fred in his cell. Fred said: "What I did all the time, and I'm still trying to do it now, is cover up for Rose". "Everything was so blatantly cruel," he confessed. "The main problem I've had is that I swore on the kids' lives that I wouldn't shop Rose for what she did. That's the only way I could get her to tell me what she done to Heather, 'cause she wouldn't tell me what she'd done to her." He was afraid that his wife had "tortured her" and hoped "that she hadn't been sent to the niggers in Bristol", concluding: "At this time I knew nothing about any other girls. Nothing. Only Heather."

He said that his home in Cromwell Street "was more secure on secrets than GCHQ is…She never told me nothing. That was her policy in life. She told nobody nothing." He then went further and said that Rose threatened him by saying: "If you drop me in it, you won't last long, and they'll make sure you die a horrible death." He then claimed to his solicitor that when he suggested to his wife that she could not have acted alone, and there must be "somebody else mixed up in it", she had told him: "You don't need to know that."

1ˢᵗ June 1994

Fred West was visited by his Probation Officer, R. W. Anderson. "I went and was able to spend over two hours with West. He talked at length about the offences, the background to them and his involvement but asked me not to record any of that as he is currently denying any personal knowledge of or involvement in the murders."

When the police interviewed Shirley Giles, the neighbour who lived above Fred and Rose at Midland Road, she told them: "Rose would comment that she could not cope with Charmaine. My impression was that Anne Marie had been browbeaten whereas Charmaine had a rebellious nature. Anne Marie was pretty timid; Rose said she could cope with her. She was no problem." Mrs Giles added that she felt Rose could not curb and control Charmaine in the way she wanted. By the time the Giles family were ready to move out, Rose was saying that she could not wait to get rid of Charmaine. She told her that she was waiting for the child's mother to arrive and take her away. "I told Rose that Charmaine and Anne Marie should not be separated."

She recalled the day she and her family moved out and into their new home in Cinderford. "Charmaine and Tracey were hugging one another and in tears." She also remembered the day she came back to see everyone, bringing Tracey along with her new baby sister, Claire. It was April 1971. Fred, she said, was still in prison. "Rose let us in and said Charmaine was no longer with them. Her mother had come to Midland Road and taken her to Bristol. My daughter Tracey cried and Anne Marie comforted her."

Shirley's daughter Tracey was also interviewed. She told the detectives that Charmaine had become her best friend. She described Anne Marie as 'always quiet, and she seemed like Charmaine's shadow.' The day Tracey returned to Midland Road was etched in her mind. She remembered her tears when she realised she would never see Charmaine again and what Rose had said as she sobbed in dismay. 'She's gone to live with her mother

373

and bloody good riddance.'

Tracey also told the police of an earlier incident that had occurred when her mother had run out of milk and sent her downstairs to borrow some: "I knocked at the door and went in. I barged straight in and stopped. Charmaine was standing on an old wooden kitchen chair. She seemed calm and unconcerned. Her hands were behind her back with a belt tight around the wrists. The image is clear in my mind. The lady with long hair was standing there with a large wooden spoon. I was very shocked and upset. Anne Marie was standing by the door, expressionless."

2nd June 1994

Fred West appeared at Gloucester Magistrates' Court, where nine murder charges had now been amended to joint charges with his wife Rosemary West. He was remanded in custody to reappear on Thursday 30th June 1994. He was then checked over at HMP Birmingham Health Care Centre.

The reinstatement at 25 Midland Road was complete and the property returned to the possession of the owner.

3rd June 1994

Rosemary West appeared at Gloucester Magistrates' Court where she was remanded in custody to reappear on Thursday 30th June 1994.

The excavation continued at Kempley which was now the only site being worked on by the police.

Rose wrote a couple of letters to Mae:

My dearest Mae,

Well here I'am, settling down in a new place. It's very nice here and everyone is being so good to me. how are things with you? I was so pleased to see you Tuesday. I know how hard it was for you, and how nither of us said half the things we wante to. Visiting should be much easier for you here. You can come anytime, as I'm allowed visit's every day. I just can't wait to see you, and have a good chin wag! It will be good to see

Steve too! as I hav'nt seen him for a long time. I can't tell you how much I appreciate you being there for me. Did you have a good birthday. I do hope you didn't have to work that day. You know you said you didn't like the sound of the key's rattling, well they don't rattle here, they jingle like the sound of bells on father christmas's raindeer. If this letter get's to you before Tuesday would you bring down with you, a very small radio and the batteries for it. They have to be DURACELL.

DON'T bring cloths?, I don't need them yet. Guess what, I'm smoking tobacco, that's all I can afford. But it does'nt matter, I'm quite happy, as long as I can see you. you and Steve can write to me as well, if you have time. I'll leave you now and get this letter on it's way.

Love you so much, Mum

P.S. send Steve my love.

Three days later, Rose wrote again to Mae:

My dear Mae,

Hope this letter finds you well and happy. I'm settling in OK, and I'm keeping fit and occupied. English lessons are under way and I hope to learn how to spell a lot better. I go to the Gym everyday, sometimes before breakfast. Sofar I'v had a go at Badmington yesterday and table-tennis today. Couldn't imagine me playing games, could you? How's Steve. You can tell me what you've been doing as well. And not to forget about Tara, and how thing's are with her. the weather's not been to good here, only a few hour's of sunshine, but the birds love it when it does arrive. I have a wall outside one of my window's, and the pidgeon's have been using it to mate on. They get feed from the canteen, so there's lots of fat one's about.

When you write would you give me Steve's full address the phone number, if he has one. I'm reading a book called 'THE SHELL SEEKERS' it realy is good. It's all about a painting and the family that own's it. I'v got loads more to read and I hope their as good as the one's I'v already read. Mae, I need money to buy thing's with, but it has to be sent by post. If you can send me 3 five pound notes in an envelope plus 40 Silk Cut, I would be very gratefull. Make sure the Envalope has my number, name and address on it. I'm sorry love, I forgot to tell you, that you maybe searched when you come to see me. just so that you know. Have you got access to a garden where you live? It would be nice for you to have somewhere to sit out in the sun, and maybe even to hang your washing out in the fresh air. It dries so quick in the nice weather, and smells really fresh. I'll leave you now, and send this letter on.

Love you allway's

Mum

xxxx xxxxx

7th June 1994

11:00

As hope was beginning to fade in the search for the remains of Ann McFall, a pool facility for the media was organised in Kempley. The police had become annoyed by the press' insistence on being told and shown more so DSI Bennett and DCI Moore met the chosen representatives from the media at the gate to Fingerpost Field and escorted them to the site. DSI Bennett began his short statement: "Our search at Fingerpost Field is beginning to draw to a close…We will move to another site in the immediate vicinity – highlighted by a number of local people and this should not take long at all…At this stage we do not plan to search any other areas…I am not prepared to say why we have searched in the locations so far, but I can assure you that if my plans change in the future I will let you know." They had no idea how close they were to discovering Ann McFall's remains.

Excavation at Fingerpost Field

18:22

Two members of the search team, PC's Robinson and Skinner, discovered the remains of Ann McFall in Fingerpost Field (Kempley B). They had unearthed part of a skull and other remains. Professor Bernard Knight was then called for.

20:00

Professor Knight commenced the removal of the remains of Ann McFall but could not finish the task because darkness fell. Inside the pit, the bones seemed to be jumbled and there were signs of cloth or clothing. Bernard Knight: "In the last few hours of that excavation a dump truck had taken up a load of earth and 'hey presto' there was a skull in it. So I was called up there to look at this skull and it was sitting on the edge of this dumper truck and we had to dig away at the bank and found the rest of this body."

Police re-opened old files of unsolved sex attacks from 30 years ago, believing the serial killer could have been responsible for many more murders.

8ᵗʰ June 1994

10:30

A news conference was held outside Gloucester Police Station. DSI Bennett said: "At 6.15pm last night the police search team at Kempley were working in the search area when they discovered what they thought were human remains. The work stopped and Professor Bernard Knight went to the scene that evening and confirmed they were human remains."

Rose wrote to Mae:

Hi Darling,

I thought I would drop you a few lines just to apologise. I felt I was insensitive and rather rash on Tuesday. I might even say I was being a tiny bit selfish.

Please thank Tara for my watch and tell her Mum will allway's treasure it. Tell her I will write to her as soon as I can get things sorted out with Social Services.

I'v been to the gym this-morning. We have two new computerised rowing machines. They cost a bomb! Their good though, it's a sort of all-in-one exercise machine. The teachers realy excited about them.

Thank you for my fags, in fact thank you for everything you do for me. I hope I will never take you for granted. I can't tell you how wonderfull it is to know that I am loved no-matter what sort of dreadfull situation I might find myself in.

Remember I will love you allways.

Mum.

xxxxx xxxxx

In an interview with Howard Ogden, Fred reiterated that his first wife Rena had killed Ann McFall "and Rena must have told Rose that she was in the pond". Rosemary West had "no feelings at all", he maintained.

378

9th June 1994

09:45

Professor Knight returned and completed the removal of the remains of Ann McFall. The skull was split in two parts but there was no way of knowing whether it had been buried like that or if the excavation work had caused the damage. The body had been placed in a roughly rectangular pit dug in the clay and covered with loose topsoil. It was lying face down and the facial bones were virtually intact. Her legs were removed at the hip. She had been decapitated. 36 of her finger and toe bones were missing, as well as both kneecaps. Her wrists had been held by some type of cord, like a dressing-gown cord or rope. Scattered near the pelvic area of the body were bones from a foetus described by the pathologist as those of an immature infant. The baby had still been inside its mother when she died. She had been 8 months pregnant with a girl. In addition, there were a number of other artefacts discovered in two plastic bags including a discoloured, round-necked, long-sleeved cardigan and a number of pieces of material, including one that was quite large, discoloured and floral, like a curtain or quilt. Fred West used to claim that Ann McFall used to be waiting for him in bed at her caravan every night wearing only a cardigan. There were also long and short pieces of rope, one of which was knotted, and a length of cord that bound the wrists together and was laid over the ribs.

When the Professor had finished he could see marks on both femurs that, along with how the remains were positioned, indicated the body had been dismembered. The only sizeable bone not recovered was part of the left fibula and a right twelfth rib. The remains were taken to the University of Wales, College of Medicine at Cardiff for examination.

Examination of the remains revealed them to be those of a woman 5ft 2ins tall, aged between seventeen and twenty-three, who had a very high, smooth forehead. The body was identified as that of Ann McFall. Old photographs were compared to the computer reconstruction from the skull to confirm this.

Sir Bernard Knight would go on to say after the trial: "There was a lot of hand and toe bones missing, but you actually rarely find every bone if you dig up a skeleton. One reason why there may be a sinister aspect is that two foetus's present and they had tiny little bones and they were there…most of them…even tiny rib bones, the size of a matchstick. And yet there were bigger bones missing from the adults. There was one shoulder blade missing and it's a bit difficult to imagine how if you can get a tiny foetal bone surviving, where has this big shoulder blade gone? Of course, the sensational aspect or explanation would be that they were taken off as some sort of fetish and even cannibalism was mentioned but that is pure speculation. But there were a lot of bones missing."

Two further sites, which had been pointed out by local people, were excavated but nothing more was found.

Howard Ogden interviewed Fred West in Winson Green prison and told him about the police discovery:

Howard Ogden: We've learned this morning that there's been a find at Kempley.
Fred: Yeah
Howard Ogden: The police…the suggestion is going to be that this is Ann McFall
Fred: I want it to be Ann
Howard Ogden: Yeah?
Fred: Really…I want her found
Howard Ogden: Right
Fred: Because I don't know how she died. I don't know anything about what happened to her.

Rose wrote to Stephen and Andrea:

Dear Steve and Andrea,

I can't tell you how wonderful it was to see you both on Saturday. You both looked so well, and I hope you look after yourselvs all the time. I'v just realised that I don't have your address, so you will have to send it to me sometime. It's been a lovly day here today, I have a nice view from my window. You want to see the sky sometimes, beautifull colours. Sometimes the clouds are white and fluffy again'st a clear bright blue sky. We have a airbase nearby. We get allsorts of aircraft come over. The other day a micro-light was hoovering around the sky. Sometimes you get a loud, drawing noise and a jet will whiz overhead. Or a wrilling sound and it will be three choppers. It's surprising what comes over here. One day it was the 'Red Arrows', we've had plenty of air balloons, come right close over the rooftops. I could see the people quite clearly in the baskets. Or you get jets making patterns, again'st the sky. Nice when you've got time to look out your window! To my great surprise, the teacher's came up the other day, I stood there with my mouth open for a couple of minute's, wondering what to say. Then they asked me daft questions like, Would you like to learn a language like Hungarian or German! Someone wrote to me saying, 'think how proud the Grand children will be when Granny gets a P.H.D. for nuclear phisic's'.

What a laugh. Crumbs, granny! old age crepping up on me. but I like the game's of table tennis and badmington when I go to the gym, but one of the gym teacher's makes me do five miles on the exercise bike as-well. But we do get a lovly shower afterward's.

There was some babies clothes at home. but I don't know what's happened to them. I don't know if you could make use of them, if you could find them. And there was some other stuff that might be usefull if you wanted. Have you both been through it all? There's been some great music on the radio today. I'v been quite happy now I'v got things to do. Well my darling's, I will leave you now and go to bed. Once again, Thanks for coming, I know how difficult it is, when you have so much to do. At least you know where to find me!

Lots of Love and Kisses.

Mum

Xxxxxxxx

10th June 1994

Rose wrote to Mae:

My dear Mae,

It realy was wonderful to see you. I still didn't tell you all I wanted to. So please come again soon, I realy do miss you to talk to. I love you, and there's no one I trust more. Thanks for my radio. It's great to have it back. I received the money, but I did ask Steve to put a letter in with the money and said that he had sent them, but they didn't get here, do you know why? I can have them, but they have to be sent in by post. Oh it's *allright, they've just got here. Ignore what I'v just said! I still need time to work out how things are done here, I'll learn, slow, but I'll learn. By what you've told me, sometimes I think I'm the lucky one to be here away from all the shit. You realy are a very strong person, and you are a constant source of comfort and delight in my life.*

Started a new book last night, it's called 'THE PRINCE OF TIDES'. It's got realy big words, so I asked for a dictionary. It's flippin massive.

Well darling, It's bedtime, so I'll snuggle down. I hope you can make sense of my letters. Give Baggy? A kiss for me. Can't wait to see you again.

Lots of Love

Mum xxxxx

xxxx

xxxx

15th June 1994

In an interview with his solicitor Howard Ogden, Fred West again suggested that there may have been more victims and was asked why he thought Rose's killing had "stopped after Heather". He paused before replying: "Did she stop?" He then went on: "There's a farm somewhere that Rose had a lot to do with." A few minutes later he told Howard Ogden: "I don't even know if they got them all."

He then tried to get praise for telling all he knew. "I knew that you wouldn't get anything out of Rose. If she went down that police station, they'd never have found any of 'em, if I hadn't got it off her, 'cause she'd never have said a word. She can just shut herself off, and you can carry on for evermore." He insisted to his solicitor: "Rose is the only person who knows the names of the people, what went on, what it was, what she was getting these girls for, and everything." But Fred also told his solicitor that he still thought "the world of Rose", even though "these things have happened."

16th June 1994

Rose was seen at the Fromside Clinic in Bristol. Fromside was an 80 bed medium secure service caring for people with a mental illness and/or personality disorder who also have a criminal history or have risks and behaviors that mean they cannot be treated in mainstream mental health services. She recalled that her and Fred had been invited to a wedding one Saturday. She looked forward to it as they rarely went anywhere together, and because her routine life had become predictable. She made sure earlier in the week that she had sexual relations with all the regular partners assigned to her by Fred in order to keep the Saturday free. Still, however, he insisted on dropping her off at another man's house, a new customer he had made arrangements with that day. She said she sat in the corridor of the house weeping.

17th June 1994

The search at Kempley finished and the equipment was taken away. This marked the end of that part of the investigation.

19th June 1994

Rose wrote a letter to Mae:

Hello Darling,

Thanks for my cigarette's and your letter. Mae, what yo do is your business, I'm just pleased you have someone, and that they care for you so much. Like our friend say's, you're a very level-headed person, I'm sure you can make your own decisions. As long as your happy, that's all that matters.

I was so pleased to hear that Tara has had her baby and that everything's allright. You can tell me all about it, when I see you next. And at least you know now, that it's a boy you have to buy for. I wondered why I was so restless last night. I woke up at 2 o'clock, and tried to make out why. I tossed and turned for a bit, and then went back to sleep. An hour later I'm awake again this time with stomach ache. By the time the mornings got here, I'v got stomach and back ache, and even my legs ached. But then again I could of just had a bad night and I'm blaming it on poor old Tara. I know the time because I have the radio on in bed at night. I put the ear-phone in, and I even fall asleep with it still switched on. I listen to radio 2 all day and then turn it to the oldies station at night. I think I'm a bit old-fashioned. Well I'll get this terribly bad spelt letter of to you, and you can have a jolly good laugh about it. I would of, wrote it all over again, but I just can't be bothered.

Love you so much,

Mum.

xxxx

xxxx

P.S. Send EMMA my love

Fred West was visited by his Probation Officer, R. W. Anderson. "Spend about two and a half hours with West who was much more forthcoming and began to talk about the likelihood of a life sentence and his feelings about the offences."

It is noted that after lock up, Fred West was crying. Asked if he was OK, he replied 'Yes'. His prison notes said to 'keep an eye' on him.

30th June 1994

Fred West was arrested for the murder of Ann McFall by DC Barnes. Fred and Rose West then appeared together for the first time at Gloucester Magistrates Court. This was the first time they had seen each other since he was arrested in February. He was charged with eleven counts of murder, she with nine along with two charges of rape and one of assault. Rose refused to speak or look at Fred. Rose asked for a police officer to be placed between them, and this was repeated on all subsequent occasions when they appeared together and were remanded. As police attempted to lead Fred from the hearing, he resisted their efforts, and again attempted to move towards Rose, who again winced and attempted to get away from his grasp. He leaned over to stroke the back of her neck and whispered in her ear. But Rose refused to even look at him and stared straight ahead as she cowered from his touch. Fred was crushed. "This clearly quite perturbed him" said Detective Superintendent John Bennett. Fred West was remanded in custody to police cells until Monday 4th July. Rose West was remanded in custody until Thursday 28th July.

Howard Ogden: "Fred had really been looking forward to seeing Rose and he was sure and convinced that she would be supportive of him. Reassuring to him. She was cold as ice. She ignored him. Every time he looked in her direction she turned away and he realised at that point that he didn't have that support."

Doug West: "I think that he was prepared to take the wrap for her, but then when they appeared in court, she snubbed him in court and once she'd done that she might as well have pleaded 'guilty' then 'cause he turned. I mean, once he turned that was it."

During 3 days of interviews with his solicitor regarding Ann McFall, Fred maintained his innocence. He also admitted that at least one of his 'experiences' of ghosts coming out of the ground was a lie.

Fred: I don't know what happened to Ann. All I know, I thought the world of her, look…No way would I have anybody touch her…You know, I spent more time, every minute I could with her and most of the time combing her hair, you know… I mean I'd never had a relationship like that before, not with one girl that wanted me and nobody else.
Howard Ogden: I asked you if there was any psychic-type experience that wasn't real and you gave me a one-word answer.
Fred: Yeah, Ann

He would later go on to give an account of Ann McFall's death to Howard Ogden. He had denied all knowledge of it up until this interview:

"I had this battle in me 'ead from then on…Ann and Rose, and I mean Ann had just completely pushed Rose out of my mind. I mean, I've got no feeling towards Rose, fucking crazy because Rose had always been Ann, in a way, to me and that's how she got away with everything 'cause I couldn't see no harm in her, you know, I couldn't see nothing wrong with her. Ann, to me, was perfect. She would give her life for me, let alone anything else. She was quite prepared to give her life for me. I mean, when you got somebody to that extent in your life, you've got somebody…But she used to accuse me of thinking of Rena all the time. We had plans for me and Ann to just disappear…drift away."

But Fred did not have the courage to leave his wife and children and lied to Ann about it. "When I was with Ann I was all for it, but I wasn't, I wasn't, if you know what I mean…I didn't know what to do." He told Rena that Ann McFall had 'gone and left me', even though he had simply moved her to Sandhurst Lane. One night, he "got back to Sandhurst, must have been about half-past eleven at night. I parked the lorry in the road…and came through the back way straight into the caravan. There's Rolf and Rena in there. Rena's absolutely out of her brains. She hadn't got a clue where she was, what she'd done. So, of course, I said, 'Where's Ann?' and Rolf said, 'Come outside'. So we went round the back of the caravan and he said, 'Rena's stabbed Ann – by mistake.' Now, I quite believed that. I don't think that Rena would have done it absolutely deliberate. I think she was so drugged out of her brains and everything else, drink and everything else, that she stabbed Ann. Anyway, I said to Rolf: 'What the bloody hell we going to do?' And he said: 'You ain't got no choice.' And I thought, Fuck me. I knew exactly what he meant. Whether Rolf was actually there when Rena stabbed Ann, I don't know. Or whether she rung him and he came to her, and bring that case to her. I'd never seen that case…It was a massive bloody case. He said: 'We're going to take her and put her on the tip, Gloucester tip.'

By this time I am literally brain dead. The mind's just gone. I hadn't got a clue what I was thinking, or saying, or nothing." However, Fred was capable of saying, according to his version of events: "No, the only place you can put her is in our special place at Marcle. We drove out there, and me and him dug the hole together, and Rena was sat in the car, watching Ann. Then we both walked back up the field, and then him and Rena went down with the car and put Ann in and covered her up, and come back to me. I was sat on the tank beside the gate splashing water on me face. And that was it. As far as I know she wasn't touched".

The following day he contradicted himself: "I went to my father and told him what had happened. I asked him to go up there with me, 'cause I couldn't go up there on me own. So he walked up there with me, and we're stood there talking. I set myself up round me father. My old man was great. Me and him got on ace. He was my God, like. Me and him never fell out in our life. If I ever had a problem – straight to Dad. When I buried Ann I went straight to Dad. Same thing. I wanted to be my father. I admired all he stood for." Note how he had just said that Rolf and Rena had buried Ann while he waited at the entrance to the field.

"I went to my father and I told him what had happened. I asked him to go there with me. So he walked up there with me and we stood there talking and that and he said 'Look, Son, I'm your father. I'm not going to turn you in or nothing', he said, 'but if you can live with it I'll say nothing, leave it. How mother found out I don't know, whether Dad had told mum or what, but mother knew, and I knew that mother knew."

Fred wrote a letter to his son Stephen:

To Stephen and Andrea

Watts going on With May and anna and Rose I was told by Mr OGDEN that Rose approve of Tara, had Watt she wonted and to see watt left and have the money to help her out so watt as anna got, When are you coming to see me bring andrea with you cum soon son, a lot has hapend since I saw you last I have a new barrister, I get on With him My case is in a mess. have you seen May tell her dad love her and give her a x from dad all my love to
Stephen and andrea

See you soon DAD xx
I have got tobacco
I need R6 battery get Rayovac VIDOR Longer Life alkaline

He seemed to miss Mae, or what Mae could do for him, and in his letters to his family he kept asking for her to come and see him. She had decided after he admitted to the murders and was charged that she no longer wanted anything to do with him, but believed that her mum was innocent of the murders.

1st July 1994

The third of Caroline Owens' statements that was to be used in court was written.

Fred West told his solicitor Howard Ogden, that Rose had murdered Charmaine by accident: "She grabbed her by the throat and killed her". This may very well have been true, although later in interviews he would claim that Rose had told him that she had given her an overdose of aspirin.

He went on to tell Howard Ogden that Rose had explained the killings as "sex acts that went wrong, bondage that went wrong" and that "Rose hated Heather, right from an early age".

He also told his solicitor that his daughter was a lesbian: "Heather hated men. There's no doubt about that. She made it quite clear to me, she hated men near her". This was probably clear in Fred's mind because she had always tried to push away his sexual advances and wasn't grateful that he had raped her on numerous occasions. "I had nothing against Heather being a lesbian, if that's what she chose to be. She was floating between one and the other all the time, and I always said that if you get a good man it'll settle you down ... 'cause all Heather said when I picked her up from school was what knickers the teachers had on". He also told Howard Ogden the lie that he had "always suspected" that Heather was not his daughter, "and that Rose was already pregnant when she came to me at Lake House. That's why she was in such a hurry and that".

At 15:20 that afternoon, Fred discussed his wife's promiscuity: "There were so many girls and blokes going in and out of that house that I hadn't got a bloody clue…She was having casual sex with some of them, I realise that. I mean they'd been drugged out their brains and they wouldn't know what time of day it was. Whether they were girls or boys, they hadn't got a clue what they were doing. See, this thing didn't start yesterday, right? This…imagination. I lived in a world of my own on it for a reason, because when I went in to work and places like that, I mean half the blokes had shagged my wife, and I knew they had! She'd either fuck off with somebody else and be fucked in the car park right by the side of me with half the pub knowing or fucking say summat or get the loose 'ead with me 'cause I was saying 'look, I thought you were with me, like. Fucking stay here."

Howard Ogden: "Fred then said that he was convinced that there are a lot more bodies to be found. He said it had been going on for 30 years."

The police enquiries were still going on to trace further possible victims, and victims of sexual assaults who had survived. Janet Leach: "Fred said that there was another two bodies in shallow graves in the woods but there was no way they'd ever find them. Fred said that there were 20 other bodies, not in one place, spread around, and that he would give the police one a year." He told her that one of those women killed was while he worked on a Birmingham construction site.

Janet Leach: "He classed it like a cult, he said. Where they'd all go to the farm. The girls would be picked up and taken there and some of them would be there for days and they'd subject them to different forms of abuse."

Janet also said that in regards to Mary Bastholm: "He had actually said that he had actually picked her up from the bus stop. He did say that she had been murdered."

Howard Ogden: "Fred said in relation to Mary Bastholm that she had been buried at Bishop's Cleeve."

The killers Modus Operandi had become obvious early on. All victims were buried in a small hole, were dismembered and were naked. In interviews with Fred West, DC Harris said: "Every single piece of information would indicate that one person must have had at least a part in all twelve". DC Barnes added: "The person that was responsible for Ann McFall is likely to be the person responsible for all of them". Since the beginning Fred had told police that there would be coal found with Charmaines' body, that there would be a knife found with Lucy Partington's remains and that it was he who had left the 'signature' on every set of remains that had been found, DC Harris said "I think our investigation to date has tended to confirm what you originally said to the police".

3rd July 1994

Fred West was charged with the murder of Ann McFall, bringing the total number of murder charges against him to twelve.

Rose wrote a letter to her daughter Mae:

Hi Mae,

How are things with you? I don't really know what to write about, as these letters seem to take so long getting to you. I was writing in my diary, and it came to me that I hav'nt told you to much latly, how much I love you. so hears my feeble atttempt:-

I love you like a part of myself,

I love you like the dawn,

I love you like the moon & stars,

And the sun on a summer's morn.

I love you like the birds and bee's

I love you like flower's sweet,

I love you like deep blue sea's,

And memories dear to keep.

I love you like your made of glass

I love you like your gold,

I love you like the rarest diamond

To precious to be sold.

In all seriousness though, you are very precious indeed, and it's not only me who thinks so. I'm very proud of you, you realy are a wonderful person.

Love you allways

Mum

xxxxx   xxxx

6th July 1994

Fred West's probation officer, R. W. Anderson: "I have now seen West on two occasions at H.M. Prison, Winson Green. The first time I saw him alone for about two and a half hours. The second time I saw him with ***** my 'pair' and we were joined by the prison Probation Officer **** when the interview had been underway for some time.

14th July 1994

Fred's probation officer visited him: "****, Probation Officer, Prison****. She says Fred seems to be suggesting there are more bodies and seeking advice on whether to tell the police. She is seeing him today with a prison officer and will do whatever seems appropriate."

Fred had also hinted to a prison officer that he had killed more than the dozen victims, more than the dozen for whose murder he was awaiting trial. He had hinted that there might be eight "extra" girls, and had rambled on about his wife wrapping their bodies in white plastic mackintoshes. He suggested that although some were in Gloucester and Cheltenham, others were further afield, in places where he and his wife had been on holiday, including Snowdonia.

Fred West retracted his earlier version of events where he said that Rose had strangled Charmaine to death, instead claiming that Rose had told him: "I gave her an overdose of aspirin or something because you were trying to find Rena".

20th July 1994

A letter was sent by Janet Leach to Winson Green prison requesting permission to visit Fred West:

Dear Sir/Madam,

I am writing this letter to request permission to visit prisoner won 3617 west fredruck walter stephen. I believe he has asked to see me. When Mr West was brought to the police station in Gloucester I was called in as a volunteer appropriate adult to sit in on interviews as an observer, and to see that he was being fairly treated. I did say to Mr West that when he was transfered to prison that I would try to arrange a visit as soon as was possible.

Yours Sincerely

Janet Leach (JANET LEACH)

Howard Ogden visited Fred West. Fred told him that he had to "tell the truth". "If I'm to have any chance in this case at all, I gotta go back to the police and tell the truth. I know exactly what the truth is…What was killing it before was that I wasn't prepared to admit to knowing about Ann." He then blamed Rose and her father for the deaths at Cromwell Street. "Why should I take the rap? Rose broke every promise she made to me." He went on: "I don't know if the girls were cut up at Cromwell Street, or somewhere else", but he suspected that it was "somewhere else" and he denied that he had ever buried anyone at his house. "I didn't know anything about any of the girls in Cromwell Street." Minutes later he contradicted himself: "All the girls I got on great with. But there was never any sexual relationship with them…I used to talk fucking dirty to them and they'd talk dirty back."

He told Howard Ogden how he met Ann McFall in Scotland: "There's this young lady sat on the step crying her pissing eyes out and looked like a tramp and I stopped…when I pushed the window open, I called her over and said 'what's up?' She turned around and she was fucking beautiful and she was absolutely in rags and her hair all matted and the long fucking hair, but she looked beautiful to me…So I got talking to her and I said 'do you want an ice cream?' 'Yes', she said. So I made her up a bloody Sundae, one of them big Sundaes, and I said 'well come and sit in the van and have it' and generally got talking to her and I said 'you can come with me if you like?' And then I got to find out what the problem was. Her mother was an alcoholic and was selling her body for drink and I said 'well, you gotta get out of that'. I said, 'I tell you what I'll take you home with me and I'll sort something out for you.' Anyway, I took her home and told Rena all about it and Rena said 'Yeah, she can come and stay here'…So Ann had a bath and cleaned herself up and Rena washed her hair for her and she looked bloody gorgeous then, with this long silky hair."

Of the other women, he insisted that he had never even met Lucy Partington or "the Dutch girl", suggesting that "Rose's father" must have picked them up on his way home.

He blamed Rose for Heather's murder, claiming that his wife had confessed to him on their last night together at Cromwell Street that she alone had been responsible. "I didn't ask any details", because "I didn't want to know what had happened. I thought the world of her. The main problem I've had is that I swore on the kids' lives that I wouldn't shop Rose for what she did.

She always had this thing against Heather, that Heather smelled. She always used to say: "You can smell that little bitch, that dirty bitch."…Rose hated Heather, right from an early age…She didn't kill her on the spur of the moment, that's obvious, because she moved her out of the house. She did exactly the same with Stephen, after she attacked him, moved him out without me knowing." This is known to have been a lie as Heather never left Cromwell Street, as witnessed by the other children.

On the night before the police started to excavate their garden, Rose West had told him: "That thing's out in the garden... "I said: "What do you mean?" She said: "Heather, I killed her."

"Well, I must have sat there for ten minutes, absolutely shocked, gone. I couldn't even think. I couldn't speak. I couldn't think of a thing to say. Me mind had gone...I thought Rose was just going to say: "I strangled her and buried her in the garden, fully clothed, dressed, everything." Then she says: "Oh she's cut up. Her head's cut off." I gave a few deep breaths and said: "What do you mean?" She said: "I had to cut her up to get her back home in a dustbin...I brought her home in a pushchair." That was the trolley she used for shopping."

This time Fred explained that Heather had left Cromwell Street with a girl "with a red mini skirt on". But "What I didn't know was that Rose had offered Heather £600 to go away", but that Heather had rung him a week later "because the money hadn't arrived". In this version he claimed that it was only then that "Heather was killed somewhere else". In this version he insisted that it was his wife – and not he – who had been in contact with Heather after she left Cromwell Street, and that she had told him to tell the children, and anyone else who asked, that he had seen Heather regularly over the years. "I just followed through what Rose told me" he claimed.

"It would be easier if people asked me who Rose didn't have sex with, not who she did. I mean, there were so many...This making love to her after every nigger. Load of fucking rubbish. I had less sex with Rose than anybody, because she was at it all day with different blokes, at it all night with different blokes. When I did join the queue...Rose provoked me all the time. If I'd attacked anybody it would have been Rose...It never stopped. It didn't stop at all."

22nd July 1994

Fred was interviewed by Howard Ogden once more: "Rose knows the answer to it all. Even the police don't think I done it on me own." He denied that he knew anything at all about ritual killing – "never had anything to do with it" – he went on to explain: "There's no video of Rose touching a girl, for a simple bloody reason – 'cause Rose didn't want to show the bloody cruelty of what she was doing to these girls." He said that Rose kept a green hardback diary behind the meter box in which she kept a sheet of paper which marked where the girls were buried. "Rose wanted it wrote down, she enjoyed this. Rose wrote everything down, always." There was also, he insisted, an audio-tape attached to the back of the diary "for her ears only". Neither of these items were ever found.

Towards the end of July, Fred's desperation became more evident and he felt alone and depressed. "I don't put in to see nobody", he told Howard Ogden. "I don't want to see nobody. I've got nothing to say to nobody." He did not know anything about the killings. He had made it all up to protect his wife, and now she had abandoned him. "All I am worried about is Rose getting out, because if Rose is out, Rose is gone, and they ain't gonna find her. What she thought is that they'd have left her at the house, and she'd have just vanished." He was convinced that she would kill again. "She can't stop."

He said he knew nothing about the dismemberment of the bodies, nothing about the abuse of his children and nothing about incest. "You didn't put a bull to a calf that was his child and all that", he told his solicitor. "To touch your own kids, your own daughters, it was disgusting." He denied attacking Anne Marie and maintained that the attack on his other daughter, the 13-year-old Louise, had been carried out by his wife with a vibrator. "Rose tried to break her in. Got too close to me coming home. Walked out and left her there in disgust."

23rd July 1994

Stephen West married Andrea Davis at St. George's Church, Brockworth. The front row in the church was left vacant "out of respect" as Fred and Rose were barred from attending by the authorities. Instead, they both sent letters to the couple:

Congratulations on Your
Wedding

May your Wedding be a day
Filled with special memories.
Congratulations and Best Wishes
        To STEPHEN AND ANDREA
    WISHING YOU BOTH THE VERY
BEST FOR THE FUTURE
BOTH OF YOU ALWAYS
IN MY THOUGHTS
                ALL MY LOVE
    FROM STEPHEN DAD
    X X X Y Y Y X X X

To my dear Son and his
    lovely new wife.

Congratulations.

Although I can't be with you,
you know my thoughts and my
love, are with you today, and
everyday of your new life together.

I wish you every happiness
for the future, take care of
each other, and learn to love
each other a little more each
day.
            Have a Great time
            Love
                Mum.

Stephen: "I was really chuffed when dad's card arrived. There were a couple of mistakes in it but he tried his best. It must have taken a lot of effort. He obviously got someone else to write it out then copied it."

Rose sent them a multi-coloured cushion as a gift that she had made in Pucklechurch Prison and a note that was read out at the ceremony (above). Stephen told the guests at the reception: "Although this is the happiest day of my life, it is tinged with sadness because my mum and dad can't share it with me. But I know their thoughts are with us."

Stephen also revealed that his new bride was 14 weeks pregnant with twins. "I cried my eyes out when I heard. The hospital think we may have a boy and a girl. They even said there might be a third baby hidden behind the other two."

<u>**27th July 1994**</u>

<u>**11:00**</u>

HM Coroner David Gibbons opened inquests at Dursley Magistrates Court for identification of the remains of Charmaine West, Catherine West (Costello) and Ann McFall. The inquests were for identification purposes only and evidence was given by Detective Superintendent John Bennett, Professor Bernard Knight and Doctor David Whittaker.

Anne Marie: "I had been visiting Dad at Winson Green on and off over the months and he regularly telephoned me. He had a cell to himself and every opportunity to do himself harm if he wanted to. On one of my last visits he had talked about taking his own life and I became concerned that he might mean to do it. I told the police and they in turn informed the prison authorities. Dad was put on special watch, whereby they checked on him every fifteen minutes, but his behaviour seemed normal and after a while they went back to checking on him at the same intervals as other prisoners.

The day Dad told me he wanted to end his own life he cried for a long time. We sat in the depressing visitor's room and he talked about arrangements for his funeral and what he wanted done with his things. He had his elbows on the table between us and he leaned forward as he spoke to me."

Fred: I've told them here I want you down as my next of kin. Rose don't want me no more. She don't want to know.
Anne Marie: Dad, don't. Don't talk about it
Fred: No, I want to. I've told them my girl is next of kin. She'll sort things out. Your dad's had enough, love. I'm going to finish it myself. I've had enough
Anne Marie: Dad, don't talk like this. You'll be alright. You don't want to do anything like that. Don't be silly!
Fred: (Crying) I want to be buried with your mum. I want to be with her. I don't want to be on my own. And I want Charmaine there too. Put me with them, love. You'll see to it won't you?...I want you buried there too one day.

With me.

Anne Marie: No, dad. It's not right. You can't do that and I won't do it for you. You can't be buried with Mum and Charmaine. Think of Mum's family. There's been too much hurt already.

"I could see that he wasn't taking in what I was saying. He had made up his mind that that was what he wanted and he really thought I would do it. He was still crying, but he didn't say much more about it. He looked really depressed when I left and I was convinced then that he might try to kill himself.

Yet earlier during that visit…he had seemed quite cheerful. He asked me what I was doing with his tropical fish, which he had insisted I looked after…

He told me he wanted me to have a lock of his hair and said that I would have to smuggle it out in my knickers. Then he made a crude joke – the sort of humour dad specialised in, which had always embarrassed the girls in the family.

During that last visit my father also asked me to go and see a woman he knew who, he claimed, would give him an alibi which would help his case. I hated it when he asked me to do things like that. He should have known I wouldn't. 'I can't do that for you, dad.' I said. (It is believed that this woman was Janet Leach).

That was when his mood began to change. The humour disappeared and he sounded more morose and depressed. 'Well, I'll get out of here one way or another.'"

28th July 1994

Anne Marie had mentioned Fred's mood to DCI Terry Moore and the information was sent from Gloucester Police to Winson Green Prison saying "that Mr West had told his daughter to arrange his funeral. It was not established whether this implied any suicidal intent or whether it was said simply in the expectation that he and his wife would get very long sentences and that such arrangements would therefore naturally fall to his daughter. In any event, Mr West's demeanour remained normal."

Fred West was checked over at HMP Birmingham Health Care Centre in regards to the conversation above. His prison notes state: "Information received that West has been discussing his funeral arrangements. On interview with West he stated he was not suicidal. Staff please be aware!!"

Fred gave Howard Ogden his last interview, the fifteenth in ten weeks. They discussed, as they had on many occasions, some of the witness statements made to the police during the case, and Fred told him that he could not "see anything in rape." He went on to confess: "If a girl says no, the only thing I had out of it was more of a challenge to get her". Then, quite suddenly, he paused in the middle of the interview and said: "Fuck me, I should go to hell for what I've done."

During these interviews with his solicitor, Fred had given many differing accounts of the events that had lead him to being in prison. Some of these are listed below:

In one interview, he gave another version of how Ann McFall was killed and said his brother John had killed her. He told Howard Ogden, tearfully, "John killed her, my fucking brother. And he fucking buried her an' all, bastard." He went on: "I wouldn't face it. And he got her so fucking easy, I told him where she was. Trusting my own fucking brother." He said that his brother had gone round to the caravan "late at night" to kill her. "Our voices are much the same, 'cause she would never let John in. She must have went to scream or summat and he fucking had her." Then he said that his wife Rena would never have thought to bury Ann at Fingerpost Field. That would have been his brother John's idea. "It was a cold time of year (When he was first sleeping with Rena) so we wouldn't have had a beauty-spot outside". "John had been fucking all of my wives", he added, "and probably half of my fucking family as well…If a girl rejects John he gets very fucking violent towards them." This was due to his brother's jealousy: "because I had all the birds and he couldn't get 'em." He went on to say that his brother had no respect for life or animals. "When John was about three or four our cat had kittens, and John got these kittens and buried them – alive…I've seen him kill cats with a stick. Grab 'em and choke 'em. Rose started doing the same thing – getting it off John. He's ruthless." He added: "John used to do the burying on the farm – sheep and that…Where Ann was buried John used to bury sheep and that…because it used to be an easy patch to dig and that."

In a different interview, Fred gave another account of the attack on

Caroline Owens, this time putting all of the blame on Rose. "When Rose attacked that girl that night in that car, I mean I didn't know what to bloody do. I mean, Rose had tape in the car, ready to tape her mouth up, and she tied her hands with the whatsername. So when Rose attacked the girl that night, I didn't know what to bloody do." He confirmed that his wife had suggested they give her a lift. "I was busting for a pee, that's what it was, and when I turned towards Cinderford there's a big lay-by, which I knew, and I pulled in there, got out, walked to the gate, dropped me zip, and next minute she screams. I run back to the car, and Rose said, "I got me hand up her cunt." I said, "What?" She got her over on the side, wrapping tape round her and God knows what 'er ain't doing. What can I do? Take the blinking girl home like that?" He then insisted that he took Caroline back to Cromwell Street to cut off the tape. But when he went to get a knife, "the next minute when I come back through the door Rose has got her legs open beating her between her legs. I said, "For fuck's sake, keep away from her, leave her." I got her together, and sorted it out, and apologised and everything. That's why we only got fined twenty-odd pound."

In a separate interview, Fred West gave a further account of the death of Carol Cooper and blamed Rose completely: "The first I seen of her was at home, at my place. I didn't pick her up nowhere. I took her back on a motor bike. I don't know how she got back to Cromwell Street...She was only at the house, as far as I know, one day...I came home from work and she was there...These girls were always in the bloody bedroom with Rose, that's what I couldn't understand. It seemed a peculiar place to keep girls. I said to Rose, "That's a schoolgirl, she can't stay here." I took her to Worcester and dropped her. That was the first time and the last that I'd ever seen her." But then he added: "Rose told me it was kinky love sessions that went wrong. That's how the girls came to get killed."

He would insist that her death was just one example of his wife's attitude towards sex and to women. "I think the cruelty bit in her was for women, she wanted to hurt women. She'd have to, to do what she's done to them." In his own words, Rose West was "fucking strong. I had a fucking job to handle her at times, mind, when she got rough with me", and she had become addicted to sado-masochistic sex. "I'd be making love to Rose and all of a sudden she'd smack me in the bloody face, nearly take your bloody head off. Then she'd say, "Do the same to me! Do the same to me!""

He said that he was at first surprised by his wife's enthusiasm for bondage: "Rose wanted to be tied up, hung up, left in the fields, everything."

Fred remained adamant that he knew Lucy Partington well. "I mean, I ought to know when I met somebody…We used to meet in the park…and then whatever we'd be doing we done, and that was it, and then she would go off up across the bank." "She knew me as Steve…I used the name Steve quite often…Never used no surname."

He then changed tact in another interview and tried to put the blame on Rose: "I never seen her before in my life. Rose's old man picked her up on the way through". He then went on to suggest that Lucy had been "supplied" by his father-in-law and his wife "to a fucking party or something. I don't know if Rose was supplying these girls to the same lot that Rena was in Bristol." But he maintained: "Half the time I didn't know who was in the bloody place. Rose was putting them in and taking them out, letting them stay, enticing them. They were bloody young girls…Rose was having casual sex with some of them but she never mentioned that to me."

Fred would then admit to making up stories to the police and why he kept changing his story: "This is where we got a hell of a problem 'cause I gotta get it all out, all sorted out because I have mixed it up deliberately for the police.

"I am working out what I'm gonna tell the police. How I'm gonna handle it, right? One body, fully clothed or I thought…but now I know she's cut up so I have to make up, to think up why the bloody hell did I cut her up? I mean, what reason for that did I cut this girl up? So I said at least it's just one. So I mean, you know, you could accidentally kill one but you wouldn't get away with accidentally killing two, like. So I said 'Well is that it?' 'Oh no' she said. 'There's another 7, 8, 9, summat like that.' So Rose told me where the ones in the basement was. I said to Rose 'Well fuck me you ain't done bad have you. I said fucking, you know, you've got a fucking 'nuff here ain't you?"

Fred went on to recall when Rose told him that Heather was buried in the garden. "I can remember taking a breath and swallowing it and I said 'what the flaming hell do you mean?' She said 'Heather's out there.' Well, I mean I just fucking died for a minute. I had to sit down and have a fag and

I was trying to light it and god knows what. So I said 'what do you mean Heather's out there?' She said 'yeah Heather's buried out there'. So I said 'where?' She said 'at the end of the fence where the other fence used to go across' and I said 'fucking hell.' It seemed as though my whole life stopped there. Finished, you know? And I couldn't think of nothing. Heather, I mean I thought the bloody world of Heather. So anyway, I got to grips with it after a while and the first thing that comes into my mind was 'I'm going to have to take this and sort it out', which I did with all the messes Rose got herself in to. I took the fucking wrap for them and helped her out. So anyway, I said 'Look, you'll have to tell me exactly what happened.' She said that, erm, 'Heather was cut up.' Well, I never felt so ill in all my life for a few seconds, a few minutes before I could get a grip of myself again. And I said 'What on Earth did you cut her up for?' She said 'She wouldn't fit in the dustbin.' Now, the thing that makes it hard, that she cut Heather up and chucked her in a fucking dustbin. Her daughter. In a dustbin!" He said Rose then told him about Charmaine:

"She said 'and Charmaine'. I said 'what Charmaine?' Hang on a fucking minute, where's Charmaine? She said 'Charmaine's buried in the coal cellar at Midland Road'. 'Yeah, she's buried in the corner', she said. I said 'she's not cut up? I mean, you haven't cut a fucking child up for God's sake? I mean, that was the fear that's come in to me. 'Oh no' she said 'oh no, she's not cut up' she said. 'She's fully clothed and wrapped in a blanket.'" Crying, Fred then went on to say: "Rose lied to me which hurt me as well about Charmaine. She said that Charmaine was an accident or summat. She grabbed her or summat, by the throat or summat and killed her. I can't think exactly what she did say, but Heather, I mean Charmaine. She said she killed her and buried her in the basement at the back of the house. And I said 'you didn't cut her up?' and she said 'Oh no, no, I wouldn't, no, no, nothing like that.' She said she's fully clothed and I wrapped her up in a blanket and buried her…when the police found her she was naked and whether she'd been cut up I don't know…Rose never liked Charmaine really. I turned a blind eye to it because I couldn't do nothing about it."

Fred went on to describe how Rose told him she'd killed Lynda Gough: "She said 'what about Lynda Gough'. I said, 'you bitch!' As soon as she said that I thought 'fuck me, she'd killed her and had her fucking clothes on!' She's wearing the girls shoes and she'd killed her for fuck sake. And her dressing gown. I mean, how fucking far can you go? I said 'you wore her fucking clothes after you'd killed her!' she said 'I washed it!' I said 'fucking hell, what are you?' So anyway, I said 'where the fucking hell did you bury her?' she said 'you remember where the pit is under the garage where you used to work on the cars?' I said 'yeah'. She said 'well that's where she is, in there.' I said, 'fuck me, I remember you fucking filled it in, or somebody did'. 'Well', she said, 'somebody filled it in'. That was the first one at Cromwell Street. There ain't no doubt about that."

In a separate interview, he told Howard Ogden that he had taken "the Mott girl back to Stroud Road several times, and to Newent…Juanita used to come and talk to me quite regular." He insisted that he had not picked her up thumbing a lift to Gloucester from Newent. "I took the Mott girl out to Newent. She had been staying on and off for a considerable time, I think…She wanted to go to America to see her father, and I was helping her to make some money to go…giving her money when I could get a few bob on the side, without Rose knowing."

He did not deny that some of the young women who found their way to Cromwell Street suffered a terrible fate. "We used to get loads of girls – but what I didn't realise was that Rose was enticing them there…I believe the girls ended up at these parties in Bristol. They were drugged. They were sexually abused. But I don't believe they were killed there. They were taken back to wherever Rose had 'em – and then they were tortured and killed by somebody else."

He described a very different version of how Shirley Robinson died to the version he had told police, and for the first time admitted that he had done something out of jealousy. He explained clearly that he had only been trying to make his wife jealous by getting Shirley pregnant. In fact, he confessed that if Rose had not been pregnant with a black child, "Shirley probably wouldn't even have got the one she got. It was a way of getting even with Rose, I suppose, not intentionally, but that was the way it went." He went on to say: "Shirley and me had a good relationship. She loved the idea of having a baby…but Shirley conned me, and I realised after, but I never quarreled with her over it." He even confessed that she was "much like Ann McFall – happy-go-lucky, carefree – I belong to Fred and I don't care who knows it" and confirmed that he had indeed made love to her one day while they were stripping wallpaper at 7 Cromwell Street. But he added:

"What I didn't realise was that Shirley had grown fond of me…The next thing I finds out, she's only gone and told Rose…From that time on Rose fucking hated her, and you could see it. Let's be fucking honest. Shirley was madly in love with me, and I knew that. But I was trying to cool it down with her. Because it could never be nothing. From the time she said about her pregnancy I said if it ever happens it is your child…I'm not leaving Rose. I wouldn't leave my kids for another woman. That's the thing I've fought all my life – to give my kids a mother." He also knew that "Rose fucking hated Shirley. She was always going to belt her face in if her ever got hold of her. Made that quite clear to everybody."

He said that Shirley Robinson wanted him "to go to Germany with her – to meet her father, who was going to send the money for the trip", but he thought: "I ain't fucking getting mixed up with that, and that was that we had the few words about." Shortly afterwards, he recalled, the girl had turned up outside the Wagon Works factory, saying: "There's me carrying your baby and you're not bothered about me at all."…Straight in front of everybody." She also told him: "Once I have the baby, you don't want me with you." He maintained that that had been "the last time I ever seen Shirley." He then tried to blame Rose for her murder: "Rose was after Shirley… give her a good hiding. I didn't think she'd kill her. I thought she'd just give her a fucking pasting, and get rid of that baby or summat." He insisted that Rose never gave him the details of exactly how Shirley met her death. "Rose never had the time to kill Shirley at home…I am a hundred per cent sure that Shirley was not attacked at home. So where she was I don't know. Where she was killed. And how she got back there…Rose wouldn't tell me…All she said was "I sorted that bitch out. She had the full length of my arm up her cunt, and that sorted her…I had the fucking head off that bitch. I hated the look on her fucking face. It gave me great pleasure cutting her head off."

He went on to give another version of how Alison Chambers was killed and insisted that Alison, whom he still described as 'Shirley's mate', had, in fact, lived with him and his wife for "a month or more after she'd left Barnwood in Gloucester", and that she had befriended one of the lodgers. He was still placing all of the blame for the killings at his wife's door, explaining only that: "When I caught them young girls there, they'd

405

have to fucking go." He also said: "If the girl did stay at all at our place, I mean, I'm not saying she didn't because if anybody was in trouble…I helped them out the best I could with…no bad intentions whatsoever. I mean, I like people to look upon me as somebody they can trust."

Fred would stick to his story that Rose was the murderer and not him, and in what may have actually been the truth, offered how they had met their deaths. "I know how they were killed" he explained towards the end of his life. "Vibrator. Pushed in with Rose's foot. That big bastard. That's why Shirley's baby was fucking up the wrong place. I seen Rose do that to a girl once. Obviously she bound their mouths up with that fucking tape round their gobs … she'd push that vibrator in as far as she could into them, then get hold of their legs and just push it in with her foot." The vibrator in question was more than a foot in length and four inches in diameter. "She did so much damage to them with that, that she had to fucking kill them" he claimed. He said that it was this that killed Alison Chambers. He said that Rose had told him: "I put her on a bloody vibrator and let her wriggle on that" and had then confessed "And she was a beautiful young juicy thing … She hadn't been fucked much". He then asked: "Why did you kill her?" She replied: "Oh, I fancied her". He continued: "She wanted to hurt women. She'd have to, to do what she's done to them."

He then maintained that, unlike his wife, he did not enjoy group sex: "I only ever tried it once, and I didn't like it, because Rose acted too bloody vicious. What she did to that little girl (Alison Chambers) was unreal. I was making love to the girl, and Rose got a vibrator and shoved it straight up her arse. Fuck me, the girl nearly went right through the fucking wall.

I would never allow Rose to tie me up. She fucking tried for years…No way was I going to let her tie me up. I didn't believe in it, and I didn't have anything to do with it…But there was blokes doing it to her, and sometimes she'd come home and she's been well beaten, mind. She'd have no knickers on, like. She'd been fucked all day, and I'd come home from work and she'd sit deliberately on the edge of the settee with her legs wide open and…say: "Look at that…I bet you wish you had something that could fill that."…It never stopped. It didn't stop at all. There was no let-up. She used to run around naked in front of Stephen and that. She used to run around…flaunting it…She did it everywhere. "It's my cunt and I'll show it to who I want to"…She'd go and pick up any old tramp…She thought every bloke would want to fuck her, and if they didn't, she got nasty about it.

Rose didn't want the gentle part of it. She wanted some big nigger to throw her down and fucking bang on top of her, and treat her like a dog…that was sex to Rose. "I don't want any of that soppy shit," she said. "I want fucking. Not fucking about with. Or chatting up… And she'd get aggressive. Rose didn't have many women friends, because she made it too blatantly obvious she was after other things…She used to have spates in which she just couldn't get enough."

Fred had previously admitted to Howard Ogden that he "tried bondage once", when he "made that harness out of plastic, so it didn't break. The red one. I put it on her once, and even then I didn't like it."

The police approached 'Miss A' during their investigation. The first person to whom she told of her experience was Detective Constable Williams on 28th July 1994, five months after the arrest of Frederick West.

29th July 1994

Fred and Rose West appeared together at Gloucester Magistrates Court and were remanded in custody until Thursday 25th August 1994.

Fred's Probation Officer, R. W. Anderson: "Attended Gloucester Magistrates Court when he was present with Rose – mainly so I could see how they relate. Interesting both to see her reaction to him and that of his 'fan club' in Court."

Anne Marie: "Dad often wanted to talk about Ann McFall…he would tell me time and time again how much he had loved Ann. They had been planning to buy a house together and live there with me and Charmaine. I asked him: 'And did you love Mum too?'
'No,' he said. 'It was different with your mum.'
He claimed Rena hadn't loved me or Charmaine; that she didn't look after us properly and kept us filthy dirty. I didn't believe him.
Whenever Dad talked about Ann McFall he would cry. He said he was going to write a book about her. At first he wanted to write a book about my mum and said he wanted me to help him. 'I don't want anything to do with it, Dad,' I responded. 'You murdered my mum. I can't help you write

about her.'

He upset me most when he claimed that my mother had killed Ann. He said he had got home late one night from his job as a delivery driver. It was about 10 p.m. when he reached the Timberland Caravan Park in Brockworth, Gloucester, where he had been living with Ann. He said Rena and a black man were there and killed Ann between them. He told me they had cut her legs off and were trying to fit the body into a suitcase. They were hysterical and wanted to dump it on a council tip. Fred said he told them that was stupid and they begged him for help, so he took the body to Much Marcle and buried it in Fingerpost Field. I repeated that story to the police but they assured me it was nonsense.

Occasionally he would deny any involvement in the murders and say simply, 'I didn't do it. It wasn't me.'

He would never go into much detail when he did discuss the murders, but once he did tell me about a ruse Rose had used to ensnare one young girl. She told the teenager she was a seamstress and could make her a dress. When the girl came to the house Rose said: 'I can't fit you for a dress unless you take all your clothes off.' I don't know who that young girl was, or if she survived."

Fred West was advised by his legal team to refuse further police interviews.

30th July 1994

Fred West wrote to his probation officer asking him to visit. He believed that his solicitor Howard Ogden had been tape recording his interviews to sell on or release as a book at his expense and had dispensed with his services. Representation was taken over by Tony Miles of Bobbets and Mackan of Bristol.

1st August 1994

Fred West was put on 15 minute watch, as he appeared distressed after dispensing with the services of his solicitor Howard Ogden. A prison report stated: "Mr West had a serious disagreement with his solicitor and dispensed with his services. He became tearful. A Self Harm at Risk form was raised and he was seen by a Medical Officer. He was not overtly depressed and had no intent to harm himself. However, as a precaution, on Doctor James McMaster's instructions, he was placed on a 15 minute watch and returned to D3 landing."

"He said he felt his solicitor had manipulated him", Dr McMasters was to recall more than a year later. "He felt uncertain as to how he was going to cope with the court case", and "protested his innocence", claiming that "he had been telling lies to the police and not giving them full information about who he suspected was involved." As the interview wore on, Dr McMasters watched him become "calm and quite rational". After visiting Fred thirty-nine times during the next five months, he reached the conclusion that he "was not mentally ill and was not at risk of harming himself."

Janet Leach continued to visit and speak regularly with Fred West even after she had ceased to be his appropriate adult. She believed that Fred would divulge further details of victims but he never did. "Because he was having all these thoughts about Ann McFall I said to him 'well why don't you write it?' It'll be good for you to get it off your mind and it will be good to improve your writing and that's what he started to do."

Fred West would significantly confide in her. He told her that all the dead girls at 25 Cromwell Street were "some of Rose's mistakes. It was all sexual. It wasn't meant to happen". He also claimed that his younger brother John had been involved "a lot" in the abductions and murders. He even told her that there were "another twenty" victims, including the missing Mary Bastholm, whose remains were "on the farm".

Speaking in 2011, Anne Marie said: "One newspaper report claimed Janet Leach "won my father's confidence", but this was never the case. She was merely a toy, an audience to his sickness, someone new to manipulate. She was completely out of her depth dealing with a master of deceit". Rose West would get through six appropriate adults: they couldn't handle hearing all the details.

Fred West's Probation Officer, R. W. Anderson: "Telephone conversation with Howard Ogden, who has been 'sacked' by West. In fact the Court may not agree to a transfer of legal aid."

Fred wrote a letter to his son Stephen:

To Stepen and andrea

Hi Stev long time no see have you forgot your DAD I have not heard from you FOR a long time 4 week I sent you a letter, ann has cum to see me 2. Janet is cuming to see me 1 A week so cume and see me soon I have lots to tell you a bout Mr Ogden. Janet got me new solicitors My new one ar Bobbetts Mackan 20A Berkeley Square Clifton Bristol BS8 1HP Telephone 0272,299001 Mr TONY Miles, send in tobacco, My new Solicitors dont send in tobacco. I have got all My thing back the fish ar at Mr Ogden. Office and is going have them for the Girls she Will hav to Get them dont till Rose or May.

all my love DAD

see you soon SON

Fred was also being tormented by other prisoners who were harassing him. He narrowly missed being seriously injured when an inmate making tea threw boiling water at him. "Build us a patio, Fred" and "Kids getting under your feet?" they would shout at him in the exercise yard. He told someone, "I can't take it anymore." As he appeared distressed a self-harm at Risk Form was again raised.

3rd August 1994

Fred West was visited by his probation officer, R. W. Anderson. "I asked if that was a wise decision (sacking Howard Ogden) and he said it was – and not before time. I felt the reason he has sacked his solicitor was because he wanted to go back to the beginning and start again developing a new story which he did. While he rambles at length he is now clearly suggesting that Rose,**** concreted the cellar and probably did all the murders. He denies any involvement with any of it at all. He seemed to me to be trying out a new story.

4th August 1994

Fred West's Probation Officer, R. W. Anderson: "****rang to say she has contacted the police as he had been talking to her and prison officers about assisting in the disposal of some bodies but denied this in front of me yesterday."

By now, Fred's demeanour had improved. He was cheerful, communicating well with staff and it was felt safe to withdraw the 15 minute observation.

Fred wrote a series of letters to Stephen:

To Stephen and andrea

Hi Boy you lette me down on satday it you cant cume to see me Ring the Prison and say you cant Make it. it makes it look bad on me. so please Boy ring in, hows andrea gitting on with the Babys its not long be for she will have them I did not see you in court have you seen May When you do tell her dad love her and tell her to Wite to me or cum and see me do you no mum is going for a Oldstill trial so she cud get out of it cud you send me sum moor tobacco and Batteries in When you can, do you see Tara if you do tell her to write to Dad and tell me all a bout her son and her and give her a kiss and cuddle from Dad Will Love you Boy give andrea My love and tell her it not long now be for she Will have the babys to play With. Well Boy Write soon or cum and see me

all my love to you

and andrea

all Ways in my thoughts

Dad.

Fred again wrote to Stephen:

To my Boy Stephen

I no you love your DAD he loved you I have a new Solicitors Bobbetts Mackan I have a team of 7.

have you seen May tell her, dad wood lick to see her I ham her DAD and I love

411

her. but she no that I forgive her for watt she said to THE police a bout me but I no
Rose did that. cume and see me soon (Two sentences removed on legal grounds.)
I Wanted to tell the truth give my love to May tell her to cum and see me soon. X

give me love to ANDREAx

love DAD.

Two investigative reporters from the Daily Mail, Paul Henderson and
Stephen Wright, reported that Fred's former solicitor Howard Ogden had
been offering the tapes he had made of conversations with Fred West, as
well as photographs of Cromwell Street, to filmmakers and agents.
According to them, the asking price for the material was £500,000.

Fred instructed his new solicitors to take out an injunction preventing
Howard Ogden from using the information and the courts ordered him to
hand over the tapes, letters, clothing and photographs in his possession.

14th August 1994

Scott Canavan, Howard Ogden's legal clerk who had sat in on some of
Fred West's police interviews, gave an interview to The News of The
World. He told the newspaper that he had quit the practice and he had no
legal qualifications but had been convicted of burglary, assault and criminal
damage. He claimed that he had only been employed by Howard Ogden a
matter of days before being asked to sit in on the interviews. "I was
surprised to be left in charge of such a big case. It was nerve-racking. My
only experience of court was sitting in the dock. Yet I was present for about
80% of the interviews and Mr Ogden about 20%."

He said he was offered the job after Howard Ogden represented him
in court on a charge of stealing potatoes. "He once said to someone else
who came to work for him who was good looking that he was hoping he
was gay. Then he turned to me and said 'That's why I employed you'.

When I first started I had one day's training in Bristol. All it
compromised of was a lecture given by a lawyer and a couple of workshop
sessions on what to do when people were arrested. Then I was on my own.
The job entailed sitting in with clients who had been arrested usually for
fairly petty crime.

412

I was with Fred more or less every day for the first six weeks or so that he was in custody. During interviews I was stunned by what I heard. It was nothing like the cases I had been dealing with. I couldn't grasp the enormity of it. And I was shocked when I heard some of the details.

Howard would pop in and see him sometimes but was hardly ever there. I was surprised he was not with him. Even at that time, right at the beginning, Howard was talking about how it was going to make him a fortune. Howard bought a diary and was keeping notes of witty comments that Fred made. He was gathering anecdotes ready for when the story was sold. Howard had dollar signs in his eyes from the start. He was talking about books and film rights. He used to mention it in front of Fred.

There was one Sunday night early on when Fred called Howard to see him at the police station. He was worried that Howard was more in it for himself. But Howard talked him out of sacking him that time.

I was present for about 80% of the police interviews, but the tapes Howard's been trying to sell were recorded privately by him much later when Fred had been charged with all the murders and was in custody in prison. Howard would visit him there and make the recordings. I was not present and I haven't heard what's on those tapes."

Scott Canavan then said that Howard Ogden got Fred to sign a confidentiality waiver two or three weeks in to the case. "Howard thought he'd landed the big one and the world was his oyster. Howard told him he would write the book and Fred said 'Do it then. Tell the true story and make sure the kids are okay with the proceeds'."

He went on to state that the stress of the case led to him drinking. "Howard noticed that I was not doing the job up to scratch at this time. It was at the bank holiday at the end of May and he told me he thought I had a problem with the drinking and I should have the rest of the week off." It was during this week off that the letter written by Howard Ogden to Fred West was stolen and he was later arrested.

While Scott was on police bail, he was suspended from his job without pay and he never returned to work for him. "I was never dismissed, we just sort of parted company." Scott later began five weeks of psychiatric counselling at Charlton Lane Hospital in Cheltenham.

Howard Ogden, however, said that he took Scott off the case "because of his drinking. He admitted he was an alcoholic and had a history of psychological problems, none of which he had revealed to me when I employed him." When he was asked if it was true that Scott had represented Fred West 80% of the time he replied: "No way was it anything like that."

Mae West claimed that her dad was tricked by his solicitor. "I think Howard Ogden is just a money-grabbing git. He tricked my father into signing an agreement when he was at his lowest ebb. It was at a weak point when he was giving statements to the police. Dad thought Ogden would get him off the murder charges and he would have given him anything. But how could Ogden be doing his best for my dad when his deals would almost certainly have hinged on him being convicted?"

24th August 1994

Fred's probation officer received a letter from him informing him of his change in solicitors. His probation officer had been busy and unable to visit after Fred's last request so Fred outlined the reason for his previous letter and blamed Howard Ogden for not letting him tell 'the truth'.

25th August 1994

Rose and Fred West again appeared at Gloucester Magistrates Court and were remanded in custody until the 22nd September. Fred was checked over at HMP Birmingham Health Care Centre on his return.

In a meeting, Fred informed Dr James McMaster that Rose had been running a brothel and had tried to murder him. He also said that Heather had dug her own grave and that Rose had been burying people without his knowledge and preparing the children for prostitution.

Fred wrote to Stephen:

To Stephen & andrea

Watt you Boy I have not herd from you have you seen May or Rose or Tara have you got a car of van, how is andrea getting on with the Babys is she Having problems With her pregnant How far pregnant is she a Boy and a Girl Wood be nice have you got names for them, how ar you gating on With Derek as he still got cowboy Working for him, can you send me sum Batteries R6 and sum tobacco When you can have you seen

Tara Baby anna cam to see me and Janet, I Wood love may to Write to me May nows about Rose, I Was her true friend never mind I have got you and Tara, I Wish andrea all the Best and send my love to her see you soon, all my love

DAD

Fred later wrote to Stephen again:

To Stephen – andrea

you Wer not in court on thursday it Went Well, My new Solicitors brilliant he sorted that court out Rose Luckd Well, is MAy seeing Rose tell May to Write to me. I did not see Anna in court to see Janet. Well congratulate on twins first time that's one up on your Dad dont mack habit of it babys cost Money lots of Money Make shor you love them. and your Wife, dont spend all your Time at Work. I did that and luck What went on at home. Money is not everything your home and family is. Well congratulation on pasting your driving test the first time have you told the Police. I had a visit from Janet on friday morning anna is cuming to see me see you soon all my love DAD.

give you a x from me

Stevphen tell May to tell Rose the thing anna has is for Me so no one sell it, it Will be sorted out after the court case Mr Ogden was going to keep it for me but he Was going to sell it, tell May I love and and I Wont her to cume and see me or Write to me I Will Write to her if she sends me her address or PHONE number I Will ring her it Will be after 700 till 830 at night, a buout the fish no one Wanted them so Way cant Carol and Michelle May loves anna Michelle and Carol I no that and May no it to, it time all of you got to gather and protect your own brother and sisters that all you got of your passed, so Boy see May and tell her to stop I love you all. Rose is Bracking you up and you all helping Rose to do it. Rose love Rose not you lot. You no that.

8th September 1994

Gloucestershire Police applied to the Home Office for financial assistance (£651,000) in relation to the Cromwell Street enquiry.

Stephen: "Near the end, he was still sticking to the story that someone else had done it, but said he'd had a little part to do with it. The truth was mixed with so many lies. He said he had stabbed Ann McFall in the caravan

415

site at Brockworth because he loved her and couldn't have her, or something.

The next time I saw him I mentioned I had seen the brother of one of the victims, Mary Bastholm, on the TV. I said: 'You don't know anything about it do you?' And he looked to the ground. I said they were going to go into the café and knock this wall down which he had built. He said: 'It's a waste of time looking there.' I went really cold. I didn't know what he meant. I said: 'Why's that?' and then Dad said he didn't know anything.

We carried on talking and he said they are just going to have to carry on finding the rest out themselves. 'I'm fed up with helping them…I'll be out of here in 12 years and we'll all go back to live again in Cromwell Street. If they find any more bodies I'll never get out. Why should I help them? What are they going to do for me?'

Rose wrote to Mae:

Hi Darling,

Thought I would drop you a line and tell you I love you, and how much I really enjoyed your visit. It's just great chatting to you, and you leave me with a wonderful feeling of warmth and security. You not only tolerate me, but believe in me too! You are very special to me. I hope you had a nice break in London, but of course you did. Being close to the one you love makes the world a much better place. I can't tell you just how happy it makes me to know you have someone for whom you care so much. He's a lovly person.

There's a lovly song they play on the radio, it's called You Don't Know, sung by Helen Shapiro, I think it's very apt. Every now and then they play a piece of music from Wathering Heights. It's called Tara's Theme, it's beautiful and I allway's think of you know who. Who's going soft then. Thanks for the poster, it's great and I'v put it up on my pin board. So now I can show you off. I was wondering, if you could give Barb's? address, she's a loving person, and we have been good friends in the past. I thought I might write to her and let her know I'm O.K. I'll leave you now, take care of yourself.

Love as allway's

Mum

Xxxxx

416

Xxxx

P.S. Has Steve sent a card.

22nd September 1994

Fred and Rose West appeared at Gloucester Magistrates Court. Both were remanded in custody until 20th October 1994.

29th September 1994

Fred West's Probation Officer, R. W. Anderson: "His new solicitors rang me. Basically wanted to know why probation are involved. Explained function and Home Office Instruction. Also concerned that I was friendly with previous solicitor who is charged with malpractice – explained I knew him for many years as colleague on Cheltenham Courts but have never been to his home or had a drink with him – i.e friendly professional relationship. Confirmed I have had no contact with him since he was sacked by Fred.

Visited H.M.P. Birmingham where I saw him for well over two hours (1.15 – 3.45pm) with **** Probation Officer at the prison. He talked at length about his childhood and younger years. Seemed more depressed, more likely to cry for no apparent reason and more into a Mills and Boon vision of the world. I think his personality grows ever more fragile."

Fred West's cell was searched by prison officers who were looking for contraband. They found 2 pepper sachets, one photo and excess tablets which were removed and destroyed.

6th October 1994

A fourth statement intended to clarify Caroline Owens' relationship with the other lodgers (in other words to admit sexual contact) was given.

Fred West's Probation Officer, R. W. Anderson: "I have now seen him on four occasions and since he changed his solicitor these interviews have been able to run from 1.15pm until 3.45pm as I am the only visitor on the day. I have also regular liaison with ****, Probation Officer at

H.M.P.Winson Green who sits in on all the interviews. In addition, despite his claims to be illiterate, I have two letters from Fred.

During interviews he rambles somewhat, usually talking about his early life, childhood, loves and relationships. He tells stories in great detail, elaborating on exact locations, car number plates etc. I tend to let him ramble because it gives me an opportunity to listen to him, establish some rapport and extract some of the repetitive strands to build a picture. This is still largely impressionistic but nonetheless useful.

There are some difficulties in the joint interview approach as **** tends to be confrontative whereas I prefer to leave him to say whatever he wishes while I build a picture of him.

My gut feeling is that he is becoming more depressed and more fragile. I feel he rushes more easily to tears and his professed view of the world is becoming ever more 'Mills and Boon'. A world in which he is ever the stereotypic gentleman, opening car doors for young ladies, helping them courteously, making love but never having sex.

In his early country years he relates to his 'friends' the badgers and foxes.

Fred sacked his original solicitor (Howard Ogden), who contacted me at the time knowing I was visiting that day but I have not heard from him since. I have known (Howard) for years as a colleague working the Cheltenham Courts so I shall miss that contact. However, it is probably better to have a more clearly formal relationship with the defence solicitor.

I will continue to visit about every six to eight weeks to establish a relationship and gather information. I liaise with the prison Probation Officer, with Social Services where appropriate and other agencies. I am largely playing it by ear at this point and my main worry is that Fred will escape into total fantasy before I can put together a balanced view of him and events."

Two days later, surveyors from Gloucester City Council listed 25 Cromwell Street as dangerous.

20th October 1994

Fred and Rose West appeared at Gloucester Magistrates' Court. Both were remanded in custody until 15th November 1994. Fred West was checked over at HMP Birmingham Health Care Centre on his return from court.

During November, Fred wrote more letters to his children:

Fred wrote to Mae:

To may West

   Hi May it your Dad Writeing to you. or lette me have your telephone number I can phone you at night from 700 to 800 or Write to me as soon you can, please may I have to sort out what Mr Ogden did to me, my new solicitors are Brilliant I Read What you seas about me in News of the   that was loylty you read watt Scott canavan sead He had 1 day training 3 weeks be for. ar you Working Stevphen sead you have a car Watt is it, about anna I now Watt anna is doing I Will sort that out I gave the fish to Michelle and carol, the Bar is in storage I did not no your address, Steven was on honeymoon, that how anna got to no about it I did not no anna had thing from Cromwell ST you or stevphen nos about Watt see wonted I was told Rose sed yes to Tara having it, I have not herd Watt Rose Wanted to do With the House I have been told By my solicitors not to sell it Till after the court, Give, Tara, my Love and her Baby Boys May Dad love you We had go time   all I Love and x

Fred also wrote to Stephen and Andrea:

To Stephen & Andrea

   I got your photos of you wedding thy ar Beautiful son. andrea and May looks stunning you were or Write. HA, HA, son have you seen Tara and hur babys son if you see them give them all my love I got the batteries and tobacco and £20 thankyou son. have you sent your mum photos of your Wedding I bet andrea is getting very bige is it 2 babys or moor HAHA that my Boy, get may to Write me I hame allways thinking of you all. I may be in High Court in London to give evidence against Mr Ogden in December.

Gave My love to

Andrea,

Love Dad xxx

PS My Book is cuming on Well tel you moor about it When I see you have you and May dun your, the Books called I Was loved By an angel

9th November 1994

Fred West's cell was searched by prison officers again looking for contraband. They found excess food which was removed.

15th November 1994

Fred and Rose West reappeared at Gloucester Magistrates' Court. Both were remanded in custody until 13th December 1994. Fred West was checked over at HMP Birmingham Health Care Centre on his return.

Fred wrote to Stephen:

Hi son

I got your letter and the batteries and tobaco. I ham sorry to hear that andrea has been in hospital there no need to cum to see me you need to stay with andrea, she needs all the help you can give hur. andrea cand go in to premature labour at anytime so you need to be with her son and When she has the babys no Working all day and night like I did or you cud end up in hear, all ways no What going on in your home pliase son all Ways spend as much time With your Wife and children as you can and love your Wife and children, there the most valuable thing you will ever have in your life so look after it son, When you see May or Tara tell them to Write to me and tell them I love them. so please son look after andrea and tell her it will be all worth it give my love to andrea,

I Will be all Ways thinking of you

all my love son

Dad

25th November 1994

DSI Bennett arranged a meeting at Winson Green Prison to discuss

Fred West's security. Also in attendance was DCI Terry Moore, the Constabulary's Prison Liaison Officer, Detective Sergeant Jan Blomfield, and Home Office Prison Liaison Officer, Detective Inspector John Kerr. Their meeting was with Deputy Governor Polkinghorn. DSI Bennett raised a number of issues about Fred and his custody before moving on to his conversation with Anne Marie and their concerns over his mental state. The Deputing Governor assured DSI Bennett that Fred West was a model prisoner. He had settled down well, was the 'best pool player on the landing' and went by the name of 'Digger'.

Fred's mental health was failing and he wrote a journal which addressed Janet Leach of his impending suicide: "I have gone to Anna, Heather, Charmaine, Rena, Shirley and my two unborn children who never had a chance to see life or I to see or hold them ... I know how the families feel, I lost 5 in this tragedy". He also wrote a letter to Rose, declaring: "The most wonderful thing in my life is that I met you. How our love was special to us" and he told her that he wanted to be buried beside her and asked: "Lay Heather by us, we loved Heather". Neither of these were ever posted.

27ᵗʰ November 1994

Fred and Rose West's solicitors were concerned as to how their clients were being portrayed in the media. The comedian Billy Connolly released a video which contained references and jokes about the West's which insinuated that they were guilty, and as such, they tried to get the video banned. Rose's solicitor Leo Goatley said: "I am very concerned. My client, who denies all charges against her, deserves a fair trial – and Billy Connolly isn't helping. It seems needless to make these wisecracks about our clients at this time. It's disgraceful and shocking. As far as I am concerned it's a fragrant breach of the contempt of court laws and the video should be withdrawn and edited, removing references to the Wests."

Mae West commented: "It's terrible. It's not a joking matter. I want my parents to have a fair trial. That is their right."

December 1994

Fred wrote letters to Stephen and Tara:

To stephen and andrea

Will Boy Been a father is not so easy is it, nut the babys Will make it all Worth it Will Boy I was allways on to about Been to hard on your girl friends by wonting to no what they were doing all the time Will you got it right I had it Wrong look What your Mother Was up, you were telling me to sort her out or throw her out, and you Wood not have a Wife like her. but not one of you told me What was going on at home. if I hade not Work all day and night I did What I thought was right for you all. Well that enough of my problems just mack sure andrea gets all the help she wonts but remember a mother nose her baby Best, and don't you work all day and night spend has much time as you can With your children by the time you get this letter you will be a dad gave my love to andrea and all my Best Wishes to her and tell andrea it Will be Worth it all I Will be thinking of you all

all my love Dad.

The second letter read:

to Tara

Well Tara your baby son is Beautiful just like you darling pleas look after my grandson allways be With him tell him is grampy love him and give him a big kiss and cuddle for me, thank you Tara for the PHOTOS of you and (Boy F). it Will take me about twelve to eighteen months Well Tara you no your Dad as never harm anyone I loved you all and that May and I will Write to you soon

Aa my thoughts ar With you

Tara, love Dad.xxxxxxxx

(a big x) FOR (BOY F)

6th December 1994

Chief Constable Tony Butler was informed that the Home Office would not provide any financial help for the Gloucestershire Constabulary in respect of the Cromwell Street investigation.

9th December 1994

Stephen's wife Andrea gave birth to twins, a boy and a girl, on December 9th. They gave an interview to The News of the World which was published on the 11th December. Stephen said: "The girl has got Mum's long thin fingers and the boy has got Dad's pointed-up nose. We've decided to call the girl Jessica Rose after Mum and the boy Andrew James. Despite everything, I didn't see why I shouldn't. She will always be my mum. Andrea and I agreed it would be nice. I didn't feel I could so easily do it on my dad's side. I thought about it, but it could have led to problems."

10th and 11th December 1994

On the 10th and 11th of December, the coroner wrote to the families of the victims and stated:

"I have reluctantly to write to tell you and all other relatives and next of kin of the victims concerned in the Frederick West enquiry, to say that despite repeated attempts to reach agreement for the release of the remains, I have so far been unsuccessful... Unfortunately I shall have to leave the matter over the Christmas period in view of the contentions put forward by those acting for Mr West but you may rest assured that I will reconsider the position early in the New Year and may well take further advice as to whether, notwithstanding the lack of agreement, in view of my duty to all the relatives and indeed, of course, to the public at large, grounds may exist for me to release the remains irrespective of the wishes of those defending Mr West."

13th December 1994

Fred and Rose West appeared for the last time together at Gloucester Magistrates Court and were remanded in custody. They were separated by two female police officers and Rose West ignored her husband. She refused to even make eye contact with him. She went so far as to inform the officers to tell her husband that she did not wish to speak to him. The Committal hearing date was fixed for 6th of February 1995 at Dursley Magistrates' Court.

When Rose came into the court, Tina West, one of the officers in the dock separating her and Fred, had tried to draw DSI Bennett's attention to a length of wool that was tied in a large bow in the buttonhole of her cardigan. When the two women were out of sight of the court the police officer asked what it meant. "It's to help me remember something!" was all Rose would say but it led to speculation that it might have been a sign to her husband that she had not betrayed him and to remind him to stay faithful to her. While no one knew for sure, it remained a topic for debate, as the couple were known to communicate by sending signals to one another.

Until now, the families of the victims had been told nothing except their daughters had been murdered and buried. They had been spared the detail of dismemberment, tape masks and rope. DSI Bennett had always promised he would tell the relatives when the time was right. With the committal a matter of weeks away, that time was fast approaching.

20th December 1994

Fred West's prison notes state: "Gov. Polkinhorne's instructions from 25th December 1994 and each <u>Sunday</u> thereafter. His telephone tape will be submitted to security and replaced by a new tape and so on. The tape will be signed over to security i.e. DW Staff and security to sign for it."

22nd December 1994

Fred West was visited by his Probation Officer, R. W. Anderson. They spent about three hours talking. According to the probation officer: "On that occasion, he talked at length about his time in Scotland with his first wife and others. Discussed his time in Scotland with Rena, Ann McFall, who was Rena's nanny,**** who worked for Fred on his Mr. Whippy van. Talked about accident where he reversed his Mr. Whippy van over a four year-old child he was fond of. Also charge of assault on Rena he was cleared of. He also mapped out his childrens' names and ages for me. My record states of that visit: …He was also not happy when I told him I could now only visit once every three months – he said he enjoyed talking to me, could trust me and felt he was being cut off from everyone he could talk to. I said I would see if I could negotiate more frequent contact. Overall he seemed in good spirits and perhaps more lucid and focused than he had been before."

Just before the turn of the year, Fred wrote a note to Rose, but never sent it:

To Rose,

I loved you forever. I made mistakes. I am so upset about you being in prison. Please keep your promise to me. I have kept mine.

I can't tell what I know. You are all free to go on with whatever you want to, but think of what I did for you all, and never complain. I love all of my children. They were all mine.

All my love and kisses to you darling,

Fred.

1st January 1995

Fred West was found dead in his cell at HM Prison Winson Green, shortly after 1pm. In the morning, Fred had acted perfectly normally. He ate his breakfast and was seen by a doctor. He had no problems or complaints. At lunchtime he collected his meal and returned to his cell. He was last seen at around 12.30 by prison officer Lee Hutchins, who said that Fred had been cheerful and had made a joke about the small size of the chicken legs that were served for lunch. On unlock after the lunchtime patrol period he was discovered at 13.05 hanging by his neck behind the door. Prison Officer Martin Harrison tried to open his door as normal but felt something behind the door obstructing him. He called for assistance. They managed to push the door open between them. They found him hanging by his neck behind the door. His feet were off the ground. A third prison officer arrived almost immediately. He lifted Fred West by the legs, while one of the other two untied the ligature. A third officer returned to the landing office to summon medical assistance urgently. The two officers with Fred West put him on to the bed and began resuscitation. A Staff Nurse was the first to arrive from the health care side. She entered the cell and felt for a pulse. She could see that Fred West was grey and his lips blue.

She judged that there was nothing more they could do. They all withdrew from the cell. Shortly after this, a Health Care Senior Officer arrived, entered the cell and checked Fred West for vital signs. There were none and she withdrew. At 13.30, a doctor arrived and examined Fred West. Although the body was still warm and there was no sign of rigor mortis, there was no sign of life. At 13.40, he pronounced Fred West to be dead.

During the afternoon the Police attended the prison and began their enquiry on behalf of the coroner. Fred West's body left the prison at 18.22.

He had stitched strips of the green blanket from his bed into a rope using the needle and thread he had been given for his job of sewing buttons on prison shirts. He hanged himself from a bar on the ventilation shaft above the door. He did not die at once, but strangled himself "for a minute or two", hanging a few feet above the floor. At 13.54 Gloucester Police were informed. At 14.20 Rose West was informed at Pucklechurch.

In Fred's cell, a note was discovered:

To Rose West, Steve and Mae,

Well Rose it's your birthday on 29 November 1994 and you will be 41 and still beautiful and still lovely and I love you. We will always be in love.

The most wonderful thing in my life was when I met you. Our love is special to us. So, love, keep your promises to me. You know what they are. Where we are put together for ever and ever is up to you. We loved Heather, both of us. I would love Charmaine to be with Heather and Rena.

You will always be Mrs. West, all over the world. That is important to me and to you.

I haven't got you a present, but all I have is my life. I will give it to you, my darling. When you are ready, come to me. I will be waiting for you.

At the bottom of the note found in his cell was a drawing of a gravestone, within which was written: 'In loving memory. Fred West. Rose West. Rest in peace where no shadow falls. In perfect peace he waits for Rose his wife.'

Scrawled on the wall of the cell were the words "Freddy, the mass murderer from Gloucester".

The Governor, G Gregory-Smith gave a detailed report on the level of surveillance on the day:

Along with other Category A prisoners Fred West was regularly checked by landing staff when in his cell (on average every ¾ hour – sometimes less).

On the day of his death West was physically checked at the following times:

07.15 – Checked at unlock
07.20 – Approximately – clothing box given to him.
07.40 – Approximately – opened for breakfast
08.15 – Approximately – opened for cleaning of eating utensils and cell.
West was regularly checked by 3 landing staff at least once every half hour until: -
10.15 – Exercise (rub-down search) – supervised on exercise
11.15 – Returned to his cell (rub-down search)
11.15-11.45 – Cell opened up and served with dinner.
12.00 – Physical roll check
12.30 – A physical check for staff handover.
13.05 – Found dead in cell when opened up for cleaning utensils.

A later report said that after collecting his lunch: "There is just a chance that he may have seen an article published in The Mail…In any event it is less sensational than much other media coverage, although it does present Mr West's previous solicitor in a favourable light."

The doctor who attended the prison cell where Fred West was found stated: "I am not a regular Doctor at the prison. I provide on call cover particularly at the weekend. I have seen Mr West several times during my routine visits. I saw Mr West on Saturday and Sunday this weekend. There was nothing unusual. I was very surprised that he hanged himself. When I arrived he was lying on the bed. There was no pulse – no breathing – no movement. There was no sign of life although his body was warm. He did not respond to painful stimuli. His pupils were fixed and dilated. I pronounced him dead. I arrived at the prison within 15 minutes or so. From my knowledge of Mr West he was not a suicide risk."

Paul Leach, Janet's 18-year-old son, later recalled when Janet Leach had just been informed that Fred West had hanged himself. He said he found his mother sobbing in her bedroom. "I've never seen a woman so heartbroken. She was hysterical, screaming and crying her eyes out. She disappeared for a couple of days after finding out about his death. She couldn't handle it.

Later, I found all my mother's papers in the house. They included the diary where he drew the map of where the bodies were. It was so revolting to see that. I couldn't handle it. My life has been tainted by my mother's involvement with Fred West".

Janet Leach insisted she broke down "not in grief but in pure unadulterated anger" because Fred had told her there were at least 20 bodies to be found and she was overcome with anguish that she would never get to the truth of the matter. She said that all the time she spent with him listening to his perversions and feeling sick at the thought of them she thought she was helping. "I was desperate. I couldn't sleep at night. I kept having nightmares about all those poor girls in the cellar. But I felt I had to keep talking to Fred. Otherwise, how would their families ever know what had happened to them?"

Mae West heard the news of her father's suicide on the car radio as she drove to Oxford to meet a friend. She pulled in at a layby and sobbed for half an hour. "I got bored with the tapes I was playing and turned on the radio. I heard the name Fred West and thought it was just something about the case. Then they said, 'He was found dead in his cell this morning'. I thought I'd misheard it but it was repeated and I can't describe how I felt. I was crying, crying so hard. Luckily, I saw a layby and pulled in immediately. I sat there in a daze hoping I hadn't heard the news correctly. I went completely white. I was shaking. I shouted out 'No, dad, why?' I cried uncontrollably for half an hour. I tried to hate him, but I don't think I can. It's as if we can't escape the past. Our destiny is always to be haunted by tragedy and death. It seems like a curse has been put on the family which will never be lifted.

I don't know what normal is anymore. I reckon normal would bore me. My life is going to seem pretty dull when everything has settled down again. Sometimes I feel as if I've lived 100 years. I look in the mirror and find it hard to believe how short a life I've had but how much has happened. If this is all a nightmare then, please God, let me wake up now."

Mae would later say: "I refused to see Dad in prison. I thought that I'd wait until after the trial and when he gets life, I'll visit him just the once, but after I found out he killed himself I felt a bit guilty because I didn't reply to any of his letters and I wouldn't speak to him."

Anne Marie only found out that her father had died via a phone call from one of her mother's relatives. She was so upset she started to drink a mixture of spirits to numb the pain and took double her prescribed medication by mistake. She insisted on seeing her Uncle Doug and his wife Christine in Much Marcle and her partner Phil eventually agreed to take her.

When they arrived Christine gave her another drink and all she could think to do was to apologise to everyone there.

When her partner eventually got her home she took yet more tablets and not long after her partner Phil took her to Gloucester Hospital to have her stomach pumped. The hospital psychiatrist didn't want her released and threatened to have her committed, but later her doctor's wife, also a psychiatrist there, agreed that she would be better off at home.

Chris Davis (Anne Marie's estranged husband): "He will rot in hell for what he did. He deserves everything that is waiting for him. They say 'an eye for an eye, a tooth for a tooth' and Fred West has had what was coming to him. Personally, I think they should have thrown him to the parents and relatives of the victims."

Katherine Halliday recalled: "I was angry when I found out about Fred topping himself because he had taken the cowards way out. He wasn't going to get his bit of just rewards."

Doug West: "He was a fool to do it. He took the easy way out, didn't he?"

Christine West: "We are devastated. What a terrible way to start the New Year. We still can't believe all that has happened. The Fred we remember is a kind, gentle family man."

Samantha West recalled: "I saw my dad's face when he got the phone call and it broke my heart. No matter what he did he was still his brother and he never got the chance to talk to him. He never got the chance to find out why or ask him anything."

Joan Owen, Alison Chambers' mother, gave an interview to the Daily Mirror: "This is the only good thing Fred West ever did. I don't think he will go to hell because you need to have a spirit to go there. Anyone who can do what he did and then walk around and act as if nothing happened is truly evil.

The police have still got my Alison's body and we haven't been able to bury her properly. I'm hoping this may speed things up a bit. I was really shocked when I heard West was dead, but now it is beginning to sink in. In a way I would have preferred him to come to trial because then he would have been confronted with what he did. But although I consider myself to be a good Christian, I have to say I am glad he is dead."

Fred's solicitor Tony Miles said: "When we saw him just before Christmas there was nothing in his manner which gave us cause for concern. Anybody facing charges of this nature is understandably under considerable pressure and would require close supervision, particularly over Christmas and the New Year. It is very surprising that at lunchtime on a supervised wing a tragic event of this nature can occur."

John McLachlan, Rena's former lover in Glasgow, told The Sun: "I'm glad the bastard did it. He should have hanged himself years ago. I'd have done it myself if I'd got near him in court. I'd have cut his throat. What he has done is the coward's way out, but he knew he had no chance in court."

Ruth Brazier, the great aunt of Carol Cooper, said: "News of West's death is the best possible start to the New Year. Carol's end at his hands does not bear thinking about. I'm pleased he is dead but suicide was too good for him."

Peter Bastholm, Mary's brother, said: "It is almost as if he has cheated everyone. I never wished him dead – I wanted him to stand trial and rot in jail."

Isa McNeil, now 47 and friend of both Ann McFall and Rena Costello, said: "I can't believe it. He deserved everything that was coming to him. Now he won't stand trial."

2nd January 1995

In interviews with various newspapers, many people had come forward and were openly shocked that Fred West had been charged with such crimes and had then committed suicide. To them, he seemed just an ordinary, hardworking man.

Charlie Keen, who lived at 21 Cromwell Street, said: "I've been here 32 years. Fred had been here for 21 years. I've known him ever since he's been here. If you asked anybody in the street you couldn't wish for a better fellow. He's quiet. He'd do any jobs for anybody. Fred was very quiet spoken, he never raised his voice, never got in a temper. He was a kind man. He thought the world of his kids…I think the children were happy, they all sounded very jolly."

Michael Newman became friendly with Fred West when they were neighbours at Lake House Caravan Site. "I recall him as very hardworking. We used to call him the man who couldn't stop working".

Christine West: "The odd times when we went there (25 Cromwell Street), Fred was always playing with the kids. He was gentle and he would scrabble around on the floor giving them piggybacks. He would shout at his kids to correct them if they had done wrong. But there was no violence. He wouldn't slap them."

Doug West: "I spoke to him on the phone at Christmas last year. He was working almost round the clock as a service heating engineer for some firm but nothing seemed to get him down. If he had work to do he would do it. He was not someone who would sit in the house. He was always on the go. He used to do a lot for the ethnic minorities and half the time he was being paid in food because they couldn't spare the money. Fred would do anything for anybody. If he had a shilling and you wanted it, Fred would give it to you. He didn't seem hard up. He always seemed to have money and if he wanted something he always seemed to get it. Everything that has happened is a mystery to me."

Christine West: "Fred and Rosemary seemed to get on well. Fred was a real family man. He always seemed to be proud of his kids. He was always talking about them. He used to take them off for weekend caravan holidays in Wales. He had a camper van with a caravan on the back and they went to the South Wales holiday resorts. Very often Fred would take the children to school before he went to work. If they came home with a good school report he would praise them. Sometimes they came out to the country to see us and we used to play football or cricket in the orchard behind the cottage. Fred was very quiet, like Heather. He didn't drink and seemed to worship his wife. The worst thing of all was Heather. Shocked isn't the word. We just thought she had gone away to a holiday camp to work. Her name was not mentioned much but Fred's dad used to ask after her. I was watching the TV news when they said police were digging up a garden in Cromwell Street. I thought – Fred lives in Cromwell Street. Then the next bulletin showed a digger in his garden with the fence ripped up. I still can't believe it. I think we are in a never-ending nightmare."

Doug West said: "I would like to say how sorry I am to all those who have suffered as a result of what my brother did."

In the New Year's honours list, DC Hazel Savage was made a Member of the Order of the British Empire.

Rose West's solicitor, Leo Goatley, claimed the charges against Rose West were now "even flimsier" following her husband's death. He said: "I have always felt that the case against her was flimsy and it is even flimsier now. Because they were jointly charged, everything that Fred has said would have come out in court and would have challenged Rose. If it had been put to a jury it could have prejudiced her case. He started out saying he knew nothing about it, but when he was confronted with the reality of what was buried at Cromwell Street, he made a truthful and candid admission and that included a statement that Rose had nothing to do with it."

He went on to tell how Rose said: "Now there's no-one left to hate", when he told her of Fred's suicide. "She didn't want anything more to do with him. I think death has exorcised her anger."

He then told of the effects the recent events had on their children Stephen and Mae. "It is a very difficult time for them – they have got very mixed emotions about their father's death. They have always stood by Rosemary and they were certainly not going to be prosecution witnesses against her. She had rationalised that Fred was a split personality and there was a dark side to him which she had not known anything about. She did know he was a rascal, he used to get into trouble in one way or another over the years, but she also knew him as a hard worker and a breadwinner."

A report in The Sun quoted Anne Marie as saying: "Dad was sick. He had to be sick to do those things. He was my dad and I loved him. No matter what people do you cannot turn away from your own parents. Keeping in touch with him does not mean in any way that I condoned anything he might have done. But he had no one else so I had to stick by him. My feelings have always been for the relatives of the victims because after all I am one too. My father stood accused of killing my sister Charmaine, half-sister Heather and the mother I believed had abandoned us all those years ago." She said she was not shocked at his suicide. "I thought this could happen. He was more and more unstable every time I saw him."

Stephen Palmer, an engineer who had been in Winson Green Prison with Fred West but was released just before Christmas, said: "I just can't believe he was given the chance to do himself in. West was watched day and night by the screws and wasn't given any space. West wore standard-issue prison uniform and had a Category A cell to himself. It had a toilet and sink, but the rest was virtually bare. He was detested by all the other inmates and almost every thug in the place was dying to get their hands on him. At lights-out his cell was carefully checked and sometimes it was turned over with a fine tooth comb. The first time I plucked up the courage to speak to him I asked him how he was and he just looked up at me with an icy grin and said: 'Go away!' Then he smiled like a maniac and continued polishing his boots. He was so unemotional. He never seemed particularly depressed, but then again he never seemed particularly anything at all. He was just sort of neutral. I was surprised to hear he had killed himself."

Marie Gardner, 22, told the Daily Express how she had made a pact with Heather not to say anything about the abuse she had been suffering. "I wish I had done something at the time – then Heather might still be alive. I think she knew something was going to happen to her when she left school. She was the best friend anyone could have wished for. We told each other secrets. One day we were talking about our fathers. She said that what she was about to tell me wasn't to go any further – it was to be our pact. Then she told me that her dad used to touch her sexually and when she complained he would hit her. Sometimes I saw the bruises on her legs and I had an idea where they came from but I never did anything about it. She told me she hated her father so much that sometimes she couldn't bring herself to go home. She would ring home and say she had a detention – but she didn't really. It was an excuse to just get away and stay with me. The last time I saw Heather was just after our exams and she seemed fine. A few months later, I saw her brother Stephen and he told me she had run away to work in a holiday camp. I didn't suspect anything because she always said she would run away and I thought that's what she had done."

Another school friend, Sharon Sellick, said: "It's all such a long time ago but one thing I do remember is that she used to say her dad was a real bastard. She said she was going to run away because she couldn't stand it at home and was frightened. She would sometimes miss PE – whether it's because she didn't want us to see her bruises I don't know. It seemed as if her father had a real hold over her and she was really terrified by him. I only went to her house once and it was really creepy. It was dark and musty and I didn't hang around for long. When Heather disappeared after our exams, I believed she had finally run away and thought 'good on her'.

Another school friend, Amy Perrins, recalled: "We were close because we were the only two girls doing metal-work at school. Heather used to tell me how she was scared of both of her parents and how she was hit by her father. But we didn't do anything about it – we didn't really know what to do as we were only children. She was always going on about how she wanted to leave home and join the army. She told me she was going to pack a suitcase and leave in the middle of the night so her father wouldn't know anything. To be honest, when they discovered her body in the garden I wasn't really surprised. She was always terrified of having to leave school."

In regards to Heather, Graham Letts (Rose's brother) said: "She was a lovely girl but when she was about 14 Fred used to taunt her about not having a boyfriend. He would say 'Why haven't you got a man, you've got to prove yourself. I think you're a lesbian'." He told how he never believed the story of Heather running off with a lesbian girlfriend. "I feel partly responsible because she was my niece. When I went round she would always smile and chat, but before she vanished she became withdrawn and quiet. Fred would rip her towel off when he caught her coming out of the bathroom and shout 'that's my body. I produced you – show it off.' Sometimes Heather would look at me as if to say, 'Please help me'. But I didn't know what was going on. If I did I would have gone straight to the police and maybe Heather would still be alive today. All the time she was growing up, Fred pushed more and more for her to have sex with men. He taunted her about being a virgin and a lesbian. It was all rubbish because she was every mother's dream child – pretty, polite, well-behaved and helpful. But I think she was going to spill the beans on everything going on in the house, so he killed her. The awful truth is that hindsight is a wonderful thing.

Fred said he wanted to improve the garden and when he had finished the patio he invited us round to show it off. He was just evil and sick. We feel ill now we know what went on in that house."

3rd January 1995

A fellow 'Category A' prisoner made a statement to West Midlands Police. In it, he stated: … "I was aware that Fred was unhappy that we were no longer in the same association group and I know that Fred approached the prison officers and asked if we could again be on the same association group. The officers refused. Fred didn't know why, but he thought it was because that neither of us were trouble makers and they kept us apart to keep things easier. Fred was concerned because there had been violence during his association groups amongst other members of the group against each other or against staff, although Fred was never attacked personally. Generally Fred thought that the prison officers were conspiring against him because he felt he was getting better treatment than the other category A prisoners. Things like the staff used to spend a lot of time talking to him, they used to call him by his first name rather than his surname… We discussed all these things during the exercise periods and we both thought that the prison staff were softening him up in order that he would open up about the Gloucester murders and the staff would put statements in against him. He also stated that his solicitors had informed him that some prison officers had already put statements in against him. He told me that part about the officers' statements during exercise on Sunday 1st January 1995. On that Sunday Fred didn't seem his usual self. He wasn't his usual talkative self. I put it down to the fact that it was very cold because Fred commented that it was too cold to think and that he wanted to get back into his cell.

On or around the 26th December 1994 myself and an inmate **** were playing pool during association and **** went over and looked into Fred's cell. He came back over to me and told me Fred was crying…On 30th and 31st December 1994 Fred didn't come out for his exercise period and I was concerned about that. As a result during association on 31st December 1994 at about 7.30pm I went over to Fred's cell and asked him if he was alright. Fred said that he was alright and would see me the next day for exercise.

I have been thinking hard about the last conversations I had with Fred during the exercise period on the 1st January 1995. We spoke about the following: First of all we spoke about what we heard on the radio news that morning. Fred mentioned about an attack when a hound was killed during an alleged animal rights incident. I asked Fred about if he had heard about a £120,000 Ferrari that had been trashed during a Round Table charity event. He would normally have made some comment but didn't. We discussed the two new Chinese lads in the exercise yard as they were searched with a metal detector and we wondered what they were in for. Fred was joking on about martial arts and stuff. We briefly spoke about the animal rights prisoner that got 14 years last week. In a previous conversation Fred had said that he should appeal. On the morning of 1.1.95 I told Fred that the man was going to appeal but he didn't seem interested. We again spoke about the officer's attitude towards Fred and about the officer's making statements against him. Fred said he would find out the context of those statements next Thursday (5.1.95). He was very interested about that. He also started talking about the old days when he was 9 or 10 and some gypsies used to go to a particular site each summer to work on Fred's family's farm and they taught him basket weaving. That's about it, what we spoke about during the exercise period. Fred didn't seem depressed."

Another inmate on the same wing told the media: "He kept saying over and over again that he had had enough. He kept saying: "I'm going to hang myself". Sometimes he would shout it so everybody, including the staff, could hear."

Robert Bashford, a builder, told the Daily Mirror of the time Fred West gave him a tour of his house: "He bragged about his handiwork and pointed out all the improvements he had made. We went in to the main bedroom and he proudly showed me his four-poster bed with a mirror under the canopy. There was no doubt what went on in that room. Then he took me down to the cellar. West told me he had hundreds of dirty videos and a video camera which he used to film women while they were making love."

6th January 1994

The inquest into the death of Fred West was opened and adjourned by Birmingham city coroner Dr Richard Whittington.

7th January 1994

A police source told the Daily Express that they were linking Fred West to rapes and indecent assaults on eight young women aged 15-22 in Gloucestershire in the mid-1960's. "None of these cases was solved at the time but the description of the man involved in each case appears to fit that of West and we believe he was responsible."

During the following week, DSI Bennett and DC Russell Williams embarked on a tour to visit all of the relatives of the victims and to disclose what they believe happened to the girls and also what was found for the first time. Knowing of the West's children's dealings with the papers, it was decided to leave them until last, in case any of the details should emerge in the papers before the police had visited.

On the evening before they were due to set off, DSI Bennett received a call informing him of an article in the Sunday Express alleging that DC Hazel Savage, 50, was trying to sell her story for up to £1,000,000. According to the report, a go-between had approached Chelsea literary agent Gloria Ferris and although the details of the conversation were secret, Ms Ferris had apparently confirmed 'She is our client' and the manuscript could be worth a considerable amount. It even appeared that a reporter had spoken to Hazel Savage. John Bennett was devastated.

He had dismissed earlier rumblings against her as malicious rumour; now there was mention of a book, an agent and quotations that seemed to give it substance.

The following day, she accepted the story was basically true, though at the same time making it clear she had neither entered into an agreement nor divulged any information. As a result she was transferred to other duties and an internal investigation began.

In due course, the investigation conducted by Wiltshire Constabulary confirmed that quite early on in the enquiry, DC Savage and her solicitor had met an agent on two occasions for preliminary talks, but cleared her of passing on confidential information. When she appeared before a disciplinary hearing for falsehood and prevarication and discreditable conduct and pleaded not guilty, the allegation of falsehood was thrown out but she was found guilty of discreditable conduct. Chief Constable Tony Butler described this as 'an error of judgement', one that while not intending to bring discredit on the force had shown a 'degree of naivety' that warranted an official reprimand. He disclosed that the detective was nearing retirement in the spring of last year and considered the possibility of writing a book on her career. She had discussions with a literary agent when her involvement in the alleged Cromwell Street murders was raised. But after two meetings she decided, after taking independent legal advice, not to take the matter further. She paid for that advice herself. She made clear in writing to the agent that she was not proceeding further. That letter was some seven months before the newspaper allegation. Mr Butler said: "It is important to point out that no confidential information was disclosed by DC Savage during the discussions. No money was received by DC Savage." He said it was wholly accepted that there was no intention to bring discredit upon her force. Mr Butler added: "This was an unfortunate but single event which should be seen in the context of a distinguished career of more than 30 years in public service." DC Savage maintained she had done nothing wrong and DSI Bennett could not believe it when she appealed, although without success.

8th January 1995

Stephen West gave an interview to The News of the World. In it, he described his visits to Fred when he was in prison. "On my last but one visit he said he had stabbed Ann McFall in the caravan site at Brockworth because he loved her and couldn't have her or something like that. He used to tell me a machete was found buried with one of the bodies. He asked me if I knew where it had come from."

He went on to say that the reason Fred stopped co-operating with the police was because he would then no longer be in control. "They needed him and he knew it. The police didn't give him one ounce of space. They were bombarding him with questions. He was keen at first to get it off his chest, but once he was in his cell at Winson Green he thought to himself 'I've helped them and I'm stuck in here, so I'm going to tell them nothing more'. He was trying to tell me the truth, but he didn't want me to be shocked by it. I think that one day I'm going to be so pissed off with him for screwing up my mind by telling me what he did and destroying my feelings for him as a real father. I'm going to say to myself 'you fucking murdering bastard'."

Stephen said that Fred claimed he knew the name of the "real murderer" and wanted to protect him. "He was just trying to cover up the fact that at other times he had slipped up. At the end of the day I wish he hadn't told me anything, but if there was one thing about him it was that you couldn't stop him talking. I just feel he wanted to tell someone. He wanted someone to know before anyone else did. He just had to get it out really. But there are things that will never be known now. There are many more bodies no one will ever know about or ever find. I think he was waiting until the court case was sorted out, until after he'd got life meaning life. Then he would have played with the police, saying every so often 'There's another one buried there'. He would have played cat and mouse with them. But in the end he couldn't last out that long. I think he knew his fate."

He then told how Fred had been worried that other inmates would beat him up or kill him. "Dad told me that if he didn't do away with himself someone else in there was going to do it. He said other prisoners shouted and swore at him and called him names.

I told him he had to think of us before he did anything silly, because he wouldn't just be killing himself, but us as well. He was crying floods of tears at the time. I don't think he could accept that life as it was at Cromwell Street was over."

Stephen said that Fred used to ring him every Sunday, but "when he didn't call me before Christmas, I realised he must be a bit down. I wrote him a letter but it's still on the side. I forgot to send it. I was just waiting for him to call. And when he didn't I thought he would call in the New Year."

He said that he had warned the prison authorities about Fred's state of mind. "I told them I was worried about his state of mind, and how his will to live seemed to be ebbing away. The prison service knew he was high risk. He really should have been checked every quarter of an hour rather than once an hour. I'd like to know why they can't design prison cells so it's impossible to hang yourself. Surely that can't be too difficult? There are a lot of unanswered questions about my father's death."

In regards to Rose, Stephen and Mae said that they had visited her in Pucklechurch Prison after the death of Fred. Rose told them "He's sold out to the devil, he really should have died a long time ago. I prayed to God he would die. He can't hurt anyone else now."

Stephen said: "I expected her to be crying and really upset, but she wasn't. She was just Mum. She grabbed me and cuddled me. Then she said 'Sorry Son'.

Mae: "When Mum prayed that Dad would die, she really meant it. She hated him. Mum feels God has done it and taken him for what he has done. She feels Dad's in the best place. She thinks they will sort him out wherever he is.

It's definitely for the best that Dad's dead. We talked about what we remembered about him, some good and happy things really. And how he worked all the time to block out from his mind what he had done. Mum said he should have died in the motorbike accident he had when he was young. She won't go to the funeral, but said that Stephen and I should if we really wanted to be there. There's no doubt, though, that mum doesn't want us to go."

Stephen told of how he first learned that his father had taken his own life, in a phone call from Mae. "I was doing some decorating at my mother-in-law's house when the call came through. I didn't know who it was at first, because the person at the other end of the phone was hysterical and in floods of tears. I just said 'slow down and tell me'. She said 'Dad was found dead in his cell'. I told her 'stop messing around' and she said 'I ain't' and started crying all over again. She said someone had rung her and told her they were sorry to tell her the bad news…then wished her a Happy New Year. By this time I was shaking. I tried to phone the prison but got the number all jumbled up. My fingers couldn't hit the right buttons. Finally I got through and spoke to someone in the governor's office. He said 'I'm sorry to tell you but your father died at seven minutes past one. I know it's a horrible way to find out. Have a good New Year'.

My legs gave up on me when I put the phone down. I was on the floor and crying. My wife Andrea started cuddling me. I had to be on my own for a while, and sat outside on the top of the drain in the pouring rain. Andrea's dad Les took me back inside, sat me down, and gave me a cup of tea. I was in a state of shock and couldn't think or do anything.

We had a family get-together to discuss what we should do, and to comfort each other. Despite everything he was still our father."

He then told how Fred had been looking forward to meeting his new grand-children. "He begged me to take his grandchildren in to see him, but I couldn't because the children were under-weight and one was quite seriously ill. It never happened and I'm sad about that." He went on to say he felt guilty that he didn't name the boy after Fred. "I partly blame myself for what's happened. He would have been so desperately upset that I didn't use his name. Dad knew I supported him 100 per cent, but he suddenly must have stopped believing in me. I took a conscious decision not to call my son after my dad. I thought about it for a long time but decided it would only cause trouble if I did. But ever since I was young I wanted to call my daughter after my mum, and despite all the circumstances I don't see why I shouldn't. Andrea and I both agreed that it would be nice."

He said that he would now add one of his father's middle names, also Stephen, to his son's. "I only found out this week when I saw my grandfather's name on a gravestone that our family traditionally uses the name Stephen. I know dad would have wanted me to carry it on. I think he would have expected it."

Stephen told how he had been to see Fred's body at Birmingham Coroner's Court three days ago with his wife Andrea. "It made everything sink in. It made me realise he was really dead." He said that his father was laid out on a table behind a glass screen covered by two white sheets with only his face visible. "He looked so tense. When I looked at his face I could see the stress he had been under. I just wish he had apologised to all the families of the victims. I would have found it better to cope with….When I looked at him lying there I said a prayer in my mind. I just said how much I cared for him and how much I wanted to stick by him."

13th January 1995

Rose West was charged with the murder of Charmaine West at Pucklechurch remand Centre near Bristol. She replied: "I'm innocent". She had previously denied all knowledge of her murder, insisting that her mother Rena had come to collect her. Before his suicide, the police had only charged Fred with her murder.

15th January 1995

Stephen and Mae West gave an interview to The News of The World, talking about Fred's strange sexual practices. Stephen: "Dad took stuff (semen) from himself and injected it into other girls. He wanted to see if he could make a baby. I couldn't take in a lot of what he was doing. There

441

were always test tubes over the house. They had strange substances in them and they were sealed with superglue. It was weird, but you learned not to ask too many questions because almost certainly you wouldn't like the answer. Dad believed you could muck around genetically with people."

Mae talked about how Fred would perform abortions. "He was more than capable of doing something like that. It would have been child's play to him. Dad bragged to his workmates that if ever they got a girl into trouble he could help them out by doing an abortion. I think in his own way he thought he could play God. That he was in control and could take life whenever he felt like it. He'd have this big, horrible grin on his face whenever he talked about something he knew was unpleasant. It was more than wanting to shock you, it was very real and evil…almost like a man possessed."

Stephen explained how he believed that Fred's near fatal motorbike crash when a teenager had been to blame for his later actions. "That's apparently when Dad turned really weird. One of his brothers told me that before the crash he'd been quite pleasant when spoken to. But after the accident he'd bite people's heads off. He had a bad attitude and didn't care about anyone. His legs were in a really bad way and he was apparently in a great deal of pain. He'd sit for hour after hour saying nothing. Then, when he'd recovered, he got up, said 'I'm going' and left home."

He gave another version of how the 'joke' about Heather being buried under the patio came about. He said that when the police first came to Cromwell Street looking for Heather in 1992, one of the members of the police search team was looking over the patio. "As a joke I said to this copper 'The next thing, you'll be looking for Heather in the garden'. He laughed and said, 'If necessary'. He smiled when I said it, but I don't think he took it as a joke. That was the beginning of the rumour. I had started it, but not from anything I knew, just coincidence.

A female detective, Hazel Savage, who knew our family well wouldn't let it rest. She did everything she could and it took her a year to do it. She looked into national insurance, abroad, everything she could do to trace Heather. She drew a blank at everything. Then she went to the courts and got a warrant to dig the garden."

He said that when the police came back with a search warrant in 1994 to dig the garden "We still didn't take it seriously. As we weren't allowed in the garden, we watched from windows, sitting on stools eating crisps and drinking tea. One of them found a small bone, it was only about three inches long and it clearly wasn't human, but they were making a big fuss and came to look at it. It turned out to be a chicken bone and I started making clucking noses in the kitchen and jumping about. Mae did the same and we thought it was a great laugh."

24th January 1995

Juanita Mott was buried at St. Oswald's Church in Coney Hill, Gloucester after the bodies were finally released by the coroner.

6th February 1995

Rose West's committal proceedings at Dursley Magistrates Court began in front of the most senior Metropolitan Stipendiary Magistrate in the land, Mr. Peter Badge.

The proceeding lasted for over a week as Rose had elected for an 'old style' committal, which meant that the Crown would need to present its evidence to the magistrate before it could decide whether it warranted sending for trial. It was Rose's firm belief that she did not have a valid case to answer.

14th February 1995

Rose West was committed for trial on ten charges of murder. The previous charges of the rape of Anne Marie against her and two other Gloucester men (Whitley Purcell, 64, and the other jointly with William Smith 67) were withdrawn by Chief Metropolitan Stipendiary Magistrate Peter Badge. The men left as free citizens.

Mr Badge said that Rose West would also face two further charges of rape alleged to have been committed jointly with Fred West, one between 1 January 1976 and 31 December 1977 and the other between 1 June and 31 December 1977 (Anne Marie and 'Miss A'). She was also charged with two indecent assaults between the same dates.

Rose's solicitor, Leo Goatley, said after the hearing: "Mrs West maintains her innocence, she strenuously denies all the charges that have been laid against her and we will be defending the matter when it comes to trial. We have not disclosed our defence but we will certainly be putting forward a very strong defence." He said that he would be seeking a judicial review of Mr Badge's decision to commit Rose for trial because of the time that had elapsed since the alleged offences and the prejudicial effect of media coverage. "These are matters which will be pursued at the outset of any trial. The kind of circumstantial evidence being relied upon is of no value at all," he said. He added that his client, who showed no emotion when Mr Badge announced his decision, was maintaining "pretty reasonable" morale and had tempered any disappointment at the decision.

Detective Superintendent John Bennett, who was leading the police inquiry, said after the hearing: "The inquiries in relation to this investigation are continuing and this will continue during the next few months."

16th February 1995

Lucy Partington was buried in Exeter, Devon. Marian Partington recalled: "The requiem mass, hosted by the Catholic Chaplaincy at Exeter University, and celebrated by Lucy's priest, was full of the beauty and love that she deserved."

23rd February 1995

It was announced that Rose West was to stand trial at Winchester Crown Court in October.

15th March 1995

Mae West made a statement to the police, telling them that in regards to the sexual abuse she and Heather suffered, when Fred West would make casual remarks about it being "your turn next", Heather would freeze. She told how she shared a bedroom with Heather when they were both in their early teenage years, and the sisters protected one another against Fred's suggestions and innuendoes. He touched both of them indecently and repeated his adage that a father's rights included the taking of his daughter's virginity, whereupon Heather and Mae promised each other that they would leave home as soon as they reached the age of sixteen, and that meanwhile they would fight him off if he ever tried anything.

28th March 1995

Anne Marie formally identified her fathers' body at Birmingham Mortuary and took charge of the funeral arrangements. "The last time I saw him he was laid out on a slab at Birmingham Mortuary. They asked me to identify him as Fred West and I did, but he wasn't the dad I knew, the one I remembered from my early childhood who used to ruffle my hair and tell me he loved me. That moment in the cold, bleak place will stay with me forever. He didn't look at rest or at peace – and I don't suppose he ever will be."

Stephen West: "He didn't die a happy man that is for certain. I just wish he had admitted to it and apologised to all the families. I would have found it better and easier to cope with if he had done that before he had gone."

Anne Marie: "I knew people were asking questions about why Fred had not yet been buried or cremated, but I had made it clear soon after his death that I wanted all the victims buried first as a sign of respect for the families. Those victims included my own mother and sister. I had no control over when Heather would be laid to rest – I was not her next of kin. That decision fell to Rose and upon her arrest to Stephen and Mae. They had already told me that Heather's funeral would not be held until Rose was free and could attend the service."

However, The News of The World had paid Stephen West for exclusive coverage of Fred's funeral and forced him to remove the body from Birmingham Morgue on the quiet in order to keep Anne Marie and The Daily Star away from the opportunity for the most dramatic pictures. The Sun newspaper had got wind of the funeral due to take place the following day, so The News of The World tried, unsuccessfully, to have the funeral postponed.

29th March 1995

Frederick West was cremated at Cranley Crematorium, near Coventry. Several crematoria had refused to accept his body. The service eventually took place at short notice without anyone else being told. When the photographer from 'The Sun' took pictures of the hearse, his rivals grappled with him to tear the camera from his hands. Anne Marie was not told of the funeral, and only Stephen, his wife Andrea, Mae and Tara West were present to represent the family, although Anne Marie arrived after lunchtime when the cremation had already taken place.

The ceremony lasted only a few minutes and there were no hymns. The Reverend Robert Simpson read from the 23rd Psalm, and added: "We should have a quiet moment of reflection for the life of Fred West and pray for his family. We must also remember in our prayers everyone else who has suffered because of these tragic events." Bereaved families who attended funerals on the same day at the crematorium were outraged when they discovered that services for their loved ones had taken place within hours of Fred West's cremation.

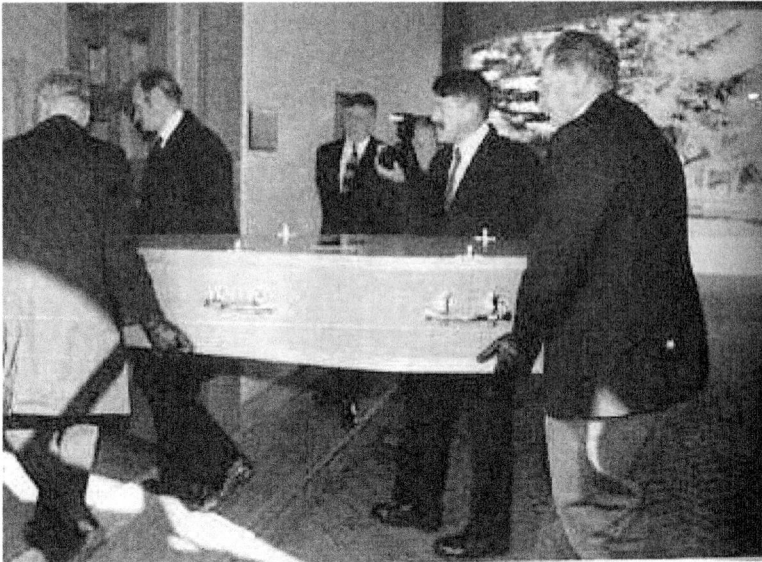

Fred West's body is taken in to the crematorium

Reverend Simpson would later recall: "I understood that Fred West had named his son Stephen executor, hence he was in charge of the funeral arrangements. As a vicar, I felt it was a job that had to be done and undertook the task without question. When I arrived at the crematorium I met up with a small group of family members awaiting my arrival. I must say I was quite surprised to find a few camera-carrying members of the media there. It's now some twenty years since this all took place. The memory has faded a little but the service as I remember, was a quiet unassuming occasion carried out in the way funerals are. With the exception

446

of a few flashguns going off, it was otherwise a normal funeral service, only the name Fred West made it an unusual occasion."

After the death of Fred West, Janet Leach had been asked to tell the police exactly what he had said to her in their meetings both in prison, and after/inbetween police interviews when they were alone. Oddly, she declined to do so and immediately consulted a solicitor.

Eventually, she revealed what Fred West had told her and put it in writing. She claimed that Rose had killed the Cromwell Street victims and that Rose's father Bill Letts, her brother-in-law John West and her black friends were all involved. Fred had not even known where they were buried until the night before he was arrested and after that he was protecting his wife. Rose, according to this version, had killed Charmaine when he was still in prison. The couple had a pact and he was upset when she was arrested because the plan had not worked. According to Janet Leach, Fred had described a farm at Gloucester where other victims were concealed, where their hands had been removed to prevent them being identified, and that Rose was involved in mutilation, too.

Stephen West later claimed: "Dad said that he used to drive up here, get out of his van, jump over the wall and come to here. He said it used to be dark when he came down here so nobody saw him and he never got interrupted and that he brought people here and buried young ladies here."

Berkeley Mill, Gloucester, where Fred West claimed other victims were buried

It was agreed that each witness should be seen by their liaison officer and further statements taken from them, showing exactly how much they had been paid and by whom, along with the details of any contracts they had signed or were negotiating, with signed permission for those who had made the payment or offer to fully disclose the details of the arrangements and what they had been told. When the statements were in it was hard to believe the five-figure sums of money on offer but easy to understand why, in the light of what they had been through, they probably felt they deserved every penny.

In the spring of 1995 the remains of Charmaine West and Rena Costello were cremated in the town of Kettering, near the home of one of Rena's sisters. At the insistence of Anne Marie, both mother and daughter shared the same coffin, and no roses were to be brought to the service by any mourners. The song 'Memories' was played at the ceremony. DSI John

448

Bennett and DC Nick Barnes, who took Anne Marie's statements, also attended as well as other members from Gloucester Police.

A few days later, over the Easter weekend, vandals desecrated the graves of both Walter and Daisy West in the churchyard of St Bartholomew's, Much Marcle. Doug West had recently paid for a new headstone for Walter and was distressed to find that both this, and Daisy's older memorial, had been pulled up and taken away during the night.

10th May 1995

On authority of the Official Solicitor Peter Harris and Leo Goatley, both defence and prosecution counsels visited 25 Cromwell Street. The house was then resealed.

12th May 1995

Rose West attended a pre-trial review at Winchester Crown Court in front of Judge Mantell for the first time and formally pleaded 'not guilty' to all ten murder charges, two counts of rape and the indecent assault of two young girls in the 1970's.

At a separate court, Barbara Letts, Rose's sister-in-law, pleaded guilty to assaulting a police officer who had gone to her Gloucester home to investigate a reported burglary. She was later given a one-year conditional discharge.

13th June 1995

A psychiatric assessment from the Fromside Clinic in Bristol found Rose West to be "pleasant, open and friendly, with a quietly spoken voice, readily forming rapport". She manifested "no sustained abnormality of mood, thought or perception" and "no evidence of mental disorder". She was visibly upset when reference was made to her husband's abuse of children, to Charmaine, or to Heather, whose departure had 'shattered' her. When she reiterated that Fred's strict instructions could never be disobeyed, she added that he sometimes turned the children against her, in order to make her feel ostracized and stupid, so that she would obey him to make him desist. She said that he treated her 'like shit'.

It was around this time that Stephen West and his wife Andrea broke up due to Stephen's violent nature. Andrea took the children and moved to the Midlands.

7th July 1995

Mr Richard Ferguson appeared before Mr Justice Mantell with an application that the four additional charges of rape and indecent assault be 'severed' from the main charge of ten murders, as being too complex for the jury to understand. The judge agreed immediately. Giving his ruling, Mr Justice Mantell said "I am content to adopt the approach of Mr Justice Garland in the Birmingham Six trial, who faced a similar application and refused. I bear in mind the power of the judge to regulate the admissibility of evidence during the course of the trial and to direct the jury accordingly. I have come to the conclusion that a fair trial may still take place, but that the clearest possible direction to the jury will be necessary". The date for the trial was set for 3rd October.

11th July 1995

The inquest began in to the death of Fred West at Victoria Law Courts, Birmingham in front of coroner Dr Richard Michael Whittington

It was around this time that Anne Marie took another overdose. Her eldest child, Michelle, had been taken into care and she had had to give up her job as a dinner lady at the local school. She fell into a deep depression. "Once again I did something stupid in my attempt to cope with what life was throwing at me. I took too many of my tablets. They made me feel like I was floating away from my troubles so I took some more. It was Phil who realised I had overdosed. He phoned my GP, who called an ambulance, and I spent another night at Gloucester Hospital. We told Carol and people locally I had dehydrated from the heat. It wasn't a serious attempt to kill myself. Again, I just wanted to blot out my problems for a while. I just didn't know when I was suffering from depression…
When I came out of hospital that day in July I felt the same way as I

had when I ended up in hospital after my father killed himself. I was ashamed of what I had done even though I knew I wasn't in my right mind when I did it.

I began drinking in the evenings to try and calm my nerves and build my courage. I couldn't eat or sleep. I was walking an emotional tightrope trying to appear calm and normal for my daughters and friends but constantly re-living the nightmare years in my mind.

One weekend I drank too much and took Phil's car out. Not a wise thing to do considering I don't drive – or at least have never passed my test. What I didn't know was that Phil had slipped a sleeping tablet in my coffee in the hope I would get some rest and relax…

A frantic and worried Phil called DC Nick Barnes, the officer assigned to look after me, and the local police force was asked to keep an eye out. They found me but not until I had bumped into someone else's car and then into one of their police cars…The court case was heard about a month later, after I had given evidence at Winchester, and I was banned from driving for 18 months and fined £250."

12th September 1995

Mr Richard Ferguson wrote to Mr Justice Mantell, objecting to the proposed inclusion of evidence of Mrs West's sexual proclivity, which was subsequently denied.

By the 20th September, the following had been recorded on the HOLMES police computer: 1,230 Statements, 5,343 Enquiries completed, 2,108 Reports, 2,159 Items of property, 4,690 Named persons and 3,059 other documents.

Additional computer equipment was obtained to produce the file of evidence for the Crown Prosecution Service. These papers compromised 31 lever arch files. Six copies of the file were prepared, totaling 186 lever arch files.

Towards the end of September, Rose was transferred from Durham Prison to Winchester gaol, where she would be held for the duration of her trial. Her cell was a tiny cubicle sparsely furnished with a bed, chair, locker and combined washing and toilet fixture. It was within a suite of seven rooms intended to become a drug rehabilitation unit. Because Rose was a Category 'A' prisoner, and could not associate with the gaol's 505 other inmates, all these rooms were dedicated to her care alone. They included a shower room and an association area, where she was allowed to watch TV and play cards with the two female warders assigned to watch her round the clock.

10 THE TRIAL

3rd October 1995

Rose West's trial on ten counts of murder began at Winchester Crown Court.

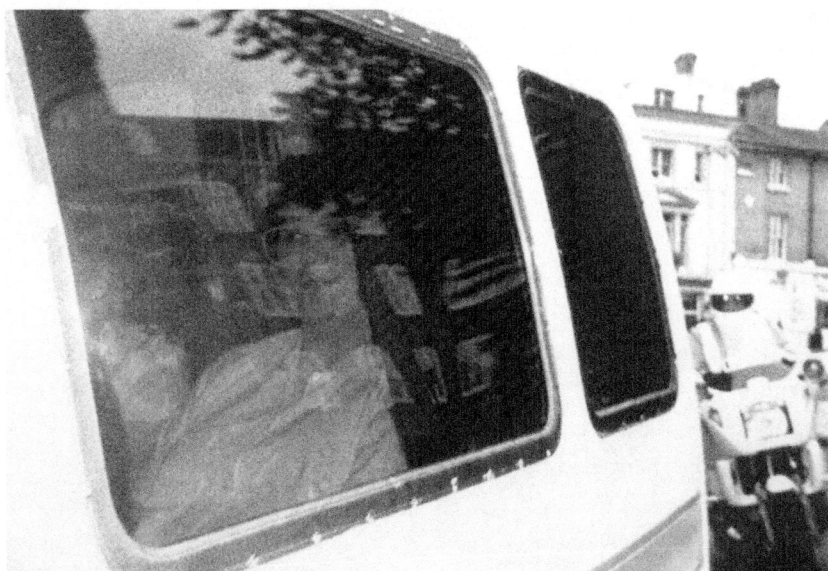

Rose West arrives for the first day of her trial

Prosecution witnesses and the relatives of victims who indicated they did not wish to be photographed by the media met at a rendezvous point and were then taken under police escort to Winchester Crown Court by car or minibus with darkened windows. The witnesses were accompanied by a relevant Police Liaison Officer and an independent member of the Victim Support Service or the Witness Support Service from the Crown Court. On arrival at court the witness was cared for by the Witness Support Service until they gave evidence and then taken back to the rendezvous point.

Mae West was on stand-by as a witness for the defence and was therefore excluded from the court. Stephen West was not called due to his dealings with the newspapers.

In court, the jurors were told by Mr Justice Mantell: "The trial which is about to begin is of Rosemary West, and it would be foolish to pretend you haven't heard about it. This case has received a certain amount of publicity and it is going to receive a lot more. Each of you have taken an oath to try the case according to the evidence and that's precisely what your duties will be – to try the case. The evidence is what you will hear in this courtroom and you won't hear it anywhere else. You must put out of your mind all preconceptions, prejudice and sentiment. You have a responsibility to be unaffected by anything you read about this case, which certainly has its sensational aspects. It is very important to bear in mind that anything you read or hear is not evidence in the case. You try this case, nobody else does. It is your job to try it according to the evidence you hear in this courtroom." The jury was then stood down while he heard legal submissions in their absence.

Mr Ferguson, for the defence, asked for a ban on any media interviews with witnesses until after the trial was over, a request that was not disputed. Then he made an application to exclude the 'similar fact' evidence which the Crown wished to introduce. "I call it disputed evidence rather than similar fact. It is prejudicial in the extreme. It cannot be admissible if its only purpose is to prove propensity". Mr Justice Mantell intervened to tell the story of Bluebeard, who murdered his wives. If one of them had escaped, he said, he would have regarded her evidence as relevant.

Mr Ferguson then said that there were two murders in which the Crown did not suggest that Rosemary West was involved and of the total of 12 sets of remains, five of them bore none of the striking similarity which the Crown suggested should allow in similar fact evidence. "These five counts present grave problems for the Crown. They cannot pick and choose. They cannot say that of the twelve instances they will pick seven and draw inferences from their common features, then blithely ignore the other five where they cannot". On the matter of Rose's sexual assault against Caroline Owens in 1972, Mr Ferguson said that evidence from other witnesses would be admissible if the defendant was being tried for sexual assault. But she was not. "Evidence of sexual abuse is NOT probative of any allegation of murder".

Mr Ferguson asked the judge to exclude the five Crown witnesses (the only five who were important to their case, as it happened), on the grounds that their 'similar fact' evidence went only to previous bad conduct and character of the defendant, and only then in respect of five counts of murder. "If you do allow these five to testify, my lord, then they will talk about sexual abuse and in so doing will raise the question of a fair trial in respect of the other seven counts. It is very problematic".

In reply for the Crown, Brian Leveson QC said, with regard to the murder of Rena, "I do not concede that Mrs West was not involved". And with regard to the murders of Heather, Charmaine and Shirley Robinson, "We admit that motive distinguishes these three from the other seven". He then responded to Mr Ferguson's objections. "The fact that the victims are dead and the witnesses as to similar fact are alive is neither here nor there. Similar facts in a murder case are likely to be from live witnesses".

The following day, Court could not sit so Brian Leveson could observe the Jewish Day of Atonement, Yom Kippur.

5th October 1995

Mr Justice Mantell said the evidence of the five witnesses illuminated both the purpose for which the victims were brought to the house and the complicity of the defendant in that purpose, and was 'of such probative value that fairness does justify its admission'.

Mr Ferguson then returned to his other application. That three counts of murder be 'severed' from the other seven. "The jury cannot reach an unbiased view on these three counts if they have heard similar fact evidence on the other seven. You would be asking them to perform a series of mental gymnastics. They will be influenced by the evidence on seven counts which is prejudicial when they are deliberating on the other three counts where such evidence is irrelevant". The judge refused this. Provided always that clear direction be given by himself, there need not be the prejudice which Mr Ferguson anticipated.

6th October 1995

It was announced that 46 witnesses were due to appear, and then the jury was brought in. They were handed a bundle of exhibits, photographs, plans of the house and maps, to consult when following Mr Leveson's opening statement.

9th October 1995

Mr Leveson continued his opening address after the weekend break and then it was time to hear from the witnesses.

The first witness to be called was Daisy Gwendolyn Letts, Rose's mother. She told the court that she had only met Frederick West once before Rose moved in with him and did not take to him. He had boasted of owning a string of hotels, which she knew could not be true, and she didn't trust him.

Daisy: I didn't have time to get on with him. He only came to the house once. My husband and I didn't think he was telling the truth. We didn't take to him very well at all. He said he had a hotel in Scotland and a caravan site in Scotland and of course he was rather older than Rosie. Our view of him was not very good and as a result my husband went to social services and she went in to care. That lasted until she was 16, then they let her out to come home to us. I think her father gave her a good talking to but she decided she wanted to go with Fred. My husband did everything in his power to break off this relationship. He threatened Fred but he did not strike him.

Her husband had placed Rose in care when she was 15 in order to keep her away from Fred, but she had run to his caravan as soon as she was legally free to do so. Daisy said she was not told when her daughter became pregnant, nor when she gave birth, nor when she married. She had not known of Heather's existence until Rose brought her home one day, aged about 4 months.

Daisy: Rosie came home with the baby who was then about four months old. That was Heather. I gathered she had fallen out with Fred, and assumed she wanted to stay at home. But she didn't say she had fallen out with him. She had only come for the day and was very quiet. Fred came to the door and asked for Rosie. My husband stood in the door. I stood behind Rosie because I didn't really want her to go back with him. Fred was saying: 'Come along Rosie, Come on home'. Rose turned to her father and said 'You don't know him, you don't know him. There's nothing he wouldn't do – even murder' or something to that effect. I heard those words. But we thought they were the words of a highly strung girl. We didn't take it seriously. Eventually she went, because her father had tried so hard to get her to stay at home. He said: 'If you've made your bed, you lie in it'. I was very upset about it.

Cross examining, Mr Richard Ferguson encouraged Daisy to recollect Rose's childhood and her affection for children. Daisy confirmed that Fred was especially close to his daughter Anne Marie, and that Rose was still a child herself, "so babyish in her ways". Nevertheless, she said, the little girls were in a much better state than they had been when she first took them in; she "kept them looking nice".

Daisy: Fred cared more for Anne Marie than for Charmaine. Charmaine was a lovely, happy little girl and Rose always seemed to make them look nice. I think she looked after them to the best of her ability. She was still a child herself. It was like a child looking after a child.
Ferguson: Was she frightened of him?
Daisy: Oh yes
Ferguson: But she went back to him?
Daisy: Yes
Ferguson: Can you remember Fred West saying to Rose something like if she didn't come back to him within 10 minutes her place in his bed would be occupied by another woman?

Daisy: He may have said such things. He used to talk very fast, and I couldn't always catch what he said.
Ferguson: Did she seem frightened of him?
Daisy: She sounded frightened of him, yes
Ferguson: Did she mention she was in love with this man?
Daisy: She didn't say. I thought the children attracted her. She loved smaller children. Charmaine was a lovely little girl – a happy little girl. Rose always seemed to keep the children nice and their hair nice. They seemed alright when they were with her. I always thought Fred made more of Anna

Marie than he did of Charmaine. I can't say that Rosie treated Charmaine any different.

Daisy Letts then went on to tell the court of the last time she saw Charmaine, at Midland Road.

Daisy: Charmaine answered the door. I didn't see anybody else in the house at that time. Rose wasn't there. I went in and asked Charmaine 'Are you on your own?' I was surprised. I don't think I ever went back to Midland Road again. Not that I can remember.

Asked if she had asked anyone about Charmaine:

Daisy: Oh, yes. I asked my daughter. She said that Charmaine had gone back with her mother. I said to her 'Does Charmaine's mother bring her to see Anna Marie at all?' She said 'No'. I understood she'd gone back to Scotland. I just thought the child had gone back with her mother, and she might be better with her. I could see she had a foreign look about her.

Daisy added: "I wasn't at my daughter's wedding. I learned of it sometime later. Could have been a year or two."
She went on to say that she had had very little contact with her daughter over the years. She had been to Midland Road 3 times, and to Cromwell Street probably about 7 times. They had not met for the past 7 years.

Daisy: First of all my husband and I used to go in the evenings to see if Rosie was all right. We were worried about her with Fred. Always when we went Rosie was there, but not Fred. She'd say Fred was out working.

She then said that Rose had visited her home on two occasions in the late 1980's.

Daisy: Heather wasn't there. I believe one of my children said Heather had left home.

The second witness was the defendant's sister Glenys Tyler. In cross-examination Mr Ferguson got the witness to confirm that Rosemary West had been childish for her age and 'absolutely devoted' to her two younger brothers. She was then asked about Heather and said she last saw her in 1987.

Glenys: Certainly on the last occasion she appeared unhappy.

As to Heather's disappearance:

Glenys: Heather told my daughter that as soon as she was sixteen she would leave home.
Ferguson: So it came as no surprise to you when she did?
Glenys: Absolutely not. She (Rose) said that Heather had left home and if that was the way she wanted it she (Rose) didn't want to know and that was the end of it.

Richard Ferguson asked what she thought of Fred West.

Glenys: I can't say as I took to him.

Mr Ferguson then suggested there was a stage when he made a sexual advance towards her.

Glenys: I would hardly say that! He gave me a lift in his van to Gloucester and talked about Rose and himself having an open marriage and had I ever thought of trying it – no more than that.

She thought it a "smutty" remark. She said she had not had much to do with her sister Rose since leaving home in 1967, but had visited both Midland Road and Cromwell Street. Asked about her impression of Charmaine:

Glenys: She was just a very pretty, normal seven or eight year old. A little bit highly strung.

Brian Leveson asked her about Charmaine's relationship with Rose:

Glenys: I think it was a little bit troubled in as much as Rosemary was quite young and Charmaine was highly strung and there were problems. I knew there was a problem with bed wetting, something like that. It seemed normal for a child like that. She was under stress because she wasn't with her natural mother.

Miss Tyler was then asked how Rose had dealt with the bed-wetting:

Glenys: It would obviously be annoying for a young person of Rose's age, which was about 16 or 17, to change bed clothes for a child of 8 when you don't expect that sort of thing. She was annoyed and it irritated her. I remember at some stage we were told Charmaine had gone back to live with her mother. That came via my mother. I don't think I thought an awful lot about it. Rose had obviously had problems with her, and so it would seem to be the best thing all round.
Leveson: Did you ever hear about Charmaine again
Glenys: No
Leveson: Did you ask?

Mrs Tyler replied that she had not but her mother Daisy had.

Glenys: As time went by it concerned me and we never heard any more.

Mr Leveson then asked if she had ever thought of doing anything about it.

Glenys: Mum and I discussed whether or not to get a private detective to find out, but we never did anything about it, no.

Mrs Tyler then told how she helped out at the café her father had bought. She said Fred West was a frequent visitor there. She remembered he was usually with a woman called Shirley and thought her second name was Robertson. She was asked whether Fred had said anything about Shirley's condition:

Glenys: At some point he did tell us Shirley was pregnant and it was his child. It certainly wasn't something he tried to hide. I was appalled.

The third witness was Shirley Ann Giles. She had lived above Frederick and Rosemary West at 25 Midland Road. Her daughter Tracey was the same age as his step-daughter Charmaine, and they were 'first best friends'. One day before breakfast Mrs Giles sent Tracey downstairs to ask Rose if she could borrow some milk. Tracey went downstairs as asked and saw something which upset her. When Tracey went back up to her mother she was in "a very distressed" state, so Shirley went downstairs herself and had it out with Rose.

Shirley: I asked her what was happening and why she had upset my daughter very much by what my daughter had seen in the kitchen. I told Rose my daughter had gone in for milk and had come back very distressed because Charmaine was stood on a chair or a stool with her hands tied behind her back and that Rose West was stood with a wooden spoon in the air as if she was going to smack her with it. I asked her why, and Rose said that Charmaine had been naughty and she had to be taught a lesson – she had to be taught wrong from right.

Mrs Giles agreed that she had not seen the wooden spoon incident herself, and told Mr Leveson that she had never seen Rose hit the children.

Shirley: She ruled her children with a steel rod, not like my girls were. My girls would run around and play but she would speak to hers and that would be it. I never saw her hit a child though.

Mrs Giles then described Charmaine as a 'wilful' character. She explained that Rose would complain that Charmaine "was very wilful" and it used to get her down. While Anne Marie was "on the timid side", Charmaine was "quite a handful".

Shirley: There was a clash of personalities between them and it caused a lot of problems.

Richard Ferguson questioned the reliability of the sequence given by the witness in regards to the year she wrote to Fred when he was in prison asking him to make her a match stick caravan:

Ferguson: There is no reference to Charmaine in this very friendly letter you wrote to Mr West. No expression of regret, no question as to where she is, no request for an address where she could be written to. Why is that?

Shirley: I didn't think of it

Ferguson: You have changed your evidence about the date of this visit. Why is that?

Shirley: Because I wasn't sure.

Ferguson: I'm trying to test how accurate your memory is, Mrs Giles. Once Rosemary accidentally got the kitchen on fire and came upstairs to you for help. Do you recall when that was?

Shirley: I can't remember dates, no, it was too long ago.

Ferguson: The police sought a second statement from you to change the dates on the first. They told you you got your dates muddled. Confusion arose. You discussed it with your daughter, and your recollection changed as a result of what your daughter said.

Mrs Giles agreed that the police had called upon her to change her statement.

Ferguson: Charmaine was still alive in June 1971, but you were told she had gone in March. You were getting muddled again. Could your visit have taken place in September?

Shirley: No.

Ferguson: Rosemary lent you Heather's baby clothes for the baby you were then expecting, Claire, and asked you to return them when she was expecting Mae. Right?

Shirley: I don't remember.

Ferguson: It was after the birth of Claire that you visited Midland Road

Shirley: I don't think so

Mrs Giles' daughter, Tracey Hammond took to the stand next. She looked frightened and asked to be allowed to sit. She recalled when she was younger "bursting in" to the Wests flat below to borrow some milk:

Tracey: I didn't knock. Then, in front of me, I saw my friend Charmaine

462

standing on the chair. There was a lady beside her and she had this spoon in her hand. Charmaine had her hands tied behind her back. She was sideways on and I could see this huge brown leather belt wrapped round her wrists.

On the wooden spoon incident she told Mr Leveson: "I still find it quite disturbing", and she remembered Rosemary's reply when, on the return visit, she asked what had happened to Charmaine – "Gone to her mother and bloody good riddance".

Mr Ferguson established two points in cross-examination: first, that by the time Tracey Hammond made her statement to the police on 1st July 1994 she already knew that Charmaine's remains had been found (and her recollection was not, therefore, as free from emotional influence as it would have been had she not known she was dead); and second, that there was a baby in a pram on the visit to Midland Road, which would place it after Claire was born in August.

Mae: "I'm getting a bit paranoid about everything. It's getting to me. The prosecution case is really having a go at Mum. Witness after witness is making her out to be evil beyond belief. She was bad, but she's no killer and I believe her – I've got to… it's hard to know what to do with myself. I've started reading books about serial killers – God knows why, but I suppose it helps me to think other families have been through the same thing."

10th October 1995

The day opened with a reading to the court of 3 letters between Fred and Rose during his 1971 custodial sentence served at Leyhill Open Prison, and followed with the establishment of the dates of that custody, given by prison officer David Whitcomb. The index card of Frederick West 401317 confirmed that he had arrived on 21st January 1971, and been discharged on 24th June of the same year. That was his earliest possible release date, which would have been delayed had there been cause for any disciplinary action. There was no evidence of absconding, though Mr Whitcomb agreed that it was not difficult to abscond. Richard Ferguson wanted him to go further and admit that absconding was a frequent occurrence. Prisoners were at liberty within the open prison between 5pm and 9pm, and there was nothing to stop people leaving, he said.

Ferguson: Prisoners sometimes went out all night leaving their clothes under the bedsheets?

Mr Whitcomb: It has been known.

Elizabeth Agius took to the witness stand next. She had been summoned from her home in Malta for the hearing. Answering Brian Leveson, Mrs Agius recalled how she had met Fred West one day when he offered to help her as she struggled up the steps with her pram. He introduced himself as the man who lived next door. Her husband was abroad at the time. She accepted an invitation to go to his flat for a cup of tea. There she met Rose, who she thought was his daughter because she looked about fourteen-years-old. They got to know one another very well, and Mrs Agius used to go into their flat about twice a week. Twice she baby-sat for them when they were out in the evening. But it was a particular conversation she had with them on the second occasion which brought her to give evidence.

Elizabeth: Fred said they had been riding around looking for young girls. He said having a woman in the car made it easier to pick up a girl as she would think it was safe. If he could get a young girl between 15 and 17, hopefully she would be a virgin and he could get more money for a virgin. They had the opportunity to come to live with them and be on the game if they wanted to, and he preferred young runaways because they had nowhere to go.

She was asked who was present in the room.

Elizabeth: He made one approach to me once about it. I couldn't believe it. But Rose had told me it was true what he said. They brought it up together when I was there. They said it when they were both in the room. He sometimes went as far as London, but said the best place for pick-ups was Bristol way.

Cross examined by Richard Ferguson about these incidents:

Elizabeth: To be honest I couldn't believe it. I never saw anybody. I

464

thought it was a joke. Everything Fred said he was always laughing about. You could not believe it was true because they were such nice people. Fred brought up the subject of sex when Rose was not there, but later she admitted that he wanted to have sexual intercourse with me. It's the truth, she said. She would have liked me to go to bed with him. They wanted three in a bed as well...he told me Rose was a prostitute and that he liked to watch or listen to everything she did. If he wasn't there, she would tell him exactly what had happened...he said if he got me into bed he would tie me up and I could do the same to him, but nothing happened. It was all just talk. If he was following me up the stairs he would flip my backside with his hands."

When Mrs Agius' husband returned from abroad, she introduced him to Fred and Rose. As she sat on the arm of a chair, and her husband put his arm around her, Fred stormed off in to the kitchen. The Wests then hurriedly left. A few weeks later, Mrs Agius called around to see them:

Elizabeth: I went in to see if they were all right. Rose gave me a cup of tea. Then Fred turned round, and said my husband should be 'six feet under fucking there'. He was pointing to the floor. All I said to him was 'don't be stupid'.

In 1972, said Mrs Agius, she had visited Fred and Rose at Cromwell Street:

Elizabeth: There was a little trap door in the floor and you had to lift it up. Fred said it would make a playroom for the children – if they had any parties they could stay out of the way down there. Then he said: 'Or else I could make this my torture chamber'. My reply was 'You're dreaming'.

She then said that she moved abroad but came back to visit:

Elizabeth: Fred was on about letting rooms off to single mothers or single girls, or people who were on social security. But they had to be women.

Asked how Fred and Rose got on together:

Elizabeth: They were such a close couple, really close. They were the type of people who didn't hide anything from one another.

Richard Ferguson pointed out that the trap-door she claimed to have seen at Cromwell Street was not there until 1975.

Elizabeth: It was. That's the truth.

He implied she had made it up. Why? Because she had been to the press before going to the police.

Elizabeth: I tried to phone the police. My mum said phone The Sun.

She said she had tried the police three times, but they were always engaged. The Sun sent a man to visit her. By this time, she had seen about the West enquiry in the newspapers. Mr Ferguson put it to her that she had tailored her memory and testimony according to the allegations she had read, but she said she hadn't paid attention to what was in the newspapers.

Ferguson: You weren't curious?
Elizabeth: You wouldn't have believed it, they were such a nice couple.

Going back to the conversation about picking up girls, Mr Ferguson asked why she hadn't repeated it before.

Elizabeth: I was shocked
Ferguson: Did you continue to be friendly with the Wests even after this 'shocking' conversation? Did it not affect your friendship?

Elizabeth: No, because I didn't believe it.
Ferguson: You thought it was a joke?
Elizabeth: Yes
Ferguson: Was it said in a joking fashion?
Elizabeth: In a certain way, yes. I didn't take it seriously. They did no harm to me. They were such a nice couple.
Ferguson: And you were friends with them right up to the very end.

He then went on to undermine the witness's credibility with a surprise question:

Ferguson: Did you ever have sex with Fred?
Elizabeth: I don't know
Ferguson: What do you mean?
Elizabeth: No, never.
Ferguson: You're not telling the truth.
Elizabeth: (Shouting) I've never done anything what you're suggesting!

Richard Ferguson reminded her that she had told a police officer, in what she took to be a confidential conversation not to be alluded to in court, that she had been three in a bed with both the Wests. A statement by Detective Constable Gerard Watters was then read to the court:

"Elizabeth Agius said she had been a neighbour of the Wests when they lived at 25 Midland Road. They were not long married and she visited their home on a regular basis. During the interview she became distressed and started to cry. She said something had happened to her involving both the Wests which she had never spoken about and was afraid because if her husband found out he would leave her. She said she needed to get this incident out. She did not wish it to be recorded in her statement in any way.

She told me that during one of her visits to Midland Road in which she had her usual cup of tea, she had started to feel drowsy. She said she had felt really strange and the next thing she remembered was coming round naked in bed with Fred and Rose, also naked. Fred indicated he had had full sexual intercourse with her when she was unconscious. She had not been aware if sexual intercourse had taken place, but agreed it probably had, if he said it did. She was drowsy and felt sick. She said Fred and Rose dressed her and took her and her baby back to her home address. Next day she still felt strange and didn't know what they had given her."

He added: "I feel somewhat embarrassed in betraying the trust that she had placed in me in revealing this incident." Mrs Agius' husband was abroad at the time. "She said she had been afraid to speak because if her husband found out he would leave her."

Elizabeth: (Shouting) I have never ever been three in a bed with the Wests!

Richard Ferguson told her that he knew she had promised she would deny having sex with Frederick West if challenged in court.

Ferguson: You're frightened that if you admit to having sex with Fred it will destroy your marriage. I suggest to you that you did have intercourse with Frederick West at a time when Rosemary West was expecting her daughter Mae, who was born in hospital when you were at Midland Road. Do you remember her coming back from the hospital, the third day after the baby was born, and hammering on the door of your flat – the bedroom door? And that you and Fred West were in your bedroom at the time?

Elizabeth: I have never been in bed with Fred West – only my husband.

She also denied ever visiting Fred West in the night, and said:

Elizabeth: I'd never leave my children in the middle of the night. Wherever I went, my children went with me.

During Liz Agius' examination, she denied receiving any money from The Sun newspaper, but acknowledged that she had found £750 on her mantelpiece following a TV interview.

Elizabeth: Even today, I don't read newspapers.

Asked why she had not told the press to go away when they knocked on her door:

Elizabeth: They don't know what going away means, do they?
Ferguson: I suggest that what has happened in order to make your story more news-worthy and therefore more valuable…
Elizabeth: (Interrupting) I want to get out of here and go back to my husband and children. I don't want to be here – not for money or anything.

Caroline Owens took to the stand next. She explained how she came to work as a nanny for the West's and why she left. She stated:

Caroline: I tried to stick up for her (Rose), and he (Fred) told me to mind my own business. I left because I didn't like Fred.

She said she got in to the car on the night of December 6ᵗʰ, 1972, because there was a woman inside and "that made it better, safer." It took nearly an hour for Caroline to tell what happened to her on that night, when Fred and Rose assaulted her.

She said she accepted a lift from them. The couple then suddenly started talking in a filthy manner.

Caroline: Fred asked me if I had had sex with my boyfriend that night. I said 'No'. Rose had her arm round the back of me. She started touching my breasts over my clothes. I said 'get off' and pushed her away. Fred said 'what are her tits like?' Rose was just grinning and laughing – not a nice laugh. She was grabbing hold of my chest and trying to grab between my legs. I was panicking and struggling. Then Fred pulled on to a grass verge near a gate. Rose was still trying to touch me. He (Fred) turned round in his seat as we were struggling with each other. He started punching me round the head. He was calling me a bitch and things like that. I was trying to fight her (Rose) off as well. There were around three blows. They got me on the head and mouth. I was knocked out. I didn't know how long. When I came round, my arms had been tied round my back with my scarf. They were putting tape round my head, round my mouth and back of my hair. It was a gag – brownish coloured, gummy and sticky. I was able to breathe through my nose. Rose was holding me and Fred was putting the tape round. My reaction was terror and panic. I couldn't open my mouth even if I tried. Rose sat on me to keep me down. Fred started driving back towards Gloucester. She (Rose) was holding me down, and they were talking and laughing. She kept grabbing at me between the legs. I was taken back to 25 Cromwell Street.

I was taken to the first floor front room. I was still bound. He (Fred) told me to keep quiet and cut the tape off. Rose was in the room at the time. The knife cut me slightly. Fred apologised. My arms were still tied up. They sat me on a sofa, then Rose started trying to kiss me. She was touching my breasts over my clothes. I told them to get off and leave me alone. She just continued. Then Rose went and made some cups of tea. I had a cup. I was untied when I had the tea. Then they undressed me.

They tied my arms again, grabbed me and gagged me with cotton wool. They put me on the mattress, or bed, on my back. I was blindfolded. Rose got undressed. My hands were tied by Fred, I think. Fred blindfolded me. I couldn't see. It was like being examined in the genital area by both of them. I was scared that they might put something inside me or even operate. Then Fred got a belt and Rose held my feet apart while Fred beat me with the belt.

Brian Leveson then intervened and asked what part of the belt was used. Caroline replied that it was the buckle and there were 10 strikes. Caroline said Rose then performed oral sex on her. Asked what Fred was doing at this time, she replied:

Caroline: Watching. Then he took his clothes off, went behind Rose and started having sex with her at the same time. I felt sick and scared. I couldn't believe it was happening.

Rose then went to the bathroom. When she left Fred raped Caroline. After the act was over Fred wept, and apologised for hurting her.

Caroline: He said I was there for Rose's pleasure

The Wests then went to sleep, naked. Caroline, still gagged, tried to force open a window. At about 7am there was a knock at the door downstairs. Fred answered.

Caroline: There was a man's voice outside. I tried to make a noise.

But Rose, she claimed, had placed a pillow over her head.

Caroline: When Fred came back into the room, they were really angry with me. He (Fred) told me he would keep me in the cellar and let his black friends use me and, when they were finished with me, bury me under the paving stones of Gloucester. He said there were already hundreds of girls there and the police wouldn't find me.

Rose was present at the time.

Leveson: Who was he saying was going to kill you?
Caroline: I'm sure it was 'we'.

The Wests then made tea for her and Rose left the room. After the attacks, the Wests asked her to come back and work for them.

Caroline: I was amazed. I thought this would be my chance to get away from them. I said I'd have to go home and get my stuff.

Afterwards, Caroline said she played with the children and helped Rose clean the room. She then joined the couple on a trip to the launderette and escaped.

Caroline: I just walked out and kept walking.

After getting a lift with a friend to another friend's house, she went home. But she could not tell her mother of her ordeal.

Caroline: I was too ashamed. I went to bed and hid under the covers. The attack shattered my life and it's taken me years to put it back together again. At the time I was afraid to give evidence in case they made it look like I was to blame.

She was then asked about that case going to court:

Caroline: Prior to the case of my abduction coming to court I was told by police that I would be cross examined in the witness box and it would be hard to handle. I felt I could not cope with this. When I first spoke to the police I did not say I had been raped. I had forgotten this had happened, along with all the other nasty assaults, so I did not mention it straight away. I did not think about it because what Mrs West did was something I had not come across before and I was shocked and upset. What Fred did was over in seconds. I was told the Wests would plead guilty to assault and I would not have to go to court so I settled for this.

Mr Leveson made her admit dealings with the press. She had

telephoned the police immediately news broke of the arrest on 24th February 1994, and her first statement was dated 26th February. A further two statements were given on 22nd April and 1st July, but in advance of these, then days after the first interview, she began her negotiations with newspapers, using a local reporter to pose as a friend in order to advise her on how to obtain the best price. She was due to receive £20,000.

In cross-examination, Mr Ferguson went straight to the 1972 assault and wondered why she had sustained no injuries. Within an hour of her escape from 25 Cromwell Street she was with her friend Doreen Bradley, when her injuries would be "at their most visible", yet there was nothing to show. No obvious black eye, no bruises. Part of her evidence told how Frederick West had whipped her genitals with the buckle end of a two-inch-wide leather belt.

Ferguson: How many times had he hit you?
Caroline: About six.
Ferguson: On your exposed body, in an overhand manner, coming down with strength? (he continued, lifting his arm above his head and bringing it down with a whoosh). Did it draw blood?
Caroline: No.
Ferguson: Six blows delivered, and no blood?
Caroline: Just bruises.
Ferguson: Bringing it down from behind his back, and no blood?
Caroline: There were weals.
Ferguson: Did you show them to Doreen?
Caroline: No.
Ferguson: To the doctors who examined you?
Caroline: Yes, they would have seen it.
Ferguson: And did they make any comment?
Caroline: No.
Ferguson: Was the area raw?
Caroline: It hurt.
Ferguson: Not bleeding?
Caroline: No.

Counsel employed the same tactics about the punch that Caroline

Owens alleged Fred West had given her in the van, knocking her out. "Was it with a clenched fist"? "Did it leave any marks"? "A cut on your face"? "Why doesn't it show on the photographs"? "Is there any mark that you can show us"? "Any bruises"? "Any way you can help us"? "Were there any injuries to your mouth"? In the wake of negative replies to all this, he said, "Is that because there was nothing to be seen"?

He then moved on to the photograph of Caroline Owens which appeared in the centre pages of The Sun dated 2nd January 1995 and said:

Ferguson: You told the court that you were deeply upset when you heard that Frederick West had hung himself, yet you don't look too upset in this photograph of you in The Sun, the day after his death! Can you tell me what date this photo was taken?
Caroline: That photo was taken in 1985.
Ferguson: Can you repeat that please?
Caroline: Yes, that photo was taken in 1985! The photo was taken in 1985 when I was 29. I am now 39.

Having failed to show that Caroline Owens was lying about her ordeal, Mr Ferguson then went on to read some of her 1973 diary to herself and the court:

Ferguson: You hitch hiked again just after the attack. You write on one page that you 'Laughed your head off!"
Caroline: Yes, I did. (Caroline then went on to explain what had happened on the day in question.)

Quoting from her diary, defence counsel was able to show that she had accepted lifts from strangers no less than eight times in the weeks and months following the ordeal which was alleged to have scarred her; one entry, in March 1973, proved she had got into a car in which there were 'two fellows'.

Mr Ferguson had tried to imply that Caroline Owens wasn't raped, but she had written in her diary on the page dated 12th January 1973 that "Fred and Rose were going to Court today for the rape, indecent assault and ABH on me."

He then went on to suggest that the witness had not been the innocent, inexperienced girl she portrayed. When she was forced into the house, bound and gagged, the lodgers Alan and Ben were there.

Ferguson: Prior to this you had had sex with both of them?
Caroline: Yes.
Ferguson: Were they friends of yours?
Caroline: Not close.
Ferguson: Close enough for you to have sex with them
Caroline: That was a mistake.
Ferguson: Two mistakes, Mrs Owens?

Mr Ferguson also established that she had had sex with another boyfriend when she had been living at 25 Cromwell Street, who had stayed overnight, and that on the day following her ordeal she had made no complaint to Ben Stanniland, who had found her using a vacuum cleaner with apparent nonchalance.

Ferguson: Were you able to use the Hoover despite the physical trauma inflicted upon you?
Caroline: In pain, but able to manage.

Mr Ferguson then got her to admit that Rose had made no attempt to restrain her when she did eventually leave the house later that day.

He then turned to Caroline Owens' dealings with The Sun, and in particular her withholding one page of detail as a bargaining counter. The judge intervened "Does this have relevance, Mr Ferguson? "If it doesn't, I shall stop it". Counsel replied that it showed how the witness had exaggerated for commercial gain. "Your attack upon the character and use of this material will not be justified unless there is a gap between the witness's account and your account of what occurred", said Mr Mantell. Mr Ferguson persisted in regarding it as central to the way the case had been brought. He told the witness in blunt terms that, though it was accepted that sexual advances were made, she had added details to make her story more dramatic and more commercial. "You were not beaten, you were not knocked out".

When he had finished, the judge leant forward again. "I did not hear you challenge the evidence that she was raped, Mr Ferguson".

Mr Leveson resumed questioning. He took the opportunity to lay emphasis that it was Rose who had been the first to lay hands upon her and that she had done so without coercion from her husband. Caroline Owens concurred. "She seemed evil to me", she said. Counsel also made it clear that when the witness had made her first statement to the police, no bodies had been found and she was therefore in no position to realize that her story would have any commercial value. He invited Mr Ferguson to admit that there was no discrepancy between her statement to the police and her account sold to The Sun. "The discrepancy is between her 1972 account and both her 1994 accounts", said Mr Ferguson.

Mr Leveson asked his final question:

Leveson: If you did not come here for commercial advantage, why did you come to court?

Immediately she started to cry.

Caroline: I want to get justice for those girls who didn't make it, because I feel it was my fault.

Mae: "It's still difficult. Mum is up there in the dock charged with ten murders. I can accept what Dad did – he was an evil monster and nothing about him surprises me. But Mum – well, that's different. I can't accept she would ever murder. I know I'm going to collapse when it's all over, whatever the verdict. We're going, myself and Stephen, at the end of the trial. I know I've coped well without Mum being around, but I don't know how I could manage thinking she was going to be in jail for the rest of her life. I know Mum will never accept being in prison. She will kill herself – and has said so. The thought of her being unhappy makes me unhappy. I know people will say how stupid I am to stand by my Mum, but she's all I've got. Mum herself is finding it tough. She said to me: "I just want it over".

Mum has now completely disassociated herself from my father. She calls him Fred West. Mum says she's finding out so much about him from statements made by witnesses. She says of Dad: 'He's an animal.'

Mum's solicitor Leo has broken many things about Dad which she didn't know about. At times she has to go to the toilet to get a breather because she says it's such a shock. I'm going to see Mum in Winchester jail tomorrow. I'm nervous about seeing her and hearing first-hand how things are going. She's become institutionalised inside prison and very much used to the life. She doesn't fight the system."

11th October 1995

Lynda Gough's mother took the stand.

Mrs Gough: Lynda was cheerful, happy and friendly. She was not withdrawn. She seemed to get along with most people quite easily. She accepted some advice but as she got older, I would say 18 or 19, she started to rebel, against our advice – like a lot of teenagers. They think they're clever, but really they're only just beginning their lives.

Brian Leveson asked her when she last saw Lynda.

Mrs Gough: The last day I saw her was 19th April 1973. That is something that has always stayed in my mind and that is not likely to be something I will ever forget.

She went on to tell how Lynda had left home and left a note saying:

Dear Mum and Dad,
Please don't worry about me. I have got a flat.
I will come and see you some time.
Love Lyn.

Two weeks earlier Lynda had said she was going for drinks with friends. That evening there was a knock at the door and Mrs Gough saw a woman standing there and a car waiting. She described the woman as:

Mrs Gough: Dark haired, proportionate build, five feet four or five – however, I thought a bit older than Lynda. I would have thought she was in her early twenties.

She said that her reaction after Lynda went missing was of:

Mrs Gough: concern and worry. Her father and I felt, 'Let her have her head for a bit – she'll be back. (Lynda had taken some savings with her but) we did not think she was earning sufficient money to take herself a flat to live on – the pay she was getting was not very much. I was just anxious. I wanted to know how she was. I wanted to know how she was living – if she could afford it. We wanted to know if she was all right.

Mrs Gough visited the Co-Op where Lynda worked, but she was not there. She learned she was living in Cromwell Street. One Saturday morning about two weeks after Lynda went missing she knocked at 25 Cromwell Street:

Mrs Gough: A lady came to the door and I immediately recognised her as the lady that called for Lynda when she went out for a drink. (A man joined the woman and they talked) as a couple would. I said I had come to see Lynda. They said she was not there – that she had left.

(She was told that Lynda had gone to Weston-Super-Mare).

Mrs Gough: I immediately noticed she was wearing Lynda's slippers and other articles of her clothing – either a blouse or a cardigan. I said, 'But those are Lynda's slippers you're wearing'.

There was washing on the line, some of which Mrs Gough thought was Lynda's.

Mrs Gough: She said that Lynda had left them behind when she left.

She continued to question the couple:

Mrs Gough: but I got no feedback – there was nothing coming back. I remember it flashed through my mind that she wouldn't have had enough luggage to take everything with her. We were feeling very hurt, almost abandoned if you like, that Lynda went off and didn't keep in touch, although she promised she would.

She contacted a policeman friend "but whether he reported Lynda as missing I don't know. The thing was, she was over 18."

She went on to tell that her and her husband had gone to Weston-Super-Mare in search of her but were told by the unemployment office there that information was confidential and even if Lynda had registered they would not say so.

Mr Ferguson put only one question to her, whether she had ever returned to 25 Cromwell Street since that day:

Mrs Gough: I went past the house five years later and saw the cellar doors had been bricked up. I shuddered. I don't know why, but I shuddered. I never went past that house again.

Mae: "I've seen Mum and feel much better for it, although she seems even harder than she was before she went inside prison. There's something about her which is so uncompromising…Mum seemed really strong. It's as if she can take anything that's thrown at her. It's scary, really. We do have a rapport, although Mum is very demanding.

Mum is on a 24 hour lock-up where she is continually watched at all times. She's shattered after a full day in court and can only manage a bit of reading and sewing. She sees her solicitor Leo at the end of the day and then wants to sleep. She says she gets very mentally tired."

Stephen: "I'm working hard at the moment doing construction work, which means I can, at times, stop thinking about the trial. I don't know when it's all going to stop. The stories the witnesses are telling are very frightening and revealing horrors we wouldn't have thought possible. I've got a lot on my mind at the moment. I'm patching things up with my wife Andrea after we had a bust up and split."

12th October 1995

Ben Stanniland, now forty-one, gave evidence. He had been a lodger at 25 Cromwell Street for nearly fourteen months, throughout the Wests first year in residence and covering the period of Caroline Owens. Mr Stanniland told how on the first night that he and Alan Davis moved in to occupy a room on the top floor, they had gone to the pub for a drink with Fred and Rose.

Ben: Then we went back for coffee. The conversation was mostly sexual innuendos.

Mrs West then came upstairs and got in to bed with both of them.

Ben: It only happened on that occasion.

They were 'dubious' about going down to face Mr West in the morning, but

Ben: He made it obvious it was OK.

He confirmed that he and other lodgers regularly brought girls back to the house, and that Fred West was constantly engaged in building work of one kind or another.

He told the court that he met Lynda Gough in a café in Gloucester and brought her back to Cromwell Street where she became a regular visitor over the next six to seven months. Their affair ended, but she then had sexual relationships with other lodgers there. Lynda did some babysitting for the Wests. But eventually he noticed she was no longer going to Cromwell Street.

He said that he also remembered Caroline Owens. She was their former nanny and was held captive by the couple at the house overnight. He remembered Caroline being there with the Hoover, and meeting her at the launderette later the same day, when he neither noticed anything odd about her appearance nor heard her allude to anything unpleasant that had occurred.

Leveson: Did you see her after she had stopped living at the house?

Ben: Only on one occasion. I went downstairs to bang on Mrs West's door to borrow the hoover to do some cleaning up and on opening the door she was there.

He said that Rose was in the room with her and:

Ben: the reaction was shock and that I should not have been there, it was the wrong time to knock on the door.

Cross-examined by Richard Ferguson, he said Caroline was not crying and that he did not notice any bruising on her face.

He moved out in March 1973, just before the disappearance of Lynda Gough. He again told the court that they had had a sexual relationship.

Ferguson: Afterwards, when you said she became friends with some of the rest of your friends, did the same apply to them?
Ben: I believe so, yes.

He was then asked if he had been intimate with Caroline Owens:

Ben: Yes, on one occasion. I had known her for two or three weeks, not very well.

Ben Stanniland said that during the period of about 14 months he spent at Cromwell Street in 1972-73, Gloucestershire police had raided the house looking for drugs.

David Evans, another former lodger, gave evidence next. He said he had been arrested seven or eight times down the years for possession of cannabis and that all of the men living at 25 Cromwell Street while he stayed there had had sex with both Lynda Gough and Rose West.

David: She was the landlady but she would come upstairs now and again because she liked sex.

He said they had sexual intercourse once. He said he had also had a sexual relationship with Lynda Gough for a time, but she suddenly stopped visiting the house.

David: Rose came up one morning and said that Lynda Gough had hit her daughter while babysitting and that she would not be coming back.

The last time he saw Lynda was when she had an argument with Alan Davies, another lodger, and it was after that that Mrs West told him she had been sacked as the babysitter. For the rest, his evidence was a repeat of Ben Stanniland's.

Charles Jones, another lodger, confirmed that up to six or eight young men could be living at 25 Cromwell Street at once, each of them bringing girls back. He also told of a "surprising" encounter in the Wests' ground floor living room. When he went to pay his £3-a-week rent, he found Rose West and another woman semi-naked.

Terence Davis, a lodger, told the court how much he liked Fred West and how he spent half a day helping him clear out the damp and muddy cellar. "I'd do a bit of work for him and he took us for drinks." He was cross examined because he had seen a girl coming to the house late one night and spotted her again the following morning in the doorway of the landlord's bedroom. This was, he said, "nothing unusual", and the girl might have been Caroline Owens. She was not bound or gagged.

Elizabeth Brewer gave evidence next. She was Shirley Robinson's closest friend in the house. She had been living there when Shirley moved in and stayed as a lodger for a further four years. She said of 25 Cromwell Street:

Liz: If you were someone who'd been on the road, someone who was a bit lost, it could be like a security. Many of us wanted to belong to this, an extended family.

She took a room in April 1977 when she was 17-years-old.

Liz: The bedroom on the left was always called 'Rose's Special Bedroom'. The one opposite was the Wests mutual bedroom. The special bedroom was always kept locked and as far as I know nobody was allowed in there apart from Mr and Mrs West. When I first moved in the Wests were very friendly but they did embarrass me by talking about their open marriage and sex. Either one or other of them would talk about it constantly.

They used to embarrass me quite a lot by talking about their open marriage or sex. I would constantly be informed about their open marriage and that Rose had her boyfriends and Fred had his girlfriends. They were quite happy to have an open marriage. There would be times when they mentioned that they knew about people's personal sex lives and Mrs West said that when she retired she was going to spend her whole retirement engaged in sexual activity.

There were three other female lodgers at the time – Shirley Robinson, Clare Rigby and Gloria Langdon. She said that both Shirley Robinson and Rose West were pregnant at the same time and that one day she saw Shirley and Rose West kissing and cuddling outside the girl's room. She became friendly with Shirley who asked if she could stay in Liz Brewer's room. She recalled that everything had been happy and carefree at first, but that the atmosphere deteriorated seriously in the spring of 1978.

<u>Liz</u>: She (Shirley Robinson) became frightened of Mr West and wanted to keep away from him.

Eventually, Shirley shared Liz's room for her own safety.

<u>Liz</u>: She needed to keep away from Mr and Mrs West. There was a breakdown in communication.

She said that Fred West had told her that Shirley was becoming too possessive towards him. She said that when she last saw her:

<u>Liz</u>: Shirley seemed depressed. I asked her to come along (she was on her way to work as a lunch-time waitress), to meet some friends, but she was too tired, she just wanted to go back to sleep. I said 'see you later' and left. When I came back that afternoon, she'd gone. I thought that perhaps she was downstairs making it up with Mr and Mrs West. I did not want to go down and get drawn into one of their explicit conversations about sex. I was sure she would be there in the morning and would tell me how everything was normal and happy again with them".

Liz went on to tell how Fred had stopped her and her boyfriend Peter at the foot of the stairs the next morning and told her that Shirley had left and moved to Germany to stay with her father. Rose was present. She said that later in the day, Fred made a special visit to her room to tell her privately that Shirley had to go because she was getting too randy and was planning to rip Liz's knickers off her.

<u>Liz</u>: He went on so much about her wanting to get my knickers off. After that, to be honest, I was quite glad she'd gone.

Weeks later, Fred told Liz that Shirley had given birth in Germany to a boy and called him Barry. He said that Rose was going to look after the baby for a while to give Shirley a break.

She described the Wests as "friendly and generous", although their constant theme of sex as a subject of conversation embarrassed her. She remembered two specific remarks. Mrs West had told her that "When she retired she would spend her whole time having sex", and on another occasion she said "no matter what Fred did she would never leave him".

She admitted that she was due to receive £10,000 from a newspaper.

In cross examination Mr Ferguson concentrated on domestic matters. Mrs Brewer recalled that Anne Marie was frequently with boyfriends considerably older than herself, who came and went. Two of them, she said, more or less lived with her. They created problems and Fred had to throw them out.

The next witness gave evidence. Kathleen Ryan said she went to view a bedsit with her sister in 1978 and was taken into the living area by Fred West. There she saw a lot of children, Rose West and Shirley Robinson.

Kathleen: I was introduced to them by Mr West who said 'These are the children, this is my wife, and this is my lover'. I just looked at my sister and thought 'God, it's a bit weird'. My sister took the bedsit and stayed there for a couple of months and I used to stay with her two or three times a week.

Gillian Britt, another lodger, remembered 'Rose's Room' on the ground floor and told the court that she:

Gillian: saw men going in to that room, sometimes two or three at a time, after midnight. At night I heard thumping, crashing about and wails which I would describe as of a sexual nature. The wails were a sort of noise – shrieks perhaps.

Mr Ferguson objected:

Ferguson: Enough of this. It is accepted that Mrs West slept with other

483

men, but it is highly irrelevant and panders to the worst possible element of salaciousness.

The judge did not agree, so Mr Leveson continued. He asked the witness what she thought about it all:

Gillian: I thought it was amusing to hear shrieks coming from this room. Really, I did take it as part of a joke. I was only 17 but I felt it quite amusing. My imagination would stretch. I thought it was just basically somebody doing something of a sexual nature. But sometimes it got beyond a joke and I had to turn up the radio to drown them out. The noises didn't seem to me to indicate and kind of pleasure, if I could put it like that.

She later added:

Gillian: It disturbed me. I didn't want to live like this and I left after six months. I did not think it was any of my business. If that is the way they wanted to carry on their sex life it is up to them. It was their home.

She described how in the summer of 1979 she talked with a smartly dressed girl she found sitting on the stairs at Cromwell Street. The teenager called herself Ali or Al. From police photographs she now knew the girl was Alison Chambers.

Clare Rigby lived in the room opposite Shirley Robinson and gave evidence next.

Clare: Fred answered the door and took me into the living area. Some of the children were there and Mrs West was there. Later, I met other lodgers including Liz Brewer and someone called Gloria. Shirley Robinson was there and she used to spend a lot of time downstairs with Fred and Rose. She never mentioned she was going to leave but then had apparently left.

She had been living there for about 2 months before Shirley Robinson vanished. She said she saw:

Clare: Mrs West in Shirley's old room after she had left – perhaps a week or two later. The door was ajar and Rose West saw me. As I looked in she was there with piles of clothes bundling them into bags – carrier bags. There were three or four bags but it was quite momentary and when Rose saw me she pushed the door to. Fred West told me 'Shirley Robinson has done a bunk'.

Jane Bayle, Liz Brewer's cousin and a community nurse who had visited 25 Cromwell Street as a young girl, told the court:

Jane: To be honest, Rose West unnerved me because she stared at me a lot and dressed like a child. I met Shirley Robinson and she was heavily pregnant. Shirley slept in three different rooms to my knowledge. Shirley had her own room, then she went in to the Wests bedroom, then she moved in to my cousins' room.

Asked how Shirley got on with the Wests, she replied:

Jane: She was having a sexual relationship with both.

A former staff member of Jordans Brook House, Enfys Davies, said in a statement:

Enfys: Alison Chambers was very clingy to me – it was as if she wanted constant affection and wanted to belong to something secure. I found it rather stifling at that time.

She said that Alison shared a room with a girl called Sharon (probably Compton) from Somerset, until they absconded at the same time.

Enfys: They were close and shared each other's clothes. She went on: During the Summer evenings there would be a van regularly parked by the entrance to Jordans Brook. It was a Transit type van, scruffy. Some of the girls would hang around the van.

The jury then heard of the last known sightings of some of the victims:

Carol Ann Cooper's boyfriend Andrew Jones said he watched her catch a bus at 9.15pm on November 10th 1973.

Andrew: Carol waved and I waved back. It was 9.15pm. I have not seen her since.

Helen Render, a school friend of Lucy Partington, said in a statement written before she passed away that they spent the evening of December 27th, 1973 discussing Christmas. Her mother, Margaret Partington, said:

Margaret: I did not expect her to be home until 11pm. She did not come.

Edith Simmons said she last saw her friend Therese Siegenthaler late in 1973 when she stayed over at her flat in Deptford, South East London, the night before leaving for Ireland.

Edith: I was surprised not to get a postcard or phone call from her. It was out of character.

Daniel Davies said he last saw Shirley Hubbard on November 14th 1974.

Daniel: I saw Shirley on to a bus to Droitwich and the next day I waited for her to arrive but she never came.

He also said that another of the victims found at 25 Cromwell Street, Carol Ann Cooper, had gone out with his older brother Alan in 1972, but the two girls had never met.

Timothy Davis took to the stand. He told how he was a boyfriend of Juanita Mott's. He told the court that about 1974-1975 she moved to 25 Cromwell Street as a lodger for a time.

Timothy: She was a lively, spirited girl and I used to pick her up and drop her off there but never went inside.

Mrs Jennifer Baldwin told how Juanita Mott disappeared the day before she was due to get married:

Jennifer: The arrangement involved Juanita looking after my children. The night before, Juanita left in the early evening to go to Gloucester. By the following day she had not returned. It was totally out of character.

13th October 1995

Stephen West: "I'm trying to keep my life together at the moment, while coping with the trial. I've been done for careless driving, fined £300 and given six points on my license. I told them I'd had it rough because of everything and they accepted that. I could have been banned, which would really have screwed up my building work."

Mae: "Mum's alright. She gave me a call. It's funny hearing her voice over the telephone. She sends me one letter a week these days. The letters used to be a lot longer, but Mum only has the time, and I suppose the energy, to write a few lines saying how much she loves me and everything. I get a bit upset because everyone hates her inside prison. The guards are really offish with her, but Mum manages. She's tough beyond belief. Nothing will break her."

16th October 1995

'Miss A', 33, gave evidence. She told how she had been placed in care at the age of thirteen and ended up a resident at Jordans Brook home for girls in Gloucester. She hated being in an institution as it made her feel unwanted and embarrassed. Shortly after her 14th birthday she was introduced to 25 Cromwell Street, where she met Rose West. She said that Rose was a combination of young mother and big sister, somebody to whom you could tell your troubles to and from whom you could expect sympathy.

Miss A: She told me I could go there any time, there would always be a shoulder to cry on. I felt that there was somebody who really cared at last.

She went to the house about nine times, usually on a Friday on her way to spend the weekend with her mother. She said she was never introduced to the children. Several times she absconded from Jordans Brook and lived on the streets. On one of these occasions she and another girl called Yvonne went to Cromwell Street and asked if they could stay the night. They were made very welcome, given hot drinks, and slept on the sofa. Nothing untoward happened.

It was on a subsequent visit that her terrible experience occurred. It began with fondling by Rose and developed in to something far worse. She was taken, she said, into a room where there were already three other people. One was Fred West. The others were two adolescent and unidentified girls.

Miss A: A blonde aged 13 or 14 and a girl of 15 or 16 with dark spiky hair and an arm tattoo. Everything seemed it was supposed to be normal, like we were all girls together. She was caressing this girl on her forehead and down her body.

She cleared her throat frequently and was close to tears as she recalled what had happened. Rose West had produced some packing tape, she said, which Fred West applied to the girl, wrapping it around her wrists "as though bandaged". Then some group sex took place.

Miss A: The other girl didn't resist. It was as though this was all normal to her.

Of Rose, she said that she was one minute aggressive, and another all motherly again. She made encouraging remarks to her husband, such as, "Is it turning you on, Fred? Are you enjoying it?" After this, said the witness, it was her turn, and she described to the court in graphic detail a series of acts performed upon her body.

Miss A: The young girl got up and just went over to the other girl and sat and wept. I was then approached by Rose and led to the bed. She held my wrists and led me to the bed. I kept wanting to cry. I just felt numb. Rose started undressing me. I didn't know what to do.

Several times she broke down when she was recalling her experience.

'Miss A' said she sat on the bed while Rose told her: 'Enjoy, relax, it's fun.'

Miss A: She started caressing, and touching my shoulders and neck. She was just stroking. I just kept quiet. I just thought 'why?' The other girls were against the wall – the dark one was sitting as she was before and the little one was sat, just crying, sobbing.

She told how Fred returned, and Rose bound her hands and ankles with brown packing tape before using a dildo on her. Then Fred raped her.

She felt "panic, discomfort – it seemed like forever". Fred then left the room and "Rose got a tiny pair of silver scissors and snipped one side of the tape and pulled it." 'Miss A' then held up her thumb to show the judge where she had been cut by the scissors as the tape was ripped away. She said she picked up her summer dress and hurried to the bathroom before leaving the house without her bra and shoes and hitchhiking to her mothers' home in Tewkesbury, Gloucestershire.

She said that she felt "so ashamed, sick and just stupid" and did not tell anyone what had happened. She said she felt betrayed by Rose.

Miss A: She was like a big-sister-cum-mum. I never had a sister so it was nice. I could talk to her – I could not talk to my mum. It was like somebody really cared and it did not matter that you were in care.

Asked what was her attitude towards the defendant following this incident?

Miss A: Hate - I felt that she really cared. I trusted someone and she used me.

Leveson: Did you tell your mother or anyone else about it?
Miss A: No, because I felt so ashamed. Besides which, I presumed I would be called a liar. Because you were in care you were regarded as bad.

She had not much left. She didn't want to see everything else taken from her. About six weeks later, she said, she went back to Cromwell Street with petrol and matches, intending to set the house on fire.

Miss A: All I had in my mind was revenge.

Mr Leveson then asked if she had gone through with her plan, her voice strangled with regret and said:

Miss A: No. I got to Cromwell Street and stood by the front gate and I wanted to do it so much.

The first person to whom 'Miss A' told of her experience was Detective Constable Williams on 28th July 1994, five months after the arrest of Fred West. The police had approached her.

Miss A: I heard something on the news about what was happening at Cromwell Street. I remember feeling cold. I knew there were bodies found there, but not how old they were or if they were boys or girls.

At the committal in February 1995, her identity was inadvertently revealed by counsel in the course of a remark to the magistrate and immediately retracted. But it was too late. A newspaper contacted her and she had a friend negotiate on her behalf. She entered into a contract in March. She was due to receive £30,000 from Express Newspapers.

Ferguson: £30,000 Miss A?

Having first exposed her deceit in giving spurious reasons for wishing to make deals with the press, he turned to her confusion. In her first statement to the police she said that she had never visited Cromwell Street. Now she says she had, up to nine times, but she could not describe anything in the house.

Ferguson: I apologize, but I must ask some things. Were you abused as a child by your father?
Miss A: Yes, not long before I went to Cromwell Street.
Ferguson: Your father had sex with you?
Miss A: Yes.
Ferguson: And your brother?
Miss A: Not full intercourse, no.

Ferguson: You've had a very unhappy medical background?

Miss A: In what sense?

Ferguson: I'll try to help as best I can.

Mr Ferguson revealed that she had attended a clinic to be treated for gonorrhoea at the age of fourteen, and was about to launch upon her psychiatric history when Mr Justice Mantell intervened to put a stop to the ordeal. What was the relevance, he asked, and how far do you intend to go?

Ferguson: It is relevant to her knowledge and ability to fantasize, My Lord. She has had the experience, unfortunately, on which to draw for this account.

He intended to go as far as was necessary to show that she invented stories, mixing up personal history with imagination, and even that she was motivated by "understandable rancour and malice". He was given leave to continue.

Counsel passed immediately on to the love affair between 'Miss A', aged fourteen, and Graham Letts, brother of Rosemary West.

Ferguson: You were infatuated with him, weren't you?

Miss A: Yes, I had a crush on him

Ferguson: And you ran away with him?

Miss A: Yes, I did.

Ferguson: You stayed with him in a flat above a tea-shop in Cheltenham, and you were having sex with him regularly.

Miss A: Only a couple of times.

Mr Ferguson then gave the witness her statement of 13ᵗʰ March in which she agreed she had been sleeping with Mr Letts on a regular basis. The statement included the lines: "There are events from my life which I find difficult to talk about...why I distrusted adults when I was a child...I thought that no-one would believe me no matter what I said or what happened to me". It went on to mention another man called Tom, aged about fifty, also living above the tea-shop in Cheltenham, who "sort of looked after us both. I let him have sex with me three or four times. He threatened to call the police and tell them I was under age if I didn't". At no time had Rose West revealed to her that Graham Letts was her brother.

Mr Ferguson built up a portrait of a forlorn, abject, misused and manipulative young girl. She made up stories about boyfriends. She had several phantom pregnancies, three within one year. She attended maternity hospital continually for a period of four years with imaginary gynaecological complaints. She sent a photograph of a baby to Graham Letts falsely claiming it was his. At the age of sixteen she entered into a horrifyingly violent marriage which ended with her spending some time in a home for battered wives after her husband had tried to smother her with a pillow. She had tried to commit suicide and had sought psychiatric help, spending time in the psychiatric wing of a hospital.

Most alarming of all were the records of her history and background as revealed to the psychiatrist. She told him of the sexual abuse she had suffered at the hands of her father and brother, of her loneliness and despair, her disastrous affair with Graham Letts and her promiscuity, and of her violent marriage. But she had not once mentioned the ordeal which she now claimed she had endured at the West's home:

Ferguson: Why?
Miss A: I didn't know how to talk about it.
Ferguson: I suggest that when you were told what had been found at 25 Cromwell Street you fantasized that you were yourself involved...it was a figment of your imagination...you made up the story of masking tape after reading about it.
Miss A: No. I know what happened and so do they. I know what happened is not a fantasy. It is something that I have kept inside for 18 years. I feel people are looking at me even now and thinking I'm dirty.

Counsel finished with the revelation that' Miss A' had suffered from hallucinations. She imagined seeing people with other people's heads on their shoulders, and was haunted in particular by a man in black who followed her around. He did not exist. She had undergone six sessions of electroconvulsive therapy. On occasions she walked out of her home and was found wandering in a state of blankness somewhere distant; only a year ago she had idly caught the first train from Basingstoke, which happened to go to Southampton, and been assaulted there at two in the morning. Ferguson's final remark was addressed directly to the judge:

Ferguson: Mrs West has no recollection of ever having met this woman. She never went to Cromwell Street at all, ever.

Mr Leveson rose to point out that the witness did not discover that Graham Letts was related to Mrs West until after she had made her statement to the police, and also to elicit from her that the man in black she imagined was following her bore the face of Fred West.

The final word belonged to Miss A. Defiantly, she said:

Miss A: I know what happened. It wasn't a fantasy, and they know it wasn't.

She had been in the witness box the whole day.

Mae: "I'm still trying to come to terms with reading about my sister Heather's murder. I didn't know the details of what happened to her – I can't really cope with thinking about her final moments. It does horrify me to think what became of Heather and those poor girls. Their final moments must have been agony. It's incredibly sad. God knows what their families must be feeling…"

Stephen: "Like Mae, I've thought a great deal of what became of the victims. I listened to Dad's confession of what he did. It was so mechanical, so monstrous, that maybe I couldn't take it in. Hearing about the bodies and the dismemberment reminds me of what actually went on…"

17th October 1995

Mrs Ruth Owen told the court how she had attended the same grammar school as Lucy Partington between 1967 and 1970 and had been friendly with her. It was her habit to walk with Lucy to the bus-stop on Evesham Road in Cheltenham, because she lived just round the corner from it. She told Mr Ferguson that she vividly recalled an odd incident one evening as she was walking between her home and the bus-stop. A car pulled up by her and the driver offered her a lift. She declined the offer because she was almost home anyway, but his manner was very friendly and persuasive and she felt she was being put under pressure to get into the car. She was anxious to move on and the possibility that the man might not take no for an answer frightened her. Eventually he gave up and drove away up the hill. She told her parents what had happened and never forgot the fear of that night. She said the driver was about ten or fifteen years older than she was, with white skin and thick, dark hair, and though the evidence she put before the court could not be conclusive, it seemed very likely that she had been on the point of being abducted by somebody who could well have been Frederick West. He was alone in the car.

Mrs Jane Hamer told the jury how she and her boyfriend went to live at 25 Cromwell Street after her 16th birthday in 1976 and left in early 1977. Asked if she heard anything unusual, she replied:

Jane: I heard children screaming and shouting "stop it daddy" and "no…no…please". I believe it was from the cellar area. They were female shouts – either Heather or Mae.

She said that Rose seemed to be dominant in character and told everyone what to do and when to do it. She said that Rose West hardly ever left the house.

Ferguson: Did you report the screaming which you heard to anyone?
Jane: No.

Mr Erwin Marschall described how he had been a boyfriend of Anne Marie and had stayed at 25 Cromwell Street one evening in 1980. Anne Marie was no longer living with her parents by this time, so it was not clear why they should have spent the night at Cromwell Street.

Erwin: I couldn't sleep, being in a strange place I heard some noises and I thought I heard a scream and someone shout. It went on for about 10 to 20 minutes – something like that.

The screaming seemed quite long, then there was a break and it began again. He heard cries of "no, no, please". He had seen Heather earlier that night. She seemed to be a shy girl. The following morning Rose West explained them away by saying her daughter Heather was having one of her regular nightmares. In 1988 Mr Marschall was working as a window cleaner and his job took him to the house next door to No. 25. He was told by Rose West that Heather had run away from home. He asked if she had told the police and she said that she had. The witness said Rose West claimed Heather had become uncontrollable and that there was nothing much she could do about her running away. At the time, Fred West was laying foundations for a patio in the garden and he never saw her again. Counsel for the defence reminded the witness that in his statement he said that the screaming had lasted five to ten minutes, and that now it had expanded to between ten and twenty minutes. Mr Ferguson asked, "Are you just guessing Mr Marschall"? "You didn't time it did you"? "You are guessing, aren't you"? The witness agreed that he was.

Ronalzo Harrison, a life-long friend of Fred West and with a daughter the same age as Heather, was called next. He said that Fred had told him that Heather had run away after Rose had given her a good hiding, but kept in touch by telephone. Fred had also made the strange comment that Heather had 'put scratches on the faces' of the younger children. Mr Ferguson tried to make two points, and succeeded with one of them. In the twenty-five years that the witness had known Fred West, he agreed that he had had nothing to do with Rose, and had rarely even spoken to her. On the other hand, he had had countless conversations with Fred over the years, and a vivid gesture of the hand to indicate that Fred was boringly talkative brought a smile to the many faces in court. Mr Ferguson wanted the witness to agree that, from so many conversations, it was not possible for him to be sure that Rose West was present when one in particular took place, but Mr Harrison was adamant that she had been.

Margaretta Dix, a neighbour who lived opposite at number 29, told of the day she found her husband dead on the bathroom floor following a heart attack. She turned to the Wests for help.

Margaretta: Fred did everything in his power to save my husband and Rose took me over to her house, tried to calm me down, offered me endless cups of tea and reassuring talk.

She said that Rose was the boss in that house and that she used to walk her grandchildren to school with Rose, who took Heather.

Margaretta: Fred thought the world of Rose, I know that. I think she felt the same.

Told that Heather had left home, she asked Rose if she had made enquiries. "No", Rose was alleged to have responded. "I am not bothered if she is dead or alive. She has made her bed and she must lie in it".

Margaretta: Had it been one of mine, I'd have been worried sick. Rose didn't seem to care at all.

Linda Tonks remembered that her daughter's boyfriend Stephen West got in to trouble when he went home with his muddy football boots and Rose berated him for ruining her clean floor. She recalled how Rose used to phone her house to make sure Stephen came home on time. She went to see Rose about it, and they sat in the kitchen chatting about the unreliability and ingratitude of teenagers. On another occasion, the witness told the court that Fred had said that Charmaine had been sent to live with her mother in Scotland because Rose had her little ones and could not cope with them all. She said Fred had described how Anne Marie had run away from home and he had found her working as a prostitute. He brought her back and he had punched her in the face and carried her into his van quite easily. On another occasion, in a discussion about videos, Rose told her that they had videos at home and said it was "the real McCoy".

A friend of Mae's and Stephen's said that Heather was often spoken about in the house after her departure, and that her brother and sister were keen on trying to find out where she was. This same witness saw Rose after a beating from her husband. Her glasses had been broken and she had a black eye. "All the things I've done for that man and he treats me like this", she apparently said.

Mrs Linda Greening, a neighbour who lived opposite 25 Cromwell Street, told the court she was pregnant at the same time as Rose West and

Shirley Robinson and was invited over for a cup of tea. She said that she was shocked when Rose told her that Fred was the father of Shirley's unborn child and that he later came in and confirmed this. She added that Rose did not seem upset by this.

Mr Arthur John Dobbs described how he met Rose West at 25 Cromwell Street after answering an advertisement in a contact magazine. She had given her name as Mandy. He was taken in to a small bedroom by Rose with her husband following. He did not object to what was going on. He told the court that Rose was "very friendly". He paid frequent visits to Cromwell Street for 18 months and sometimes as much as three times a week. He paid £10 a time at first, but there was no charge later as he carried out repairs on Fred's van. He told how, once, over a cup of tea, Rose made a speech during which she said that her husband had been having sex with the children. Mr Dobbs said he thought that was odd and that something had slipped out which was not meant to. He was an inquisitive sort of person and kept it in his mind, thinking one day it would be "a little armour of mine". He said that he had telephoned social services anonymously between 1986 and 1988 to tell them of his discovery.

Kathryn Halliday, 38, had shared a room at 11 Cromwell Street with another woman after leaving her husband. When a leak appeared in her ceiling, she was advised to get Fred West down the road to have a look. He repaired it immediately. There was no secret about her sexuality, she said, and Fred said she should "see my missus – she'll sort you out". She visited Rose every morning for months to chat about teenagers and knitting. The lesbian affair began within minutes of her first visit to number 25. She says she was immediately ushered upstairs to the sitting-room and bar on the first floor, where

Kathryn: Fred asked me if I wanted to see any videos – pornographic videos. Anything I wanted he could put on for me.

She asked if he had a "straight video – showing ordinary sex", and Fred promptly put one on.

Kathryn: Rose came straight into the room and sat down beside me. She was wearing a miniskirt and a low-cut top. Nothing else. No underwear at all. She began to undress me very quickly. I must admit I was very taken aback. I'd never been in a situation like this. I was dragged upstairs to the front bedroom. It was very, very quick, very forceful. There were mirrors on the wardrobes and there was a double bed. I was pushed down on the bed, and Rose West joined me. She was quite aggressive. She proceeded to make love to me.

Fred, meanwhile, disappeared for ten minutes, then came back with a tray of drinks and a video camera. He was now naked and he started to film the two women.

Kathryn: It appeared that Rose was trying to get me sexually excited, and then Fred joined in. He made love to me while Rose was sitting astride me, on top of me. Mr West climaxed very quickly, and went downstairs to get another drink...Rose became very aggressive. She held me down on the bed very hard. She gripped my wrists and began to taunt me. She was saying, "Are you woman enough to want to do all the things that we want to do to you?

Rose wanted to use a variety of vibrators and dildos on Kathryn Halliday, and then for Kathryn to use them on her. She tried, but

Kathryn: I couldn't use them all, even though the session went on until one o'clock or one-thirty in the morning.

Even then, Rose was not anxious to bring it to an end. "But Fred didn't join in again, after the first time." She would occasionally have sex with Rose while Fred was at work.

Kathryn: I'm not naïve, but I've never in my entire life been in a situation where it all happened so quickly.

The two women met "about once a day, mostly during the day – but some evenings as well" for months.

Kathryn: Rose would knock on the window at number 11 after taking the children to school.

She was not allowed to go to 25 Cromwell Street on Thursday mornings, because that was kept for Rose's male clients. Each time she went, she remembered, "vibrators were there", to be used "very, very physically", along with "dildos of different shapes and sizes." One of the dildos was eighteen inches long and covered with nodules. Rose called it her Exocet, the name of a missile used during the Falklands conflict, but there were many others. One was called The Eiffel Tower and then there was Fred's favourite. A 14" rubber phallus that he called "the cunt-buster". Their meetings always started:

Kathryn: very gently and she was very persuasive. But once she had got you into the bedroom she wanted to make you vulnerable. When she got you into a vulnerable position physically and mentally, she would use that against your person.

When Fred West was there, he would:

Kathryn: Often put on videos while we were having a drink, like most people would put on background music. They were all to do with bondage and sadism. They were amateur videos. There was one of a girl in a black rubber suit having sex with a man. There were others with girls who were tied to a bed with chains and straps"

And in one of them Kathryn even recognised the Wests' front bedroom. "A girl with fair hair was being whipped and tied to the bed" by a man who might possibly have been Fred West himself.

Kathryn: She was forcibly being made love to – very, very forcefully.

A large dildo was being used, and the camera focused specifically on the young girl's distress.

During the evening sessions:

Kathryn: Fred would watch rather than take part…He took part sometimes, but not very often at all.

On one occasion he ejaculated into his wife so quickly that she told him "you needn't have bothered." If Fred West took part at all, it was usually only when

Kathryn: I had my hands and feet tied. Rose would sit across me. She would hold me down and Fred would make love to me. She was quite a big woman and very, very physically strong. Most times I went in the evening, it would end up with me being tied up.

Fred and Rose then began to increase their sexual demands.

Kathryn: She wanted orgasms all the time, like a machine. They wanted me to do more and more. They pushed me beyond my personal limits, and they hurt me. The first time was making love – the second time had become more forceful, more aggressive, more demanding. Rose West wanted me to do things to her which were very, very aggressive.

They blindfolded her "several times" and Rose put a pillow over her head and whispered: "What does it feel like not to be able to see?" Then, after leaving the pillow in place for some time, she whispered again: "Can't you breathe? Aren't you woman enough to take it?" She said that Fred and Rose enjoyed causing her pain, and that Rosemary West in particular:

Kathryn: had no limit to what she would do. They played with me and the idea that I was frightened. They got their thing from seeing other people frightened.

On one occasion, she was taken into a bedroom which contained a four-poster bed with two hooks on a pelmet. She was shown a collection of short leather skirts and lingerie. In a suitcase beside them "there were black rubberised masks and suits. There were all-in-one suits with slits for the nose". There were also masks with no nose or mouth holes, which offered "no physical means of being able to breathe." The masks and suits had obviously been worn, "because they smelled of sweat". She was also shown whips. When the Wests asked her if she would wear one of the suits:

Kathryn: I said no and I edged out of the room. I was frightened. I never ever went back into that room.

On another occasion Fred actually punched her in the face while Rose was holding her down, and on another she felt a sharp stabbing pain in her stomach which she discovered was a half-inch cut in her navel.

Kathryn: Each time they pushed me a little further. They became more and more violent, physically and mentally. Fred would beat me around the head with his fists and Rose slapped me."

Gradually, Fred and Rose got bored "because a lot of the time I couldn't take any more." Finally, she accepted:

Kathryn: I was getting out of my depth. I realised how dangerous things were getting. I never returned to Cromwell Street. I was very, very vulnerable. The scenario was very much like a moth to a flame. You kept going back until you burned yourself…I kept going back until I could take no more.

She went on to tell the court that she had often met the West's children.

Kathryn: They put little children to sleep above the bodies that were found at Cromwell Street. I find that absolutely… They knew that they were there and they let children sleep on top of them.

She admitted to being paid £8,000 by Mirror Group.

Mr Ferguson began his cross-examination by telling the witness that she had negotiated with newspapers and refined her story for them before she made her first statement to the police, and that she managed to extract another £1,000 out of them after the suicide of Frederick West. Why had she done this?

Kathryn: Because I wanted the world to know I'm a survivor

Did she realize that there would be no publication unless the trial resulted in a conviction? Yes she did.

Ferguson: You have cashed in on sexual activity which you enjoyed, then exaggerated that activity and tried to present yourself as a victim. The truth is that between October 1988 and June 1989 you kept going back to 25 Cromwell Street for more sex.

Defence then argued in the absence of the jury that repetition of this kind of evidence was salacious and added nothing to the case. He further objected to the Crown's intention to introduce Frederick West's advice that the holes in the cellar beams were meant to suspend living bodies. A distinction must be made between inference and speculation, he said. The judge ruled in his favour.

18th October 1995

Three more witnesses, one of them in the form of a statement read out by junior counsel, were heard. 'Miss X', whose statement was read out, said she had had two lesbian sessions with Rose West.

One seventeen year old girl who found her way back to Cromwell Street in the second half of 1975 said she was first taken there by a friend. She thought that Fred and Rose were a "very pleasant couple", especially when Fred offered "to run her home" in his A35 van. She went back a few weeks later, and Rose invited her to her bedroom to see a jacket she had been making, and then persuaded the girl to take off her clothes and lie down on the bed. As Fred explained himself years afterwards: "Rose had terrific powers of persuasion over these girls. If you could persuade a girl to undress in a bedroom, and that you're measuring her up for a dress, you've got some power." When the girl was naked, Rose proceeded to kiss her neck, and then work down her body until she was sucking and licking her vagina.

"I was bewildered by it all", the girl remembered later. But, a few weeks afterwards, she returned to Cromwell Street, and on this occasion Rose took her down into the cellar and laid her on a "single mattress on the floor." The rest of the room, she remembered, "was full of toys." Once again, Rose persuaded her to take off her clothes, and licked her vagina, but this time she went on to insert a vibrator into her. "She did it so quick, it hurt me a lot", the girl told the court "and she held it up there inside me. I had to ask her to take it out because it was hurting so much."

The seventeen-year-old was a virgin. She ended up bleeding so badly that Rose West handed her a baby's nappy to use as a sanitary towel. But the girl did not complain. She simply put on her clothes and left.

Just after lunch time, Anne Marie took to the stand. Mr Leveson talked her through her early childhood and the love of her father and Rosemary's often physical beatings of her.

She said her last memory of her mother, Rena, was when she was about seven.

Asked how she got on with Charmaine, she replied:

Anne Marie: I was a daddy's girl. I loved my dad a lot. I was a cry-baby. Charmaine wouldn't cry. She felt it was giving in.

She recalled seeing Charmaine tied to a bed – but she didn't know the reason. Finally, she was told that Charmaine had been taken away by their mother.

She told how Rosemary had hit her over her head and drawn blood because she had been angry with Charmaine.

Leveson: Do you remember your first sexual experience?
Anne Marie: Yes I do
Leveson: How old were you?
Anne Marie: I was eight.

Leveson: Where was it?
Anne Marie: It was at 25 Cromwell Street. In the basement, the cellar.
Leveson: Who was involved?
Anne Marie: My stepmother and my father. I was taken downstairs, my father in front, me in the middle with my stepmother behind. We entered the room and on the floor there were some cloths and tape. I was very frightened. I didn't know what was happening. I asked what these things were for. There was no answer.

Anne Marie later recalled: "Mr Leveson let me tell the story in my own words only occasionally interrupting."

Anne Marie: I had my clothes removed.
Leveson: Do you remember who did that?
Anne Marie: Rosemary did.

Anne Marie later recalled: "There was a gasp from the public gallery as I began to tell the judge and jury about what happened to me that day."

Anne Marie: I was crying. I was asking 'what's going on? What's happening?' I was told that I should be very grateful I had such caring parents who thought of me, who were going to make sure that when I got married I would be able to satisfy my husband. I was struggling. I had my legs crossed. I was screaming and crying. Because I was struggling so much I had my hands bound and was gagged. Rose was sitting across me. I remember this excruciating pain. I wished I was dead. I also felt I shouldn't be so ungrateful because they were doing this to help me. My stepmother watched my father have sexual intercourse with me. It seemed to go on for a long time. Then they were whispering a lot.

She was asked if Rose did anything other than restrain her during the first assault.

Anne Marie: She was laughing and smirking and joining in. She was saying to me it was for my own good, and to stop being silly.

Rose then assaulted her. Anne Marie said that she never told anyone.

Anne Marie: I was told I should be very grateful, and was lucky I had such loving parents. I was led to believe all loving parents acted the same.

On another occasion, she said, Rose told her to tidy up toys in the basement.

Anne Marie: I was very apprehensive about going down there. I did as I was told, and this object (a U-shaped device) was against the wall. I went to turn around and go back up. Rosemary was behind me. I think she said something like 'Where are you going? I told you to tidy up'. I said I didn't want to. I felt frightened because my dad wasn't there.

She said she was ordered to undress, then strapped to the instrument.

Anne Marie: I was gagged because I started screaming…Rosemary started hitting me

Asked what she had been hit with, she replied:

Anne Marie: Her fists and hands…and swearing at me. Calling me names. Hitting me with a belt. Then I remember my father being there. He had his work overalls on, and I remember looking at him pleading with him with my eyes. My father had intercourse with me and then he went. I presume it was his lunch hour.

Asked how the incident finished, she said:

Anne Marie: Rosemary sexually abused me.

Afterwards, she said Rose ran her a bath. "She'd make me a cup of tea – she was so kind to me."

She told how she had regular sexual intercourse with her father, and that he gave her a few pounds not to tell Rose. Except once. Rosemary took her out for the evening when she was thirteen, helped dress her nicely and put make-up on.

Anne Marie: My father took us in the green van we had. Rose was laughing and joking. I felt happy. She was very nice to me, a different person. I drank barley wine and ate crisps, and by closing time I was a bit tipsy.

After they left the pub, Fred pulled up in the van and Anne Marie was pushed in.

Anne Marie: Rose started clawing at me and hitting me with her fist. She was saying 'If you think you're going to be friends with me, you must be joking'. I kept thinking, what have I done? Why? I haven't done anything wrong. Then my father came in to the back, and was hitting me. My father had intercourse with me. My step mother was just laughing, taunting me, hitting, fondling and pinching me. I was frightened.

Anne Marie said that whenever she had been abused, Fred told Rose to make sure the bruising didn't show. Once, a teacher called at the house after seeing a bruise.

Anne Marie: When she went, I got the biggest hiding in my life. But I never said anything. I thought it was right and I must not make a fuss. I was told I was being ungrateful.

Asked what the relationship between Fred and Rose was like, she replied:

Anne Marie: They doted on each other. Rose would have done anything for my dad. They used to talk a lot and used what was called their office – the bathroom – and talk with the door shut. I believe they always told each other what they were doing and had total trust in each other.

After being questioned about lodgers at Cromwell Street, Anne-Marie said:

Anne Marie: Sometimes people would stay a few days and then go, it was the normal circumstances we lived in. No-one questioned whether people stayed or left.

Anne Marie then told she remembered her father patting Shirley Robinson and saying "There's a baby in there."

Anne Marie: They didn't make any secret of their relationship. As Shirley's pregnancy started to show more, she would sometimes walk around with just a bra and pants on. He taunted my stepmother by saying 'Shirley is going to be my next wife.' I remember I thought 'I can't believe what I am hearing.'

She was then asked how Rose reacted:

Anne Marie: She was very upset, and it was understandable. He was humiliating her. After that it became very tense, and Shirley would go upstairs and stay up there. There were a lot of rows between my step-mum and father.

When Shirley vanished, Anne Marie recalled:

Anne Marie: I remember I came home from school one day and it was very close to when Shirley's baby was due and I was told Shirley had gone to Germany.

At the end of the afternoon the defence barrister Mr Richard Ferguson QC, said he was not ready to cross examine Anne Marie and the judge adjourned. Before doing so, he warned Anne Marie not to talk to anyone about the evidence she had given.

Mae: "Hearing about Anne Marie's evidence is really hard. I'm torn really. I don't really get on with her. We're very different people and she hates Mum with a vengeance. I think it's because Mum isn't her real mum, though I accept completely she had a very, very rough time as a child. We all did in our own ways. Yet, I suppose we've taken sides. Anne Marie against Mum and me."

Stephen: "…I'm trying to get myself together. I'm seeing psychiatrists to try to control my temper and understand what I'm all about. I'm not a bad person, it's just that things happen to me. I need to get myself on the straight and narrow."

Anne Marie: "I didn't go home after giving evidence the first day. Instead I was put up in a hotel on the South Coast. It was unfortunate that the day after I gave evidence the jury were going to go on a planned visit to 25 Cromwell Street.

19th October 1995

The judge, jury, counsel and court officials visited 25 Cromwell Street. Rose West chose not to attend and said that she thought it would be too distressing. The judge and his clerk went in a limousine; the jury were in a coach with curtains drawn at the windows and motorcycle police escort before and behind; and twelve people from the media followed in another coach, also with police escort but without the secrecy of curtains.

Upon arrival, the jury coach disappeared beneath a canopy behind 25 Cromwell Street before the jurors got off, so that they weren't seen by anybody. Once the jury had left, the media representatives followed exactly the same route through the house as they had, in single file, silently, prohibited from asking questions or making remarks. They started on what remained of the patio, bare now apart from three chalked circles to mark where the remains of Heather West, Shirley Robinson and Alison Chambers had been found. Marching down the side of the house, they entered by the front door, walked in and out of the two lower rooms and up the pale-green staircase to the bar-room and the former lodger's rooms above. They finished with a grim viewing of the dark and dusty cellar.

25 Cromwell Street

Mae: "I've been watching the news and it doesn't look good. Everybody seems so shocked by what is coming out in the trial. I know it's awful. There's been evidence which has really hurt me. Mum had admitted she did things to Caroline Owens – "I was a bit over the top," she said."

Anne Marie: "The fear once again began to build in my mind…in the evening I wanted to be alone and refused all offers from the police for company. I needed space and I felt no one could help me. I spent a substantial amount of the evening drinking and then took some of the drugs the doctor had given me. It was stupid but I wasn't thinking straight. I made a call for help and the police got to me in time. I had my stomach pumped at Southampton Hospital and spent part of the night there.

The next day they could not release me without the permission of a psychiatrist. There wasn't one present and a doctor had to be rushed from Winchester to pass me fit before I could leave the hospital. I was ready and waiting at eight o'clock, determined to finish my evidence. Somehow word had got out and when I left the hospital the press were there."

20th October 1995

It was announced to the court that Anne Marie was unable to continue with her testimony because she was 'indisposed'.

Her estranged husband, Christopher Davis, took to the stand and recalled the birthday party in 1987 to which the entire West family came and at which Heather seemed more and more "into herself, withdrawn and morose". It was the last time he saw her. He also confirmed the existence of a suitcase in the bar-room containing sex videos and snapshots of Rose West naked. He was not cross-examined.

There followed legal arguments concerning the admissibility of these videos, not that they should be seen, but that they should be described to the jury. Mr Ferguson objected on two grounds. The home-made videos which depicted the defendant were "of an extremely personal nature, very private, and not relevant to issues in this case. They did not include bondage". As for the commercial video which Mr Leveson wished to introduce because it depicted a woman tied to beams in a cellar and whipped by two men, Mr Ferguson pointed out that this dated from 1992, whereas the events the jury were considering occurred twenty years before; there was therefore no probative connection.

Mr Justice Mantell ruled that he would not allow the description of a video showing suspension from beams, because no witness had ever mentioned suspension, hence there was no basis for it. (The only reference was by Fred West himself in police interviews, about which the jury as yet knew nothing). Others, however, he would allow. Mr Ferguson's reflection on this was that "I accept there were home-made videos, but dispute they were ever shown to anyone. Also, one may find videos of many things in many homes, but it does not follow that people who have them behave in the same way".

The jury was handed pieces of beams cut from the cellar of the Wests house. Each section had a hole drilled through it. A door was also brought in to court and a large removable screw was taken out and handed to the jury.

Anne Marie was back in the witness-box to face Richard Ferguson at 12.20pm.

Ferguson: I have a few questions to ask about your relationship with your father. I'm sorry, but it has to be done.

It was then that she told just how extensively she had been her father's lover over a period of years, and that she had been made pregnant by him when she was fifteen.

Anne Marie: When I used to go out in the van with my father I used to remember there was a purple light that would come on in the dashboard. I would get a funny feeling in my tummy and when this light came on I knew we would have intercourse.

She said she had sex many times with her father - in woods, places where he was working and his green work van.

Ferguson: You were devoted to your father?
Anne Marie: Yes, I did love my father
Ferguson: You would have done anything for him?
Anne Marie: I would have done anything for both Rosemary and my father.

He passed on to her promiscuity and then to her contract with The Daily Star. He told her that she had put her stepmother into the story because she found it difficult to face the fact of her father's abuse.

Anne Marie: I do know right from wrong.
Ferguson: I suggest to you that your stepmother never bound or gagged you.
Anne Marie: Yes, my stepmother did.
Ferguson: I suggest to you that she never sexually abused you or was present when you were.
Anne Marie: Yes, my stepmother was.

He suggested the incidents in the cellar never took place.

Anne Marie: The things that I have said in court have been the truth.

Brian Leveson then re-examined Anne Marie. She told how sex with her father had been in the "straight missionary position", with nothing unusual or unorthodox demanded of her. She said that her stepmother beat her for no reason, with whatever happened to be at hand, and that on one occasion Rosemary had asked her to stay home from school to keep her company when Fred came home. Rose had told her that Fred would be very angry with her when he came home and wanted Anne Marie there.

Anne Marie: I wanted to be with her because she had been good to me. I stood between her and Dad when he came home, trying to protect her. But she hit me and said: 'that'll teach you to be so cocky'. I was trying to be good to her, I thought.

After Anne Marie had finished giving her evidence, a tape recorder was set up and four small speakers were arranged on the court clerk's desk. Recordings of several of Rose's police interviews were to be played.

The very first words the jury heard Rose speak formed a belligerent answer to a routine request from the police to state her name for the benefit of the tape. "You don't know who I am?" mocked Rose. The next forty-five minutes continued in the same shrewish, often foul-mouthed way. Apart from her constant swearing, Rose's vocabulary was odd – she frequently repeated odd words, like 'tricky', as in boys 'got up to tricky things'. The nature of what she said was also bizarre: she claimed to know Heather was a lesbian partly because the child "knew exactly what kind of knickers the women teachers had on."

The second interview tape ended dramatically, with Rose being told that Fred had confessed to Heather's murder. Her response was a loud shriek. In the dock Rose clutched a tissue as if she were distressed.

She had recovered sufficiently by the next interview, taped just hours after the last, to offer her alibi: Fred had often made her spend the night with black men so she could not know what he was doing. She said Fred was the dominant partner in the relationship and "what he says goes". He made her sleep with other men even though she used to fight with him over it.

On another matter, Rose persisted with the story of giving £600 to Fred for Heather to go away with, but was told that Fred had said it was only £100. When put under pressure like this, Rose's memory failed her. It seemed that there was a great deal which she simply did not remember, but the fate that awaited her appeared to be sinking in. Towards the end of the interview, she said: "I ain't got a lot to live for now, have I?"

Despite her aggression, in the next tape the jury learned something of Rose's extraordinary alternating personality – the concerned mum and the foul-mouthed prostitute. She was asked about Heather's dentist (so the police could find dental records for identification of remains) and, like any mother, instantly remembered not only the name, but the full street address. Yet within the same interview she made harsh allegations about Heather, claiming that her daughter had hurt the other children, trapping their fingers in doors, giving them black eyes and making them drink obnoxious mixtures of "vinegar and salt and stuff". In fact, what she was describing was the abuse her children said she meted out to them.

In the tape Rose told the police that she was now certain she had spent the night with a black lover when Heather had vanished. Rose had to do what Fred told her: she claimed she had been hit when she was younger, and had once had her jaw twisted by Fred. Going with other men was something she was doing "for our marriage…He can be very persuasive, put it that way", she said. But when asked for the name and address of this boyfriend, she could only remember that he was "Jamaican…big chap, I think", and in his fifties. His name escaped her; it was one of those "awkward" names.

DS Terence Onions: What satisfaction did he, or you, get in seeing black men?
Rose: Best ask him that. I used to get things like 'You're not doing enough for our marriage'.

When Rose was informed on tape that the police had actually found Heather's bones, she was heard to wearily complain, "Why have we got to go through this again?" She went on to repeat the lie that she had last seen Fred's first wife, Rena, when she came to take Charmaine away (the prosecution had already gone to some trouble to prove that Fred was in prison when Charmaine was murdered).

Sergeant Peter Maunder took to the stand and told the jury Fred West had visited the house three times with officers after his arrest.

Maunder: When Fred West was in custody he indicated the presence of two sites of what transpired to be remains in the garden. He returned to the house on two other occasions while I was there. On the second occasion he went round the basement area of the house and indicated possible places where we may locate further sets of remains. We subsequently found the remains.

Describing the search for Heather, he said he was digging in the barbecue area of the garden when he came across a length of bone. Scientific aids, including X-ray machines, ground penetrating radar and quasar optics, were used to help detect bodies buried at the house, as well as traces of blood and semen.

DC Bob Beetham then took to the stand and said Fred was also taken to sites at Much Marcle in Gloucestershire. There the bodies of his first wife Catherine and former nanny Ann McFall were found in Letterbox Field and adjacent Fingerpost Field.

Sir Bernard Knight, CBE, consultant pathologist to the Home Office for thirty years and Professor of Forensic Pathology at the University of Wales College of Medicine for twenty-five years took to the stand. He explained the difficulty of excavation at Cromwell Street, due to the fact that the water table was often higher than the floor of the cellar, which meant that the diggers had to work in waterlogged soil. No sooner was a cavity emptied than it filled with water again. This suggested that it was possible for bones buried there to have moved around in a semi-liquid medium and changed position relative to one another. He then told how everything was carefully removed and examined by him and all remains precisely counted. That was why he was able to tell, in the case of Heather (the first to be excavated), that 22 finger and toe bones were missing out of a total of 76, and that one knee cap was missing. Describing the chop-marks made on thigh bones, he held a femur aloft in court by way of demonstration. Passing through the sequence of remains as they were excavated, with five skeletons uncovered in nine and a half hours, Professor Knight gave details on each and also detailed what he found. This included descriptions of the tape wrapped around skulls, a knotted cloth, lots of hair, some hair trapped in the knot, some degenerate brain tissue, a black-handled knife, a plastic rope similar to a clothes line and much more. When he came to the baby that Shirley Robinson was expecting, most of whose bones were matchstick size and very brittle, the jury were visibly shaken. Professor Knight gave details of the exhumation of Charmaine as well, confirming that both her kneecaps and 47 bones were missing. He declared that it was impossible to say whether any of the dismemberments had taken place before or after death.

Leveson: Could the knife (found in the grave of Lucy Partington) have been responsible for the cut marks you saw?
Knight: Possibly some, but not all. Not for removing the thighs.
Leveson: How difficult is it to disarticulate legs and remove a head? How long would it take?
Knight: A good many minutes if you're not used to it.
Leveson: While the victim is still alive?
Knight: There would be massive arterial blood loss.

Leveson: And if she was dead?

Knight: The blood would be oozing, but not that much.

Leveson: Is it easier after death, or before?

Knight: After.

Leveson: Easier two or three days, or immediately after?

Knight: It would not make much difference, except for rigor mortis.

The jury looked through books of photographs taken of the bones and the instruments of torture. One showed Professor Knight holding the skull of Shirley Hubbard, the masking tape and tube still in place. The mask was slack, he explained, because the flesh had rotted away. Questioning soon moved on to the bones which were not there. Professor Knight said that this was not the first time he had found skeletons with some bones missing. He said there were four possibilities:

1) Degeneration. "Eventually, most skeletons will disappear as the bones disintegrate over time, and usually the smallest and most fragile bones will disappear first. That was not the case here however. If those which remained were in very good condition, there was no reason why others should have disintegrated. It was just not possible."

2) Failure to excavate properly. This was quickly discounted by Professor Knight, who had been present at Cromwell Street and had seen for himself that the police search was thorough to a fault, recovering even some fingernails. Every centimetre of ground was carefully sifted until there could be no doubt that nothing of interest remained.

3) Bodies removed and re-buried. Professor Knight pointed out that bones are held together by strong ligaments and tendons, over which there are muscles, fat and finally skin. The ligaments are much more resistant than soft tissues and will survive much longer. If the bodies had been buried elsewhere and then moved to Cromwell Street, there would have been the possibility of animal predation. Professor Knight looked specifically for evidence of animal interference (tooth marks) and found none. He said that it would take a couple of years for a skeleton to reach the stage of consisting only of dry bones, besides which the black soil which surrounded the remains proved that there had been a substantial quantity of soft tissue present, which meant that the limbs must have been whole when buried, that is to say with flesh and gristle intact. Asked how strongly a patella (kneecap) was attached to the leg, Professor Knight replied that it

515

was very strongly indeed.

Knight: It cannot become detachable until the thigh muscles and shin muscles have rotted away. Most of this would have had to go before the kneecap could come off.

4) Bones removed as a result of deliberate mutilation. "Fingers and toes are very easy to remove and a kneecap is quite possible to remove with a sharp knife". The shoulder-blade, on the other hand, would have been very hard, and the Professor found it difficult to explain why such a huge bone should be missing, attached as it was by lots of tendons to shoulder-joints and the end of the collar bone. "Is it possible to cut out a shoulder-blade?" Mr Leveson asked. "I could do it" replied Professor Knight.

Dr Whittaker took to the stand and gave a demonstration of how he identified the remains using Facial Superimposition. The curtains in the court-room were closed and a photograph of Charmaine as an eight-year old child was projected on to a screen. Dr Whittaker then overlaid the photograph of the child's skull as it had been when found at Midland Road in 1994 – broken and discoloured. He pointed out the exact fit of the empty eye-sockets and jaw-line, and where the court could see teeth previously shielded by gums now matured and unprotected in the most naked way.

DSI Bennett was next in the stand and he confirmed that all the remains, apart from those of Lynda Gough, still gave off an odour. He was asked about Mary Bastholm, and replied that he had compared her case with that of Lucy Partington but there had never been enough evidence to charge Fred with involvement in her disappearance. He admitted that the 'safe houses' occupied by Stephen, Mae and Rose West for six weeks after Fred West's arrest had been bugged.

Leveson: The purpose of the operation, Mr Bennett, was to try to obtain further evidence if you could against Mrs West?

Bennett: No, sir, it was for the purpose of seeking intelligence to gain the truth

Police had been able to listen to every word of conversation in the houses, and at no time had Rose West said anything to indicate her implication in any of the ten murders.

25th October 1995

The Crown rested its case against Rosemary Pauline West. Mr Ferguson asked that he and Miss Sasha Wass be given time to prepare the defence, and the judge rose until the following Monday. It was then that permission was sought by the defence to introduce four of the taped interviews with Fred West. Mr Leveson warned that, to respond to four tapes he would need to play another thirty-one.

Mae: "I can't give evidence to support Mum and I'm devastated. Mum's lawyer has read a proof of our book and he says there are details about what Mum did to us which could really hurt Mum's case. I've been in tears since being told and feel I've let Mum down very badly. I feel incredibly guilty. I'm meant to be supporting her, yet I won't be called as a defence witness. Giving evidence on my Mum's behalf was going to be very important to her. I'm the only member of the family who's stood by Mum. She was counting on me and I don't know how she's going to take the news that I'm not going to say nice things about her in court. No one is going to say anything good about her.

I don't want to be caught lying in the witness stand. That wouldn't do me or Mum any good. There are things they could ask me which would make Mum look really bad. I don't want to talk about them in court because they'll make Mum out to be a psychopath.

If Mum goes down then I'm going to feel really guilty. I think Mum has forgotten the beatings she gave me as a child and how she treated us. She would deny it ever happened in court, I know she would...

I've been truthful in the book and there are incidents which happened I've told no one else. If I thought Mum was a murderer then I'd have nothing to do with her. I certainly don't think she's an angel. Neither is she whiter than white. She was hard when we were young, but I've got to believe she's innocent. I don't think I could live otherwise.

Just because Mum is weird and into kinky sex doesn't make her a criminal."

29th October 1995

Mae: "Leo Goatley, Mum's solicitor, gave Mum the first 160 pages of our book to read, because he said it was relevant. She won't admit a page of it is true, because we have hurt her so much. I was hoping she would never read it, or at least not until the dust had settled on the case. The timing is lousy. She is just about to give evidence and she's read everything I've said about her. She was very offish with me when I went to visit her in Winchester today.

I don't know why Leo gave it to her. I would like to have talked him out of it… She's had it for four days. Now she feels totally let down because none of us have stood up for her…All I have said is the truth. She doesn't like that though. In our family it's an unwritten rule that you shut your gob and the only way you show you love someone is to let things lay and not tell the police or anybody.

There's a gap there now I will never be able to patch up with her.

I've cried a lot over this but now I think: fuck it- I should never have been put in this position. If she was more of an angel, she wouldn't be facing all this.

Leo said it would help Mum's situation and that he would get a feel of what Cromwell Street was like if he saw the book. But he never said anything about showing it to Mum.

My visit lasted two hours and it was the hardest time Mum and I have ever spent together. Usually we talk endlessly about everything, but she was much harder and just said she was on her own. She seemed to have lost a bit of hope. She didn't seem bothered either way what happened. She said she's not got complications if she came out or stayed in jail. She won't face the truth. She never has.

For all those years she's saying that she never knew that I had one complaint. Now, suddenly she's facing the lot, having read it all in the book, and she can't take it all in."

30th October 1995

Over the course of the weekend, one of the jurors had been arrested on a minor charge and released on bail. Mr Justice Mantell asked him to

stand and told him that he had automatically disqualified himself from
service and was immediately discharged. Rose West was then to be tried by
eleven people instead of twelve.

Richard Ferguson QC opened the case for the defence by reminding
the jury that they had heard only half the evidence so far and they must
suspend their judgement until they had heard it all. Speaking directly to
them for the first time, he said:

Ferguson: Some of what you have heard is shocking and some of it
irrelevant to the issue which you have to decide… I want to tell you as
loudly and as clearly as I can that Rosemary West is not guilty. She neither
knew of nor participated in any of the murders, nor did anything to hide or
conceal those murders. There is no evidence and can be no evidence about
how the victims died, and so the Crown has filled the void with prejudice
and speculation. We are here because we believe in a system which holds
you innocent until proven guilty. The Crown must prove guilt beyond all
reasonable doubt. I do not wish to be presumptuous, but all they have are
allegations, accusations and a superficially attractive theory. You do not
have to accept it, and we place our trust in your integrity and independence.
You will be fair and impartial.

He told how Fred West was a murderer. He had told everyone he was
and had pointed out where to look for the remains of his victims. Two of
these died before he met the defendant, and Mary Bastholm could well
have been a third.

Ferguson: If you think it is a fair assumption that Frederick West
murdered even before he met Rosemary West, then the consequences are,
1) that he was capable of murder without her assistance
2) that he was capable of dismemberment and disposal of bodies without
her knowledge, help or assistance.

You have heard evidence of sexual bondage, ropes and gags and so on.
The same sort of articles were found with the remains of Ann McFall. What
does that say? The Crown has built a careful but speculative case. The stack
of cards on which it rests is that all the victims were sexually abused and
that Rosemary West was a necessary ingredient in that mix. She must have
enticed a number of victims to 25 Cromwell Street, lured them in to a car.

Who lured Ann McFall? … Even if you accept that Rosemary West was perverted, that is proof of that, and nothing more… Because there can be no evidence as to how these girls met their deaths, the Crown have filled that void with prejudice and speculation… The defendant fell under the spell of Frederick West at the age of fifteen. He abused her as he abused everyone else during his evil life. It is because of her marriage to him that she is before this court now.

Mrs West may have been a lesbian, but that does not make her a murderer. She may have had sex with her lodgers, but that does not make her a murderer. She may have been forced into prostitution, but that does not make her a murderer. She may have had sex aids in the house, but that does not make her a murderer. What is the relevance of all this, except to excite prejudice against this defendant, and incidentally to provide interest to those whose appetites are so satisfied by it? These matters may offend your moral sensibilities, but they are not crimes. They may satisfy the media, but they do not add to the evidence with which you have to grapple.

If it is a fair assumption that Fred West murdered before he even met this defendant, then some consequences become apparent. Members of the jury, you should remember that Ann McFall, a babysitter, was murdered before Frederick West met Rosemary. It is apparent, is it not, that he was capable of murder without her assistance? It is also apparent, is it not, that he was capable of dismembering and disposing of the bodies without her knowledge, help or assistance?

The Crown's second point was that the defendant was bound to know what her husband was doing in the home which they shared.

Ferguson: This is an argument of doubtful validity in many marriages, but in this house and in that marriage it is utterly without any substance whatever. The jury must not be tempted to compare Cromwell Street to their own domestic situation.

The absence of a familiar face would gain your attention. Not so at No. 25, a refuge for the flotsam and jetsam of modern life. The sounds of digging, demolition and excavation would be a matter for comment in your homes. Not so at No. 25.

He conceded that the Crown was on firmer ground with the evidence of four witnesses – Caroline Owens, 'Miss A', Kathryn Halliday and Anne Marie.

Ferguson: Let us look dispassionately at what they had to say. One thing they have in common is involvement with the media. I'm not unduly cynical, but you may think perhaps they are not as unworldly as they would have you believe. There may have been an element of amateur dramatics in the way some of them gave evidence. One cannot blame these young women for selling what they have to sell, but it has this effect: you may think that, consciously or unconsciously, they are aware that the more sensational their evidence, the more the media will pay for their stories. No newspaper is going to pay out large sums if Rosemary West is acquitted…I accept the maxim that justice must be seen to be done and that there is legitimate public interest, however. These proceedings alone will serve it.

Taking the four witnesses in turn, Mr Ferguson identified what was lacking in each.

Ferguson: All we have for certain about Caroline Owens is the fact that Mr and Mrs West were fined £50 each for what they had done, and that at a magistrate's court. She underwent no medical treatment whatever as a result.

'Miss A' made no complaint for over twenty years, and then could remember nothing that would substantiate her account of having been in that house. She had been infatuated by the defendant's brother, had run away with him, had pretended to be pregnant by him. Pause before you accept the evidence of this witness.

Kathryn Halliday kept going back for more.

Anne Marie was a tragic figure by any account and on any showing, irrespective of what the defendant did or did not do. She had always been resentful of Rosemary West coming in to her family. Mrs West denies emphatically that she was ever party to the sexual exploitation of that sad woman.

You have heard her on tape. You have heard her shocked response on being told that her husband had confessed to murdering her daughter Heather. 'So she's dead, is that right?' she said.

You are now going to hear from her in person. She will tell you, not me. For the first time in public she will say what actually did take place during her years at 25 Cromwell Street. This will be a considerable ordeal for her. This was her family, her home. I call Rosemary Pauline West.

Rose West took to the stand, and responding to questioning from her own counsel, told of her childhood.

She described the break-up of her family, when she went with her mother and younger brothers to live at the home of her married sister, Glenys, in Cheltenham.

Rose: I had a job by this time and I came back to my sister's after work, and my mum and my brothers were not there. I asked my sister where they were. They were gone, they had moved on. It had a devastating effect on me at that time. I had left my father's home and I expected the support of my mother, and she just left me, she abandoned me.

She went to live with a friend of her sisters, a 30-year-old man. They had a sexual relationship.

Of her younger brothers, her first job in a bakery, the two rapes she suffered before she was fifteen, and her meeting with Fred West, Rose told the court that when she was 15 she was the victim of two rapes. The first was when a stranger gave her a lift home from a Christmas party, shortly after her 15th birthday which she accepted reluctantly.

Rose: The man in question had been watching me during this party and I was expecting a lift home with my friend. But my friend went off with her boyfriend and I was abandoned. I knew I had missed the last bus home. I was looking around for a taxi when this fellow approached me and more or less forced me into the car. I felt I had to get in. He said he was going to take me home. Instead he went on past my home into the hills beyond where we lived. I felt very threatened by this man. I honestly thought he was going to kill me.
Ferguson: What happened next?
Rose: He raped me

The second rape took place when a man approached her as she was waiting for a bus.

Rose: He approached me, he was chatting me up. I resisted his advances. I was not interested in men at the time – I had enough problems with my family. He was very forceful. I was hoping the bus would come along quickly so I could get away from him. He grabbed me. He was very strong

– it got out of hand. I got away and ran down towards the park in Cheltenham. I was hoping there was somebody around who could help me, but there was nobody. When I looked around this man was gaining on me. He grabbed me by the arm. The gates to the park were padlocked. He just smashed the lock off using his fist because he was so strong. He said he had been in the army. He dragged me down to the lake by some trees and raped me.

Ferguson: Did you tell your parents or anyone else about this?

Rose: No I didn't.

After that she decided always to catch the bus home from the main depot at Cheltenham. It was there she met Fred, who asked her out.

Ferguson: What was your reaction?

Rose: Shock, horror, at first

Ferguson: And then?

Rose: He asked me out three times. I made it clear I was not interested, but he was very persistent. Then he came in to the bread shop one day and asked me out to the local pub in our village near our home. I said yes because I knew it would be safe. It was a small distance away. If anything went wrong I could run home.

She told the court that on her first date with Fred, when she was just 15, he gave her a fur coat and a lace dress.

Rose: I wanted him to take it back because I had no intention of getting involved with him, but he insisted. I took it, and I said there was no way I could take it home because my parents would not agree to it. So he kept it in the caravan he lived in. He was living in a caravan with his two children, Anne Marie and Charmaine. The caravan was fairly scruffy and untidy and I cleared it up and babysat when Fred was out.

Rose said she enjoyed looking after them. Within weeks she had begun a sexual relationship with Fred West, to her parents' horror.

She said that she was appalled by Charmaine and Anne Marie's condition when she first agreed to baby-sit for Fred and immediately cleaned them up as she couldn't bear the idea of them being taken away and put in to care yet again.

Rose: I felt sorry for them because their mother was not there. I wanted to look after them. I loved them straight away. I felt sorry for them and wanted to look after them. It was his children that really interested me, I suppose, more than him. He was just a boyfriend, somebody I knew.

She went on to tell how her family disapproved of her relationship with Fred and of her being pregnant.

Rose: They tried to put a stop to it in every way they thought possible. They threatened and tried to intimidate me and threatened Fred. They even told the authorities a man was having sex with a girl who was under age.

Asked what her feelings were towards Fred at that stage, she said:

Rose: He promised to love me and care for me, and I fell for it. I was nursing old wounds. I just wanted someone to love me. He had promised me the world, promised me everything and because I was so young I fell for his lies but because I was so young I did not realise they were lies at the time. I am afraid I was nursing old wounds from my past history of my family, particularly when my mum left me. I had been devastated by the thought that my mum could walk away and leave. I loved my mum very much – and still do – and she just left me, and I don't know why. I thought 'well, my mother left me, and my dad abused my mum, and I just wanted somebody to love me'.

She said that when her parents put her in to care:

Rose: My family came to see me. I promised I would do as they wished and they took me back home. My father told me I could stay at home as long as I went to work and earned money, and had an abortion and had no boyfriends. Or I was told I could go off with this Fred West and never see my family again. I did not believe it was much of an ultimatum for a young girl to just go to work and come home and not have any life. Anna-Marie and Charmaine needed looking after. They were in a home. I did not want them to be. I wanted them to have parents and a better home life, and I wanted my baby. So I left home.

After she had moved in with Fred and they moved to Midland Road, and she had given birth to Heather, she was asked how she regarded her step-children.

Rose: I loved them. In fact, I did all I could as a young girl to look after them. I did not want to see them back in homes again.

When Fred was imprisoned for nine months, she was asked how she coped with the children. She said all went well at first but then Charmaine started playing up. After Charmaine started to become difficult, Rose said:

Rose: I was perfectly willing to keep Char on but if it was best for her to be with her mother, then I understood. She was resisting me, not eating, running away. I had nobody else to discipline the children. It was my job. I would smack their bottoms, or their legs.

She denied that she had ever stood Charmaine on a chair with her hands tied behind her back, and hit her with a wooden spoon.

On one of her visits to see Fred in prison Rose discussed with him Charmaine's wish to be back with Rena, and he agreed it might be a good idea.

Rose: Fred sympathised with me, and also with Charmaine, because I had made it abundantly clear that I was perfectly willing to keep Charmaine on and did basically love her even though we did not get on. But if it was the best thing for her to be with her mother, which for me is quite understandable…Fred agreed with me. He said he would 'sort it out'.

It was shortly after he came out that she disappeared. Fred said that he had got in contact with Charmaine's mum and she had agreed to have Charmaine if that was what Charmaine wanted. He said she was coming to the house to pick Charmaine up. He advised me that I would be better off if I was not around, as his wife would not be too pleased that I was looking after her children. I was too young to have anything to do with decisions like that. It was their past life.

Mr Ferguson asked if Charmaine's mother had come to the house at 25 Midland Road.

Rose: Yes she did

Asked if she had spoken to her:

Rose: No, sir. I walked straight past her. I took Heather and Anne Marie and we went over to my mums. It was late in the evening when I came back.

Ferguson: When you came back, was Charmaine there?

Rose: No sir, she was gone. Fred told me Charmaine had gone with her mum and that she was very happy about it…In a way I was pleased for her. Fred said she had gone back to Scotland with her mum.

Ferguson: Had you any reason to disbelieve that?
Rose: No sir

She said that at first, Anne Marie was:

Rose: just a little girl who needed looking after…the child I left home for. I thought she would accept me as she got older, but obviously she never did. I tried to make rules, but was condemned for it. Fred said I had 'no right'. Anne Marie was quite settled. She wanted to stay with her dad, and she made that quite clear.

Rose said Fred had asked her if she had been with other men while he was in prison.

Rose: I said no, of course not. He asked me why not. He told me he wanted me to go with other men. He always brought the subject up. It was a daily thing. He gave me assorted reasons. He was very, very persuasive. He said I was a young girl and I couldn't just dedicate myself to looking after children and doing housework. He said I needed a break. I needed to go out. I would miss my young life and it was my right, more or less, to be able to go out in the evening and have some fun like most young girls do.

She told how the couple rarely went out together. Fred would stay at home with the children while she went out at night. Asked why, she replied:

Rose: Normally to pick up other men. That is what Fred wanted me to do. That is what I was out there to do. By this time I had got used to him keeping on about it. If I put up a barrier, said I didn't want to do it, then he would make my life miserable. I knew I had to go. There was no choice with him.

When she was questioned about the time she had come home from hospital and allegedly discovered Fred and their former neighbour Mrs Agius together, she told of how she barged into Elizabeth Agius' house 'very angry', shouting and banging on the doors –

Rose: I was getting louder and louder demanding either of them – I was angry.

Questioning moved on to Cromwell Street.

Rose: Whatever you put down there (the cellar) would get soaking wet. It looked like a cold, wet, damp cave. It was dark and gloomy and wet.

She said she rarely helped her husband renovate the cellar because she was so frequently pregnant.

Rose: He used to say it was not a place to have pregnant women or small children. He would just lock off the doors and do whatever he was doing. It was nothing unusual for us to hear him digging up the floors.

Her son Stephen was born in August 1973. "Our first boy…I spoiled him very much". She told how after the birth she would sleep during the day and Fred thought she was anaemic so she went to the doctors. She told how it had been Fred's idea for her to go with other women, and that she had not been attracted to other women when she was younger. She said she "didn't entertain it as a sexual thought" until she was pregnant with her first son Stephen.

Rose: My sexual relationships with other women were very special to me. They were entirely different to when I went with a man. They were warm, close and I would say they were more fun and because of that I also felt closer and more satisfied in a sexual way.

When she was questioned about being a land lord, she said that she tried to leave that to Fred:

Rose: I didn't believe I was capable of taking on that sort of responsibility.

She went on to call the first group of lodgers "drop outs". Within a few months 6 of them crowded into 3 rooms.

Rose: They stripped the wallpaper and painted the walls in psychedelic colours, black and purple. The drug squad raided the house regularly. Fred seemed to revel in the upheaval. The police coming was just a joke to him. He was always upstairs with the lodgers, never downstairs with the family.

She said that lodgers would often leave bits and pieces behind, and it was "up to me to clean up the mess and prepare the room for the next person".
She said that Fred persuaded her to have sex with some of the lodgers.

Rose: He was always on about other men. He would use emotional blackmail. He could be very, very persuasive.

Rose said that at the time of Mae and Stephen's births, in 1972 and 1973 respectively, her and Fred were "More or less living separate lives. I was pregnant and he got on with his work."
After they got rid of the male lodgers, Fred suggested they take in women.

Rose: He said they were cleaner and show more respect to other people in the house, and pay their rent more regularly. For a while I resisted, I wanted the house to myself but as always he won the argument and we had the girls in. He was always doing things for them – giving them lifts, taking them to see their mums, redecorating their rooms or doing something for them.

Rose said she felt "exhausted all the time" struggling to cope with the children. Asked if Fred could be supportive, she replied:

Rose: Sometimes he could be very, very good then other times exactly the opposite – very difficult and very bloody-minded. When he was in a bad mood it was as if he was jealous of the other men he had forced me to go with. He was always having a go at me. We could never agree. If he was losing an argument he would use his fists and hit me. It was a regular thing but when he was good he was very, very good. He bought me presents and took the children out and bought them presents like a swimming pool or swings. He could just be so extreme."

She recalled how Fred forced her in to prostitution:

Rose: He told me he wanted me to go with other men. He was always bringing the subject up, and giving me reasons why I should. He was very persuasive. He persuaded me to jump in to bed with the boys upstairs, that was his idea, and he would use emotional blackmail if I argued. He said that you're not doing enough for the marriage, you've got to play your part. He went on and on, it was an everyday thing.

Rose West told the court that shortly after Fred came out of prison he started pressurising her to have sex with other men. She said her husband forced her to go out to pubs to pick up men.

Rose: There was no money involved – if money came into it at all, it was only at Easter or Christmas. They would say 'have a drink' or to 'get something for the kids'. But sometimes they bought me flowers or chocolates. I told him all the time I was not prepared to go on with this. He said 'You have definitely got to do this'.

Rose was then asked to describe her 'special room' where she took men for sex while Fred watched through a hole in the door. She told how she would meet men in pubs and clubs around Gloucester and take them home.

Rose: I would have sex with these men more often than not. It was straight sex, not kinky or anything way out. I would like to make friends with people, and we would talk and have a drink and maybe play records. There would be noises coming from the room. If you were not in that room and could not see what we were doing, you could interpret things in a different way. If a young girl had heard those noises maybe she would be a bit frightened about them.

Asked if Fred objected to her giving birth to other men's children, she replied:

Rose: No, it was in fact his idea. In his usual persuasive manner he would recall I loved children. I believed he loved them very much. We were pleased to have them. He called them our love children. I certainly don't regret having them. He knew who the fathers were. There was no secret about it. I didn't want the fathers to know. I wanted the children to be part of my family and didn't want the fathers to know – but Fred told them anyway.

Richard Ferguson then asked her what she remembered about Caroline Owens. She insisted she was "as much of a victim". She said she was frightened by her husband and had tried to stop him.

Rose: I don't remember Caroline working for us as a nanny. I remember Fred saying to me about getting involved with Caroline Owens in a lesbian relationship which would have been my first experience with a woman. He did persuade me that Caroline Owens was willing to try it out. We talked it over. I told him that Caroline was not that way inclined. It was like he was acting as a middle man. But still I allowed myself to be persuaded she was willing.

She also told the court that she had tried to stop the sexual assault on Caroline Owens in 1972 when she realised that the girl had not consented to sex with herself and her husband.

Rose: I remember I was terrified at the time. I was frightened. I knew in some way I had done wrong. I had made a mistake…I have tried very hard to remember these events but I just can't. I was a young girl, I had been conned into this situation. I don't have a clear memory whatsoever. I remember being with Caroline in the car. I remember putting my arm around her and touching her on the outside of her clothes. As soon as she put up resistance, as soon as I realised that she was against this, that she did not agree with it in any way, I stopped. All I can remember is being very frightened. Fred was a threat at this moment in time. I can't remember Fred punching her, I just remember it got out of hand. I was pleading with Fred all the time for it to stop. I didn't want to get involved in anything like this. I didn't want Caroline to get hurt. It was just a mess. I don't remember tape being put round her face. I don't remember her being brought to Cromwell Street. I was a young girl. I realised I had been conned into this and I just wanted over with it. I believe I was as much a victim as Caroline was. I was frightened on her behalf and I felt frightened for me. I think the whole situation was so traumatic for me. Fred had promised me faithfully that nothing like this would ever happen again, that he would never put me in that sort of situation again. I was vulnerable to his persuasion and his promises. He had the gift of the gab. I was a young girl, I believe nineteen at the time, and he had a lot of influence over me.

When she was asked what she had said to Fred after the assault:

Rose: I asked him what the hell he thought he was doing.

She said Caroline Owens, who told the court about being raped by Fred, had exaggerated "for her own reasons".

Rose: I have never forced anybody to do anything in my life. There was no pleasure to force anybody to do anything.

Asked to remember her court case in 1973, she said:

Rose: Obviously I remember being charged but I don't remember my time in court. I just remember being frightened that I would be in trouble. I remember afterwards when me and Fred had a row about it. I didn't want my children being put in a home. All I ever wanted in my life was my family.

After the incident involving Caroline Owens, she revealed that she had tried to leave her husband:

Rose: I knew in some way I had done wrong. I wanted it all to go away, and was terrified I would lose my family because we were in trouble. I wanted out of the marriage, to take my children away. I had them in the pram and was ready to walk out of the door. Then I thought, where am I going to go? Who would help me? Where would the money come from? I just felt so alone. Anne Marie loved her dad very much. If I took her away she would never forgive me.

In the end, her husband promised her he would never put her in that kind of situation again. "I did not see that side of him before or since". She said they had kept a newspaper clipping of the court case as a reminder for him to keep his promise. The clipping was found in their home when the police searched it both in 1992 and 1994.

At the end of the day Rose was shown photographs of the dead girls and was asked, in turn, whether she had known them or had had anything to do with their deaths.

When asked about Lynda Gough, she disagreed with Lynda's mother having visited 25 Cromwell Street and suggested she may have gone to a different house. When she was shown a photograph of her, she said:

Rose: I remember her very, very vaguely. I remember her in the early years when there was only one bathroom up on the middle landing. I went upstairs to use the bathroom and she was on the landing. She was just one of the girls who came in with the boys who were lodging and that's all I remember. I remember her because of her hair. She wore it over the front of her face. And I remember her glasses because they looked particularly old-fashioned. The sort my grandfather would wear, with heavy rims. I had nothing to do with the death or disappearance of Lynda Gough.

Asked about the evidence of Lynda Gough's mother, she said:

Rose: It wasn't me. I wouldn't even have known if her slippers would have fitted me. This lady doesn't even remember if I was pregnant at the time.

She was shown a photograph of Carol Ann Cooper and simply said:

Rose: No, I have no recollection of her at all.

She was then shown a photograph of Lucy Partington.

Rose: I never saw her at 25 Cromwell Street. I've never seen her before.

She was shown a photograph of Therese Siegenthaler.

Rose: I've never seen her before. I've never, to my knowledge, seen her in Cromwell Street.

Shirley Hubbard?

Rose: I've never seen her before

Juanita Mott?

Rose: No, no sir!

Rose became more and more aggrieved as the afternoon wore on, and her solicitor Leo Goately later said that this was due to his client becoming progressively more tired.

Richard Ferguson asked Rose about her relationship with Fred. She said he was a workaholic who frequently carried out work in their basement. She said Fred would never let her or the children go down there, and when he went down he would bolt the door behind him. He used to say: "I'm going down to see to the drains to try to stop the water coming up." She said: "It wasn't unusual for us to hear him digging up the floor."

She said Fred had mood swings, with his behaviour ranging from petting her to hitting her with his fists during arguments.

Rose: Things weren't very good between us. We literally did lead separate lives. He did what he wanted to do. He could walk in and out of the door as he wanted. He did not have the ties that I had. When he walked in the door, I walked out and that was it.

Mae: (regarding Rose's lack of memory about the attack on Caroline Owens) "She's honest about that. She's got a terrible memory, it's like a sieve – she can't even remember what she did last week. She said to me: 'if I can't remember, that's what I will have to tell them.'

I think in the 70's she just did as she was told. She was only 16 and Dad stopped her going out and that. If she made him a cup of tea he would throw it at her. He was a right bastard.

Mum did tell us when we were kids that she had been raped. When we got to adolescence she'd say never go in strange cars, and she told us that story about the bloke who raped her. She said if you are ever in that situation, being raped or he might kill you, then give in. I didn't know about the other rape."

31st October 1995

Richard Ferguson began the day by asking Rose about her attitude towards Fred after his admission of murdering Heather.

Rose: I hate him. I just couldn't believe that anybody...

Then she broke down in tears. She told the court that she never spoke to Fred about his admission "No, I didn't want to know him." She said she avoided opportunities to speak with him.

Rose: I didn't trust myself. I would have at least had a go at him. The worst thing for me was going backwards and forwards to court to be remanded, and we were actually sat in the dock together, and I requested that there be police officers between us.

Asked if her feelings had changed since Fred's death:

Rose: No, certainly not. I am still very angry with him. I think it will take many years for that to go. I just feel such a fool because he had fooled all of us for all these years. I just don't know how he managed it. How did he get those poor girls in and out of the house without being seen? The houses around our house were always full. Anyone could have seen him at any time. There were tenants in the house, the doors were open, people just came and went.

When questioned about 'Miss A', there was no truth whatsoever, she said. It didn't happen. She said she had never even met the girl. But then contradicted herself:

Rose: Why didn't she tell someone if it was so terrible?

She contradicted herself even further by telling the court that 'Miss A' had been about to marry at the time of the assault.

Rose then denied that she had grown jealous over Shirley Robinson. She claimed that neither Fred, or herself, had had sex with her. It never caused them arguments. Questioned about why she and Fred told people that he was the father of Shirley Robinson's baby:

Rose: Fred told me he was covering as the father of the baby to help Shirley out until she got on her feet. I believed it. I believed she was silly enough to get herself in a scrape like that. The real father was a businessman, and Fred was protecting her. I never had a clue it was Fred's baby.

Asked what she would have done if the baby had been her husband's:

Rose: I would have asked her to leave, as simple as that. I had no need to harm Shirley. She had no hold over Fred or my family. It was my house. I was the one that was married to Fred.

When questioned about the fate of Shirley Robinson and her foetus:

Rose: It would take a really sick mind to do something like that.

When questioned about her disappearance:

Rose: It was an everyday occurrence for us, people came and went. She was only there on a temporary basis. She just wasn't around one day.

She said that Fred had told her that Shirley had left and gone to Germany, where Rose knew she had relatives.

Asked about Heather, Rose said that she loved her "very, very, very much". She told how Fred had loved her too.

Rose: Fred always loved Heather. He always made such a fuss of her and called her 'his big girl'. I just didn't believe he would hurt any of the children.

Asked how she had gotten on with Heather in the early years:

Rose: Very well, really. She was rather shy and nervous of other people, but she seemed happy enough when she was with me or her brothers and sisters. But when she left school she would just sit around the house and didn't want to make any particular effort in doing anything. I wanted her to take some interest in getting a job and the normal things with children but she didn't want to know. When I did try to talk to her she seemed very offhand and very quiet and didn't seem to want to communicate with me.

She described how Fred had commented on her sexuality:

Rose: He said that because Heather didn't get on with boys and didn't like the male visitors to the house he thought she might have been a lesbian.

Asked about Heather's job offer in Torquay, and her mood after it had been withdrawn:

Rose: To be honest I felt sorry for her because it was the first time she'd shown an interest in anything since she left school.

She said that she and Heather had not been getting on too well around the time she vanished. She believed Heather disliked her because of the men in her life. She said Fred had told her Heather might be a lesbian and she was concerned about the affect it would have on her other children.

Rose: I really couldn't understand how she could find men so repulsive. I believe she was a true lesbian. I have had lesbian relationships but I don't consider myself a lesbian. I consider myself bisexual.

She went on to tell the court how she withdrew £600 from her accumulated family allowance and gave it to Fred, who was to have one last talk with her to try and dissuade her from leaving so abruptly. He wanted to tell her that she was too young to go just like that, and to talk it over with her.

Rose then said that she went shopping, having first got a promise from Fred that if he failed to stop Heather from leaving, he would at least delay her until she came back so that she could say goodbye. Her things were in the hallway, ready. Rose estimated that she was gone for two or three hours.

Rose: When I got back, she had gone. Fred was there. I immediately hit the roof because he promised he would not let her go without saying goodbye and she was gone. He just said he couldn't stop her. I was led to believe that she had left with some woman in a mini.

She then started to sob in the dock. Rose was asked how Fred appeared when she had come back from the shopping trip:

Rose: I thought he appeared to be – well, rather ashamed of having let her go before I got back home. He was rather coy and making excuses.

She said Fred had told her that Heather had promised to keep in touch. He then announced that he had arranged for Rose to spend the night with a regular man in Pembroke Street.

Rose: I didn't want to leave the house, because I thought the kids would miss her, but nevertheless followed Fred's instructions and did not return until seven the next morning, in time to see to the kids' breakfast. We were expecting to hear from her. Fred said she'd promised to keep in contact. I thought she's bound to get in contact at Christmas, she wouldn't let it pass without saying Happy Christmas to Mae and Stephen. But we heard nothing. I thought she'd turned her back on us. I didn't think I was that bad a mother. I was so upset I told my mother. She said these things happen in families.

Ferguson: Did you hear from her?
Rose: I feel a fool about it now. I believed I did. Fred said he had heard from her on the telephone. One time he said it was Heather. I was given the phone and there was somebody drunk and shouting on the other end. I thought it was Heather. It was a very sort of blurred voice. It seemed like a young voice to me. There was a lot of noise and stuff in the background, like it was in a very busy public house or a club or something.

She said Fred would tell her that he had seen her but not been close enough to speak to her.

Rose: I just kept hoping she would get in contact. I thought once birthdays and things came along she would be in touch. Then with Christmas coming up I thought she was bound to get in contact.

As the years went by, Rose said she became angry with Heather, believing she had turned her back on her and forgotten the family. Questioned about the search for Heather:

Rose: The first I knew about it was when the police came round with a warrant to dig up the garden. I thought the police were being bloody-minded, going too far. It seemed so silly at the time. They were in the house and I tried to get hold of Fred on the telephone. He had a mobile phone on the van then. I eventually got hold of him and told him to come straight home and sort this mess out. The time was going by but it was hours before he came home…There had been some trouble with the police in 1992 and I just thought they were being bloody minded and going over the top with their harassment. I thought 'what the hell's going on? Detective Sergeant Onions interviewed me in the room upstairs. They were asking questions about Heather. At that time I didn't know Fred had done anything to Heather.
Ferguson: Up until then, did you know what had happened to Heather?
Rose: No sir, I didn't know he was a murderer, sir.

She went on:

Rose: Fred didn't tell me he was going to the police. Steve came in (to the room) shouting, where's dad? I said he was here a minute ago. His girlfriend (Andrea) said she'd just seen Fred leave with a police car. I didn't know what was going on…I have had no part in murder whatsoever. I'm not a murderer. I wouldn't take anyone's life from them, especially my own daughter.

When asked about Fred being a murderer:

Rose: He fooled everybody. I don't know how he managed it, to actually get those poor girls in and out of the house. I don't know how he did it without being seen. The houses were always full around our house, anybody could have seen him at any time.

Ferguson: Did you have any part to play in the death of any of these victims?

Rose: I had no part in murder whatsoever. I am not a murderer. I couldn't take somebody's life from them. I wouldn't want it done to me and I couldn't do it to anyone else, especially my own daughter.

Ferguson: Did you ever suspect that Fred West was a murderer?

Rose: Not for one minute, sir. If I had thought that, I could never have lived with a murderer. I would never have known when it was going to be my turn. I would have been too scared. I would have had to have gone to the police, I couldn't have lived like that. I was not aware of anything at the time.

Rose was asked why she had blanked Fred at their joint court appearances. She declared that she saw her husband as the devil after he confessed to murdering Heather:

Rose: I hated him. I just couldn't believe I could hate anyone so bad. I didn't see the man I had known all those years. I saw a walking figure of evil. I saw him - it might sound daft - but I saw him with horns and complete with a satanic grin. He never looked sorry for what he did or anything. He just used to grin, like it was all a joke or something. I'm still very, very angry with him. I think it will take me a long time to get over that.

Ferguson: Did you ever do anything after the death of any of these young women either to hide or disguise the fact that they had been murdered?

Rose: No, sir, I didn't know, I wasn't aware of it.

Ferguson: At any time?

Rose: At any time.

Brian Leveson then began his cross-examination. He seemed to ask a lot of questions with yes or no answers, probably so he could fire off question after question and get Rose to confuse and incriminate herself. To a certain extent it worked perfectly.

Leveson: Mrs West, between 1971 and 1994 you never saw anything which alerted you to the horror of what had been happening in your home?0

Rose: No, Sir
Leveson: You never saw a body?
Rose: No, Sir
Leveson: You never saw human remains?
Rose: No, Sir
Leveson: Blood-stains on your husband?
Rose: No, Sir
Leveson: On his hands?
Rose: No, Sir
Leveson: On his clothes?
Rose: No, Sir
Leveson: In the bathroom after he left?
Rose: No, Sir
Leveson: Never heard any screams?
Rose: No, Sir

Even before she had married Fred West, said counsel, she had told her mother that he was capable of murder, hadn't she?

Rose: Will you let me explain?

She said that she and Fred had argued over his insistence that she sleep with other men, which she had refused to do; he had grabbed her by the throat, and when she realized that he was not going to let go, she had taken her words back, then fled to her mother with the children. That was why she had said, "Mum, you don't know what he's like".

After lunch, Mr Leveson turned to the alleged collaboration between husband and wife in every regard:

Leveson: You remained in love with him, utterly and completely devoted, at least until the moment of your arrest. You presented to the world at large as a perfect couple.
Rose: I don't know how I presented. I wanted a home, and Fred to provide... We only connected when we came to decisions about the house or the children, when it was needed.

Mr. Leveson then produced love letters which she had sent to Fred while he was in prison. Asked about having written "Remember, I love you always" in one of them, she replied that at that time she had been having an affair with another man:

Rose: I was in a difficult position. I had had an affair with a man. I wanted this man but I was not sure whether I could split up my home without hurting the children.

Mr Leveson suggested to her that even at the age of 15 or 16 it was she who took the initiative in the relationship:

Leveson: You were the one with the ideas…You remained devoted to Fred West until the moment of your arrest.

He suggested that her husband had been totally devoted to her throughout:

Rose: I don't believe he was capable of loving anyone

Turning to her sexual proclivities:

Leveson: Sexually, you would do anything with anyone – male or female?
Rose: No sir.

She also denied having seen a commercial sex video which police had found at the house, and which showed a distressed naked girl being taken to a cellar and suspended from a beam in the ceiling.
Mr Leveson then asked her about the holes in the beams in the ceiling in the cellar. Rose said that the children used to put string through the holes to make a swing.

Leveson: You knew the true purpose of those holes only too well?
Rose: No sir

To clarify whether she had access to the cellar, Brian Leveson asked if she had a key to the door. She clearly lied in her answer and replied:

Rose: We had a main key that opened a lot of doors, what we called the master key at the time because they were all the same locks.

Leveson: So you could get into the cellar whenever you wanted to?

Rose: No sir, they were bolted from the inside

Leveson: Well, they could not be bolted from the inside if there was not anybody in, could they?

Rose: I don't understand, sir.

When asked about Mrs Giles's evidence:

Rose: I remember her coming when Charmaine wasn't there and it was after Fred came out of prison, but she could have well come to see me before that as well.

Leveson: We can dance around this all afternoon, Mrs West, the fact is that she came once and Charmaine was not there, is that not the truth?

Rose: No, she is mistaken, sir.

Leveson: Because if it was only once and Charmaine was not there, she was already dead, was she not?

The court was reminded of the love letter Rose had sent Fred, in which she had talked about how Charmaine like to be 'handled rough': Mr Leveson suggested to Rose that she had killed Charmaine.

Leveson: Was it an accident because she was 'treated a bit rough'?

Rose: Certainly not sir, she did not die under my care.

Leveson: You abused that girl, didn't you?

Rose: Not to the extent that you would like to think I have.

Leveson: You tied her arms?

Rose: No sir.

Leveson: Tied her to the bed?

Rose: No sir

Leveson: You beat her?

Rose: No sir.

Leveson: You pushed her around and killed her …and from that moment on you were tied together forever.

Rose: No, sir, I couldn't have killed a little girl at that time, or at any time.

Leveson: And you kept her body for Fred to bury?

Rose: Sir, no. Please sir, how could I have kept the body in Midland Road?

Could you please explain how I could have kept a little body there?

Leveson: Underneath your flat there was a coal cellar, was there not?

Rose: I wasn't aware of it, sir – to me it looked like a vent.

1st November 1995

Mr Leveson asked Rose West about the allegations involving her treatment of Anne Marie.

Rose: She obviously loved her father very much. Even when Fred was arrested and he was admitting all these terrible things he had done, she didn't turn against him. She went and visited him in Winson Green Prison and she was still loyal to him then. Even when she knew what he had done – he had killed her mother and two half-sisters – it didn't seem to matter to her at all.

Rose denied taking part in any sexual assaults and denied 'smirking and laughing' as her husband assaulted Anne Marie and then raped her.

Rose: Even after she left home and started having the children, I was still there for her. She knew she could rely on me if ever she needed me, just as I knew that in a dire emergency I could rely on her to help me as well. In lots of ways she was a good girl. I was very proud of her. I believe she resented me coming between her and her father. I thought she would accept me as she got older, but obviously she never did. She really must hate me.

Brian Leveson then questioned her about her trips out with Anne Marie:

Rose: She was going to do it anyway. I believed she was better with me than on her own. We liked to drink Malibu and coke and halves of cider.

Rose told the court that Anne Marie was a "good drinker – she could hold her drink".

Leveson: At 12 or 13?

Rose: She looked much older than she was.

Asked if she used to find men for her stepdaughter:

Rose: Anne Marie was quite capable of finding fellows for herself…there was an occasion when we went out and I found them for her. We were together.

Leveson: When Anne Marie was 12?
Rose: She was very grown up for her age.
Leveson: After what you had done to her it wasn't surprising, was it?
Rose: I didn't do anything to her.
Leveson: You were concerned to improve her sex life, weren't you?
Rose: No, sir. It was me that took her to the doctor's when she was ill.
Leveson: You shoved a vibrator up a little girl aged eight.
Rose: No, sir, that's not right.
Leveson: You certainly did assist in the examination of the genitals of Caroline Owens, didn't you?
Rose: I don't know.
Leveson: Are you saying it didn't happen, you can't remember, or what?
Rose: I can't say either way.
Leveson: Because of what you claim are the limitations of your memory.
Rose: Are we talking about Caroline Owens?
Leveson: We most certainly are.

Rose said her memory of the night of Caroline Owens attack was "practically non-existent."

Rose: I would like to say that, yes, there was an incident with her; yes, it was a mistake in my life and obviously now I tremendously regret it. I'm going to pay dearly for the one mistake I made in my life. I was charged with indecent assault, not attempted murder. I'm here charged with murder, not abuse.
Leveson: You're not going to pay for one mistake now at all, as well you know

She said she wanted to put the "traumatic" event out of her mind. She denied remembering Caroline being taped up. She said she was "terrified" at the time.

Leveson: Let me make this abundantly clear, this was the start of your career of sexually abusing girls, wasn't it?
Rose: No sir.
Leveson: Girls that you picked up in some way or another
Rose: No, sir. It didn't happen like that.

Rose went on to deny that she was a shoulder to cry on for girls who went to Cromwell Street.

Having established that lots of young girls came in to the house for a chat, then that the defendant could have no idea what 'Miss A' looked like fifteen years ago, Mr Leveson said "Then how do you know she wasn't one of the girls who came in for a cup of tea?"

Mr Leveson then passed around more photographs of the victims found at 25 Cromwell Street. When asked if she had seen a photograph of Lynda Gough's skull with adhesive tape wrapped round it, she said: "It was Fred, not me". She was then asked if she wanted to see the gag found by Lucy Partington, she replied: "I have seen enough of the horror, thank you."

On Shirley Robinson:

Leveson: She was carrying his child, wasn't she? Your life could have come tumbling down if Fred had gone off with Shirley, because of the extent of your devotion to Fred. By now you were perfectly used to it, weren't you?
Rose: What?
Leveson: Killing people
Rose: The girl was pregnant, Sir. I wouldn't kill her baby. I wouldn't kill anybody. It would take a really sick mind.
Leveson: And you must have made it very clear to Fred, the prospect of your risking your relationship with Fred was just too great.
Rose: No, sir. Shirley was not a threat.

Rose became angry and blamed everybody apart from herself for what had happened. Most of all, she blamed Fred. Peevishly she complained:

Rose: It's all very well for someone to say I did this or did that, because I'm the one now in the spotlight. Fred West is dead and I've got to take responsibility for what he's done. It's just gossip and rumour and getting things wrong. It's been done a lot in this case!

Leveson: It's not everybody dumping everything on you. It's you dumping everything on Fred West, isn't it?

Rose: Fred West is responsible for these murders. I wasn't mixed up in murder, especially of my own daughter!

Mr Leveson suggested that she had been lying and was trying to put all the blame on Fred; they had contrived a story the night before Fred was arrested, talking it over for hours.

She was asked about the last night her and Fred spent together at Cromwell Street.

Rose: He joked that once the police dug up the garden they'd find nothing and have to put it back again.

When questioned about Heather's disappearance, she admitted that she might have said that she didn't care if her daughter was dead or alive because she was angry that Heather had "abandoned us." But she believed her husband when he said their daughter was safe. She then broke down in tears and claimed she and her children toured the streets of Gloucester hoping to bump in to Heather. Rose was then asked about a family row in which Anne Marie said: "I bet Heather is under the patio".

Leveson: That must have appalled you
Rose: That's right.
Leveson: Did it worry you?
Rose: No Sir, because I thought it was said in a fit of anger

Rose was then asked about the discrepancies between her police reports given in 1992 and 1994 regarding Heather's disappearance. Mr Leveson pointed out that she had said at the time that her other children had kept in touch with Heather, and suggested this was a lie. Rose then practically agreed with him:

Leveson: Was it an honest answer?
Rose: I can't answer that, Sir. I just would have been very confused at the time, Sir.

Mr Leveson then suggested that evidence she had given – saying a neighbour had seen Heather leave home – was false. He further suggested that Rose, if she was a mother with a mother's feelings, would have gone straight to a neighbour in an attempt to find out where her daughter had gone. Rose admitted she hadn't.

He then pointed out further discrepancies. He told how in her 1994 interviews, she had told police that Heather was her father's confidante and would not have confided in her. Yet in 1992 she said that Heather would not speak to Fred, only her.

Rosemary West was released from the witness-box at lunch-time. She had claimed a faulty memory at one moment, a clear one the next; she had been caught telling lies; she had been stroppy; and she had denied any accusation of child abuse.

2nd November 1995

A string of witnesses testified for the defence to having been approached by or assaulted by Frederick West acting alone and trying to abduct women in his car. These witnesses were introduced as the defence were trying to show that Fred West did not need Rose's help in abducting women.

Janette Clarke, sixteen at the time, recalled that she was stalked by Fred West in Gloucester in November or December 1966. On her way home, she found herself walking close to his car and glanced at him.

Janette: He just glared at me. I did not feel comfortable because there was nobody else about.

Moments later he pulled up in front of her, flung open the door and said: "Have you got the time?"

Janette: I felt uneasy and I ran. I didn't know what fear was until then.

Two nights later Fred West followed her again in his car, and she froze.

Janette: I didn't know what to do. I just froze. I couldn't move. I couldn't scream.

It was only the arrival of her younger sister that frightened him away.

547

Janette: She ran up and banged on the car and told him to bugger off.

When shown a photograph of Fred West in court she said:

Janette: Oh God, that's the one.

She said she screamed at the TV in February last year and dropped some tea mugs when his face was flashed on the TV screen.

Janette: I have never forgotten him. It was something from the past, and I never forgot his face.

At about the same time, in 1966, another young woman (Known only as Mrs C in court) accepted a lift from Fred West when she was hitchhiking from a bus stop to Cheltenham to see her boyfriend. During the journey he pulled into a lane and stopped the car. He told the girl to remove her knickers, but she refused. He then exposed himself, but when she tried to get out of the car to run, he hauled her back by throwing his arm around her throat.

Mrs C: He pulled into a lane. He grabbed my body. I can't remember the precise details but it was a sexual and physical attack ... I managed to get halfway out of the car and he had his arm around my throat dragging me back into the car.

She told how he had then masturbated in front of her. Afterwards:

Mrs C: He was charming, pleasant, laughing.

Alison Clinton said she had been grabbed by a man in 1968, when she was aged thirteen, and that she thought he was Fred. She said she was walking home alone when a car passed her and pulled up in front. The driver got out and opened the bonnet. As she walked past:

Alison: He grabbed my wrist. I got free and ran to the nearest house.

Twenty-six years later she recognised Fred West's face on television after his arrest.

Caroline Langman said in a statement that in 1972 when she was 16 she was repeatedly followed by a blue van as she cycled home from school in Gloucester and that she later received an obscene telephone call. Her brother answered the phone to a man who asked for her by name. The caller subjected her to a stream of sexual abuse, using words such as "I would like to do to you." She said she was once too terrified to ride past his van. She went to a nearby house where police were called. When she saw Fred West's photograph last year she:

Caroline: went very cold and felt very strange. All of this incident immediately came back to me. The photo was that man who followed me all those years ago.

Julie Coulson described in a statement how she was attacked in Tewkesbury, Gloucestershire, in 1975, aged 15.

Julie: The man grabbed hold of my arm and tried to pull me into the car. I managed to get away and ran home.

A statement from Theresa Davies, 24 at the time, was read out in which she said she was assaulted by a man who gave her a lift near Stroud, Gloucestershire, in 1975 and who last year she recognised as Fred West. She said she was hitchhiking and he gave her a lift. Suddenly he stopped the car and lunged towards her. She started struggling and he locked the passenger door.

Theresa: I continued to struggle and he became more and more violent, punching me in the abdomen several times. Somehow I managed to unlock the door and struggle free.

She flagged down a lorry driver who took her to a friend's home where the police were called.

A woman referred to only as 'Mrs D' said she had recognised Fred

West on TV last year as the man who had masturbated in front of her and then assaulted her in Gloucester in 1975.

Vincent Oakes said he had seen Fred West in a car with Mary Bastholm who disappeared in Gloucester in January 1968 on four or five occasions. He knew Mary, who was a neighbour, but did not recognise Fred West until after his arrest.

3rd November 1995

Stephen West decided to carry out his father's wish and scatter his ashes over his parents' graves. Wanting to avoid cameras and publicity, he set off from Gloucester with Anne Marie and Tara in the early hours of the morning, taking the urn containing the ashes, but something went wrong.

Stephen: "Anna (Anne Marie) is nuts, she's flaming bananas. She knew what she was doing. She just wanted Dad. She rang me, begging me, pleading to me, if she could just hold Dad's ashes. I said: "No, 'cos I don't trust you to give them back.". I said "Dad's wishes were to have his ashes scattered over his Mum's and Dad's grave. Let's go and do it and get it over with. Then we will both know where Dad is." So I picked Anne Marie up and we drove off to the cemetery in Much Marcle. It's pitch black, no lights or anything. I can't find the cemetery, and Anna is saying: "Keep going, keep going," then she says "Stop here". So I pull over and she jumps out of the car.

Suddenly I look in the back of the car and saw the ashes had gone. She runs across this grass verge and in to this house, which I realised belonged to Dad's brother Dougie. I started shouting, and we had an argument. We waited about 20 minutes until Anne Marie came out and started screaming and crying.

Then she goes running across the fields in the pitch black. We're trying to find her and can't. The police turn up and they get this helicopter with heat seeking equipment and dogs.

The police found Anna and then got the ashes back from inside the house. I put them in the boot of the car and for some reason Anna started kicking the car and bashing on the windows saying: "I want to see Dad." I said: "He's in the car. You get in the car and I'll take you home." She said: "I want to see him" and I said: "He's in the boot." I opened up the boot and said: "There he is," and suddenly she grabbed him and goes legging it down the road.

We waited an hour-and-a-half, it was 4.30am, and I rang the police who said the ashes were with her and nobody knows who they belong to. I said I could prove they belong to me. I am going to report they've been stolen out the back of my car. Anne Marie said she wanted to pour Dad's ashes into the same pot as his victims, Rena and Charmaine. I can't believe she'd want to mix the ashes of the man who killed his wife and child.

Dad wanted to be scattered there and she's caused all these problems. She said she's got this little room in the house with a low wattage bulb and she's got the ashes in a corner with other memorabilia.

It broke my flaming heart. I just wanted to put Dad where he wanted to go. It's unbelievable. She's got no respect."

Mae: "I've had a bust up with Stephen. We don't think the same and I get really angry when he goes on about Mum. We fight all the time over this. I am sorry what happened over Dad's ashes. Stephen was heartbroken. He tries to do things for the best but they don't work out. It's not his fault."

Fred West's ashes were eventually scattered at Barry Island in Wales by some of his children, after objections were raised to them being scattered over his parents' graves in Much Marcle.

Permission was given for four taped interviews of Fred West, selected from a total of 145, to be played in court.

The first to be played was interview No 3, dated 25th February 1994, in which Fred West gave his description of the murder of Heather, complete with her loss of bladder control and his decapitation of her.

There followed the interviews in which he claimed to have been having affairs with all the girls who died, in which he described the ambushing of his wife Rena and killing of Charmaine as an afterthought, in which he claimed Lucy Partington, who he knew as 'Juicy Lucy' because her vaginal juices were so plentiful, and that when she told him she was pregnant she had said: "I've been bloody looking for you – I want a thousand quid for an abortion" and how she wanted him to meet her parents and in which he described how girls would start messing about undoing his fly-buttons and threatening to tell Rose. He described how

Lucy was "just a girl I was knocking off". He said "I grabbed her by the throat and then I drove back to Gloucester. I brought the van up over the pavement, then I knocked the engine and lights out and let him cruise down to the back."

DC Geoff Morgan was heard telling other officers that he had become upset in a previous interview when they asked about Rose's involvement. They then asked him about bondage. "The bondage side of it was mine – Rose never had nothing to do with it", he said. Asked about Caroline Owens, he indicated that she had indeed almost died. "I think I would have went too far with it if Rose had been willing." He added that he had been "trying to get Rose involved with my sex life". Fred also claimed that Caroline Owens had wanted to have intercourse with him the night they abducted her.

DC Savage: Are you saying she agreed to it?
Fred: Well, she didn't do a lot about it, put it that way. I mean she could have screamed and the whole house would have heard her.
DC Savage: Women don't always scream when they're being raped – they're terrified very often.
Fred: Rubbish!

His attitudes both to rape and to murder were revealed further in this exchange with Hazel Savage:

DC Savage: You find things like that very difficult to cope with, don't you?
Fred: What?
DC Savage: Allegations of rape.
Fred: Well, yeah, 'cos I never raped nobody.
DC Savage: And yet you killed people.
Fred: You see, you've even got the killing wrong. You're trying to make out that I just went out and blatantly killed somebody…
DC Savage: No I'm not…they went through hell actually.
Fred: No, nobody went through hell. Enjoyment turned to disaster.

After the tapes had been played, Brian Leveson's junior, Andrew Chubb, questioned the interviewing police detectives for the prosecution to establish that these excerpts had only been part of what Fred said, and that he also told many insane lies. Fred had told police 'lie after lie', for example that Shirley Robinson had sexually abused Anne Marie; that he had killed her because she was jealous of Rose having a 'black babby' and that she had called Rose 'that bitch, that slag, that cow'. Fred told police that after this insult to his beloved wife he had 'lost all sense' and strangled his lover.

The interview that assumed most importance took place on 29th April 1994, when he proclaimed, following a meeting with solicitor and counsel the night before, that he was protecting other "person or persons". It was this contention that was to let in a surprise witness the following week.

Mr Ferguson completed on Friday afternoon, but did not formally rest his case until 10.30am on Tuesday, 7th November (the court did not sit on Monday in order to permit a juror to see a spouse in hospital).

6th November 1995

Mae West: "Tomorrow the prosecution will be answering the evidence from Dad's tapes, and that's it. The trial's almost over.

Mum's happy with me. I saw her Sunday and she's fine. She's not forgotten about the book, though.

She says about the verdict: "it's 50/50." At the moment she's up because Dad is saying on the tapes that it's him. But she's worried about the prosecution tapes. She told me: "as long as there is a bit of doubt they've got to acquit me."

She has told us what we've all got to do for the verdict. She doesn't want me there. She said medically I shouldn't be there. (*Mae was 7 months pregnant*). I'm happy I'm not going. I wouldn't mind if I knew Mum was going to get out, but if she didn't I couldn't take it. I don't want to break down in front of people so I'd rather stay at home. She's asked the nun who befriended her to sit with me when the verdict is announced. I'm not sure what to do really. I don't want to upset Mum.

When Mum talks about being acquitted, she says: "How can I ever get on with my life knowing Stephen will be telling people what I'm doing...we are going to fall out over this," because she knows how much I think of Stephen.

Mum loves us, which she makes obvious, but she's as tough as old boots. We have these strict rules with her and you are either for her or you're nothing.

553

She said to me: "If you're mixed up with the fucking press I'm leaving you behind." Mum told me to do the book, and then she has a go at me. Mum has a fairy tale idea of what it's going to be like. She can't walk into a dole office and say – give me housing benefit. She's Rose West for God's sake. I'm going to wait until she gets out and talk to her.

Mum holds my hand all the time when I'm talking to her. I can't just abandon her, even though she's charged with these horrible murders. There's evidence from this Janet Leach woman, who was with Dad in prison, saying he told her Mum did it with him. That's not good. I wish she wasn't giving her evidence.

7th November 1995

Mr Leveson made five applications to call evidence in rebuttal of the assertions made by Frederick West. These were

1) To hear the probation officer George Guest, who made a social enquiry report at the time of the Caroline Owens incident, lost it, but recalled some of the details. Mr Ferguson objected due to the lapse of time since the event, but the judge allowed it anyway.

2) To read the whole statement of Lucy Partington's mother, showing in detail all her daughter's movements throughout 1973, when it was literally impossible for her to have been having an affair with anyone. There was no objection.

3) To hear the evidence of Detective Constable Harris, to whom Frederick West on tape No 132 said he had nothing to do with any of the twelve deaths and asked him "for God's sake to put it all together" as he would not tell whom he was protecting. There was no objection.

4) To hear the evidence of Dr James McMaster, who interviewed Frederick West at Winson Green Prison in Birmingham in August 1994, when he had become fearful after a disagreement with his then solicitor Howard Ogden regarding book and film rights to his story and claimed Howard Ogden had manipulated him into saying things to the police which he ought not to have said. There was no objection, but Mr Ferguson reserved the right to cross-examine.

Before the fifth and last application was made, exhibits 64 and 65 were admitted without dispute. They were letters written by Fred West and taken from his cell after the removal of his body. "Well Rose, it's your birthday and you will be 41 he wrote. "The most wonderful thing in my life was when I met you. Keep your promises to me. You know what they are. You will always be Mrs West all over the world. I have no present. All I have is my life. I give it to you. Come to me, I'll be waiting".

The last application, which was granted without argument, was that the 'appropriate adult' who had sat in on eighty of the interviews police officers conducted with Fred West, and had formed a friendship with him outside of these interviews, be called in rebuttal of his own tapes.

The jury heard more statements from Lucy Partington's mother – whose detailed accounts of her daughter's movements in the months before her disappearance proved that Fred West's obscene claim he and her daughter were lovers was a work of fiction – and the equally damaging testimony from a former probation officer, who revealed that in the assault on Caroline Owens, Fred West confided in him that Rose had been the instigator and prime offender.

A retired probation officer named George Guest, who had interviewed Fred West at the time of the rape of Caroline Owens, recalled that he had admitted freely that Rose was involved, and had taken a leading part. The account he remembered Fred giving of the attack was quite different to the one heard in Fred's tapes. Mr Guest remembered Fred saying Rose had taken a very active, if not a leading part in the abduction and sexual assault. "He said Rose West asked her husband to stop the car and invited somebody into it. The young lady got into the car, Mrs West got into the back with her. Soon after they set off, Mr West noticed in his rear mirror that she was interfering with the lady." They took her to Cromwell Street where the two women engaged in sexual activity for "a considerable period. I got the impression he was not present all the time while this was going on." He said the girl was bound and tied up and Fred West had sex with his wife. "He said that when his wife was pregnant their sexual behaviour was normal but when she was not she was like a raging queer."

DC Steven Harris, who had interviewed Fred in May 1994, recalled him saying that he was protecting somebody, but was not prepared to say who because he felt that his life, and the lives of his children, were in danger. Fred insisted that he was quite innocent: "I had nothing to do with these girls' deaths at all. I have lied through the statements and at this moment I am not prepared to change that…I am not prepared to say who I am protecting in this case."

Even more importantly the jury heard from a Winson Green prison psychiatrist, Dr James McMaster, who had seen Fred West when he was on remand. Not having spoken to the media, and not paid by them, he referred to his notes. Warders became concerned about Fred when they heard he was making arrangements for his own funeral, and on 1st August 1994 Fred sat down with Dr McMaster to talk about his feelings. "I was asked to see him because he had become tearful following a disagreement with his solicitor, and staff were concerned about his mental state. At first he was distressed discussing problems with his solicitor and then he became calm and rational towards the end. He started by complaining his solicitor had sold the film and book rights to his story without his consent.

He felt uncertain as to how he was going to cope with the court case. He protested his innocence and felt he had already lost enough – meaning two daughters, his wife, etc."

The conversation turned to Fred's interviews. "Fred said he was innocent of the charges and had been telling the police lies to protect another person. He then said that Rose was responsible for restraining his daughters while they were raped. He said his wife was, to quote him, running a brothel from the house. He claimed that he was protecting her and prepared to go to jail for life."

He said that Fred claimed Rose used a sex aid to abuse young women. "He also claimed that his wife enjoyed cruelty and abused his daughters with sex toys. He also said that one daughter, Heather, helped to dig a hole in the back garden. He said it was her grave, but at the time she thought it was a paddling pool she was helping with."

He said that Fred told him that Rose buried people in the basement without his knowledge and he unwittingly laid concrete over the graves. He had been away on a building job and when he returned the floor had been dug up and Rose asked him to concrete it over.

He said Fred also told him that Rose had tried to once murder him with a knife. "The last thing he said was he blamed his wife for sexual abuse of children and for using them for prostitution."

He considered Fred to be rational, not mentally ill and was at no risk of harming himself when he made these allegations.

Under cross-examination McMaster agreed that he saw Frederick West two or three times a week between August and December 1994 and had determined that he presented no danger to himself.

The trial was rounded off with the appearance of Janet Leach in the middle of that morning. Mrs Leach had been registered with a young homeless project in Cheltenham and her name placed on the rota of those likely to be summoned to act as an independent non-participatory witness at police interviews to ensure that no duress is applied during interrogation. When she drew the straw of Fred West she had never heard of him, although it later became clear that she had known his brother John.

In edited form, here is what she told Brian Leveson: "It was important to Fred that Rose be released from custody because they had made a pact that he would take the blame for everything. He told me that on 27th February 1994 and did not change it over several months. Other things he did change his mind about, but not the pact. Rose would never say anything, he said. Before the interviews he told me he was going to say a lot of nonsense, and went through it with me before he saw the police. I did not divulge all this to the police because it was not my place. I was told in confidence. When Rose was released, he said the pact was working, and when she was re-arrested he said the police were getting too close to her being involved. He told me he waited for the police to come up with something, and then would weave a story to fit round it. He was always at work when Rose killed, though he sometimes helped to dispose of the bodies afterwards. The deaths were all sexual, mistakes, they weren't meant to happen. The fingers were chopped off during dismemberment to prevent identification. He didn't say what he did with the bones."

Mrs Leach frequently sniffed, blew her nose or broke into sobs during her testimony. She revealed that Fred West often contradicted himself, first saying he murdered Heather, then that Rose had killed her by accident, or claiming to have been in prison when Charmaine died, then confessing to having killed her when he came out. It began to look as if he altered his accounts to her in exactly the same way as he said he altered them to the police – as a result of ideas suggested to him during interrogation. On the events of 24th February 1994, when the warrant to search 25 Cromwell Street was served, he told Janet Leach that he was five hours late getting home because the van had broken down, and that Rose had told him that evening where the bodies were buried.

She described conversations over the death of Charmaine. Mrs Leach told the court that Fred West had given two accounts. Initially, he insisted he was in a remand hostel when she disappeared. Later, he said he had murdered Charmaine's mother Rena and then, having forgotten Charmaine was in the back of his car, killed her too. She told the court she asked Fred which was the true story. He told her he was in a remand hostel at the time Charmaine disappeared. Mrs Leach told the court how Fred West described how he, Rose, and another person would pick up young girls who were hitch-hiking and from bus stops. During their conversations, he denied that he knew bodies were buried under the cellar at 25 Cromwell Street. He came back from work one day and was told by his wife to concrete over the floor. At other times, he contradicted his story by saying he had helped dispose of the remains. It was at this stage he suggested that the deaths were all Rose's mistakes.

During one police interview, Mrs Leach said, Fred was told that the remains of victim Shirley Robinson's unborn child had not been found "where they were supposed to be." Mrs Leach said: "He was upset. He said 'Rose would have done that'.

Leveson: Done what?
Leach: Would have took the baby from where it was supposed to be, inside Shirley. He kept asking if he was shocking me. I was actually devastated, but I didn't want him to know how upset I was, because I was just doing a job to the best of my ability. I told him he would have to cope by himself if he thought there was anything between us. I was not prepared to put up with that.

Asked why she kept in touch with Fred after her official duties had finished:

Leach: He said there were other people. I couldn't leave it like that. If there was somebody else out there, they had to be found. The last time I saw him was on 16th December 1994, and I spoke to him by telephone on 23rd December to cancel a visit due to bad weather. I was very angry that he killed himself and left me with all that knowledge, because he had promised me he would tell the truth. He said he was going to tell his barristers and solicitors about it and it would all be sorted out.

Asked if Fred West had mentioned bones that were missing from victims, Mrs Leach said he told her Heather's fingers were taken off so nobody could identify her. The only other explanation for bones missing from other bodies from him was: "It was just the way they chopped them."

In cross-examination Richard Ferguson reminded Mrs Leach of other things she had forgotten to mention, as for instance that Fred West had told her it was Anne Marie who brought young girls to Cromwell Street for him and knew what was going on, that he liked to break them in, and that many other people besides Rosemary West had been involved in the murders, including his brother, her father and several black men.

Ferguson: Did you not think he was having you on?
Leach: He didn't come across that way.

She agreed that she had taken no notes of conversations which took place when she and Fred West were alone.

Ferguson: In police interviews, did you never interrupt?
Leach: No.
Ferguson: You sat there listening to hours and hours of lies and never told the police they were at variance with what he told you?
Leach: Yes.
Ferguson: You told the police you were concerned about his solicitor not being good enough for him, but you were not concerned about his lies to them?
Leach: It wasn't my place.
Ferguson: Was he using you?
Leach: I suppose he was, but I didn't think so at the time.

When the court rose for lunch, Mrs Leach collapsed and was rushed to hospital in an ambulance. It appeared she had suffered a stroke some months before, and was exhibiting signs of a recurrence. She had lost the power to speak or move her lips, and was completely immobile.

After lunch, Mr Ferguson told the judge he still had questions to put to Mrs Leach, and since the jury had heard her testimony thus far, and since it was potentially extremely damaging to the defendant, it was essential she be fully cross-examined. "It is impossible to over-estimate the impact of her evidence, which was a severe blow to the credibility of the defence". She had been presented to the jury as the first utterly honest and trustworthy witness who had refused to have any dealings with the press, whereas the defence intended to show that she was already under contract to a newspaper. Court rested until Mrs Leach was able to return.

Mae: "When this is all over I'm definitely going away. I'm moving away from Gloucester and starting again."

Stephen: "Mum took a bashing over the evidence from Janet Leach, who said what Dad had told her. I don't know why they played the tapes, where Dad admitted he's guilty, and then allowed Mrs Leach to say Dad was only saying that for the benefit of the police. It's a mistake and doesn't look good for Mum at all.

I want to go and see the end of the trial. It's important for one of us to be there. I don't really get on with Mum. I've heard a lot of things about her which have left me feeling dazed and angry. But I've got to be there when it's all over."

9th November 1995

Stephen West: "I took James Weatherup and Gary Jones from News of The World to the farmhouse where Dad said he tortured the victims. It's actually an old flour mill, about 20 minutes' drive from Cromwell Street, down on the Severn estuary.

It's very eerie being there. I didn't believe Dad at first, but he did give me very precise directions. Dad told the police about it, and it would have come out at his trial had he lived.

I think the police will start looking there next year. I was told they won't even think of stopping until they find Mary Bastholm, whose body has vanished. They know there are more bodies, a lot more, but they don't really know how many. There's a large area to cover and I don't think they know where to start.

I know the police have gone back into the history of the place, and have looked at old photographs of the area. They told me it was empty around the times Dad was saying. But that's all they have got to go by. Until they get the imaging camera around and see if the ground has been moved, nobody will know.

There are two great wells which have been blocked off, capped. I should think they will look in there. The police told me about them.

Nobody knows what Dad did here. He told me he did Heather at Cromwell Street, but he took the others out. He said that he tortured some of them at the mill, and they were found gagged and bound. Dad was very strong he could have easily put them in the back of the van.

When Dad confessed to me, he was really crying all the time and very vague on the detail. He was so distressed, and I didn't really want to hear it either. He admitted to me he had killed Mary Bastholm, and he also admitted it to a lot of other people. I was told he had boasted about it to the blokes in prison in Birmingham. Apparently he was saying he had killed loads of them, but he was never going to say where they all were. A copper told me they had interviewed the inmates and that's what they had all been saying. Dad was seen with Mary before she disappeared, but no one knows where she is.

I don't know how long Dad was up at the mill for, but he did say he had bricked up a doorway when he first went there. I think I can recognise his work. It looks like one door was bricked up about 10 or 15 years ago. All the bricks bow in the middle. That's the sort of stuff he would do."

13th November 1995

Janet Leach was brought into the witness-box in a wheelchair, with Dr Christopher Gordon from the Royal Hampshire County Hospital sitting behind her in case she should suddenly collapse. Mr Ferguson established immediately that the meetings which took place between the witness and Fred West were unsupervised, and accused her of complicity with him. He rehearsed the various matters Fred had revealed to her, and which she had kept to herself, including a confession to the murder of Mary Bastholm who he said was buried in a field. He had also implicated other people with the allegation that girls were murdered outside the house and brought there for burial, and said one person in particular (not the defendant) had helped him murder Heather.

Leach: I didn't ask things. He just talked all the time. By talking to me he was getting things straight in his mind.

She told how Fred had told her that the girls found at 25 Cromwell Street had died accidentally, and that he had never intended to kill them. They had been killed away from the house, and then brought back to the family home either by himself or by another person for burial.

Leach: Fred said he had to dispose of the bodies quickly because there were people in the house. I said to him that if there were bodies out there, then wouldn't the families want to know? He just said that he wasn't the only one responsible. Other people were involved.

Questioned by Richard Ferguson, defending, Mrs Leach said Fred West had told her that he knew Mary Bastholm, who disappeared in Gloucester in 1968. He said he picked up the 15-year-old at a bus stop.

Ferguson: Did you ask him about where Mary Bastholm was? Did you gather that she was dead?
Leach: Yes
Ferguson: Did you ask him where her remains were?
Leach: He said that they were on a farm.

She said Fred told her that the victims found at 25 Cromwell Street had died by accident and that someone else had brought their bodies back there.

He also told her that his first wife, Rena, and another person had killed Ann McFall, whose remains were found near his home village of Much Marcle, Herefordshire. Fred West was charged with her murder, but Rose West was not.

She admitted that she knew that Fred was telling her one thing and the police another.

Ferguson: You did nothing about it?
Leach: I couldn't
Ferguson: Why was he prepared to take responsibility for these killings?
Leach: Because he would do anything for Rose.

Mr Ferguson asked why she continued to maintain contact with him after she had been released from duty and after the police had objected to her interventions and expressions of disapproval about the advice Fred

West was receiving from his solicitor. She had visited him privately once every week and he had telephoned her three times a week.

Leach: I just wanted the other girls' bodies to be found
Ferguson: No, you wanted to get more information out of him. Did you work your way into his confidence?

Mrs Leach denied that Fred West was emotionally attached to her after a letter was read in which the builder referred to her as 'kid'. The letter said: "It was lovely to see you on Friday, you looked well, keep it up kid. You looked great. I will have to wait till Friday to see you. When you read this, remember me and bear me in mind and let the world say of me what it will. But speak of me as you find me. Will you be in court on Thursday? Well, kid, if the police let you and me have two weeks together we would sort this out and have all the right people in prison where they should be".

Asked about any romantic attachment:

Leach: None whatsoever. I said if he thought there was something, he would be sadly mistaken.

Mr Ferguson then announced that a woman had telephoned the Daily Mirror to ask how a friend of hers, another woman, should go about getting a book about Frederick West's revelations published. Mrs Leach admitted that she had made the call.

A reporter arranged to meet this mysterious woman for discussions. "You were that woman, Mrs Leach. You were the woman who planned to write a book", he said. She was barely able to reply, so he went on, quoting from the letter of 2nd August 1994 which The Mirror wrote in reply to her proposal to pen an account of her dealings with Fred West and offering £7,500 for the exclusive first option.

Mrs Leach agreed that in August MGN had provided a chalet in Somerset for herself and her family, and in September she had personally received £5,000 from The Mirror. He further revealed that payments were made in August, October and December to a man called Brian Jones so that they could not be traced to her. "Brian Jones is your boyfriend" he said. "It was his idea" that she could deny receiving any money, whispered Mrs Leach. Mr Ferguson told the court that she and Brian Jones and three children had been provided with a chalet by the newspaper, that further payments had been made in the interim, and that in the course of a meeting with three men she had verbally agreed to accept £100,000 from them to tell all. She replied that she had signed no contract.

Mr Ferguson told the witness she had been lying, and her reply was so faint that neither the microphone nor the court typist picked it up, but she said "sorry about that". He then attacked her loyalty to the confidentiality of her role.

Ferguson: You continued to see Frederick West even after entering into this agreement with the press.
Leach: Because he asked me too.
Ferguson: Because you needed to continue the relationship for profit. You were unhappy when his solicitor advised him to make no comment, because you needed him to talk. You made conditions before giving a statement to the police to avoid being identified in the media as someone who had made a statement, as that would breach your agreement with the newspaper. You were prepared to assist the police to ensure a conviction against Mrs West. Did you help Frederick West make up his account? Did you assist in developing that account? Did you want to make it as vivid and lurid as possible to make a more valuable commodity to sell?

Mr Levseon then re-examined Mrs Leach:

Leveson: Last lap, Mrs Leach.

She said he told her that the remains of some girls had been buried at a farm.

Leveson: Did you ever get to the bottom of these others?
Leach: Only as to what happened to them and how many but he did not give me specific areas.
Leveson: How many people was he talking about?
Leach: Another twenty
Leveson: Did Mr West ever reveal to you who else was involved in the killings?
Leach: Rose, another person, himself and some coloured men
Leveson: In which killings were you being told that these other people were involved?

Leach: There was a few involved in the ones at Cromwell Street, but others were involved in the ones at the farm.

Leveson: Are you in the position to evaluate or judge whether whatever he said to you was true or not?

Leach: No.

14th November 1995

Mr Leveson and Mr Ferguson gave their closing speeches.

16th November 1994

Mr Justice Mantell began his summing up across the next two and a half days. Mae, Stephen, Stephen's friend Ian and Tara went to hear the summing up. They had two policemen assigned to them who sat either side of the group in the gallery. They were warned not to try to communicate with Anne Marie and if they tried they would be instantly arrested. It was the first time that Mae had found out that Caroline Owens had lived in the house with the family. She had always been told that she was just picked up out of the blue. She also found out about the number of rapes Fred was purported to have committed.

20th November 1995

The jury retired to consider their verdict at 11.44 and the judge told them that if they had not reached a verdict by 16.30 he would send them to a hotel overnight. The jury were handed thick folders containing transcripts of interviews with Rose and Fred West, photographs of each of the victims, forensic details of their remains, and maps, plans and diagrams of 25 Cromwell Street, plus a photograph of the sharp knife found with the remains of Lucy Partington and the long plastic rope found knotted around the remains of another victim.

"Let me know when you have finished. Consider each count or charge separately. You will be required to return a separate verdict for each. For Rose West to be guilty of murder you will have to be sure that she participated in the killings and was responsible herself or did it jointly with some other person, Fred West for example. You have to be satisfied that what was done was deliberate and unlawful, and that she had the intention to cause harm at the time.

To find her guilty of manslaughter it would have to be shown that she engaged in a joint plan with somebody else in something that resulted in death. Your verdict in each case will have to be unanimous. You will all have to agree about it."

He then reminded the jury that in seven of the counts, where it was alleged the victims were objects of sexual torture, the Crown relied on the evidence of three women. He said they were Caroline Owens, 'Miss A' and Anne Marie. "There is no suggestion of collusion between these three. The Crown says that the evidence these three have been able to give you explains why in seven of the cases the victims had been gagged or taped and bound. It also shows the Crown that Rose West was one of those who helped to do it. It shows the purpose for which it had been done and it shows you who did it.

There are no eyewitnesses apart from those who committed the crimes or any direct evidence. The bodies were not found for many years.

This evidence is not applicable or relevant to three of the charges – those relating to Shirley Robinson, Charmaine and Heather. That is because the Crown do not say there is a sufficient coincidence of circumstances between that which must have happened or did happen to Caroline Owens and others, and that which they can prove happened in the case of any one of these three."

He then told them that in the case of Charmaine the Crown were saying that Fred West was in prison when she was killed and that she was in the sole charge of Rose who had shown antipathy to the child.

Shortly before 16.30, the judge called the jury back in to the court room and told them that they had "worked hard enough for one day. I am going to ask you not to talk about this case at all. The last thing we want to happen is for you to talk about it in small groups."

21st November 1995

Just after 3.05pm, the jury unanimously returned two verdicts of guilty (Charmaine and Heather) and then at 4.30pm they found her guilty of the murder of Shirley Robinson.

The judge then asked the jury "Do you think if I allowed you further time tonight you would be able to reach any more verdicts, or are you too tired?" The foreman of the jury replied: "I don't think we would reach any further verdicts tonight."

They again retired to consider the remaining seven charges. Rose West was helped out of the dock and was crying after the first two guilty verdicts. After the third, she just looked stunned.

Stephen and Mae waited for the verdicts at a hotel near Cheltenham, with James Weatherup and Gary Jones of News of the World. Gary and James broke the news to them.

Mae: "I can't cope. It's all too much. People keep saying life is going to get better, but it isn't. It never will. I didn't think there would be these guilty verdicts. I just didn't. I believed in Mum's innocence.

We've had everything taken away from us. It's been no life. Now I've got to bury Heather…Mum won't see me again after this, that's for sure. She said she'd cut us off. She said she wouldn't give anyone the satisfaction of knowing she was going to be inside prison for life."

Stephen: "Mum will commit suicide, there's no way she'll want to live…If they watch her 24 hours a day she'll still find a way to kill herself. She's got it all planned. She just won't have any will to live.

Dad did himself in for nothing. He was trying to protect her, but what was the point? He thought that, with him out of the way, they would never prove anything.

The jury seemed reasonable people, but I can't see how she had anything to do with Heather's death.

I think maybe she might have known and covered up for Dad. She loved him beyond the bounds of what is normal – more than someone should.

Whenever we've tried to talk to her about Dad, she won't have it. She tells me to shut up. She says she doesn't love him. But I believe she loved him more than anyone knows…What would you do if someone you loved said they had lost their temper momentarily, and killed someone? You'd help them somehow, definitely.

The television reports said Mum was sat motionless in court, and I know why. I think she was just waiting for a massive heart attack to strike her down. She had talked about that. I just know she doesn't want to go on.

I thought it would be 50/50 if Mum got convicted but I never thought the jury would come back so quickly.

I'd love to know what they were saying in there, what points they were arguing over. She wasn't like Dad. He was ill, sick. He needed help. Mum wasn't as bad as he was."

22nd November 1995

The foreman of the jury asked two questions:

1) "Is the total absence of direct evidence other than the presence of their remains linking a victim to 25 Cromwell Street an obstacle to bringing in a guilty verdict"?

2) "Is the jury entitled to rely on a combination of the presence of the remains together with conclusions drawn from the evidence of other actions taken by the defendant with, for example, Caroline Owens, Miss A, etc"?

In reply, Mr Justice Mantell re-read that part of his summing up which dealt with similar fact evidence presented by the prosecution. The answer was no, the absence of direct evidence did not constitute an obstacle, and yes, they could rely on similar fact evidence allied to the discovery of human remains. The jury returned to their room.

The jury then returned twenty-three minutes later at 12.53 and unanimously returned a further seven guilty verdicts against Rose West.

Mr Justice Mantell: Stand up. Rosemary Pauline West, on each of the ten counts of murder of which you have been unanimously convicted by the jury, the sentence is one of life imprisonment. If attention is paid to what I think, you will never be released. Take her down.

After a momentary pause as Rose West had been taken away, the judge addressed the court:

Mantell: Mr Leveson and the Gloucestershire Police deserve to be commended for the meticulous way in which they have conducted the investigation of this case, as do Professor Knight and Dr Whittaker for the part they have each played.

Members of the jury, you will never have had a more important job to do in your lives. I am fully aware of the sacrifices each one of you has made in giving your time and great effort in helping to decide this case. I am also aware of the great stress that it must have placed each of you under. You deserve my thanks and your country's for the part you have played. If it is what you wish, but only if it is what you wish, you are excused from ever serving on a jury again.

The four other charges Rose West faced, two of rape and two of indecent assault, remained on the file.

Anne Marie: "I just sat there. I was glad I had been vindicated. That people had accepted the truth of what I had said in the witness box. I felt glad for the families of the victims who must have felt they had justice at last."

Rose was incarcerated at HMP Bronzefield as a Category A prisoner and given prisoner number GJ0017.

Rose being taken away from court after the 'guilty' verdict.

Kathryn Halliday: She is an evil, wicked woman. And she's going inside and she should never, ever come out.

She later said: "They knew what they were doing. They knew what they were going to do and they would've carried on and make no mistake about that and I for one just hope she rots in hell and in prison and I hope she never gets out because she's as wicked as he is. They were both as bad as one another."

DSI John Bennett: Rosemary West has never, ever admitted any culpability to any crimes she was charged with. Certainly not at the time of her conviction or appeal so she is in total denial. That is my view.

Caroline Owens: I don't think she should ever be set free again 'cause she lured a lot of them young girls to their deaths. I think for some of them it was most probably a blessing ending for them, from what they'd been through, if my experience was anything to go by.

Liz Agius: I look at it that I'm one of the lucky people to be alive today, because when I think about it I think were they trying to find out if I was going to be one of the people that if they picked on me would I be missed? 'Cause Fred used to come out with "where do you go every day?" "If you didn't go to your mums and things like that where would I go?" And I used to tell him that if I didn't go to my mums every day she'd be on my doorstep.

Belinda Moore (Juanita Mott's sister): We are relieved in one way, but we all feel absolutely sickened in the way she's met her death. If she'd been ill with a serious illness or she'd had an accident I think we would have come to terms with it a lot quicker but I don't think we'll ever come to terms with this.

Stephen West: You just can't prepare yourself for it. It makes things a lot worse, having seen Mum last Saturday. I told her they didn't have the evidence to convict her and no one could be 100% sure that she was involved. She held me, cuddled me, kissed me and said: 'thanks son, I feel a lot better now.' ...I felt like I had let her down by saying all that.

We talked a lot of things out, because we hadn't been getting on that well. So we were able to remind each other that we still loved each other. She said she was worried that she would be found guilty because people would want to convict somebody for these murders and now Dad's gone there was only her left to convict. She felt that might force them into it. She was very nervous, you could see it, but more placid. She wasn't cold, she was fine.

We're quite amazed by the verdict. We couldn't believe they could find her guilty on all the charges, if any. We just didn't think they had the evidence.

Mae West: I really believe she's innocent. I shall carry on supporting her. I intend to see her in prison. Most people in their lifetimes have ups and downs and bad times but I feel we've had more than our fair share.

Mum's solicitor told me she was shocked and devastated when she heard the verdicts. At first she didn't know what was happening, when she heard the first two verdicts, but after the third she was beginning to adjust to what was going on.

Richard Ferguson: She was incoherent. There were no tears. She was just numb. Another member of the legal team said: "She was slumped in a chair, as if in a trance."

Leo Goatley (speaking outside the court): My client is totally devastated. She wept uncontrollably at the verdicts which she contests. She continues to maintain her innocence and retains the love and support of her children.

Mae West: I know they won't let Mum go to Heather's funeral. She said about the funeral: 'If it all goes wrong, you will sort things out on your own.' We want to give Heather a decent funeral. That's something we feel very strongly about. It's time for her to be laid to rest properly.

I feel the police and social services are to blame for letting things slip through their fingers. The police caught Dad loads of times, and if they'd sorted him out all those years ago he wouldn't have killed all those women.

Dad used to flash and pick girls up and do things to them when he was stalking them outside the Top Rank cinema, near where he used to live. But the police just moved him on without sorting the situation out.

They didn't see the signs. Dad was into everything and it was amazing the social services also didn't notice what was going on with us kids. They didn't do anything. One of Mum's clients said the kids were being abused, but they did nothing.

Stephen West: If I had got caught with what Mum and Dad did in the seventies with that girl Caroline Owens I would have expected to be put away. But all they got was a fine. It was like a green light. You know, go for it.

I even spoke to the NSPCC when they came to the school once when I was 14-years-old. Mum and Dad had worked me over one night and my girlfriend told the school, who told the NSPCC. I spoke to them a few times, but then they asked me did I want to take it further? I said no. What did they expect me to say? I wanted them to do something about it.

Dad showed me once where he met Mum at a bus stop in Cheltenham. He took me there when we were stealing bikes together. There was a whole row of bus stops and he first saw Mum when they were standing together at No.13. Dad told me: 'that's where me and your mum met,' as we stood at the exact spot where he picked her up. I don't know why he took me there. Maybe he thought to himself this will be part of history and I should know about it."

Mae West: He should have said to you Stephen: 'That's where I stalked your mother.' It's frightening to think that's where it all started to go wrong. It's uncanny, No.13, who'd believe it.

Graham Letts: I punish myself every day for not asking enough questions, for not finding out more and maybe stopping it before it happened, and you can't put that in to words.

Details of nine girls so far not traced who had visited 25 Cromwell Street were mentioned in press conferences and press packs released by the police. They show how little the officers sometimes had to go on in finding people who had either stayed at or visited the house:

1) Marilyn, who was in her late 30's in 1973. Possibly lived in Gloucester.
2) Donna Lynn Moore (or similar) who in 1973 was 13 or 14. Father believed to be a US serviceman.
3) Name unknown. Visited Cromwell Street, pictured there in 1975.
4) Marieka or similar. In 1977-78 was in late 20's
5) Maria Ann, in early 20's in 1991, possibly student.
6) Name unknown. In 1978 was 18-20
7) Name believed Ingrid, who in 1978-79 was 18. Possibly German.
8) Marilyn, who in 1973 was 18-19. Possibly from The Forest Of Dean
9) Name unknown. In 1973 was 17-20. Blonde

That evening, a press conference was held by DSI John Bennett, along with Chief Constable Tony Butler and the Chief Executive of Gloucestershire County Council, Michael Honey.

The Chief Constable praised the courage of witnesses who had themselves been victims of the Wests and without whose personal sacrifices the police could not have pursued the case. He paid tribute to the strength shown by the victims' relatives and the work of Victim Support, but reserved the highest praise for the man who had headed the inquiry from the beginning.

"It is impossible for me to overstate the dedication, leadership and compassion of Detective Superintendent John Bennett, ably supported by Detective Chief Inspector Terry Moore and a number of officers and members of the civilian staff. The work that they have undertaken has been beyond the call of duty but underlines the compassionate nature of British policing at its best."

He also credited the Gloucestershire Social Services and the whole of the legal team.

DSI John Bennett then praised the resilience and dedication of all his staff and the excessive demands the investigation had made on their personal lives.

He said that there was no evidence of any more victims, and that all lines of inquiry in the case would be re-examined in two weeks. "Fred West has never admitted to us any other offences whatsoever. We have no intention to search or dig in the immediate future. The file is still open."

He went on to say that the Wests were psychopaths. "They were Jekyll and Hyde characters who appeared to people who knew them to be an ordinary couple. People who met Fred West thought of him as a friendly braggart. You are really talking about Jekyll and Hyde characters with multiple personalities. The court heard tapes of Fred West talking in a very glib fashion about things that would seem to ordinary people utterly disgusting, yet he was able to do that."

Asked about the missing bones, he said: "I don't know what happened to them. And I think it is a matter that is best left alone. It is not for me to speculate."

He touched on the considerable scientific help needed to identify victims dating back twenty-seven years and how their families' uncertainty had been replaced by the terrible circumstances of their deaths. He also took a dig at the press, saying that the victims' families had been continually visited and harassed by reporter after reporter and that had only added to their distress.

"No one can appreciate the pain and suffering they have been through over the past eighteen months and I now appeal again that the families be left alone to rebuild their lives."

A report in the Plymouth Evening Herald quoted Joan Scobling, Rosemary's neighbour as a child in Plymouth:

Scobling: It was very, very rare that Rosemary was let out to play, and she seemed quite happy to stay in after school and help her mother with the chores. Rose was remembered as a "good little girl" and "obedient." She went on: I find it all totally unbelievable. If someone had told me Rosemary had become a nun, I would have found it easier to believe.

Andrew Letts: I can't forgive because Rosemary knew right from wrong. I'm her brother, but I can't possibly forgive anyone for cruelty to children, let alone murder.

Graham Letts: I think she will be in tremendous shock. I know she thought she was going to get off. She was really convinced she was going to walk away from this. I fear she'll hang herself just like Fred. She's a tough person but I don't think she will be able to cope.

Anne Marie: I believe the only reason I'm here is because I was a coward. I never stood up to them. I wish deep down I hadn't been so gutless.

She said she felt guilty over her father's death and how Fred begged her to give him an alibi: "Then he hanged himself and I felt really bad. But I couldn't help him. There have been too many lies".

She told of her experiences growing up: "Whenever I approached my father he would say every family goes through the same thing. He said it was for our own good, to teach us to be better and to have respect for people."

She described how her sister Heather had begged to join her after she ran away from home at the age of 15: "I said no because I was concerned my stepmother and father would come and get her and she'd end up being hit. I thought I was doing right. I'm not proud of what I have done and I don't suppose my children will be proud of me. People say I'm lucky, but I don't feel it. I feel guilty and ashamed that I'm here. I have lost my life."

Some people still believe that Rosemary West is innocent of the murders as there was no direct evidence of her involvement. No-one saw her murder anyone. No-one saw her dispose of any bodies.

No-one had more access to her after her arrest than her solicitor Leo Goatley, and I think it's apt that he is given the final word on Rose West's conviction:

Leo Goatley: Put it this way…I wouldn't sleep at night if I was convinced she was innocent…and I do, I do sleep quite well at night.

11 THE AFTERMATH

Stephen West said after the trial: "He told me that he tortured them in the basement of our house. He told me he took some of them away to a farmhouse and abused them and cut them up there and brought them back in dustbins in the van and buried them in the house. He said that he raped all of them and that he kept them alive because he just wanted to be with them. He said he only did it when they tried to leave him. He said he didn't want nobody to leave him and he wanted them to stay with him.

He said he only told the police what they needed to know. He said he told them about the ones in Cromwell Street because they were always going to find them, so to release the pressure off him, he told them where they were. He promised he would die without them ever knowing the full extent of what he did. I said to him that people believed that you didn't stop. The 7-year gap between the last one and Heather, people believed you didn't stop, you couldn't stop and he said: "I didn't". He said we would never believe the extent of what he did."

He told a very similar story to Janet Leach when she visited him in prison. He told her that at least four other men belonged to The Cult. "They're still walking the streets and they'll kill again when all the fuss about this case has died down."

"Fred would tell me these horrible things as if he was discussing the weather." Fred told her that the girls were kept in a barn. She said that Fred told her: "We had them there for days. We used to go round to children's homes for some of them. Some were from the Hereford area. We would give them a good time and they all enjoyed the sex. We used to tie them up. They had tubes coming from their noses. Some suffocated, we did not mean to kill them but we did. Some were hung up like pigs and their throats were slit. There was blood everywhere. We used to hang them up and leave them there."

He told her that some of the girls were left hanging so long that they became "mummified". All the victims had their fingertips cut off and burned ceremonially. "One of the other men liked the smell of burning finger nails".

Janet Leach said that Fred told her that the girls were tortured even more brutally, and kept alive for longer, than the victims at 25 Cromwell

Street. Their bodies were slashed with knives, although The Cult were not involved in black magic.

He told her that the victims were given nicknames, such as 'knockers' and 'snake'. He told her that the farm was "across the river at Over – next to the electricity station with two cooling towers."

Janet: "He told me 16 were buried in the barn and around the farm." She asked: "What about these other people out there, still at liberty after carrying out the most appalling crimes?" He replied: "Oh, they will be caught because someone is going to slip up somewhere. I'd tell you who they were, Janet, but I don't want to put you or your family at risk. Best you don't know." Janet added: "He said many times 'There are a lot of very frightened people out there'." And she said that Fred had warned her "If Rose gets out she will come looking for you."

A possible site for this 'farm', other than at Berkley, was a former power station called Castle Meads which was closed in 1976 and was demolished a few years later. It has since been turned into a car park. Fred told Janet that there was a pub nearby called 'The Dog'. The power station had a high perimeter fence and could be seen from the farm.

Following her conviction, Rose's daughter Mae and son Stephen and separately, her stepdaughter, Anne Marie, visited her in prison on a regular basis.

Stephen West recalled how, when the police said they were still looking for possibly another nine victims, Rose commented "God knows what will happen if they're found". She said that she wanted to use her "mother's instinct" to become a nursemaid inside. "I want to take them under my wing, I want to look after people like I looked after my children. And I want to use that instinct in prison to help them come to terms with being in there, help them through their sentence. I've got to come to terms with it. I'm here for the rest of my life."

Stephen said: "Mum's got quite a few friends in Durham so she won't be lonely. She's also got one special friend – actually it's a bit more than a friendship, if you know what I mean. Mum knows a woman in there and can't wait to see her when she gets over the other side. She's in H wing and they became really close."

Rose told him "I hate it in there (the hospital wing). I want to be with my friends. It's stupid – I'm being watched, but I'm not going to do anything. I don't do drugs. The light is on in the night so they can watch me. I feel very tired. Shattered. I'm angry."

She then contradicted herself and said "I worry about you. I want you to cope with it all. I'm still numb and may never come to terms with it for years. I could be in here for another 30 years. I hope I don't live that long. I'd prefer to die young. This may be it. This will be it. I've got no hope for an appeal. I don't want to build myself up again only to be knocked down."

She told Stephen that she was worried about a gang on her wing once she was released from the hospital wing. "I am worried about a gang in the prison who are not very friendly. When I was on remand people would shout abuse and 'child murderer' at me. I'm trying not to let this affect me. I can look after myself. I don't see these people who are saying these things as bad people, but people I could help."

Stephen said: "Mum made me a cup of tea from a flask of hot water. She held back from crying until the end. She cuddled me and the tears started coming out of her face. She said: 'Even though I was hard on you kids I loved you more than anything in the world'. That was difficult to take. She maintains she never murdered anyone. She said: 'Look at me – do you think I could murder a child?' She never mentioned Dad. She thinks the judge was biased because of what he said about Mum never being released. She said: 'Throughout the trial he was against me'. I asked what she wanted to do about Heather's funeral and she said: 'I'll think about it and that's it'. Her eyes filled with tears. She kept saying: 'I don't understand how the jury could convict anyone of murder from what they heard. There's no direct evidence. I could never kill a child'."

She told Stephen: "When I stood up to hear the verdicts I felt all numb. I couldn't hear or see anything around me and I couldn't move. I heard what was being said, but couldn't take it in. A police woman said to me 'Come on Rose' and tried to take me away, but I just couldn't move…I'm innocent and I believed I was going to get off. All I heard was abuse, saying I abused them, and whether the statements are right or wrong, that doesn't make me a murderer. I know things were not good at home. I accept I lost my temper a lot but it doesn't make me a murderer."

Stephen then went on to tell of his visits to Fred in prison and of his confessions. He told how Rose was his accomplice. "I want the police to think I did it all but I didn't. The bodies are spread far and wide." Stephen said: "I put it to Dad when he was in prison. 'You did more, didn't you?'

578

and he replied: "I didn't stop when it seemed like I stopped. After I'd killed these girls I'd sit on the steps of Gloucester police station and think about giving myself up – but I couldn't do it. I can't tell you where some other girls are, because it would lead to bigger things." Stephen added: "He also told me about his time in Scotland when he drove an ice-cream van and hinted that there were some bodies up there too. He was nervous whenever Scotland was mentioned. He said: 'As long as the bastards stay out of Scotland I'm alright."

Stephen then told of some of the instruments Fred kept at home. "Dad had everything razor sharp. There were big axes, a scythe, a thick-bladed knife he made himself, a horrible looking ice pick, and an incredible tool for pulling out cow's horns. It's terrifying to think these things could have been used on the victims."

DSI Bennett gave a press conference in Cheltenham, where he told the waiting press that the police were following up 12 fresh lines of inquiry, but they did not include searching for more bodies. He said one line of inquiry concerned a devout Christian known only as Marilyn who was in her late 30's in 1973.

Gloucestershire Chief Constable Tony Butler said: "We have not got a shred of evidence to say there were any other victims. We have had some lines of inquiry from our appeal on Wednesday to help us identify the people we want to trace. But these are not victims. They are just nine people mentioned by others in our inquiry who we have not yet been able to identify. We have no intention of searching or digging in the immediate future.

Fred West had never admitted any other offences. There is no evidence on which we would take further action to search in locations in Gloucestershire for the recovery of any human remains. But it is our duty to tie up all the loose ends of this case."

DSI Bennett added: "There is nothing to support the idea that these persons are victims. We have 12 lines to follow. One is quite an interesting line of inquiry which could lead to the first woman, Marilyn."

Alan Rice, who ran Jordans Brook residential home in the late 1970's with his wife Rosemary, told the Daily Express: "My conscience is clear. We knew nothing about 25 Cromwell Street or girls visiting it until the murder inquiry. We ran that home to the best of our abilities. The girls were like our own children to us. I did all I could to help the police. For some reason social services refused to give them certain information regarding certain residents and staff. I think they had not dealt with such a large-scale inquiry before and they just panicked."

A former resident of Jordans Brook at the time recalled: "Fred and Rose used to hang around outside the gates of the home in a dirty van. Word soon got round amongst the children that it was an open house at Cromwell Street where we could always go for tea and toast and a shoulder to cry on. Rose would offer us the chance to nanny for their children too."

Rose's Appeals, Cutting Off The Children and Letters To Penpals

On the 17th January 1996 Rosemary West decided to appeal. Her grounds for the plea were:

- The trial judge had wrongly exercised his discretion in refusing to stay the indictment.
- The trial judge erred in law in admitting the similar fact evidence. Alternatively, he wrongly exercised his discretion in allowing this evidence to go before the jury.
- That having admitted the similar fact evidence, the trial judge wrongly exercised his discretion in refusing to sever the murders of Charmaine West, Shirley Robinson and Heather West.
- That the verdicts in respect of Lynda Gough, Carol Cooper, Lucy Partington, Therese Siegenthaler, Shirley Hubbard, Juanita Mott and Alison Chambers are unsafe and unsatisfactory in that the evidence of similar fact witnesses was tainted by the interference of the media.
- That the trial judge erred in law in failing to remind the jury of the defence case on 22nd November when they sought further direction on the similar fact evidence.

On the 18th March 1996 The Court of Appeal heard Rose West's application to appeal against her conviction. Lord Chief Justice of England, Lord Taylor of Gosforth, Mr Justice Newman and Mr Justice Mitchell were in charge. Once again, Richard Ferguson QC spoke on her behalf, and Brian Leveson QC who responded for the Crown. Ferguson submitted that there were seven separate grounds for appeal.

Two weeks later Rose West's appeal was rejected. Lord Taylor gave a statement which in full read:

"Mr Ferguson argued that there was a dearth of evidence against the appellant. We cannot agree.

At the heart of the case was the incontrovertible evidence of the bodies buried at 25 Cromwell Street, of the sadistic sexual abuse they had suffered in life and of the fact that the applicant and Fred West lived in the house together throughout the period. Given, as we have held, that the similar fact evidence was admissible, it showed that the applicant and Fred West were sadistically abusing young girls in the cellar of their house for their joint pleasure. There was the evidence of Fred West's admissions coupled with his late confession that he had been protecting the applicant.

The jury had the advantage of hearing and seeing the applicant give the evidence and be cross-examined. Clearly they rejected her evidence. We fully understand their doing so. The concept of all these murders and burials taking place at the applicant's home and concurrently grave sexual abuse of other young girls being committed by both husband and wife together, without the latter being party to the killings is, in our view, clearly one the jury were entitled to reject.

The evidence in its totality was overwhelming. For the reasons we have given in detail, we had no doubt that the verdicts were safe and accordingly we refuse the application."

In July 1997 the then Home Secretary, Jack Straw, subjected Rose West to a whole life tariff, effectively denying her any possibility of parole. This was the second instance of a whole life tariff imposed on a woman in Britain in modern times. The first was serial killer Myra Hindley, convicted in 1966 and issued with a whole life tariff in 1990 before dying in prison in 2002.

Reports in The Guardian on the 22nd October 2000 said Rose West had made a formal application to have her conviction reviewed by the Criminal Cases Review Commission. Rose's legal representatives claimed the judge, Mr. Justice Mantell, had misdirected the Jury and that pre-trial media coverage as well as witnesses being approached by journalists had prevented her from receiving a fair trial. Rose again announced her intentions to appeal her sentence via her solicitor Leo Goatley in October 2000. Rose,

46, submitted a skeleton argument to the CCRC, the body responsible for referring suspected miscarriages of justice to the Court of Appeal. Her legal team was seeking to prove she did not receive a fair trial when she was convicted of the killings in the house she shared with her husband, Fred, in Cromwell Street, Gloucester. It is understood that part of the argument submitted centred on crucial photographic evidence that could prove that Fred - who killed himself in prison - was the sole killer. The Polaroid pictures, contained in an album, were allegedly not disclosed at her murder trial at Winchester Crown Court. At the time it was claimed they had been destroyed, which the defence team say prevented them from using them in evidence to possibly exonerate her. Lawyers also claimed that under the terms of the new Human Rights Act, the pre-trial news coverage and approaches by the press to witnesses prevented her from getting a fair trial. Possible misdirection by the trial judge, Mr Justice Mantell, in relation to payments to witnesses, was another issue raised by the defence.

Rose West's solicitor, Leo Goatley, confirmed he had faxed a skeleton argument supporting an application to the CCRC. He said: "The casefile documents are so extensive that I cannot put them in the post. I am going to have to drive to Birmingham to deliver them to the commission in person."

On the 29th September 2001, Rose West announced her intention to cancel her appeals in her first public comments since her trial. Rose West, 48, said she would drop her appeal against the sentence in hope of "reconciliation" with her family stating she would never feel free, even if released. Nonetheless, Rose maintained her innocence in any of the murders for which she was convicted.

In October 2005 Rose West was moved from HMP Durham, to the new state of the art HMP Bronzefield, in Ashford, Kent.

In 2006 Rose West cut off all ties with her children, except for Anne Marie. Mae wrote a letter to Rose asking her a number of 'uncomfortable' questions. In response, she received a letter asking her not to get in touch again.

Rose also wrote to her pen-pal about the subject:

"Well a lot has changed for me recently. I'm not having contact with my children anymore. For two reasons mainly – one because I have simply been in prison too long and two because of my son Stephen. He's sick, and because I can no longer be out there he's been able to certain of the children under complete control."

Rose entered in to correspondence with a mature student from Oxford. "My innocent children and grandchildren are the ones that must be cared for and protected. For them, life will prove to be hard, painful sometimes, and full of pitfalls, for they carry a dreadful inheritance. My role can only be that of someone who can offer only some of the answers to the questions. For I believe in the truth – no matter how difficult – it is always better than having to 'exist' in the shadows of others' sick fantasies", Rose said.

In regards to her court case: "There is so much more to all of this than meets the eye! Only once I had actually entered the prison system did I start to learn 'what' it was that was motivating the authorities to act in such an appalling manner. When I started to receive the 'paperwork' on which to build a 'defence' and started to read certain pieces of 'evidence', it started to become clear that for those in the position of great power and control there was a lot of stuff that could never become public knowledge. Not only were they responsible for the most abominable inadequacy, neglect and incompetence, that in my view would undermine the public's confidence in them, but they were also shown to be corrupt and evil.

It certainly made clear for me just why after more than 20 years of asking for authorities 'help' with the terrible situation I and my children found ourselves in, not once did they 'respond'. We were being systematically used, abused and tortured and they could only find it in their hearts to threaten us! This is nothing new to me – we were treated just the same when myself and my siblings were very young. It is my belief that because of this, plus the fact that there is no one else left to stand for these terrible crimes, the 'judicial system' will always have their hearts and minds closed to an appeal from me."

Put simply, Rose West believed that she bore little responsibility for the killings. She also clearly believed that she has been made a scapegoat for her husband, and that, had he not hanged himself, the case against her might not have been proved.

Detective Superintendent John Bennett who led the investigation said:

"The whole case was about Rose being sexually insatiable. There were huge amounts of pornographic material and sex objects in the house. I firmly believe that Rose murdered those girls and Fred disposed of the bodies".

Rose claimed she had chosen not to appeal further as "Life is too precious to waste on a futile 'cause' despite the undeniable voices from deep down inside ourselves, urging us to make the truth known. We are learning to live with the frustration and despair, to keep the turmoil at bay – for it's this that will give us life. Even when we have to look the Devil in the eye, we count our losses and still we are unable to be heard. Ours is a lonely path, the rewards are small, but, I believe, are still worth clinging onto! Being a model prisoner is the only thing that has afforded me any kind of dignity over the years."

More of Rose's letters became accessible later in 2006. Talking to a pen pal, Rose said: "What I've been wrestling with mainly is trying to come to terms with this natural life sentence. It has thrown up all kinds of thoughts and feelings, stuff I wasn't even expecting."

A few weeks later: "Learning to accept my natural life sentence is one thing – living with it is another. It leaves me empty sometimes, lonely, sad, angry, frustrated. I am restricted in just about every direction possible!"

A family friend gave an interview and said: "Anne Marie is incredibly compassionate and sees herself as the person who keeps the link alive between Rose and the family. There are eight surviving siblings and a lot of them have changed their names and are living all around the country, but she wants to retain some kind of contact with Rose on behalf of them. Rose is kept informed if she has had a new grandchild or that sort of thing, and that has kept her going for more than ten years in prison."

In a letter to a pen pal written from prison in 2005, published in the News of the World, Rose West said: "My parents were sick people who should never have had children in the first place. They were control freaks and at their hands we suffered mental, physical and sexual abuse…No one cared for us EVER!"

In October 2008, Rose West was moved to HMP Low Newton in Brasside, near Durham, after prison officers discovered a plot to beat her with pool balls.

In a newspaper interview, Rose apparently admitted sexually abusing children with her husband Fred - but still denied murder – to another former prisoner. She said she believed she has been in jail long enough and should be freed. The former inmate who befriended her in prison told the Mirror: "Rose says she has been locked up for long enough for the crimes she actually committed. She knows she is a twisted and depraved child abuser but thinks her time has been served". The ex-inmate, named Jenny - not her real name - went on: "Rose confided in me that she abused children. She said on several occasions Fred would call her upstairs and there would be a naked child held in their bedroom. She admitted going ahead with sickening, depraved acts. Yet she made out she was going along with what Fred told her to do. Although she is a paedophile, she insists she never killed anyone."

Jenny said she struck up a relationship with Rose at Bronzefield prison, Middlesex. She said: "Rose opened up to me and told me things because we were neighbours and talked a lot. Rose sometimes opened up about Fred and her part in their crimes. Rose certainly knew her husband was a killer or at the very least capable of murder. She said she lived in fear of her life when he would take her out in the car to a remote farm. Fred often lived out a warped fantasy of his which involved tying Rose to a gate on a farm in the middle of nowhere, removing her clothes and having sex. Rose said she thought each time it happened he might kill her. It meant she knew he was a sick and evil man and she was under no illusions about his character."

Jenny said she knows Rose will never apologise to the families of her victims. She said: "I would play Scrabble regularly with her ... I went cold one night. She had been mentioning Fred and her past. At the end she had beaten me by a large margin and I quipped, 'Don't worry, you don't have to feel sorry'. She looked me in the eye until I knew she wasn't talking about Scrabble, then replied, 'Don't worry, I don't ever feel sorry about anything'. My blood ran cold."

Jenny, from Southampton, who was jailed for six years, told of her horror when Rose had made several lesbian passes at her. She said: "It's well known that Rose is a lesbian inside jail but I never believed she would make a beeline for me. I was absolutely appalled." Jenny said Rose revels in her notoriety: "Rose is always moaning about her press coverage. It's remarkable, as if she has pushed her crimes from her memory. But when there are stories in the newspapers Rose learns of, she often said, 'Well at least they all still know who I am'.

Rose West's life behind bars was revealed in newspaper articles. She had been kept in the special segregation wing at Low Newton. The other inmates in the unit are Tracey Connelly, the mother of 'Baby P', with whom she is said to have had a lesbian fling; Kemi Adeyoola, just 17 when she butchered her elderly neighbour in 2006; Clare Nicholls, sentenced to at least 28 years in 2010 for killing her boyfriend; and fellow child abuser Valerie Walsh, who is in her 50's. The sixth segregated prisoner is Kayley Boleyn, 20, another child killer who occupies a cell just yards from Rose West.

Nicholls and Walsh are in Rose West's cross-stitching class. Adeyoola is an orderly in the gym where Rose goes every morning between 8am and 9am. She is also Rose's regular opponent at Monopoly.

Outside this little circle, the only people to visit her behind bars are a Christian couple, in their 60's, who have been performing the unenviable task for a number of years. They spend two hours with her in a private room at Low Newton once a month. Rose has grown so close to them that she refers to them as 'mum and dad'.

On the 15th October 2016 Rose West was pinned down and attacked at HMP Low Newton in a fight with a fellow inmate. Rose, 62, suffered a black eye and facial swelling after she was "pummelled" by a younger prisoner. Her attacker was dragged off by guards.

"It was a very nasty attack and Rose was quite shaken," a source told The Sun. "The girl gave her a bit of a pummelling. Rose was OK after a while and didn't need hospital treatment. She is a big woman, but is getting on a bit, and this other girl is younger and caught her by surprise. No one knows what it was about, whether it was to do with a fling or anything and Rose has kept quiet about it. But a lot of the inmates hate her because of her crimes and for what's seen as her 'celebrity status' inside."

On the 30th September 2017 Rose West's struggles with her health became evident. She has had problems with her knees and complained that she's kept in cells on the upper landing which she finds hard to get to. She is not allowed a corner cell as it has two outside walls which could increase her chances of escape.

An insider said: "Rose has really bandy legs that give her constant pain. She's always moaning about them and really struggles to get up and down stairs."

She is now on F wing at HMP Low Newton prison in Durham and classed as Restricted Status, the female equivalent of a high security Category A male prisoner.

The source said: "In theory all prisoners of that level are supposed to be moved every 28 days but in reality it doesn't happen due to lack of resources. It's a mark of how Rose is still seen that she most definitely gets moved every 28 days." She added: "People used to be scared of Rose. She still thinks she's the boss of the wing but she's pretty frail now. She has this issue with her legs and her eyesight is failing. She couldn't boss anyone about any more."

She was moved to HMP New Hall, Wakefield, West Yorkshire in June 2019.

Howard Ogden

On the 1st March 1996 Fred West's former solicitor, Howard Ogden, was suspended for a year for unbecoming conduct, but cleared of trying to cash in on his former client's notoriety. Howard Ogden was also ordered to pay half the costs of the solicitors' disciplinary tribunal hearing, which were believed to be several thousand pounds. The tribunal was told that he got Fred West to sign a form which waived his right to professional confidentiality.

The tribunal also heard that Fred West and Howard Ogden jokingly discussed a film of the murder case and talked about which actors and actresses would play the various parts.

The case arose out of the decision by Fred West to sack Mr Ogden in August 1994 amid allegations that the solicitor was trying to sell the book and film rights to the case for £1,000,000. Howard Ogden admitted two allegations that he had behaved in a way which compromised or impaired his professional reputation and that the waiver agreement had caused a conflict of interest between himself and Fred West, but he denied that the agreement either gave him or might have acquired him an interest in publication rights in the West case and the tribunal found in his favour on this allegation. In March 1994 Mr Ogden visited Fred West and produced a form for him to sign in which, Fred West "agreed to waive his rights to confidentiality as a client in favour of the respondent [Howard Ogden]". The form stated Howard Ogden "may write a book concerning my case" and meant that neither Fred West nor his family would benefit from the sales of such a book. The agreement which was signed by both Fred West and Janet Leach "represented a serious example of misconduct" and breached the solicitor-client relationship.

Howard Ogden initially denied the existence of such an agreement but was eventually forced to hand over all material relevant to the case by a court order obtained by Fred West's new solicitor. A statement from Fred West was read to the tribunal which said: "It became clear that Mr Ogden's main concern was to get information from me to write a book."

Howard Ogden told the tribunal that he accepted that he should not have put Janet Leach in the position of becoming a witness and that he should have allowed Fred West access to another lawyer. But Howard Ogden denied that he intended any financial gain from a book adding: "All I set out to do was to follow my client's instructions which were to be in a position to discuss this with somebody. I believe that that was all the waiver of confidentiality was about." But Philip Hodson, chairman of the tribunal, told him: "With the exceptional circumstances of the West case it was important for the respondent to take exceptional care and ensure he dealt with all matters in a scrupulous professional manner. This he failed to do."

"That case changed my life. I contracted a rare form of leukaemia during it, as a result of the stress. I've since had special chemotherapy treatment and been given the all-clear. Seeing that horrible evidence had a big effect. I still get terrible nightmares and awful flashbacks. If I read a newspaper headline which contains the word West, I still shudder", Howard Ogden later said.

John West, William Hill, Steven Letts and David & Pauline Williams

On the 25th November 1996 Fred West's brother, John West, went on trial at Bristol Crown Court for the Rape and Sexual Assault of his nieces Anne Marie Davis and Mae West. Mae was living with Tara and her two children at the time and didn't want to give evidence but was told she had no choice.

John West arriving for his trial

The jury of seven men and five women at Bristol Crown Court were repeatedly told that they should ignore the murders committed at the Cromwell Street address. Trial Judge Mr Justice Cresswell was determined to be scrupulously fair during the trial and ruled that this evidence should not go to the jury. It was not alleged that John West had been involved in those events.

Mr Brian Leveson, QC, told the jury that he could not be deprived of every citizen's entitlement to a fair trial because he was linked to the Wests and that notorious address.

The jury was told that the charges John West faced concerning Anne Marie were only sample counts. The alleged rape of Mae referred to only one occasion.

Anne Marie took to the stand, where she claimed she was raped at least 300 times from the age of 10 or 11 by her uncle at 25 Cromwell Street, Gloucester. She told the court that John West became a frequent visitor to 25 Cromwell Street. Most of the time she was made to stay at home and not go to school. She told the jury that she was only 10 or 11 when John West first had sexual intercourse with her, in a ground-floor bathroom at Cromwell Street. Later attacks took place in a toilet.

After the first alleged attack by John West, Fred's younger brother, Anne Marie spoke about it to her stepmother, Rosemary, who laughed it off. "It was of no consequence and it was perfectly all right" was the response from the convicted mass murderer, the court was told. She told the jury she accepted her stepmother's response that the alleged rape was perfectly normal. "I was never ever aware that anything going on was wrong. It was the way I was brought up. I didn't know any different. It was just accepted by him that he was allowed to have sex with me."

In the dock, John West sipped a glass of water while staring intently at his niece in the witness box. Earlier, he had heard Mr Leveson say that at the time of the alleged attacks he was "big, strong, rough, and someone not be argued with".

Asked if she had given consent to Mr West, Anne Marie replied: "No, sir."

She told the jury that she was repeatedly raped by her uncle several times a week until she fled Cromwell Street shortly before her sixteenth birthday. Her uncle had raped her twice a week, almost every week, for at least three years.

"On your account you were raped by John West on more than 300 occasions?" asked Nigel Pascoe, QC, defending. "Is that the truth?"

"Yes," Anne Marie replied. She said 25 Cromwell Street was very much a sexually orientated address. Rosemary dominated – "You did never go against her wishes."

Asked how long the alleged attacks by her uncle continued, she told the court: "Until I went away from home." She had spoken to no-one about the alleged incidents until the arrest of Rosemary and Fred West, because she had presumed it natural. After she fled Cromwell Street, she was only allowed to return if she made an appointment with Rose.

She sobbed in the witness box as she described how she had been abused by perhaps 10 or more people - apart from her parents - before her teenage years. She also revealed that two years before Fred and Rose were first questioned on murder charges she had made a statement alleging abuse by them. She withdrew it because the police would not offer her protection against her father and his wife. As a consequence of this withdrawal, the police threatened to prosecute her for wasting their time.

Mae denied to the court having said that Rose West was going to have her own back on those who had not stuck up for Fred. She said she had been raped by John West in the bathroom at Cromwell Street after being called in from the garden of the house where she had been playing with children, including Heather. John West's solicitor quizzed Mae and said that she was a liar. John West said that he had caught her smoking and had threatened to tell Fred and Rose and Mae had made this story up to get back at him.

Both witnesses admitted receiving payments from newspapers for their stories.

Anne Marie claimed that the money would go to her children and that a book she had helped prepare was not for financial gain. It was written so that her children might understand when they became older what she had gone through during her childhood

27th November 1996

John West, a refuse collector, denied raping and sexually assaulting Anne Marie over a period of up to five years. He also denied raping and sexually assaulting Mae West once.

He strongly rejected Anne Marie's story and told the jury: "I did not rape her at all. We had a very friendly relationship…Honest, you can bring a stack of Bibles. I swear on them all, I've never laid a finger on either of them."

John West explained that "My brother used to phone me up and asked me to chuck a few bags on the dustcart."

He told the court that he would collect his young son Anthony from school in Gloucester after September 1983 and take him to Cromwell Street for an hour or so until his wife had finished work. He explained that at Walter West's funeral "I told him (Fred) to his face that I didn't like the way he'd treated his father and as far as I was concerned I was never going to speak to him again."

Until the allegations of rape, John West was a man of good character who had no previous convictions. Relatives of John West described him as "kind and gentle". His wife Anita told the court that they had been to Cromwell Street together "occasionally" for weekend visits, evenings and children's birthdays, from "just after" the birth of her son Anthony until "five or six years' ago." She described her husband as "very loving, very caring" and a "good father, good uncle and good grandfather", a view repeated to the court by his son Andrew, who called his father "a gentle giant really", and then echoed by three of his nieces, as well as one of their husbands.

His niece Lorna Gatfield, 18, who went on holiday with him as a child, said: "I felt safe with him. Uncle John was always known as a gentle giant. He was big on the outside, but soft and gentle on the inside. He is a very down-to-earth, friendly person." Another niece, Theresa Poole, daughter of John and Fred's sister Kitty, said she had no concerns about leaving her children with him. She said: "I don't think he would do anything to harm children."

28th November 1996

John West was found hanged in his garage in Curlew Road on Gloucester's Abbeydale estate. At the time of his death he was a grandfather and he had fathered five children - two from his first marriage which ended in 1970 after five years; two from a long term relationship; and a son from his last wife, Anita, a nurse whom he married in 1976, after they met in hospital where he was a patient. Until the end Anita West was standing by her husband.

Neighbour Ann O'Reilly said: "I saw a police car at his house at about 9pm but I didn't realise why it was there. I knew John West as a very nice, reliable, friendly neighbour who was there when we needed him."

By law the judge called the jury back into Court No 2 at Bristol, and told them they were no longer required to deliver verdicts. During the brief hearing, Mr Brian Leveson QC prosecuting, said that it was with "great regret" that the accused had apparently taken his own life. Mr Nigel Pascoe QC, defending, said: "The death of Mr John West is first and foremost a dreadful tragedy for his wife and his family to whom I wish to extend our deepest sympathy on behalf of the defence and on behalf of all in court. He had a conspicuously fair trial."

The judge then formally directed that the indictment against John West should be declared "of no legal effect". He said the file should be closed unless there was a further court order.

Stephen West said of his uncle John: "I believe he knew that the odds were stacked against him and there was no way he would get out of this." He believed his uncle took his life because he knew it would be difficult to do so in prison. "It is just a way of taking your life and it is a quick way. They have escaped justice by taking their lives. My father was guilty and I certainly believe my uncle was," he said.

Anne Marie said: "I never wanted this to happen, but please believe me - what I said was true." Of the shock felt by John West's family at his suicide, she said: "I can honestly say I know how they feel. I have lost my family, lost my mum and dad. I know what they are going through and I am very sorry."

Doug West, brother of the late Fred and John said: "He should have waited to see what the verdict was. It should have been up to the 12 members of the jury. I haven't seen John for two years and I have not spoken to him since he phoned me on New Year's Day 1995 and told me

Fred had hanged himself. He was upset then and I'm very surprised that he would do the same thing."

John West's solicitor, Mr Steve Young, a partner in Cheltenham-based Smith Robinsons, spoke to his client less than an hour before his death. He said: "It's a great shock, a terrible shock. The trial went very well and we were confident John would be acquitted. He was fine when I spoke to him last night not long before he did this, and he gave no hint that he had anything like this in mind."

On the 19th May 1998, William Hill (Fred and John West's cousin) was jailed for 4 years on one count of rape and three counts of indecent assault against three teenage girls between 1976 and 1984 at his Much Marcle home. He was cleared of rape and indecent assault of a fourth girl.

William Hill appearing at court

But William Hill, 45, was cleared at Birmingham Crown Court of another charge of rape and three other counts of indecent assault. William Hill, known to his victims as John, had been charged with attacking four girls and was convicted of incidents relating to three of them. He showed no emotion in the dock as the guilty verdict was read out. His wife Ruth sat just feet away in the public gallery. One of his convictions for indecent assault related to a girl who was just 15, although he was cleared of another charge of indecent assault against her. The attack on the girl for which Hill, of Putley, near Ledbury, was convicted, happened in 1980 or 1981. He was originally charged with raping the 15-year-old but after legal submissions the trial judge substituted this with "indecent assault by having sex."

The victim, who cannot be named for legal reasons, had told the jury Hill had had sex with her on a number of occasions in an upstairs bedroom at his former home.

The other offences for which he was convicted took place between 1976 and 1983 when the two girls visited Hill's former home in Much Marcle, Herefordshire. The court heard that Hill, who has three children, had visited Fred West's home at 25 Cromwell Street, Gloucester, frequently until he married in 1985. Hill tried to commit suicide while on remand at Gloucester prison. He was later moved to a mental health unit at Hereford County Hospital.

On the 14th October 2015 the trial of David and Pauline Williams began at Exeter Crown Court. The court heard how they became child abusers in their own right - subjecting youngsters to rapes, sex assaults and beatings. David, 56, terrified his young victims - six girls and four boys aged 7-15 - by boasting of his connections with the Wests.

David Williams would even tell his victims "I knew the Wests". The voyeur also set up cameras to watch his wife having sex with pub customers, friends and some of the children they both abused. He also filmed himself having sex with some of the female victims who had been lured to their home. He was encouraged in his campaign of child abuse by his wife Pauline, who mocked the victims during their ordeals.

The court was told how his wife carried out her own sexual assaults on several of the traumatised children.

Their campaign of rape and sexual assault began in the late 1980's, when they were running the Prince Albert pub, where the Fred and Rose West drank. Detective Constable Dow, who worked on the case, said (speaking about the first woman to tip the police off): "This woman was brave enough to speak to me. The investigation then soon progressed when a number of other people came forward to uncover the abuse they had all been subjected to at the hands of David and Pauline Williams."

The married couple continued the abuse when they moved to Exeter and Tiverton in Devon in the 1990's and 2000's.

Jurors heard how they initiated sex with their victims - some who were as young as seven - through sordid games of strip poker and truth or dare. David Williams even told some victims that he could speak to the dead and would terrify them with stories about the Wests. They also used violence to bully the victims into compliance, beating some of them with sticks or strangling them. David Williams told some of the children he was possessed by the devil and had received messages from his dead father telling him to abuse them.

During their six-week trial, he admitted knowing the Wests but denied using the connection to threaten anyone. He told jurors: "Fred had a drink in our pub before he became infamous and so did his wife Rose. From what I remember he was a very friendly quiet man who would sit at a corner table and have a drink. It was Rose who was the mouthy one. She was the one with all the chomps. I did not mention them to anyone but sometimes people asked me if I knew them because I came from Gloucester. The pub was round the corner from Cromwell Street. I never worked for Fred West."

David Williams was found guilty of ten rapes, 13 indecent assaults, five counts of gross indecency, two of cruelty, and one of sexual activity with a child. Pauline Williams was found guilty of two rapes and five indecent assaults. The couple, from Bradninch, Devon, were warned to expect "very long" jail terms when they were sentenced the following month. Judge Erik Salomonsen told them: "You have been convicted of appalling behaviour that you meted to these children over a long period of time. You have been convicted on overwhelming evidence of a campaign of abuse simply for your own sexual satisfaction. This is very serious sexual offending which has damaged the lives of the children."

Despite his assertions that he did not know Fred or Rosemary West that well, the postcard they received (dated from October 1990) shows that the Wests knew them well enough to send them a postcard from their holiday. It was addressed to 'The West Williams Menagerie', and appears to show that the West's children were staying with the Williams' at the time.

November 2015

David Williams was jailed for life (with a minimum term of 23 years) after being found guilty of offences including 11 counts of indecent assault, 10 counts of rape and two counts of gross indecency with a child. He was also convicted of three counts of indecency with a child, two counts of cruelty and two cases of aiding and abetting an indecent assault.

Pauline Williams was sentenced to 12 years in prison with four years on extended licence after being found guilty of two counts of aiding and abetting rape, two counts of aiding and abetting an indecent assault and three counts of indecent assault.

Judge Erik Salmonsen told David Williams: "Your behaviour towards children was sick. You had no conscience in using young people for your perverted sexual pleasure." He told Pauline Williams: "You aided and abetted your husband to rape young girls on several occasions."

Detective Constable Dow said after the trial: "The strength of these victims, both men and women, in finding the courage not only to come forward to the police, but to give evidence at the trial, was incredible. They have had their childhoods stolen, and all suffered difficulties throughout their adulthood following this abuse."

David and Pauline Williams

After the trial, allegations came to light from a source close to the abuse that years previously a baby was murdered and cut in half by the Williams'.

4th May 2016

Police began excavating the former home of David and Pauline Williams, who were jailed at Exeter Crown Court in November for a string of sexual offences dating back to the 1980's.

Their catalogue of abuse started in Gloucester, where they met the Wests, and continued when they moved to Devon in the 1990's. Devon and Cornwall Police confirmed excavation work had started at an address in Bradninch in Cullompton, Devon. A spokeswoman said: "Following intelligence received, Devon and Cornwall Police are undertaking excavation work at a property on Cullompton Hill, Bradninch, Cullompton, Devon. This relates to historic intelligence connected to the address and its former occupants. It is expected to take up to four days to complete. Specialist officers will be involved in the excavation, which we hope will have as little impact on the local community as possible."

The abuse on victims as young as seven years old was both physical and sexual. The investigation into the pair, named Operation Abbey, began in July 2013 when a woman disclosed to a mental health professional that she had been raped and sexually abused by David Williams when she was 15. She then spoke to Detective Constable Debbie Dow, from the force's child abuse investigation unit, and made a complaint against David

Williams. A number of other people then came forward to uncover the abuse they had been subjected to at the hands of Williams and his wife.

The couple denied all allegations against them throughout the investigation and the trial, despite overwhelming evidence against them. Speaking after the pair were sentenced, DC Dow said: "David and Pauline Williams carried out a string of sickening and callous sexual attacks on children and teenagers without remorse over a 15-year period. Their campaign of abuse started in Gloucester and continued when they moved to Devon and lived in Exeter and Tiverton. The abuse was both physical and sexual and undertaken by both David and Pauline Williams; one victim was as young as seven years old when this started. These victims, both men and women, had their childhoods stolen by David and Pauline Williams and all have suffered difficulties throughout their adulthood following this abuse as they struggled to live normal lives."

A neighbour, who asked not to be named, told the Press Association: "It is pretty gruesome, terrible really. I think they only lived there for a couple of years at most. An old lady lived there before, she was a church-going lady, she would be turning in her grave if she knew. They obviously moved here as a hideaway because it is a villagey place where nobody would know them. The man spoke to me once at a bus stop and I saw the lady a few times, but I didn't know them."

She said nobody knew about the horrific crimes the couple committed until it hit the headlines when they were convicted and jailed. "We found out they were friends of Fred West, they are terrible. It is terrible. You don't expect it, do you? No-one has lived in the house since they were jailed - it has been empty."

A local said: "Some people say they looking for a baby's body, but we just don't know. The thought makes you feel numb. It's horrific. Mr and Mrs Williams used to encourage children to come and play in their garden. I thought they were creepy, so I never had anything to do with them."

No remains were found.

On the 6th March 2017 Steven Letts, 39, who is the son of Graham and Barbara Letts, and nephew of Rose West, abducted and raped a 12-year-old girl after plying her with cocaine, cannabis and vodka.

They met in the street when the girl asked him for a cigarette and he offered her a joint. Letts spoke to the youngster after she approached a number of adult men asking them if they had a cigarette. The girl, who was in care, was with her support worker when an argument broke out between them. The support worker warned him that the girl was underage but he still left with her.

When they got back to his flat, he gave her apple vodka and allowed her to smoke cannabis. He let the girl smoke cocaine through a pipe "to see how her body copes with it" because it was her first time trying the Class A drug.

Steven Letts had a friend present – but he is said to have left the flat when the girl declared that she was underage.

He then kissed the girl in the kitchen, where she reiterated her age. "He kissed me and I said I can't do this because I'm only 15. He told me sad stories like a couple of months ago he tried to strangle himself. I think he said that so that I'd feel bad and kiss him. I did tell him I was 15 (instead of 12) because I thought I had more of a chance of getting drink and drugs."

The girl then became tired and went to sleep under a blanket in Letts' bed. He then climbed in and began "cuddling" the child before initiating sex. The girl said: "It went from cuddling to just like too far" and the sex lasted for 30 minutes. She said that the sex "started to hurt" and she wanted him to stop but felt guilty asking because he had earlier provided alcohol and cocaine.

The rape only came to light when the girl asked a social worker "how long it'd take to find out if you're pregnant".

Despite claiming that the girl told him she was 16, police arrested him and found DNA matching the girl inside his underwear.

On the 6th November 2017 Steven Letts, of Barton Road, Gloucester, was found guilty of kidnapping and raping a 12-year-old girl. He pleaded not guilty to abducting the girl on March 6 and raping her in his flat between March 6 and 8.

Steven Letts' mother Barbara - who was present in the public gallery throughout the trial - shouted: "I will still fight your corner" as he was taken down.

Detective Constable Lindsay Tomkinson of Gloucestershire Constabulary who lead the investigation praised the victims' courage. She said: "I would like to thank the young victim who showed great courage and bravery in coming forward and for our partner agencies which provided invaluable assistance and support to the victim along the way. This has been a difficult case for the young victim to relive in court and for the witnesses who gave evidence during the trial. We will strive to do everything we can to bring offenders to justice and Letts is due to be sentenced for his crimes later this month."

The panel returned a unanimous verdict with all 12 jurors finding Letts guilty of both charges. Prosecutor Sarah Regan said the victim wanted Letts to stop, but "felt guilty" because he had given her alcohol and drugs.

Steven Letts claimed he believed the girl was 16 when they met. The "troubled" child had already tried heroin and spice despite her young age, the court was told.

Police were tipped off by the support worker, but the girl did not immediately divulge the details of what had happened. The following day, the child told a support worker that Letts assaulted her. When police quizzed her, she said she had not told them because she did not want to get him into trouble.

14th November 2017

Steven Letts was sentenced to jail for 18 years for kidnapping and raping the 12-year-old girl. Jailing him for, Judge Jamie Tabor QC branded him a "volatile compulsive liar" and revealed he was a career criminal convicted of offences related to drugs, weapons and an armed burglary.

At court he was sentenced not only for those offences but also for an earlier aggravated burglary of a house in Gloucester when a young couple and their two children were threatened with a knife. He also had to be sentenced for a series of other unrelated crimes of possessing a knife in public, theft of bicycles, going equipped for theft, possessing heroin, having an offensive weapon, handling stolen goods, and breaching a suspended jail sentence. He was given eight years, plus one year on extended licence, to run concurrently with a two year sentence for abduction. He was also sentenced to 10 years for aggravated burglary which was to run consecutively to the eight years. He will also serve a slew of concurrent short sentences for petty crimes including three months for bicycle theft, one month for possession of heroin, six months for possession of an offensive weapon and six months for a possession of a bladed article.

Steven Letts refused to be transported to court for sentencing and instead watched via video link from Bristol Prison. But during the hearing he got angry and started ranting when Judge Jamie Tabor QC suggested he was lying about having himself been the victim of assaults before both the rape and the burglary offences. The judge ordered Letts' microphone be turned off and the hearing continued with him apparently still shouting until he stormed out of the prison video suite.

Announcing Letts' sentence the judge said he had studied him during the course of two trials and had concluded that "he is a very volatile man, he is a compulsive liar and a man steeped in the use of drugs. He walked out of his first trial when he started to be asked awkward questions by prosecuting counsel and he refused to come to court today. He did appear by video link but then, after a relatively short period, he lost his cool again and started ranting over the video link before going back to his cell," said the judge. He said he accepted that the rape victim looked and sounded much older than 12 and her foul language "would have made a sergeant major blush." But he said that the young woman was "highly vulnerable".

The court heard that Steven Letts should be classed as "dangerous" - meaning that he will not be released from his rape sentence until the Parole Board rules that he is safe.

"I am satisfied that Letts believed she was 15," he said. "But that is the only mitigation I can devine. He told the jury he felt he had a duty of care to her because he was being verbally abused by her carer but I reject that entirely. This was a fairly remarkable comment because he deliberately caused her to leave her carer while in the docks and then a matter of hours later he had taken her back to his flat, given her cocaine, cannabis and alcohol and proceeded to have intercourse with her. To say he had a duty of care towards her was nothing less than remarkable. She was highly vulnerable. Paradoxically, one of her vulnerabilities is that she looked older than she was."

An NSPCC spokesperson for South West England said: "This is a disturbing case in which Letts preyed on a vulnerable young girl for his own sexual gratification. Not only did he abduct her from a street, he plied her with drink and drugs with the sole intention of taking advantage of her. The victim has shown huge bravery in speaking out and we hope she is being given appropriate support to recover."

Fred's Inquest

On the 11th July 1996 the inquest into Fred West's death began in Birmingham. Anne Marie told the court that her father had seemed at ease when she visited him in prison. "He said you wouldn't think he was a prisoner, the way they treated him. It was so good. If you asked for anything, you got it."

Just before Christmas 1994, she had called her father and asked him what he would like as a Christmas present. "He said he would like a helicopter. He said I could smuggle it in. I said I couldn't do that." She had noticed something different in her father's manner, and he had insisted on talking to her young daughter. At the end of their conversation he had said: "I've got to go now, my angel." He had blown a kiss to her over the telephone, which he had never done before. "I felt somehow uneasy," she said.

Her father had told her that he wanted her to arrange his funeral. He had wanted all the family to be buried in Much Marcle in Herefordshire. He had said: "I'll get out of here one way or the other." He had also told her that his wife, Rosemary, was "the main person" involved in the crimes.

Stephen West told the inquest that his father had talked about suicide for months. He said he had told a senior police officer about it, but, at his father's request, had not told prison staff. He was found hanging from a grille over the door by a 7ft strip of green blanket.

Stephen West: "I watched him slowly deteriorate. He cried a lot and talked jumbled-up rubbish. He was trying to think of ways of getting out of prison. He asked me to help him get out. He had it all planned in his mind." He told the coroner, Richard Whittington, that his father had talked about suicide during October 1994. He had said he would kill himself to protect his wife, Rosemary. "He said he loved her so much he was willing to give his life for her." Stephen West said he told a senior police officer early in December about his father's plans. "He said it would be quick and simple and he was sorry he would let us all down." Asked by the coroner about the date of his father's death, Stephen West said it was typical that he should choose New Year's Day. "I thought it would be around Christmas. He loved the publicity. He always wanted to be remembered."

The court also heard from James McMaster, a medical officer at the prison, who had spoken to Fred West on a number of occasions and had placed him on a 15-minute watch after reports that he had been talking about his own funeral. He said the watch had been withdrawn when it became apparent that Fred West was not depressed.

The following day the inquest jury at the Birmingham Victoria Law Courts decided that Fred West killed himself. A jury of six men and three women, sitting before Dr Richard Whittington, decided - by a majority of eight to one – that Fred West did indeed kill himself.

The jury had heard the "infinite pains" Fred had gone to in his determination to take his life. He had volunteered to mend his fellow prisoners' shirts, thereby giving him access to a needle and thread. He had secretly sewn a thick eighty-eight-inch long rope from the hem of a green prison blanket and then attached that rope to plaited loops made from the handles of the laundry bags the shirts for repair had come in using his poacher's knots. Slipping the noose around his neck – moments after a prison officer had glanced into his cell – he had not risked standing on a chair. Instead, he had climbed on to the laundry bag full of shirts, tied the thin white strips attached to his thicker, sewn rope to a ventilation grille above his cell door, and silently pushed the bag away from beneath his feet, leaving his body suspended two feet above the floor of his cell.

In the words of the pathologist Dr Peter Acland, Fred West was "dead almost instantaneously", certainly "within one or two minutes", the supply of blood and oxygen to his brain fatally cut off causing cerebral anoxyia.

The Prison Service released a short statement following the inquest of Fred West:

"Every death in custody is regrettable and the Prison Service is committed to preventing, wherever possible, suicide and self-harm in custody.

Staff at Birmingham Prison are trained to identify prisoners felt to be at risk and procedures involving prison staff and experts such as the Samaritans play a vital part in our work. Sadly, however good our support, some suicides are not preventable.

The outcome of this inquest will be carefully considered to see whether and further lessons can be learnt."

Caroline Owens

In an interview with *The Independent* in 1998, Caroline Owens said: "Not a day goes by when I don't think about the girls who didn't make it. Just three months after I escaped, the Wests killed their first victim - their baby-sitter, Lynda Gough. If I had gone through with a rape charge against Fred West back in 1972, Lynda and the other girls would still be alive. When they started finding the bodies I felt terrible. I just kept thinking, why didn't I say something?"

In 2014, Caroline Owens revealed that she had forgiven Rose West and written to her in prison. "I have forgiven Rose West. I had to do that for my emotional recovery and I am glad I have. I wanted to write to her to tell her she has my forgiveness" said Caroline. "I asked her once more to reveal what she knows about the murders. I think that would help a lot of people." But she also said that it was the police who snubbed her claim that has caused her the "most distress". "I blame them for the fact Rose and

Fred didn't get a prison sentence for what they did to me. I am certain that would have saved some of their victims."

On the 12th August 2016 Caroline Roberts passed away following a short battle with cancer at the age of 61. Close friend Andy Jones, who worked with her on a West exhibition at his 'Crime Through Time' museum, said Caroline had always been 'guilt-ridden'.

He said: "Having personally known Caroline for a great many years, she was always a very brave, caring, much loved lady and mother who had survived appalling torture and abuse at the hands of evil serial killers Fred and Rose West. Caroline would never shy away from telling her traumatic life story and always felt a strong sense of guilt that she survived whilst many others did not. In her own words: 'I Survived 25 Cromwell Street, God bless those who didn't.' He added: "This is very sad news for her family and for those she has left behind. They all had to live through this life that she had. She spoke to me privately on many occasions and she has always been guilt-ridden because she felt that she could have done something."

Andy Jones described her as "a very brave, kind, thoughtful and forgiving woman" and praised the way she had the courage to deal with her past. He said: "It is just such a shame. She was feeling poorly so she went to the doctors and she was found to be riddled with cancer. Her family are absolutely grief-stricken. It is a really sad situation. Her illness was very swift as she was only diagnosed a few weeks ago. It is very, very sad but she is at peace now."

Funerals

On the 19th December 1995, the funeral of Heather Ann West took place at St Michael's parish church at Tintern, on the Gwent border with Gloucestershire in the Forest of Dean, an area she had loved as a child. The funeral marked the end of a "terrible nightmare" said Stephen.

"We want to give Heather a decent funeral. That's something we feel very strongly about. It's time for her to be laid to rest properly" Mae added.

Heather's funeral was postponed until the end of her mother's trial. Rose West had allegedly wished to attend the service but was not granted permission to leave Durham prison.

Stephen led the small group of mourners, together with his sisters Mae and Tara. Also present at the service were Rose West's solicitor Leo Goatley and his wife Catherine. Anne Marie was not present. The service was conducted by the Reverend Julian White.

In February 1996 inquests into the deaths of Ann McFall and Rena West took place in Gloucester and were conducted along the same lines as all the others, essentially to complete the formalities as no one had been convicted of their murders. The coroner formally returned verdicts of unlawful killing.

On the 2nd June 2004 a newspaper reported that the brother of Carol Ann Cooper, Nigel, was angry that her grave was still unmarked, 10 years after her remains were found under floorboards in the House of Horrors. A family estrangement meant the 15-year-old girl's grave, at Worcester's Astwood Cemetery, remained anonymous. The only item marking her resting place are a few plastic flowers, whose fading petals had been scattered by a lawnmower.

Her mother had died when she was very young and half-brother Nigel was born after her father, Colin Cooper, remarried. But, when the marriage failed, he moved out of the area. Her friends and family only discovered that he had secretly cremated her remains when they made a claim to police for them. "My father Colin has the rights to the grave and we don't even know where he lives. I haven't seen him for years," said half-brother Nigel, of Ronkswood, who was two when his sister vanished. "It's sad and I'm still angry at her not having a gravestone, but there's nothing we can do. If there was a gravestone, I'd be able to lay flowers on it and think about her, but I can't. I can't even rely on memories because I was only a baby. It's almost like she didn't exist."

Demolition

Shortly before dawn on the 7th October 1996, Anne Marie paid one last visit to 25 Cromwell Street before the demolition of the house began. Not long after, Stephen, Mae and Tara left flowers with a hand written card attached containing a poem for Heather:

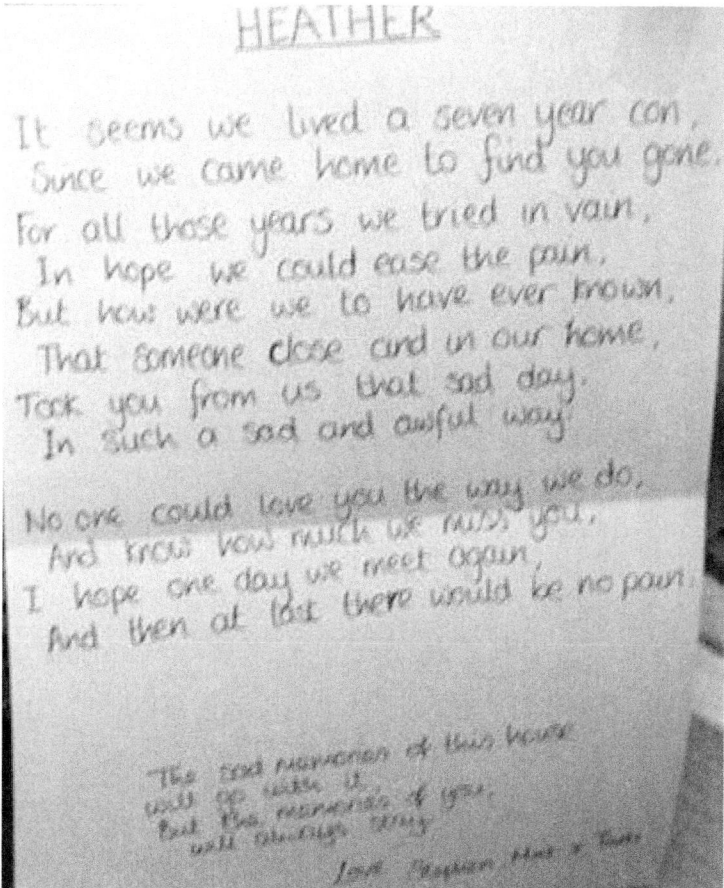

HEATHER

It seems we lived a seven year con,
Since we came home to find you gone.
For all those years we tried in vain,
In hope we could ease the pain,
But how were we to have ever known,
That someone close and in our home,
Took you from us that sad day.
In such a sad and awful way

No one could love you the way we do,
And know how much we miss you,
I hope one day we meet again,
And then at last there would be no pain

The sad memories of this house
will go with it.
But the memories of you,
will always stay

love Stephen, Mae + Tara

The Police supervised the five-day demolition of 23 and 25 Cromwell Street; the fabric was reduced to rubble and ground to dust and placed deep in a landfill site. Other items were burnt. In July 1997 a pedestrian walkway replaced 23 and 25 Cromwell Street.

This image really shows how small the property was.

The walkway where 23 and 25 Cromwell Street once stood.

Further Searches

By April 1996 eight of the nine outstanding girls named in the police press conference after Rosemary West's trial were traced, leaving only Donna Lynn Moore unaccounted for. Described in 1973 as white and 13 or 14 years of age, the slim pretty girl spoke with an American accent and may have been the daughter of a US serviceman from East Anglia. She was also known as 'Yankee Doodle.' While there was no doubt that a girl of that name and vague description had visited 25 Cromwell Street at some time, continued enquiries over the years by both the police in the United Kingdom and the armed forces in America had failed to find either her or any other member of her family.

"There are a lot of girls who went missing and the families all want to know the truth," said Mary Bastholm's brother, Peter. "Mary has never been found, but I would love the chance to lay my sister to rest. I'm sure Rose West could help us do that if she wanted to. She is probably living a better life in prison than many people do on the outside."

In January 2012, Gloucestershire's Chief Constable Tony Melville was confronted with an online petition instigated by Chris Roberts. The petition, containing 329 signatures, called on the police to excavate the cellar of the Oasis Café (formerly known as the Pop-In Café) in Southgate Street, Gloucester in a search for the remains of Mary Bastholm.
Mr Roberts presented several 'facts' in support of his case but these were strongly refuted by Tony Melville in an open letter via the media, addressed to Mr Roberts and the petitioners. He explained why his officers would not be digging up the café. This is the essence of his reply to questions raised regarding the petition:

Dear Mr Roberts,

We have reviewed the information in your letter in conjunction with material we hold from the 1994 investigation regarding Fred and Rosemary West and the 1968 inquiry into the disappearance of Mary Bastholm.
Your letter refers to 'six known irrefutable facts' concerning the relationship between Mary and Fred West and you call on us to explain why the Pop-In Café was not forensically analysed following the discovery of Mary's exercise book in the toilet area in 1994.

It is unusual for us to give the level of detail that follows but we do so because of the scale of public interest and at the request of Mary's family, who relive the trauma of her loss with each public airing of the facts, often intertwined with varying inaccuracy and urban myth.

Petition: Fred was a regular customer of the café and knew Mary

Reply: The 1994 inquiry found evidence of this but it was always denied by Fred West

Petition: Mary was seen in West's car on more than one occasion

Reply: There is evidence from the 1994 inquiry which tends to suggest this but it is in no way categoric.

Petition: West admitted to his son Stephen and to Janet Leach that he killed Mary.

Reply: **Fred West was and remains the only suspect for the abduction and murder of Mary Bastholm**. In interview he denied it. No information of Mary's whereabouts has ever come to light.

Petition: West did the basement building work at the Pop-In Café around the time of Mary's disappearance, a major part of this work was laying a concrete floor.

Reply: This is not true. The owner of the café was in possession of the property long before Mary disappeared and no work took place in the building until the late 70's. None of that work was conducted by Fred West.

Petition: West's known modus operandi was to bury his victims

Reply: This is correct

Petition: At the time of West's arrest in 1994 the tenant of the café told police he'd found a school exercise book belonging to Mary, secreted behind brickwork in the toilet area. This book was collected by the police but the Bastholm family were not informed of its discovery.

Reply: The tenant contacted police in 1994 about a book he discovered amongst junk and rubble in the basement – not in the brickwork. It was an old café diary which was not connected to Mary. It had no relevance to Mary or her family.

On the basis of the above facts it is our view there is simply no evidence to support the idea Mary is buried in that location. A search of the Pop-In Café would be entirely disproportionate and without foundation and I would politely make a request for the petition calling for the café to be searched in relation to Mary's disappearance to be removed. We have visited Mary's family and they are wholly supportive of this course of action.

Having furnished you with the full facts, you will now be aware some of your information was flawed and is misleading to the people who signed your document.

I agree entirely with the sentiment you express at the end of your letter – that is your desire to find and return Mary to her family. I don't believe there is one of us in Gloucestershire Constabulary who wouldn't want the same conclusion.

Yours Sincerely

Tony Melville

Daisy Letts and The Children

Daisy Letts, Rose's mother, had had to move home and change her name. "I have had a bad time through my life. I was just beginning to feel that I had my own home, where I was happy and then all this came about. I thought of doing away with myself because I didn't think I could make it. I don't know how my family is going to cope with it – my son has lost his job and my daughter has lost hers. It seems to be all the stress what done it."

She said Rose was "not an aggressive child – she was too dense. There was nothing odd about her; she's a great big baby and a bit slow. One of my daughters said Rosie was hard. I didn't know she was hard. She may have become hard with this Fred, because she obviously became caught up in it. To think my daughter has been pulled into something like this is terrible."

She hoped Rose's disturbed upbringing might win her a more lenient sentence and possibly psychiatric help. "I thought that maybe they would put her in a mental place like Broadmoor and give her a lot of counselling. But if she has done all these wicked things, they must put her in prison. I was told there was threads of rope in some of the graves. Someone said there was orgies going on, where they sacrifice victims. How could she?

How could she? Isn't it dreadful?

I want to go and see Rosie, and I'm afraid to go and see her. I don't know if it would be a good thing or a bad thing."

Mae

By the end of December 1995, Mae was 23-years-old and 8 months pregnant with her first child. She was living with Tara and her small son Nathan. Once a month, she visited her mother in Durham prison. They would write most days. She had not changed her appearance, but had acquired a new name, she explained, for practical reasons. "I couldn't get a bank account, or a loan or anything. You would fill in 25 Cromwell Street as your previous address, and they either thought it was a joke and chucked the form away or didn't want to know."

Mae was no longer with the father of her baby. She said: "I don't really trust anyone any more. A lot of men won't ever want to know me now, and there are others who just want to go out with you so they can say they've been with Mae West.

When I say something like, 'Oh, my mum taught me that', I can see people thinking – 'God, what else did she teach you?'"

Of Rose she said: "She's more like a normal mum, now. Which is a shame, because she's locked up."

In 2011 Mae revealed that she had never managed to lose the fear that one day someone would discover who she really was. She had not spoken publicly for seventeen years and had changed her identity - she had plastic surgery to remove a birthmark from her face. She had a child from an earlier relationship and had taken the child's father's name. Mae felt that she had not dealt with the horror, yet couldn't be open about it either, because she had to protect her privacy and her own children. "Not talking doesn't make it go away," she said. "I don't think people realise how a mum and dad are really important in your life. You can't just say, 'They're not there anymore. They never existed. I've just appeared on this Earth with no parents.' No one knew what it was like for us, living with those sorts of parents. I'm not sure, do people care or not?" Mae carried misplaced guilt as many survivors of serious abuse do. "You worry all the time. You're never really at peace. You'll do something nice and then beat yourself up afterwards for hours, because that's what we do. We're people that try and plod along. As long as I think I'm plodding, I'm happy."

Mae had remained loyal to her mother. But Rose eventually cut her out of life after she wrote her a letter outlining how she felt. Rose came in to some money when she was in prison and decided to distribute it amongst her children, but instead of distributing it equally, she gave more to those who she got on with. Mae had had enough of Rose's behaviour and wrote her the following letter:

Dear Mum,

I have spoken to Tara and she said that she does not want the kids to have the money; she feels she will give the kids all they need for their futures. I have had a long talk to her and she has made me see sense in a lot of what she has said.

Firstly I want to tell you how I feel. You may not agree with any of it but I still think it needs to be said. I feel that you separate us all and you treat us differently, take Steve for instance. He has never felt that you really ever loved him.

Sometimes I feel unless we are making something of our lives you don't want to know us. If we go to work, bring our kids up well, own property etc., then you want to know us, but if we struggle – and let's face it I think with what we have been through the likelihood is that we were never going to be able to live a normal life – then you just shy away. Maybe it makes you feel better to know that at least one or two of us made good but the truth is all of us have made something of our lives however small. It's as if you judge us and we feel you have no right to do that.

It's like this money; you did not sit down and think I have 7 children (8 if you want to include Anne Marie) and say well I want to give them all an equal amount, however small, because they are my children. No you judge us over whether we criticised you in the press, got compensation or just never stuck by you and we all got written off. But I suppose you can write us off and hope the grand-children make more of their lives and you can feel good about what you did for them. Oh and I only mean a select few of them as well, because of Steve, his kids lose out and so on, it's just a power thing at the end of the day. Well none of us want it.

I hate doing this but it's time I stuck up for myself and for the family. Ever since we were kids you have tried to separate us. When it suited you the family had to stick together, but individually if we wanted to spend time with each other it wasn't allowed. I won't turn my back on Amy no matter what she does. Like I am with you, Mum, when you love someone it should be unconditional, I have always been there for you ever since I was young, even though you can be so hard sometimes. It's not about the money but what it could have symbolised – that for once we all counted and we were equal.

Mae

"We have to accept that good and bad happens. There are many people who don't want to know that there are evil people in the world, that bad things happen."

In reply a couple of days later Rose replied:

When I came to prison I never intended to try to become a 'parent' to you children. I know that with all that has happened in my life and later in 'our' lives that I would never be capable of such a 'feat'. I was never a parent and could never be now! You have always 'been there' for me and I have counted myself as a very privileged person indeed!! I was hoping and still do that it was a choice you made rather than a feeling of expectation that I could live up to your hopes of having a 'good mother'. I have mentioned on several occasions that if you wanted to break contact with me I would understand perfectly. I am sorry Mae – I can't be something different now. My intention was to make myself available, to allow you children to have someone to come to and maybe get some answers to your unanswered questions. As it is I can see that I have only made matters worse. I can only assure you that was genuinely NOT my intention. I truly do not have the skills to be a parent and although I am sad and ashamed of this, it is something that has to be accepted.
Love as always,
Mum xxxxx"

Mae wrote back telling her about her daughter's new secondary school uniform and chose not to respond to what Rose wrote in her letter. She didn't receive a response and Mae hasn't heard from or seen her since.

Anne Marie

Anne Marie: "In life I would say there's only two fears I have. One is if my partner left me and the other one is Rosemary. She said that if she ever saw me again she would kill me. Rosemary's going for an appeal, and this sounds absolutely horrible, but if she ever comes out then I would go. I would sooner take my own life than let her because there would be nothing left of me. I have that much fear for her, but yet in another way I miss her so that is confusing in itself."

Anne Marie described how Fred's brother John raped her more than 300 times when she was a child. Two weeks previously she said she wished she had died with the Wests' other victims. She told a national newspaper:

"People say I'm lucky to have survived, but I wish I'd died. I can still taste the fear. Still feel the pain. It's like I'm going back to being a child again. I have always had to be strong but I'm not. I'm really scared."

On the 17th November 1999, just a few days after her last interview, Anne Marie was found in The Severn, having jumped from Westgate Bridge. Anne Marie, 35, was unconscious when she was found tangled in reeds close to the riverbank. She was taken to Gloucester Royal hospital but was allowed to return home after treatment. She had been diagnosed as suffering from depression. A passer-by saw her jump from the Westgate Bridge in the centre of Gloucester late on Wednesday and called the police. She was swept half a mile downstream before being rescued.

Assistant divisional officer Simon McMillan, who led the 15-strong search team, said: "She was blue when we got to her. It was extremely cold... You couldn't last very long in those conditions."

In 2009 Anne-Marie, 41, worked at a supermarket and, after divorcing her pub landlord husband Chris, lived with partner Phil and her two teenage children in Gloucester.

Phil said: "Life has been a nightmare for Anne-Marie, because she keeps reliving the trauma. What she's been through is unimaginably hard for anyone to cope with, but I'm so proud of her. It's a heavy burden, but she's just trying to lead an ordinary life now. With me and the kids supporting her, I think she can see a light at the end of the tunnel."

Speaking in 2011, Anne Marie said: "My mother Rena and my sisters Charmaine and Heather, are my heroes. I was an eight-year-old coward and I was still a coward when I ran away. But my mother and siblings stood up to them and paid the ultimate price." She described the lasting effect that the horrifying experiences had on her life: "There was no doubting the overwhelming sense of emptiness and loss. Justice had been served and now it was time to try and pack away the memories of past and present, except it was not that easy. There was little support available locally and the NHS just didn't know what to do with me and I am ashamed to admit that I attempted to take my own life on a number of occasions and I am lucky to be alive. It would take years before I got the kind of counselling and professional support that I desperately needed.

I was like a little mother to Heather, changing her nappies when she was a baby. I'm still devastated by the loss of Heather because I didn't realise how much danger she was in. That is always in my mind

Lucyanna

In July 1996 Lucyanna West, aged 13, remembered her childhood as a "mixture of happy and unhappy times", although she was less sure whether Fred loved her. "I wasn't his best daughter, like Rose or Tara. He didn't really show if he loved me, or I can't remember." She remembered her parents' arguments. "I suppose they must have loved each other at least a little bit, but I'm not sure how much." She concluded firmly: "I think it is obvious he wasn't a good man."

Louise

Not long after Rose was convicted Louise managed to get back in contact with Mae. She had stayed in contact with Tara but due to the care order Mae and Stephen were not allowed contact. Louise was in a desperately unhappy state after being shifted from care home to care home. She still wanted things to go back to how they were before they were all split up. Mae and Louise met up and Louise told her how she blamed herself for splitting the family up. "It's because of me, because I told what Dad had done to me, the others lost their home, their mum and dad." She told Mae how she had been separated from the other children almost as soon as they were taken by social services.

She also told Mae for the first time how Fred and Rose had done everything they could to intimidate the younger children into not backing up her story by telling them that it would break up the family.

Louise kept running away from her care home and turning up at Tara's and wanted to stay with her and Mae. When her care order expired, she was legally allowed to see Rose if she wanted. Although hesitant, along with Tara, Mae and their children, she made the trip to Durham. Rose was pleased to see them all but was reluctant to accept any blame or responsibility; instead blaming either Fred or social services for everything. As she was unwilling to accept responsibility for her actions Louise decided not to see her again.

Although their first trip went OK on subsequent trips she was negative and hostile about Louise and Tara. Rose told Mae that Louise was an emotional wreck and as such she wouldn't make a success of work, relationships or motherhood.

In November 1996, aged 18, Louise West talked publicly about her father for the first time: "He kissed me goodnight as any other father." For her, "he was just my dad and I loved him." She explained: "His bad side was a bit extreme, as in what I know now from the press, not as how I knew him then. On his good side, he was good and nice because he was my dad. If he gave you anything you treasured it."

The memory of her father that Louise West treasured most was "the funny side". He "was rude and morbid, but always had a sense of humour", with jokes that he "used to kick in when you were beginning to think he was getting serious." She did not recall ever feeling "sad or depressed around him", remembering that he used to sing 'I want to be Bobby's girl', and used to "take the piss out of people." Most of all she recalled her father as a man who was "always doing something. When he was at work we were at school, and when we were at home he was always at work."

Louise West remembered her childhood as "very up and down. Dad wasn't around all the time. He had to go out late and earn money. He was the bread-winner, and therefore demanded respect. He was rather old-fashioned." But she also acknowledged that "things could change drastically at times, up and down, depending on the money situation." The Wests "signed her birthday cards together – although they were written by Mum." Her parents argued, but even though "they had fights, they got on. They argued like parents and they kissed like parents. They loved each other."

Rosemary Jr

Rosemary Jr, 14, like Louise, now spoke about her family for the first time. She remembered "some happy times and some bad", although she added, "but doesn't every family have bad times?" Even though Fred was not her natural father, Rosemary Jr spoke of him as if he were. "I felt my father loved me. He cuddled me, cared for me and looked after me. I can remember his face and smile when he gave me money for all of us to get some sweets down the shop."

Rosemary Jr accepted that she "didn't really know my dad. I thought I did, but no. I don't really know what to think. He was my dad, and what I knew of him was good. Then I hear what he had done, and I'm not so sure." "I think my mum and dad did love each other. I suppose they had bad times as well."

Tara

On the 24th November 1996 Tara gave birth to her second son. Tara visited Rose on occasions with Mae and Louise. Although the first visit went well, on subsequent visits Rose was hostile towards her. She told Tara that she would make a bad mother and have her children taken away from her by social services.

On the 22nd October 2000, Tara West gave an interview to a national newspaper. It told how last year she went back to 25 Cromwell Street. The house had been demolished - there was only the garden left where she used to play with her brothers and sisters. But she still broke down and cried: "Why us? Why did it happen to us?" Since the trial, Tara tried to rebuild her life and to bring up her sons. She moved out of the Gloucester area, changed her name and did her best to form relationships. But the flashbacks to a home where it was normal for the children to watch pornographic films with their father, to a home where her prostitute mother entertained her clients, had made it difficult for Tara to love anyone.

"I hate showing my tender side to men," she said. "I think it is a weakness. I pretend I am hard. I just can't say, 'I love you'. I fear rejection because of my upbringing. I never said, 'I love you' to Mum, and the love I gave Dad was just used by him."

Not surprisingly her record with men had been disastrous. She had a string of broken relationships behind her. Her last boyfriend split with her two months before the interview. "A lot of men just can't handle the fact that my mum and dad are Fred and Rose West. I told one bloke, and he literally ran out of the house, he was so scared."

Tara moved 10 times in the six years since 1994 to avoid the pointing fingers and the searching questions. "As soon as somebody gets too close I either drop them or move on. I have very few real friends outside the family. I panic when somebody asks me about my past."

Tara, 22, lived in a neat semi- detached house in a quiet town in the North of England. Her sitting room was full of the normal children's clutter of toys and games - but there were no family photographs on the walls. Her home was her refuge.

"I close my front door and lock out the world. I don't open the front door to anybody. And I don't let the children out to play. I am probably over-protective, but I fear them being taken by somebody like Dad. If the children go to a party, I go. If they go out to play, I go. I know what evil is out there. I lived with it for many years."

Tara was seven years old when she realised she was different from the other West children. It was this difference which was to save her from a childhood of even worse abuse. "You're darker, Tara," said her sister, and for the first time Tara wondered why. It was years later that she was to find out the truth. Fred was not her real father. Her father was a black man who paid for a single sex session with Rose at Cromwell Street.

Despite this, Fred seemed to accept Tara as his own child. He would lie, saying: "You're a throwback. Your great-great-grandmother was black." Tara believed Rose felt guilty that her father was a client. "She often spoilt me. I was allowed to stay up late and was given treats." But even she felt her mother's cruelty.

"Mum used to hit me with a wooden spoon - I think she just had too many kids and couldn't cope." Tara clearly found it hard to blame her mother – "it's not like we were hospitalised...she didn't break any of our bones. And Mum always made sure we went to the doctors, dentists and were smartly turned out. She wasn't all bad."

However, the beatings got worse as Tara got older. "She would end up throwing bits of the furniture at me." The violence and abuse had a brutalising effect on Tara. She became a bully at school in a desperate attempt at getting attention. "I was angry at the world," she explained. "It was a cry for help, but none of the teachers recognised it. They just thought I was a naughty girl."

Although she suffered at the hands of her mother, Tara was saved from the advances of her step-father. She became aware of her father's growing interest in her sisters. But it was only when she was 12 that she discovered the extent of his depravity.

One evening, her sister walked into the bedroom she shared with Tara, crying in pain. "All she said was, 'He's raped me'. She was hysterical. I couldn't get a word out of her."

Tara had been only 10 when Fred sat the family down to watch a porn film. "He called it sex education. I was a bit uncomfortable with it all." But Tara and her siblings also had to get used to their parents having sex in front of them at any time of the day. "Dad would come into the kitchen and Mum would be cooking dinner. They would start having sex. We would just ignore them."

Then there were Rose's 'clients'. Tara said: "They had their own bell to ring. We didn't see many - but we heard quite a lot."

Fred would even listen to his wife having sex on speakers as the family watched children's TV. When Tara told her mother about Fred's treatment of the 13-year-old, "she just said, 'Are you sure? He's always messing around'. Dad was allowed to go on raping her." Tara herself escaped her father's attentions. "I realise now that Dad was only interested in his natural daughters. He thought they were his property. Because I wasn't his daughter he left me alone.

Once she was taken into care, Tara began to struggle with her sexual feelings. At 14 she lost her virginity to a 19-year-old and instantly regretted it. "I hated every moment of it and cried all the way through. I only did it because I wanted a cuddle. It was horrible and dirty."

Two years later 16-year-old Tara and her then boyfriend, a 19-year-old shop worker, had a baby together. "I deliberately got pregnant. I just wanted something to love." The romance foundered, but two years later Tara began a relationship with a social worker twice her age. In 1996, she gave birth to a second boy but her relationship collapsed. She began to worry what kind of mother she was. "I was told by social workers that the abused becomes the abuser. And the family say I am very like my Mum in personality, so that worries me. But I think that is because I am outgoing like Mum. I don't think I have her nasty streak. I have never hit the children and never would. I want them to have a better life than I did. The social workers and police keep telling me to face up to facts, but I can't. I never refer to Dad as a murderer or killer. It's too painful. I just say he did some wicked things. They also tell me to accept that Mum is guilty. But I don't believe it. I really believe Mum never killed anybody."

Tara visited Rose twice a year and wrote frequently. Tara, her elder brother Stephen, and her sister Mae, often met at a secret address to discuss their past. "But we don't talk about the sad things. We try to remember the good times." Her relationship with Louise, who is a single parent, is strained. "Louise thinks it's her fault we were taken into care." Two other sisters, Rosemary Junior and Lucyanna, who were not Fred's children, have started new lives. Tara occasionally sees Barry, the Wests' youngest son. Anne Marie has been ostracised because she gave evidence against her stepmother. Tara said of her step-father: "I hate him for the murders, and feel so sorry for the victims' relatives. But I am too tired to be angry any more. Now I have the children to look after, I haven't time for anger."

Barry

In 2004, one of the Wests' youngest children, Barry, claimed to have witnessed the murder of his sister Heather. According to Barry (who was just seven at the time), both Fred and Rose had restrained, then sexually and physically abused Heather, before Rose had repeatedly stamped on her head until Heather ceased to move. The little boy was standing behind the door when Heather came home in the early hours of the morning:

"It was about 3 a.m. I heard mum slap her and I saw my dad walk round behind her and put his leg out. Then my mum just booted her. She was kicking and kicking her and calling her a slag. Then when my dad tried to get her to do things to him (these would be sexual), she refused. I think that's why she ended up dead. When my dad finished with her, Heather was too weak to get up and my mum kicked her in the head. I could see blood coming out of her head and her mouth. Then my mum stamped on her head five times and Heather didn't move again. Finally mum rubbed her hands together saying matter-of-factly, "Right, let's clear this up. Let's get rid of this fucking whore." I could hear my dad wrapping her in some plastic and I could see my mom scrubbing the floor with a bucket and brush.

My mum continually lies about her involvement in the hope that one day she'll be free," added Barry West, "But she knew every detail of what took place ..."

The account appears in *Rose West: The Making of A Monster* by Jane Carter Woodrow and is repeated in other places but is not corroborated by what has been established about Heather's death. According to the account Heather had come home in the early hours of the morning yet it has been accepted that she died on the morning of 19th June 1987 and is corroborated by Mae West who remembered seeing her before she left for school. Both Mae and Stephen remembered coming home around 5 p.m that afternoon and finding Heather gone. It is possible that the events became jumbled in the boy's mind. He would have been at school on the morning Heather died. But the violent way in which he claims Heather died rings true.

Stephen

Stephen hardly visited Rose in prison. She blamed him for leaking stories about the family to the press during the police investigation and because he visited Fred when he was in prison she accused him of taking his side. "Sometimes I can hardly believe he's my son!" Rose would say. Mae doesn't believe that she ever loved him.

In January 2002, Stephen West attempted suicide at his home near Stroud, Gloucestershire, after his girlfriend left him - he had tried to hang himself but survived when the rope snapped.

On the 19th October 2004 Stephen West appeared at Worcester Crown Court and pleaded guilty to seven counts of unlawful sexual intercourse with a 14-year-old schoolgirl. He was arrested in Worcester in June, where he was living at the time, and quizzed by West Mercia Police. But he gave officers a "no comment" interview. Stephen, aged 31 and then living at Water Lane, Oakridge, Stroud, admitted to the crimes between October 2003 and May 2004. He was remanded on bail for psychiatric and pre-sentence reports. Judge Michael Mott told him: "You are in a very serious position, doing this to a child."

Stephen West denied an eighth charge of sexual activity with a child and the prosecution asked for it to lie on the court file. His barrister, Stephen Mooney, told the judge: "You may not be aware of the background, but the defendant is the son of Fred and Rosemary West. Due to the notoriety of the case, he has concerns about being misrepresented. He is prepared to liaise with a counsellor."

The defendant had already had a preliminary meeting with a psychiatrist. The judge bailed Stephen on condition he lived at his home address, did not enter Worcestershire - except to see his solicitor - and was not left alone with any child under the age of 18.

It is understood that talk about his illicit relationship leaked out at the victim's school and teachers alerted the police.

On the 3rd December 2004 Stephen West was jailed for nine months after admitting underage sex with a 14-year-old girl. Judge Michael Mott said he had no option but to jail him because of the seriousness of the offence. He also imposed a five year prevention order on him which forbade him taking any job working with children, not living at any place where there are 13 to 16 year old girls present other than his own children and not to contact his victim until she was 16. But the judge added: "You went through an experience when you were younger that no one would wish on anybody. If it's not unique it's in the highest degree unusual. You had a terrible childhood and the tragedy is that you have done a great deal to live that down. You have led a hard-working life, you have not got yourself into any trouble with the law. You were not in any way responsible for what happened in your childhood, I understand all that. I also understand that it must have had a marked effect on you and your development. On the other hand ... she (the victim) was a child and quite clearly a virgin. You were her first sexual experience. You allowed yourself to have intercourse with her in such a way that you got her pregnant. Instead of coming to your senses ... and owning up, you took her secretly to the clinic to have an abortion. You continued to have sex with her. That, frankly, I think, is one of the worst features of the case."

Judge Mott said he did not consider Stephen West had "groomed" the schoolgirl and it was "quite clear" that she felt she was in love with him. But he should have realised the relationship was wrong being the adult, he added. Stephen Mooney, defending, urged the judge not to impose a custodial sentence because of the effect his client's "traumatic" and "distressing" childhood had had on his emotional development. Referring to psychological reports, the lawyer said there was a "chronological difference" between his real age and his emotional age, and that he had not matured when it came to developing relationships. The court also heard he was suffering from Post-Traumatic Stress Disorder because of the events that took place at 25 Cromwell Street in Gloucester, where he was brought up. He was also undergoing psychotherapy to deal with his severe childhood trauma. Mr Mooney said Stephen West was still "very much an adolescent" emotionally and was therefore more likely to relate to teenagers. The offences arose out of a "relationship for relationship's sake". He added: "He related to (his victim) on a very similar emotional level to herself. He felt she could confide in him and he could confide in her. This was not an attempt on behalf of Mr Stephen West in order to target her or groom her. This was a meeting of minds. He appreciates, however, that he, being the older person ... had such experience of life to know that the responsibility for the relationship was his and his alone. By allowing himself to become involved in a sexual relationship with this young girl, he is entirely at fault."

By 2011, Stephen had been married twice and had five children.

<u>MORE VICTIMS?</u>

On the 1ˢᵗ July 1974, Elizabeth Swann, 23, went missing in Birmingham. She was last seen where she was staying with her brother. She had told friends that she had got a receptionists job in Gloucester and intended to hitchhike there. She had a young daughter at the time, who is now believed to be living in Australia. She was 5'7" and slim with blue eyes and long, blonde hair worn in a ponytail which gave her the appearance of a schoolgirl.

Fred West told his appropriate adult Janet Leach that there were as many as 20 bodies "not in one place, but spread around." He told her that one of those women killed was while he worked on a Birmingham construction site.

To date, no evidence has ever come to light of what has happened to Elizabeth. A West Midland police spokesman said in 2018 that: "To date, the investigation in to her disappearance remains unsolved. The case is subject to periodic review, and any new evidence from the public will be thoroughly investigated."

Whilst no evidence exists to prove that Elizabeth became a victim of the Wests, it remains a distinct possibility that Fred may have had something to do with her disappearance. Although a couple of years older than any of the Wests known victims, she looked a lot younger and was known to have told people she was going to hitch hike from Birmingham to Gloucester.

Donna Lynn Moore was aged 13 or 14 in 1973. She was described as 'slim and pretty' and was known to have visited 25 Cromwell Street on many occasions. She spoke with an American accent, and it's believed that her father may have been a US Serviceman based in East Anglia. Throughout the police inquiry, many attempts were made to trace her and her family, but none proved to be successful. Her whereabouts are still unknown.

CONCLUSION

So here we are, currently 25 years since the police knocked on the door of 25 Cromwell Street looking for the remains of Heather West. What they discovered was something that none of them expected. Multiple murders, sexual abuse, incest, rape, kidnap, theft and suicide were all discovered to have gone on over the previous 30 odd years. Even after Fred West's suicide and Rosemary West's trial and incarceration, the effects on and of that family have been far reaching. Even today, members of the West and Letts families are in trouble with the law, and some have followed the path, to a certain extent, of Rose and Fred. Stephen West, Steven Letts and Fred's cousin, William Hill have both been jailed for sex with under-age girls. John West hanged himself before the verdict of his trial for raping his nieces Anne Marie and Mae. Violence and sexual gratification seem to be a theme that runs through the heart of some members of these families.

But other members of these families are normal, friendly, approachable people. Anne Marie, for example, has been through more in her life time than anyone can ever imagine. There are probably even parts that have been blanked out by her memory, such as the attack on 'Miss A', which from the description she gave of one of the girls in the room at the time, must have been her. What else could she have blanked out?

Mae said that her father never raped her or Heather, but Stephen claims to have been in the room when he did. From all probability, and from what happened to Anne Marie and Louise at such young ages, he almost certainly did. Perhaps Mae has blanked it out, as many victims do.

Alarmingly, when Mae was a youngster she could recall some advice her mother had given her about men. Rose told her that if she ever found herself in a situation with a man who wanted to touch, or do anything else to her, whatever it was, she shouldn't resist. "Just let them get on with it. It'll hurt less and be over quicker." Could this be a reason why some girls were killed and others let go? Had the girls who had become buried in the basement and garden of 25 Cromwell Street fought back and been killed because of it? And had others such as Caroline Owens been released because once she had been abducted she was unable fight back?

It is easy to say that all of the West family knew what was going on in that house. That all of the West and Letts family members are the same, but that is unkind, and I believe, not true. I'll leave you with these words from Doug and Christine West's daughter Samantha:

"People say 'how do you feel about the victim's families?' Well hello, it's nice to meet you because I am one of the victim's families. I lost two cousins and when I say my name people look at me like I am evil and I don't want to hurt anybody."

Further Reading

The Corpse Garden – Colin Wilson

She Must Have Known – Brian Masters

An Evil Love - The Life of Frederick West – Geoffrey Wansell

Happy Like Murderers – Gordon Burn

The One That Got Away – Caroline Roberts

Inside 25 Cromwell Street – Stephen & Mae West

Fred & Rose – Howard Sounes

The Missing – Andrew O'Hagan

Rose West – Jane Carter Woodrow

The Cromwell Street Murders – The Detective's Story – John Bennett and Graham Gardner

Seasons of Death – Michael Charity

If You Sit Very Still – Marian Partington

Out of The Shadows – Anne Marie West with Virginia Hill

Love as Always, Mum xxx – Mae West with Neil McKay

Did you enjoy this book? Please leave a review on Amazon

Did you enjoy this book? If so, please leave a review on Amazon

Printed in Great Britain
by Amazon